THE CAROLINA RHETORIC

For English 102

Spring 2017

USC Columbia
The Department of English

Editor: Ben Harley

macmillan learning
curriculum solutions

10 9 8 7 6 5 4 3 2 1

ISBN 978-0-7380-9025-2

Macmillan Learning Curriculum Solutions
14903 Pilot Drive
Plymouth, MI 48170
www.macmillanlearning.com

Fisk 9025-2 W17

Acknowledgements (listed in order of appearance)

Adamson, Joni. "Indigenous Literatures, Multinaturalism, and *Avatar*: The Emergence of Indigenous Cosmo-politics" from *American Literary History*, vol. 24, no. 1, pp. 143–149, 153–157, 159 + notes through page 162. Reprinted by permission of Oxford University Press.

Banaji, Mahzarin R. and Greenwald, Anthony G. "On Stereotypes." Excerpt(s) from *Blindspot: Hidden Biases of Good People* by Mahzarin R. Banaji and Anthony G. Greenwald, copyright © 2013 by Mahzarin R. Banaji and Anthony G. Greenwald. Used by permission of Bantam Books, an imprint of Random House, a division of Penguin Random House LLC. All rights reserved. Any third party use of this material, outside of this publication, is prohibited. Interested parties must apply directly to Penguin Random House LLC for permission.

Acknowledgements and copyrights are continued at the back of the book on pages 515–517, which constitute an extension of the copyright page.

Sustainability
Hayden-McNeil's standard paper stock uses a minimum of 30% post-consumer waste. We offer higher % options by request, including a 100% recycled stock. Additionally, Hayden-McNeil Custom Digital provides authors with the opportunity to convert print products to a digital format. Hayden-McNeil is part of a larger sustainability initiative through Macmillan Learning. Visit http://sustainability.macmillan.com to learn more.

bedford/st. martin's • hayden-mcneil
w.h. freeman • worth publishers

TABLE OF CONTENTS

Part One—Rhetorical Concepts

Part Two—Professional Essays

Unit One—Media and Technology

Unit Two—Gender and Sexuality

Introduction

Welcome to *The Carolina Rhetoric*, the textbook for ENGL 102 at the University of South Carolina. Like the English 101 textbook, *The Carolina Rhetoric* is a collaborative project of the USC English Department. Over the last year faculty and graduate students have volunteered their time and expertise to create the rhetorical definitions, questions, and exercises that constitute Part One; to choose the essays that constitute Part Two; and to holistically edit the book. It was an arduous process, but we are proud to have a collection that both represents our collective knowledge in the field and caters specifically to our students' needs. I would like to dedicate a few pages here at the beginning of the book to highlight some of its most important features.

The most prominent organizational feature of this book is the split between Part One and Part Two. Part One is filled with rhetorical terms that should be useful to you both as you analyze texts and as you engage in your own research and writing. Part Two, then, is made up of professional essays that you can analyze for rhetorical devices, cite in your Researched Argumentative Essay, or use as models for your own work. Ideally, the two parts work in tandem, with each informing the other. For instance, learning about stakeholders in Part One should help you both to identify the different people and institutions you want to consider as you develop your research project and to rhetorically analyze an essay in Part Two, such as Blake Hurst's "The Omnivore's Delusion." Considering how Hurst includes the concerns of various stakeholders in his argument should help you to invent ways to discuss stakeholders in your arguments. In short, both parts of this book work together to help you become a stronger writer.

Of course, not all instructors teach students to become stronger writers in the same way; your class will have a learning environment unique from every other class on campus. Uniqueness is good because it allows instructors to focus on the contents and methods in which they are most expert. With this principle in mind, we left the decision about what essays pair best with what terms to the discretion of your instructor, which is why the terms and the essays are separated into two distinct sections. Perhaps your class will not pair terms with essays at all, but instead choose to read through the terms all at once and then read through the essays all at once. This method works well too, and the choice is up to your instructor.

PART ONE

Part One is based on the ancient Roman philosopher Cicero's **five canons of rhetoric**—invention, arrangement, style, memory, and delivery—which were developed to explain the process of composing an oration. "In contemporary education, the canons are also used to explain the process of composing other texts such as essays, lab reports, videos, songs, etc. The editors of this book hope the canons serve as a useful guide to thinking about how to compose, but we realize that the actual process of writing is not as linear as Cicero's model often seems to be.

Cicero's cannons are not meant to be static. They are not simple steps for composing but rather the different components of creation that overlap, coalesce, and double back on one another during the process of composition. The dynamic quality of the canons, and all rhetorical concepts for that matter, is one of the reasons that many of the ideas you read in the definition for one rhetorical concept in Part One will also be discussed in the definition of other concepts. Ideas transcend both terms and canons. Important concepts cannot be contained; they are instead diffused throughout the composing process. Some might call this repetitive, but those who study rhetoric (i.e., rhetoricians) call it recursive; we believe that ideas keep popping up because they are important and because no part of the composition process is an entity unto itself. Creating anything requires the author to constantly be negotiating, searching, thinking, renegotiating, researching, and rethinking.

The Carolina Rhetoric welcomes this type of recursivity not only because it helps to remind us of important concepts throughout the composing process but also because different authors in this textbook think about and articulate these same ideas differently. For example, both John Bailes and Mark Schaukowitch discuss *stasis*, but the former discusses this concept as an issue-centered method of invention while the latter discusses it as different steps within an argument. Both of these are "correct" ways of understanding the term, but the differences between them add important nuance and subtlety. This textual richness is why we are so lucky to have a variety of authors for this book; each person is bringing their own perspective, expertise, and personality to the text. When compiled, this book represents the best rhetorical understanding USC can impart to its students. This book is stronger because of its diversity in authorship, and we believe your education will be richer for it as well.

PART TWO

The editors of this book tried to keep the idea of diversity in mind as we compiled Part Two as well. The predominant feature of Part Two is that it has been broken into four units—Media and Technology; Gender and Sexuality; Food; and Race, Ethnicity, and Heritage. The idea behind this organization was to allow instructors either to teach a sampling from each unit throughout the semester or to focus solely on one unit throughout the entire term. For this reason, each unit not only has a diversity of opinions but also a diversity of writing styles. We hope you will read essays in this class that will challenge you with both new ideas and new ways of writing. Some of the new formats you will encounter may include scientific articles, academic essays, podcasts, memoirs, and investigatory journalism. Some of the ideas and forms you encounter in this class will challenge you, and you might dislike them; still, we hope you take them seriously, and they help you grow as a writer.

Because of the different genres, styles, and formats, the essays in Part Two often do not resemble one another. They use different types of citations, notations, and quotations. They have different ways of indicating topic shifts, pauses, and emphasis. Such a diversity of styles can be disorienting for freshman readers, but we believe that it is important for you to be introduced to as many different ways of writing as possible. It is only through introduction to a wide variety of diverse texts that you can come to appreciate the multitude of ways the rhetorical concepts in Part One influence actual texts. To highlight this connection between Part One and Part Two, the editors have only made minimal changes to the texts in Part Two; we tried to keep each reading as true to its original published version as possible. We didn't force them into an academic style but instead printed them complete with stylistic peculiarities, idiosyncratic formats, and typos. One edit we did make, however, was to shorten some pieces; if you encounter an ellipsis (e.g.,...) that is not within a quotation, it means that we decided to cut a section of the original essay rather than print it. We would have liked to keep every piece fully intact, but doing so would have made the size and cost of this book unreasonable.

To help you make some of the connections between Part One and Part Two, we begin every unit in the former with suggested essays from the latter that we believe speak to the concepts you will be discussing in that unit. These suggestions are only recommendations; our route through this book, the route your teacher assigns, and your own personal route may end up being very different from each other. We encourage you to break the boundaries of the units. You will find that many essays in Part Two could be categorized differently than they are. For instance, Haiming Liu's and Lianlian Lin's "Food, Culinary Identity, and Transnational Culture" is in the Race, Ethnicity, and Heritage unit, but it would be comfortable in the Food unit as well. Other essays—such as Susan Schneider's "*Mindscan*" and Katrina Karkazis's "Taxonomies of Intersexuality to the 1950s"—lack conceptual connections but have methodological, generic, or ideological connections. We urge students not to be limited by the organization we have produced, but rather to follow these other connections when they seem productive.

THE EVERYDAY WRITER

Finally, the department could not have written this book if not for *The Everyday Writer*. While *The Carolina Rhetoric* provides you with rhetorical concepts for consideration and essays for analysis, *The Everyday Writer* provides you with the practical information that will allow you to write your essays and various other compositions. The value of this information as regards success in this class cannot be understated, which is why every unit in Part One includes suggested readings from *The Everyday Writer* that we believe pair well with that unit. These readings will help you as you invent, arrange, stylize, remember, and deliver your own compositions. Like our Part Two suggestions, these are simply recommendations; unlike our Part Two recommendations, however, it would be very difficult for you to read everything we suggest from *The Everyday Writer*. Your teacher will make decisions about which chapters to have you read, which to have you skim, and which to have you skip. We make recommendations, but only your teacher can make them mandatory.

Good luck, and good writing!

Editor:
Ben Harley

Managing Editor:
Nicole Fisk

Section Editors:
Christopher Holcomb (Part One)
Adam Lerner (Part Two)

Writers:
John Bailes (Topoi, Voice)
Kevin Brock (Style)
Candace Cooper (Audience, Stakeholders)
Alana Hatley (Opportunities and Constraints)
Joseph Hendryx (Poetics)
Andreas Herzog (Exigence)
Sebastian Ivy (Arrangement, Genre)
Amber Lee (Classical Arrangement, Memory)

Writers *continued*:
Trevor Meyer (The Rhetorical Situation, The Appeals)
Ashley Moore Walker (Delivery)
John Muckelbauer (Invention)
Kimberly Overmier (The Toulmin Model)
Adam Padgett (Kairos)
Melody Pritchard (Rogerian Argument)
Mark Schaukowitch (Stasis)
David Stubblefield (Deductive Reasoning, Inductive Reasoning)
Kelly Wheeler (Design)

PART 1

RHETORICAL CONCEPTS

Invention

Invention is the first of the five canons of classical rhetoric; it refers to the process of discovering or creating arguments on a particular topic. This process can refer to both figuring out the position you want to support and/or coming up with the arguments that support that position. In other words, invention can begin when you don't know what you actually think about a topic (am I for or against gay marriage?) or when you know your conclusion but want to figure out good reasons for various audiences to support it (how would I convince my grandparents to agree with me on gay marriage?). The classical tradition offers a number of different strategies for inventing arguments, including inartistic appeals (evidence and examples) and artistic appeals (ethos/pathos/logos), topoi (commonplaces), and stases (questions for identifying disagreement)—all of which will be discussed in more detail in this first unit.

To get a sense for invention, imagine you have been asked to give a toast at a wedding. You might start the process of writing your speech by thinking about how you want to come across to the audience (funny, irreverent, sincere, romantic, etc.) or by brainstorming the attributes of the couple you want to mention (What are they good at? What are they bad at? etc.). In this case, you invent arguments by first considering your rhetorical situation—another idea that will be discussed in this unit.

Determining what you want to write can be difficult, yet many types of writing instruction in the twentieth century skipped this step of the writing process. Instructors simply assumed that students knew what they wanted to argue, or would come up with reasons on their own. Such writing instruction therefore focused more on other canons such as arrangement and style. However, the late twentieth and early twenty-first-century writing pedagogies are frequently characterized by a revitalized focus on invention and a commitment to training students in the process of discovering and creating persuasive arguments; *The Carolina Rhetoric* is no exception to this trend.

Suggested Essays from Part Two

- Mahzarin R. Banaji and Anthony G. Greenwald "On Stereotypes"

- Cordelia Fine "The 'Seductive Allure' of Neuroscience"

- Roxane Gay "Daniel Tosh and Rape Jokes: Still Not Funyy"

- Blake Hurst "The Omnivore's Delusion: Against the Agri-intellectuals"

- Robert Paarlberg "Attention Whole Foods Shoppers"

- Eric Schmidt and Jared Cohen "Our Future Selves"

- Christina Hoff Sommers "The Boys at the Back"

- George Yancy "Dear White America"

Suggested Chapters from *The Everyday Writer*

- Chapter 3 "Rhetorical Situations"

- Chapter 4 "Exploring Ideas"

- Chapter 9 "Critical Reading"

- Chapter 10 "Analyzing Arguments"

- Chapter 12 "Preparing for a Research Project"

- Chapter 13 "Doing Research"

- Chapter 14 "Evaluating Sources and Taking Notes"

The Rhetorical Situation

About 2,500 years ago, the ancient Greek thinker Aristotle defined rhetoric as "the ability to see in each case the available means of persuasion." For Aristotle, rhetorical principles and techniques helped citizens defend themselves and accuse others in law courts, advocate for and against policy in the Assembly, and praise or blame each other on ritual occasions, like a eulogy at a funeral. While designed specifically for oral arguments, we can use these ancient rhetorical principles in many different media besides speeches, as they provide a useful foundation for rhetorical inquiry and invention.

While writing and rhetoric have changed in the millennia since Aristotle's time, his work still has useful things to teach us. While Aristotle's definition is not the first, only, or best, it does provide a very important idea: **the rhetorical situation.** The rhetorical situation asserts that language does not exist in a vacuum, as "any given case" can vary widely from any other. Simply, we do not talk to everyone about the same things in the same ways (e.g., talking about weekend plans is very different if we are talking with friends, classmates, teachers, or parents). We already change our language implicitly, but reflecting on these choices actively and critically makes us much more effective. Therefore, we must consider the four primary elements of any given rhetorical situation: the **rhetor** is the one making the message, the **audience** is whoever receives the message, the **text** is the message itself, and the **purpose** is the goal the rhetor hopes to achieve with the message.

Different texts work differently on different audiences; what persuades one audience at one time could fail miserably with the next audience, and what is persuasive coming from one person may not be persuasive coming from another. That is, what is "good writing" or "effective rhetoric" depends on who the rhetor is, what they are writing about, and to whom they are writing. To be effective therefore requires many considerations of the part of the rhetor. Before you enter a rhetorical situation, some questions to consider include: Who is the intended audience? What does the audience care about or want? How does the audience perceive you? How do you perceive them? What are you trying to achieve? How are you relating your purpose? What kinds of texts work for that purpose? For that audience? For you as a rhetor?

Paying close attention to these details and thinking deeply about them will help you shape your texts to the situations that call for them. However, remember that what is persuasive in one case may not be persuasive in another. This is a problem that opens up many philosophical questions.

Discussion Questions

1. This text asserts that the rhetorical situation is applicable to a wide variety of texts, that everything is written by someone(s) for someone(s) for some purpose(s). Are there any texts that would not fit into the situation? If so, what texts are they, who is involved, and what are they for?

2. Since we change our language use based on audience, purpose, and context, can we ever actually be honest? If so, what does *honest* mean within the context of rhetoric? If not, why do we value honesty in our society? What is *truth* anyway?

3. If the quality of rhetoric is judged by its effectiveness, is there any such thing as "bad" rhetoric? Is anything permissible as long as the rhetor achieves her results? If not, how do we determine what is permissible and what is not? Who gets to make those rules, and how would they enforce them?

Exercises

1. In a short writing assignment, think about your Researched Argumentative Essay for this class. What is the rhetorical situation into which you are entering? What is your purpose? Who is your audience? What kind of text are you creating? And what version of yourself do you want to show through your writing? Write detailed answers to all of these questions, and keep them to use as a map for your future writing—though your answers to these questions may change as you move forward.

2. In a small group, choose a popular commodity, such as a food, drink, garment, game, or entertainment show. Using the internet to find commercials or print ads for this commodity, brainstorm the demographic audience to whom this commodity is usually sold: gender, class, ethnic background, social group, age, education, etc. Identify specific elements of the ad that point to the audience, and outline how you might change the ad so that it might cater to a different audience. For example, beer commercials are heavily oriented toward a male audience, so how might a beer commercial targeting women be different? Present this to the class.

3. Read an essay from Part Two, and then draw a map of the rhetorical situation of which it is a part. Identify not only the rhetor, audience, text, and purpose but also other actors, media, messages, and background information that you think are important. Try to make your map so detailed that someone with no knowledge of the topic could understand the rhetorical situation and the argument being made. Be prepared to show your map to the class.

Exigence

In 1968 the American rhetorician Lloyd Bitzer defined exigence as "an imperfection marked by urgency" and "a thing which is other than it should be." You can think of exigence as any event, condition, incident, etc. that requires a response. Bitzer elaborated that "an exigence is rhetorical when it is capable of positive modification and when positive modification requires discourse or can be assisted by discourse." In this way, we can consider an exigence rhetorical when it is possible to influence it through the use of language. Any time a speaker is able to influence the course of events through rhetorical means, we can say that he or she is responding to a rhetorical exigence. For example, a commencement speech is based on the exigence of students graduating, a political speech shortly before a politician is about to resign from office is based on the need for an explanation, and an acceptance speech after a person receives an award is based on expressing thanks and honoring those who helped that person to succeed. Each of these speeches is brought about by a specific event, and the speech itself attempts to make an impact on future actions—a student's comportment to their new vocation, how the public understands a politician's legacy, or maintaining comradery among friends, family, and colleagues.

According to Bitzer, exigence not only determines what a rhetor will say but also "specifies the audience to be addressed and the change to be effected." In other words, the exigence determines the kind of audience the rhetor will address because not all events or incidents are relevant to a large audience. Political speeches, for example, are sometimes only broadcast in the country, state, city, or town where they are relevant. In such cases, public availability of the speech could be limited to just one radio station in one town. However, the president of the United States condemning an act of terrorism will likely be featured in the news around the world. A terrorist attack may not initially seem like a rhetorical exigence, but a speech after such an attack does demonstrate compassion to the families of the victims and a resolve to respond to the perpetrators. In this way, the speech will create action in the world. Often in such a speech the president will address various specific audiences—community leaders, citizens, Congress, etc.—and ask them to take specific actions—remain calm, remain hopeful, pass a certain bill, etc. In this way, we can see that all situations are to some extent rhetorical, even if the rhetorical response does not have an *immediate* effect in the world.

Despite this holistic argument, not all rhetoricians agree with Bitzer or his ideas about exigence. Famously, Richard Vatz argued "meaning is not intrinsic in events, facts, people or 'situations,' nor are facts 'publicly observable.'" For Vatz, situations do not have meaning in and of themselves; rather, meaning is constructed through individual interpretation of events. In a linguistic sense, the rhetor herself creates the exigence to which she responds. Instead of a problem in the world forcing a rhetor to speak and determining what she should say, the rhetor creates reasons for speaking by interpreting the world in a particular way. This understanding of exigence is different from Bitzer's because it considers that different people can interpret reality differently, that there are no such things as "problems" beyond the ones people construct, and that rhetors can use language to affect the way others understand reality. In this understanding of exigence, the rhetor frames actual events in the world as problems so that she can make her arguments; whether or not these events are actually problems is not certain.

Discussion Questions

1. Write a paragraph that explains your personal understanding of exigence. As a class, discuss how you understand the term and its importance for writing.

2. Some modern rhetoricians think Bitzer's definition of exigence is outdated. Do you think it functions well in a contemporary society that has many diverse modes of communication? Write a brief response to the question, and give an explanation for your answer.

3. The second paragraph claims "all situations are rhetorical to some extent." Do you agree with that statement? In small groups brainstorm some non-rhetorical exigencies. Be prepared to share your answers with the class.

Exercises

1. Read an essay from Part Two of this book, identify the author's exigence, and evaluate her argument as a response to it. Does she begin with an exigence people care about and believe to be problematic? Do you think her framing of the situation is accurate and ethical? Does her argument respond well to the problems she identifies?

2. Using the same essay you chose for the first exercise, write a paragraph that explains whether the author is using a Bitzerian exigence (responding to a situation) or a Vatzian exigence (creating a situation so she can respond). How can you tell which method is being used? Does the method being used matter for how you read the argument? Be prepared to share your paragraph with the class and defend your answers.

3. Take the following argument: "free speech is a cornerstone of this country and must be protected at all costs." Compose three short essays (500 words) that each make this argument but in response to completely different exigences. Afterwards, get into groups and discuss how changing the exigences changed the effectiveness of the argument.

Topoi

Starting a writing project can have different pitfalls, such as freezing up with writer's block or rushing ahead in various directions. In high school or English 101, you may have used prewriting activities either to "warm up" or "get organized" for an essay assignment. You may have tried brainstorming, clustering, free writing, charting, or outlining. But even as these prewriting techniques helped, they may not have called forth the ideas you needed to respond to an exigence in a particular rhetorical situation. In fact, rhetorical considerations may not have even entered the process. So how does invention work in rhetoric?

A relevant place to start is in the past with Aristotle, an ancient Greek thinker whose book on rhetoric is still used today. According to Aristotle, invention operates in "discovering the best available means of persuasion in a given case." In other words, invention is at the core of rhetorical activity. To assist his students with invention, Aristotle compiled the **topoi** (Greek for "places") to produce logical ideas that could serve an argument. In rhetoric, the topoi provide places in the mind, or mental shortcuts, for accessing information helpful in developing an argument. Aristotle divides the topoi into two categories: common places (general) and special places (specific). You will most likely focus on the common topoi, which can be used to analyze or to invent any argument, whereas the special topoi are used to discover knowledge for experts (such as engineers, lawyers, or physicians). Although Aristotle listed many common topoi, here are seven particularly useful ones to help on your path to discovery. Each of these seven topoi serve as questions that will prompt you to discover and examine key information that can then be used to develop a claim. In the following examples, I use the topoi to ask questions about chess. These questions prompt me to identify key information, which then allows me to create a claim about the game:

1. **Topic of Definition**—To what group does it belong? How does it fit into this group? What are the group's characteristics?

   - *Key information*: Chess is a two-player board game that has a long history as highly challenging. It requires complex logical strategies and tactics when playing. The objective is to "checkmate" the opponent's king.

   - *Claim:* Chess is the most challenging board game for the mind, requiring a player to use complex logical strategies and tactics in outthinking and outmaneuvering an opponent.

2. **Topic of Division**—What parts make up this thing or idea? How do they relate to one another?

   - *Key information:* Chess has six types of pieces that are placed on the board. Each player begins with eight pawns, two knights, two bishops, two rooks, a queen, and a king. The pieces may also be put in order of importance from weakest to strongest. Although the king is the most important piece, the most powerful is the queen.

- *Claim:* Chess pieces have retained the hierarchal order of a medieval society, which demonstrates the values represented in the game.

3. **Topic of Similarity/Difference**—How is it similar to other things? How is it different from those same things? To what can we compare and contrast it?

- *Key information:* Chess uses the same 64-checkered board as checkers. But the two games have different pieces, different rules about movement, and different objectives.

- *Claim:* Chess demands more thought, intelligence, and cunning than checkers.

4. **Topic of Degree**—In what way is it *more* or *less* than similar things? Is there abundance of it? Is there scarcity?

- *Key information:* Across the world chess has different degrees of popularity. Chess has been highly popular in Russia and Eastern Europe over the past century, producing most of the world champions. In Europe, chess has been more popular than in the United States, which prefers board games like Monopoly instead.

- *Claim:* If chess had the same popularity in the United States that it does in Russia, then Americans might produce more world chess champions.

5. **Topic of Cause/Effect**—What causes it to exist? What causes it to behave a certain way? What effects does it cause? What consequences?

- *Key information:* The earliest origin for chess is as a strategic military game in ancient Persia. The game's pieces were based on army divisions. As the game developed, it kept its combative play while adding more sophistication over the years.

- *Claim:* The militaristic culture of ancient Persia shaped the combat-oriented rules of chess.

6. **Topic of Negation**—If it or a part of it is negated, what happens?

- *Key information:* In chess, clocks are used to intensify play by creating time constraints that pressure players to move quickly. When chess clocks are removed, the game can move at a leisurely pace.

- *Claim:* Without chess clocks to keep time, some New York City street hustlers would be less effective at luring bystanders into betting on "speed chess" matches and pocketing easy cash.

7. **Topic of Substitution**—If it or part of it is replaced by something else, what is significant?

- *Key information:* If we substituted checker pieces for chess pieces, the pieces would be indistinguishable.

- *Claim:* Unlike other games with pieces as markers, chess marshals pieces that have special significance and power because of their shapes and sizes. The variety of pieces is one of the things that makes the game so unique.

We should mention another method of invention used by classical thinkers. Ancient Roman statesmen Cicero and Quintilian define invention as a process for generating and sharpening an argument before making it. This special method for preparing an argument is called **stasis** (Greek for "stand"). Stasis provides a more issue-centered approach for producing a research problem or preparing for a debate. Below is an outline of the four key questions to be asked in stasis.

1. **Facts**—Did it happen? What happened?

2. **Definition**—What is the nature of the problem or issue?

3. **Quality**—How serious is the issue or problem? Whom did it affect?

4. **Policy**—Should a solution be provided? What needs to happen to solve it?

Discussion Questions

1. Aristotle's topoi seek logical answers to questions about any subject. Which of these two topoi seems better at discovering why something exists—*topic of negation* or *topic of substitution*? Explain with examples.

2. Each of the topoi offers a different perspective on a single object of study. What is the advantage of gaining multiple perspectives? What might be the problem with this approach to invention?

3. What important similarities and differences exist between topoi and stasis? In what situations would topoi be useful for invention? In what situations might stasis be useful? Could you imagine a rhetorical situation in which the two could work together? Try to create as specific examples as possible.

Exercises

1. Using the seven common topoi above, find seven arguments for each element in the list below. Be sure to compose each of your thirty-five statements as argumentative.

- Choose a sport (football, hockey, rugby, soccer, etc.) to invent arguments about.

- Choose a geographical location (Florida Everglades, Rocky Mountains, Sahara Desert, etc.) to invent arguments about.

- Choose a hobby (scrapbooking, knitting, stamp collecting, etc.) to invent arguments about.

- Choose an economic issue (higher minimum wage, college tuition, national debt, etc.) to invent arguments about.

- Choose a digital issue (social media, texting, gaming, etc.) to invent arguments about.

2. Using the Internet, search Aristotle's common *topoi*. List at least five other common topoi you discover. Be sure these five are not the seven mentioned above. Then, explain how these other five topoi might be effective for inventing arguments. Provide some examples.

3. Using stasis, analyze the following excerpt from President Barak Obama's speech on receiving the Nobel Peace Prize in 2009. In this excerpt, Obama tackles a major conflict of interest between being at war as commander-in-chief of the most powerful military in the world while accepting the peace prize. Identify what *facts* he provides, how he *defines* his conflict, what *problems* exist because of this conflict, and what his *solution* is.

> *Perhaps the most profound issue surrounding my receipt of this prize is the fact that I am the Commander-in-Chief of the military of a nation in the midst of two wars. One of these wars is winding down. The other is a conflict that America did not seek, one in which we are joined by 42 other countries—including Norway—in an effort to defend ourselves and all nations from further attacks. Still, we are at war. And I am responsible for the deployment of thousands of young Americans to battle in a distant land. Some will kill; and some will be killed. And so I come here with an acute sense of the costs of armed conflict—filled with difficult questions about the relationship between war and peace, and our effort to replace one with the other. Now these questions are not new. War, in one form or another, appeared with the first man. At the dawn of history, its morality was not questioned; it was simply a fact, like drought or disease—the manner in which tribes and then civilizations sought power and settled their differences. And over time, as codes of law sought to control violence within groups, so did philosophers and clerics and statesmen seek to regulate the destructive power of war. The concept of a "just war" emerged, suggesting that war is justified only when certain conditions were met: if it is waged as a last resort or in self-defense; if the force used is proportional; and if, whenever possible, civilians are spared from violence.*

Stasis

The word **stasis** comes from the ancient Greek word for *standing* or *stoppage*. Both meanings are relevant for our purposes, but we'll start with *stoppage*. In this understanding, a stasis functions as the agreed upon topic of discussion, the limit to the range of topics an argument may address.

When speaking and writing, rhetors generally make one overarching claim—in academic writing we call this a thesis. To support this thesis, a rhetor will break it down into a series of smaller claims that make an argument. We can refer to these various small claims as a set of stases. They limit the field in which the conversation is taking place, ideally to one issue or location in academic speaking/writing. Stases function as the borders of an argument. Rhetors and audiences are discouraged from moving beyond the well confined space of debate, though often they do so anyway in order press their opinions, values, or beliefs.

> *Ex: If a speaker were to claim, "Illegal immigration on the southern US border is a problem. I will build a wall, and make Mexico pay for it," then someone else may counter by saying, "No. Mexico will not pay for a wall." It would be less appropriate for someone to counter with, "Mexico has the largest population of whale sharks off its borders, and a wall will hurt them."*

In the argument above, the first two claims address one another directly. However, the third claim does not directly participate in the same argument as the initial speaker. Whale sharks may be important, but they have little to do with the act of building a wall or who pays for it. In other words, the whale sharks are part of a different argument outside the limits defined by the first speaker. Still, some activists will bring up whale sharks in an attempt to shift the argument to their terms.

To determine the topic of debate in ways that will make it productive and help rhetors to determine precisely about what it is they disagree, ancient rhetoricians developed four questions to help debaters identify the main point at issue:

1. **Fact**—The question of fact is the first to consider. It asks whether something happened or if something exists. Keep in mind that facts are not self-explanatory. Facts are historical and change over time. For a long time, it was a fact that the earth was flat, but the fact eventually changed due to overwhelming evidence to the contrary. When a rhetorician says *fact*, then, what they mean is a frequently repeated idea that is understood by a culture or group to be true.

    Ex: Did Chris steal Mark's bike? Yes or No.

2. **Definition**—The question of definition asks about the exact meaning of a term in a particular situation. Definitions are based on agreement between

two parties as to what the facts of the situation are. Definition builds on the first stasis question by interrogating how we categorize specific actions.

> *Ex: Chris definitely took Mark's bike, but he said it was borrowed. Mark says it was stealing. So was the action of taking Mark's bike stealing or borrowing?*

3. **Quality**—The question of quality examines whether an action or situation, once properly defined, is good/bad, productive/unproductive, moral/immoral, etc.

> *Ex: Chris's taking of Mark's bike was definitely theft, but did he have a justifiable reason for stealing the bike? What if the bike was needed to escape a bully?*

4. **Policy**—The question of policy asks what should be done about the situation at hand. We may say not only that certain actions need to be taken but also that certain actors need to take them.

> *Ex: Chris did not have a good reason to steal Mark's bike. What should Mark do about the situation? Is Mark the best person to handle this situation?*

Ancient rhetoricians used the stases as an exercise to determine the main point of dispute between two parties, and you too can work through these questions as a brainstorming strategy to determine where any disagreements may lie between you and the texts with which you disagree. You can also use these questions as a framework for organizing your argument. This is where stasis's second meaning of *ground* is useful.

Using the stases—starting with fact and ending with policy—the rhetor invents the ground on which their argument stands. In modern composition these questions are usually worded as claims that need to be evidenced. This creates a specific problem for the rhetor because if any of these layers is not solid, the following layers will lack stability. Still, if you use all the stases, you do not need to deal with them all equally. It is up to the rhetor, after deeply researching the rhetorical situation and its various components, to determine where in an argument interventions need to be made.

> *Ex: If you were writing a paper on whether or not Run DMC should have been admitted into the Rock & Roll Hall of Fame, you may choose to briefly discuss the facts of the situation, while focusing mainly on the definition of rock and roll and the qualities of Run DMC's music that would determine whether or not it is part of the genre; then, you may choose to only briefly discuss what should be done about the situation and by whom. In this case, the intervention is mostly one of definition and quality, but all of the stases are represented.*

Finally, knowing that most arguments either implicitly or explicitly follow the stases can accelerate your research because if you know the stases and their order, you can locate the claims that are relevant to your project much faster. Many contemporary compositions follow Cicero's original modes of interrogation, though they are worded as claims, not questions. Authors will often begin by stating the facts of their rhetorical situation and citing the sources that verify those facts. Then, authors will define any ambiguous terms or uncertain aspects of those facts as they pertain to the specific situation. Then, they will explain why these facts are good/bad, problematic/unproblematic, reassuring/concerning, etc. Finally, they present a proposal as to what should be done about the situation and by whom.

Discussion Questions

1. A rancher in Nevada states, "The US federal government should not own any ranching land. All federal land should be privately held." Based on these two claims answer the following:

   a. On what type of stasis is each sentence based?

   b. What is the general quality of the US federal government that is being implied, and how can you tell?

   c. Based on the general qualities derived from the last question, how might the US federal government be loosely defined?

   d. Based on that definition, what is the assumed fact that the rancher must make of the federal government, which may or may not be true, in order to arrive at his statement?

2. A lobbyist for the South Carolina historical society says, "The Hunley submarine is the greatest historical artifact in Charleston." Based on this sentence, answer the following:

   a. What type of claim is this?

   b. What does an audience need to have defined to understand this argument?

   c. Now, do some research and provide a definition for what is currently vague, confusing, or unknown. Based on your research and your definitions, do you agree that the Hunley submarine is the "greatest historical artifact in Charleston?" Be prepared to defend your answer in class.

3. Consider your own identity. Make a claim to fact based on your identity. Then, develop a paragraph that further refines that claim using sub-claims of definition, values, and policy.

Exercises

1. Read through one of the essays in Part Two. As a class, identify the different stases the author uses. Does any particular stasis feature more prominently than the others? Are all the stases represented?

2. Watch the following debate: http://www.intelligencesquaredus.org/debates/free-speech-threatened-campus. At the end of each speech, identify the different stases the speaker used and in what order.

3. Choose one of the articles you have found this semester during the course of your research for the Researched Argumentative Essay. Preferably, choose an article with which you disagree. Then, go through the stasis questions with the article, writing down short versions of the article's answers (e.g., What does the article say the facts are? How does the article define the important Words?). Next, go through the responses to the questions you derived from the article and ask yourself if you agree with the answers; if you disagree, write down your position (e.g., What do you think the facts are? How would you define the important words?). Finally, write a brief paragraph reflecting on this exercise. Did it help you to clarify where you disagree with your opponents? Did it help you to think about the focus of your essay? Did it help you to consider the organization of your paper or how you will use sources?

The Appeals

As you begin to think about the rhetorical situation in which you compose, the exigence to which you are responding, and the type of intervention you plan to make, you may also want to consider the two modes through which rhetors can act persuasively, which Aristotle referred to as the **artistic appeals** and the **inartistic appeals**. This is not "artistic" in its usual sense of "creative," but rather a definition that is closer to the contemporary word "artificial." Artistic appeals are those *made* by the rhetor in the text, while inartistic are those *found* and brought into the text.

Artistic Appeals

There are specific ways that rhetor, audience, purpose, and text affect the way we persuade and are persuaded; these are famously known as the artistic (*entechnic*) appeals: **ethos**, **logos**, and **pathos**. Traditionally, *ethos* is appeal to belief, *logos* is appeal to thought, and *pathos* is appeal to feeling. Often, ethos, logos, and pathos are understood as discrete and mutually exclusive parts, but they are far subtler than that.

We can better understand the artistic appeals as types of *motivation*, and Aristotle's frame as one of the first attempts at psychology: literally "studies of the soul." We are persuadable because we believe, we think, and we feel. A good piece of rhetoric makes the audience *believe, think,* and *feel* all at once. The appeals are like instruments in a symphony, members of a sports team, or spices in a meal: only when they work together do they really work well. Still, there is an ease in looking at them each individually.

- **Ethos** is the credibility of the rhetor as they present themselves in the text. To seem credible rhetors must demonstrate virtue, goodwill, and practical wisdom, each of which is discussed below. When these elements are combined together, we have an effective ethos, a rhetor who is a good person who cares about the audience and knows what they are doing.

    - **Virtue** (*arête*): a "good person" performs and embodies qualities that are valued by the audience. These can vary and even contradict, making this quite difficult. How partisan politicians describe the "other side" is a prime example of how virtue can be vice, depending on the audience. Tolerance for one audience is weakness to another, so too with passionate/hateful, principled/stubborn, humorous/cruel, etc. <u>We do not believe those we perceive to be "bad people."</u>

    - **Good will** (*eunoia*): caring about the audience is not just being nice (or not being mean); instead, caring is about relating that you as a rhetor have their interests in mind. Even in situations with a hostile audience, demonstrating that you want the best for them, rather than self-promotion, is necessary to be effective. <u>We do not believe those we perceive not to care about us.</u>

- **Practical wisdom** (*phrōnesis)*: effective rhetors have a solid and detailed understanding of the topic at hand, the assumptions of their argument, and the consequences of their proposals. You do not have to know everything, but knowing what you do know and what you do not know is vital. <u>We do not believe those we perceive not to know what they're doing.</u>

- **Logos**: While formal logic is mathematical in rigor, most of our arguments are judged by less rigid standards, such as whether or not they are "reasonable" or "probable." This standard is generally sufficient. You must have a thorough and defensible line of reasoning, but it does not *necessarily* have to be formally logical.

  - The **syllogism** is an important basic logical form consisting of premises and a conclusion that is judged by its validity and soundness. An argument is **valid** if the conclusion *necessarily* follows from the premises, regardless of the truth of the premises. However, if a valid argument also has true premises, it is **sound.** <u>It is important to differentiate truth and logic, but even more important to use them together.</u> Consider the following examples:

All zebras are jellybeans, and John is a zebra, therefore John is a jellybean.	Valid, not Sound
All humans will die, and Socrates is human, therefore Socrates will die.	Sound, Valid & True

  - **Enthymemes,** unlike the syllogisms, skip a premise—the one that "goes without saying" or "most people know to be true." These kinds of *commonplaces* are both widespread and various, so <u>knowing what premises your audience already accepts and those your argument relies on are very important</u> for effective *logos*. Consider these examples, modified from above:

John is a jellybean because he is a zebra.	"zebras are jellybeans" is implied
Socrates will die because he is human.	"all humans die" is implied

When the premise is omitted, it's up to the audience to supply it, and it is this audience participation, even if unconscious, that makes enthymemes so powerful. The audience helps create the argument, sometimes without realizing it. Because the commonplace is unstated, you need to be especially reflective about the validity of your enthymemes; often what people assume to be true is actually false.

- The **example** is another important part of rhetorical reasoning; an effective example can be a story, image, chart, or an outside source cited and quoted. Since lots of reasoning and argumentation can be abstract, presenting clear and concrete examples is vital. Be critical and reflective in what examples you use and how you use them because <u>evidence is not self-evident.</u>

- While premises can change, the logical process operates on the level of necessity. If a conclusion does not *necessarily* follow from the premises, it is a **logical fallacy**. However, because rhetoric does not rely strictly on necessity, fallacious arguments are common and even usefully persuasive. Fallacies are persuasive because a certainly reasonable and common justification for doing something is not always logical. Consider the following examples of fallacious arguments:

  > *This car is the best because it's the most popular model (ad populum)*

  > *He is wrong about immigration policy because he is a racist (ad hominem)*

  > *He's right about my illness because he's a doctor (ad verecundiam)*

- **Pathos** concerns the bodily affect of the audience, and for this reason it is the most challenging, most powerful, and most dangerous of the appeals. Making the audience feel things can be manipulative; however, if an audience doesn't feel, then believing and thinking will never turn into action. Consider the following types of pathos, but remember feeling is complex, intertwined, and messy. It may be confusing, but feelings often are.

  - **Emotions** are the most intellectual of the pathetic appeals; they are the feelings that are later named as anger, happiness, sadness, and all the nuances, degrees, and combinations of them. While Aristotle outlines some, and psychologists like Robert Plutchik have developed more complex schemes, there is no definitive guide to emotions. Therefore, try to think about <u>specific kinds, intensities, and targets of feelings, rather than ones that are simply "good" or "bad."</u>

  - **Bodily desire** is the most base of pathos; some even consider emotions and values to be illusions that hide from us our desirous, bodily being. This can be desire for food and water, safety and security, sex and reproduction, adrenaline, or even just <u>"gut feeling."</u> Advertising relies heavily on this type of pathos, and it is best to avoid it unless you are very specific, critical, and reflective about it.

  - **Moral values** are different from emotions and desires, but they are not less strongly felt. Whether they come from a particular creed, culture, or "common sense," feelings about right and wrong are especially powerful.

However, since these are deeply involved in people's ideas of identity, do not assume that your values are the right or only ones; instead, try to find common ground with your audience. <u>No one believes a villain, but patronizing isn't effective either.</u>

Inartistic Appeals

Inartistic (*atechnic*) appeals are the counterpoint to artistic appeals and refer to anything found outside and brought into the text (e.g., finding, analyzing, and integrating outside research and previous arguments on the subject). Even though each text occurs in a rhetorical situation, not everyone in the situation has the same information, background, or sources; in response to these differences, you will have to use the resources and arguments that came before you to make your own arguments recognizable, coherent, and effective. Consider the following as some types of evidence you might use:

- **Anecdotal evidence** is any story or narrative presented from your own or another's experience. Be careful because singular experiences may not resonate with general cases.

- **Testimonial evidence** is using the words of another, usually in direct quote or paraphrase. Generally, you'll want to find established authorities on the subject and think deeply about what gives them that authority.

- **Numerical evidence** is using specific statistics, measurements, dates, and times that have been established as true. However, while "numbers don't lie," people with numbers often do. Numerical evidence must be made to support your claims, which requires reflective framing and thorough explanation.

- **Graphical evidence** is any image, chart, or diagram through which you illustrate your claim. Because we generally believe what we see, images can be very powerful, but they are subject to the same framing, explanation, and scrutiny as other types of evidence.

If this all seems difficult, that is because it is. The rest of this book is dedicated to looking at the ways rhetors can navigate the different aspects of the rhetorical situation and persuade audiences. There are many risks in entering discussion, but many possible rewards as well. With a strong understanding of the rhetorical appeals and thorough practice in composition, you will have valuable tools and techniques for your future rhetorical projects not only in this course but also in your university career and other future endeavors.

Discussion Questions

1. What kind of evidence is the most persuasive? Why? Does it depend on the situation? In what cases might a scientific study be more persuasive than an anecdote? Are there times when the anecdote might be more persuasive

than the study? How does the source of either type of evidence affect its strength? In other words, how do you know what to believe, especially when evidence exists to support multiple beliefs?

2. As we see above, "logic" is a much more specific term than we might commonly understand. Except for cases of formal logic above, what do people commonly mean when they call something "logical" or reject something as "illogical"? What is the purpose of such labelling, and is it effective? Is it logical?

3. Aristotle himself was very distrustful of pathetic appeals to emotion since they could lead people to be persuaded against their own interests or promote harmful ideas and policies. Does emotion have to be suppressed, controlled, or directed? Which emotions seem particularly dangerous? Are some feelings inherently destructive or inherently beneficial?

Exercises

1. In a short writing assignment, outline what values you think define a *good person*, and explain how such a person can perform these values in their writing. Then, with a partner, compare your values and discuss how they are similar, whether they're different, and why you chose the values you did.

2. Find the course outcomes from your English 102 syllabus. In a full-class discussion, deliberate on the reasons behind these outcomes, the assumptions they rely on, whether the reasons you discovered are logical or fallacious, and whether such logicality matters.

3. Use the internet to find Aristotle's emotions from the *Rhetoric* and Plutchik's wheel of emotions. In small groups compare the similarities and differences of the two frameworks, as well as this entry. Do the models seem complete and reasonable? After you have discussed the models, combine them into a unique framework of emotions, making changes and improvements as needed. Share your framework with the class.

Audience

When writing anything—even something as trivial as a grocery list, an email, or a text message—an audience is involved. Lisa Ede and Andrea Lunsford have argued that in any rhetorical situation there are two types of audiences to be considered: **audience addressed** and **audience invoked**.

Audience addressed refers to the actual physical audience in the world to whom a rhetor is trying to communicate. It is the people gathering to hear a speech, driving past a billboard, or purchasing a book. To persuade this audience, a rhetor should research their attitudes, beliefs, values, reading habits, media consumption, and preconceived notions of the issues being discussed. Of course, the rhetor cannot know everything about every audience member, but research can help her to connect with a majority of her audience.

Audience invoked, on the other hand, refers to the audience that the rhetor invents for her text. Rhetors bring about these audiences through composition. The goal is for the rhetor to create an ideal subject for her argument, and through her language, get her addressed audience to understand themselves that way. The rhetor creates a way for her audience to perceive themselves.

Considering both your addressed audience and your invoked audience is vital to composing an effective essay. Ask yourself who needs to hear your message and who would be sympathetic to it. For example, if you are writing about the need to institute a needle exchange program in Austin, IN, you may need to address the city's principled and stubborn city council members; however, you may want to invoke an audience that is pragmatic and willing to set aside their disdain for enabling drug users in order to stop a serious HIV outbreak. The goal in this case is to get your addressed audience to see themselves as your invoked audience—to see themselves not as stubborn and principled but as reasonable and pragmatic. This strategy can be very persuasive if done with a light touch; going too far with it can come across as pandering, naïve, or insulting.

Many rhetoricians believe that the addressed audience is the most important aspect of the rhetorical situation because they are the ones who ultimately judge the effectiveness of an argument. For this reason, such rhetoricians suggest that rhetors dedicate much time and effort to researching their audiences. However, a broader version of audience complicates this idea because the texts rhetors produce are often engaged by audiences beyond the ones they intended or anticipated. For example, a scholarly essay about the impact global warming has on coral reefs would likely be intended for an audience of scientists—the author's peers who read the journal in which the article is published—however, you may end up using that article if you write an essay on coral reefs. In this situation, you would become part of the article's audience, even though the writer of the piece did not write it with you in mind.

In the digital age, it is increasingly likely that anything you write will be found by unintended audiences; consider all the times politicians have said something in "closed events" only to have their messages recorded and distributed to much larger audiences. Because of the ability for anything and everything to be shared and recorded, the digital age makes it vital for us to think deeply about what we write. In our contemporary cultural moment, it is important for rhetors to consider their intended audiences and their invoked audiences, but they should also be aware that they can never know the vastness of their possible audiences.

Discussion Questions

1. In a rhetorical situation, audience consideration is very important. However, it shouldn't always be the rhetorical element with the most focus when writing a paper because, depending on the situation, other elements could require more attention. What are some other elements in a rhetorical situation that could sometimes be just as, if not more, important than audience? What is an example of such a situation?

2. When writing an essay for class, do you ever consider an audience other than the person who will be grading it? Think about the Researched Argumentative Essay for this course, and consider who might be your audience outside of your instructor. How will you consider the audience's needs/expectations in your paper? What kind of audience would you want to invoke your instructor to be, and how would you go about invoking that identity?

3. Think of one of your personal favorite texts—poem, essay, song, etc.—what is the person/audience that the writer is invoking you to be? When you engage with that text do you see yourself as that type of person? What strategies does the author use to make you understand yourself that way? Be as specific as possible.

Exercises

1. Find an article in Part Two of this textbook, and determine who the intended audience is. For whom is the author writing? How can you tell? Are there particular phrases that identify or allude to certain people or groups? Can you point out certain instances of the audience being addressed and the audience being invoked? If so, what are the differences between the two? Write a 5–7-sentence-long paragraph that analyzes the audience of the article you found.

2. Create a list of the types of composing/writing that you do in a normal week during the semester (this may include class work, emails, to do lists, etc.). In small groups discuss the types of composing you came up with. Identify both who is the addressed audience and the invoked audience for each type of writing.

3. Think about an embarrassing situation/moment in your life. It could be from a long time ago, or it could be from yesterday. Write a short letter to your best friend recounting this incident. Then, write a short letter to your mom/dad/guardian recounting that same incident. When you're done, ask yourself what changes you made when writing about the same incident to your mom/dad/guardian and consider why you made them. Next, turn to a peer and discuss your changes with each other. Are their changes similar to yours? Why did you feel the need to make the changes you did when the audience changed?

Stakeholders

When you hold a stake in something, you care about what happens to it. For example, if you buy a new car, you care about its upkeep and maintenance; you invest time, effort, and money into the car. You have, in other words, a stake in it. People with a stake in something are referred to as **stakeholders**. They are people who affect or are affected by an issue or object. As a stakeholder in your car, you have the power to affect your car in good and bad ways. You can wash your car regularly, vacuum out the interior once a week, and conduct regular maintenance. Conversely, you can ignore these issues. Either way, you affect your car; perhaps more interestingly, your car also affects you. If your car doesn't start, you're not going anywhere. If your car radio breaks, you have nothing to listen to on your commute. Further, you are not the only one with a stake in your car's ability to function. A brief list of other stakeholders in your car includes mechanics who rely on fixing cars like yours for their livelihood, your friends who may rely on you when they need a ride to school, other drivers on the road who might be harmed if your car malfunctions, and the car manufacturers who would like to eventually sell you a new car.

When it comes to less concrete things like issues, arguments, and debates, the stakes are still important and the stakeholders as tangible. Take for instance the issue of gun rights in the United States. This controversial issue is constantly debated in part because of mass shootings such as those at Sandy Hook Elementary School in Newton, CT; Emanuel African Methodist Episcopal Church in Charleston, SC; and Pulse nightclub in Orlando, FL. People with a stake regarding gun rights and gun regulation—those who affect and/or are affected by this issue—include gun owners, law makers, the president of the U.S., gun sellers, and gun manufacturers. Of course, this list does not represent all of the potential stakeholders in this issue, just some who are immediately affected. When thinking about an issue, it can be helpful to list both who the stakeholders are and what positions they hold; doing so will help you get an idea of the whole situation. Considering the variety of stakeholder positions present in an issue will enable you to present a more complete and informed picture of the issue at hand, which will vastly improve the effectiveness of any argument you create.

When you are writing, one of the stakeholders is always you; you are invested in what you're saying and how you're saying it. Having a strong stake in an issue can make what one writes a bit biased, so it is important to take other positions seriously when doing research in order to make an informed and intellectually honest argument. In addition, understanding the stakeholders can help you determine both your addressed and invoked audience. Ask yourself: Who is affected by this issue? Who has the power to affect this issue? How do these stakeholders affect my view or argument about this issue? If I wasn't writing this argument, would I still be a stakeholder, and if so, how does that affect my writing on this issue?

Once you have answered these questions, you will have a good place to start in terms of the direction you want to take your argument, as well as in terms of how you will organize and compose your thoughts on that particular issue. Keep stakeholders in mind throughout the writing process because what you write and how you write it can make a difference to them.

Discussion Questions

1. Consider the issue of gun rights mentioned above. Besides those immediately affected by this issue (gun owners, law makers, the president of the U.S., gun sellers, and gun manufacturers), who else could have a stake in this issue? Think of all the ways in which gun rights can impact people (both negatively and positively). Who is included on the list of people you created? Are you one of them?

2. Who has a stake in you? Family and friends, of course, but in the grand scheme of things, who else could be a stakeholder in your life and in what ways? Write a paragraph explaining some of the ways in which people have stakes in you.

3. In this unit you are being asked to invent arguments. How can considering stakeholders help you to invent an argument? Consider the two purposes of invention mentioned in the unit introduction when you answer this question. Also, consider pairing a consideration of stakeholders with other types of invention such as topoi or stasis.

Exercises

1. In small groups create a list of stakeholders for the cost of college education in the United States. Then, create a graphic that illustrates the relationship(s) between these stakeholders. What does this graphic tell you about the cost of college education?

2. Imagine two stakeholders having an argument about social media's impact on interpersonal, real-world relationships. One may argue that it has a positive impact, while the other may argue it has a negative impact (or one stakeholder could even argue it has had no impact at all). Create a brief dialogue between these two people based on their individual stakes in the issue. Who are these people? What are some points they might bring up based on their stakes in the issue? Is there a "winner" in your dialogue? Should there be?

3. Brainstorm a list of the issues/ideas in which you have a stake. Make sure to choose not only political issues but also more mundane issues. Choose the issue/idea you find most interesting and write a brief paragraph on why this issue/idea matters to you and what your stake is in it. Then, write three paragraphs that take the position of another stakeholder in the issue. Finally, turn to a peer, share your paragraphs with each other, and brainstorm ways to negotiate the needs of the different stakeholders.

Kairos

The word **kairos** is one of several words the Greeks had to refer to time. Specifically, kairos expresses the sense of time as *timing* or *timeliness*—the quality of time that makes certain moments ideal for certain actions; kairos is the time in which elements come together to create opportunity. However, not everyone agrees as to when something is kairotic. For example, consider the public dialog that occurs whenever a mass shooting makes national news. Often, there is a debate as to when exactly it is appropriate to have discussions about public policy as it pertains to relevant topics such as mental health and gun control. Immediately following such a tragedy, are people too emotionally distraught to engage in a productive discourse? Is immediately having these conversations too disrespectful to the victims? Or, for fear of losing public concern and media coverage, is the best time the soonest and most emotionally ripe moment?

When considering our rhetorical situations, we have to think about how to utilize the most appropriate language at the most appropriate time. Have you ever sat in class and wanted to say something but didn't, soon feeling your ideal moment drift by along with your opportunity to make an important point? Sure, you could speak up later, but your message would certainly lose some of the rhetorical punch it otherwise would have had. Life is full of these moments, rhetorical or not, where timing seems crucial.

Since ancient Greece, kairos has been closely associated with sport because it combines timing with skill, knowledge, instinct, movement, awareness, and training. In baseball, for instance, the batter has at least three pitches to hit the ball. If the batter swings too early or too late, he'll miss, earning a strike. Of course, he could abstain from swinging altogether. So, how does the batter know when to swing and when not to swing? For one, it has to do with commonsense and deductive reasoning. But it also has to do with the athlete's prior experience, the batter's ability to recognize a bad pitch, and the ability to know when a pitch is worth hitting. The batter often has many opportunities to connect with the baseball, but he is looking for the best moment—not necessarily the only moment—to swing. But it is not only the batter who needs to consider kairos. The pitcher pays attention to other players on the field, weather conditions, his own energy levels, previous plays, the catcher's signals, and a myriad of other factors to know when, how, and where to throw the ball. All of the stakeholders in the game—players, coaches, fans, etc.—are concerned both with and about kairos.

Successful rhetoric is a balancing act among all the elements involved (writer, reader, subject matter, medium, situation, etc.); attention to kairos allows the rhetor to take full advantage of a given rhetorical situation. As the adage goes, timing is everything. How might an election year sway legislation? What does arriving late to an interview communicate to an employer? And when exactly do you make a phone call after a first date? While working through a research project, you might want to ask if any current events or upcoming anniversaries might inform how you plan to present your argument. Perhaps your research will reveal something about the history of your topic and how other writers have made use of kairos in the past. Moments tend to be fleeting, especially the best or most appropriate ones, and a poor sense of timing runs the risk of dissuading an otherwise persuadable audience.

Discussion Questions

1. Think of a moment in history (recent or distant) where the timing of a major issue was especially important. Name a specific moment or event that propagated a particular action such as passing of legislation, actions of war, political/social movements, etc. Think of famous speeches with timing that was especially apropos. What made the timing for that issue so key?

2. How might kairos affect any one of Aristotle's three artistic appeals? In other words, how might timing affect a rhetor's ethos, pathos, or logos? Offer a specific example with your answer.

3. Can a rhetor create kairos? Like with exigence, can she use the world around her to manufacture a kairos that makes others see her argument as timely whether or not it objectively is? Try to consider ways in which a rhetor might do that.

Exercises

1. Choose an essay from Part Two and examine how the author(s) utilize kairos. Is their use explicit, implicit, or both? To answer this question, you may have to do some outside research on the author(s), the subject, the sources used, or when the piece was written. Write an in-class essay that explains both how kairos functions in the essay and how you can use it as a model for mobilizing kairos in your own writing. Be as specific as possible.

2. In a group, collectively compose a fictional email to your ENGL 102 professor. In this email, you will ask for an extension on your next paper, an extra credit opportunity, or forgiveness of an absence due to extenuating circumstances. Your choice. After you have collectively composed this email and crafted it as persuasively as possible, look over the course syllabus. Choose a specific date you would hypothetically deliver this email. Why did you choose that particular date? What role did kairos play in that decision? Would there have been a time too early? Or a time too late? Explain.

3. Choose one of the various monuments on the USC campus or the Statehouse grounds. Conduct some quick, online research and familiarize yourself with the history of the monument and the person/group/event for which it was erected. Finally, write a short essay that explores the following questions:

What rhetorical purpose does the monument serve? In what way, do you think, did kairos influence the construction of these monuments? Would these buildings or monuments be erected today? If so, would they look the same or different? What events, ideologies, or beliefs would change how the monument would look if built today?

Arrangement

At the most general level, **arrangement** (*Taxis* in Greek and *Dispositio* in Latin) refers to the way the different parts of a composition are ordered. Because of the spoken context of the earliest rhetorical practice, arrangement originally concerned ordering the sections of a speech. Like the other canons of rhetoric, however, modern arrangement deals with any type of composition. While this canon may not immediately seem as important as some of the others, like invention, ancient and modern composers know that even an inventive, well written, extensively researched composition can fall flat if it is disorganized or arranged in a confusing way. As you learned in the last chapter, kairos is concerned with "the opportune moment" for an argument; in a similar way, arrangement asks you to think about "the opportune" placement of the various aspects of your composition.

While the "standard" academic essay you may have learned in high school (introduction, opposing views, point one, point two, point three, conclusion) can be a very effective organization, there are also many other options, and this unit encourages you to explore several of them. But arrangement is not just concerned with the ordering of paragraphs; rather, it includes all different levels of a composition. Within your paragraphs arrangement will help you think about the placement of your topic sentences, your claims, your supporting evidence, your transitions, and more. At certain points in history, arrangement has even been considered an important part of style because it includes the ordering of the parts *within* a sentence—the words, clauses and phrases that work together to express your ideas. The knowledge you gain about arrangement here is also applicable to compositions in any number of media and genre; whether you're working with fiction, poetry, newspaper articles, text messages, PowerPoint presentations, etc., how you arrange your arguments is vital to their effectiveness.

When thinking about and experimenting with different arrangements in your compositions, the most important thing to remember is that organization should be *effective.* More specifically, think about what kind of experience you want to orchestrate for your readers through your composition's organization. You already know that in order for your audience to be engaged with an argument, it must be timely, but kairos isn't always enough to keep them interested. An effective arrangement is one that keeps your audience engaged all the way to the end. As such, it also helps you to think through your argumentative choices. These choices include, among other things, the type of logic or reasoning you want to use, the best placement of your examples, which of your sources should go where, and which aspects of your argument are the most important. As you work through this chapter and learn about arrangement, you will explore two common types of reasoning, a contemporary model for argumentation, the classical arrangement scheme, and a number of modern strategies for arranging your arguments. As you learn about these different forms, try to identify them in the things you read (in and out of class), experiment with them in your own writing, and pay attention to what works best where—each one will have its opportune use!

Suggested Essays from Part Two

- Donald L Barlett and James D. Steele "Monsanto's Harvest of Fear"

- Jennifer Cockrall-King "Chicago: The Vertical Farm"

- Naomi Gerstel and Natalia Sarkisian "The Color of Family Ties: Race, Class, Gender, and Extended Family Involvement"

- Ken Gillam and Shannon R. Wooden "Post-Princess Models of Gender: The New Man in Disney/Pixar"

- Katrina Karkazis "Taxonomies of Intersexuality to the 1950s"

- Michael Kimmel "'Bros Before Hos': The Guy Code"

- Matthew Salesses "Different Racisms: On Jeremy Lin and How the Rules of Racism Are Different for Asian Americans"

- Constance Steinkuehler and Sean Duncan "Scientific Habits of Mind in Virtual Worlds"

Suggested Chapters from *The Everyday Writer*

- Chapter 5 "Planning and Drafting"

- Chapter 6 "Developing Paragraphs"

- Chapter 7 "Reviewing, Revising, and Editing"

- Chapter 8 "Reflecting"

- Chapter 11 "Constructing Arguments"

- Chapter 15 "Interrogating Sources and Avoiding Plagiarism"

- Chapter 16 Writing a Research Project"

Inductive Reasoning

Induction is a species of reasoning that involves making probable generalizations about the future from particular empirical instances or facts from the past. This move from particular to general is also commonly described in rhetoric textbooks as an inference from sample to population. Since we inevitably can have only a finite sample and can never be sure of the future, our conclusions are always probabilities rather than certainties.

Within this context, it makes sense to speak of the relative strength of a given inductive argument. For example, consider the following cases:

Ex: My roommate never studies and has a 4.0 GPA; therefore, studying is not a necessary part of being a successful student.

Ex: In a survey of one hundred American universities, it was found that students with a 4.0 or higher studied an average amount of 30 hours a week; therefore, putting in lots of hours studying is essential for being a successful student.

In the first case, while the premise may be true—the author's roommate may, in fact, be excelling in school without studying—the conclusion is not warranted since this is a very limited sample.

In the second case, we can see that a much more extensive sample was taken, making the conclusion much more probable; however, once again, the conclusion is not certain since it is always possible that there is a genius that doesn't need to study.

While sample size often provides some indication of a good inductive argument, things are not always that simple. Sometimes a particularly significant example can be very persuasive for a specific audience. For example, from the fact that one person was able to hack into a computer system, a group of computer engineers might infer that the computer's security system is not acceptable. Likewise, within some communities a single expert's testimony might be very convincing, as when a world-renowned scholar shares her opinion on a certain matter. In other words, though sample size is certainly something to consider, there are many cases where sample size fails to fully capture the persuasive capacity of an inductive argument.

When thinking about induction it is important to remember that we make inductive generalizations every day of our lives and would not be able to function effectively without them. Indeed, many of our decisions—from deciding where to eat or what route to take to work—rely on inductive reasoning. But these kinds of generalizations can also go awry.

We may have had our instructors write something like "generalization" on our papers when the inference from particular evidence to general conclusion does not seem warranted. In real life, we are likely to call such hasty generalizations **stereotyping**. For example, we may reason inductively that since the best students we have known in the Mechanical Engineering department are men, women do not make good mechanical engineers. Of course, such an erroneous conclusion is not only based on a small sample size but also neglects other factors such as the social emphasis on femininity, sexism in education, discrimination in STEM fields, the process we used to determine the "best students," and noteworthy exceptions to our conclusion. Thus, we can see that inductive arguments cannot only be evaluated in terms of their reasonableness but also in terms of their ethicalness. In the light of such potential for bad or unethical uses of induction, you might ask what constitutes good, effective, and ethical uses of inductive reasoning.

While there is an answer to this question, it is neither simple nor steadfast; rather, like most things in rhetoric, it is complex and contingent. According to *The Stanford Dictionary of Philosophy*, "There is no comprehensive theory of sound induction, no set of agreed upon rules that license good or sound inductive inference, nor is there a serious prospect of such a theory." In the absence of any consensus on this matter, we can think of making good inductive arguments as a situated art form. And while there is no definitive method that can guarantee good inductive arguments, as we analyze and participate in specific rhetorical situations, we learn more about what constitutes a good inductive argument within those situations.

Discussion Questions

1. Consider how induction works in your own life. For instance, when you decided to attend University of South Carolina, did you conduct a poll of everyone you knew, or did you seek out specific opinions that seemed to matter more than others? Describe what it was that made some voices louder than others. How much evidence did you need before you were comfortable making the decision? Alternatively, was your conclusion to attend USC reached deductively? If so, write out the syllogism.

2. Inductive reasoning can be very persuasive; how do you utilize it without engaging in stereotyping, making hasty generalizations, or choosing poor examples? Give specific examples (either hypothetical or from real life) in your response.

3. This entry is situated in a unit about arrangement. What is the relationship between inductive reasoning and arrangement? What is the relationship between inductive reasoning and invention?

Exercises

1. One of the most common problems with using inductive reasoning is confirmation bias, the phenomenon in which the conclusions of research

simply confirm the initial beliefs of the researcher. Confirmation bias has been used to explain why people unconsciously cherry pick examples, interpret neutral information as supporting their opinion, over-value the importance of outliers in their data sets, refuse to change their minds in the face of insurmountable contradictory evidence, and create correlations where none exist. Considering the power of confirmation bias, is persuasion even possible? Do some research on confirmation bias before writing a short essay that answers this question.

2. Using the internet, research different types of inductive fallacies. In a small group, prepare a presentation for your class that names one inductive fallacy, explains it, provides an example of it, and explains what makes it both problematic and persuasive.

3. Think about your Researched Argumentative Essay. Does it rely on inductive or deductive reasoning? If inductive, go through every element in your data set (each example, analogy, etc.) and evaluate its specific strengths. If deductive, write it out as a syllogism and test both its soundness and validity.

Deductive Reasoning

A **deductive argument** is one that relies on general premises thought to be universally true, and through valid forms of reasoning, leads to a conclusion that does not claim to be merely probable, like inductive arguments, but rather certain. You may have encountered deductive arguments in your geometry class when you were asked to prove certain theorems. In these cases, various premises could definitively prove certain conclusions beyond a shadow of a doubt. This is precisely the kind of certainty that deductive arguments attempt to provide.

Perhaps the most common type of deductive argument is called the *syllogism.* A syllogism consists of a general statement called the major premise, a specific statement called the minor premise, and a conclusion.

A famous example of a syllogism can be found below:

> *All men are mortal (Major Premise)*
>
> *Socrates is a man (Minor Premise)*
>
> *Therefore, Socrates is mortal (Conclusion)*

Notice that this argument tries to move to a particular conclusion based on a general, or universal, truth: "All men are mortal." This is the important difference between deductive arguments and inductive arguments. Deductive arguments use general principles to reach conclusions about specific cases, whereas inductive arguments use specific examples to reach a general principle.

While it is certainly important to be able to identify deductive arguments, it is also important to know how to evaluate them. Deductive arguments are evaluated on two criteria: **validity** and **soundness**. To illustrate how this works, let's consider an example. The argument above about Socrates's mortality is an example of a well-known form of deductive argumentation called *Modus Ponens.* As you can see, the form is as follows:

> All P's are Q
>
> S is P
>
> Therefore, S is Q

This is an example of a deductive argument that is valid. An argument is called valid if the form of the argument is such that the conclusion logically follows from the premises. Validity is purely a formal criterion of arguments, it does not establish that the argument is, in fact, true or false. It simply establishes that if the premises do indeed turn out to be true, then the conclusion will be true as well. In other words, the following argument is valid despite its premises being untrue:

> *All men are immortal*
>
> *Socrates is a man*
>
> *Therefore, Socrates is immortal*

This argument is still valid, but it is not *sound*. An argument is called sound when its form is valid and the premises have been found to be true. The soundness of an argument is established by interrogating the premises in terms of their truth or falsehood and determining that the premises are indeed true.

When one reads deductive arguments, often the first task is to establish whether or not the argument is valid by looking at the form of the argument and then proceeding to ask whether or not it is sound by looking at the actual content of premises and interrogating them in terms of their truth and falsehood. Keep in mind that when your instructor reads your paper, she will most likely go through some sort of process like this and will likely attempt to flesh out the argument being made and evaluate it. Sketching the deductive argument that you make or want to make is often a good idea at the pre-writing stage, at the revision stage, or at a conference with your instructor. Getting clear about exactly what you are arguing is an important step in writing a successful persuasive essay.

It should be obvious by now that there is much attractive about deductive arguments. We all would like to be able to prove our conclusions beyond a shadow of a doubt. However, despite this appeal, deductive arguments have their limitations. For example, in everyday affairs they can sound unnecessarily mechanical or formulaic since very few people argue this way. For this reason, Aristotle argues that leaving the major premise out often increases the audience's attention, and since the major premise is often something that would be obvious to the audience, there is little risk of confusion. Further, he surmises that the shortened or "truncated" syllogism that results from omitting the major premise, which he calls the **enthymeme**, forces audiences to supply this major premise. Supplying the premise, then, psychologically pre-disposes the audience to accept the truth of the argument. However, even with these advantages, the enthymeme is, in the end, still based on a deductive argument that can, in theory, be made explicit and discussed. Therefore, understanding deduction is an important part of learning to read and write effective arguments.

Discussion Questions

1. Consider the following argument:

   If it is sunny in Columbia, then he won't be wearing a coat.

   It is sunny in Columbia.

   So, he won't be wearing a coat.

   What is the major premise? The minor premise? The conclusion? Do you think this argument is valid? Why or Why not? Do you think this argument is sound? Why or Why not? If you wanted to argue against the certainty of this conclusion, how would you do it? Explain.

2. Deductive argumentation attempts to create certainty on specific issues by reasoning from general truths, but how do we know for sure any general truths are correct? As a class, create a list of truths with which you think everyone would agree and could serve as sound major premises. Then, interrogate these general truths to see if they really are certain or not. By what criteria do you judge truth?

3. This entry is situated in a unit about arrangement. What is the relationship between deductive reasoning and arrangement? What is the relationship between deductive reasoning and invention?

Exercises

1. Use the internet to find forms of deductive arguments other than *Modus Ponenus*. Create arguments using these various forms. In small groups discuss these arguments, their validity, and their soundness. What is useful about these forms and what is limiting?

2. Think about the readings you have done from Part Two of this book. Have those arguments been deductive or inductive? What kinds of arguments lend themselves to deduction and which kind lend themselves to induction?

3. Find a deductive argument in Part Two of this book, and write it as a syllogism or series of syllogisms. Then, write a paragraph explaining both the benefits and limitations of constructing arguments in this manner.

The Toulmin Model

British philosopher Stephen Toulmin developed his model of argumentation in the twentieth century after realizing that syllogisms failed to accurately represent arguments as they took place in the world. Instead of focusing on formal validity, the goal of **The Toulmin Model** was to illustrate how arguments *move* at a micro-level and how each action in an argument serves to constrain and extend the argument in a particular direction. In doing so, his model comes closer to capturing the ways people in everyday situations make arguments. For this reason, the Toulmin model is an excellent analytical tool that allows both audiences and rhetors to understand how a particular argument works, how each part of an argument functions, and what an argument's strengths and weaknesses are.

Toulmin's model begins by identifying the three basic components of an argument: the **claim**, the **data**, and the **warrant**.

- **Claim** refers to a conclusion or thesis that a rhetor seeks to establish as accepted knowledge, course of action, or value.

- **Data**, also known as evidence, is the facts, statistics, examples, or expert testimony upon which the claim is based.

- **Warrant** refers to a "general, hypothetical statement, which can act as [a] bridge" between the data and claim.

Toulmin argued that it is not enough when arguing to simply make a claim and provide evidence for it; rather, an additional step is necessary for audiences to make the jump from evidence to claim. This extra step is the warrant. Warrants explain how the data is connected to the claim. They are usually very simple statements, and in many cases they are not explicitly expressed by rhetors because the audience's cultural practices and values often allow them to infer the connection between the claim and the data on their own.

Rhetors aware of their audience's values and prejudices need not make their warrants explicit because the audience has the knowledge to infer what they mean, but identifying these moments was key for Toulmin because warrants expose cultural values and open space for deliberation of their merit. To put the first three steps together and see how an argument moves, let us consider a recent argument demanding free college:

Data		Claim
Increasing tuition prices are keeping many people from pursuing a college education in the U.S.		College in the U.S. should be free.
	Warrant	
	We should remove obstacles to a college education.	

The argument seems simple enough, but analyzing it can be difficult when the warrant is hidden. When "we should remove obstacles to a college education" is not stated, it is difficult to critique it. In other words, if warrants are not stated, then the underlying assumptions and values they represent will often be passively accepted, misinterpreted, or confused. By identifying the warrant, one opens up the space for informed debate and disagreement about the values it presupposes. Stating the warrant allows the assumption of the argument to be investigated—to have its quality, relevance, validity, and soundness critiqued.

Besides allowing us to critique the assumptions that underlie many arguments, the Toulmin model also acknowledges the conversational nature of arguments by mapping the series of moves speakers often make after laying out their claim; these moves serve to strategically anticipate and address opposition to the rhetor's claim. Toulmin identifies three such moves: the **backing**, the **rebuttal**, and the **qualifier**.

- **Backing** refers to the additional evidence provided to support the warrant.

- **Rebuttal** refers to phrases the rhetor uses to acknowledge what weaknesses or conditions the argument possesses. It is utilized in anticipation of potential refutations.

- **Qualifier** refers to the way a rhetor tells her audience how certain or strong her argument is by using words such as *mostly*, *absolutely*, *possibly*, etc.

When this additional set of moves is added to the first set, it is easy to see how the Toulmin model maps all the moves a rhetor typically makes in a single argument.

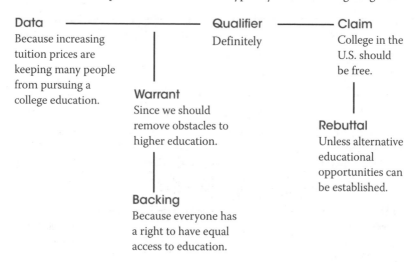

Remember, the Toulmin model maps arguments at the micro-level; it demonstrates how, though a rhetor often has an overarching claim that directs her work, the argument she provides is made up of a series of minor claims, data, and warrants. When reading and listening to arguments, try to keep track of how each argumentation chain works to move the audience to the thesis of the piece.

When attempting to apply the Toulmin model to a rhetorical act, there are a series of steps you use:

1. **Identify the claim or thesis**. Understanding where the rhetor wants the argument to go will help you start identifying the directions she has available to get there.

2. **Identify the data, or evidence, the rhetor deploys to support her thesis**. Are there statistics, expert testimony, or facts being used? If so, where does each piece of information come from, and is it both sufficient and relevant to her claim?

3. **After looking at the claim and data presented, look for a justification or explanation of why the evidence is applicable to the claim, keeping in mind that the rhetor may not have provided an explanation.** The warrant is in many cases implied. If that is the case, then think about what value or action you have to accept in order to follow the evidence to the claim. (This is in many cases the hardest thing to identify in arguments.)

4. **Once you have identified the first three steps of the Toulmin model, look to see if the rhetor offers backing, or additional evidence, to support her warrant.** Especially if the warrant is not a widely held cultural value, but rather something contested, the rhetor will more than likely try to support why she made that particular "jump" of reasoning.

5. **Next, see if the author addresses any weaknesses her argument may have by limiting the scope of her argument in a rebuttal**. Rebuttals help demonstrate the rhetor's cognizance of the rhetorical situation.

6. **Finally, look to see if the rhetor qualifies the strength of her argument.** Often, rhetors include a word or phrase in their claim that softens or boosts its force or an assertion that tells audiences how much trust they should put in the claim.

Discussion Questions

1. Does the Toulmin model successfully capture how arguments function/ move at the micro-level? Before you answer, think about a recent discussion, debate or argument you have been involved in, and use that experience to help guide your answer.

2. What do you think is the usefulness of this model—analysis, invention, arrangement? What challenges do you foresee with using it? What benefits do you think will come from using it?

3.	The Toulmin model replaced the syllogism as the way rhetoricians under-stand argumentative structure, but is it a model only for deductive reason-ing? Can this model represent inductive arguments? Could you modify the model so that it could work for both types of reasoning?

Exercises

For the following exercises, as a class, choose one paragraph from an essay in Part Two of this book to analyze. Once you have selected your paragraph, complete the following exercises in small groups. Be prepared to discuss your maps and short answers with the class.

1.	Map the argument using the Toulmin model (note: there are multiple pos-sible maps).

2.	What precisely about the argument is strong/weak? Highlight where exactly in the model the argument's strengths/weaknesses show up for you, and then write a few sentences explaining why.

3.	How would you counter argue against the author's position, or what would you add/shift to improve their argument?

Classical Arrangement

Classical arrangement incorporates the six parts of discourse that ancient rhetoric teachers believed were necessary for persuasion, especially when presenting in front of diverse audiences whose members may range from mildly skeptical to hostile.

While classical arrangement may seem to be a cookie-cutter way to structure an essay, it is not necessarily a static template: that is, simply filling in the elements does not itself constitute a successful essay. However, if you use this overall structure as a guideline, it can be a useful heuristic for developing effective arguments.

The classical arrangement consists of six parts:

1. **The Introduction (Exordium)** usually begins the essay and should engage the interest of a particular audience and focus that audience's attention on a specific argument. An effective introduction should introduce your topics, state your position on that topic, and establish your credibility to your particular audience. As you develop your exordium, ask yourself:

    - What, really, is my argument?

    - Who is my particular audience?

    - What image of myself and my stance do I want to project?

2. **The Statement of Facts (Narratio)** follows. It is necessary to provide an exigence for your audience to believe that there really *is* a problem demanding concern; rhetors often combine this step with the introduction. The statement of facts should provide background information necessary to orient your particular audience to the problem and your argument. As you develop your narratio, ask yourself:

    - What is the situation to which this argument is responding?

    - What elements of background or context do I need to present for this particular audience?

3. **The Division (Partitio)** is, according to the Roman rhetorician Quintilian, the most effective way to continue. The division summarizes the argument(s) you are about to make. Think of it as a plan or map of your argument, which will allow your audience to know in advance where you are headed, even if they do not know the particular proof, or ways in which you will escort them through your argument. As you develop your partitio, ask yourself:

    - What is my thesis?

    - Where do I want my argument to end?

    - How do I want to take my audience to this particular end?

4. **The Proof (Confirmatio)** presents the essential claims and evidence that support and substantiate the thesis of your argument. These claims are often made and evidenced through rhetorical appeals. In other words, the proof provides the answer to "why should anyone agree with me?" As you develop your confirmatio, ask yourself:

- What proof supports my thesis? *Is my audience likely to respond to this support?*

- To what proof would my audience be *least* likely to respond?

- How can I demonstrate that my proof is valid and applicable to my argument?

5. **The Concession and Refutation (Refutatio)** allows you to acknowledge other viewpoints and appeal to an audience that may be particularly skeptical. That is, usually you will be making an argument toward an audience who doesn't necessarily agree with your point of view: why would you be making an argument to an audience who already agrees with everything you say? Therefore, because both arguments and audiences are multi-faceted, this part of the classical arrangement gives you the chance to address the complexities of your argument and audience while pointing out the shortcomings of other points of view. As you develop your refutatio, ask yourself:

- What counterarguments or hesitations is my audience likely to harbor?

- How can the weaknesses in my argument be modestly acknowledged without undermining my entire stance?

- What shortcomings in opposing arguments might I highlight?

6. **The Conclusion (Peroratio)** reiterates your argument as forcefully and memorably as possible. This means that, if you want your audience to remember what you have said, simply restating your thesis or repeating your proof isn't enough. Ancient rhetoricians often advocated for using pathos heavily in the conclusion to forge an emotional connection between your audience and your argument. Creating this emotional investment provides a different type of force than facts alone and, often, makes your argument more memorable. As you develop your peroratio, ask yourself:

- What do I want my audience to remember most about my argument?

- Am I simply repeating what I have already said? What are the broader implications of my argument?

- Is my conclusion doing the rest of my paper justice? (That is, is it furthering all of the work I've done by memorably driving home my point?)

Discussion Questions

1. When would classical arrangement be beneficial to an argument; in other words, what types of arguments would be best articulated through this form of arrangement?

2. What are ways of molding or playing with classical arrangement that would allow it to work differently? In order to answer this question, you should consider how classical arrangement works as delineated above, how it might work differently, and the ways you would have to change it in order to make it work differently.

3. While the above outline illustrates the different components of classical arrangement and their purposes, it does not explain how much space should be dedicated to each section in relation to the entire argument. What sections do you think would take the longest to write and why? Which sections do you think would take the longest to read and why? Ultimately, what section do you think is the most vital for persuasion?

Exercises

1. Go online and listen to Dr. Martin Luther King Jr's speech, "I Have a Dream." Outline the classical moves he makes in this speech. Then, in a separate paragraph, answer the following questions: Are his movements all classically arranged? Does he rearrange any of the classical elements? What might be the purpose for the arrangement he uses?

2. Using a paper you have written in the past (whether for this or a previous class) outline the arrangement you've done. Is the arrangement working for your purpose and your intended audience? (Do you know what your purpose is or who your intended audience is?) Rearrange your paper to follow the classical arrangement guidelines. How does the argument work differently after you've rearranged it?

3. While outlining your next paper, first outline it following the classical arrangement structure, then consider:

   a. How is this outline working toward your purpose and intended audience?

   b. Do you think this is a structure that will do your paper justice?

   c. Should any of the elements be rearranged in a way that will better serve your argument? Why?

Rogerian Argument

A **Rogerian Argument** is another format writers use to craft effective arguments. It operates on the belief that a writer's presentation of goodwill and her willingness to compromise are sometimes the quickest route to solving a problem or easing a disagreement. Rogerian arguments persuade by highlighting the common ground between opposing positions and using that common ground to work toward a solution to some, if not all, aspects of the issue.

A Rogerian argument often consists of five sections. Keep in mind that one section does not necessarily equal one paragraph but rather can include as many paragraphs as necessary:

1. **Introduction:** In this section, the writer provides an overview of the problem or topic about which she is arguing. The overview should include any background information an audience needs to understand the depth and complexity of an argument and its rhetorical situation. For example, a writer arguing in favor of the Black Lives Matter movement would likely compose an introduction summarizing the historical and cultural contexts that shaped what she sees as a demand for justice and equality, the contemporary situations that led to the birth and proliferation of the movement, and the types of actions and initiatives in which the organization is involved.

2. **Summary of Opposing Positions:** Here, the writer describes the opposing sides' arguments. The purpose of this section is to inform rather than persuade, so all positions must be presented with as much objectivity as possible. The writer of the Black Lives Matter argument mentioned previously could use this section to define the perspectives contrary to her own—such as people associated with the Blue Lives Matter movement and people who generally disagree with social protest. Not only will fair treatment of different viewpoints help build her credibility as an informed speaker, but also it will serve as a powerful gesture of goodwill and sympathy towards those with whom she disagrees.

3. **Statement of Understanding:** After outlining the argument, the writer establishes common ground between opposing positions by acknowledging aspects of her opponents' beliefs that she considers valid. The writer focusing on the Black Lives Matter movement could ground her argument in how most people invested in this issue—whether for it or against it—believe that non-violence is the best way to effect change and their shared dedication to building safer communities. By building her argument on points of agreement, the writer increases the likelihood that her readers will listen to, and thus potentially be persuaded by, her ideas.

4. **Statement of the Writer's Position:** This section allows the writer to argue in favor of her position. This section includes the evidence (outside sources,

inductive/deductive reasoning, examples, etc.) needed to establish her points. Although the purpose of this section is to persuade, it should do so with the goal of reconciling with the opposition, not defeating it. Remember, the strength of the Rogerian Argument is its ability to connect with the opposition, not to alienate it. During this section the writer should build her argument on the shared values she described in the previous section. The writer focusing on the Black Lives Matter movement, then, would want to reach out to those who are skeptical of the movement and invoke their best natures rather than alienate them by using negative labels or ignoring their concerns.

5. **Conclusion:** Finally, the writer presents a solution that appeals to everyone. An effective conclusion should highlight how accepting the writer's position on the issue-at-hand would benefit all parties, even if total agreement cannot be reached. To draw from the Black Lives Matter example once more, the argument may not fully solve the issues it addresses, but it should suggest ways to move forward and bring about mutually beneficial change.

Discussion Questions

1. The Rogerian format is based not only on demonstrating the goodwill of the rhetor but also assuming goodwill on the part of those with whom she disagrees. Many people find this latter step difficult. Why is it so hard to see those with whom we disagree on political and social issues as good people? Why is it so much easier to see them as stupid, ignorant, or nefarious? Think of several specific examples to discuss while answering this question.

2. Think of an issue that would work well with the Rogerian format. Explain your choice. Conversely, think of an issue that would not work well with the Rogerian format. What are the differences between the two issues?

3. Thinking of the issues you identified in question two as inappropriate for the Rogerian format, could you think of ways to modify the Rogerian argument so that the topic would fit well with the arrangement?

Exercises

1. Find an article in Part Two of this book. Conduct a reverse outline of the article to get a clear sense of its arrangement. Consider how effective the author's arrangement is—both its strengths and weaknesses. Then, restructure the argument to follow a Rogerian format. What does this shift in arrangement change? Does it make the argument more or less persuasive? Why?

2. In small groups pick an issue or problem that is highly divisive. Outline the main points of argument for each position and find places of possible consensus. Discuss the areas of agreement between opposing parties and

develop a "Statement of Understanding" that meets the goals of the Rogerian format. Make sure your paragraph treats both sides fairly and ethically while finding common ground and pointing towards shared goals.

3. As a class, discuss some of the different arguments you are writing for your Researched Argumentative Essays. Then, choose one person's argument that you all think will work well in the Rogerian format and create a Rogerian outline for it. Then, choose one person's argument that you all think will not work well in the Rogerian format and create a Rogerian outline for it. Reflect on the process of outlining each argument. What did you learn about the Rogerian format, the arguments, or yourselves?

Poetics

If you were to define poetry as potentially anything not written in a conventional paragraph or prose form, you wouldn't be far off. One difficulty in thinking about and trying to define **poetics** as a whole is that there are countless variations. Most of us are familiar with poetry written in traditional forms—sonnets, haiku, monologues, story-telling epics, etc.—that are written about cliché topics—love, personal identity, the meaning of life, etc.—but beyond this is a massive, and potentially overwhelming, variety of compositions. Experimental poetry creates new and interesting interactions between imagery, metaphors, subject matter, language, syntax, and a host of other elements. With all of this variety, sometimes poetry seems to have no recognizable form at all. If the concept of poetics includes everything up to formless poetry, what's our next move in working to read and understand poetry?

The difficulty with any particular poetic form is when it strays into the unfamiliar—away from characters, descriptions, or plot lines; away from sentences, clauses, or phrases; away from clear communication, purpose, or point. Poems often break and create rules at the level of language itself, refusing to give the audience something they usually take for granted, like a recognizable complete sentence. Such language manipulation often forces us to think outside of familiar structures. But even the most frustrating and inaccessible forms are not merely random nonsense; instead, they are working to push our brain into new and unfamiliar, often uncomfortable, modes of thinking. And in the world of reading poetry and confronting poetic forms, confusion and frustration are actually good things. Broadly speaking, poetry serves to question, critique, or actively oppose mainstream norms, dominant ideas, and systems in order to explore other possibilities, and poetics does this work not only through its content but also through its innovation of form and language.

This innovation can be thought of as a poem's rhetoric or rhetorical strategies. Poems differ from academic research and argumentative writing in that they are not expected to follow (and often don't follow) a clear logic or arrangement that is accessible to a large audience. Poetry tends to make its business the opposite, but in doing so, it allows for creative rhetoric that may appeal to an audience in ways that logical, researched writing may not be able. It can be productive to think of poetry as achieving a different kind of rhetorical status or effect by refusing the things traditionally associated with a good argument (clarity, accessibility, logic) and replacing them with something else.

Once you identify this fundamental difference, you can consider ways in which these defining characteristics and effects of poetry can, in turn, complement your research and argumentative writing. Academic writing after all still incorporates narrative, creative metaphors, and vivid imagery; it still engages the reader with dynamic syntactic and structural choices. After you've gotten a sense of the new, unusual, and possibly bizarre places that poetics can take you, consider how you might make these forms your own in order to enliven and innovate your research and writing.

Incorporating poetics into your argumentative prose adds a depth, richness, and texture they might otherwise lack. Sure, we could just "tell" our audience in "clear, understandable sentences" what we want to say; we could just "get to the point," but this notion of getting to the point isn't always as central as it might seem; this is true in your argumentative prose and even in a simple, everyday scenario like traveling from point A to point B. For example, when you go to school, you probably drive a car, ride a bicycle or moped, or maybe you walk. Maybe you go on a skateboard, a unicycle, a magic carpet, or a jet pack. Maybe you teleport to school, jump in a wormhole, or carpool. However you got there, the *point* is that you are now at school. But points are easy and don't always tell us much. The *experience*, the thing that really begins to define your day or say something about your life and the world you live in is, in this case, your form of transportation. The sounds, the structure, the feeling of form is important to the human experience. Each iteration of these elements offers different experiences and perspectives of the world; each has different interactions with and effects on the environment; each establishes you in a particular relation to other people; each expresses certain values and possibilities. Poetics do the same; whether in poetry or prose.

Discussion Questions

1. Based on your own personal experiences with and memories of reading poems, what are the main characteristics of poetry? What are poems supposed to do? What is it like to read poetry? For whom are poems written?

2. Poetry can approach a subject matter or argue for a perspective indirectly—without following a familiar line of logic or using peer-reviewed statistics or evidence. Do you think this is an ethical problem? As a class, read a poem and explore different answers to that question.

3. Is there anything poetic about your Researched Argumentative Essay? What overlap do you see between these two seemingly disparate genres? How might we consider poets to be rhetors? How might we consider rhetors to be poets?

Exercises

1. Using the internet, find a complex poetic form; do some research on its origins and nuances. Then, rewrite your argumentative essay for this class in that form. What changes about your argument when it is remediated into

poetry? What are the benefits of this form to your argument? Conversely, what are the drawbacks?

2. Since many poets make up their own rules and restrictions out of thin air, there is no reason you can't do the same. Try writing with your own rules through this exercise:

    a. Create five of your own rules for writing a new poem; perhaps you want to specify line length, require only words with a certain number of letters, make each line have one more syllable than the previous, or dictate certain predetermined words to be used a certain number of times. These are your rules, and they can be *anything*.

    b. Write your poem. As you do, pay attention to how the rules you've created force you into new ways of thinking and using language, even on just a small scale.

    c. Exchange rules with a classmate. Try to write a second poem—on the same topic as your first—that uses their rules. Compare the experience of obeying your own writing rules and obeying theirs.

3. Go through the sources you've gathered for your Researched Argumentative Essay, paying attention to the relationship between authors and arguments. Then create a collage—it could be textual, visual, sonic, or tactile—that represents your rhetorical situation without your voice intervening. In other words, try to accurately describe the field of discussion without using any of your own language. How would you describe what you have created: rhetoric, poetics, art, remix, garbage?

Style

Despite being one of the five canons of rhetoric (and thus supposedly central to the art of persuasion), **style** often gets underestimated and undersold as "mere ornamentation" or worthless decoration to be layered on top of the more important ideas or concepts that make up our writing and speaking. However, style involves all of the performances we make in our language; it is how we connect to audiences through particular choices of words, tone, gestures, and ideas. Style is the glue that connects the other canons to one another. We invent arguments while considering how we want to style ourselves and our beliefs through them. We anticipate delivering claims to certain audiences, and we identify with those audiences—just as we help those audiences identify us—through the values we make apparent through our stylistic decisions.

This doesn't mean that style is all about "pretending" or otherwise acting artificially or inauthentically. Rather, we usually recognize that there are often better (or worse) ways to go about persuading certain audiences. For example, you may face skepticism or resistance if you tell people you're a Gamecocks fan while you're dressed in orange and purple. Or, if you've ever asked family for money, you might have found that certain approaches worked better than others, depending on who you asked (e.g., politeness, forthrightness, compliments made before the request, etc.). Similarly, you probably haven't turned in many assignments for your college classes in neon green, 17-point Comic Sans text printed on cardboard. These decisions are tactical but they are not disingenuous.

To put it another way, style is a part of everything we do in the world and everyone with whom we communicate. You can't escape style, although there are certainly times when you might not, or definitely do not, know you're infusing certain kinds of style into your words and actions. Part of becoming a more skilled rhetor, then, is recognizing how to employ style more effectively when communicating with others—highlighting or emphasizing those stylistic decisions we think might be most appropriate and useful while downplaying or avoiding those that might not be so helpful.

In this section, you'll learn about some concepts that are tied very closely to style. It's not accurate to say that they're hierarchically subordinate to style, but it's impossible to consider either of these concepts without keeping style clearly in mind. First, you will read about **voice**, which refers to the means by which authors identify themselves in connection to others and makes themselves stand out; attitude, orientation, language choice, and other qualities all contribute to the construction of an effective and recognizable voice. Then, you will read about **genre**, which refers to kinds, or types, of communication that have recognizable rhetorical and formal features; when multiple authors work toward similar ends, they often build on established conventions as well as on each other's ideas and forms (although, as with everything else related to communication, these resemblances are context-specific and change over time). Through these two readings, then, you will get a sense of how to both mobilize your personal style and utilize conventional styles developed through tradition in order to create effective arguments.

Suggested Essays from Part Two

- Michael Idov "When Did Young People Start Spending 25% of Their Paychecks on Pickled Lamb's Tongues?"

- Ariel Levy "Either/Or: Sports, Sex, and the Case of Caster Semenya"

- Haiming Liu and Lianlan Lin "Food, Culinary Identity, and Transnational Culture: Chinese Restaurant Business in Southern California"

- Bill McKibben "The Only Way to Have a Cow"

- Pepper Schwartz "The Social Construction of Heterosexuality"

- Margaret Talbot "Brain Gain: The Underground World of 'Neuroenhancing' Drugs"

- David Treuer from *Rez Life: An Indian's Journey Through Reservation Life*

- Taylor M. Wells and Alan R. Dennis "To Email or Not to Email: The Impact of Media on Psychophysiological Responses and Emotional Content in Utilitarian and Romantic Communication"

Suggested Chapters from *The Everyday Writer*

- Chapter 17 "Academic Work in Any Discipline"

- Chapter 18 "Writing for the Humanities"

- Chapter 19 "Writing for Social Sciences"

- Chapter 20 "Writing for the Natural and Applied Sciences"

- Chapter 21 "Writing for Business"

- Chapters 26–29 "Language"

- Chapters 30–35 "Style"

Genre Conventions

Science fiction, action, romantic comedy, drama. These categories of movies—or **genres**—are pervasive in popular culture and make regular appearances in our everyday conversations. Similarly, the idea of musical genres is so commonplace in twenty-first-century American society that you will more than likely be familiar with at least a few *sub-genres*, like gangsta rap or indie rock. While these everyday uses of genre are probably familiar to you, you may not have heard the term used in reference to literature or academic writing. In fact, genre ("a kind" in French) is applicable to any compositional endeavor—including English essays, lab reports, and even business presentations. As such, understanding how genres work is important for developing your skill in composing.

When we think of different genres of movies or music, we usually think of certain characteristics that the genre tends to include. For instance, science fiction movies often concern time travel, and many country songs include references to pick-up trucks. In an academic context, we call these tendencies **conventions** of the genre. When reading (or viewing or listening to) a composition, **genre conventions** help the reader understand what an author is trying to do, as well as the context in which they are composing. In an academic essay, one genre convention is to place the thesis statement at the beginning or end of the introduction; this practice helps readers to understand the purpose of the essay. In fact, because this is expected, placing your thesis statement somewhere else runs the risk of confusing your reader and making your arguments less effective. These conventions are what allow your audience to recognize your arguments, so in a certain sense, the genre conventions actually help you to *create* your composition. That said, it is important to remember that genre conventions are not hard-and-fast; they are not rules. In other words, not all compositions in a genre will use every convention. Some science fiction doesn't use time travel at all; instead, it may rely on futuristic or seemingly impossible technology. In the same way, not every country song includes pick-up trucks but is still identifiably country because of its instrumentation and chord patterns. Most compositions, no matter their medium, will use enough conventions that the reader can easily identify their genre.

While categorizing a composition is often an easy task, composers also experiment with conventions, sometimes using multiple genres to create new (and strange) effects. Because of this experimentation, genre conventions are constantly changing. Think of pop music from the 1980s—one of its conventions was the heavy use of synthesized instruments. But as music preferences changed—as hip hop, rap, grunge, and even punk music became more mainstream—pop music changed as well (or it wouldn't be popular anymore). For pop composers who were trying to evolve their genre, one of the most effective tactics was to incorporate aspects of other genres; they used more hip-hop beats, the overdriven guitar of grunge, and different vocal techniques to keep up with their audience. When we get to the twenty-first century, then, we recognize the pop genre by a vastly different set of conventions, and '80s pop often feels dated (at least until it becomes fashionable again). Academic writing has developed in similar ways. For instance, because the internet is such a ubiquitous resource, academic citation practices have had to adapt, incorporating URLs and online databases. Further, with the development of online journals, scholars can now publish articles as web pages, which use a set of conventions quite different from traditional academic journals. Paying attention to these changes, and especially the different tactics composers use to address them, is an effective strategy for gaining insight into their work. In your own compositions, too, being aware of how you are using genre conventions—whether you are conforming to them, ignoring them, resisting them, or helping them grow—is an invaluable tool for crafting your arguments and creating a relationship with your audience.

Discussion Questions

1. How does the use of genre conventions change the legitimacy of a composition? As an example, in the movie *Sean of the Dead*, how does the incorporation of the comedy genre affect the movie's legitimacy as a Zombie flick?

2. Other than musical tastes, what are some of the factors that can influence the way genre conventions change? Are some of these factors more powerful than others?

3. What are all of the conventions of the academic research essay? Do these conventions change due to academic sub-genres? Can you think of any examples?

Exercises

1. Choose your favorite genre and list out as many of its conventions as you can. If you were to compose your own genre piece, which of these would you use? Leave out? Why?

2. Take a piece that you've read for this course and pretend you're going to "translate" it into another genre. In order to do this, what conventions of the new genre will you use? How do the new conventions change the original piece? Keep in mind genre transcends medium, so it is possible to have a hip-hop essay or a science fiction album.

3. List as many different written genres as you can. Do any of these overlap? If so, in what ways? Why do you think this is the case?

Voice

When we talk about **voice** in rhetoric, we are referring to the way an author expresses his or her attitude towards a *topic* and an *audience*. For instance, let's say a physicist has written a scholarly article in the field of physics, and the article discusses the complexities of string theory in explaining our universe at its earliest stages of development. Here might be an excerpt:

> String tension T is the only dimensionful quantity in string theory, using the parameter called the Regge slope.

What is clear right away is that the voice of the physicist expresses a scholarly attitude towards the topic. It is also clear that the voice assumes the audience understands the highly mathematical language of physics (*"tension T," "dimensionful quantity," "parameter," "Regge slope"*). But what if the physicist were to give a talk about string theory to a class of third graders? To be effective, her voice would have to modulate so that it is much less scholarly and technical and a bit more entertaining. The physicist might say something like this:

> To understand what string theory is about, imagine the universe full of billions of guitar strings being played at once. Isn't that cool?

Here the physicist's voice shifts to a more engaging, playful attitude towards both the audience and the topic (*"imagine the universe," "billions of guitar strings," "Isn't that cool"*). As a result, the physicist's voice may accomplish less technical precision, but it gains more for third grade attention. Now consider if the physicist had switched voices for her audiences. That is, the first quote above is said to the children, and the second quote is written in a scholarly journal. The third graders' reception of the topic would have certainly fallen flat, and no scholarly journal would have published her article.

For voice to be most effective rhetorically, it is important to understand that you must carefully calibrate your attitude towards topic and audience based on your *purpose*. As in the physicist's two quotes, one was meant to inform and discuss, the other to entertain and motivate.

Voice can be difficult to control if an author has an inflexible attitude about the topic and audience. Take, for example, a Black Lives Matter activist writing about racial injustice in a conservative newspaper. For the voice of this author, we might assume that the activist is already passionate about the topic and extremely angry towards the audience. The author will have to decide what the purpose is for engaging a conservative audience so as to determine what type of voice to use. For instance, is the purpose to enrage the audience or connect with the audience? In the following two quotes, clearly the first is meant to anger the audience while the second is meant to find common ground.

- *Until America locks up its murderous cops for destroying our black communities, blacks will never be free in a land of white terrorism.*

- *As we fight for justice together, let us work to achieve more fairness in how neighborhoods of color are policed, while seeking cooperation and peace between law enforcement and black citizens.*

Discussion Questions

1. Discuss the importance of voice in your English class—both when you speak and when you write. What changes in voice do you notice in yourself and your peers as you converse, peer edit, and revise? Are these changes due to the topic, the audience, and/or the purpose? Explain your answer and give specific examples.

2. Gauge and discuss the style of your written voice in this English class. What aspects of the class should you be considering as you modulate your voice? Explain.

3. Do you have an authentic voice—one that represents your truest self? Can you have multiple authentic voices? Is it possible to have an inauthentic voice? How do you gauge authenticity?

Exercises

1. Consider how the previous two examples above shift the voice of the activist. How does each indicate the author's attitude towards policing in America (*topic*) and towards law-and-order readers (*audience*)?

2. As you examine the two examples of the activist's voice, note the word choices (the first's *murderous cops* and *land of white terrorism* versus the second's *fight for justice together* and *seeking cooperation and peace*). What attitudes does each example express? What role do pronouns play in these examples, and how can you incorporate that into your own writing?

3. Read the following excerpt from the Oscar-winning movie *Norma Rae*, and explain how voice is used and expressed by the lead character, Norma Rae Webster. Norma Rae was a real-life union organizer in North Carolina. In the film depiction, she is shown fighting for better wages at her hometown textile plant in Roanoke Rapids in the 1970s. Below is part of her speech in which she calls her fellow laborers into a strike for better wages. Be sure to consider word choice, topic, and audience as you describe and explain Norma Rae's voice. After you have analyzed the passage, use the internet to find the scene. Watch the clip, and consider what else occurs that makes Norma Rae rhetorically effective. Can we consider these things as voice as well?

    - (After pursuing plans to unionize her plant, Norma Rae walks to the middle of the textile plant while being followed by a plant security guard who has been ordered to remove her from the premises. As she turns around, she makes this speech to both the guard and other workers in the plant, and then stands on a table, holding a sign that says, "UNION." Within minutes all the laborers have shut off their textile machines and joined Norma Rae in a strike.)

NORMA RAE: *I'm staying put! Right where I am! It's gonna take you, and the police department, and the fire department, and the National Guard to get me outta here! I'm waitin' for the sheriff to come and take me home! And I ain't gonna budge till he gets here!*

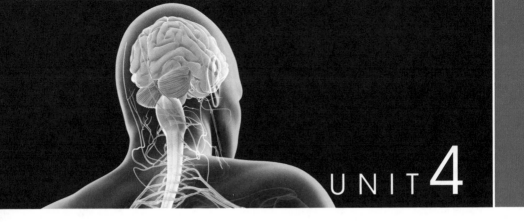

Memory

As the fourth of the five rhetorical canons, memory is essential to rhetorical study; however, it also exceeds rhetoric in the sense that it is a foundation for other disciplines such as history, psychology, and more recently, neuroscience. Rhetorical memory was valued in antiquity, as Aristotle delineates in his influential work *On Memory and Reminiscence* where he claims that memory is both "an object of contemplation and a mnemonic token" both of which have been "conditioned by the lapse of time." In other words, for Aristotle, memory is usually conceived of as both the *ability* to remember (our brain function of memory) and *what* is remembered (our memories of the past).

As is perhaps made obvious by Aristotle's dedication of an entire work to the canon, memory's rhetorical value stems from the classical tradition in which arguments and other forms of communication were performed aloud in a public forum. Memory was essential for an effective orator; that is, ancient orators needed to memorize their speeches in order to deliver them to the public. For the Greeks, a strong memory was indicative of intelligence, and relying upon written notes or reminders was not only frowned upon, but it was a sign of a weak mind. In Plato's *Phaedrus*, for example, Socrates claims that "If men learn the art of writing it will implant forgetfulness in their souls: they will cease to exercise memory because they rely on that which is written, calling things to remembrance no longer from within themselves."

Traditionally, rhetorical memory is valued for three main capacities, the first of which is that it **allows us to remember our argument** as well as **how we want to deliver that argument**. Usually this applies to speeches and other oral communication. Think about speakers you've witnessed (for example, the president of the United States giving a speech or your teacher delivering a lecture). Are those speakers more powerful if they read verbatim from a script or if they make eye contact with the audience, engaging what they are saying with how they are saying it in both tone and body language?

Memory's second function refers to our **words themselves being memorable**. That is, in tandem with the other four canons, which work together to make our arguments persuasive, memory is what allows the audience the ability to remember (in order to apply) what we have said. That is, there would be little value in being persuasive if our audiences would forget what we persuade them to do.

The third traditional element of this canon is that **memory can act as a storage space** or bank for archiving important information. Classical rhetoricians described this as a treasury through which the orator navigates, saving valuable facts, quotes, or anecdotes for later use.

It is important to note that in these three elements of classical memory, memory operates as a *tool for humans*: that is, memory is a capacity which humans possess (the ability to remember), the thing itself that is remembered, as well as the storage space from which what is remembered is retrieved. The central force surrounding memory in the classical conception, then, is the human. Overall, this understanding has changed very little since its inception and is still the most widely accepted. However, some philosophers have explored memory in a different way. Friedrich Nietzsche, for example, valorizes forgetting over remembering in claiming that "there could be no happiness, cheerfulness, hope, pride, immediacy, without forgetfulness." Others—such as Henri Bergson and Paul Ricoeur—deviate from the classical understanding of memory by exploring memory's potential for productively functioning **outside human control**. That is, this scholarship attempts to view memory as that which is not *simply* memorization: it explores what is made possible through forgetting, or through *not* remembering.

While these philosophers are perhaps most well-known within rhetorical memory studies itself, more contemporary scholarship (in trauma studies and neurorhetorics, for example) has begun to overlap and develop in tandem with memory studies. And while this cross-pollination and consideration of forgetting has not detracted from the importance of a classical understanding of memory, it has provided alternate and perhaps more productive ways of conceiving memory's rhetorical potential.

That is to say, memorization is certainly a crucial strategy for our education system today: how would you have survived elementary school without remembering the sequence of letters that would allow you to pass spelling tests? Or high school without being able to memorize a few history dates or mathematical sequences? However, while this type of memorization is certainly valuable, it is not the only way memory can be productive. In fact, an over-fidelity to memorization can be detrimental to the composition process. For example: in order to analyze another text, event, problem, etc.—we must be able to both consider what we *do* remember (what we think we "know" based on observation) as well as the possibility for alternate solutions—ones that are speculative, or, perhaps, ones which we have forgotten and then, in the process of forgetting, recreate.

Discussion Questions

1. What do you think memory is? How is it valuable to your compositions?

2. In what ways might remembering be valuable for your writing process? Conversely, in what ways might forgetting be valuable for your writing process?

3. It is clear that memory used to be very important for composition, but in contemporary society—with our ability to take notes, save documents, copy and paste information, bookmark websites, and mark e-books—is memory still as valuable? Is memory different than it used to be?

Exercises

1. Compose a short paragraph to deliver orally (to a roommate, friend, classmate, etc.) Try to memorize the paragraph for its delivery. What do you notice about your composition process (i.e., because you know you will have to memorize this paragraph)? What are some benefits of memorizing your own composition? What are some drawbacks?

2. Write down three topics you feel confident discussing on a piece of paper and exchange topics with a partner. For five minutes, research one of your partner's topics you'd like to know more about and develop three questions for your partner. Ask each other your questions. Neither is allowed to use research materials in answering questions; you must rely on your memories. After exchanging and answering questions, reflect on the process.

3. Compare a studio version of one of your favorite songs to a live version. What are the differences and similarities? How does memory play into the performance itself? How does memory play into your experience as an audience member?

Suggested Essays from Part Two

■ Joni Adamson "Indigenous Literatures, Multinaturalism, and *Avatar*: The Emergence of Indigenous Cosmopolitics"

■ Petra Doan "The Tyranny of Gendered Spaces: Reflections from Beyond the Gender Dichotomy"

■ Linda Holtzman and Leon Sharpe "Theories and Constructs of Race"

■ Barbara Kingsolver "You Can't Run Away on Harvest Day"

■ Marion Nestle "Eating Made Simple"

- Jesse J. Prinz "Gender and Geometry"

- Akiba Solomon "Thugs. Students. Rioters. Fans: Media's Subtle Racism in Unrest Coverage"

- Marcelo M. Suárez-Orozco and Carola Suárez-Orozco "How Immigrants Become 'Other'"

Suggested Chapters from *The Everyday Writer*

- Chapters 57–60 "MLA Documentation"

- Chapters 61–64 "APA Documentation"

- Chapters 65–67 "Chicago Documentation"

Delivery

Delivery, the fifth and final canon of rhetoric, focuses on the ways in which messages are presented, conveyed, or displayed. When thinking about delivery, you're focusing on *how* you say what you intend to say. After all, there are many ways to convey a message without using words, such as wearing black at a funeral to signal mourning or crossing your arms when you feel defensive. Aristotle, one of the fundamental philosophers who wrote about rhetoric, describes delivery as having "as much to do with oratory as with the poetry . . . It is, essentially, a matter of the right management of the voice to express the various emotions—of speaking loudly, softly, or between the two; of high, low, or intermediate pitch; of the various rhythms that suit various subjects." In this way delivery focuses on the medium of a message, while also acknowledging that the medium expresses meaning.

As the rhetorical canons were once used predominantly for the crafting of oral speeches, delivery focused on the speaker's tone of voice, volume, stance, hand gestures, and so on; today, delivery can refer to many different aspects of your message, depending on the media with which you are working. For example, when crafting a written piece, your choices of font, paper style, and paragraph breaks can all affect how your message is delivered and what additional or supplemental meaning is carried along with it. When putting together a short film, choices such as music, camera movements, and transitions should be considered. If you create a poster, colors, lines, and images are additional things to think about. Each medium comes with its own considerations.

All of the possibilities can be a little overwhelming, but the important thing to remember is to be **purposeful** in your decisions. Each method of delivery provides **opportunities and constraints**; keeping your goals in mind will help you choose your medium based on its unique characteristics. For example, if you want to share your message with a global community, a digital video would afford you the ability to reach more people than a poster, but the video will also make your message less spontaneous, since people will have to choose whether or not to access it rather than having it appear unsolicited as they walk by.

After choosing a medium, the question becomes how to utilize its opportunities and constraints when you **design** your argument. As you consider how you want your audience to interact with your message, you are thinking about delivery. For example, if you choose to make a video you may want it to be fun, frustrating, interesting, disorienting, or something else entirely. The medium creates opportunities and constraints, but it is up to the rhetor to design the argument within these parameters so as to persuade her audiences in certain ways.

Suggested Essays from Part Two

- Diane Goldstein "I'm a Cop and I Support Black Lives Matter: How Can We Heal These Wounds?"

- Jane McGonigal "Becoming Part of Something Bigger Than Ourselves"

- Ruth Padawer "When Women Become Men at Wellesley"

- HRH the Prince of Wales "On the Future of Food"

- S. Sayyid "A Measure of Islamophobia"

- Susan Schneider "*Mindscan*: Transcending and Enhancing the Human Brain"

- Nicola Twilley and Cynthia Graber "Why the Calorie Is Broken"

- Bryan Wuest "Stories like Mine: Coming Out Videos and Queer Identities on YouTube."

Suggested Chapters from *The Everyday Writer*

- Chapter 22 "Making Design Decisions"

- Chapter 23 "Creating Presentations"

- Chapter 24 "Communicating in Other Media"

- Chapter 25 "Writing to Make Something Happen in the World"

- Chapters 36–46 "Sentence Grammar"

- Chapters 47–56 "Punctuation and Mechanics"

Opportunities and Constraints

Imagine you walk into your English classroom for the first time, and your instructor hands you a full outline of a paper, including a thesis statement, point-by-point paragraph breakdown, and a bibliography of sources. Not only must you adhere to standard requirements such as page or word count, but you must also use exactly this thesis statement, exactly these supporting paragraphs in exactly this order, and exactly this set of sources and no others. It's hard to imagine an assignment that affords fewer **opportunities** than the one described above. In such a scenario, most people will produce a paper that is uninteresting to read and downright torturous to write. However, it would be equally problematic if you came in the first day of class and your instructor simply said, "Write." Your response might be, "Write? About what? For how long? Can I write down my grocery list? How would you even grade my grocery list?" In other words, in the absence of any **constraints**, most of us would immediately ask for some; after all, an infinite number of choices can make it very difficult to choose.

Whether we're aware of it or not, we negotiate opportunities and constraints each time we sit down to write. Some are *situated*, while others are *generated*. *Situated* means that they preexist your own writing choices. For instance, perhaps the assignment sheet asks for an essay, thereby constraining you from writing a poem. On the other hand, *generated* means that the choices you make while writing generate new opportunities and constraints that didn't exist before. For instance, you may decide to include a personal anecdote in your essay, which affords you the opportunity to humanize your issue; however, if you've chosen to construct an overtly formal ethos, it may constrain you from relying too heavily on this kind of emotional argument. In an English class, many of the "dos and don'ts" that seem to be rules of writing are actually the opportunities and constraints afforded by the medium/genre of a written academic essay—in other words, they can and do change when your argument takes another form.

For example, a written academic essay constrains you to an academic audience of some kind and affords you the opportunity to cite an in-depth sociological study on the relationship between violence at home and violence at school in order to support your proposal for counselling as a deterrent to bullying. If you choose to reimagine this argument as an interpretive dance, you are no longer constrained to an academic audience, and you also no longer have the opportunity to describe the compelling study that was so convincing to you. Now, you are constrained from using words and are afforded the opportunity to visibly demonstrate the visceral impact that violence can have on real human bodies and minds. Neither medium is "freer" or "more confining" than the other; instead, each medium affords *different* kinds of opportunities and constraints.

It's important to remember, too, that "opportunities and constraints" is not simply synonymous with "possibilities and impossibilities." It's perfectly *possible* to video yourself slowly turning the pages of a paper you've written so that the watcher can read it, but doing so doesn't really take advantage of any particular *opportunity* offered by the medium of video. Likewise, it's not *impossible* to include large chunks of text within an image collage, but breaking the *constraint* of using only images would defeat the purpose of choosing to do an image collage in the first place.

As you practice thinking about opportunities and constraints, you will begin to notice that the same thing can be thought of as both an opportunity and a constraint, depending on your perspective. Having a required number of sources in an academic essay is both an opportunity and a constraint, in that it allows you to weave many voices together into a rich conversation while simultaneously curbing your impulse to describe only your own position. Rethinking your argument as a puppet show affords you the opportunity to bring your message straight to the kids, while simultaneously constraining you to simplify your message so that it both appeals to and makes sense to children—a notoriously difficult-to-please audience.

Thinking about opportunities and constraints is useful throughout the composing process, from invention all the way through to re-envisioning. The worst position to find yourself in as a writer is not knowing what to do next; considering opportunities and constraints shifts the question from "What do I do next?" to the much more productive and answerable question, "What do I *get* to do next?"

Discussion Questions

1. Consider the opportunities and constraints afforded to you as a college student. What do you get to do now that you couldn't before (or won't be able to do later)? What is harder for you to do now that was easier before (or will be easier later)? How might you separate these opportunities and constraints into the categories of *situated* and *generated*?

2. Think about a fictional character from a film you are very familiar with. How would you describe the opportunities and constraints that he or she faces? Which are situated and which are generated? How does the character use both to his or her advantage (or fail to do so)?

3. Reflect on the process of composing your Researched Argumentative Essay. What are some situated and generated opportunities that stand out in your memory of that process, and how did you take advantage of them? What about situated and generated constraints? How did you use these to your advantage?

Exercises

1. Find a celebrity that frequently uses at least two different social media platforms: Facebook and Twitter, Twitter and Instagram, etc. Analyze some of their more recent posts on both platforms. What seems to be the reason they choose one platform over the other? In other words, if they post different kinds of things to different platforms, each platform must be offering them some opportunities and constraints that the other platforms don't offer. How might you articulate these differences?

2. As a way to begin choosing the medium and/or genre you will be using for your Public Turn assignment, look back at your Researched Argumentative Essay. Make a list of the situated and generated constraints that you would like the opportunity to redirect. (For instance, maybe you were aware that an academic essay would probably not reach a particular audience that you would like to include in the conversation, or maybe you had trouble making your project sound as fun as you know it can be.) Then, make a list of the media and/or genres that might afford you the opportunities to achieve those goals. Finally, for each of the media and/or genres you have in this second list, what *new* situated constraints would you encounter if you were to choose that option? Write out as many as you can foresee.

3. In small groups analyze the assignment sheet you were given for the Public Turn assignment. Consider what constraints it puts on you and what opportunities it allows. Now, rewrite the assignment sheet so that it works differently. What constraints might you add to help your classmates complete the assignment? What opportunities might you allow that are currently closed off? Be prepared to share your rewritten assignment sheet with the class.

Design

Thought of in its broadest context, **design** refers to the planning and construction of any object or system. Massive projects such as the layouts of cities, the organization of governments, and the creation of artificial islands are intentionally designed to facilitate certain actions, thoughts, and feelings in those who interact with them. Likewise, miniscule projects such as the construction of drink coasters, board games, and bottle caps also require design decisions. Regardless of the magnitude of the project, good design focuses on the economic, aesthetic, functional, social, political, and emotional relationship users will have with the object being designed. As such, to think about design rhetorically is to think about all the possible ways in which an audience will interact with a text.

When the rhetor considers design, she focuses on the interaction an audience will have with a text—the relationship between the message and its recipients. As you learned earlier, the rhetor cannot be aware of every possible audience, and some audiences may not react to texts in the way a rhetor may wish. Nonetheless, good rhetors consider not only who their audiences are but also how their audiences will be interacting with their texts materially, ideologically, socially, etc. Thus, an effective rhetor chooses from her rhetorical toolbox—the various media, arrangements, formats, logics, styles, and arguments with which she is familiar—the tools she believes will allow her to create the most suitable argument for her intended audience. The argument may take any number of forms (e.g., a game, movie, art installation, album, elevator, etc.), but no matter its form it will be designed to get an audience to act a certain way in the world.

Design manifests itself differently depending on the **modes of meaning** being used. In other words, the different elements through which a rhetor constructs meaning—spoken language, alphabetic text, photography, gesture, texture, sound, temperature, spatial orientation, or any combination thereof—help to determine how she will design her argument and persuade people to engage with the world differently. For instance, when looking at printed alphabetic text, design features such as document size, font choice, font size, font color, paper color, paper texture, ink opacity, margins, and text orientation play a part in conveying a message to the audience. With other media, different elements need to be considered. For instance, if we were creating an argument using only soundscapes, we might consider speaker placement, the room in which the project will be presented, how people can move about that room, the kinds of sounds we are recording/creating, the ways we edit the sound, the pitch, timber, rhythm, speed, volume, etc. In both these examples, the medium helps to determine the design just as the design helps us to determine the medium.

Audience and medium are not the only factors to consider when thinking about design; the contexts in which rhetors present their arguments also influences their design decisions. Spaces have their own logics, structures, and constraints. For example, we all know that typing in only capital letters is intended to convey EMPHASIS in some situations but intended to denote YELLING in others. Likewise, an interpretive dance may not be an appropriate medium for a eulogy at a Catholic funeral, and a subway station might not be the best place for a lecture on quantum physics. Messages must be designed to fit into the situation and space in which they are delivered; this does not mean that texts must follow predetermined ideas, conventions, and layouts; rather, it means that rhetors should think both about the physical space of delivery and the social context of the situation while designing their projects.

As you can see, then, design is always much more complicated than it first appears—especially in contemporary society where most media combine several different modes of meaning. Videos, for instance, combine elements of audio design, visual design, spoken language design, textual design, etc. Further, the systems that allow us to format, save, and distribute the video need to be designed. Making these decisions and understanding these structures can be difficult, but we can make them easier by always keeping our audience in mind. Ask yourself: how do these choices impact how the audience will interact with my text? Do these choices do what I wish them to do in relation to my message?

The diagram below shows some—though by no means all—of the rhetorical design choices we make when creating and delivering messages. It is good to become familiar with all of these tools because the more diverse tools we have the better choices we can make and the more we can tinker with our arguments so that they work the way we wish.

Some Elements of Design

Table 1. Modes of Meaning

Linguistic Design	Audio Design	Gestural Design	Visual Design	Spatial Design
■ Delivery	■ Music	■ Behavior	■ Colors	■ Ecosystem and Geographic Meanings
■ Intonation	■ Sound Effects	■ Physicality	■ Contrast	■ Architectonic Meanings
■ Stress	■ Noises	■ Gesture	■ Complementary	■ Layout
■ Rhythm	■ Ambient Noises	■ Sensuality	■ Saliency	■ Proximity
■ Speed	■ Silence	■ Kinesics	■ Perspective	■ Direction
■ Accent	■ Volume	■ Proximics	■ Framing	■ Place Identity
■ Vocabulary and Metaphor	■ Pitch	■ Patterns	■ Distance	■ Navigability
■ Transitivity	■ Tone		■ Angle	
■ Types of process of participants in the clause	■ Rhythm		■ Vectors	
■ Positioning			■ Foregrounding and Backgrounding	
■ Information Structures			■ Scale	
■ Clauses			■ Layout	
■ Sentences			■ Balance	
■ Local Coherence Relations			■ Symbols	
■ Cohesion between clauses			■ Still versus Moving Image	
■ Logical relations between clauses			■ Camera movement	
■ Global Coherence			■ Subject movement	
■ Overall organizational properties of texts (e.g., genres)			■ Screen format	

Discussion Questions

1. What does design add to your conception of rhetoric that other concepts don't? In other words, how might considering design help you compose your Public Turn assignment in a way that considering style, voice, genre, delivery, or opportunities and constraints wouldn't?

2. Design decisions are often subverted by the audience; that is, people interact with objects in unintended ways—e.g., they jump turnstiles, record the sounds of escalators, sleep on park benches, and produce memes from news stories. In what ways is it important to you as you create your Public Turn assignment to prevent or invite such subversive interactions? What are some ways you can design your project to meet these goals?

3. This entry discusses texts that use multiple modes of meaning to make their point. Are there any texts that only use one mode? If so, what are they, and how do they function on their own?

Exercises

1. Listen to this podcast about the game Monopoly: http://99percentinvisible. org/episode/the-landlords-game/. After considering the game's design weaknesses, its history, and the reasons for its longevity, redesign the game so that it espouses your own beliefs about economics, gamesmanship, and fun. In other words, rethink Monopoly so that it not only reflects your economic ideals but also is fun to play. Create rules, a board, and pieces for your new game. Then, present your game to the class explaining both the rules of the game and the ideology behind it.

2. Read an essay in Part Two of this book while thinking about design. Ask yourself how the text invites you to interact with it and the ways it encourages you to take action in the world. Then, make a list of different design elements in the text, each with a brief description of how they function within the argument as a whole. Be as thorough as possible when you make this list; be thorough to the point of ridiculousness. Finally, discuss what, if anything, you learned from this exercise.

3. Think of a human-created object you find miniscule and unimportant. Then, research its history and design. How much work went into creating that object? What are some design elements that allow it to function the way it does? Does understanding the object's design make you think about it differently? Be prepared to share your research with the class.

PART 2

PROFESSIONAL ESSAYS

Media and Technology

Joni Adamson is a Professor of Environmental Humanities in the Department of English and a Senior Sustainability Scholar at the Julie Ann Wrigley Global Institute of Sustainability at Arizona State University. Through analyzing contemporary media culture in relation to current advancements in science and technology, her work focuses on both the material and the social effects of global warming.

Indigenous Literatures, Multinaturalism, and *Avatar*: The Emergence of Indigenous Cosmopolitics
Joni Adamson

Light and color are often the only signs of these lives invisible to the unaided eye.

Stefan Helmreich, Alien Ocean

James Cameron's *Avatar* (2009) premiered to some predictably scathing reviews comparing the film to Kevin Costner's *Dances with Wolves* (1990) and Disney's *Pocahontas* (1995). Set 145 years in the future, the film tells the story of the Na'vi, 10-foot-tall blue-skinned humanoids living on an Earth-like moon called Pandora in a monolithic "Hometree." Humans have come from Earth intent on mining "unobtainium," a rare mineral located beneath Hometree and considered the solution to Earth's energy crisis. Hero Jake Sully, a parapalegic ex-marine, is hired to gather intelligence and given a genetically engineered Na'vi body, or avatar, to pilot in the alien Pandoran atmosphere. When he is attacked by wild animals, he is saved by Neytiri, the daughter of the Na'vi chief, and they later fall in love. Neytiri teaches Jake that Hometree and all living beings are alive with the spirit of "Eywa," described as a "network of energy" represented as bioluminescent, brightly colored seeds, trees, and animals. Given this romantic plot and luminous setting, it is not surprising that most reviews referenced the commonplace figure of the "ecological Indian" in movies that seek absolution for the sins of industrialization and evoke desire for the re-enchantment of nature (Newitz n.p.).

What *was* surprising about some of the first responses to the film were the number of cautiously positive responses from indigenous groups, political figures, community leaders and scholars. For example, Evo Morales, the Aymara President of Bolivia, praised *Avatar* for its imaginative portrayal of an indigenous group fighting a greedy corporation ("Head of State" n.p.). Morales's comments resonate with the language of the 2010 Universal Declaration on the Rights of Mother Earth written at the World Peoples' Conference on Climate Change in Cochabamba, Bolivia. Organized by Morales after the failure of the United Nations climate talks in Copenhagen, delegates declared that they would no longer be silent and would make themselves visible in international spaces of political negotiation (Eshelman n.p.). Their authority as politicians was based on a "cosmic spirituality linked to nature" thousands of years in the making and they would no longer support the economic models promoted by industrialized countries that had radically transformed their relationship to Mother Earth or "Pachamama."[1]

Throughout Latin America, Pachamama is understood *not* as a female-gendered planet but as "Source of Light" or "Source of Life" (de la Cadena 335, 350). Indigenous peoples and nations are mobilizing around the concept of earth-beings that "concentrate energy and life"; "being" is defined as "ecosystems, natural communities, species and all other natural entities which exist as part of Mother Earth" (UDRME Art. 4.1 n.p.). The resonance between notions of sentient earth-beings and Cameron's representation of Na'vi relationship to Pandora's networked energy may be one reason for Morales's positive response to *Avatar*. Another might be explained using Rob Nixon's work on the concepts of "slow violence" (6) and "spectacle" (16). Nixon, who is noted for bridging postcolonial and ecocritical studies, analyzes the work of writer-activists in the Global South, including Ogoni organizer Ken Saro-Wiwa, a prolific creative writer, novelist, screenwriter, and politician. Saro-Wiwa's work helped to illuminate an inattention to the attritional lethality of environmental disasters which exacerbate the vulnerability of ecosystems and people who are poor, disempowered, and often involuntarily displaced. In an increasingly globalizing world, this is a pattern that is often repeated, with transnational corporations based in the Global North promising to contribute to the progress of modern society, then managing to evade resolution of "matters of environmental injury, remediation, and redress" for decades (Nixon 6). Since there is a deficit of spectacle or of "recognizable special effects that fill movie seats" in these communities, there is nothing to draw the global media's attention to their plight; consequently, slow violence often remains hidden (6).

---

1. See the "Universal Declaration on the Rights of Mother Earth," hereafter cited as UDRME.

Nixon has illustrated how a deficit of spectacle in Nigeria led to the 1995 execution of Ken Saro-Wiwa on trumped-up charges. The Ogoni are an indigenous and ethnic minority group that has been subjected both to racism by Royal Dutch/Shell Oil and discrimination by an elite faction of dominant ethnic groups profiting from oil extraction. For their resistance to the degradation of their lands and water, the Ogoni were being murdered, raped, and tortured. Saro-Wiwa had been attempting to call the world's attention to this violence and to oil spills the size of the Exxon Valdez spill that had been occurring in the Niger Delta every year since 1958. But lacking the sudden spectacle of oiled Alaskan wildlife, no one seemed to care. By 1993, when he began traveling his country to give speeches for the United Nations International Year for the World's Indigenous People, Saro-Wiwa was only just beginning to imagine how he might capitalize on new forms of international organizing and attention. In his speeches, he outlined Ogoni territorial boundaries and settlement in terms of "six kingdoms" formed in a time in the past (Saro-Wiwa 11). His purpose was not to suggest that his people were "closer to nature," but to extend the world's gaze across time, to articulate the long-term perils lurking in 50 years of spills. Shortly before his execution, Saro-Wiwa learned that indigenous peoples in Ecuador had sued Texaco-Chevron for decades of oil and chemical spills. He thought this might be the kind of "spectacle" that could draw the world's gaze to the slow violence in Ogoniland. Soon after, Ogoni villagers sued Shell for spillages that had "robbed them of their livelihoods" as subsistence farmers and fishers (Nixon 119).[2]

On the other side of the Atlantic, 10 years after Saro-Wiwa's execution and several decades after the lawsuit in Ecuador had been filed against Texaco-Chevron, the case was still pending. The plaintiffs had learned that simply entering a courtroom was not "spectacular" enough to draw the world's gaze. So, in 2005, the legal team representing the plaintiffs persuaded famed documentarian Joe Berlinger to try to fill movie seats with a dramatic account of their David and Goliath battle. The result was *Crude: The Real Cost of Oil* (2009), an award-winning documentary which tells the story of substandard oil drilling practices, gas flaring, and untreated toxic wastes in the territory of the indigenous Cofán. Berlinger follows Pablo Fajardo, a young Cofán lawyer taking his first case, and his associate, Cofán environmental activist Luis Yanza, as they gather evidence of cancers, rashes, and death. They form an alliance with US human rights and criminal lawyer, Steven Donziger, himself just out of Harvard Law School, and his backers who include powerful US class action law firms. Berlinger also records the statements of Chevron and Ecuadoran politicians who deny causal links between contamination and ill health. Rock star Sting's wife, Trudie Styler, brings a missing element of celebrity to the jungle as she flies in to be the eyes

2. Today, these two groups are formally organized and linked; see *Justice in Nigeria Now!*, 25 May 2011 http://justiceinnigeria.wordpress.com/ and *Amazon Defense Coalition*, 25 May 2011 http://www.texacotoxico.org/eng/node/.

of the Global North. The buzz created around the film undoubtedly drew the world's gaze to the Andes. In February 2011, an Ecuadoran court awarded the plaintiffs over $18.1 billion in compensation. However, Chevron has appealed the ruling and sued Berlinger, Donziger, and Farjardo for fraud. The Cofán, and the multiple species with which they coexist, must continue waiting for remediation and redress.

The notion, as Nixon has phrased it, that there is an ongoing, crude" battle over spectacle taking place in the world points to the reasons why blockbuster films and documentaries are playing an increasingly important role in global environmental justice struggles and why Evo Morales, as I will discuss below, is not the only indigenous leader to link a political struggle to *Avatar* . . . . This analysis will allow me to explore further why indigenous groups are linking their movements to a blockbuster film that features a coalition of humans and bioluminescent nonhuman species fighting to shift audience focus from the spectacle of war and corporate greed to the ontology and agency of the material world.

Cosmopolitism and Ecocriticism

Questions of citizenship have long been at the heart of the field imaginary in American studies and central to recent ecocritical debates about the interrelations of cosmopolitanism, nationalism, localism, and environmentalism. In a special issue of the *Journal of Transnational American Studies*, Günter Lenz surveys key texts and scholars that have been at the center of a rich discussion of the meaning and promises of new versions of cosmopolitanism.[3] He observes that this work is energizing the potential for "newly defined conceptions and practices of governance, justice, [and] citizenship...in a multi-polar world of unequal distribution of power and resources" (9). In the same issue, Alfred Hornung praises *Ursula Heise's Sense of Place and Sense of Planet* (2008) as a key example of this new work. Heise urges literary critics and environmentalists to consider how studies of globalization suggest new possibilities for "ecocosmopolitanism," a term she coins as a kind of shorthand for ecologically inflected notions of "world citizenship" (10). Heise surveys the tensions and contradictions that theories of globalization and cosmopolitanism present for ecocriticism, which she defines as environmentally oriented literary and cultural studies. She urges ecocritics to recognize the limitations of an "excessive investment in the local" (10) while cautioning that academic theories of globalization and cosmopolitanism must always be enriched by "environmental justice fieldwork" (Heise 159). Both Hornung and Lenz suggest that new work exploring cosmopolitanism and environmentalisms is revealing "new options for forging more complex, multifaceted" and "localized visions of communal politics and cultural practices in a globalizing world" (Lenz 7).

---

3. See especially page 5, note 5.

Lenz notes that new versions of cosmopolitanism are leading to a recognition of multiple new dimensions of "cultural citizenship, minority rights, [and] the right of ecological citizenship" (6). Rob Nixon's work on slow violence (which brilliantly answers Heise's call for environmental justice field work that forges more complex, multifaceted visions of localized communal politics) offers excellent examples of how some of these new concepts of ecological citizenship are developing. For example, in the after-math of the chemical spill at Bhopal, nuclear disaster at Chernobyl, and oil spills in the Niger Delta, new "varieties of biological citizenship" are produced when some of the survivors gain "official recognition as sufferers" while others are "dismissed as nonsufferers because their narratives of injury are deemed to fail the prevailing politico-scientific logic of causation" (Nixon 47). Stacy Alaimo and Susan Hekman's coedited work in *Material Feminisms* (2008) also addresses the ways in which mobilization around environmental justice issues is forging new possibilities for coalition and communal politics. Alaimo and Hekman analyze the "traffic in toxins," showing how toxic substances released into a community can bring together interest groups heretofore imagined separately (9). An oil spill, for example, studied from a cultural–natural perspective that does not separate the two realms, reveals how a toxin may affect the workers who produce it, the community in which it is produced, and the humans and animals (domesticated and wild) that ingest it. Saro-Wiwa's connection of Ogoni resistance to Ecuadoran indigenous groups through his work with the United Nations and Berlinger's *Crude* provide innovative examples of how coalitional groups can form around the siting and practices of extractive industries or environmental accidents.

Marisol de la Cadena's ethnographic study of indigenous organizing in Latin America also illustrates how coalitions are forming around the notion that multiple species and "things" that have heretofore not been considered deserving of the same rights and protections as humans should be granted the "right to regenerate…biocapacity and continue…vital cycles" (UDRME n.p.). De la Cadena draws from Isabelle Stengers's work to explicate an emerging "indigenous cosmopolitics" focused on recognition of the rights of "Pachamama." Stengers extracts from the word "cosmopolitan" its two constituents: cosmos and politics. Cosmos "refers to the unknown" constituted by multiple, divergent worlds and politics "to the articulation of which they would eventually be capable" (Stengers 995). Stengers argues that a cosmos detached from politics is irrelevant, then dives deep into the philosophies of politics and science to explore how "our modern world," to use Latour's phrase, separated humans from nature (27). The Declaration on the Rights of Mother Earth counters this separation by urging all the world's citizens to become more aware of multiple, divergent worlds and to build a politics that would support the "recovery, revalidation, and strengthening" of "cosmovisions based on ancient and ancestral indigenous knowledge" (UDRME Art. 1 n.p.).

Political rallies and events across Latin America are illustrating what an "indigenous cosmovision" might look like in practice. At a protest in 2006 organized to oppose a proposed mining concession in Peru, for example, a coalition of indigenous peoples, environmentalists, and academics enlisted Ausangate, a mountain considered a "powerful earth-being, the source of life and death, of wealth and misery," as an ally (de la Cadena 338). They argued that Ausangate should have the right to exist in proper relationship with its surrounding mountains. A mine sited at Ausangate would prevent the maintenance and continuance of this relationship. But in the modern world, writes de la Cadena, the notion that a mountain can be sentient is dismissed as "anti-capitalist nonsense" (340). The President of Peru, Alan García, denied that Ausangate was sacred and described it as *tierra ociosas*, or "idle land" that could be developed for the "common good" of the "nation" (340). In dismissing the legitimacy of the protest, García calls upon ideas accepted by modern societies that agree that unscientific indigenous or "ethnic beliefs" block "progress." Despite García's views, protestors at the rally included indigenous people, many educated and already elected to political office, who believed in sentient entities. They were working to prevent unfortunate accidents that might be caused by the ire that would be triggered by a sentient mountain subject to desecration. Other protestors, some academics and some environmentalists, did not believe in sentient entities and were at the rally to protect local rivers and agriculture from the harm that erosion and pollution might cause. What was notable, observes de la Cadena, is that despite many differing views and opinions, indigenous politicians and nonindigenous academics and activists were able to commit to a politics of nature that included "disagreement on the definition of nature itself" (de la Cadena 346). This kind of commitment is emerging throughout Latin America....

Multidimensional Relationship and Multinaturalism

"[W]hat forces—imaginative, scientific, and activist," asks Rob Nixon, "can help us extend the temporal horizons of our gaze not just retrospectively" to past environmental injustices but prospectively to worlds we might see if we knew what to look for (62)? Many indigenous groups, scholars, and politicians around the world have raised *Avatar* like a red flag to begin suggesting answers. In eastern India, the Dongria Kondh tribe posted a YouTube video titled "The Real Avatar" that narrates their (successful) battle to stop mining giant Vedanta Resources from siting a bauxite mine on their sacred mountain, Niyam Raja. At an Ecuadoran fundraising event posted on YouTube, Shuar, Achuar, and Waorani tribal members enter a movie theater decked out in their plumes, feathered crowns, and jewelry, then watch *Avatar* wearing 3-D glasses. Achuar leader Luis Vargas objects to the main character being a "white guy [who] sweeps in to the rescue" but allows that such plot devices are to be expected from Hollywood (Spitzer n.p.). Vargas is more interested in the film's potential for calling attention to the plans of multinationals to drill for oil in Yasuni National Park, home to some of the world's still uncontacted tribes (Spitzer n.p.). At a fundraiser attended by James Cameron, near the site of a proposed dam which will dry up a 60-mile stretch of the Xingu River in Brazil and displace the Arara people, the media asks the chief for a response to the film and he says simply, "*Avatar* is happening here" (Barrionuevo A1).

In a review subtitled "An Indigenous Woman Considers *Avatar*," Julia Good Fox analyzes the connections that indigenous communities are making to the film and argues that it is a willful oversimplification to reduce the film to "white savior" or "going native" metaphors. She is more interested in whether or not the imaginative, scientific, and activist forces portrayed in the film can move audience members toward better understanding of issues that indigenous groups face in a globalizing world. Jake Sully, she wryly observes, is no "savior" since he would be powerless, and literally unable to move, without the alliance formed between the Na'vi's ceremonial elder, Mo'at and her daughter, Neytiri, and without the scientist in charge of the Avatar program, Dr. Grace Augustine. This kind of alliance is typical in the context of Cameron's *oeuvre*: from *The Terminator* (1984), to *Aliens* (1986), to *Titanic* (1997), this director has spent his career exploring the "ways that representative individuals and cultures misconnect….abuse connection, and, of course, connect" (Good Fox n.p.). He *wants* viewers to think of cowboys and Indians, militarization, and genocide and colonization. The film is a "deliberately pieced together metatext" whose embedded history encourages the audience to explore the possibilities of individuals "to connect to each other's humanity despite overwhelming hurdles" (Good Fox n.p.).

Good Fox explains that diverse tribes have various characteristics that differentiate them from other tribes, but indigenous peoples share a general recognition of "multidimentional relationships," often referred to as "all my relations," or the notion that all life is connected.[4] Cameron represents this notion when Neytiri's mother, Mo'at, charges her daughter with leading Jake Sully from "insanity to sanity." In a scene in which Neytiri upbraids Sully for not fully understanding that hunting is not just a sport and animals are not just food, she emphatically teaches him the phrase "Oel ngati kameie" or "I see you," which implies, argues Good Fox, not just a glance, but an accurate and encompassing recognition, an insightful and respectful acknowledgment of connectedness or "relatedness" to elements of the world that cannot be seen by humans. Neytiri's extensive knowledge of the brightly colored, iridescent species of Pandora points to emerging fields of study that focus on multispecies relationship. Led by scholars such as Donna Haraway, Stacy Alaimo, and Stefan Helmreich, this field has gone well beyond the work of famed anthropologists such as Claude Lévi-Strauss to show that other-than-human species are not just "good to think" or "good to eat" but are also, in Haraway's formulation, "entities, and agents, 'to live with'" (qtd. in Kirksey and Helmreich 552). As Helmreich has observed in his "anthropological

---

4. For a book-length consideration of this concept, see Winona LaDuke's *All Our Relations* (1999).

voyages in microbial seas," at the smallest of scales, light and color "are often the only signs of these lives invisible to the unaided eye" (187). Neytiri commandingly teaches Jake that interpreting light and color takes committed apprentice-ship. Jake, whose last name, "Sully," means "to mar the luster of something," is secretly working to gather intelligence on the Na'vi for use by the mining corporation. This deceit is clouding his gaze and blinding him to the lustrous networked energy of Eywa that connects all the species and "things" on Pandora.

The relationships between Mo'at, Neytiri, and Grace illustrate that "all our relations" also encompass relations between various human groups (Good Fox n.p.). This is the element of the film, writes Daniel Heath Justice, another indigenous scholar and reviewer, that prevented the Indigenous Studies community from dismissing the film (Justice n.p.). Grace's research on the Na'vi offers what Justice calls a "muted critique of academic colonialism" which focuses a spotlight on the danger—and potential—of historical "legacies of interface"—between indigenous peoples, colonizers, armies, teachers, preachers, and scholars (Justice n.p.). Grace's corporate funding has produced a bestselling ethnography that is offering humans insight into the Na'vi, but the information is also being used by the corporation to plan the forced removal of the indigenous population from Hometree. This aspect of the film highlights historically problematic relationships between indigenous peoples and other human groups, including today's academics, NGOs (non-governmental organization), and others, who may have good intentions, but whose activities lead to harmful consequences.

Grace's research on the bioluminescent botany of Pandora is also meant to show how alliances between academics and local populations might extend human vision to different scales of time and space. Cameron became interested in bioluminescence while filming *Abyss* (1989), a deep-sea sci-fi thriller, and several documentaries on deep-ocean volcanoes, animals, and plankton. Because bioluminescence occurs only in marine life on earth (with a few exceptions, like fireflies), Cameron hired botanist Jodie Holt to ensure that the representation of Pandora's "networked energy" would be scientifically credible and adhere to "known laws of physics and biology" (Kozlowski n.p.) Plants do not have a nervous system, Holt told Cameron, so they cannot literally "communicate" with each other; however, communication among plants could credibly be explained with the language of the emerging field of biosemiotics, and, more specifically, with reference to the process of "signal transduction" (Kozlowski n.p.). Biosemiotics and signal transduction are areas of research, writes Stefan Helmreich, that deal with how living things "perceive and interpret their environments" through chemical gradients or intensities of light (187).

Before the corporation begins forcibly removing the Na'vi, Grace tries to convince the head executive that the real wealth of Pandora is not "under the ground" but in understanding how signal transduction works. Her words fall on deaf ears and the corporation sends in bomb-dropping planes and missile-launching robots. As the sentient Hometree is violently blown apart and the Na'vi are scattered and killed, Cameron shows how blindness to scales of time and space prevents a precautionary approach that might have averted socionatural disaster or mitigated its effects. While humans see only a "thing," Hometree is actually a grove of mangrove-like trees that have grown and intertwined from just a few bioluminescent seeds over the course of 10,000 years. Each increases the strength of the whole and expands Hometree's ability to shelter a host of species. The Na'vi's relationship to Hometree and knowledge of the other species that live there offers insight into the meaning of "deep time" and phrases like "a cosmic spirituality in the making for thousands of years" (UDRME n.p.).

What is astonishing about indigenous groups linking their own regionally specific movements to *Avatar* is not that a block buster film is playing in India or the Andes or the Amazon; it is that the "things" that *Avatar* is helping to "make public," to use the language of Bruno Latour, are living systems (mountains, rivers, forests, deserts) that may help inaugurate a politics that is more plural not because the people enacting it are bodies marked by race or ethnicity demanding rights, or by environmentalists representing nature, but because they force into visibility the culture–nature divide that has prevented multiple worlds and species from being recognized as deserving the right to maintain and continue their vital cycles (de la Cadena 346). The alliance between Mo'at, Neytiri, and Grace, observes Good Fox, calls upon the audience to consider how "independent thinkers and question-ers" possess traits that allow them to move away from a "monolithic mindset" of profit and enter into coalitions seeking solutions to seemingly insurmountable cultural, territorial, and environmental conflicts (Good Fox n.p.). The plurality being called for, then, does not stop at multiculturalism, but is a project that de la Cadena suggests might more accurately be called "multinaturalism" (347)....

Allowing earth-beings to count in politics, writes de la Cadena, does not remove other proposals for economic growth and development from the table (de la Cadena 362). People, citizens—indigenous or not—can still side with a mine or dam, and choose jobs or money, depending on local needs. Opening a space for the contemplation of earth-beings would allow for recognition of nature's multiple and heterogeneous ontologies (including its possibility as repository of mineral wealth). Multiple possibilities might weigh into discussions of dif-fering, even competing political proposals without any of these proposals being dismissed as "right," "left," "superstitious" or "unscientific." Cameron imagines this kind of increasingly plural politics, or cosmovisions, that would allow for more innovative interpretations of "citizenship" for the culture–nature entity known to many as "Source of Light."

Works Cited

Alaimo, Stacy. "Trans-Corporeal Feminisms and the Ethnical Space of Nature." *Material Femi-nisms*. Eds. Stacy Alaimo and Susan J. Hekman. Bloomington: Indiana UP, 2008. 237–64.

Avatar. Dir. James Cameron. Perf. Sam Worthington, Zoe Saldana, Sigourney Weaver. Twentieth Century Fox Film Corporation, 2009.

Barrionuevo, Alexei. "Tribes of Amazon Find an Ally Out of *Avatar*." *New York Times* 11 Apr. 2010: A1.

Crude: The Real Price of Oil. Dir. Joe Berlinger. Entendre Films. 2009.

De la Cadena, Marisol. "Indigenous Cosmopolitics in the Andes: Conceptual Reflections beyond 'Politics.'" *Cultural Anthropology* 25.2 (2010): 334–70.

Eshelman, Robert S. "World Peoples Conference on Climate Change and the Rights of Mother Earth Kicks Off in Bolivia." *Huffington Post* 19 Apr. 2010 17 Sept. 2010. <http://www.huffingtonpost.com/robert-s-eshelman/worldpeoples-conference_b_543211.html>.

Good Fox, Julia. "*Avatars* to the Left of Me, Pandora to the Right: An Indigenous Woman Considers James Cameron's *Avatar*." 21 Jan. 2010. 2 Mar 2010 <http://lastwoman. wordpress. com/2010/01/21/48_Avatar/>

"Head of State Fights for Environment: Evo Morales 'Identifies' with *Avatar* Film." *Buenos Aires Herald* 12 Jan. 2010. <http://www.buenosairesherald.com/article/22287/evo-morales -identifies-with-Avatar-film> 9 Aug. 2010.

Heise, Ursula. *Sense of Place and Sense of Planet: The Environmental Imagination of the Global*. New York: Oxford UP, 2008.

Helmreich, Stefan. *Alien Ocean: Anthropological Voyages in Microbial Seas*. Berkeley: U of California P, 2009.

Hornung, Alfred. "Planetary Citizenship." *Journal of Transnational American Studies* 3, 1 (2011): 37–46.

Justice, Daniel Heath. "James Cameron's *Avatar*: Missed Opportunities." *First People: New Directions in Indigenous Studies*. 20 Jan. 2010. 2 Mar 2010 <http://firstpeoplesnewdirections. org/blog/?p=169/>.

Kirksey, S. Eben and Stefen Helmreich. "The Emergence of Multispecies Ethnography." *Cultural Anthropology* 25.4 (2010): 545–76.

Kozlowski, Lori, "*Avatar* Team Brings in UC Riverside Professor to Dig in the Dirt of Pandora." *Los Angeles Times* 2 Jan. 2010. 25 Jan. 2010. <http://latimesblogs.lat-imes.com/ herocomplex/2010/01/avatar-team-brought-in-uc-riverside-professor-to-dig-in-the-dirt-of-pandora.html>.

Lenz, Günter H. "Symposium: Redefinitions of Citizenship and Revisions of Cosmopolitanism— Transnational Perspectives." *Journal of Transnational American Studies* 3.1 (2011): 1–17.

Latour, Bruno. *We Have Never Been Modern*. Cambridge: Harvard UP, 1993.

Nixon, Rob. *Slow Violence and the Environmentalism of the Poor*. Cambridge: Harvard UP, 2011.

"The Real Avatar: Mine—Story of a Sacred Mountain." *Survival International* 31 Mar. 2009. 10 May 2011. <http://www.youtube.com/ watch?v=R4tuTFZ3wXQ>.

Saro-Wiwa, Ken. *Genocide in Nigeria: The Ogoni Tragedy*. Lagos: Saros International, 1991.

Spitzer, Melaina. "Avatar in the Amazon." *Public Radio International* 29 Jan. 2010. 8 Aug 2010. <http://www.youtube.com/watch?v=Qh_dFfoE6wo>.

Stengers, Isabelle. "The Cosmopolitical Proposal." *Making Things Public: Atmospheres of Democracy*. Eds. Latour Bruno and Weibel Peter. Cambridge: MIT P, 2005. 994–1004.

United Nations Declaration on the Rights of Indigenous Peoples. *The United Nations Permanent Forum on Indigenous Issues* 13 Sept. 2007. 11 Aug 2009. <http://www.un.org/esa/socdev/ unpfii/en/declaration.html>.

Universal Declaration on the Rights of Mother Earth. *World People's Conference on Climate Change and the Rights of Mother Earth* 22 Apr. 2010. 17 Sept 2010. <http://www. globalresearch.ca/index. php?context=va&aid=18931>.

Roxane Gay is an Associate Professor of English at Purdue University where she teaches creative writing—both fiction and creative non-fiction—at the graduate and undergraduate levels. She is better known as an opinion writer for the *New York Times*; the author of *Bad Feminist, Difficult Women*, and *Hunger*; and an award-winning short-story writer.

Daniel Tosh and Rape Jokes: Still Not Funny

Roxane Gay

The furor over Daniel Tosh's rape jokes reminded me of the morning the space shuttle Challenger exploded. When I was in the sixth grade, there was a kid in my class, we'll call him James, who was really funny, the class clown. James joked about everything and we all loved him for it because his wit was so sharp, even at such a young age. You never wanted James to turn his humor against you, but you always wondered what he might say next. You always laughed.

On Jan. 28, 1986, we watched the Challenger lift off in science class and it was a really big deal to have our traditional class activities set aside. Our science teacher was particularly excited because Christa McAuliffe, a teacher from New Hampshire, was one of the seven astronauts onboard. The mysteries of outer space felt a little more within his reach that day.

Shortly after liftoff, the Challenger exploded. We watched on the small television screen as the shuttle burst into flames and thick, spiraled plumes of smoke filled the air. Debris began falling into the ocean. It did not seem real. The classroom was silent. Our science teacher's eyes reddened and he kept trying to speak but could only clear his throat. James snickered and said, "I guess there are a lot of dead fish now." Our science teacher lost it completely and gave James a serious dressing down. The rest of the year was rough for James. He had finally crossed an invisible line about what one can or cannot joke about. James suddenly became an outcast because he went too far, because it was too soon, because joking about tragedy was too much.

Inappropriate humor is often the best kind, as Tosh knows. Everyone has at least one joke they find funny even though they know they probably shouldn't. Humor that makes us laugh and makes us uncomfortable also makes us think. In a profile of the late Patrice O'Neal for *New York* magazine, Adrian Nicole LeBlanc wrote about how O'Neal was deliberate and merciless in testing boundaries and saying the unspeakable. She characterized his willingness to do this by saying, "The transformative power of the ugly truth was, for O'Neal, a form of grace." Most comedians seem to be reaching for that form of grace, trying to talk about the complexity of these lives we lead in ways that can make us laugh and think and feel.

Daniel Tosh's humor, however, is utterly lacking in grace. The star of Comedy Central's "Tosh.0" does not possess the transformative power of his betters, so when he tries to be edgy and transgressive, it tends to fall flat. In April, the unapologetic misogynist encouraged his audience to film themselves touching women softly on their stomachs. I am not quite sure how this encroachment on personal space and ignorance of appropriate boundaries constitutes humor, but it takes all kinds. (I'm also a woman—we are, from what I hear, not funny.) Nonetheless, the incident gave me pause, particularly when his ardent fans actually began filming themselves touching women softly on their stomachs and posting the videos to YouTube. Somehow, they thought this behavior was acceptable because the comic they admired told them so. You'd be amazed what people are willing to do when they are given permission, either implicitly or explicitly.

Given Tosh's brand of humor and his general history of immature, frattish humor, I wasn't really surprised when I heard he made inappropriate statements about rape at the Laugh Factory last Friday. Rape jokes are part of his shtick. During his Laugh Factory set, a young woman in the audience yelled, "Actually, rape jokes are never funny." Tosh is said to have maturely responded, "Wouldn't it be funny if that girl got raped by like, five guys right now? Like right now? What if a bunch of guys just raped her . . ."

What if, indeed.

There's no better follow-up for a rape joke than a gang rape joke. Because if rape is funny, gang rape is funnier . . . .

Rape humor is designed to remind women that they are still not quite equal. Just as their bodies and reproductive freedom are open to legislation and public discourse, so are their other issues. When women respond negatively to misogynistic or rape humor they are "sensitive" and branded as *feminist* a word that has, as of late, become a catch-all term for "woman who does not tolerate bullshit."

Humor is subjective but is it *that* subjective? I don't have it in me to find rape jokes funny or to tolerate them in any way. It's too close a topic. Rape is many things—humiliating, degrading, physically and emotionally painful, exhausting, irritating. It is never funny for most women. There are not enough years in this lifetime to create the kind of distance where I could laugh and say, "That one time, when I was gang raped, was totally hilarious, a real laugh riot."

We are free to speak as we choose without fear of prosecution or persecution, but we are not free to speak as we choose without consequence. The woman who called Tosh out on his comments walked out of the club and a friend posted about it on Tumblr. The Internet picked up her story. Tosh has since offered a small act of contrition qualified by his assertion that his comments were shared out of context, he was heckled, and that you can still make jokes about the awful things in the world. (He added the hashtag #deadbabies to that tweet.) He clearly doesn't think he has done anything wrong. His half-assed apology is the kind where he is merely sorry someone has taken offense rather than taking responsibility for his actions. He will never think it is wrong to joke about rape. Like I said—it takes all kinds.

Many comedians are very proud of themselves for saying the things others are supposedly *afraid* to say. They are at the forefront of this culture of entitlement where we get to know everything, do anything, think anything and say anything. People don't use humor to comment on the "awful things in the world," because they are afraid. Maybe, just maybe, they have common sense; they have conscience. Sometimes, saying what others are afraid or unwilling to say is just being an asshole. We are all free to be assholes but we are not free to do so without consequence.

What Tosh calls heckling, I'd call taking a stand. All too often, when we see injustices, both great and small, we think, "That's terrible," but we do nothing. We say nothing. We let other people fight their own battles. We remain silent because silence is easier.

Qui tacet consentire is Latin for, "Silence gives consent." When we say nothing, when we do nothing, we are saying we consent to these trespasses against us.

When that woman stood up and said, "No, rape is not funny," she did not consent to participating in a culture that encourages lax attitudes toward sexual violence and the concerns of women. Rape humor is what encourages a man to feel comfortable tweeting to Daniel Tosh, "the only ppl who are mad at you are the feminist bitches who never get laid and hope they get raped so they can get laid," which is one of the idiotic, Pavlovian responses a certain kind of *person* has when women have the nerve to suggest that they don't find sexual violence amusing. In that man's universe, women who get properly laid are totally fine with rape humor. A satisfied vagina is a balm in Gilead.

We know the appalling statistics. We know sexual violence is embedded within our culture so deeply that there exists a website where women regularly report street harassment. Sexual violence is so problematic that there is a Sexual Assault Awareness Month and there are countless organizations whose sole function is to support victims of sexual violence. We live in a society where the phrase "rape culture" exists and where the culture itself exists. This climate is staggering. Either you recognize that or you don't. Rape humor is not "just jokes" or "stand-up." Humor about sexual violence suggests permissiveness—not for people who would never commit such acts, but for the people who have whatever weakness that allows them to do terrible things unto others. If any number of young men were willing to film themselves touching women lightly on their stomachs, how many were encouraged to ignore a woman's no because Daniel Tosh finds rape amusing? What are the consequences if the answer is even one?

What surprises me, what really troubles me, is that only one person stood up and had the strength of conviction to say, "Enough."

Ken Gillam is an Associate Professor and Director of Composition at Missouri State University; his research focuses mainly on composition and rhetoric. **Shannon R. Wooden** is a Professor at Missouri State University who researches the relationship between literature and science.

Post-Princess Models of Gender: The New Man in Disney/Pixar
Ken Gillam and Shannon R. Wooden

Lisping over the Steve McQueen allusion in Pixar's *Cars* (2006), our two-year-old son, Oscar, inadvertently directed us to the definition(s) of masculinity that might be embedded in a children's animated film about NASCAR. The film overtly praises the "good woman" proverbially behind every successful man: The champion car, voiced by Richard Petty, tells his wife, "I wouldn't be nothin' without you, honey." But gender in this twenty-first-century bildungsroman is rather more complex, and Oscar's mispronunciation held the first clue. To him, a member of the film's target audience, the character closing in on the title long held by "The King" is not "Lightning McQueen" but "Lightning the queen"; his chief rival, the always-a-bridesmaid runner-up "Chick" Hicks.

Does this nominal feminizing of male also-rans (and the simultaneous gendering of success) constitute a meaningful pattern? Piqued, we began examining the construction of masculinity in major feature films released by Disney's Pixar studios over the past thirteen years. Indeed, as we argue here, Pixar consistently promotes a new model of masculinity, one that matures into acceptance of its more traditionally "feminine" aspects.

Cultural critics have long been interested in Disney's cinematic products, but the gender critics examining the texts most enthusiastically gobbled up by the under-six set have so far generally focused on their retrograde representations of women. As Elizabeth Bell argues, the animated Disney features through *Beauty and the Beast* feature a "teenaged heroine at the idealized height of puberty's graceful promenade ... [f]emale wickedness ... rendered as middle-aged beauty at its peak of sexuality and authority ... and [f]eminine sacrifice and nurturing ... drawn in pear-shaped, old women past menopause" (108). Some have noted the models of masculinity in the classic animated films, primarily the contrast between the ubermacho Gaston and the sensitive, misunderstood Beast in *Beauty and the Beast*,[1] but the male protagonist of the animated classics, at least through The *Little Mermaid*, remains largely uninterrogated.[2] For most

---

1. See Susan Jeffords, "The Curse of Masculinity: Disney's *Beauty and the Beast*" for an excellent analysis of that plot's developing the cruel Beast into a man who can love and be loved in return: "Will he be able to overcome his beastly temper and terrorizing attitude in order to learn to love?" (168). But even in this film, she argues, the Beast's development is dependent on "other people, especially women," whose job it is to tutor him into the new model of masculinity, the "New Man" (169, 170).

2. Two articles demand that we qualify this claim. Indirectly, they support the point of this essay by demonstrating a midcentury Disney model of what we call "alpha" masculinity. David Payne's "Bambi" parallels that film's coming-of-age plot, ostensibly representing a "natural" world, with the military mindset of the 1940s against which the film was drawn. Similarly, Claudia Card, in "Pinocchio," claims

of the early films, this critical omission seems generally appropriate, the various versions of Prince Charming being often too two-dimensional to do more than inadvertently shape the definition of the protagonists' femininity. But if the feminist thought that has shaped our cultural texts for three decades now has been somewhat disappointing in its ability to actually rewrite the princess trope (the spunkiest of the "princesses," Ariel, Belle, Jasmine, and, arguably, even Mulan, remain thin, beautiful, kind, obedient or punished for disobedience, and headed for the altar), it has been surprisingly effective in rewriting the type of masculine power promoted by Disney's products.[3]

Disney's new face, Pixar studios, has released nine films—*Toy Story* (1995) and *Toy Story 2* (1999); *A Bug's Life* (1998); *Finding Nemo* (2003); *Monsters, Inc.* (2001); *The Incredibles* (2004); *Cars* (2006); *Ratatouille* (2007); and now *WALL•E* (2008)—all of which feature interesting male figures in leading positions. Unlike many of the princesses, who remain relatively static even through their own adventures, these male leads are actual protagonists; their characters develop and change over the course of the film, rendering the plot. Ultimately these various developing characters—particularly Buzz and Woody from *Toy Story*, Mr. Incredible from *The Incredibles*, and Lightning McQueen from *Cars*—experience a common narrative trajectory, culminating in a common "New Man" model:[4] they all strive for an alpha-male identity; they face emasculating failures; they find themselves, in large part, through what Eve Sedgwick refers to as "homosocial desire" and a triangulation of this desire with a feminized object (and/or a set of "feminine" values); and, finally, they achieve (and teach) a kinder, gentler understanding of what it means to be a man.

Emasculation of the Alpha Male

A working definition of *alpha male* may be unnecessary; although more traditionally associated with the animal kingdom than the Magic Kingdom, it familiarly evokes ideas of dominance, leadership, and power in human social organizations as well. The phrase "alpha male" may stand for all things stereotypically patriarchal: unquestioned authority, physical power and social dominance, competitiveness for positions of status and leadership, lack of visible or shared emotion, social isolation. An alpha male, like Vann in *Cars*, does not ask for

---

that the Disneyfied version of the nineteenth-century Carlo Collodi tale replaces the original's model of bravery and honesty with "a macho exercise in heroism [. . . and] avoid[ing] humiliation" (66–67).

3. Outside the animated classics, critics have noted a trend toward a postfeminist masculinity—one characterized by emotional wellness, sensitivity to family, and a conscious rejection of the most alpha male values—in Disney-produced films of the 1980s and 1990s. Jeffords gives a sensible account of the changing male lead in films ranging from *Kindergarten Cop* to *Terminator 2*.

4. In Disney criticism, the phrase "New Man" seems to belong to Susan Jeffords's 1995 essay on *Beauty and the Beast*, but it is slowly coming into vogue for describing other postfeminist trends in masculine identity. In popular culture, see Richard Collier's "The New Man: Fact or Fad?" online in *Achilles Heel: The Radical Men's Magazine* 14 (Winter 1992/1993). http://www.achillesheel.freeuk.com/article14_9.html. For a literary-historical account, see Writing Men: *Literary Masculinities from Frankenstein to the New Man* by Berthold Schoene-Harwood (Columbia UP, 2000).

directions; like Doc Hudson in the same film, he does not talk about his feelings. The alpha male's stresses, like Buzz Lightyear's, come from his need to save the galaxy; his strength comes from faith in his ability to do so. These models have worked in Disney for decades. The worst storm at sea is no match for *The Little Mermaid*'s uncomplicated Prince Eric—indeed, any charming prince need only ride in on his steed to save his respective princess. But the postfeminist world is a different place for men, and the post-princess Pixar is a different place for male protagonists.

Newsweek recently described the alpha male's new cinematic and television rival, the "beta male": "The testosterone-pumped, muscle-bound Hollywood hero is rapidly deflating .... Taking his place is a new kind of leading man, the kind who's just as happy following as leading, or never getting off the sofa" (Yabroff 64). Indeed, as Susan Jeffords points out, at least since *Beauty and the Beast*, Disney has resisted (even ridiculed) the machismo once de rigueur for leading men (170). Disney cinema, one of the most effective teaching tools America offers its children, is not yet converting its model male protagonist all the way into a slacker, but the New Man model is quite clearly emerging.

Cars, *Toy Story*, and The *Incredibles* present their protagonists as unambiguously alpha in the opening moments of the films. Although Lightning McQueen may be an as-yet incompletely realized alpha when *Cars* begins, not having yet achieved the "King" status of his most successful rival, his ambition and fierce competitiveness still clearly valorize the alpha-male model: "Speed. I am speed… I eat losers for breakfast," he chants as a prerace mantra. He heroically comes from behind to tie the championship race, distinguishing himself by his physical power and ability, characteristics that catapult him toward the exclusively male culture of sports superstars. The fantasies of his life he indulges after winning the coveted Piston Cup even include flocks of female cars forming a worshipful harem around him. But the film soon diminishes the appeal of this alpha model. Within a few moments of the race's conclusion, we see some of Lightning's less positive macho traits; his inability to name any friends, for example, reveals both his isolation and attempts at emotional stoicism. Lightning McQueen is hardly an unemotional character, as can be seen when he prematurely jumps onto the stage to accept what he assumes to be his victory. For this happy emotional outburst, however, he is immediately disciplined by a snide comment from Chick. From this point until much later in the film, the only emotions he displays are those of frustration and anger.

Toy Story's Buzz Lightyear and Sheriff Woody similarly base their worth on a masculine model of competition and power, desiring not only to be the "favorite toy" of their owner, Andy, but to possess the admiration of and authority over the other toys in the playroom. Woody is a natural leader, and his position represents both paternalistic care and patriarchal dominance. In an opening scene, he calls and conducts a "staff meeting" that highlights his unambiguously dominant position in the toy community. Encouraging the toys to pair up so that no one will be lost in the family's impending move, he commands: "A moving buddy. If you don't have one, GET ONE." Buzz's alpha identity comes from a more exalted source than social governance—namely, his belief that he is the one "space ranger" with the power and knowledge needed to save the galaxy; it seems merely natural, then, that the other toys would look up to him, admire his strength, and follow his orders. But as with Lightning McQueen, these depictions of masculine power are soon undercut. Buzz's mere presence exposes Woody's strength as fragile, artificial, even arbitrary, and his "friends," apparently having been drawn to his authority rather than his character, are fair-weather at best. Buzz's authority rings hollow from the very beginning, and his refusal to believe in his own "toy-ness" is at best silly and at worst dangerous. Like Lightning, Buzz's and Woody's most commonly expressed emotions are anger and frustration, not sadness (Woody's, at having been "replaced") or fear (Buzz's, at having "crash-landed on a strange planet") or even wistful fondness (Woody's, at the loss of Slink's, Bo Peep's, and Rex's loyalty). Once again, the alpha-male position is depicted as fraudulent, precarious, lonely, and devoid of emotional depth.

An old-school superhero, Mr. Incredible opens *The Incredibles* by displaying the tremendous physical strength that enables him to stop speeding trains, crash through buildings, and keep the city safe from criminals. But he too suffers from the emotional isolation of the alpha male. Stopping on the way to his own wedding to interrupt a crime in progress, he is very nearly late to the service, showing up only to say the "I dos." Like his car and toy counterparts, he communicates primarily through verbal assertions of power—angrily dismissing Buddy, his meddlesome aspiring sidekick; bantering with Elastigirl over who gets the pickpocket—and limits to anger and frustration the emotions apparently available to men.

Fraught as it may seem, the alpha position is even more fleeting: In none of these Pixar films does the male protagonist's dominance last long. After Lightning ties, rather than wins, the race and ignores the King's friendly advice to find and trust a good team with which to work, he browbeats his faithful semi, Mack, and ends up lost in "hillbilly hell," a small town off the beaten path of the interstate. His uncontrolled physical might destroys the road, and the resultant legal responsibility—community service—keeps him far from his Piston Cup goals. When Buzz appears as a gift for Andy's birthday, he easily unseats Woody both as Andy's favorite and as the toy community's leader. When Buzz becomes broken, failing to save himself from the clutches of the evil neighbor, Sid, he too must learn a hard lesson about his limited power, his diminished status, and his own relative insignificance in the universe. Mr. Incredible is perhaps most obviously disempowered: Despite his superheroic feats, Mr. Incredible has been unable to keep the city safe from his own clumsy brute force. After a series of lawsuits against "the Supers," who accidentally leave various types of small-time mayhem in their wake, they are all driven underground, into a sort of witness protection program. To add insult to injury, Mr. Incredible's diminutive boss fires him from his job handling insurance claims, and his wife, the former Elastigirl, assumes the "pants" of the family.

Most of these events occur within the first few minutes of the characters' respective films. Only Buzz's downfall happens in the second half. The alpha-male model is thus not only present and challenged in the films but also is, in fact, the very structure on which the plots unfold. Each of these films is about being a man, and they begin with an out dated, two-dimensional alpha prototype to expose its failings and to ridicule its logical extensions: the devastation and humiliation of being defeated in competition, the wrath generated by power unchecked, the paralyzing alienation and fear inherent in being lonely at the top. As these characters begin the film in (or seeking) the tenuous alpha position among fellow characters, each of them is also stripped of this identity—dramatically emasculated—so that he may learn, reform, and emerge again with a different, and arguably more feminine, self-concept.

"Emasculated" is not too strong a term for what happens to these male protagonists; the decline of the alpha-male model is gender coded in all the films. For his community service punishment, Lightning is chained to the giant, snorting, tarspitting "Bessie" and ordered to repair the damage he has wrought. His own "horsepower" (as Sally cheerfully points out) is used against him when literally put in the service of a nominally feminized figure valued for the more "feminine" orientation of service to the community. If being under the thumb of this humongous "woman" is not emasculating enough, Mater, who sees such subordination to Bessie as a potentially pleasurable thing, names the price, saying, "I'd give my left two lug nuts for something like that!"

Mr. Incredible's downfall is most clearly marked as gendered by his responses to it. As his wife's domestic power and enthusiasm grow increasingly unbearable, and his children's behavior more and more out of his control, he surreptitiously turns to the mysterious, gorgeous "Mirage," who gives him what he needs to feel like a man: super hero work. Overtly depicting her as the "other woman," the film requires Elastigirl to intercept a suggestive-sounding phone call, and to trap her husband in a lie, to be able to work toward healing his decimated masculinity.

In *Toy Story*, the emasculation of the alpha male is the most overt, and arguably the most comic. From the beginning, power is constructed in terms conspicuously gender coded, at least for adult viewers: As they watch the incoming birthday presents, the toys agonize at their sheer size, the longest and most phallic-shaped one striking true fear (and admiration?) into the hearts of the spectators. When Buzz threatens Woody, one toy explains to another that he has "laser envy." Buzz's moment of truth, after seeing himself on Sid's father's television, is the most clearly gendered of all. Realizing for the first time that Woody is right, he is a "toy," he defiantly attempts to fly anyway, landing sprawled on the floor with a broken arm. Sid's little sister promptly finds him, dresses him in a pink apron and hat, and installs him as "Mrs. Nesbit" at her tea party. When Woody tries to wrest him from his despair, Buzz wails, "Don't you get it? I AM MRS. NESBIT. But does the hat look good? Oh, tell me the hat looks good!" Woody's "rock bottom" moment finds him trapped under an overturned milk crate, forcing him to ask Buzz for help and to admit that he "doesn't stand a chance" against Buzz in the contest for Andy's affection, which constitutes "everything that is important to me." He is not figured into a woman, like Buzz is, or subordinated to a woman, like Lightning is, or forced to seek a woman's affirmation of his macho self, like Mr. Incredible is, but he does have to acknowledge his own feminine values, from his need for communal support to his deep, abiding (and, later, maternal) love of a boy. This "feminine" stamp is characteristic of the New Man model toward which these characters narratively journey.

Homosociality, Intimacy, and Emotion

Regarding the "love of a boy," the "mistress" tempting Mr. Incredible away from his wife and family is not Mirage at all but Buddy, the boy he jilted in the opening scenes of the film (whose last name, Pine, further conveys the unrequited nature of their relationship). Privileging his alpha-male emotional isolation, but adored by his wannabe sidekick, Mr. Incredible vehemently protects his desire to "work alone." After spending the next years nursing his rejection and refining his arsenal, Buddy eventually retaliates against Mr. Incredible for rebuffing his advances. Such a model of homosocial tutelage as Buddy proposes at the beginning of the film certainly evokes an ancient (and homosexual) model of masculine identity; Mr. Incredible's rejection quickly and decisively replaces it with a heteronormative one, further supported by Elastigirl's marrying and Mirage's attracting the macho superhero.[5] But it is equally true that the recovery of Mr. Incredible's masculine identity happens primarily through his (albeit antagonistic) relationship with Buddy, suggesting that Eve Sedgwick's notion of a homosocial continuum is more appropriate to an analysis of the film's gender attitudes than speculations about its reactionary heteronormativity, even homophobia.

Same-sex (male) bonds—to temporarily avoid the more loaded term *desire*—are obviously important to each of these films. In fact, in all three, male/male relationships emerge that move the fallen alphas forward in their journeys toward a new masculinity. In each case, the male lead's first and/or primary intimacy—his most immediate transformative relationship—is with one or more male characters. Even before discovering Buddy as his nemesis, Mr. Incredible secretly pairs up with his old pal Frozone, and the two step out on their wives

---

5. Critics have described the superhero within some framework of queer theory since the 1950s, when Dr. Fredric Wertham's *Seduction of the Innocent* claimed that Batman and Robin were gay (Ameron Ltd, 1954). See Rob Lendrum's "Queering Super-Manhood: Superhero Masculinity, Camp, and Public Relations as a Textual Framework" (*International Journal of Comic Art* 7.1 [2005]: 287–303) and Valerie Palmer-Mehtan and Kellie Hay's "A Superhero for Gays? Gay Masculinity and Green Lantern" (*Journal of American Culture* 28.4 [2005]: 390–404), among myriad nonscholarly pop-cultural sources.

to continue superheroing on the sly; Buddy and Frozone are each, in their ways, more influential on Mr. Incredible's sense of self than his wife or children are. Although Lightning falls in love with Sally and her future vision of Radiator Springs, his almost accidentally having befriended the hapless, warm Mater catalyzes more foundational lessons about the responsibilities of friendship—demanding honesty, sensitivity, and care—than the smell-the-roses lesson Sally represents. He also ends up being mentored and taught a comparable lesson about caring for others by Doc Hudson, who even more explicitly encourages him to resist the alpha path of the Piston Cup world by relating his experiences of being used and then rejected. Woody and Buzz, as rivals-cum-allies, discover the necessary truths about their masculine strength only as they discover how much they need one another. Sedgwick further describes the ways in which the homosocial bond is negotiated through a triangulation of desire; that is, the intimacy emerging "between men" is constructed through an overt and shared desire for a feminized object. Unlike homosocial relationships between women—that is, "the continuum between 'women loving women' and 'women promoting the interests of women'"—male homosocial identity is necessarily homophobic in patriarchal systems, which are structurally homophobic (3). This means the same-sex relationship demands social opportunities for a man to insist on, or prove, his heterosexuality. Citing Rene Girard's *Deceit, Desire, and the Novel*, Sedgwick argues that "in any erotic rivalry, the bond that links the two rivals is as intense and potent as the bond that links either of the rivals to the beloved" (21); women are ultimately symbolically exchangeable "for the primary purpose of cementing the bonds of men with men" (26).

This triangulation of male desire can be seen in *Cars* and *Toy Story* particularly, where the homosocial relationship rather obviously shares a desire for a feminized third. Buzz and Woody compete first, momentarily, for the affection of Bo Peep, who is surprisingly sexualized for a children's movie (purring to Woody an offer to "get someone else to watch the sheep tonight," then rapidly choosing Buzz as her "moving buddy" after his "flying" display). More importantly, they battle for the affection of Andy—a male child alternately depicted as maternal (it is his responsibility to get his baby sister out of her crib) and in need of male protection (Woody exhorts Buzz to "take care of Andy for me!").[6] *Cars* also features a sexualized romantic heroine; less coquettish than Bo Peep, Sally still fumbles over an invitation to spend the night "not with me, but..." in the motel she owns. One of Lightning and Mater's moments of "bonding" happens when Mater confronts Lightning, stating his affection for Sally and sharing a parallel story of heterosexual desire. The more principal objects of desire in *Cars*, however, are

---

6. Interestingly, Andy and *Toy Story* in general are apparently without (human) male role models. The only father present in the film at all is Sid's, sleeping in front of the television in the middle of the day. Andy's is absent at a dinner out, during a move, and on the following Christmas morning. Andy himself, at play, imagines splintering a nuclear family: when he makes Sheriff Woody catch One-Eyed Black Bart in a criminal act, he says, "Say goodbye to the wife and tater tots...you're going to jail."

the (arguably) feminized "Piston Cup" and the Dinoco sponsorship. The sponsor itself is established in romantic terms: With Lightning stuck in Radiator Springs, his agent says Dinoco has had to "woo" Chick instead. Tia and Mia, Lightning's "biggest fans," who transfer their affection to Chick during his absence, offer viewers an even less subtly gendered goal, and Chick uses this to taunt Lightning. It is in the pursuit of these objects, and in competition with Chick and the King, that Lightning first defines himself as a man; the Piston Cup also becomes the object around which he and Doc discover their relationship to one another.

The New Man

With the strength afforded by these homosocial intimacies, the male characters triumph over their respective plots, demonstrating the desirable modifications that Pixar makes to the alpha-male model. To emerge victorious (and in one piece) over the tyrannical neighbor boy, Sid, Buzz and Woody have to cooperate not only with each other but also with the cannibalized toys lurking in the dark places of Sid's bedroom. Incidentally learning a valuable lesson about discrimination based on physical difference (the toys are not monsters at all, despite their frightening appearance), they begin to show sympathy, rather than violence born of their fear, to the victims of Sid's experimentation. They learn how to humble themselves to ask for help from the community. Until Woody's grand plan to escape Sid unfolds, Sid could be an object lesson in the unredeemed alpha-male type: Cruelly almighty over the toy community, he wins at arcade games, bullies his sister, and, with strategically placed fireworks, exerts militaristic might over any toys he can find. Woody's newfound ability to give and receive care empowers him to teach Sid a lesson of caring and sharing that might be microcosmic to the movie as a whole. Sid, of course, screams (like a girl) when confronted with the evidence of his past cruelties, and when viewers last see him, his younger sister is chasing him up the stairs with her doll.

Even with the unceremonious exit of Sid, the adventure is not quite over for Buzz and Woody. Unable to catch up to the moving van as Sid's dog chases him, Woody achieves the pinnacle of the New Man narrative: Armed with a new masculine identity, one that expresses feelings and acknowledges community as a site of power, Woody is able to sacrifice the competition with Buzz for his object of desire. Letting go of the van strap, sacrificing himself (he thinks) to Sid's dog, he plainly expresses a caretaking, nurturing love, and a surrender to the good of the beloved: "Take care of Andy for me," he pleads. Buzz's own moment of truth comes from seizing his power as a toy: holding Woody, he glides into the family's car and back into Andy's care, correcting Woody by proudly repeating his earlier, critical words back to him: "This isn't flying; it's falling with style." Buzz has found the value of being a "toy," the self-fulfillment that comes from being owned and loved. "Being a toy is a lot better than being a space ranger," Woody explains. "You're *his toy*" (emphasis in original).

Mr. Incredible likewise must embrace his own dependence, both physical and emotional. Trapped on the island of Chronos, at the mercy of Syndrome (Buddy's new super-persona), Mr. Incredible needs women—his wife's super-powers and Mirage's guilty intervention—to escape. To overpower the monster Syndrome has unleashed on the city, and to achieve the pinnacle of the New Man model, he must also admit to his emotional dependence on his wife and children. Initially confining them to the safety of a bus, he confesses to Elastigirl that his need to fight the monster alone is not a typically alpha ("I work alone") sort of need but a loving one: "I can't lose you again," he tells her. The robot/monster is defeated, along with any vestiges of the alpha model, as the combined forces of the Incredible family locate a new model of postfeminist strength in the family as a whole. This communal strength is not simply physical but marked by cooperation, selflessness, and intelligence. The children learn that their best contributions protect the others; Mr. Incredible figures out the robot/monster's vulnerability and cleverly uses this against it.

In a parallel motif to Mr. Incredible's inability to control his strength, Buddy/Syndrome finally cannot control his robot/monster; in the defeat, he becomes the newly emasculated alpha male. But like his robot, he learns quickly. His last attempt to injure Mr. Incredible, kidnapping his baby Jack-Jack, strikes at Mr. Incredible's new source of strength and value, his family. The strength of the cooperative family unit is even more clearly displayed in this final rescue: For the shared, parental goal of saving Jack-Jack, Mr. Incredible uses his physical strength and, with her consent, the shape-shifting body of his super-wife. He throws Elastigirl into the air, where she catches their baby and, flattening her body into a parachute, sails gently back to her husband and older children.

Through Lightning McQueen's many relationships with men, as well as his burgeoning romance with Sally, he also learns how to care about others, to focus on the well-being of the community, and to privilege nurture and kindness. It is Doc, not Sally, who explicitly challenges the race car with his selfishness ("When was the last time you cared about something except yourself, hot rod?"). His re-formed behavior begins with his generous contributions to the Radiator Springs community. Not only does he provide much-needed cash for the local economy, but he also listens to, praises, and values the residents for their unique offerings to Radiator Springs. He is the chosen auditor for Lizzy's reminiscing about her late husband, contrasting the comic relief typically offered by the senile and deaf Model T with poignancy, if not quite sadness. Repairing the town's neon, he creates a romantic dreamscape from the past, a setting for both courting Sally ("cruising") and, more importantly, winning her respect with his ability to share in her value system. For this role, he is even physically transformed: He hires the body shop proprietor, Ramone, to paint over his sponsors' stickers and his large race number, as if to remove himself almost completely from the Piston

Cup world, even as he anticipates being released from his community service and thus being able to return to racing.

Perhaps even more than Buzz, Woody, and Mr. Incredible do, the New Man McQueen shuns the remaining trappings of the alpha role, actually refusing the Piston Cup. If the first three protagonists are ultimately qualified heroes—that is, they still retain their authority and accomplish their various tasks, but with new values and perspectives acquired along the way—Lightning completely and publicly refuses his former object of desire. Early in the final race, he seems to somewhat devalue racing; his daydreams of Sally distract him, tempting him to give up rather than to compete. The plot, however, needs him to dominate the race so his decision at the end will be entirely his own. His friends show up and encourage him to succeed. This is where the other films end: The values of caring, sharing, nurturing, and community being clearly present, the hero is at last able to achieve, improved by having embraced those values. But Lightning, seeing the wrecked King and remembering the words of Doc Hudson, screeches to a stop inches before the finish line. Reversing, he approaches the King, pushes him back on the track, and acknowledges the relative insignificance of the Piston Cup in comparison to his new and improved self. He then declines the Dinoco corporate offer in favor of remaining faithful to his loyal Rust-eze sponsors. Chick Hicks, the only unredeemed alpha male at the end, celebrates his ill-gotten victory and is publicly rejected at the end by both his fans, "the twins," and, in a sense, by the Piston Cup itself, which slides onto the stage and hits him rudely in the side.

Conclusion

The trend of the New Man seems neither insidious nor nefarious, nor is it out of step with the larger cultural movement. It is good, we believe, for our son to be aware of the many sides of human existence, regardless of traditional gender stereotypes. However, maintaining a critical consciousness of the many lessons taught by the cultural monolith of Disney remains imperative. These lessons—their pedagogical aims or results—become most immediately obvious to us as parents when we watch our son ingest and express them, when he misunderstands and makes his own sense of them, and when we can see ways in which his perception of reality is shaped by them, before our eyes. Without assuming that the values of the films are inherently evil or representative of an evil "conspiracy to undermine American youth" (Giroux 4), we are still compelled to critically examine the texts on which our son bases many of his attitudes, behaviors, and preferences.

Moreover, the impact of Disney, as Henry Giroux has effectively argued, is tremendously more widespread than our household. Citing Michael Eisner's 1995 "Planetized Entertainment," Giroux claims that 200 million people a year watch Disney videos or films, and in a week, 395 million watch a Disney TV show, 3.8 million subscribe to the Disney Channel, and 810,000 make a purchase at a Disney store (19). As Benjamin Barber argued in 1995, "[T]he true tutors of our children are not schoolteachers or university professors but filmmakers, advertising executives and pop culture purveyors" (qtd. in Giroux 63). Thus we perform our "pedagogical intervention[s]" of examining Disney's power to "shap[e] national identity, gender roles, and childhood values" (Giroux 10). It remains a necessary and ongoing task, not just for concerned parents, but for all conscientious cultural critics.

Works Cited

Bell, Elizabeth. "Somatexts at the Disney Shop: Constructing the Pentimentos of Women's Animated Bodies." Bell, *From Mouse to Mermaid* 107–24.

Bell, Elizabeth, Lynda Haas, and Laura Sells, eds. *From Mouse to Mermaid: the Politics of Film, Gender, and Culture*. Bloomington: Indiana UP, 1995.

Card, Claudia. "Pinocchio." Bell, *From Mouse to Mermaid* 62–71.

Cars. Dir. John Lasseter. Walt Disney Pictures/Pixar Animation Studios, 2006.

Collier, Richard. "The New Man: Fact or Fad?" *Achilles Heel: The Radical Men's Magazine* 14 (1992–93). <http://www.achillesheel.freeuk.com/article14_9.html>.

Eisner, Michael. "Planetized Entertainment." *New Perspectives Quarterly* 12.4 (1995): 8.

Giroux, Henry. *The Mouse that Roared: Disney and the End of Innocence*. Oxford, Eng.: Rowman, 1999.

The Incredibles. Dir. Brad Bird. Walt Disney Pictures/Pixar Animation Studios, 2004.

Jeffords, Susan. "The Curse of Masculinity: Disney's *Beauty and the Beast*" Bell, *From Mouse to Mermaid* 161–72.

Lendrum, Rob. "Queering Super-Manhood: Superhero Masculinity, Camp, and Public Relations as a Textual Framework." *International Journal of Comic Art* 7.1 (2005): 287–303.

Palmer-Mehtan, Valerie, and Kellie Hay. "A Superhero for Gays? Gay Masculinity and Green Lantern." *Journal of American Culture* 28.4 (2005): 390–404.

Payne, David. "Bambi." Bell, *From Mouse to Mermaid* 137–47.

Schoene-Harwood, Berthold. *Writing Men: Literary Masculinities from Frankenstein to the New Man*. Columbia: Columbia UP, 2000.

Sedgwick, Eve Kosofsky. *Between Men: English Literature and Male Homosocial Desire*. New York: Columbia UP, 1985.

Toy Story. Dir. John Lasseter. Walt Disney Pictures/Pixar Animation Studios, 1995.

Wertham, Fredric. *Seduction of the Innocent*. New York: Reinhart, 1954.

Yabroff, Jennie. "Betas Rule." *Newsweek* 4 June 2007: 64–65.

Jane McGonigal is an American game designer and author who advocates for the use of mobile and digital technology to channel positive attitudes, collective intelligence, and collaboration in order to improve the quality of human life and solve societal problems. Her two bestselling books *Reality Is Broken* and *SuperBetter* stress the importance video games can have in affecting non-digital lives. She maintains an active online presence with multiple websites, social networking accounts, and video presentations.

Becoming Part of Something Bigger Than Ourselves
Jane McGonigal

In April 2009, *Halo 3* players celebrated a collective spine-tingling milestone: 10 billion kills against their virtual enemy, the Covenant. That's roughly one and a half times the total number of every man, woman, and child on earth.

To reach this monumental milestone, *Halo 3* players spent 565 days fighting the third and final campaign in the fictional Great War, protecting earth from an alliance of malevolent aliens seeking to destroy the human race. Together, they averaged 17.5 million Covenant kills a day, 730,000 kills per hour, 12,000 kills a minute.

Along the way, they'd assembled the largest army on earth, virtual or otherwise. More than 15 million people had fought on behalf of the science fiction game's United Nations Space Command. That's roughly the total number of active personnel of all twenty-five of the largest armed forces in the real world, combined.[1]

Ten billion kills wasn't an incidental achievement, stumbled onto blindly by the gaming masses. Halo players made a concerted effort to get there. They embraced 10 billion kills as a symbol of just how much the *Halo* community could accomplish—and they wanted it to be something bigger than anything any other game community had achieved before. So they worked hard to make every single player as good at *Halo* 3 as possible. Players shared tips and strategies with each other and organized round-the-clock "co-op," or cooperative, campaign shifts. They called on every registered member of *Halo* online to pitch in: "This could be something big, but we will need YOU to get it done."[2] They treated their mission like an urgent duty. "We know we'll be doing our part," one game blog declared. "Will you?"[3]

It's no wonder London *Telegraph* reporter Sam Leith observed in his coverage of the *Halo 3* community that "a big shift has taken place, in recent years, in the way video games are played. What was once generally a solitary activity is now…overwhelmingly a communal one."[4] More and more, gamers aren't just in it for themselves. They're in it for each other—and for the thrill of being a part of something bigger.

When *Halo* players finally reached their goal, they flooded online forums to congratulate each other and claim their contributions. "I just did some math and with my 32,388 kills I have .00032% of the 10 billion kills," one player wrote. "I feel like I could have contributed more…well, on to 100 billion then!"[5] This reaction was typical, and the new 100 billion goal was repeated widely on *Halo* forums. Fresh off one collective achievement, *Halo* players were ready to tackle an even more monumental goal. And they were fully prepared to recruit an even bigger community to do it. As one gamer proposed: "We did that with just a few million gamers. Imagine what we could do with the full force of six billion humans!!"[6]

Halo's creators, a Seattle, Washington–based game studio called Bungie, joined in the celebration. They issued a major press release and an open letter to the *Halo* community, emphasizing the teamwork it had taken to get to 10 billion kills: "We've hit the Covenant where it hurts. Made them pay a price for setting foot on our soil. We're glad we've got you by our side, soldier. Mighty fine work. Here's to ten billion more."[7]

Perhaps you're thinking to yourself right now: So? What's the point? The Covenant isn't real. It's just a game. What have the players actually *done* that's worth celebrating?

On one hand, nothing. There's no *value* to a Covenant kill, whether you score one, 10 billion, or even 100 billion of them. Value is a measure of importance and consequence. And even the most die-hard *Halo* fan knows that there's no real importance or consequence to saving the human race from a fictional alien invasion. There's no actual danger being averted. There are no real lives being saved.

But on the other hand, just because the kills don't have value doesn't mean they don't have *meaning*.

Meaning is the feeling that we're a part of something bigger than ourselves. It's the belief that our actions matter beyond our own individual lives. When something is meaningful, it has significance and worth not just to ourselves, or even to our closest friends and family, but to a much larger group: to a community, an organization, or even the entire human species.

Meaning is something we're all looking for more of: more ways to make a difference in the bigger picture, more chances to leave a lasting mark on the world, more moments of awe and wonder at the scale of the projects and communities we're a part of.

How do we get more meaning in our lives? It's actually quite simple. Philosophers, psychologists, and spiritual leaders agree: The single best way to add meaning to our lives is to *connect our daily actions to something bigger than ourselves*—and the bigger, the better. As Martin Seligman says, "The self is a very poor site for meaning." We can't *matter* outside of a large-scale social context. "The larger the entity you can attach yourself to," Seligman advises, "the more meaning you can derive."[8]

And that's exactly the point of working together in a game like *Halo 3*. It's not that the Covenant kills have value. It's that pursuing a massive goal alongside millions of other people feels good. It feels meaningful. When players dedicate themselves to a goal like 10 billion Covenant kills, they're attaching themselves to a cause, and they're making a significant contribution to it. As the popular gamer site Joystiq reported on the day *Halo* players celebrated their 10 billionth kill: "Now we know for sure.... Every kill you get in *Halo 3*'s campaign actually *means* something."[9]

To experience *real* meaning, we don't have to contribute something of *real* value. We just have to be given the opportunity to contribute at all. We need a way to connect with others who care about the same massively scaled goal we do, no matter how arbitrary the goal. And we need a chance to reflect on the truly epic scale of what we're doing together.

Which gives us one fix for our broken reality:

Epic Scale

Compared with games, reality is trivial. Games make us a part of something bigger and give epic meaning to our actions.

"Epic" is the key word here. Blockbuster video games like *Halo*—the kind of games that have a production budget of thirty, forty, or even fifty million dollars—aren't just "something bigger." They're big enough to be *epic*.

Epic is one of the most important concepts in gamer culture today. It's how players describe their most memorable, gratifying game experiences. As one game critic writes, "*Halo 3* is epic. It empowers you the way no other game can. It doesn't have moments, but events. Experiences that tickle the soul, sending shivers down the spine."[10]

A good working definition for "epic" is something that far surpasses the ordinary, especially in size, scale, and intensity. Something epic is of *heroic proportions*. Blockbuster video games do epic scale better than any other medium of our time, and they're epic in three key ways:

They create *epic contexts for action*: collective stories that help us connect our individual gameplay to a much bigger mission.

They immerse us in *epic environments*: vast, interactive spaces that provoke feelings of curiosity and wonder.

And they engage us in *epic projects*: cooperative efforts carried out by players on massive scales, over months or even years.

There's a reason why gamers love epic games. It's not just that bigger is better. It's that bigger is more awe-inspiring.

Awe is a unique emotion. According to many positive psychologists, it's the single most overwhelming and gratifying positive emotion we can feel. In fact, neuropsychologist Paul Pearsall calls awe "the orgasm of positive emotions."[11]

Awe is what we feel when we recognize that we're in the presence of something bigger than ourselves. It's closely linked with feelings of spirituality, love, and gratitude—and more importantly, a desire to serve.

In *Born to Be Good*, Dacher Keltner explains, "The experience of awe is about finding your place in the larger scheme of things. It is about quieting the press of self-interest. It is about folding into social collectives. It is about feeling reverential toward participating in some expansive process that unites us all and that ennobles our life's endeavors."[12]

In other words, awe doesn't just *feel* good; it inspires us to *do* good.

Without a doubt, it's awe that a *Halo 3* player is feeling when he says that the game sends "shivers down the spine." Spine tingling is one of the classic physiological symptoms of awe—along with chills, goose bumps, and that choked-up feeling in the throat.

Our ability to feel awe in the form of chills, goose bumps, or choking up serves as a kind of emotional radar for detecting meaningful activity. Whenever we feel awe, we know we've found a potential source of meaning. We've discovered a real opportunity to be of service, to band together, to contribute to a larger cause.

In short, awe is a call to collective action.

So it's no accident that *Halo* players are so inclined toward collective efforts. It's the direct result of the game's epic, and awe-inspiring, aesthetic. Today's best game designers are experts at giving individuals the chance to be a part of something bigger—and no one is better at it than the creators of *Halo*. Everything about the *Halo* games—from the plot and the sound track to the marketing and the way the community is organized online—is intentionally crafted to make players feel that their gameplay really means something. And the one simple trick used over and over again is this: always connect the individual to something bigger.

Let's take a closer look at exactly how *Halo* does it.

Epic Context for Heroic Action

It's five hundred years in the future. The Covenant, a hostile alliance of alien species, is hell-bent on destroying humanity. You are Master Chief Petty Officer John 117—once an ordinary person, now a supersoldier, augmented with biological technologies that give you superhuman speed, strength, intelligence, vision, and reflexes. Your job is to stop the Covenant and save the world.

That's the basic *Halo* story. It's not that different from many other blockbuster video games. As veteran game developer Trent Polack puts it, "To look at the majority of games today, one might think that gamers care only about saving the world." He would know: Some of Polack's previous games have asked players to save the galaxy from malevolent aliens (*Galactic Civilizations II*), save the universe from evil deities (*Demigod*), and save the world from marauding Titans (*Elemental: War of Magic*).

Why *are* so many games about saving the world? In an industry article about the rise of "epic scale" narratives in video games, Polack suggests, "When games give players the epic scope of saving the galaxy, destroying some reawakened ancient evil, or any other classical portrayal of good versus evil on a grand scale, they're fulfilling gamers' power fantasies."[13]

I agree with Polack, but it's important that we be clear on exactly what *kind* of power fantasy is being fulfilled by these save-the-world stories.

Any video game that features a slew of high-powered weapons and gameplay that consists largely of shooting and blowing things up is, at one level, about the aesthetic pleasures of destruction and the positive feelings we get from exerting control over a situation.[14] This is true of any shooter game on the market today. But we don't need an epic story about saving the world to get those pleasures. We can get them quite effectively, and more efficiently, from a simple, plotless game like Atari's *Breakout*. Games that come with epic, save-the-world narratives are using them to help players get a taste of a different kind of power. It's the power to act with meaning: to do something that matters in a bigger picture. The story is the bigger picture; the player's actions are what matters.

As Polack explains, "Story sets the stage for meaning. It frames the player's actions. We, as designers, are not telling, we're not showing, we're informing the *doing*—the actions that players engage in and the feats they undergo." These feats make up the player's story, and the story is ultimately what has meaning.

Not every game feels like a larger cause. For a game to feel like a *cause*, two things need to happen. First, the game's story needs to become a collective context for action—shared by other players, not just an individual experience. That's why truly epic games are always attached to large, online player communities—hundreds of thousands or millions of players acting in the same context together, and talking to each other on forums and wikis about the actions they're taking. And second, the actions that players take inside the collective context need to feel like service: Every effort by one player must ultimately benefit all the other players. In other words, every individual act of gameplay has to eventually add up to something bigger.

Halo is probably the best game in the world at turning a story into a collective context and making personal achievement feel like service.

Like many other blockbuster video games, *Halo* has extensive online community features: discussion forums, wikis, and file sharing (so that players can upload and share videos of their finest gameplay moments). But Bungie and Xbox have taken it much further than these traditional context-building tools. They've given players groundbreaking tools for tracking the magnitude of their collective effort and unprecedented opportunities to reflect on the epic scale of their collective service.

Every *Halo* player has their own story of making a difference, and it's documented online in their "personal service record." It's an exhaustive record and analysis of their individual contributions to the *Halo* community and to the Great War effort—or as Bungie calls it, "Your entire *Halo* career."

The service record is stored on the official Bungie website, and it's fully viewable by other players. It lists all the campaign levels you've completed, the medals you've earned, and the achievements you've unlocked. It also includes a minute-by-minute, play-by-play breakdown of *every single* Halo *level or match you've ever played online*. For many *Halo* players, that means thousands of games over the past six years—ever since the *Halo* series first went online in 2004—all laid out and perfectly documented in one place.

And it's more than just statistics. There are data visualizations of every possible kind: interactive charts, graphs, heat maps. They help you learn about your own strengths and weaknesses: where you make the most mistakes, and where you consistently score your biggest victories; which weapons you're most proficient with, and which you're weakest with; even which teammates help you play better, and which don't.

Thanks to Bungie's exhaustive data collection and sharing, everything you do in *Halo* adds up to something bigger: a multiyear history of your own personal service to the Great War.

But it's not just your history—it's much bigger than that You're contributing to the Great War effort alongside millions of other players, who also have service records online. And *service* really is a crucial concept here. A personal service record isn't just a profile. It's a history of a player's contributions to a larger organization. The fact that your profile is called a "service record" is a constant reminder. When you play *Halo* online, rack up kills, and accomplish your missions, you're *contributing*. You're actively creating new moments in the history of the Great War.[15]

The moments all add up. The millions of individual personal service records taken together tell the real story of *Halo*, a collective history of the Great War. They connect all the individual gamers into a community, a network of people fighting for the same cause. And the unprecedented scale of data collected and shared in these service records underscores just how epic the players' collective story is. Bungie recently announced to players that its personal-service-record servers handled more than 1.4 *quadrillion* bytes of data requests from players in the past nine months. That's 1.4 petabytes in computer science terms.

To put that number in perspective, experts have estimated that the entire written works of humankind, from the beginning of recorded history, in all languages, adds up to about 50 petabytes of data.[16] *Halo* players aren't quite there yet—but it's not a bad start, considering that they've been playing together online for only six short years, compared to all of recorded human history.

One of the best examples of innovative collective context building is the *Halo* Museum of Humanity, an online museum that purports to be from the twenty-seventh century, dedicated to "all who fought bravely in the Great War."

Of course, it's not a real museum; it was developed by the Xbox marketing group to build a more meaningful context for *Halo 3*.

The museum features a series of videos done in the classic style of Ken Burns' *Civil War* series: interviews with Great War veterans and historians, images from Covenant battles, all set to a hymnal score. As one blogger wrote, "The videos in the *Halo* Museum of Humanity seem like they could have been pulled straight from The History Channel.... It's nice to see video game lore treated with this kind of reverence."[17]

Reverence—the expression of profound awe, respect and love, or veneration is usually an emotion we reserve for very big, very serious things. But that was precisely the point of the *Halo* Museum of Humanity: to acknowledge how seriously *Halo* players take their favorite game, and to inspire the kind of epic emotions that have always been the best part of playing it.

It's worked. The video series packs a real emotional wallop, despite the fact that, in the words of one player, "it's meant to honor heroes that never existed."[18] Brian Crecente, a leading games journalist, wrote, "It left me with chills."[19] And online forums and blogs were full of comments expressing heartfelt emotion. One player put it best when he wrote, "Really poignant. They've made something real out of fiction."[20]

It's not that the museum is such a believable artifact from the future. It's that the *emotions* it provokes are believable. The online Museum of Humanity is a place to reflect on the extreme scale of the *Halo* experience: the years of service, the millions of players involved. The Great War isn't real, but you really do feel awe when you think about the scale of the effort so many different people have made to fight it.

In the end, as one player sums it up, "*Halo* proves that you can have a shooter game with a story that really means something. It draws you in and makes you feel like you're part of something bigger."[21]

But *Halo* isn't just a bigger story. It's also a bigger environment—and this brings us to our next strategy for connecting players to something bigger: built epic environments, or highly immersive spaces that are intentionally designed to bring out the best in us.

Epic Environments—Or How to Build a Better Place

An epic environment is a space that, by virtue of its extreme scale, provokes a profound sense of awe and wonder.

There are plenty of natural epic environments in the world: Mount Everest, the Grand Canyon, Victoria Falls, the Great Barrier Reef, for example. These spaces humble us; they remind us of the power and grandeur of nature, and make us feel small by comparison.

A *built* epic environment is different: It's not the work of nature, but rather a feat of design and engineering. It's a *human* accomplishment. And that makes it both humbling and empowering at the same time. It makes us feel smaller as individuals, but it also makes us feel capable of much bigger things, together. That's because a built epic environment—like the Great Wall of China, the Taj Mahal, or Machu Picchu—is the result of extreme-scale collaboration. It's proof of the extraordinary scale of things humans can accomplish together.

Halo 3 is, without a doubt, such an environment.

The game consists of thirty-four different playing environments spanning more than two hundred thousand light-years of virtual space. From one level to the next, you might find yourself traveling from the crowded market city of Voi, Kenya, to the Ark, a desert far, far beyond the limits of our own Milky Way galaxy.

It's not just how big the *Halo* playing field is; it's also how diverse and carefully rendered the environments are. As Sam Leith observes, "The building of a game like *Halo 3* is a work of electronic engineering comparable in scale to the building of a medieval cathedral." It took Bungie three years to craft this gaming cathedral, with a team of more than 250 artists, designers, writers, programmers, and engineers collaborating together. "You get a sense of the scale and intricacy of the task," Leith continues, "by considering the sound effects alone: The game contains 54,000 pieces of audio and 40,000 lines of dialogue. There are 2,700 different noises for footsteps alone, depending on whose foot is stepping on what."[22]

And that's what players are appreciating when they get goose bumps from *Halo*: the unprecedented achievement it represents as a work of computer design and engineering. Gamers aren't so much in awe of the environment itself as they are in awe of the work and dedication and vision required to create it. In this regard, *Halo* players join a long tradition in human culture of feeling awe, wonder, and gratitude toward the builders of epic environments.

The very first epic environments were constructed more than eleven thousand years ago, during the Neolithic period, or the New Stone Age. In other words, six thousand years before humans first used the written word, they were already building physical spaces to inspire awe and cooperation.

The world's oldest known example of an epic built environment is the Gobekli Tepe. Discovered less than two decades ago in southeastern Turkey, it's believed to predate Stonehenge by a staggering six thousand years. It's a twenty-five-acre arrangement of at least twenty stone circles, between ten and thirty meters in diameter each, made from monolithic pillars three meters high.

In comparison with other stone houses, tombs, and temples from the same period and location, this building was constructed on an extreme scale: It was much, *much* bigger, taller, and more formidable in its design than anything archaeologists had seen before at the time of its discovery. One archaeologist on the scene described it as "a place of worship on an unprecedented scale—humanity's first 'cathedral on a hill.'"[23]

And it wasn't just the scale of the building—it was its particular winding design. The Gobekli Tepe features an intricate series of passageways that would lead visitors through the dark to a cross-shaped inner sanctum, almost like a labyrinth. This particular architecture seems designed intentionally to trigger interest and curiosity, alongside a kind of trembling wonder. What would be around the next corner? Where would the path take them? They would need to hold on to other visitors for support, feeling their way through the darkness.

Crucially, the Gobekli Tepe wasn't an isolated example. As researchers have discovered since, epic stone cathedrals were common across the Neolithic landscape. Most recently, in August 2009, archaeologists working in northern Scotland unearthed the ruins of a 5,330-square-foot stone structure with twenty-foot ceilings and sixteen-foot-thick walls, also of a labyrinthine design, and also dating back to the New Stone Age.[24]

"A building of this scale and complexity was here to amaze, to create a sense of awe in the people who saw this place," Nick Card, director of the archaeological dig, said to reporters when the ancient cathedral was first unearthed.

In the wake of unearthing these types of structures all over the planet, archaeologists have recently proposed a startling theory: that these stone cathedrals served an important purpose in the evolution of human civilization. They actually inspired and enabled human society to become dramatically more cooperative, completely reinventing civilization as it once existed. In an in-depth report in *Smithsonian* magazine on these Neolithic cathedrals, Andrew Curry wrote:

> Scholars have long believed that only after people learned to farm and live in settled communities did they have the time, organization and resources to construct temples and support complicated social structures. But…[perhaps] it was the other way around: the extensive, coordinated effort to build the monoliths literally laid the groundwork for the development of complex societies.[25]

In fact, as Curry quotes one scientist in his article, "You can make a good case these constructs are the real origin of complex Neolithic societies."[26]

No wonder epic environments inspire gamers today to collective efforts. They have been inspiring humans to work together to do amazing things for eleven thousand years and counting….

Johan Huizinga, the great twentieth-century Dutch philosopher of human play, once said, "All play *means* something."[27] Today, thanks to the increased scale of game worlds and advances in collective game design, gameplay often means something *more*. Game developers today are honing their ability to create awe-inspiring contexts for collective effort and heroic service. As a result, game communities are more committed than ever to setting extreme-scale goals and generating epic meaning.

When our everyday work feels trivial, or when we can't easily be of direct service to a larger cause, games can fulfill an important need for us. As we play games at an epic scale, we're increasing our ability to rise to the occasion, to inspire awe, and to take part in something bigger than ourselves.

Earlier in this chapter I quoted a *Halo* player who wondered, "Imagine what we could do with the full force of six billion humans!!"

Of course, there aren't enough Xboxes in the world to do it. Nor could everyone afford them, of course. But it does make for an interesting thought experiment: What *could* you do in a game like *Halo 3* if you had the full force of humanity playing together?

On one hand, this is an absurd idea to even consider. What would be the point of assembling 6 billion people to wage a fictional war?

But on the other: Can you imagine what it would feel like to have 6 billion people fighting *on the same side* of a fictional war?

I think it's pretty clear that such an effort would have real meaning, even if it failed to generate any real-world value. If you were able to focus the attention of the entire planet on a single goal, even if just for one day, and even if it just involved dispatching aliens in a video game, it would be a truly awe-inspiring occasion. It would be the single biggest collective experience ever undertaken in the whole of human history. It would give the whole earth goose bumps.

That's the epic scale that gamers are capable of thinking on. That's the scale gamers are ready to work at.

Gamers can imagine 6 billion people coming together to fight a fictional enemy, for the sheer awe and wonder of it. They are ready to work together on extreme scales, toward epic goals, just for the spine-tingling joy of it. And the more we seek out that kind of happiness as a planet, the more likely we are to save it—not from fictional aliens, but from apathy and wasted potential.

Jean M. Twenge, a professor of psychology and the author of *Generation Me*, has persuasively argued that the youngest generations today—particularly anyone born after 1980—are, in her words, "more miserable than ever before." Why? Because of our increased cultural emphasis on "self-esteem" and "self-fulfillment." But real fulfillment, as countless psychologists, philosophers, and spiritual leaders have shown, comes from fulfilling commitments to others. We want to be esteemed in the eyes of others, not for "who we are," but rather for what we've done that really matters.

The more we focus on ourselves and avoid a commitment to others, Twenge's research shows, the more we suffer from anxiety and depression. But that doesn't stop us from trying to make ourselves happy alone. We mistakenly think that by putting ourselves first, we'll finally get what we want. In fact, true happiness comes not from thinking *more* of ourselves, but rather from thinking *less* of ourselves—from seeing the truly small role we play in something much bigger, much more important than our individual needs.

Joining any collective effort and embracing feelings of awe can help us unlock our potential to lead a meaningful life and to leave a meaningful mark on the world.

Even if it's a virtual world we're leaving our mark on, we're still learning what it feels like to be of service to a larger cause. We're priming our brains and bodies to value and to seek out epic meaning as an emotional reward. And as recent research suggests, the more we enjoy these rewards in game worlds, the more likely we may be to seek them out in real life.

Three scientific studies published in 2009 by a consortium of researchers from eight universities in the United States, Japan, Singapore, and Malaysia studied the relationship between time spent playing games that require "helpful behavior" and the gamers' willingness to help others in everyday life. One study focused on children age thirteen and younger, another on teenagers, and the third on college students. The researchers worked with more than three thousand young gamers in total, and in all three studies they reached the same conclusion: Young people who spend more time playing games in which they're required to help each other are significantly more likely to help friends, family, neighbors, and even strangers in their real lives.[28]

Although these studies weren't specifically looking at epic-scale games, the core findings seem likely to remain consistent, or even increase, at larger scales. As Brad Bushman, one coauthor of the studies and a professor of communications and psychology at the University of Michigan's Institute for Social Research, puts it, "These findings suggest there is an upward spiral of prosocial gaming and helpful behavior."[29] In other words, the more we help in games, the more we help in life. And so there's good reason to believe that the more we learn to enjoy serving epic causes in game worlds, the more we may find ourselves contributing to epic efforts in the real world.

The psychologist Abraham Maslow famously said, "It isn't normal to know what we want. It is a rare and difficult psychological achievement."[30] But to-day's best games give us a powerful tool for achieving exactly that rare kind of self-knowledge.

Games are showing us exactly what we want out of life: more satisfying work, better hope of success, stronger social connectivity, and the chance to be a part of something bigger than ourselves. With games that help us generate these four rewards every day, we have unlimited potential to raise our own quality of life. And when we play these games with friends, family, and neighbors, we can enrich the lives of people we care about.

So games are teaching us to see what really makes us happy—and how to become the best versions of ourselves. But can we apply that knowledge to the real world?

By supporting our four essential human cravings, and by providing a reliable source of flow and fiero, the gaming industry has gone a long way toward making us happier and more emotionally, resilient—but only up to a point. We haven't learned how to enjoy our *real lives* more thoroughly. Instead, we've spent the last thirty-five years learning to enjoy our *game lives* more thoroughly.

Instead of fixing reality, we've simply created more and more attractive alternatives to the boredom, anxiety, alienation, and meaninglessness we run up against so often in everyday life. It's high time we start applying the lessons of games to the design of our everyday lives. We need to engineer *alternate* realities: new, more gameful ways of interacting with the real world and living our real lives.

Fortunately, the project of making alternate realities is already under way.

Notes

1. "13 Billion Kills: Join the Mission." *Halo 3* forum, Bungie.net, February 20, 2009. http://www.bungie.net/News/content.aspx?type=topnews&link=TenBillionKills.

2. Ibid.

3. "Players Attempt to Hit 7 Billion Kills While *Halo 3* Killcount Exceeds Global Population." Joystiq, June 27, 2008. http://xbox.joystiq.com/2008/06/27/players-attempt-to-hit-7-billion-kills-while-halo-3-killcount-ex/.

4. Leith, Sam. "*Halo 3*: Blown Away." *Telegraph*, September 22, 2007. http://www. telegraph .co.uk/culture/3668103/Halo-3-blown-away.hbnl.

5. "Campaign Kill Count: 10,000,000,000." *Halo 3* forum, Bungie.net, April 13, 2009. http://www.bungie.net/Forums/posts.aspx?postID=32064021&postRepeater]-p=3.

6. Ibid.

7. Ibid.

8. Seligman, *Learned Optimism*, 287.

9. "Bungie: 10 Billion Covenant Killed in *Halo 3*...and *Growing*." Joystiq, April 13, 2009. http://xbox.joystiq.com/2009/04/13/bungie-10-billion-covenant-killed-in-halo-3-and-growing/.

10. "*Halo 3* Review." NZGamer, September 24, 2007. http://nzgamer.com/x360/reviews/538/halo-3.html.

11. Paul Pearsall. *Awe: The Delights and Dangers of Our Eleventh Emotion* (Deerfield Beach, Florida: HCl, 2007), 193.

12. Keltner, *Born to Be Good*, 268.

13. Polack, Trent. "Epic Scale." Gamasutra, July 16, 2009. http://www.gamasutra.com/blogs/IYerit Polack/20090716/7.412/Epic_Scale.php.

14. Kuhrcke, Tim, Christoph Klimmt, and Peter Vorderer. "Why Is Virtual Fighting Fun? Motivational Predictors of Exposure to Violent Video Games." Paper presented at the annual meeting of the International Communication Association, Dresden, Germany, May 25, 2009. http://www.allacademic.com/meta/p91358_indcx.html.

15. "Return of the New Hotness." Bungie.net, August 27, 2009. http://www.bungie.net/news/content.as px?type=topnews&Link=NewHotness.

16. Kelly, Kevin. "Scan This Book!" *New York Times*, March 14, 2006. http://www. nytimes .com/2006/ 05/14/magazine/14publishing.html.

17. "Watch New *Halo 3* Ad: 'Two Soldiers Reminisce.'" Joystiq, September 22, 2007. http://www.joystiq.com/2007/09/22/watch-new-halo-3-ad-two-soldiers-reminisce/.

18. "*Halo 3* Ad Brings Battle to Reality." Escapist, September 12, 2007. http://www.escapistmagazine.com/forums/read/7.48542.

19. Crecente, Brian. "*Halo* Diorama May Tour Country." Kotaku, September 13, 2007. http://kotaku.com/gaming/gallery/halo-diorama-may-tour-country-299470.php.

20. "Watch New *Halo 3* Ad," Joystiq.

21. "Hindsight: *Halo 3*." Ascendant Justice, March 1, 2008. http://blog.ascendant justice.com/halo-3/hindsight-halo-3/.

22. Leith, *"Halo 3*: Blown Away."

23. Curry, Andrew. "Gobekli Tepe: The World's First Temple?" *Smithsonian*, November 2008. http://www.smithsonianmag.com/history-archaeology/gobekli-tepe.html #ixzz0T0oKIRQ6.

24. McIntosh, Lindsay. "'Neolithic Cathedral Built to Amaze' Unearthed in Orkney Dig." *The Times* (UK), August 14, 2009. http://www.timesonline.co.uk/tol/news/uk/scotland/article6795316.ece.

25. Curry, "Gobekli Tepe."

26. Ibid.

27. Huizinga, Johan. *Homo Ludens* (Boston: Beacon Press, 1971), 446.

28. Gentile, Douglas A., Craig A. Anderson, Shintaro Yukawa, et al. "The Effects of Prosocial Video Games on Prosocial Behaviors: International Evidence From Correlational, Longitudinal, and Experimental Studies." *Personality and Social Psychology Bulletin*, 2009, 35:752–63.

29. "Some Video Games Can Make Children Kinder and More Likely to Help." Science Daily, June 18, 2009. http://www.sciencedaily.com/releases/2009/06/090617171819.htm.

30. Maslow, Abraham. *Motivation and Personality* (New York: Harper Collins, 1987), 113.

Eric Schmidt is an American software engineer, businessperson, and the Executive Chairman of Alphabet Inc. He has had a long career in the field of technology, influencing powerful people both inside and outside that industry. Jared Cohen is the founder and president of Jigsaw (previously Google Ideas) and an Adjunct Senior Fellow at the Council on Foreign Relations. As a member of the Secretary of State's Policy Planning staff under both Condoleezza Rice and Hillary Clinton he focused on counter-terrorism, counter-radicalization, internet freedom, and fostering opposition in repressive countries.

Our Future Selves
Eric Schmidt and Jared Cohen

Soon everyone on earth will be connected. With five billion more people[1] set to join the virtual world, the boom in digital connectivity will bring gains in productivity, health, education, quality of life and myriad other avenues in the physical world—and this will be true for everyone, from the most elite users to those at the base of the economic pyramid. But being "connected" will mean very different things to different people, largely because the problems they have to solve differ so dramatically. What might seem like a small jump forward for some—like a smart phone priced under $20—may be as profound for one group as commuting to work in a driverless car is for another. People will find that being connected virtually makes us feel more equal—with access to the same basic platforms, information and online resources—while significant differences persist in the physical world. Connectivity will not solve income inequality, though it will alleviate some of its more intractable causes, like lack of available education and economic opportunity. So we must recognize and celebrate innovation in its own context. Everyone will benefit from connectivity, but not equally, and how those differences manifest themselves in the daily lives of people is our focus here.

Increased Efficiency

Being able to do more in the virtual world will make the mechanics of our physical world more efficient. As digital connectivity reaches the far corners of the globe, new users will employ it to improve a wide range of inefficient markets, systems and behaviors, in both the most and least advanced societies. The resulting gains in efficiency and productivity will be profound, particularly in developing countries where technological isolation and bad policies have stymied growth and progress for years, and people will do more with less.

The accessibility of affordable smart devices, including phones and tablets, will be transformative in these countries. Consider the impact of basic mobile

---

1. *The World in 2011: ICT Facts and Figures*, International Telecommunication Union (ITU), accessed October 10, 2012, http://www.itu.int/ITUD/ict/facts/2011/material/ICTFacts Figures2011.pdf. The above source shows that as of 2011 35 percent of the world's population is online. We factored in population increase projections to estimate five billion set to join the virtual world. [All notes are Schmidt and Cohen's, except 13 and 17.]

phones[2] for a group of Congolese fisherwomen today. Whereas they used to bring their daily catch to the market and watch it slowly spoil as the day progressed, now they keep it on the line, in the river, and wait for calls from customers. Once an order is placed, a fish is brought out of the water and prepared for the buyer. There is no need for an expensive refrigerator, no need for someone to guard it at night, no danger of spoiled fish losing their value (or poisoning customers), and there is no unnecessary overfishing. The size of these women's market can even expand as other fishermen in surrounding areas coordinate with them over their own phones. As a substitute for a formal market economy (which would take years to develop), that's not a bad work-around, for these women or the community at large.

Mobile phones are transforming how people in the developing world access and use information, and adoption rates are soaring. There are already more than 650 million mobile-phone users in Africa,[3] and close to 3 billion across Asia.[4] The majority of these people are using basic-feature phones[5]—voice calls and text messages only—because the cost of data service in their countries is often prohibitively expensive, so that even those who can buy Web-enabled phones or smart phones cannot use them affordably. This will change, and when it does, the smart-phone revolution will profoundly benefit these populations.

Hundreds of millions of people today are living the lives of their grandparents, in countries where life expectancy is less than sixty years, or even fifty in some places,[6] and there is no guarantee that their political and macroeconomic circumstances will improve dramatically anytime soon. What is new in their lives and their futures is connectivity. Critically, they have the chance to bypass earlier technologies, like dial-up modems, and go directly to high-speed wireless connections, which means the transformations that connectivity brings will occur even more quickly than they did in the developed world. The introduction of mobile phones is far more transformative than most people in modern countries realize. As people come online, they will quite suddenly have access to almost all the world's information in one place in their own language. This will even be true for an illiterate Maasai cattle herder in the Serengeti, whose native tongue, Maa, is not written[7]—he'll be able to verbally inquire about the day's market prices

2. This fisherwomen thought experiment came out of a conversation with Rebecca Cohen, and while we put it in the context of the Congo, the example belongs to her.

3. "Africa's Mobile Phone Industry 'Booming,'" BBC, November 9, 2011, http://www.bbc .co.uk/news/world-africa-15659983.

4. See mobile cellular subscriptions, Asia & Pacific, year 2011, in "Key ICT Indicators for the ITU/BDT Regions (Totals and Penetration Rates)," International Telecommunication Union (ITU), ICT Data and Statistics (IDS), updated November 16, 2011, http://www.itu.int/ITU-D/ict/statistics/at_glance/KeyTelecom.html.

5. Ibid. Compare mobile cellular subscriptions to active mobile broadband subscriptions for 2011.

6. "Country Comparison: Life Expectancy at Birth," CIA, World Fact Book, accessed October 11, 2012, https://www.cia.gov/library/publications/the-world-factbook/rankorder/2102rank.html#top.

7. One of the authors spent the summer of 2001 in this remote village, without electricity, running water, or a single cell phone or landline. During a return trip in the fall of 2010, many of the Maasai

and crowd-source the whereabouts of any nearby predators, receiving a spoken answer from his device in reply. Mobile phones will allow formerly isolated people to connect with others very far away and very different from themselves. On the economic front, they'll find ways to use the new tools at their disposal to enlarge their businesses, make them more efficient and maximize their profits, as the fisherwomen did much more locally with their basic phones.

What connectivity also brings, beyond mobile phones, is the ability to collect and use data. Data itself is a tool, and in places where unreliable statistics about health, education, economics and the population's needs have stalled growth and development, the chance to gather data effectively is a game-changer. Everyone in society benefits from digital data, as governments can better measure the success of their programs, and media and other nongovernmental organizations can use data to support their work and check facts. For example, Amazon is able to take its data on merchants and, using algorithms, develop customized bank loans to offer them—in some cases when traditional banks have completely shut their doors. Larger markets and better metrics can help create healthier and more productive economies.

And the developing world will not be left out of the advances in gadgetry and other high-tech machinery. Even if the prices for sophisticated smart phones and robots to perform household tasks like vacuuming remain high, illicit markets like China's expansive *"shanzhai"* network[8] for knock-off consumer electronics will produce and distribute imitations that bridge the gap. And technologies that emerged in first-world contexts will find renewed purpose in developing countries. In "additive manufacturing," or 3-D printing, machines can actually "print" physical objects by taking three-dimensional data about an object and tracing the contours of its shape, ultra-thin layer by ultra-thin layer, with liquid plastic or other material, until the whole object materializes.[9] Such printers have produced a huge range of objects, including customized mobile phones, machine parts and a full-sized replica motorcycle.[10] These machines will definitely have an impact on the developing world. Communal 3-D printers in poor countries would allow people to make whatever tool or item they require from open-source templates—digital information that is freely available in its edited source—rather than waiting on laborious or iffy delivery routes for higher-priced premade goods.

In wealthier countries 3-D printing will be the perfect partner for advanced manufacturing. New materials and products will all be built uniquely to a

---

women had crafted beautiful beaded pouches to store their cell phones in.

8. Nicholas Schmidle, "Inside the Knockoff-Tennis-Shoe Factory," *New York Times Magazine*, August 19, 2010, Global edition, http://www.nytimes.com/2010/08 /22/magazine/22fake -t.html?pagewanted=all.

9. "The Printed World: Three-Dimensional Printing from Digital Designs Will Transform Manufacturing and Allow More People to Start Making Things," *Economist*, February 10, 2011, http://www.economist.com/node/18114221.

10. Patrick Collinson, "Hi-Tech Shares Take US for a Walk on the High Side," *Guardian* (Manchester), March 16, 2012, http://www.guardian.co.uk/money/2012/mar/16/hi-tech-shares-us.

specification from the Internet and on demand by a machine run by a sophisticated, trained operator. This will not replace the acres of high-volume, lowest-cost manufacturing present in many industries, but it will bring an unprecedented variety to the products used in the developed world.

As for life's small daily tasks, information systems will streamline many of them for people living in those countries, such as integrated clothing machines (washing, drying, folding, pressing and sorting) that keep an inventory of clean clothes and algorithmically suggest outfits based on the user's daily schedule. Haircuts will finally be automated and machine-precise. And cell phones, tablets and laptops will have wireless recharging capabilities, rendering the need to fiddle with charging cables an obsolete nuisance. Centralizing the many moving parts of one's life into an easy-to-use, almost intuitive system of information management and decision making will give our interactions with technology an effortless feel. As long as safeguards are in place to protect privacy and prevent data loss, these systems will free us of many small burdens—including errands, to-do lists and assorted "monitoring" tasks—that today add stress and chip away at our mental focus throughout the day. Our own neurological limits, which lead us to forgetfulness and oversights, will be supplemented by information systems designed to support our needs. Two such examples are memory prosthetics—calendar reminders and to-do lists—and social prosthetics, which instantly connect you with your friend who has relevant expertise in whatever task you are facing.

By relying on these integrated systems, which will encompass both the professional and the personal sides of our lives, we'll be able to use our time more effectively each day—whether that means having the time to have a "deep think," spending more time preparing for an important presentation or guaranteeing that a parent can attend his or her child's soccer game without distraction. Suggestion engines that offer alternative terms to help a user find what she is looking for will be a particularly useful aid in efficiency by consistently stimulating our thinking processes, ultimately enhancing our creativity, not pre-empting it. Of course, the world will be filled with gadgets, holograms that allow a virtual version of you to be somewhere else, and endless amounts of content, so there will be plenty of ways to procrastinate, too—but the point is that when you choose to be productive, you can do so with greater capacity.

Other advances in the pipeline in areas like robotics, artificial intelligence and voice recognition will introduce efficiency into our lives by providing more seamless forms of engagement with the technology in our daily routines. Fully automated human-like robots with superb AI [artificial intelligence] abilities will probably be out of most people's price range for some time, but the average American consumer will find it affordable to own a handful of different multipurpose robots fairly soon. The technology in iRobot's Roomba vacuum cleaner, the progenitor of this field of consumer "home" robots (first introduced in 2002), will only become more sophisticated and multipurpose in time. Future varieties of home robots should be able to handle other household duties, electrical work and even plumbing issues with relative ease.

We also can't discount the impact that superior voice-recognition software will have on our daily lives. Beyond searching for information online and issuing commands to your robots (both of which are possible today), better voice recognition will mean instant transcription of any-thing you produce: e-mails, notes, speeches, term papers. Most people speak much faster than they type, so this technology will surely save many of us time in our daily affairs—not to mention helping us avoid cases of carpal tunnel syndrome. A shift toward voice-initiated writing may well change our world of written material. Will we learn to speak in paragraphs, or will our writing begin to mirror speech patterns?

Everyday use of gesture-recognition technology is also closer than we think. Microsoft's Kinect, a hands-free sensor device for the Xbox 360 video-game console that captures and integrates a player's motion, set a world record in 2011 as the fastest selling consumer-electronics device in history, with more than eight million devices sold in the first sixty days on the market. Gestural interfaces will soon move beyond gaming and entertainment into more functional areas; the futuristic information screens displayed so prominently in the film *Minority Report*—in which Tom Cruise used gesture technology and holographic images to solve crimes on a computer—are just the beginning. In fact, we've already moved beyond that—the really interesting work today is building "social robots" that can recognize human gestures and respond to them in kind, such as a toy dog that sits when a child makes a command gesture.[11]

And, looking further down the line, we might not need to move physically to manipulate those robots. There have been a series of exciting breakthroughs in thought-controlled motion technology—directing motion by thinking alone—in the past few years. In 2012, a team at a robotics laboratory in Japan demonstrated successfully that a person lying in an fMRI machine (which takes continuous scans of the brain to measure changes in blood flow) could control a robot hundreds of miles away just by imagining moving different parts of his body.[12] The subject could see from the robot's perspective, thanks to a camera on its head, and when he thought about moving his arm or his legs, the robot would move correspondingly almost instantaneously. The possibilities of thought-controlled motion, not only for "surrogates" like separate robots but also for prosthetic limbs, are particularly exciting in what they portend for mobility-challenged or "locked in" individuals—spinal-cord-injury patients, amputees and others who cannot communicate or move in their current physical state.

---

11. Sarah Constantin, "Gesture Recognition, Mind-Reading Machines, and Social Robotics," *H+ Magazine*, February 8, 2011, http://hplusmagazine.com/2011/02/08/gesture-recognition -mind-reading-machines-and-social-robotics/.

12. Helen Thomson, "Robot Avatar Body Controlled by Thought Alone," *New Scientist*, July 2012, 19–20.

More Innovation, More Opportunity

That the steady march of globalization will continue apace, even accelerate, as connectivity spreads will come as no surprise. But what might surprise you is how small some of the advances in technology, when paired with increased connection and interdependence across countries, will make your world feel. Instant language translation, virtual-reality interactions and real-time collective editing—most easily understood today as wikis—will reshape how firms and organizations interact with partners, clients and employees in other places. While certain differences will perhaps never be fully overcome—like cultural nuance and time zones—the ability to engage with people in disparate locations, with near-total comprehension and on shared platforms, will make such interactions feel incredibly familiar.

Supply chains for corporations and other organizations will become increasingly disaggregated, not just on the production side but also with respect to people. More effective communication across borders and languages will build trust and create opportunities for hardworking and talented individuals around the world. It will not be unusual for a French technology company to operate its sales team from Southeast Asia, while locating its human-resources people in Canada and its engineers in Israel. Bureaucratic obstacles that prevent this level of decentralized operation today, like visa restrictions and regulations around money transfers, will either become irrelevant or be circumvented as digital solutions are discovered. Perhaps a human-rights organization with staff living in a country under heavy diplomatic sanctions will pay its employees in mobile money credits, or in an entirely digital currency.

As fewer jobs require a physical presence, talented individuals will have more options available to them. Skilled young adults in Uruguay will find themselves competing for certain types of jobs against their counterparts in Orange County. Of course, just as not all jobs can or will be automated in the future, not every job can be conducted from a distance—but more can than you might think. And for those living on a few dollars per day, there will be endless opportunities to increase their earnings. In fact, Amazon Mechanical Turk,[13] which is a digital task-distribution platform, offers a present-day example of a company out-sourcing small tasks that can be performed for a few cents by anyone with an Internet connection. As the quality of virtual interactions continues to improve, a range of vocations can expand the platform's client base; you might retain a lawyer from one continent and use a Realtor from another. Globalization's critics will decry this erosion of local monopolies, but it should be embraced, because this

---

13. Amazon Mechanical Turk: A crowd-sourcing Internet marketplace that allows individuals to earn money doing tasks inside computer applications that computers are currently unable to do by themselves. The original Mechanical Turk was a chess-playing "robot" that created a sensation when it toured Europe in the eighteenth century defeating famous opponents like Napoleon Bonaparte and Benjamin Franklin. Not really a robot at all, the "Turk" actually contained a live chess master hidden behind a mechanical façade. [Eds.]

is how our societies will move forward and continue to innovate. Indeed, rising connectivity should *help* countries discover their competitive advantage—it could be that the world's best graphic designers come from Botswana, and the world just doesn't know it yet.

This leveling of the playing field for talent extends to the world of ideas, and innovation will increasingly come from the margins, outside traditional bastions of growth, as people begin to make new connections and apply unique perspectives to difficult problems, driving change. New levels of collaboration and cross-pollination across different sectors internationally will ensure that many of the best ideas and solutions will have a chance to rise to the top and be seen, considered, explored, funded, adopted and celebrated. Perhaps an aspiring Russian programmer currently working as a teacher in Novosibirsk will discover a new application of the technology behind the popular mobile game Angry Birds, realizing how its game framework could be used to improve the educational tools he is building to teach physics to local students. He finds similar gaming software that is open source and then he builds on it. As the open-source movement around the world continues to gain speed (for governments and companies it is low cost, and for contributors the benefits are in recognition and economic opportunities to improve and enlarge the support ecosystems), the Russian teacher-programmer will have an enormous cache of technical plans to learn from and use in his own work. In a fully connected world, he is increasingly likely to catch the eyes of the right people, to be offered jobs or fellowships, or to sell his creation to a major multinational company. At a minimum, he can get his foot in the door.

Innovation can come from the ground up, but not all local innovation will work on a larger scale, because some entrepreneurs and inventors will be building for different audiences, solving very specific problems. This is true today as well. Consider the twenty-four-year-old Kenyan inventor Anthony Mutua, who unveiled at a 2012 Nairobi science fair an ultrathin crystal chip he developed that can generate electricity when put under pressure.[14] He placed the chip in the sole of a tennis shoe and demonstrated how, just by walking, a person can charge his mobile phone.[15] (It's a reminder of how bad the problems of reliable and affordable electricity, and to a lesser extent short battery life, are for many people—and how some governments are not rushing to fix the electricity grids—that innovators like Mutua are designing microchips that turn people into portable charging stations.) Mutua's chip is now set to go into mass production,[16] and if that successfully brings down the cost, he will have invented one of the cleverest designs that no one outside the developing world will ever use, simply because they'll never need to. Unfortunately, the level of a population's access to technology is

14. "Shoe Technology to Charge Cell Phones," *Daily Nation*, May 2012, http://www.nation.co.ke/News/Shoe+technology+to+charge+cell+phones++/-/1056/1401998/-/view /printVersion/-/sur34lz/-/index.html.

15. Ibid.

16. Ibid.

often determined by external factors, and even if power and electricity problems are eventually solved (by the government or by citizens), there is no telling what new roadblocks will prevent certain groups from reaching the same level of connectivity and opportunity as others.

The most important pillar behind innovation and opportunity—education—will see tremendous positive change in the coming decades as rising connectivity reshapes traditional routines and offers new paths for learning. Most students will be highly technologically literate, as schools continue to integrate technology into lesson plans and, in some cases, replace traditional lessons with more interactive workshops. Education will be a more flexible experience, adapting itself to children's learning styles and pace instead of the other way around. Kids will still go to physical schools, to socialize and be guided by teachers, but as much, if not more, learning will take place employing carefully designed educational tools in the spirit of today's Khan Academy,[17] a nonprofit organization that produces thousands of short videos (the majority in science and math) and shares them online for free. With hundreds of millions of views on the Khan Academy's YouTube channel already, educators in the United States are increasingly adopting its materials and integrating the approach of its founder, Salman Khan—modular learning tailored to a student's needs. Some are even "flipping" their classrooms, replacing lectures with videos watched at home (as homework) and using school time for traditional homework, such as filling out a problem set for math class.[18] Critical thinking and problem-solving skills will become the focus in many school systems as ubiquitous digital-knowledge tools, like the more accurate sections of Wikipedia, reduce the importance of rote memorization.

For children in poor countries, future connectivity promises new access to educational tools, though clearly not at the level described above. Physical classrooms will remain dilapidated; teachers will continue to take paychecks and not show up for class; and books and supplies will still be scarce. But what's new in this equation—connectivity—promises that kids with access to mobile devices and the Internet will be able to experience school physically *and* virtually, even if the latter is informal and on their own time.

In places where basic needs are poorly met by the government, or in insecure areas, basic digital technologies like mobile phones will offer safe and inexpensive options for families looking to educate their children. A child who cannot attend school due to distance, lack of security or school fees will have a lifeline to the world of learning if she has access to a mobile phone. Even for those children without access to data plans or the mobile Web, basic mobile services, like text messages and IVR (interactive voice response, a form of voice-recognition technology), can provide educational outlets. Loading tablets and mobile phones with

17. Khan Academy: A nonprofit, online educational organization that provides micro lectures on thousands of academic topics via YouTube videos. [Eds.]

18. Clive Thompson, "How Khan Academy Is Changing the Rules of Education," *Wired Magazine*, August 2011, posted online July 15, 2011, http://www.wired.com/magazine/2011/07/ff_khan/.

high-quality education applications and entertainment content before they are sold will ensure that the "bandwidth poor," who lack reliable connectivity, will still benefit from access to these devices. And for children whose classrooms are overcrowded or understaffed, or whose national curriculum is dubiously narrow, connectivity through mobile devices will supplement their education and help them reach their full potential, regardless of their origins. Today numerous pilot projects exist in developing countries that leverage mobile technology to teach a wide range of topics and skills, including basic literacy for children and adults, second languages and advanced courses from universities. In 2012, the MIT Media Lab tested this approach in Ethiopia[19] by distributing pre-loaded tablets to primary-age kids without instructions or accompanying teachers.[20] The results were extraordinary: within months the kids were reciting the entire alphabet and writing complete sentences in English. Without the connectivity that will be ubiquitous in the future, there are limits to what any of these efforts can accomplish today.

Just imagine the implications of these burgeoning mobile or tablet-based learning platforms for a country like Afghanistan, which has one of the lowest rates of literacy in the world.[21] Digital platforms, whether presented in simple mobile form or in more sophisticated ways online, will eventually be able to withstand any environmental turbulence (political instability, economic collapse, perhaps even bad weather) and continue to serve the needs of users. So while the educational experience in the physical world will remain volatile for many, the virtual experience will increasingly become the more important and predictable option. And students stuck in school systems that teach narrow curriculums or only rote memorization will have access to a virtual world that encourages independent exploration and critical thinking.

A Better Quality of Life

In tandem with the wide variety of functional improvements in your daily life, future connectivity promises a dazzling array of "quality of life" improvements: things that make you healthier, safer and more engaged. As with other gains, there remains a sliding scale of access here, but that doesn't make them any less meaningful.

The devices, screens and various machines in your future apartment will serve a purpose beyond utility—they will offer entertainment, wanted distraction, intellectual and cultural enrichment, relaxation and opportunities to share

19. Nicholas Negroponte, "EmTech Preview: Another Way to Think About Learning," *Technology Review*, September 13, 2012, http://www.technologyreview.com/view/429206/emtech-preview-another-way-to-think-about/.

20. David Talbot, "Given Tablets but No Teachers, Ethiopian Children Teach Themselves," *Technology Review*, October 29, 2012, http://www.technologyreview.com/news/506466/given-tablets-but-no-teachers-ethiopian-children-teach-themselves/.

21. "Field Listing: Literacy," CIA, World Fact Book, accessed October 11, 2012, https://www.cia.gov/library/publications/the-world-factbook/fields/2103.html#af.

things with others. The key advance ahead is personalization. You'll be able to customize your devices—indeed, much of the technology around you—to fit your needs, so that your environment reflects your preferences. People will have a better way to curate their life stories and will no longer have to rely on physical or online photo albums, although both will still exist. Future videography and photography will allow you to project any still or moving image you've captured as a three-dimensional holograph. Even more remarkable, you will be able to integrate any photos, videos and geographic settings that you choose to save into a single holographic device that you will place on the floor of your living room, instantaneously transforming the space into a memory room. A couple will be able to re-create their wedding ceremony for grandparents who were too ill to attend.

What you can watch on your various displays (high-quality LCD—liquid crystal display—screens, holographic projections or a handheld mobile device) will be determined by you, not by network-television schedules. At your fingertips will be an entire world's worth of digital content, constantly updated, ranked and categorized to help you find the music, movies, shows, books, magazines, blogs and art you like. Individual agency over entertainment and information channels will be greater than ever, as content producers shift from balkanized protectiveness to more unified and open models, since a different business model will be necessary in order to keep the audience. Contemporary services like Spotify, which offers a large catalog of live-streaming music for free, give us a sense of what the future will look like: an endless amount of content, available anytime, on almost any device, and at little or no cost to users, with copyrights and revenue streams preserved. Long-standing barriers to entry for content creators are being flattened as well; just as YouTube can be said to launch careers today[22] (or at least offer fleeting fame), in the future, even more platforms will offer artists, writers, directors, musicians and others in every country the chance to reach a wider audience. It will still require skill to create quality content, but it will also be easier to assemble a team with the requisite skills to do this—say, an animator from South Korea, a voice actor from the Philippines, a storyboarder from Mexico and a musician from Kenya—and the finished product may have the potential to reach as wide an audience as any Hollywood blockbuster.

Entertainment will become a more immersive and personalized experience in the future. Integrated tie-ins will make today's product placements seem passive and even clumsy. If while watching a television show you spot a sweater you want or a dish you think you'd like to cook, information including recipes or purchasing details will be readily available, as will every other fact about the show, its story lines, actors and locations. If you're feeling bored and want to take an hour-long holiday, why not turn on your holograph box and visit Carnival in

---

22. The Korean K-pop star Psy's fame reached global proportions almost overnight as the video he created for his song "Gangnam Style" became the most-watched YouTube video ever within a span of three months.

Rio? Stressed? Go spend some time on a beach in the Maldives. Worried your kids are becoming spoiled? Have them spend some time wandering around the Dharavi slum in Mumbai. Frustrated by the media's coverage of the Olympics in a different time zone? Purchase a holographic pass for a reasonable price and watch the women's gymnastics team compete right in front of you, live. Through virtual-reality interfaces and holographic-projection capabilities, you'll be able to "join" these activities as they happen and experience them as if you were truly there. Nothing beats the real thing, but this will be a very close second. And if nothing else, it will certainly be more affordable. Thanks to these new technologies, you can be more stimulated, or more relaxed, than ever before.

You'll be safer, too, at least on the road. While some of the very exciting new possibilities in transportation, like supersonic tube commutes and suborbital space travel, are still far in the distance, ubiquitous self-driving cars are imminent. Google's fleet of driverless cars, built by a team of Google and Stanford University engineers, has logged hundreds of thousands of miles without incident, and other models will soon join it on the road. Rather than replacing drivers altogether, the liminal step will be a "driver-assist" approach, where the self-driving option can be turned on, just as an airline captain turns on the autopilot. Government authorities are already well versed on self-driving cars and their potential—in 2012, Nevada became the first state to issue licenses to driverless cars,[23] and later that same year California also affirmed their legality.[24] Imagine the possibilities for long-haul truck-driving. Rather than testing the biological limits of human drivers with thirty-hour trips, the computer can take over primary responsibility and drive the truck for stretches as the driver rests.

The advances in health and medicine in our near future will be among the most significant of all the new game-changing developments. And thanks to rising connectivity, an even wider range of people will benefit than at any other time in history. Improvements in disease detection and treatment, the management of medical records and personal-health monitoring promise more equitable access to health care and health information for potentially billions more people when we factor in the spread of digital technology.

The diagnostic capability of your mobile phone will be old news. (*Of course* you will be able to scan body parts the way you do bar codes.) But soon you will be benefiting from a slew of physical augmentations designed to monitor your well-being, such as microscopic robots in your circulatory system that keep track of your blood pressure, detect nascent heart disease and identify early-stage

23. Chris Gaylord, "Ready for a Self-Driving Car? Check Your Driveway," *Christian Science Monitor*, June 25, 2012, http://www.csmonitor.com/Innovation/Tech/2012/0625/Ready-for-a-self-driving-car-Check-your-driveway.

24. James Temple, "California Affirms Legality of Driverless Cars," *The Tech Chronicles* (blog), *San Francisco Chronicle*, September 25, 2012, http://blog.sfgate.com/techron/2012/09/25/california-legalizes-driverless-cars/; Florida has passed a similar law. See Joann Muller, "With Driverless Cars, Once Again It Is California Leading the Way," *Forbes*, September 26, 2012, http://www.forbes.com/sites/joannmuller/2012/09/26/with-driverless-cars-once-again-it-is-california-leading-the-way/.

cancer. Inside your grandfather's new titanium hip there will be a chip that can act as a pedometer, monitor his insulin levels to check for the early stages of diabetes, and even trigger an automated phone call to an emergency contact if he takes a particularly hard fall and might need assistance. A tiny nasal implant will be available to you that will alert you to airborne toxins and early signs of a cold.

Eventually these accoutrements will be as uncontroversial as artificial pacemakers (the first of which was implanted in the 1950s). They are the logical extensions of today's personal-health-tracking applications, which allow people to use their smart phones to log their exercise, track their metabolic rates and chart their cholesterol levels. Indeed, ingestible health technology already exists—the Food and Drug Administration (FDA) approved the first electronic pill in 2012. Made by a California-based biomedical firm called Proteus Digital Health, the pill carries a tiny sensor one square millimeter in size, and once the pill is swallowed, stomach acid activates the circuit and sends a signal to a small patch worn outside the body (which then sends its data to a mobile phone). The patch can collect information about a patient's response to a drug (monitoring body temperature, heart rate and other indicators), relay data about regular usage to doctors and even track what a person eats. For sufferers of chronic illnesses and the elderly particularly, this technology will allow for significant improvements: automatic reminders to take various medications, the ability to measure directly how drugs are reacting in a person's body and the creation of an instant digital feedback loop with doctors that is personalized and data-driven. Not everyone will want to actively oversee their health to this degree, let alone the even more detailed version of the future, but they probably will want their doctor to have access to such data. "Intelligent pills" and nasal implants will be sufficiently affordable so as to be as accessible as vitamins and supplements. In short order, we will have access to personal health-care systems run off of our mobile devices that will automatically detect if something is wrong with us based on data collected from some of the above-mentioned augmentations, prompt us with appointment options for a nearby doctor and subsequently (with consent) send all of the relevant data about our symptoms and health indicators to the doctor being consulted.

Tissue engineers will be able to grow new organs to replace patients' old or diseased ones, using either synthetic materials or a person's own cells. At the outset, affordability will limit the use. Synthetic skin grafts, which exist today, will give way to grafts made from burn victims' own cells. Inside hospitals, robots will take on more responsibilities, as surgeons increasingly let sophisticated machines handle difficult parts of certain procedures, where delicate or tedious work is involved or a wider range of motion is required.[25]

Advances in genetic testing will usher in the era of personalized medicine. Through targeted tests and genome sequencing (decoding a person's full DNA), doctors and disease specialists will have more information about patients, and

25. Robotic surgical suites are already in operation in hospitals in the United States and Europe.

what might help them, than ever before. Despite steady scientific progress, severe negative reactions to prescribed drugs remain a leading cause of hospitalization and death. Pharmaceutical companies traditionally pursue a "one-size-fits-all" approach to drug development, but this is due to change as the burgeoning field of pharmacogenetics continues to develop. Better genetic testing will reduce the likelihood of negative reactions, improve patients' chances and provide doctors and medical researchers with more data to analyze and use. Eventually, and initially only for the wealthy, it will be possible to design pharmaceutical drugs tailored to an individual's genetic structure. But this too will change as the cost of DNA sequencing drops below $100 and almost everything biological is sequenced, making it possible for a much broader segment of the world's population to benefit from highly specific, personalized diagnoses ....

The Upper Band

Connectivity benefits everyone. Those who have none will have some, and those who have a lot will have even more. To demonstrate that, imagine you are a young urban professional living in an American city a few decades from now. An average morning might look something like this:

There will be no alarm clock in your wake-up routine—at least, not in the traditional sense. Instead, you'll be roused by the aroma of freshly brewed coffee, by light entering your room as curtains open automatically, and by a gentle back massage administered by your high-tech bed. You're more likely to awake refreshed, because inside your mattress there's a special sensor that monitors your sleeping rhythms, determining precisely when to wake you so as not to interrupt a REM cycle.

Your apartment is an electronic orchestra, and you are the conductor. With simple flicks of the wrist and spoken instructions, you can control temperature, humidity, ambient music and lighting. You are able to skim through the day's news on translucent screens while a freshly cleaned suit is retrieved from your automated closet because your calendar indicates an important meeting today. You head to the kitchen for breakfast and the translucent news display follows, as a projected hologram hovering just in front of you, using motion detection, as you walk down the hallway. You grab a mug of coffee and a fresh pastry, cooked to perfection in your humidity-controlled oven—and skim new e-mails on a holographic "tablet" projected in front of you. Your central computer system suggests a list of chores your housekeeping robots should tackle today, all of which you approve. It further suggests that, since your coffee supply is projected to run out next Wednesday, you consider purchasing a certain larger-size container that it noticed currently on sale online. Alternatively, it offers a few recent reviews of other coffee blends your friends enjoy.

As you mull this over, you pull up your notes for a presentation you'll give later that day to important new clients abroad. All of your data—from your personal and professional life—is accessible through all of your various devices, as it's stored in the cloud, a remote digital-storage system with near limitless capacity. You own a few different and interchangeable digital devices; one is the size of a tablet, another the size of a pocket watch, while others might be flexible or wearable. All will be lightweight, incredibly fast and will use more powerful processors than anything available today.

You take another sip of coffee, feeling confident that you'll impress your clients. You already feel as if you know them, though you've never met in person, since your meetings have been conducted in a virtual-reality interface. You interact with holographic "avatars" that exactly capture your clients' movements and speech. You understand them and their needs well, not least because autonomous language-translation software reproduces the speech of both parties in perfect translations almost instantly. Real-time virtual interactions like these, as well as the ability to edit and collaborate on documents and other projects, makes the actual distance between you seem negligible.

As you move about your kitchen, you stub your toe, hard, on the edge of a cabinet—ouch! You grab your mobile device and open the diagnostics app. Inside your device there is a tiny microchip that uses low-radiation submillimeter waves to scan your body, like an X-ray. A quick scan reveals that your toe is just bruised, not broken. You decline the invitation your device suggests to get a second opinion at a nearby doctor's office.

There's a bit of time left before you need to leave for work—which you'll get to by driverless car, of course. Your car knows what time you need to be in the office each morning based on your calendar and, after factoring in traffic data, it communicates with your wristwatch to give you a sixty-minute countdown to when you need to leave the house. Your commute will be as productive or relaxing as you desire.

Before you head out, your device reminds you to buy a gift for your nephew's upcoming birthday. You scan the system's proposed gift ideas, derived from anonymous, aggregated data on other nine-year-old boys with his profile and interests, but none of the suggestions inspire you. Then you remember a story his parents told you that had everyone forty and older laughing: Your nephew hadn't understood a reference to the old excuse "A dog ate my homework"; how could a dog eat his cloud storage drive? He had never gone to school before digital textbooks and online lesson plans, and he had used paper to do his homework so rarely—and used cloud storage so routinely—that the notion that he would somehow "forget" his homework *and* come up with an excuse like that struck him as absurd. You do a quick search for a robotic dog and buy one with a single click, after adding a few special touches he might like, such as a reinforced titanium skeleton so that he can ride on it. In the card input, you type: "Just in case." It will arrive at his house within a five-minute window of your selected delivery time.

You think about having another cup of coffee, but then a haptic device ("haptic" refers to technology that involves touch and feeling) that is embedded in the heel of your shoe gives you a gentle pinch—a signal that you'll be late for your morning meeting if you linger any longer. Perhaps you grab an apple on the way out, to eat in the backseat of your car as it chauffeurs you to your office.

If you are a part of the world's upper band of income earners (as most residents of wealthy Western countries are), you will have access to many of these new technologies directly, as owners or as friends of those who own them. You probably recognize from this morning routine a few things you have already imagined or experienced. Of course, there will always be the super-wealthy people whose access to technology will be even greater—they'll probably eschew cars altogether and travel to work in motion-stabilized automated helicopters, for example.

We will continue to encounter challenges in the physical world, but the expansion of the virtual world and what is possible online—as well as the inclusion of five billion more minds—means we will have new ways of getting information and moving resources to solve those problems, even if the solutions are imperfect. While there will remain significant differences between us, more opportunities to interact and better policy can help blur the edges.

Susan Schneider is an Associate Professor in the Department of Philosophy, a member of the Cognitive Science Program, and a member of the Connecticut Institute for Brain and Cognitive Science at the University of Connecticut. Her work focuses on philosophy of the self, the mind, ethics, and cognition. She is perhaps best known for her work on robotic cognition and emotion.

Mindscan: Transcending and Enhancing the Human Brain[1]
Susan Schneider

Suppose it is 2025 and, being a technophile, you purchase brain enhancements as they become readily available. First, you add a mobile internet connection to your retina, then you enhance your working memory by adding neural circuitry. You are now officially a cyborg. Now skip ahead to 2040. Through nanotechnological therapies and enhancements you are able to extend your lifespan, and as the years progress, you continue to accumulate more far-reaching enhancements. By 2060, after several small but cumulatively profound alterations, you are a "posthuman." To quote philosopher Nick Bostrom, posthumans are possible future beings, "whose basic capacities so radically exceed those of present humans as to be no longer unambiguously human by our current standards" (Bostrom 2003). At this point, your intelligence is enhanced not just in terms of speed of mental processing; you are now able to make rich connections that you were not able to make before. Unenhanced humans, or "naturals," seem to you to be intellectually disabled—you have little in common with them—but as a transhumanist, you are supportive of their right to not enhance (Bostrom 2003; Garreau 2005; Kurzweil 2005).

It is now AD 2400. For years, worldwide technological developments, including your own enhancements, have been facilitated by superintelligent AI. A superintelligence is a creature with the capacity to radically outperform the best human brains in practically every field, including scientific creativity, general wisdom, and social skills. Indeed, as Bostrom explains, "creating superintelligence may be the last invention that humans will ever need to make, since superintelligences could themselves take care of further scientific and technological developments" (Bostrom 2003). Over time, the slow addition of better and better neural circuitry has left no real intellectual difference in kind between you and a superintelligent AI. The only real difference between you and an AI creature of standard design is one of origin—you were once a "natural." But you are now almost entirely engineered by technology. You are perhaps more aptly characterized as a member of a rather heterogeneous class of AI life forms (Kurzweil 2005).

So let me ask: should you enhance and if so, why? I have just given a very rough sketch of the kind of developmental trajectory that the transhumanist generally aspires to.[2] Transhumanism is a philosophical, cultural, and political movement that holds that the human species is now in a comparatively early phase and that its very evolution will be altered by developing technologies.

Future humans will be very unlike their present-day incarnation in both physical and mental respects, and will in fact resemble certain persons depicted in science fiction stories. Transhumanists share the belief that an outcome in which humans have radically advanced intelligence, near immortality, deep friendships with AI creatures, and elective body characteristics is a very desirable end, both for one's own personal development and for the development of our species as a whole.

Despite its science fiction-like flavor, the future that transhumanism depicts is very possible: indeed, the beginning stages of this radical alteration may well lie in certain technological developments that either are already here (if not generally available), or are accepted by many in the relevant scientific fields as being on their way (Roco and Bainbridge 2002; Garreau 2005). In the face of these technological developments, transhumanists offer a progressive bioethics agenda of increasing public import. They also present a thought-provoking and controversial position in philosophy of cognitive science, applying insights about the computational nature of the mind to the topic of the nature of persons, developing a novel version of one popular theory of personal identity: the psychological continuity theory.

In this chapter I shall employ science fiction thought experiments to discuss what I take to be the most important philosophical element of the transhumanist picture—its unique perspective on the nature and development of persons. Persons are traditionally viewed as being an important moral category, being the bearers of rights, or at least deserving of consideration of their interests in a utilitarian calculus. And, as we shall see, considering the nature of persons through the lens of transhumanism involves pushing up against the boundaries of the very notion of personhood. For consider again the issue of enhancement. When one wonders whether to enhance in the radical ways the transhumanists advocate, one must ask, "Will this radically enhanced creature still be me?" If not, then, on the reasonable assumption that one key factor in a decision to enhance one-self is one's own personal development, even the most progressive technophile will likely regard the enhancement in question as undesirable, for when you choose to enhance in these radical ways, the enhancement does not really enhance *you*. As we shall soon discuss, this is a lesson that the main character in Hugo award winner Robert Sawyer's *Mindscan* learns the hard way. Hence, examining the enhancement issue from the vantage point of the metaphysical problem of personal identity will thereby present a serious challenge to transhumanism. Given their conception of the nature of a person, radical, and even mild, enhancements are risky, not clearly resulting in the preservation of one's original self. Indeed, I suspect that this is a pressing issue for any case for enhancement.

The Transhumanist Position

Transhumanism is by no means a monolithic ideology, but it does have an organization and an official declaration. The World Transhumanist Association is an international nonprofit organization that was founded in 1998 by philosophers

Nick Bostrom and David Pearce. The main tenets of transhumanism were laid out in the Transhumanist Declaration (World Transhumanist Association 1998) and are reprinted below:

1. Humanity will be radically changed by technology in the future. We foresee the feasibility of redesigning the human condition, including such parameters as the inevitability of aging, limitations on human and artificial intellects, unchosen psychology, suffering, and our confinement to the planet earth.

2. Systematic research should be put into understanding these coming developments and their long-term consequences.

3. Transhumanists think chat by being generally open and embracing of new technology we have a better chance of turning it to our advantage than if we try to ban or prohibit it.

4. Transhumanists advocate the moral right for those who so wish to use technology to extend their mental and physical (including reproductive) capacities and to improve their control over their own lives. We seek personal growth beyond our current biological limitations.

5. In planning for the future, it is mandatory to take into account the prospect of dramatic progress in technological capabilities. It would be tragic if the potential benefits failed to materialize because of technophobia and unnecessary prohibitions. On the other hand, it would also be tragic if intelligent life went extinct because of some disaster or war involving advanced technologies.

6. We need to create forums where people can rationally debate what needs to be done, and a social order where responsible decisions can be implemented.

7. Transhumanism advocates the well-being of all sentience (whether in artificial intellects, humans, posthumans, or non-human animals) and encompasses many principles of modern humanism. Transhumanism does not support any particular party, politician or political platform.

This document was followed by the much longer and extremely informative *The Transhumanist Frequently Asked Questions*, authored by Nick Bostrom, in consultation with dozens of leading transhumanists (Bostrom 2003).[3]

The Nature of Persons

Now let us consider some of the ideas expressed in the Declaration. Overall, central transhumanist texts have advanced a sort of trajectory for the personal development of a contemporary human, technology permitting (Kurzweil 1999, 2005; Bostrom 2003, 2005):[4]

21st century unenhanced human → significant "upgrading" with cognitive and other physical enhancements → posthuman status → "superintelligence"[5]

Recalling the chronology of enhancements I sketched at the beginning of this chapter, let us again ask: Should you embark upon this journey? Here, there are deep philosophical questions that have no easy answers.[6] For in order to understand whether you should enhance, you must first understand what you are to begin with. But what is a person? And, given your conception of a person, after such radical changes, would you yourself continue to exist, or would you have ceased to exist, having been replaced by someone else? If the latter is the case, why would you want to embark on the path to radical enhancement at all?

To make such a decision, one must understand the metaphysics of personal identity—that is, one must answer the question: What is it in virtue of which a particular self or person continues existing over time? A good place to begin is with the persistence of everyday objects over time. Consider the espresso machine in your favorite café. Suppose that five minutes have elapsed and the barista has turned the machine off. Imagine asking the barista if the machine is the same one that was there five minutes ago. She will likely tell you the answer is glaringly obvious—it is of course possible for one and the same machine to continue existing over time. This seems to be a reasonable case of persistence, even though at least one of the machine's properties has changed. On the other hand, if the machine disintegrated or melted, then the same machine would no longer exist. What remained wouldn't be an espresso machine at all, for that matter. So it seems that some changes cause a thing to cease to exist, while others do not. Philosophers call the characteristics that a thing must have as long as it exists "essential properties."

Now reconsider the transhumanist's trajectory for enhancement: for radical enhancement to be a worthwhile option for you, it has to represent a form of personal development. At bare minimum, even if enhancement brings such goodies as superhuman intelligence and radical life extension, it must not involve the elimination of any of your essential properties. For in that case, the sharper mind and fitter body would not be experienced by you—they would be experienced by someone else. Even if you would like to become superintelligent, knowingly embarking on a path that trades away one or more of your essential properties would be tantamount to suicide—that is, to your intentionally causing yourself to cease to exist. So before you enhance, you had better get a handle on what your essential properties are.

Transhumanists have grappled with this issue. Ray Kurzweil asks: "So who am I? Since I am constantly changing, am I just a pattern? What if someone copies that pattern? Am I the original and/or the copy? Perhaps I am this stuff here—that is, the both ordered and chaotic collection of molecules that make up my body and brain" (Kurzweil 2005: 383). Kurzweil is here referring to two theories at center stage in the age-old philosophical debate about the nature of persons. The leading theories include the following:

1. The soul theory: your essence is your soul or mind, understood as a nonphysical entity distinct from your body.

2. The psychological continuity theory: you are essentially your memories and ability to reflect on yourself (Locke) and, in its most general form, you are your overall psychological configuration, what Kurzweil referred to as your "pattern."[7]

3. Materialism: you are essentially the material that you are made out of—what Kurzweil referred to as "the ordered and chaotic collection of molecules that make up my body and brain" (Kurzweil 2005: 383).

4. The no self view: the self is an illusion. The "I" is a grammatical fiction (Nietzsche). There are bundles of impressions but no underlying self (Hume). There is no survival because there is no person (Buddha).[8]

Upon reflection, each of these views has its own implications about whether one should enhance. If you hold (1), then your decision to enhance depends on whether you believe the enhanced body would retain the same soul or immaterial mind.[9] If you believe (3), then any enhancements must not change your material substrate. In contrast, according to (2), enhancements can alter the material substrate but must preserve your psychological configuration. Finally, (4) contrasts sharply with (1)–(3). If you hold (4), then the survival of the person is not an issue, for there is no person to begin with. You may strive to enhance nonetheless, to the extent that you find intrinsic value in adding more superintelligence to the universe—you might value life forms with higher forms of consciousness and wish that your "successor" should be such a creature.

Of all these views, (2) is currently the most influential, as philosopher Eric Olson underscores:

> Most philosophers believe that our identity through time consists in some sort of psychological continuity. You are, necessarily, that future being who in some sense inherits his mental features from you … the one who has the mental features he has then in large part because you have the mental features you have now. And you are that past being whose mental features you have inherited.
>
> … So magnetic is this view that many feel entitled to assert it without argument. (Olson 2002)

I will now suggest that the Transhumanist adopts a novel version of the psychological continuity view; that is, they adopt a computational account of continuity. First, consider that transhumanists generally adopt a computational theory of the mind.

The Computational Theory of Mind ("CTM"): The mind is essentially the program running on the hardware of the brain, that is, the algorithm that the brain implements, something in principle discoverable by cognitive science.[10]

Computational theories of mind can appeal to various computational theories of the format of thought: connectionism, dynamical systems theory (in its computational guise), the symbolic or language of thought approach, or some combination thereof. These differences will not matter to our discussion.

In philosophy of mind, computational theories of mind are positions about the nature of thoughts and minds; unfortunately, discussions of CTMs in mainstream philosophy of mind do not generally speak to the topic of personhood. (Perhaps this is because personal identity is a traditional topic in metaphysics, not philosophy of mind.) But upon reflection, if you uphold a CTM, then it is quite natural to adopt a computational theory of persons. For note that proponents of CTMs reject the soul theory, for they reject the idea that minds are non-physical entities. One might suspect that the transhumanist views materialism favorably, the view that holds that minds are basically physical or material in nature and that mental features, such as the thought that espresso has a wonderful aroma, are ultimately just physical features of brains. Transhumanists reject materialism, however. For instance, consider Kurzweil's remark:

> The specific set of particles that my body and brain comprise are in fact completely different from the atoms and molecules that I comprised only a short while ago. We know that most of our cells are turned over in a matter of weeks, and even our neurons, which persist as distinct cells for a relatively long time, nonetheless change all of their constituent molecules within a month....I am rather like the pattern that water makes in a stream as it rushes past the rocks in its path. The actual molecules of water change every millisecond, but the pattern persists for hours or even years. (Kurzweil 2005: 383)

Later in his discussion, Kurzweil calls his view "Patternism" (ibid.: 386). Put in the language of cognitive science, as the transhumanist surely would, what is essential to you is your computational configuration—for example, what sensory systems/subsystems your brain has (e.g. early vision), the way that the basic sensory subsystems are integrated in the association areas, the neural circuitry making up your domain general reasoning, your attentional system, your memories, and so on—overall, the algorithm that your brain computes.[11]

Kurzweil's patternism is highly typical of transhumanism. For instance, consider the appeal to patternism in the following passage of *The Transhumanist Frequently Asked Questions*, which discusses the process of uploading:

> Uploading (sometimes called "downloading," "mind uploading" or "brain reconstruction") is the process of transferring an intellect from

a biological brain to a computer. One way of doing this might be by first scanning the synaptic structure of a particular brain and then implementing the same computations in an electronic medium....An upload could have a virtual (simulated) body giving the same sensations and the same possibilities for interaction as a non-simulated body.... And uploads wouldn't have to be confined to virtual reality: they could interact with people on the outside and even rent robot bodies in order to work in or explore physical reality....Advantages of being an upload would include: Uploads would not be subject to biological senescence. Back-up copies of uploads could be created regularly so that you could be re-booted if something bad happened. (Thus your lifespan would potentially be as long as the universe's.)...Radical cognitive enhancements would likely be easier to implement in an upload than in an organic brain....A widely accepted position is that you survive so long as certain information patterns are conserved, such as your memories, values, attitudes, and emotional dispositions...For the continuation of personhood, on this view, it matters little whether you are implemented on a silicon chip inside a computer or in that gray, cheesy lump inside your skull, assuming both implementations are conscious. (Bostrom 2003)

In sum, the transhumanist's cognitive science orientation introduces a new computationalist element to the traditional psychological continuity view of personhood. If plausible, this would be an important contribution to the age-old debate over the nature of persons. But is it correct? And further, is patternism even compatible with enhancement? In what follows, I suggest that patternism is deeply problematic. Furthermore, as things now stand, patternism is not even compatible with the enhancements that the transhumanists appeal to.

Robert Sawyer's *Mindscan* and the Reduplication Problem

Jake Sullivan has an inoperable brain tumor. Death could strike him at any moment. Luckily, Immortex has a new cure for aging and serious illness—a "mindscan." Immortex scientists will upload his brain configuration into a computer and "transfer" it into an android body that is designed using his own body as a template. Although imperfect, the android body has its advantages—as the transhumanist FAQ notes, once an individual is uploaded, a backup exists that can be downloaded if one has an accident. And it can be upgraded as new developments emerge. Jake will be immortal.

Sullivan enthusiastically signs numerous legal agreements. He is told that, upon uploading, his possessions will be transferred to the android, who will be the new bearer of his consciousness. Sullivan's original copy, which will die soon anyway, will live out the remainder of his life on "High Eden," an Immortex colony on the moon. Although stripped of his legal identity, the original copy will be comfortable there, socializing with the other originals who are also still confined to biological senescence.

While lying in the scanning tube a few seconds before the scan, Jake reflects:

I was looking forward to my new existence. Quantity of life didn't matter that much to me—but quality! And to have time—not only years spreading out into the future, but time in each day. Uploads, after all, didn't have to sleep, so not only did we get all those extra years, we got one-third more productive time. The future was at hand. Creating another me. Mindscan.

But then, a few seconds later:

"All right, Mr. Sullivan, you can come out now." It was Dr. Killian's voice, with its Jamaican lilt.

My heart sank. No...

"Mr. Sullivan? We've finished the scanning. If you'll press the red button..."

It hit me like a ton of bricks, like a tidal wave of blood. No! I should be somewhere else, but I wasn't....

I reflexively brought up my hands, patting my chest, feeling the softness of it, feeling it raise and fall. Jesus Christ!

I shook my head. "You just scanned my consciousness, making a duplicate of my mind, right?" My voice was sneering. "And since I'm aware of things after you finished the scanning, that means I—this version—isn't that copy. The copy doesn't have to worry about becoming a vegetable anymore. It's free. Finally and at last, it's free of everything that's been hanging over my head for the last twenty-seven years. We've diverged now, and the cured me has started down its path. But this me is still doomed...." (Sawyer 2005: 44–5)

Sawyer's novel is a *reductio ad absurdum* of the patternist conception of the person. For all that patternism says is that as long as person A has the same computational configuration as person B, A and B are the same person. Indeed, Sugiyama, the person selling the mindscan to Jake, had espoused a form of patternism (Sawyer 2005: 18). Jake's unfortunate experience can be put into the form of a challenge to patternism, which we shall call the "reduplication problem": only one person can really be Jake Sullivan, as Sullivan reluctantly found out. But according to patternism, both creatures are Jake Sullivan—for they share the very same psychological configuration. But, as Jake learned, while the creature created by the mindscan process may be a person, it is not the very *same* person as Jake. It is just another person with an artificial brain and body configured like the original. Hence, having a particular type of pattern cannot be *sufficient* for personal identity. Indeed, the problem is illustrated to epic proportions later in the book when numerous copies of Sullivan are made, all believing they are the original! Ethical and legal problems abound.

A Response to the Reduplication Problem

Perhaps there is a way around this objection. As noted, the reduplication problem suggests that sameness of pattern is not sufficient for sameness of person. However, consider that there seems to be something right about patternism—for as Kurzweil notes, our cells change continually; it is only the organizational pattern that carries on. *Given this, materialism either leaves us with a view of persons in which persons do not persist, or it covertly depends on the idea that we consist in some sort of pattern of organization and is not really a materialist theory at all.* Unless one has a religious conception of the person, and adopts the soul theory, patternism seems inevitable, at least insofar as one believes there is such a thing as a person to begin with. In light of this, perhaps one should react to the reduplication case in the following way: one's pattern is *essential* to one's self despite not being *sufficient* for a complete account of one's identity. Perhaps there is an additional essential property which, together with one's pattern, yields a complete theory of personal identity. But what could the missing ingredient be? Intuitively, it must be a requirement that serves to rule out mindscans and, more generally, any cases in which the mind is "uploaded". For any sort of uploading case will give rise to a reduplication problem, for uploaded minds can in principle be downloaded again and again.

Now, think about your own existence in space and time. When you go out to get the mail, you move from one spatial location to another, tracing a path in space. A spacetime diagram can help us visualize the path one takes throughout one's life. Collapsing the three spatial dimensions into one (the vertical axis) and taking the horizontal axis to signify time, consider the following typical trajectory (Figure 1). Notice that the figure carved out looks like a worm; you, like all physical objects, carve out a sort of "spacetime worm" over the course of your existence.

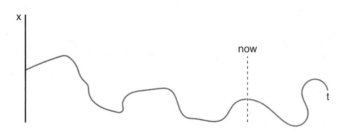

Figure 1.

This, at least, is the kind of path that "normals"—those who are neither post-humans nor superintelligences—carve out. But now consider what happened during the mindscan. Again, according to patternism, there would be two of the very same person. The copy's spacetime diagram would look like the following:

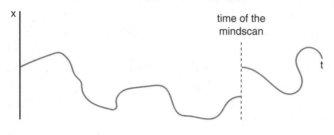

Figure 2.

This is bizarre. It appears that Jake Sullivan exists for 42 years, has a scan, and then somehow instantaneously moves to a different location in space and lives out the rest of his life! This is radically unlike normal survival. This alerts us that something is wrong with pure patternism: it lacks a requirement for spatiotemporal continuity.

This additional requirement would seem to solve the reduplication problem. For consider the day of the mindscan. Jake went into the laboratory and had a scan; then he left the laboratory and went directly into a spaceship and flew to Mars. It is this man—the one who traces a continuous trajectory through space and time—who is in fact the true Jake Sullivan.

This response to the reduplication problem only goes so far, however. For consider Sugiyama, who, when selling his mindscan product, ventured a pattern-ist pitch. If Sugiyama had espoused patternism together with a spatiotemporal continuity clause, few would have signed up for the scan! For that extra ingredient would rule out a mindscan, or any kind of uploading for that matter, as a form of survival. Only those wishing to have a mere replacement for themselves would sign up. There is a general lesson here for the transhumanist: if one opts for patternism, enhancements like uploading to avoid death or to facilitate further enhancements are not really "enhancements" but forms of suicide. *The transhumanist should sober up and not offer such procedures as enhancements.* When it comes to enhancement, there are intrinsic limits to what technology can deliver. (Ironically, the proponent of the soul theory is in better shape here. For perhaps the soul does teleport. Who knows?)

Let me sum up the dialectical situation thus far: we have just discarded the original form of patternism as false. If the transhumanist would like to uphold patternism, then she should add the spatiotemporal continuity clause. And im-portantly, she will need to modify her views on what sorts of enhancements are compatible with survival. Let us call this new position "modified patternism." As we shall now see, although modified patternism is a clear improvement, it requires far more spelling out in at least the following two dimensions.

Two Issues that Modified Patternism Needs to Address

(1) Consider: if you are your pattern, what if your pattern shifts? Do you die? In order for the transhumanist to justify the sort of enhancements needed to become a posthuman or a superintelligent being, she will need to say precisely what a "pattern" is, and when enhancements do and do not constitute a continuation of the pattern. The extreme cases seem clear—for instance, as discussed, mindscans are ruled out by the spatiotemporal continuity clause. And further, because patternism is a psychological continuity view, the patternist will want to say that a memory erasure process that erased one's childhood is an unacceptable alteration of one's pattern, removing too many of one's memories. On the other hand, mere everyday cellular maintenance by nanobots to overcome the slow effects of aging would, according to proponents of this view, not affect the identity of the person.[12] But the middle range cases are unclear. Maybe deleting a few bad chess-playing habits is kosher, but what about erasing all memory of some personal relationship, as in the film *Eternal Sunshine of the Spotless Mind*? The path to superintelligence may very well be a path through middle range enhancements. So again, what is needed is a clear conception of what a pattern is, and what changes in pattern are acceptable and why. Without a firm handle on this issue, the transhumanist developmental trajectory is perhaps the technophile's alluring path to suicide.

This problem looks hard to solve in a way that is compatible with preserving the very idea that we can be identical over time to some previous or future self. For determining a boundary point seems a rather arbitrary exercise in which once a boundary is selected, an example is provided suggesting the boundary should be pushed outward, ad nauseum. On the other hand, there is something insightful about the view that over time one gradually becomes less and less like one's earlier self. But appreciate this point too long and it may lead to a dark place: for if one finds patternism compelling to begin with, how is it that one truly persists over time, from the point of infancy until maturity, during which time there are often major changes in one's memories, personality, and so on? Indeed, even a series of gradual changes cumulatively amounts to an individual, B, who is greatly altered from her childhood self, A. Why is there really a relation of identity that holds between A and B, instead of an ancestral relation: *A's being the ancestor of B?* Our second issue relates to the issue of gradual, but cumulatively significant, change as well.

(2) Suppose that it is 2050, and people are getting gradual neural regeneration procedures as they sleep. During their nightly slumbers, nanobots slowly import nanoscale materials that are computationally identical to the original materials. The nanobots then gradually remove the old materials, setting them in a small container beside the person's bed. By itself, this process is unproblematic for

modified patternism. But now suppose there is an optional upgrade to the regeneration service for those who would like to make a backup copy of their brains. If one opts for this procedure, then, during the nightly process, the nanobots take the replaced materials out of the dish and place them inside a cryogenically frozen biological brain. At the end of the slow process the materials in the frozen brain have been entirely replaced by the person's original neurons. Now, suppose you choose to undergo this procedure alongside your nightly regeneration. Over time, this second brain comes to be composed of the very same material as your brain originally was, configured in precisely the same manner. Which one is you? The original brain, which now has entirely different neurons, or the one with all your original neurons?[13]

The modified patternist has this to say about the neural regeneration case: you are the creature with the brain with entirely different matter, as this creature traces a continuous path through spacetime. But now, things go awry: why is spatiotemporal continuity supposed to outweigh other factors, like being composed of the original material substrate? Here, to be blunt, my intuitions crap out. We'd like to find a solid justification for selecting one option above the other. Until the transhumanist provides a solid justification for her position, it is best to regard forms of enhancement that involve the rapid or even gradual replacement of parts of one's brain as being risky.

Conclusion

I hope all this has convinced you that if the transhumanist maintains patternism there are some serious issues that require working out. Indeed, as *The Transhumanist Frequently Asked Questions* indicates, the development of radical enhancements, such as brain-machine interfaces, cryogenic freezing for life extension, and uploading to avoid death or simply to facilitate enhancement, are key enhancements invoked by the transhumanist view of the development of the person. Now, all of these enhancements sound strangely like the thought experiments philosophers have used for years as problem cases for various theories of the nature of persons, so it is not surprising that deep problems emerge. Herein, I've argued that the Mindscan example suggests that one should not upload and that the patternist needs to modify her theory to rule out such cases. Even with this modification in hand, however, transhumanism still requires a detailed account of what constitutes a break in a pattern versus a mere continuation of it. Without progress on this issue, it will not be clear if medium range enhancements, such as erasing childhood memories or adding neural circuitry to make oneself smarter, are safe. Finally, the nanobot case warns against even mild enhancements. Given all this, it is fair to say that the transhumanist currently cannot support her case for enhancement. Indeed, *The Transhumanist Frequently Asked Questions* notes that transhumanists are keenly aware that this issue has been neglected:

While the concept of a soul is not used much in a naturalistic philosophy such as transhumanism, many transhumanists do take an interest in the related problems concerning personal identity (Parfit 1984) and consciousness (Churchland 1988). These problems are being intensely studied by contemporary analytic philosophers, and although some progress has been made, e.g. in Derek Parfit's work on personal identity, they have still not been resolved to general satisfaction. (Bostrom 2003: section 5.4)

Our discussion also raises some general lessons for all parties involved in the enhancement debate. For when one considers the enhancement debate through the lens of the metaphysics of personhood, new dimensions of the debate are appreciated. The literature on the nature of persons is extraordinarily rich, raising intriguing problems for commonly accepted views of the nature of persons that underlie positions on enhancement. When one defends or rejects a given enhancement, it is important to determine whether one's stance on the enhancement in question is truly supported by, or even compatible with, one's position on the nature of persons. Further, the topic of the nature of persons is of clear relevance to the related topics of human nature and human dignity, issues that are currently key points of controversy in debates over enhancement (see, e.g., Bostrom 2008; Fukuyama 2002).

Perhaps, alternately, you grow weary of all this metaphysics. You may suspect that social conventions concerning what we commonly consider to be persons are all we have because metaphysical theorizing will never conclusively resolve what persons are. However, as unwieldy as metaphysical issues are, it seems that not all conventions are worthy of acceptance, so one needs a manner of determining which conventions should play an important role in the enhancement debate and which ones should not. And it is hard to accomplish this without getting clear on one's conception of persons. Further, it is difficult to avoid at least implicitly relying on a conception of persons when reflecting on the case for and against enhancement. For what is it that ultimately grounds your decision to enhance or not to enhance, if not that it will somehow improve you? Are you perhaps merely planning for the well-being of your successor?

Notes

1. This piece is expanded and modified from an earlier piece, "Future Minds: Cognitive Enhancement, Transhumanism, and the Nature of Persons", which appeared in the *Penn Center Guide to Bioethics*, Arthur L. Caplan, Autumn Fiester, and Vardit Radvisky (eds.), Springer, 2009. Thanks very much to Ted Sider and Michael Huemer for their helpful comments.

2. Julian Huxley apparently coined the term *transhumanism* in 1957, when he wrote that in the near future "the human species will be on the threshold of a new kind of existence, as different from ours as ours is from that of Peking man" (Huxley 1957: 13–17).

3. Bostrom is a philosopher at Oxford University who now directs the transhumanist-oriented Future of Humanity Institute there. In addition to these two documents, there are a

number of excellent philosophical and sociological works that articulate key elements of the transhumanist perspective (e.g. Bostrom 2005; Hughes 2004; Kurzweil 1999, 2005). For extensive Web resources on transhumanism, see Nick Bostrom's homepage, Ray Kurzweil's newsgroup (KurzweilAI.net), the Institute for Ethics and Emerging Technologies homepage, and the World Transhumanist Association homepage.

4. It should be noted that transhumanism by no means endorses every sort of enhancement. For example, Nick Bostrom rejects positional enhancements (enhancements primarily employed to increase one's social position) yet argues for enhancements that could allow humans to develop ways of exploring "the larger space of possible modes of being" (2005: 11).

5. There are many nuances to this rough trajectory. For instance, some transhumanists believe that the move from unenhanced human intelligence to superintelligence will be extremely rapid because we are approaching a singularity, a point at which the creation of superhuman intelligence will result in massive changes in a very short period (e.g. 30 years) (Bostrom 1998; Kurzweil 1999, 2005; Vinge 1993). Other transhumanists hold that technological changes will not be so sudden. These discussions often debate the reliability of Moore's Law (Moore 1965). Another key issue is whether a transition to superintelligence will really occur because the upcoming technological developments involve grave risk. The risks of biotechnology and AI concern transhumanists, progressive bioethicists more generally, as well as bioconservatives (Annis 2000; Bostrom 2002; Garreau 2005; Joy 2000).

6. For mainstream anti-enhancement positions on this question see, e.g., Fukuyama (2002), Kass et al. (2003), and Annas (2000).

7. Because our discussion is introductory, I will not delve into different versions of psychological continuity theory. One could, for instance, appeal to (a): the idea that memories are essential to a person. Alternatively, one could adopt (b), one's overall psychological configuration is essential, including one's memories. Herein, I shall work with one version of this latter conception—one that is inspired by cognitive science—although many of the criticisms of this view will apply to (a) and other versions of (b) as well. For some different versions see chapter 27 of John Locke's 1694 *Essay Concerning Human Understanding* (note that this chapter first appears in the second edition; it is also reprinted as "Of Identity and Diversity" in Perry 1975). See also the essays by Anthony Quinton and Paul Grice, both of which are reprinted in Perry (1975).

8. Sociologist James Hughes holds a transhumanist version of the no self view. (See the Institute for Ethics and Emerging Technology's "Cyborg Buddha" project at http://ieet.org/index.php/IEET/cyborgbuddha.) For helpful surveys of these four positions, see Eric Olson's chapter in this volume (Chapter 7), and Conee and Sider (2005).

9. It should be noted that although a number of bioconservatives seem to uphold the soul theory, the soul theory is not, in and of itself, an anti-enhancement position. For why can't one's soul or immaterial mind inhere in the same body even after radical enhancement?

10. For discussion of computational theories, see Block (Chapter 14 in this volume) and Churchland (1996).

11. Readers familiar with philosophy of mind may suggest that the transhumanist could accept one version of materialism, namely, "token materialism." However, I suspect that it is not really a coherent form of materialism. Token materialism holds that every instance of a mental property is identical to some instance of a physical property. But can the instances really be *identical* if the properties themselves belong to different types? The distinct property types are instead coinstantiated by the same particular.

12. Or at least, this is what the patternist would *like* to say. The example in the paragraph after next will in fact question whether she can truly say this.

13. This is a science fiction variant of the well-known Ship of Theseus case. It first appears in print in Plutarch (*Vita Thesei*, 22-3).

References

Annas, G. J. (2000). The man on the moon, immortality, and other millennial myths: The prospects and perils of human genetic engineering. *Emory Law Journal* 49 (3): 753–82.

Bostrom, N. (1998). How long before superintelligence? *International Journal of Futures Studies* 2. Available at http://www.nickbostrom.com/superintelligence.html (retrieved Dec. 20, 2008).

Bostrom, N. (2003). *The Transhumanist Frequently Asked Questions*: v 2.1. World Transhumanist Association. Retrieved from http://transhumanism.org/index.php/WTA/faq/.

Bostrom, N. (2005). History of Transhumanist Thought. *Journal of Evolution and Technology*, 14 (1).

Bostrom, N. (2008). Dignity and enhancement. In The President's Council on Bioethics, *Human Dignity and Bioethics: Essays Commissioned by the President's Council on Bioethics* (Washington, DC: U.S. Government Printing Office).

Conee, E. and Sider, T. (2005). *Riddles of Existence: A Guided Tour of Metaphysics.* Oxford: Oxford University Press.

Churchland, P. (1988). *Matter and consciousness.* Cambridge, MA: MIT Press.

Churchland, P. (1996). *Engine of reason, seat of the soul.* Cambridge, MA: MIT Press.

Fukuyama, F. (2002). *Our posthuman future: Consequences of the biotechnology revolution.* New York: Farrar, Straus and Giroux.

Garreau, J. (2005). *Radical evolution: The promise and peril of enhancing our minds, our bodies—and what it means to be human.* New York: Doubleday.

Hughes, J. (2004), *Citizen cyborg: Why democratic societies must respond to the redesigned human of the future.* Cambridge, MA: Westview Press.

Huxley, J. (1957). *New bottles for new wine.* London: Chatto & Windus.

Joy, B. (2000). Why the future doesn't need us. *Wired*, 8: 238–46.

Kurzweil, R. (1999). *The age of spiritual machines: When computers exceed human intelligence.* New York: Viking.

Kurzweil, R. (2005). *The singularity is near: When humans transcend biology.* New York: Viking.

Moore, G. (1965). Cramming more components into integrated circuits. *Electronics*, 38 (8): 11–17. Retrieved from ftp://download.intel.com/research/silicon/moorespaper.pdf.

Parfit, D. (1984). *Reasons and persons.* Oxford: Oxford University Press.

Perry, J. (1975). *Personal identity*, Berkeley: University of California Press.

Roco, M. C., and Bainbridge, W. S. (eds.) (2002). *Converging technologies for improved human performance: Nanotechnology, biotechnology, information technology and cognitive science.* Arlington, VA: National Science Foundation/Department of Commerce.

Sawyer, R. (2005). *Mindscan.* New York: Tor.

Vinge, V. (1993). The coming technological singularity: How to survive in the post-human era. *NASA Technical Reports*, Lewis Research Center, Vision 21: Interdisciplinary Science and Engineering in the Era of Cyberspace, pp. 11–21.

World Transhumanist Association (1998). *Transhumanist Declaration.* Retrieved from http://www.transhumanism.org/index.php/WTA/declaration/.

Akiba Solomon is the editorial director of Colorlines.com, a daily news site published by the racial justice organization Race Forward. Her work predominantly focuses on the intersection between gender and race.

Thugs. Students. Rioters. Fans: Media's Subtle Racism in Unrest Coverage
Akiba Solomon

Whenever black civilians become enraged enough by police violence toward black men to set fires, loot stores and throw things at police in riot gear, I become this old, conservative black lady who asks annoying, clichéd questions like, "Why are they destroying their own neighborhoods?"

I get my faculties back by reviewing how some media describe arson, looting and projectile-throwing by predominantly white crowds. I don't do this exercise to condemn individual journalists, but the subtle differences in language and context that emerge are just too jarring to ignore.

Take these excerpts from an April 27, 2015 Associated Press piece that ran in the New York Times called "Riots in Baltimore Over Man's Death in Police Custody." Keep in mind that Baltimore is predominantly black and most of images of unrest over Freddie Gray show black men in their late teens and early 20s:

> **Rioters plunged part of Baltimore into chaos Monday,** torching a pharmacy, setting police cars ablaze and throwing bricks at officers hours after thousands mourned the man who died from a severe spinal injury he suffered in police custody.

> …**Earlier Monday, the smell of burned rubber wafted in the air in one neighborhood where youths were looting a liquor store. Police stood still nearby as people drank looted alcohol.** Glass and trash littered the streets, and other small fires were scattered about. One person from a church tried to shout something from a megaphone as two cars burned.

Now, check out how the Times characterized the overwhelmingly white mass of Penn State students who tore up State College, Pa., because they were angry about about Joe Paterno—a leader who stood by as his assistant coach, Jerry Sandusky, sexually molested boys—getting fired.

The November 11, 2011 article is titled "Penn State Students Clash With Police in Unrest After Announcement" and describes rioters and their actions:

> After top Penn State officials announced that they had fired Joe Paterno on Wednesday night, **thousands of students stormed the downtown area to display their anger and frustration, chanting the former coach's name, tearing down light poles and overturning a television news van parked along College Avenue.**

...**The demonstrators** congregated outside Penn State's administration building before stampeding into the tight grid of downtown streets. **They turned their ire on a news van, a symbolic gesture that expressed a view held by many:** that the news media had exaggerated Mr. Paterno's role in the scandal surrounding accusations that a former assistant coach, Jerry Sandusky, sexually assaulted young boys.

So in Baltimore, "rioters" and "youths" are "plung[ing] the city into chaos," and drinking liquor they looted. In College Park, "thousands of students" are expressing their anger and making "symbolic gestures" like tipping over news vans.

Let's try another one—a March 2015 Cleveland Plain Dealer story about that riot that mostly white Ohio State fans had to celebrate the Buckeyes championship win.

The piece, "Columbus police use of force against Ohio State crowds reveals training, communication problems," describes some 8,000 to 9,000 people breaking into the Ohio Stadium, throwing bottles at police, lunging at police, trying to lift police cruisers and setting at least 89 fires. About 200 National Guard members were called in:

> Columbus police reported giving differing orders **to a crowd of Ohio State fans celebrating January's championship win** before deploying pepper spray and tear gas, according to reports obtained by Northeast Ohio Media Group.
>
> ..."The one weakness in our plan, **as Generation Xers planning for a Millennials event**, was that we did not account for everyone to meet at a central location," stated Sgt. Smith Weir in his report.
>
> ..."Monday we were dealing with **drunk, happy college kids with a handful of agitators** just taking advantage of the situation," Weir wrote.
>
> ... **Some in the crowd claimed they couldn't hear the police's demands to leave**, [Commander Christopher D.] Bowling stated [in his report], so **he suggested that his department purchase better amplification equipment** ....

Compare that to this Associated Press story The Cleveland Plain Dealer ran on January 12, 2012 called "'White Only' swimming pool sign violated girl's civil rights, panel says."

> ... **Racial discrimination has particular resonance in Cincinnati, whose population is 45 percent black,** far higher than the rest of Ohio, which is about 12 percent black. Surrounding Hamilton County is 26 percent black.

Cincinnati was the scene of race riots in April 2001 when police and demonstrators clashed in a blighted neighborhood following the shooting of a black suspect by police.

A white Cincinnati landlord posts a sign that says "Public Swimming Pool, White Only" at his complex's pool to bar a black girl from "clouding" the water with her hair products and that's "discrimination." The April 2001 unrest over a police shooting of a black man amounts to "race riots."

The "racial discrimination has particular resonance" among Cincinnati's black population. But the purposeful, proudly racist landlord literally takes things back to Jim Crow segregation, but racial discrimination doesn't resonate with him?

And then, of course, there's the infamous "who's a looter?" captions from Hurricane Katrina coverage.

Now I admit that this level of examination does leave me vulnerable to becoming that big-word butchering guy from "In Living Color."

But at the same time, as my late, beloved aunt Kinyozi Yvette Smalls used to say about 15 times a day: "Words are powerful."

If they weren't, everybody would be using same language.

Constance Steinkuehler is an Associate Professor in Digital Media and Co-Director of the Games + Learning + Society Center at the University of Wisconsin, Madison. She has also served as a Senior Policy Analyst in the Office of Science and Technology Policy at the White House Executive Office. **Sean Duncan** is an Assistant Professor at Indiana University Bloomington's School of Education; his research focuses on play in informal learning environments, with a primary emphasis on gaming, game design, and gaming culture.

Scientific Habits of Mind in Virtual Worlds
Constance Steinkuehler and Sean Duncan

In 1905, at a gathering of the world's greatest minds in the physical sciences, Henri Poincaré reflected on the rapid progress of scientific inquiry and the means through which the scientific community at the turn of the twentieth century and beyond would refine our understanding of the world. In his historical address, Poincaré warned against the seduction of reducing science to a domain of seeming facts, stating, "Science is built up of facts, as a house is built of stones; but an accumulation of facts is no more science than a heap of stones is a house" (1905/2001, p. 141). A century later, his admonition against the framing of science as a "rhetoric of conclusion" (Schwab 1962, p. 24) still holds, with science scholars and educators from Dewey on repeatedly warning us against the teaching of science as only content rather than process. In Dewey's own words, "the future of our civilization depends upon the widening spread and deepening hold of the *scientific habit of mind* [italics added] ... the problem of problems in our education is therefore to discover how to mature and make effective this scientific habit" (1910, p. 127).

In today's world of massive globalization and technological interconnectivity, the need for a scientifically literate citizenry in the United States has only grown more urgent; yet, by some measures, it seems we have done a poor job at fostering the right habits of mind in our schools. Currently only one in five Americans is scientifically literate (Miller 2004), despite mandatory instruction in science. In a recent study of contemporary classroom practice, Chinn and Malhotra (2002) found that standard "inquiry" activities not only failed to engender scientific habits of mind, but in fact actually fostered epistemological beliefs directly *antithetical* to them. Recent assessment of high school laboratory activities by the National Research Council (Singer et al. 2005) reaches similar conclusions: science labs, long heralded as *the* site for engaging students in science practice, fail. Meanwhile, the public seems to grow increasingly hostile to the scientific enterprise (Elsner 2005).

Leveraging Online Play

But, if the inquiry activities used currently in education are unable to foster the right attitudes toward science, what can? Games, potentially. Despite dismissals as "torpid" and inviting "inert reception" (Solomon 2004) in some mainstream press, videogame technologies may be one viable alternative—not to the role of teachers and classrooms in learning science, but rather to textbooks and science labs as educational experiences about the inquiry process. Recent studies indicate that the intellectual activities that constitute successful gameplay are nontrivial, including the construction of new identities (Gee 2003; Steinkuehler 2006b), collaborative problem solving (Squire 2005; Steinkuehler 2006a; cf. Nasir 2005), literacy practices that exceed our national standards (Steinkuehler 2007, 2008a), systemic thinking (Squire 2003), and, as one might expect, computer literacy (Hayes and Games in press; Steinkuehler and Johnson, 2007, unpublished manuscript).

Games, however, are more than just the sum of their intellectual practices (as important as those may be); they are, in fact, *simulated worlds:*

> The first step towards understanding how video games can (and we argue, will) transform education is changing the widely shared perspective that games are "mere entertainment." More than a multi-billion dollar industry, more than a compelling toy for both children and adults, more than a route to computer literacy, video games are important because they let people participate in new worlds. (Shaffer, Squire, Halverson, and Gee 2005, p. 106)

As simulations, games allow "just plain folk" (Lave 1988) to build situated understandings of important phenomena (physical laws, for example) that are instantiated in those worlds amid a culture of intellectual practice that render those phenomena culturally meaningful (Steinkuehler 2006c). Their affordances for learning have not gone unnoticed, and the last two years have witnessed a marked rise in interest across various academies in leveraging game technologies toward educational ends: the Woodrow Wilson Foundation's Serious Games Initiative; the Games, Learning and Society program at the University of Wisconsin-Madison; the Education Arcade project at MIT; the Games for Social Change Movement; and Stanford University's Media X "Gaming To Learn" Workshop, to name a few.

One genre of videogame in particular offers distinctive promise in terms of fostering scientific habits of mind: *massively multiplayer online games.* Massively multiplayer online games (MMOs) are 2- or 3-D graphical, simulated worlds played online that allow individuals to interact, through their digital characters or "avatars," not only with the designed environment in which activities take place, but also with other individuals' avatars as well. For example, five friends or strangers could create an impromptu group and go hunting "boss" dragons in one of the virtual world's more difficult dungeons. Previous ethnography of such online worlds demonstrates their function as naturally occurring learning environments (Steinkuehler 2004, 2005), yet the forms of scientific argumentation, model-based reasoning, and theory-evidence coordination that arise in the context of MMO play warrant further investigation.

In MMOs, individuals collaborate to solve complex problems within the virtual world, such as figuring out what combination of individual skills, proficiencies, and equipment are necessary to conquer an in-game boss dragon in the example above. As part of developing efficient and effective solutions, players are customarily expected to research various game strategies and tactics by consulting on- and offline manuals, databases, and discussions, as well as by using such knowledge as the basis for in-game action. Such research might include, to continue our example, consulting collective online databases about where the boss dragon lives, what its special skills are, and what previous strategies have been successful.

Members of the group then come to the activity well-versed in known research on the problem and enter into collaborative work under the mutual expectation that each will apply known information to solving the problem. Should the solution not prove to be straightforward, the group learns from what fails, discounting some solution paths while raising others. In prior ethnographic work (2005), Steinkuehler found that it was not unusual for players to gather data about a specific monster or challenge in the virtual world in Excel spreadsheets, create models of the data in the form of simple mathematical equations, and then argue about whose model was "better" in terms of prediction and explanatory scope.

Thus, as part of standard gameplay (particularly beyond the beginning levels), individuals share their own hypotheses about what strategies work by proposing models for solutions, justifying their "theories" with evidence (such as tabulated mathematical results aggregated across multiple trials), and debate the merits of conflicting hypotheses. This collaborative construction of knowledge, parallel to what takes place in the scientific community, is not aimless contentious discussion (although there is a bit of that as well), but rather part and parcel of the *collective intelligence* (Levy 1999) amassed through patterned participatory consumption (Jenkins 1992), which is a hallmark of interactive "entertainment" media such as games.

Innovative projects such as Harvard University's *River City* (e.g., Ketelhut 2007; Ketelhut et al. 2007; Nelson et al. 2007) and Indiana University-Bloomington's *Quest Atlantis* (e.g., Barab et al. 2005; Barab et al. 2007) have begun to tackle the complexities of designing MMOs for science learning, offering proof of concept of the argument presented above. Yet, as Lave and Wenger (1991) note, understanding informal contexts for learning is crucial if we are to advance educational theory and practice beyond the contexts we ourselves contrive. Therefore, in order to extend our understanding of the forms of scientific reasoning that emerge as a natural part of gameplay in informal MMOs and the design features that appear to foster them, this paper presents an examination of discussions on the official online forum for the commercial MMO *World of Warcraft.*

In this investigation, we analyzed a random sample of nearly 2,000 discussion posts in which participants discuss various game-related topics. Using codes based on national benchmarks for scientific literacy (American Association for the Advancement of Science 1993), Chinn and Malhotra's (2002) theoretical framework for evaluating inquiry tasks, and Kuhn's (1992) epistemological framework, we highlight the scientific habits of mind displayed within the forum discussions and the features of the game—both as designed object and emergent culture—that appear to foster them. This study moves beyond arguments about the *potential* of MMOs for learning by documenting and assessing which *specific* literacy practices emerge within such game-related online communities (and which do not). Based on those findings, we then take a first step toward identifying the characteristics of MMOs that may be enabling such practices to emerge.

Data Collection and Research Methods

Context of the Research and Data Corpus

The context for this investigation is *World of Warcraft* (*WoW*), a successful MMO released in November 2004 and currently boasting the single largest share of the global MMO market with well over ten million subscribers globally (Woodcock 2008). The game is set in a fantasy world in which players of various classes (nine total, at the time of this article's writing) wander the environment hunting, gathering, questing, battling, and crafting in order to strengthen or "level" their character in various ways.

The data analyzed for this particular study consist of threaded discussions that took place early November of 2006 (before the release of the expansion, *World of Warcraft: The Burning Crusade*) on the "priest forum" of the official *World of Warcraft* website (http://forums.worldofwarcraft.com). Although there are a number of relevant online forums to be found, the official website alone featured thirty-one separate forums totaling well over 270,000 separate, active threads. Therefore, we chose to limit our data corpus by selecting a single character class-related forum rather than, say, the guild recruitment or bug report forum. Class-related forums are just like any other discussion forum, except the content is ostensibly focused on class-related topics for discussion. Content is not restricted in any way (other than by the overarching rules of the forums, such as decency), but posters are expected to discuss something related to the respected character class in some way, whether that be anecdotes, strategies, complaints, preferences, or what have you. We pulled a random sample of 1,984 posts across eighty-five threads of 4,656 threads total ($\overline{X} = 23$, $\sigma = 38$ posts per thread), resulting in a confidence level of approximately 91 percent. Data from the discussion forums were saved as text files, extraneous information and HTML markup tags were removed, and descriptive information (such as data on the "level" of each poster) was collected in a separate spreadsheet. The final corpus included discussion posts made by 1,087 unique *WoW* characters.

Method of Analysis

In order to assess the *scientific habits of mind* that characterize (or fail to characterize) the data corpus examined here, we developed a set of codes (following methods outlined in Chi 1997) based in combination on a subset of the AAAS benchmarks for scientific literacy (American Association for the Advancement of Science 1993), Chinn and Malhotra's (2002) theoretical framework for evaluating inquiry tasks, and Kuhn's (1992) framework for categorizing epistemological stances in argumentation. Both the AAAS benchmarks and the Chinn and Malhotra report have been quite influential in science education, with the former serving as the basis of the National Research Council's (1996) Science Standards and many state science standards for K–12 education in the United States. Kuhn's work has also proven quite influential in its own right in research on argumentation in informal scientific reasoning. The codes were selected from these sources based on a combination of a priori assumptions about the forms of scientific reasoning such spaces ought to generate (e.g., understanding systems and feedback among components of a system), previous games related literature (Gee 2003; Squire 2003, 2005; Steinkuehler 2004, 2005, 2006a, 2006b, 2006c), and a pilot study conducted in preparation for this investigation (Steinkuehler and Chmiel 2006).

Our goal was to focus on scientific reasoning as "the building of houses" rather than the "collection of stones," per the vision of science practice articulated by Poincaré (1905/2001) and science education forwarded by Dewey (1910) and Schwab (1962). Therefore, important aspects to scientific understanding that are specific to *content knowledge* rather than practice per se (e.g. an understanding of natural forces) are notably absent. However, given the focus of our interests (scientific practices rather than content) and the nature of the phenomenon under investigation (a simulated world that makes no claims of correspondence with the natural one), such omission was justified. Table 1 includes the full set of eighteen codes and their definitions.

Together, the coding set addresses aspects of scientific thinking as seen through three major groups of codes: scientific discursive practices (including social knowledge construction), systems- and model-based reasoning, and tacit epistemologies. The scientific discursive practices codes each addressed a different aspect of argumentation, discourse, and the use of evidence or other resources in the formulation of an argument. The systems- and model-based reasoning codes each addressed a different aspect of scientific thinking, cutting across specific scientific domains, including reasoning using systems and models; understanding feedback, prediction and testing; and the use of mathematics to investigate the problem under discussion. Finally, the tacit epistemology codes addressed the implicit conception of knowledge employed by an author in a given post—that knowledge is objective and absolute, or that it is subjective and nothing is certain, or that knowledge is shaped through evaluation and argument. Four raters, each of whom had at least 4 months of experience as participant observer within the game, coded the data; four-way interrater reliability, calculated on a subset of roughly 10% of the corpus, was 92%.

In addition, a second set of codes were developed in order to characterize the *WoW*-specific content discussed in each post. Two raters, both with over a year of participant-observer experience within the game, coded the data; two-way inter-rater reliability, calculated again on roughly 10% of the corpus, was 93%. Addition-ally, for each poster, we collected virtual "demographic" information—including character level, race, class, guild status, and player-vs.-player rank—in addition to the total number of occurrences of each scientific reasoning and content code their posts received and the total number of posts per individual made.

Table 1. The Full Set of Analytic Codes Used to Assess Scientific Habits of Mind

Scientific discursive practices	
Social knowledge construction	Scientists construct knowledge in collaborative groups; students do not (AAAS.D.12.6 & 1.A. 12.2; Chinn and Malhotra 2002)
Build on others' ideas	Participate in group discussions on scientific topics by restating or summarizing accurately what others have said, asking for clarification or elaboration (AAAS)
Use of counterarguments	Suggest alternative claims or arguments, criticize arguments in which data, explanations, or conclusions are represented as the only ones worth consideration with no mention of other possibilities, suggest alternative trade-offs in decisions and designs, criticize designs in which major trade-offs are not acknowledged (AAAS.I2.E)
Uses data/evidence	Use data or evidence in making arguments and claims (AAAS)
Alternative explanations of data	No matter how well one theory fits observations, a new theory might fit them just as well or better, or might fit a wider range of observations. In science, the testing, revising, and occasional discarding of theories, new and old, never ends. This ongoing process leads to an increasingly better understanding of how things work in the world but not to absolute truth (AAAS.1.A.12.3, AAAS.12.A.8.3)
References outside resources	References outside resources in making arguments and claims (e.g., other threads or stickies, online articles, databases) (AAAS12.D.8.3/Chinn and Malhotra 2002)

Systems- and model-based reasoning	
Systems-based reasoning	Reasons about some phenomenon or problem in terms of a system—a collection of components and processes that interact in some way (i.e., have relationships to one another of some form). Defined systems have boundaries, subsystems, relation to other systems, and inputs & outputs (AAAS.11.A)
Understanding feedback	Thinking about things as systems means looking for how its components relate to each other. Output from one part of a system can function as input to other parts of a system. A change in one component's state can result in changes in another component's state. This includes relationships among components within a system or between systems (AAAS. 11.A.8.2)
Model-based reasoning	Model-based reasoning involves the envision of a principle-based mechanism with interacting components that represents the operation of a system within the natural (virtual) world. A model may concretize phenomena that are not directly observable (Mayer 1992; AAAS.11.B)
Model testing and prediction	The usefulness of a model can be tested by comparing its predictions to actual observations in the real world. But a close match does not necessarily mean that the model is the only "true" model or the only one that would work (AAAS.11.B. 12.2)
Mathematical modeling	The basic idea of mathematical modeling is to find a mathematical relationship (e.g., algebraic equation, relationship between two quantities, etc.) that behaves in the same ways as the objects or processes under investigation. A mathematical model may give insight about how something really works or may fit observations very well without any intuitive meaning (AAAS.11.B.12.1)
Mathematical computation	Explicitly gives some form of mathematical calculation in their argument or thesis that is not given by the game itself (e.g., not merely the DPS listed on a weapon). For example, demonstrates how an algebraic equation (a mathematical model) can be solved for (or predict) the relative trade-off between two variables, or compares two groups using their mean, median, variance, standard deviation, etc. (AAAS.12.B)
Not relevant to sci reason	Social banter, non science related topics, etc.
Uncodable	Cannot tell if it is science related or not

Tacit epistemologies	
Absolutist	Knowledge is objective, certain, and simply accumulates (Kuhn 1992)
Relativist	Knowledge is subjective, dictated only by personal tastes and wishes of the knower. Nothing is certain, all opinions are of equal validity, and even experts disagree (Kuhn 1992)
Evaluative	Knowledge is an open-ended process of evaluation and argument (Kuhn 1992)
Uncodable	Cannot tell what epistemology the poster tacitly holds

Findings

The results from this analysis are presented in Figure 1, which shows the percentage of posts that exhibit each code we focused on for analysis. Here, we see the saturation of key characteristics of scientific reasoning skills and dispositions across the sample. Several interesting patterns emerge from this analysis.

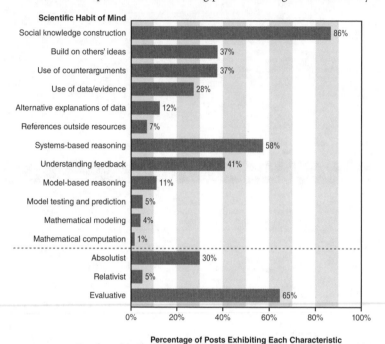

Figure 1. Proportion of posts within the data corpus that exhibit each scientific habit of mind and tacit epistemology under examination.

Social Knowledge Construction

The first and most obvious pattern is the large proportion of productive discussion found on the boards: We found that 86% of the *WoW* discussion forums consisted of talk that could be considered "social knowledge construction"—meaning, the collective development of understanding, often through joint problems solving and argumentation. In other words, in the overwhelming majority of forum talk, participants were solving problems through discussion, knowledge sharing, and debate through threads that began with posts such as "I notice that high level priests carry around a great deal of potions ... Which potions do you carry around constantly and why?" (post #3357.0) Only 8% of the discussion posts were mere social banter (the remaining 6% were uncodable with this coding scheme)—perhaps a surprising result for those who presume that discussions around videogames are a "torpid" waste of time.

One of our initial hypotheses was that only the more experienced *WoW* players would engage in higher order intellectual work on the discussion forums. In fact, we found no relationship between a given poster's character level (which represents their experience with the game) and the quality or quantity of the attributes for which we coded, other than a very mild and negative correlation ($r = -0.08$) between author's character level and social banter. Thus, while we cannot disprove the notion that only the "hardcore" gamers engage in the forms of informal science literacy investigated here, we find no evidence that such is indeed the case.

Scientific Discursive Practices

Of the 86% of the forum posts that were not social banter or simply uncodable, roughly one-third (37%) built on ideas that previous posters had raised; for example, by stating "Given your advice, I've spec'd out the following talents ..." (post #4109.29). Roughly another third (37%) used counterarguments against previous posters' ideas; for example, stating "The real question is 'Are Holy or Disc priests going to kill as much?' And the answer is no. Shadow has more offensive utility, which is just as important as the increase in damage ...." (post #2143.5) That *WoW* players either elaborated on or disagreed with previous people's comments in the context of a forum should come as no surprise given the "collectively intelligent" (Levy 1999) nature of many such communities. However, it is interesting that forms of *scientific* argumentation were also prevalent within this informal context, given previous findings indicating that such practices do not come naturally and are difficult to foster (Kuhn 1992; Osborne et al. 2004).

As another illustration of scientific argumentation, in 28% of the posts made individuals used data or evidence of some form in order to warrant their claims. For example, in a thread discussing priest healing strategies, one poster argues for his strategy by stating, "my +355 healing allows me to use Heal4 [spell] to hit around 1k+ every time, ignoring crits [critical hits]. That's good enough to spam [cast repeatedly] for most battles while throwing in a Fheal [flash heal] now and then" (post #3247.20). In another 12%, individuals challenge one another's hypotheses by providing alternative explanations of evidence used to support those suppositions with statements such as the following:

> The calculations correctly show that mind flay [spell] receives just as much +damage percentage as mind blast. However mind blast has a 1.5 second cast time, and mind flay has a 3 second cast time. And therefore mind flay receives half the dps [damage per second] boost it should. (post #2609.43)

And in 7% of the posts, participants cited a variety of information resources beyond the current discussion thread itself (see Table 2). For example, one poster: recommended a particular character configuration (i.e. "talent build," discussed below) over another with the statement "I would be more inclined to go with a build similar to: http://www.wowhead.com/?talent=bVMhzZZxOgtczR if you would like to go Shadow [one particular form of character specialization]" (post #3374.9).

What did the typical "social knowledge construction" discussion thread containing "scientific discursive practices" look like? As the example in Figure 2 illustrates, most such discussions began with an initial question about a given mechanic in the game or game-playing strategy, often coupled with the proposal of some theory. A second poster would typically then elaborate in answering the question or responding to the proposed theory, at times using data from the game to warrant the claims made. The response would then be discussed and debated by a larger group. Often a second, alternative hypothesis or explanation would eventually be offered (or, more rarely, the interpretation of the data used in the first explanation was reinterpreted), followed by an additional round of discussion and debate, and so on. Occasionally, confirming or disconfirming claims or evidence from other resources, such as collaborative online manuals to the game (e.g., WoWWiki, http://wowwiki.com) or other archived discussions on this or other forums, would be introduced into the discussion. In some threads, a comparison or synthesis of the two or more explanations would culminate the discussion; in others, the conversation simply petered out as though the participants had accepted the most recently posted theory or explanation as the preferred one or had perhaps tired of the topic and moved on.

Table 2. Types of Outside Resources Referenced by Forum Poster Within the Sample

Outside Resources Referenced	
Talent calculators/builds	Links to an official or unofficial tools for calculating talent point allocations
Personal talent builds	Links to a player's specific talent build
WoW databases and Wikis	Links to information on publicly accessible WoW databases and Wikis created by WoW players themselves
Official blizzard documents	Links to official information published by Blizzard
Other WoW forums	Links to other discussions in the WoW forums (beyond current forum)
Personal websites	Links to a player's personal website or other online material

scientific habit of mind

post #		social knowledge construction	build on others' ideas	use of counterarguments	use of data / evidence	alternative explanations of data	references outside resources	systems-based reasoning	understanding feedback	model-based reasoning	model testing and prediction	mathematical modeling	mathematical computation	absolutist	relativist	evaluative
0	Poses question: group healing strategy (A) or (B)?	•		•				•	•	•						•
1	Advocates (B) & gives strategy (C)	•			•			•	•							•
2	Compares (A) & (B) on use conditions, advocates (A)	•													•	
3	Critiques (A) & (B), advocates (C), raise issue (X)	•	•	•				•	•							•
4	Elaborates (X)	•	•		•			•	•							•
5	Elaborates (X)	•	•			•		•	•					•		
6	Argues (A) > (B)	•	•	•				•	•							•
7	Elaborates (X)	•	•					•	•					•		
8	Elaborates (A) > (B) but dependent on conditions	•	•					•	•						•	
9	Argues (A) = (B) under the right conditions for each	•	•	•		•		•	•						•	
10	Counterargues (B) > (A)	•	•	•	•			•	•					•		
11	Elaborates counterargument (B) > (A)	•	•	•	•	•	•	•	•	•	•	•	•	•		
12	Details scenario with (B) strategy & issue (X)	•		•				•	•	•						•
13	Details scenario with both (A) & (B) strategies	•		•	•			•	•	•						•
14	Details scenario with (A) strategy & new issue (Y)	•		•				•								•
15	Challenges detail of scenario with (A)	•	•													
16	Argues (A) > (B)	•			•	•		•		•						•
17	Argues (B) > (A) & details issue (X)	•	•		•	•		•		•	•				•	
18	Elaborates (A) > (B)	•	•					•								
19	Counterargues (B) > (A)	•	•													•
20	Argues (B) > (A)	•		•				•	•							•
21	Compares (A) & (B) on use conditions, advocates (A)	•		•	•	•		•	•							•
22	Original poster acknowledges discussion	•														•
23	Argues both (A) & (B) strategies	•						•	•							•
24	Argues (A) > (B)	•			•			•	•					•		
25	Counterargues (B) > (A)	•		•	•			•	•							•
26	Argues (A) = (B) under right conditions based on (X)	•	•	•	•	•		•	•	•						•
27	Details scenario w/ (A) & (B) & (C) strategies given (X)	•	•					•	•	•						•
28	Argues (A) > (B)	•		•	•			•								
29	Argues (A) = (B) under right conditions based on (X)	•			•			•	•	•						•
30	Elaborates detail of scenario with (A) & (B) & (C)	•						•	•							
31	Counterargues (B) > (A)	•	•	•	•			•	•	•	•	•				•
32	Argues (B) > (A)	•			•			•	•							•
33	Challenges initial characterization of (B)	•												•		
34	Argues (A) > (B) & raises issue (X)	•		•	•			•	•	•				•		
35	Argues (A) > (B)	•		•	•							•	•	•		
36	Details scenario with both (A) & (B) strategies	•		•	•			•	•	•				•		

A = spam PoH   B = Holy Nova   C = renew   X = FR gear   Y = FR pots

Figure 2. An example "social knowledge" construction thread (#329) of thirty-six posts detailed in terms of both the augmentative moves made within each and the codes applied to them.

System- and Model-Based Reasoning

Over half (58%) of the *WoW* forum posts evinced *systems-based reasoning*, the majority of which also demonstrate an understanding of feedback among components of the system. For example, participants discussed the game in terms of components and processes that interact in ways such that changes in one impact cause changes in another, as in the following post:

> By choosing a slower spell [variable one] and the lowest rank [variable two] you can live comfortably with (or your tank can live with, in our case), you are still making the most of your mana [variable three], given your gear [variable four]. (post #3247.12)

Roughly one tenth of the forum posts illustrated *model-based reasoning*—essentially, using some form of model to understand a given system under consideration—with about half of those (5% of posts total) including some comparison between the model's predictions and actual observations of the phenomenon it is intended to capture or explain in some way. One example of such discussion focused on a phenomenon called "scaling." Imagine that, for a level 2 priest, a given spell does ten damage; when the priest reaches to level 20, that ten damage accomplishes much less because the level 20 priest is now fighting much harder monsters. In order to balance ability with challenge, *WoW* makes higher level, stronger spells available as one's character level increases. In place of a spell that does ten damage would be a spell that does one hundred damage, for example, so that the ability to do damage to monsters using a given spell "scales" as character level increases. Scaling is not the same for every spell or character class, and one way that designers "balance" their game mechanics is to monitor and tweak scaling. In the following excerpt, a participant proposes one particular model of how the in-game scaling mechanics work and considers that model's predictions given changes in input:

> If mind flay [priest spell] actually got the full scaling of a 3 second cast spell, then by combining mind flay with both dots [priest damage over time spells] and all available talents [point system for specializing character types] to improve those, you would actually see a shadow priest's scaling maxing out at a little under 80% of what a fire mage's scaling would max out at with 40 fire and nothing more. (post #2609.51)

Thus, posters orient toward the usefulness of a model in terms if its ability (or inability) to make predictions that match actual observations. Slightly less than half of those models (4% of posts total) were explicitly mathematical, and only 1% of the total forum posts included actual computations as well. An example illustrating both is the following post excerpt raising issues about the balance of priest versus mage abilities:

By intuition, you should notice a problem...

but I'll give you the numbers anyways

For Mindflay, SW:P, and presumably VT [3 priest spells]:

Damage = (base_spell_damage + modifier * damage_

gear) * darkness * weaving * shadowform * misery

For Frostbolt [mage spell]

Average Damage = (base_spell_damage + (modifier + empowered frost)

* damage_gear) * (1 * (1 − critrate − winter's chill − empowered frost) +

(1.5 + ice shards) * (critrate + winter's chill + empowered frost)) * piercing ice

mindflay = (426 + 0.45 * dam) * 1.1 * 1.15 * 1.15 * 1.05

650.7 + 0.687 * dam

frostbolt = (530 + (0.814 + 0.10)*dam) * ((1 − crit − 0.10 − 0.05) +

(1.5 + 0.5) * (crit + 0.10 + 0.05)) * 1.06

(530 + 0.914 * dam) * ((0.85 − crit) + 2 * (crit + 0.15)) * 1.06

0.968 * (dam + 579.7) * (crit + 1.15)

Please notice the 0.687 versus the 0.968. That's the scaling factor. (post #2609.18)

In this example, the author makes an argument about the relative scaling of priest skills compared to mage skills based on a thoroughly mathematical argument, using computation as a form of evidence for the points made. His conclusion—that the scaling factor of each class type (0.687 and 0.968 respectfully) is unequal—is his climactic justification for the initial claim that the two character classes are not balanced.

What did a typical "systems- and model-based reasoning" forum post discussion thread look like? Figure 3 shows the analysis of one post-containing relevant codes.

Typically, such posts would occur in context of broader "social knowledge construction" threads (described above). In order to make an argument for one particular hypothesis or solution for some in-game system, the poster would often present a model to explain the system as evidence for their claim. In some rare cases, that model would be mathematical in nature, and fidelity between the model's prediction and actual in-game observations would function as evidence of its explanatory power. More frequently, evidence would include direct observations taken in-game and references to outside resources such as collective data sets, heuristics in the form of online database backed websites, or fan-created user manuals and guides. Generally speaking, the proportion of model-based reasoning, model testing and prediction, use of mathematics, and explicit computation (11%, 5%, 4%, 1%, respectively) were rather low; however, the sophistication of arguments that leverage such models warrants consideration. For example, Figure 4 shows the model linked in the post detailed in Figure 3.

	The unfortunate fact is that there is no shadow nuke [prior topic] …
social knowledge construction	and no shadow nuke which benefits from reduced casting time. All other casters (including holy priests) have a nuke which benefits from reduced
uses data/evidence	casting time: bane, improved fireball, improved frostbolt, divine fury, improved wrath. I have put together **my own spreadsheet** which goes into more detail and takes into account exactly what happens to **spells**
systems based reasoning	**with regard to talents** and gives a column at the end expressing **each**
understanding feedback	**spell's total scaling with respect to +dmg [damage] applied per second** (i.e. how much your gear actually improves your dps):
model based reasoning	http://geocities.com/[omitted].htm ──────▶
mathematical modeling	
mathematical computation	
	If I got anything wrong feel free to email me at [omitted]@gmail.com but if you read up at
references outside resources	**wowwiki.com** and check out the **coefficients**
evaluative epistemology	**used in the theorycraft mod** you'll find that I'm consistent with respect to them.
	You see there at the end - if you add flay and swp together you see that shadow is at 31%, where fire mages are around 48%. I have done some preliminary numbers for the expansion and shadow only improves to
model testing & prediction	35% as fire mages jump way up to 60%. **If flay were empowered to the point that it recieved 65% of +dmg then shadow would be up around 45% dps scaling.** That would be quite respectible considering that a shadow priest can swp/flay for nearly 2 minutes without interruption where other classes would peter out in a minute or less except for their mana recovery abilities. Without empowered scaling shadow priests will languish at under 50% of the endgame dps of mages and warlocks. (post #2609.6)

Figure 3. Analysis of an individual post exemplifying system- and model-based reasoning.

Tacit Epistemologies

We chose to examine the dispositions toward knowledge exhibited in the data corpus because previous pilot work indicated that, while we may find informal science reasoning and argumentation in *WoW* forum discussions, it may also be the case that the stance authors in such contexts take toward their claims is appropriate for *reverse engineering*, but inappropriate for *scientific inquiry* (Steinkuehler and Chmiel 2006). An "absolutist" epistemology, for example, might serve someone well when operating in a virtual world where there really is a single algorithm (or set of algorithms) underlying a given phenomenon and success is only a matter of finding them. However, such an absolutist approach does not serve someone well for understanding science in the real world. Instead, in science, an evaluative disposition is most appropriate, one that treats knowledge as an open-ended process of evaluation and argument of hypotheses about whether and how "algorithms" govern natural phenomena.

The epistemology tacitly displayed in 27% of the data corpus was too ambiguous to code. Of the remaining data corpus that could be coded for epistemological disposition, we found that 65% of the forum posts displayed an evaluative epistemology through rhetorical moves that treat knowledge as an open-ended process of evaluation and argument such as "Shadow Affinity [priest talent] and Silent Resolve [priest talent]: Do they stack? If so, why would a shadow priest

Constants: Crit Rate 5%

Class	Spec	Spell (+ talent conditions)	Spell Damage Scale	Damage Talents	Target Debuffs	Damage Scale	Spell Damage Total Scale	Crit Bonus	Crit Rate Bonus	Crit Scale	Damage Interval	Cast Interval	Cast Time	Casts Per Interval	DPS Scale	Time Ratio	Max Crit DPS Scale	Modified Crit Rate	TOTAL DPS SCALE	Notes
			Cast Time / 3.5	per talents	per abilities	talents * debuffs	scale * talents * debuffs	per talents (no bennefit for dots)	per talents	total scale * crit bonus	limited by dots	limited by cooldowns			total scale / dmg interval	dmg interval * cast interval / # casts	crit scale / dmg interval	crit rate + rate bonus	dps * (1 - crit rate) + crit dps * crit rate	
		Solo Caster Classes at Level 60																		
Priest	Shadow	Mind Flay	45.7%	125%	115%	**144%**	65.7%	100%	0%	65.7%	3	3	Channel	1	21.90%	100.00%	21.90%	5.00%	21.90%	Channeled
		SWP	133.3%	125%	115%	**144%**	**191.7%**	100%	0%	191.7%	18	18	1.5	1	10.65%	100.00%	10.65%	5.00%	10.65%	
		Mind Blast	42.9%	125%	115%	**144%**	61.6%	150%	0%	92.4%	1.5	5.5	1.5	1	**41.07%**	27.27%	61.61%	5.00%	**42.10%**	
	Disc/Holy	Smite	71.4%	115%	100%	115%	82.1%	150%	15%	123.2%	2	2	2	1	**41.07%**	100.00%	61.61%	**20.00%**	**45.18%**	
		Holy Fire	75.0%	115%	100%	115%	86.3%	150%	15%	129.4%	3	3	3	1	28.75%	100.00%	43.13%	**20.00%**	31.63%	Dot
		Holy Fire Dot	25.0%	115%	100%	115%	28.8%	100%	15%	28.8%	10	10	3	1	2.88%	100.00%	2.88%	**20.00%**	2.88%	
		SWP	100.0%	105%	100%	105%	**105.0%**	100%	0%	105.0%	18	18	1.5	1	5.83%	100.00%	5.83%	5.00%	5.83%	
		PI + Smite	71.4%	135%	100%	**135%**	96.4%	150%	15%	144.6%	2	180	2	6	**48.21%**	6.67%	72.32%	**20.00%**	**53.04%**	Cooldown
		PI + Holy Fire	75.0%	135%	100%	**135%**	**101.3%**	150%	15%	151.9%	3	180	3	5	33.75%	8.33%	50.63%	**20.00%**	37.13%	Dot + Cooldown
		PI Holy Fire Dot	25.0%	135%	100%	**135%**	33.8%	100%	15%	33.8%	10	180	3	2	3.38%	11.11%	3.38%	**20.00%**	3.38%	
Warlock	SM/Ruin	Shadowbolt	85.7%	110%	110%	121%	103.7%	200%	5%	**207.4%**	2.5	2.5	2.5	1	**41.49%**	100.00%	82.97%	10.00%	**45.63%**	
		Corruption	100.0%	110%	110%	121%	**121.0%**	100%	0%	121.0%	18	18	1.5	1	6.72%	100.00%	6.72%	5.00%	6.72%	
		Curse of Agony	100.0%	110%	110%	121%	**121.0%**	100%	0%	121.0%	24	24	1.5	1	5.04%	100.00%	5.04%	5.00%	5.04%	improved CoA does not apply to gear
		Shadowburn	42.9%	110%	110%	121%	51.9%	200%	5%	103.7%	1.5	10	1.5	1	34.57%	15.00%	69.14%	10.00%	**38.03%**	
		Improved Shaodwbolt	85.7%	110%	132%	**145%**	**124.5%**	200%	5%	**248.9%**	2.5	2.5	2.5	1	**49.78%**	100.00%	99.57%	10.00%	**54.76%**	Luck
	SM/DS	Shadowbolt	100.0%	125%	110%	**138%**	**137.5%**	150%	0%	**206.3%**	3	3	3	1	**45.83%**	100.00%	68.75%	5.00%	**46.98%**	
		Corruption	100.0%	125%	110%	**138%**	**137.5%**	100%	0%	137.5%	18	18	1.5	1	7.64%	100.00%	7.64%	5.00%	7.64%	
		Curse of Agony	100.0%	131%	110%	**144%**	**144.1%**	100%	0%	144.1%	24	24	1.5	1	6.00%	100.00%	6.00%	5.00%	6.00%	
	Ember/DS	Soul Fire	100.0%	125%	110%	**138%**	**137.5%**	200%	5%	**275.0%**	6	6	6	1	22.92%	100.00%	45.83%	10.00%	25.21%	Reagent
		Searing Pain	42.9%	125%	110%	**138%**	58.9%	200%	15%	117.9%	1.5	1.5	1.5	1	**39.29%**	100.00%	78.57%	**20.00%**	**47.14%**	
		Immolate	19.8%	150%	110%	**165%**	32.7%	200%	5%	65.3%	1.5	1.5	1.5	1	21.78%	100.00%	43.56%	10.00%	23.96%	Dot
		Immolate Dot	65.3%	125%	110%	**138%**	89.8%	100%	5%	89.8%	15	15	1.5	1	5.99%	100.00%	5.99%	10.00%	5.99%	
	MD/Ruin	Shadowbolt	85.7%	115%	110%	127%	108.4%	200%	5%	**216.9%**	2.5	2.5	2.5	1	**43.37%**	100.00%	86.74%	10.00%	**47.71%**	
		Corruption	100.0%	115%	110%	127%	**126.5%**	100%	0%	126.5%	18	18	1.5	1	7.03%	100.00%	7.03%	5.00%	7.03%	
		Curse of Agony	100.0%	115%	110%	127%	**126.5%**	100%	0%	126.5%	24	24	1.5	1	5.27%	100.00%	5.27%	5.00%	5.27%	improved CoA does not apply to gear
		Shadowburn	42.9%	115%	110%	127%	54.2%	200%	5%	108.4%	1.5	10	1.5	1	36.14%	15.00%	72.29%	10.00%	**39.76%**	
		Improved Shaodwbolt	85.7%	115%	132%	**152%**	130.1%	200%	5%	**260.2%**	2.5	2.5	2.5	1	**52.05%**	100.00%	104.09%	10.00%	**57.25%**	Luck
Mage	Frost	Frostbolt	81.4%	106%	100%	106%	86.3%	200%	10%	172.6%	2.5	2.5	2.5	1	34.53%	100.00%	69.05%	**15.00%**	**39.70%**	winter's chill for all ice
		Frozen + Frostbolt	81.4%	106%	100%	106%	86.3%	200%	60%	172.6%	2.5	2.5	2.5	1	34.53%	100.00%	69.05%	**65.00%**	**56.97%**	Frozen target
	AP/Frost	Frostbolt	81.4%	109%	100%	109%	88.8%	200%	3%	177.5%	2.5	2.5	2.5	1	35.50%	100.00%	71.01%	8.00%	**38.34%**	
		Frozen + Frostbolt	81.4%	109%	100%	109%	88.8%	200%	63%	177.5%	2.5	2.5	2.5	1	35.50%	100.00%	71.01%	**68.00%**	**59.64%**	Frozen target
		AP + Frostbolt	81.4%	139%	100%	**139%**	**113.2%**	200%	3%	226.4%	2.5	180	2.5	5	**45.27%**	6.94%	90.55%	8.00%	**48.90%**	Cooldown
		AP + Frozen Frostbolt	81.4%	139%	100%	**139%**	**113.2%**	200%	63%	226.4%	2.5	180	2.5	5	**45.27%**	6.94%	90.55%	**68.00%**	**76.06%**	Cooldown + Frozen target
	Fire	Fireball	100.0%	110%	115%	**127%**	**126.5%**	219%	6%	**277.0%**	3	3	3	1	**42.17%**	100.00%	92.35%	11.00%	**47.69%**	imp scorch for all fire mage
		Fire Blast	42.9%	110%	115%	**127%**	54.2%	219%	10%	118.7%	1.5	8	1.5	1	36.14%	18.75%	79.15%	**15.00%**	**42.59%**	ignite is 150% + 150% * 40% * debuffs
		Scorch	42.9%	110%	115%	**127%**	54.2%	219%	10%	118.7%	1.5	1.5	1.5	1	36.14%	100.00%	79.15%	**15.00%**	**42.59%**	
	AP/Fire	Fireball	100.0%	103%	115%	118%	**118.5%**	219%	6%	**259.4%**	3	3	3	1	**39.48%**	100.00%	86.47%	11.00%	**44.65%**	
		Scorch	42.9%	103%	115%	118%	50.8%	219%	6%	111.2%	1.5	1.5	1.5	1	33.84%	100.00%	74.12%	11.00%	38.27%	
		AP + Fireball	100.0%	133%	115%	**153%**	**153.0%**	219%	6%	**335.0%**	3	180	3	4	**50.98%**	6.67%	111.65%	11.00%	**57.66%**	Cooldown
Druid	Balance	Moonfire	20.0%	110%	100%	110%	22.0%	200%	13%	44.0%	1.5	1.5	1.5	1	14.67%	100.00%	29.33%	**18.00%**	17.31%	Dot, imp MF doesn't apply to gear
			57.1%	110%	100%	110%	62.9%	100%	13%	62.9%	12	12	1.5	1	5.24%	100.00%	5.24%	**18.00%**	5.24%	
		Wrath	57.1%	110%	100%	110%	62.9%	200%	3%	125.7%	1.5	1.5	1.5	1	**41.90%**	100.00%	83.81%	8.00%	**45.26%**	
		Starfire	100.0%	110%	100%	110%	**110.0%**	200%	3%	**220.0%**	3	3	3	1	36.67%	100.00%	73.33%	8.00%	**39.60%**	
Shaman	Elemental	Lightning Bolt	85.7%	105%	100%	105%	90.0%	200%	10%	180.0%	2	2	2	1	**45.00%**	100.00%	90.00%	**15.00%**	**51.75%**	
		Chain Lightning	71.4%	105%	100%	105%	75.0%	200%	10%	150.0%	1.5	6	1.5	1	**50.00%**	25.00%	100.00%	**15.00%**	**57.50%**	

Figure 4. An example model of an in-game phenomenon called scaling (Basic n.d.) that illustrates the complexity of the models sometimes discussed.

need a 45% reduction in threat?" (post #1937.0). Thirty percent displayed an absolutist epistemology, treating knowledge as objective, certain, and simply accumulative through statements such as: "There is a basic strategy for any one class vs any other class and whoever carries out that strategy most successfully will win" (post #415.92) [even though no such basic strategy exists]. Another 5% displayed a relativist epistemology, treating claims about the world as subjective and "to each his own" (post #215.58). Thus, the majority of posts that could be coded in terms of the attitude toward knowledge held fell into the "evaluative" category, which is consistent with scientific inquiry and inconsistent with reverse engineering. We discuss these findings in greater depth below.

Game Specific Content

What specific content areas of the game elicit these forms of informal science literacy practice? Examining the relationships among our scientific habits of mind codes (see Table 1) and our *WoW* content codes (Table 3), we found that the only moderately strong and non-obvious relationship between the two was between systems-based reasoning (and its concomitant "understanding feedback") and discussion of the priest "talent tree" ($r = 0.48$ and 0.42, respectively), shown in Figure 5, whereby players allocate "talent points" toward customizing the functions and abilities of their online character or "avatar."

In working through this system, participants are faced with the challenge of finding the best-fit solution to a problem of limited resources (talent points) for distribution across multiple variables, each with their own mathematical relationship to underlying avatar characteristics (e.g., hit points, mana points, regeneration speed). Because *WoW* is a complex system with no single obvious solution, a significant amount of time on the priest discussion boards is spent assessing how choices in one area of the talent tree affect outcomes elsewhere and debating which point allocations are best given various play styles and goals. Many of the examples used throughout this paper are a testament to the intellectual labor spent on just this one game-related content area.

Table 3. A Second Set of Codes Used to Describe the Game-Related Content of the Post

World of Warcraft *Content Codes*		
Guilds	Items, equipment, supplies	PvP content, battlegrounds
Quests, instances, raids	Talent trees, spells, abilities	Collaborative play
Other classes (than priests)	Addons, macros	Patches, expansions
Factions (horde vs. alliance)	*WoW* forums, trolling	Class/profession guides, how-to's
Reputation/experience grinding, leveling	Null/social banter	Uncodable

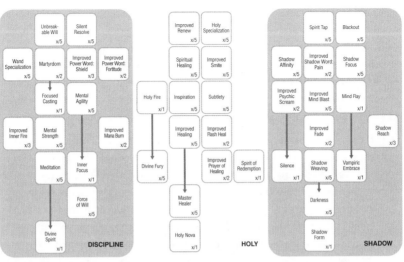

Figure 5. The *World of Warcraft* "talent tree" for the priest class (at the time of data collection), which enables players to customize their avatars.

Discussion and Implications

Our goal has been to provide empirical evidence to substantiate claims of the potential of MMOs as sites fostering learning, especially informal science literacy. Given the overall representativeness of our sample (confidence level of 91%), we are in a good position to make reasonably strong claims. Overwhelmingly, game related forums like the one examined here are rich sites for social knowledge construction. That game communities engage in productive forms of discussion and problem solving is not surprising; that such an overwhelming majority of their conversation (86%) is dedicated to such labor *is* surprising. Discursive practices include argument, counterargument, and the use of evidence to warrant one's claims. In such contexts, much of the conversation focuses on puzzling through complex systems within the virtual world and the relationships among components within those systems. At times, that inquiry includes the proposal of explanatory models of how the system under scrutiny functions. On rare occasions, posts debate the merits of their models in terms of their predictive power. On even rarer occasions still, those models take the form of mathematical equations whose computations are done explicitly and publicly.

The findings on tacit epistemology displayed throughout the discussions were also a surprise. Contrary to our initial hypotheses, the pre-dominant epistemological disposition exhibited in the forum posts was "evaluative" and therefore appropriate to science. Such findings are quite encouraging. In an earlier study of argumentative reasoning in everyday contexts that examined Americans across gender, age, class, and educational level (Kuhn 1992), only 15% of those interviewed held an evaluative epistemology, 50% held an absolutist epistemology, and

35% held a relativist epistemology. In this earlier study, argumentative ability did not differ systematically as a function of gender or age but it did differ systematically in terms of level of education. Kuhn therefore concluded that classrooms are one promising context for the development of such skills. However, she also points out the limitations of teacher led dialogues, crediting the positive impact education has on such attributes to the "social environment of peers" that school, as a byproduct, enables rather than teacher led formal dialogues per se:

> ... does school experience in fact offer the opportunity for the kinds of exchange of ideas and argumentative discourse that would enhance development of argumentative thinking? In one sense, the answer is yes; in another sense it is no. The answer is yes in the sense that from the earliest years, schooling provides a social environment of peers. In the informal social interaction that is a major part of school experience, ideas are tested and inevitably challenged; thus social experience serves as the natural challenge to individual thought. In a second deeper sense, however, the answer is no; schools do not provide this opportunity, or at least do not provide it optimally. Even in the best schools, what may appear to be genuine group debates about an issue are usually heavily controlled by the teacher ... [who] already possesses the understanding of an issue that he or she wishes students to attain ... Most often missing, even in the best of such "discovery-based" pedagogies, is genuine, open debate of complex, unanswered questions. (Kuhn 1992, pp. 175–176).

While Kuhn does not advocate the use of informal social dialogue necessarily either (in her own words, they "only occasionally leads students to think explicitly about their ideas—to reflect on their own thought" p. 175), these data suggest their efficacy, at least under certain conditions. In the context of game related forums, informal social dialogues are indeed "genuine, open debate of complex, unanswered questions" and therefore may very well lead participants toward a more reflective stance toward knowledge ultimately. Such a hypothesis is certainly worth future consideration in studies that follow. Of course, one could also argue that game forums (like the one studied here) tend to attract individuals with a more nuanced stance toward knowledge rather than fostering such a stance themselves. Regardless, we can at least say that the cultural norms that emerge in this part of *WoW* fandom preference an evaluative epistemology and that this preferencing of an evaluative disposition varies significantly from the disposition preferenced by other cultural norms, including but certainly not limited to the typical cultural norms of an American classroom.

In addition to providing empirical evidence to substantiate the potential of such play contexts for informal science literacy learning, this study sheds some curious light on the nature of collective intelligence (Levy 1999). Discussion environments such as these are best characterized as *collective* rather than *collaborative.* It could have easily been the case that a handful of verbose posters engage in extended dialogue with each other, making it a highly collaborative (albeit small) community of exceptional minds who happen to make their cognition public. This, however, was not at all the pattern we found. Rather, as Figure 6 shows, the relationship between length of discussion thread and number of players contributing to it is strongly linear.

In such contexts, solutions developed by one person are referenced, debated, and built upon by masses of other participants, not merely a handful of designated experts. Thus, a large number of posters each make one or two contributions to the discussion, with the solution to the problem or answer to the inquiry emerging as a result of swarms of thinkers, not a lonely few.

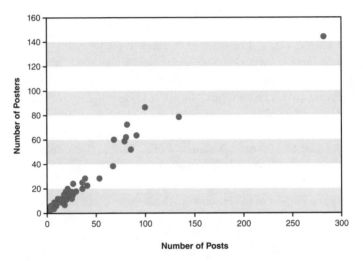

Figure 6. Scatter plot of number of posts by number of unique posters
for each thread in the data corpus.

Such findings are useful in that they enable us to more accurately characterize virtual worlds as learning contexts that stretch across both intra-game and extra-game spaces. As our study shows, forms of inquiry within play contexts such as these are *authentic* although *synthetic:* even though the worlds themselves are fantasy, the knowledge building communities around them are quite real. And, it is their designed nature that makes these communities so lively. For they were designed such that particular user-controlled configurations (e.g., how one builds her talent tree) has powerful and important implications for the success of one's game play. In fact, in these synthetic worlds designers can manipulate these dynamics so that they are most likely to breed rich conversations as users struggle with the most appropriate configurations.

What, then, are the implications for science education and future research? There are several. First, the veritable firewall against games and gaming culture within schools might erode. While virtual worlds may seem "torpid" (Solomon 2004) to a non-gaming older generation, empirical analysis of what game communities do and value indicates that this interactive medium might well be a worthy vehicle of learning for those who value intellectual and academic play. In a school system sometimes sidetracked by testing regimes that pressure teachers and students to focus on only a narrow range of topics, popular culture contexts such as these might be a nice complement to classrooms, augmenting classroom instruction by situating informal science literacy in popular culture context.

Second, we should ask ourselves how these practices are distributed across various groups by demographic variables known to be important, such as age, education level, and income. Demonstrating that game communities such as those in *WoW* engage in important forms of science literacy again raises the specter of a new form of digital divide—one not between the have and have-nots, but between the do and do-nots. We need to think deeply about what people are doing with the technologies that are becoming so ubiquitous and engaging. As educators, we have a responsibility to better understand what these different forms of technology afford and communicate this to the public more broadly.

Third and finally, we should actively seek out ways to build *bridging third spaces* (Steinkuehler 2008b) between school and home that incubate forms of academic play such as those studied here. In so doing, we might address both growing digital divides at once. We can ameliorate the generational divide by educating the keepers of the canon as to the genuine merit of games and gaming cultures, and we can close the access gap by providing rich intellectual play spaces in technically and cognitively sophisticated environments to kids and young adults who might not otherwise happen upon them. As Dewey himself once argued, good education, effective and life-enhancing education, represents life "as real and vital to the child as that which he carries on in the home, in the neighborhood, or on the play-ground" (1897).

References

American Association for the Advancement of Science (1993) Benchmarks for science literacy. Oxford University Press, New York

Barab S, Arcici A, Jackson C (2005) Eat your vegetables and do your homework: a design-based investigation of enjoyment and meaning in learning. Educ Technol 45(1):15–21

Barab SA, Sadler T, Heiselt C, Hickey D, Zuiker S (2007) Relating narrative, inquiry, and inscriptions: a framework for socio-scientific inquiry. J Sci Educ Technol 16(1):59–82. doi: 10.1007/s10956-006-9033-3

Basic (n.d.) Scaling model. Retrieved November 1, 2007 from http://geocities.com/ karlthepagan/ wow/damage_scale.htm

Chi MTH (1997) Quantifying qualitative analyses of verbal data: a practical guide. J Learn Sci 6(3):271–315. doi:10.1207/s15327809jls0603_1

Chinn CA, Malhotra B (2002) Epistemologically authentic inquiry in schools: a theoretical framework for evaluating inquiry tasks. Sci Educ 86(2):175–218. doi:10.1002/sce.10001

Dewey J (1897) My pedagogic creed. Sch J 14(3):77–80

Dewey J (1910) Science as subject matter and as method. Science 31(787):121–127. doi:10.1126/science.31.787.121

Elsner A (2005) Is US becoming hostile to science? CNN.com. Retrieved October 31, 2005 from http://www.cnn.com/2005/TECH/science/10/28/science.debate.reut

Friedman TL (2005) The world is flat. Farrar, Straus, and Giroux, New York

Gee JP (2003) What video games have to teach us about learning and literacy. Palgrave, New York

Hayes E Games I Learning through game design: a review of current software & research. Games Cult (in press)

Jenkins H III (1992) Textual poachers: television fans & participatory culture. Routledge, New York

Ketelhut DJ (2007) The impact of student self-efficacy on scientific inquiry skills: an exploratory investigation in River City, a multiuser virtual environment. J Sci Educ Technol 16(1):99–111. doi: 10.1007/s10956-006-9038-y

Ketelhut DJ, Dede C, Clarke J, Nelson B, Bowman C (2007) Studying situated learning in a multi-user virtual environment. In: Baker E, Dickieson J, Wulfeck W, O'Neil H (eds), Assessment of problem solving using simulations. Lawrence Erlbaum Associates, Mahwah, NJ

Kuhn D (1992) Thinking as argument. Harv Educ Rev 62(2):155–178

Lave J (1988) Cognition in practice. Cambridge University Press, Cambridge UK

Lave J, Wenger E (1991) Situated learning. Cambridge University Press, Cambridge

Levy P (1999) Collective intelligence. (Robert Bononno, trans.). Perseus Books, Cambridge MA

Mayer RE (1992) Thinking, problem solving, cognition, 2nd edn. WH Freeman, New York

Miller JD (2004) Public understanding of, and attitudes toward, scientific research: what we know and what we need to know. Public Underst Sci 13(3):273–294. doi:10.1177/0963662504044908

Nasir NS (2005) Individual cognitive structuring and the sociocultural context: strategy shifts in the game of dominoes. J Learn Sci 14(1):5–34. doi:10.1207/s15327809jls1401_2

National Research Council (1996) National science education standards. National Academy Press, Washington DC

Nelson B, Ketelhut DJ, Clarke J, Dieterle E, Dede C, Erlandson B (2007) Robust design strategies for scaling educational innovations: The River City MUVE case study. In: Shelton BE, Wiley DA (eds) The design and use of simulation computer games in education. Sense Press, Rotterdam, The Netherlands

Osborne J, Erduren S, Simon S (2004) Enhancing the quality of argumentation in school science. J Res Sci Teach 41(10):994–1020. doi:10.1002/tea.20035

Poincaré H (2001) Science and hypothesis. In: Gould SJ (ed) The value of science: essential writings of Henri Poincaré. The Modern Library, New York, pp 7–180 (Original work published 1905)

Schwab JJ (1962) The teaching of science as enquiry. Harvard University Press, Cambridge MA

Shaffer DW, Squire KD, Halverson R, Gee JP (2005) Video games and the future of learning. Phi Delta Kappan 87(2):105–111

Singer SR, Hilton M, Schweingruber HA (2005) America's lab report: investigations in high school science. The National Academy Press, Washington DC

Solomon A (2004, July 10) The closing of the American book. The New York Times p. A17

Squire K (2003) Replaying history: learning world history through playing Civilization III. Unpublished dissertation. Indiana University, Bloomington IN

Squire KD (2005) Educating the fighter. Horizon 13(2):75–88. doi: 10.1108/10748120510608106

Steinkuehler CA (2004) Learning in massively multiplayer online games. In: Kafai YB, Sandoval WA, Enyedy N, Nixon AS, Herrera F (eds) Proceedings of the sixth ICLS. Erlbaum, Mahwah, NJ, pp 521–528

Steinkuehler CA (2005) Cognition and learning in massively multiplayer online games: a critical approach. Unpublished dissertation. University of Wisconsin, Madison WI

Steinkuehler C (2006a) The mangle of play. Games Cult 1(3):1–14

Steinkuehler CA (2006b) Massively multiplayer online videogaming as participation in a Discourse. Mind Cult Act 13(1):38–52. doi: 10.1207/s15327884mca1301_4

Steinkuehler CA (2006c) Why game (culture) studies now? Games Cult 1(1):1–6

Steinkuehler C, Chmiel M (2006) Fostering scientific habits of mind in the context of online play. In: Barab SA, Hay KE, Songer NB, Hickey DT (eds) Proceedings of the international conference of the learning sciences. Erlbuam, Mahwah NJ, pp 723–729

Steinkuehler C (2007) Massively multiplayer online gaming as a constellation of literacy practices. eLearning 4(3):297–318

Steinkuehler CA (2008a) Cognition and literacy in massively multiplayer online games. In: Coiro J, Knobel M, Lankshear C, Leu D (eds) Handbook of research on new literacies. Erlbaum, Mahwah NJ, pp 611–634

Steinkuehler C (2008b) Massively multiplayer online games as an educational technology: an outline for research. Educ Technol 48(1):10–21

Woodcock BS (2008) An analysis of MMOG subscription growth 23.0. Retrieved April 21, 2008 from http://www.mmogchart.com

Margaret Talbot is a journalist, essayist, and current staff writer for *The New Yorker.* She is a prolific writer who has covered a variety of topics throughout her career.

From Brain Gain: The Underground World of "Neuroenhancing" Drugs
Margaret Talbot

A young man I'll call Alex recently graduated from Harvard. As a history major, Alex wrote about a dozen papers a semester. He also ran a student organization, for which he often worked more than forty hours a week; when he wasn't on the job, he had classes. Weeknights were devoted to all the schoolwork that he couldn't finish during the day, and weekend nights were spent drinking with friends and going to dance parties. "Trite as it sounds," he told me, it seemed important to "maybe appreciate my own youth." Since, in essence, this life was impossible, Alex began taking Adderall to make it possible.

Adderall, a stimulant composed of mixed amphetamine salts, is commonly prescribed for children and adults who have been given a diagnosis of attention-deficit hyperactivity disorder. But in recent years Adderall and Ritalin, another stimulant, have been adopted as cognitive enhancers: Drugs that high-functioning, overcommitted people take to become higher-functioning and more overcommitted. (Such use is "off label," meaning that it does not have the approval of either the drug's manufacturer or the Food and Drug Administration.) College campuses have become laboratories for experimentation with neuroenhancement, and Alex was an ingenious experimenter. His brother had received a diagnosis of ADHD, and in his freshman year Alex obtained an Adderall prescription for himself by describing to a doctor symptoms that he knew were typical of the disorder. During his college years, Alex took fifteen milligrams of Adderall most evenings, usually after dinner, guaranteeing that he would maintain intense focus while losing "any ability to sleep for approximately eight to ten hours." In his sophomore year, he persuaded the doctor to add a thirty-milligram "extended release" capsule to his daily regimen.

Alex recalled one week during his junior year when he had four term papers due. Minutes after waking on Monday morning, around seven-thirty, he swallowed some "immediate release" Adderall. The drug, along with a steady stream of caffeine, helped him to concentrate during classes and meetings, but he noticed some odd effects; at a morning tutorial, he explained to me in an e-mail, "I alternated between speaking too quickly and thoroughly on some subjects and feeling awkwardly quiet during other points of the discussion." Lunch was a blur: "It's always hard to eat much when on Adderall." That afternoon, he went to the library, where he spent "too much time researching a paper rather than actually writing it—a problem, I can assure you, that is common to all intellectually curious students on stimulants." At eight, he attended a two-hour meeting "with a group focussed on student mental-health issues." Alex then "took an extended-release Adderall" and worked productively on the paper all night. At eight the next morning, he attended a meeting of his organization; he felt like "a zombie," but "was there to insure that the semester's work didn't go to waste." After that, Alex explained, "I went back to my room to take advantage of my tired body." He fell asleep until noon, waking "in time to polish my first paper and hand it in."

I met Alex one evening last summer, at an appealingly scruffy bar in the New England city where he lives. Skinny and bearded, and wearing faded hipster jeans, he looked like the lead singer in an indie band. He was ingratiating and articulate and smoked cigarettes with an ironic air of defiance. Alex was happy enough to talk about his frequent use of Adderall at Harvard, but he didn't want to see his name in print; he's involved with an Internet start-up and worried that potential investors might disapprove of his habit.

After we had ordered beers, he said, "One of the most impressive features of being a student is how aware you are of a twenty-four-hour work cycle. When you conceive of what you have to do for school, it's not in terms of nine to five but in terms of what you can physically do in a week while still achieving a variety of goals in a variety of realms—social, romantic, sexual, extracurricular, résumé-building, academic commitments." Alex was eager to dispel the notion that students who took Adderall were "academic automatons who are using it in order to be first in their class, or in order to be an obvious admit to law school or the first accepted at a consulting firm." In fact, he said, "it's often people"—mainly guys—"who are looking in some way to compensate for activities that are detrimental to their performance." He explained, "At Harvard, at least, most people are to some degree realistic about it . . . . I don't think people who take Adderall are aiming to be the top person in the class. I think they're aiming to be among the best. Or maybe not even among the best. At the most basic level, they aim to do better than they would have otherwise." He went on, "Everyone is aware of the fact that if you were up at 3 a.m. writing this paper it isn't going to be as good as it could have been. The fact that you were partying all weekend, or spent the last week being high, watching *Lost*—that's going to take a toll."

Alex's sense of who uses stimulants for so-called nonmedical purposes is borne out by two dozen or so scientific studies. In 2005, a team led by Sean Esteban McCabe, a professor at the University of Michigan's Substance Abuse Research Center, reported that in the previous year 4.1 percent of American undergraduates had taken prescription stimulants for off-label use; at one school, the figure was 25 percent. Other researchers have found even higher rates: A 2002 study at a small college found that more than 35 percent of the students had used prescription stimulants nonmedically in the previous year.

Drugs such as Adderall can cause nervousness, headaches, sleeplessness, and decreased appetite, among other side effects. An FDA warning on Adderall's label notes that "amphetamines have a high potential for abuse" and can lead to dependence. (The label also mentions that adults using Adderall have reported serious cardiac problems, though the role of the drug in those cases is unknown.) Yet college students tend to consider Adderall and Ritalin benign, in part because they are likely to know peers who have taken the drugs since childhood for ADHD. Indeed, McCabe reports, most students who use stimulants for cognitive enhancement obtain them from an acquaintance with a prescription. Usually, the pills are given away, but some students sell them.

According to McCabe's research team, white male undergraduates at highly competitive schools—especially in the Northeast—are the most frequent collegiate users of neuroenhancers. Users are also more likely to belong to a fraternity or a sorority and to have a GPA of 3.0 or lower. They are ten times as likely to report that they have smoked marijuana in the past year, and twenty times as likely to say that they have used cocaine. In other words, they are decent students at schools where, to be a great student, you have to give up a lot more partying than they're willing to give up.

The BoredAt Web sites—which allow college students to chat idly while they're ostensibly studying—are filled with messages about Adderall. Posts like these, from the BoredAtPenn site, are typical: "I have some Adderall—I'm sitting by room 101.10 in a grey shirt and headphones"; "I have Adderall for sale 20mg for $15"; "I took Adderall at 8 p.m., it's 6:30 a.m. and I've barely blinked." On the Columbia site, a poster with an e-mail address from CUNY complains that her friends take Adderall "like candy," adding, "I don't want to be at a disadvantage to everyone else. Is it really that dangerous? Will it fuck me up? My grades weren't that great this year and I could do with a bump." A Columbia student responds, "It's probably not a good idea if you're not prescribed," but offers practical advice anyway: "Keep the dose normal and don't grind them up or snort them." Occasional dissents ("I think there should be random drug testing at every exam") are drowned out by testimonials like this one, from the BoredAtHarvard site: "I don't want to be a pusher or start people on something bad, but Adderall is AMAZING."

Alex remains enthusiastic about Adderall, but he also has a slightly jaundiced critique of it. "It only works as a cognitive enhancer insofar as you are dedicated to accomplishing the task at hand," he said. "The number of times I've taken Adderall late at night and decided that, rather than starting my paper, hey, I'll organize my entire music library! I've seen people obsessively cleaning their rooms on it." Alex thought that generally the drug helped him to bear down on his work, but it also tended to produce writing with a characteristic flaw. "Often, I've looked back at papers I've written on Adderall, and they're verbose. They're belaboring a point, trying to create this airtight argument, when if you just got to your point in a more direct manner it would be stronger. But with Adderall I'd produce two pages on something that could be said in a couple of sentences." Nevertheless, his Adderall-assisted papers usually earned him at least a B. They got the job done. As Alex put it, "Productivity is a good thing."

Last April, the scientific journal *Nature* published the results of an informal online poll asking whether readers attempted to sharpen "their focus, concentration, or memory" by taking drugs such as Ritalin and Provigil—a newer kind of stimulant, known generically as modafinil, which was developed to treat narcolepsy. One out of five respondents said that they did. A majority of the 1,400 readers who responded said that healthy adults should be permitted to take brain boosters for nonmedical reasons, and 69 percent said that mild side effects were an acceptable risk. Though a majority said that such drugs should not be made available to children who had no diagnosed medical condition, a third admitted that they would feel pressure to give "smart drugs" to their kids if they learned that other parents were doing so....

If Alex, the Harvard student, ... [considers his] use of neuroenhancers a private act, Nicholas Seltzer sees his habit as a pursuit that aligns him with a larger movement for improving humanity. Seltzer has a BA from UC Davis and a master's degree in security policy from George Washington University. But the job that he obtained with these credentials—as a researcher at a defense-oriented think tank, in northern Virginia—has not left him feeling as intellectually alive as he would like. To compensate, he writes papers in his spare time on subjects like "human biological evolution and warfare." He also primes his brain with artificial challenges; even when he goes to the rest room at the office, he takes the opportunity to play memory or logic games on his cell phone. Seltzer, who is thirty, told me that he worried that he "didn't have the mental energy, the endurance, the—I don't know what to properly call this—the *sponginess* that I seem to recall having when I was younger."

Suffice it to say that this is not something you notice when you talk to Seltzer. And though our memory is probably at its peak in our early twenties, few thirty-year-olds are aware of a deficit. But Seltzer is the Washington-wonk equivalent of those models and actors in LA who discern tiny wrinkles long before their agent does. His girlfriend, a technology consultant whom he met in a museum, is nine years younger, and he was already thinking about how his mental fitness would stand up next to hers. He told me, "She's twenty-one, and I want to stay young and vigorous and don't want to be a burden on her later in life." He didn't worry about visible signs of aging, but he wanted to keep his mind "nimble and healthy for as long as possible."

Seltzer considers himself a "transhumanist," in the mold of the Oxford philosopher Nick Bostrom and the futurist writer and inventor Ray Kurzweil. Transhumanists are interested in robots, cryogenics, and living a really, really long time; they consider biological limitations that the rest of us might accept, or even appreciate, as creaky obstacles to be aggressively surmounted. On the Imminst forums—"Imminst" stands for "Immortality Institute"—Seltzer and other members discuss life-extension strategies and the potential benefits of cognitive enhancers. Some of the forum members limit themselves to vitamin and mineral supplements. Others use Adderall or modafinil or, like Seltzer, a drug called piracetam, which was first marketed by a Belgian pharmaceutical company in 1972 and, in recent years, has become available in the United States from retailers that sell supplements. Although not approved for any use by the FDA, piracetam has been used experimentally on stroke patients—to little effect—and on patients with a rare neurological condition called progressive myoclonus epilepsy, for whom it proved helpful in alleviating muscle spasms. Data on piracetam's benefits for healthy people are virtually nonexistent, but many users believe that the drug increases blood flow to the brain.

From the time I first talked to Seltzer, it was clear that although he felt cognitive enhancers were of practical use, they also appealed to him on an aesthetic level. Using neuroenhancers, he said, "is like customizing yourself—customizing your brain." For some people, he went on, it was important to enhance their mood, so they took antidepressants; but for people like him it was more important "to increase mental horsepower." He added, "It's fundamentally a choice you're making about how you want to experience consciousness." Whereas the '90s had been about "the personalization of technology," this decade was about the personalization of the brain—what some enthusiasts have begun to call "mind hacking."

Of course, the idea behind mind-hacking isn't exactly new. Fortifying one's mental stamina with drugs of various kinds has a long history. Sir Francis Bacon consumed everything from tobacco to saffron in the hope of goosing his brain. Balzac reputedly fuelled sixteen-hour bouts of writing with copious servings of coffee, which, he wrote, "chases away sleep, and gives us the capacity to engage a little longer in the exercise of our intellects." Sartre dosed himself with speed in order to finish *Critique of Dialectical Reason*. My college friends and I wrote term papers with the sweaty-palmed assistance of NoDoz tablets. And, before smoking bans, entire office cultures chugged along on a collective nicotine buzz—at least, if *Mad Men* is to be believed. Seltzer and his interlocutors on the Imminst forum are just the latest members of a seasoned cohort, even if they have more complex pharmaceuticals at their disposal.

I eventually met Seltzer in an underground food court not far from the Pentagon. We sat down at a Formica table in the dim light. Seltzer was slim, had a shaved head, and wore metal-frame glasses; matching his fastidious look, he spoke precisely, rarely stumbling over his words. I asked him if he had any ethical worries about smart drugs. After a pause, he said that he might have a concern if somebody popped a neuroenhancer before taking a licensing exam that certified him as, say, a brain surgeon, and then stopped using the drug. Other than that, he couldn't see a problem. He said that he was a firm believer in the idea that "we should have a fair degree of liberty to do with our bodies and our minds as we see fit, so long as it doesn't impinge on the basic rights, liberty, and safety of others." He argued, "Why would you want an upward limit on the intellectual capabilities of a human being? And, if you have a very nationalist viewpoint, why wouldn't you want our country to have the advantage over other countries, particularly in what some people call a knowledge-based economy?" He went on, "Think about the complexity of the intellectual tasks that people need to accomplish today. Just trying to understand what Congress is doing is not a simple thing! The complexity of understanding the gamut of scientific and technical and social issues is difficult. If we had a tool that enabled more people to understand the world at a greater level of sophistication, how can we prejudice ourselves against the notion, simply because we don't like athletes to do it? To me, it doesn't seem like the same question. And it deserves its own debate."

Seltzer had never had a diagnosis of any kind of learning disorder. But he added, "Though I wouldn't say I'm dyslexic, sometimes when I type prose, after I look back and read it, I've frequently left out words or interposed words, and sometimes I have difficulty concentrating." In graduate school, he obtained a prescription for Adderall from a doctor who didn't ask a lot of questions. The drug helped him, especially when his ambitions were relatively low. He recalled, "I had this one paper, on nuclear strategy. The professor didn't look favorably on any kind of creative thinking." On Adderall, he pumped out the paper in an evening. "I just bit my tongue, regurgitated, and got a good-enough grade."

On the other hand, Seltzer recalled that he had taken piracetam to write an essay on "the idea of harmony as a trope in Chinese political discourse"—it was one of the papers he was proudest of. He said, "It was really an intellectual challenge to do. I felt that the piracetam helped me to work within the realm of the abstract, and make the kind of associations that I needed—following this idea of harmony from an ancient religious belief as it was translated throughout the centuries into a very important topic in political discourse."

After a hiatus of several years, Seltzer had recently resumed taking neuroenhancers. In addition to piracetam, he took a stack of supplements that he thought helped his brain functioning: Fish oils, five antioxidants, a product called ChocoMind, and a number of others, all available at the health-food store. He was thinking about adding modafinil, but hadn't yet. For breakfast every morning, he concocted a slurry of oatmeal, berries, soy milk, pomegranate juice, flaxseed, almond meal, raw eggs, and protein powder. The goal behind the recipe was efficiency: To rely on "one goop you could eat or drink that would have everything you need nutritionally for your brain and body." He explained, "Taste was the last thing on my mind; I wanted to be able to keep it down—that was it." (He told me this in the kitchen of his apartment; he lives with a roommate, who walked in while we were talking, listened perplexedly for a moment, then put a frozen pizza in the oven.)

Seltzer's decision to take piracetam was based on his own online reading, which included medical-journal abstracts. He hadn't consulted a doctor. Since settling on a daily regimen of supplements, he had sensed an improvement in his intellectual work and his ability to engage in stimulating conversation. He continued, "I feel I'm better able to articulate my thoughts. I'm sure you've been in the zone—you're having a really exciting debate with somebody, your brain feels alive. I feel that more. But I don't want to say that it's this profound change."

I asked him if piracetam made him feel smarter, or just more alert and confident—a little better equipped to marshal the resources he naturally had. "Maybe," he said. "I'm not sure what being smarter means, entirely. It's a difficult quality to measure. It's the gestalt factor, all these qualities coming together—not only your ability to crunch some numbers, or remember some figures or a sequence of numbers, but also your ability to maintain a certain emotional state that is conducive to productive intellectual work. I do feel I'm more intelligent with the drugs, but I can't give you a number of IQ points."

The effects of piracetam on healthy volunteers have been studied even less than those of Adderall or modafinil. Most peer-reviewed studies focus on its effects on dementia, or on people who have suffered a seizure or a concussion. Many of the studies that look at other neurological effects were performed on rats and mice. Piracetam's mechanisms of action are not understood, though it may increase levels of the neurotransmitter acetylcholine. In 2008, a committee of the British Academy of Medical Sciences noted that many of the clinical trials of piracetam for dementia were methodologically flawed. Another published review of the available studies of the drug concluded that the evidence "does not support the use of piracetam in the treatment of people with dementia or cognitive impairment," but suggested that further investigation might be warranted. I asked Seltzer if he thought he should wait for scientific ratification of piracetam. He laughed. "I don't want to," he said. "Because it's working."

It makes no sense to ban the use of neuroenhancers. Too many people are already taking them, and the users tend to be educated and privileged people who proceed with just enough caution to avoid getting into trouble. Besides, [University of Pennsylvania neurologist] Anjan Chatterjee is right that there is an apt analogy with plastic surgery. In a consumer society like ours, if people are properly informed about the risks and benefits of neuroenhancers, they can make their own choices about how to alter their minds, just as they can make their own decisions about shaping their bodies.

Still, even if you acknowledge that cosmetic neurology is here to stay, there is something dispiriting about the way the drugs are used—the kind of aspirations they open up, or don't. Jonathan Eisen, an evolutionary biologist at UC Davis, is skeptical of what he mockingly calls "brain doping." During a recent conversation, he spoke about colleagues who take neuroenhancers in order to grind out grant proposals. "It's weird to me that people are taking these drugs to write grants," he said. "I mean, if you came up with some really interesting paper that was *spurred* by taking some really interesting drug—magic mushrooms or something—that would make more sense to me. In the end, you're only as good as the ideas you've come up with."

But it's not the mind-expanding 60s anymore. Every era, it seems, has its own defining drug. Neuroenhancers are perfectly suited for the anxiety of white-collar competition in a floundering economy. And they have a synergistic relationship with our multiplying digital technologies: The more gadgets we own, the more distracted we become, and the more we need help in order to focus. The experience that neuroenhancement offers is not, for the most part, about opening the doors of perception, or about breaking the bonds of the self, or about experiencing a surge of genius. It's about squeezing out an extra few hours to finish those sales figures when you'd really rather collapse into bed; getting a B instead of a B-minus on the final exam in a lecture class where you spent half your time texting; cramming for the GREs at night, because the information-industry job you got after college turned out to be deadening. Neuroenhancers don't offer freedom. Rather, they facilitate a pinched, unromantic, grindingly efficient form of productivity.

This winter, I spoke again with Alex, the Harvard graduate, and found that, after a break of several months, he had gone back to taking Adderall—a small dose every day. He felt that he was learning to use the drug in a more "disciplined" manner. Now, he said, it was less about staying up late to finish work he should have done earlier, and more "about staying focussed on work, which makes me want to work longer hours." What employer would object to that?

Taylor M. Wells is an Assistant Professor of Management Information Systems at California State University, Sacramento; his work focuses on how individual behavior, cognition, and emotion are affected by information and communication technologies. **Alan R. Dennis** is the John T. Chambers Chair of Internet Systems at the Kelley School of Business at the University of Indiana; his work focuses on teams, designing technology for the subconscious, neurological information systems, and the internet.

To Email or Not to Email: The Impact of Media on Psychophysiological Responses and Emotional Content in Utilitarian and Romantic Communication
Taylor M. Wells and Alan R. Dennis

1. Introduction

Communication media such as email and voicemail have become ubiquitous in work and in personal life because they enable individuals to correspond asynchronously. Whether due to limitations of the technology (e.g., the inability to convey vocal tone) or cultural norms, some media are considered less appropriate for some types of communication (Kock, 2004; Sussman & Sproull, 1999). For example, email and text chat are considered poor for communicating emotion (Byron, 2008; Hancock, Landrigan, & Silver, 2007) because they may increase interpersonal conflict (Polites & Karahanna, 2013), yet other research shows they are suitable for building interpersonal relationships (Walther, 1996).

Despite the widespread use of media for work and personal communication, little is known about how the characteristics of various media lead to emotional responses among users or how they distort communication messages for work and personal tasks. In dyadic communication between two parties, message senders and receivers play different roles and may be influenced by the media differently during the communication process. In this study, we limit our examination to the individual composing and sending the message to understand how the media influences senders and the messages they compose. Specifically, our goal is to examine the effects of media use for two different types of tasks (a utilitarian work task and a personal romantic task) on 1) the senders' emotional responses and 2) the messages composed. We use psychophysiological measures because they enable us to examine emotional responses in real time without interrupting the user (Riedl et al., 2010).

2. Theory and prior research

Researchers often classify media along the theoretical dimensions of richness (Daft, Lengel, & Trevino, 1987), synchronicity (Dennis, Fuller, & Valacich, 2008), social presence (Short, Williams, & Christie, 1976), and naturalness (Kock, 2009) so that an individual medium can be differentiated from the diversity of available media. A medium's richness is its ability to change understanding in the recipient by conveying a variety of cues, enabling feedback, and transmitting language variety (Daft et al., 1987). A medium high in synchronicity enables users to work together in a synchronized pattern of collaboration (Dennis et al., 2008). Media high in social presence provide the impression of intimacy towards a communication partner (Short et al., 1976). Natural media are those closest to face-to-face (FtF) and emphasize vocal communication, facial expressions, and synchronicity (Kock, 2005b). Researchers have advanced theories using these dimensions to explain individual behavior with various media. While media richness theory (MRT)(Daft et al., 1987), media synchronicity theory (MST) (Dennis et al., 2008), and social presence theory (SPT) (Short et al., 1976) inform our research, we primarily draw upon media naturalness theory (MNT) (Kock, 2004, 2005b, 2009).

2.1. Media naturalness theory

MRT uses evolutionary biology to explain how the traits and abilities humans use to understand vocal and non-verbal communication were naturally selected over time (Cuthbert et al., 2003; Kock, 2009). MNT posits that users of less natural media will be required to expend greater cognitive effort to complete tasks (Kock, 2005b). Under MNT, a medium's naturalness is an indication of its similarity to FtF communication along several important dimensions (Kock, 2005b). Natural media offer the perception of colocation, provide synchronicity in interaction, and allow for the conveyance and interpretation of facial expressions, body language, and speech (Kock, 2004) with a particular emphasis on vocal communication (called the speech imperative proposition) (Kock, 2004). For example, videoconferencing is considered a natural media because it can convey vocal cues (e.g., tone, pace, and volume) and visual cues (e.g., body posture and gestures) synchronously much like FtF communication (Kock, 2005b). Email primarily transfers textual cues and is typically used asynchronously. Even when users add formatting or emoticons to messages (Skovholt, Grønning, & Kankaanranta, 2014), email lacks the variety of cues found in FtF communication and is considered less natural. Voicemail is ranked between email and videoconferencing in naturalness because it is used for asynchronous communication, but conveys vocal cues (Kock, 2004).

We chose email and voicemail because they are ubiquitous in business and social communication (Clore & Ketelaar, 1997) and because they allow us to examine how media that differ in naturalness influence senders and the messages they compose (Kock, 2007). The two media are similar on some dimensions of media naturalness but differ in their capability to convey vocal cues (Dennis et al., 2008; Lang & Bradley, 2010). These differences allow us to theoretically examine how different media influence emotional communication.

2.2. Emotion and emotional communication

Individual emotion has emerged as an important theoretical construct for researchers seeking to understand the use of information technologies (Adelaar, Chang, Lancendorfer, Lee, & Morimoto, 2003; Hudlicka, 2003; Stieglitz & Dang-Xuan, 2013; Venkatesh, 2000; Yin, Bond, & Zhang, 2014). In this study, we use the two-dimensional model of emotion (Potter & Bolls, 2012), where, instead of considering discrete emotions such as anger, sadness, or happiness, or joy, emotion is conceptualized and measured along the dimensions of arousal and valence (Bradley & Lang, 2000; Cacioppo, Petty, Losch, & Kim, 1986). Emotional arousal is the magnitude of the affective response, and valence is the positive or negative direction of that response. Under this model, the emotion happiness is characterized by moderate arousal and positive valence while anger is characterized by moderate to high arousal and negative valence. These emotional responses can be evaluated consciously or may also be subconscious—influencing an individual without his or her knowledge (Dennis, Minas, & Bhagwatwar, 2013).

Less natural media have been deemed by some as inappropriate or unsuitable for emotional communication (Byron, 2008; Kruger, Epley, Parker, & Ng, 2005). However, these media may not be as poor in communicating emotion in practice as once thought (Hancock et al., 2007); less natural media may be preferred when sending messages with negative emotion, such as bad news (Sussman & Sproull, 1999). People using unnatural communication media can convey and recognize emotion and develop interpersonal relationships (Derks, Fischer, & Bos, 2008; Hancock et al., 2007; Hian, Chuan, Trevor, & Detenber, 2004).

We examine the composing of individual messages which may comprise part of a larger overall task. These *communication tasks* are our unit of analysis, and we are interested in how different types of communication tasks may influence the sender's emotional response and the content of the messages composed. Different types of communication tasks have different emotional components. In this study, we consider communication tasks that are utilitarian in nature and communication tasks that are romantic. Utilitarian communication tasks are those which are focused on completing a larger task and are not addressed to a romantic partner. The tasks themselves typically have little positive or negative emotional content. With romantic communication, a sender composes messages addressed to his or her partner or romantic interest which often include flirtatious language and tone. The goal of a utilitarian message is to communicate information or coordinate behavior. In contrast, the goal of a romantic message is to increase the emotional connection between communicators.

Researchers have typically studied utilitarian communication tasks so research on media use in romantic communication is limited. High levels of cell phone use have been linked to romantic relationship satisfaction (Miller-Ott, Kelly, & Duran, 2012) and romantic vocal communication using a phone similarly strengthens couples' relationships by increasing love and commitment. The content of messages between friends differs from messages between romantic partners (Johnson, Haigh, Becker, Craig, & Wigley, 2008); however, using text messaging may impair relationships (Pizzagalli, 2007). Even with these studies, it remains unclear how the use of different media influences emotional communication.

2.3. Hypotheses

Our research model is presented in Fig. 1. First, we examine how the use of different media triggers emotional responses in the sender. Second, we examine how the use of different media influences the content of composed messages. Finally, we investigate how these relationships are moderated by communication task type.

MNT proposes that communication outcomes are influenced by the naturalness of the chosen communication media (Kock, 2005b, 2007; Vlahovic, Roberts, & Dunbar, 2012). When humans use a less natural medium, its limitations will make communicating less satisfying than using more natural media, even after senders learn to use the medium effectively (Kock, 2005b). In the case of email, senders consciously or subconsciously become frustrated at the medium's inability to convey vocal tone or other non-verbal cues and expend greater cognitive effort to overcome email's short-comings, which causes negative responses (Kock, 2004). Though a medium may have advantages (e.g., long-distance communication), its unnaturalness will be unpleasant to senders. Users of less natural media will experience more negative emotional responses when composing messages compared with using more natural media.

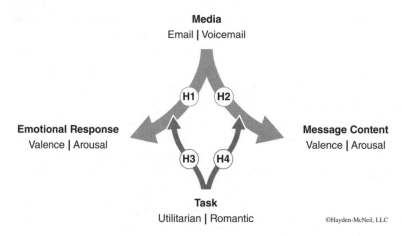

Figure 1. Research model.

H1a. The use of email will elicit a more negative valence in the sender's emotional response while composing a message than the use of voicemail.

Communication is inherently a social activity, and individuals enjoy and desire communication with others; when new media become available, they are used, in part, because of the satisfaction that comes in communicating with others (Valenzuela, Park, & Kee, 2009). In MNT, FtF communication is the most natural form of communication and humans are evolutionarily predisposed to seek communication with others for survival and procreation (Kock, 2004). As a result of this, engaging in FtF communication is more exciting and physiologically arousing because of the social interaction with other humans. The cues transmitted in more natural media such as facial expressions and body language elicit physiological arousal (Byron, 2008; Critchley et al., 2005). By comparison, less natural media are perceived as less exciting, duller, and less arousing (Kock, 2005b). As email messages are primarily textual, the level of perceived social presence is low and will elicit less excitement in the sender (Short et al., 1976). With voicemail, individuals hear and interpret the human voice, increasing social presence and leading to greater excitement.

One early empirical study used physiological measures to test whether media elicited more arousal than a FtF conversation (Kiesler, Zubrow, Moses, & Geller, 1985) and found no differences in arousal. While this empirical result is not consistent with our theorizing, those researchers examined different media (i.e., synchronous text chat vs. FtF) and the research took place early in the development of computer-mediated communication where participants may not have been familiar with the media so its novelty may have triggered different responses. We argue that email should be less arousing than voicemail to senders because email is less natural than voicemail and does not engender the degree of social presence that voicemail does.

H1b. The use of email will elicit less emotional arousal in the sender's emotional response while composing a message than the use of voicemail.

Email lacks the ability to convey vocal tone and vocal cues which makes it more difficult to convey emotion than when using voicemail (Byron, 2008; Daft et al., 1987; Kock, 2005b). Email is perceived as a task-oriented medium, which may subconsciously reduce the emotion senders include when composing messages (Dennis et al., 2008). Senders also overestimate the emotion they convey through email because they "hear" the tone of their messages in their heads during composition even though this tone is not included in the actual emails (Kruger et al., 2005). For the same type of communication tasks, we expect composed email messages to be less positive and less arousing than voicemail messages.

H2a. For the same communication task, the content of email messages will be less positive than the content of voicemail messages.

H2b. For the same communication task, the content of email messages will be less arousing than the content of voicemail messages.

Senders use media to communicate a wide variety of messages. Media researchers have most commonly examined the sending and receipt of utilitarian messages (Dennis et al., 2008). Utilitarian messages are composed and processed to accomplish tasks. However, both within and outside of organizational settings, individuals use communication media to send both mundane utilitarian messages and social messages. Differences in communication tasks may influence both the sender composing the message and the recipient processing and interpreting the message (Zhang, 2009).

Less natural media may be effective for utilitarian communication tasks that do not require the conveyance of emotion, but they may be poorly suited for social communication tasks (Byron, 2008). This is especially true with romantic communication, where the conveyance of emotion is the *raison d'être*. Romantic communication is socially-oriented and associated with the biological imperative to reproduce. For romantic tasks, senders should convey emotion better using natural media. We expect an interaction between the type of communication task and the medium such that senders composing romantic voicemail messages will experience the strongest positive emotional responses and the strongest feelings of arousal. Senders composing utilitarian email messages should have less positive responses and the lowest levels of arousal because the communication type is task-oriented and mundane.

H3a. The type of communication task will moderate the relationship between media and the valence of emotional response such that composing romantic voicemail messages will elicit more positive emotional responses and composing utilitarian email messages will elicit less positive responses.

H3b. The type of communication task will moderate the relationship between media and the arousal of emotional response such that composing romantic voicemail messages will be more arousing, and composing utilitarian email messages will be less arousing.

Embedded in MNT is the concept of compensatory adaptation, where individuals can compensate for the limitations of a medium by applying conscious and subconscious cognitive effort to a problem (Kock, 2004). Compensatory adaptation explains how less natural media perform better in some tasks: individuals overcome a medium's limitations by over-utilizing its capabilities. Compensatory adaptation has been used to explain performance outcomes in individual and group tasks, but has not been applied to emotional communication (Kock, 2005a).

When engaging in romantic communication, senders convey positive emotion using the available cues (Egland, Spitzberg, & Zormeier, 1996). When using email for romantic communication, individuals consciously or subconsciously recognize the limitations of the medium and compensate by composing emails that are more positive in content. Senders of utilitarian emails do not need to compensate because there is less need to communicate emotion. When leaving a romantic or utilitarian voicemail message, senders will use vocal tone to convey emotion and will not need to compensate by altering the content of the message.

H4a. The type of communication task will moderate the relationship between media and the valence of message content such that romantic email messages will have more positive content than romantic voicemail messages and all utilitarian messages.

H4b. The type of communication task will moderate the relationship between media and the arousal of message content such that romantic email messages will have more arousing content than romantic voicemail messages and all utilitarian messages.

3. Method

3.1. Participants

Seventy-two undergraduate participants were recruited from a technology course. All were experienced users of email and voicemail with participants reporting using voicemail weekly and email daily. Participants were randomly assigned treatment conditions.

3.2. Independent variables

Each participant composed four messages (two media × two communication tasks) with the media and communication task combinations randomized for each participant. We chose to have participants compose four messages to minimize hypothesis guessing and participant fatigue. Participants used simulated email and voicemail that were designed for realism to maintain control over this manipulation. The simulated email and voicemail allowed us to maintain the precise timing required in psychophysiological recording (Bradley, Lang, & Cuthbert, 1993; Potter & Bolls, 2012; vanOyen Witvliet & Vrana, 1995). When instructed to compose email, participants were presented with an email interface with the same appearance and functionality of Google Mail. This was chosen because the university uses this email provider for all undergraduates as their official university email account, and students are highly experienced with the interface. When leaving voicemail messages, participants were presented with an automated message instructing them to leave a message after a tone. After the tone sounded, participants could record the voicemail message.

We manipulated the communication tasks (utilitarian or romantic) by asking participants to send messages for specific scenarios. In the romantic communication tasks, participants were asked to send a romantic message expressing feelings for an individual he or she was interested in romantically. In the utilitarian communication tasks, participants were asked to send a message coordinating the work of a course group project with other team members or giving feedback to a friend about a well-crafted résumé (Sussman & Sproull, 1999). These communication tasks were chosen because in pilot testing they were found to be equivalent in difficulty and valence, familiar to our target population, and respectively rated as utilitarian or romantic. These simulated communication tasks also enabled us to maintain control over exogenous variables such as familiarity that might have influenced the results (Carlson & Zmud, 1999; Straub & Karahanna, 1998).

3.3. Dependent variables

Psychophysiological measures from cognitive psychology have strengths which can complement traditional measures and techniques to help researchers better understand phenomenon (Riedl et al., 2010). The measures used in this study were collected while the participants were interacting with the media. We followed established guidelines on psychophysiological recording from the media literature (Potter & Bolls, 2012).

The valence of emotional response was measured by Corrugator supercilii muscle response (Hazlett & Benedek, 2007). Facial electromyography (EMG) is the recording and testing of the electrical activity brought on by the activation and deactivation of muscles in the face. We measured the Corrugator supercilii muscle on the eyebrow because it has been used in many studies as a valid, sensitive measure of emotional valence (Bolls, Lang, & Potter, 2001; Cacioppo et al., 1986; Hazlett & Benedek, 2007). People furrow their eyebrows by activating this muscle when experiencing negative emotion.[1] Facial EMG is sensitive enough that even if participants do not display visible muscle contractions, the equipment can measure the minute activation and deactivation of these muscles as they respond to stimuli (Cacioppo et al., 1986).

Corrugator response was measured using two Beckman mini-Ag/AgCl electrodes filled with standard amplification jelly. The signal from these electrodes passed through a Coulbourn bio-amplifier with high- and low-pass filters, then passed through a contour follower for digital time smoothing and was sampled 20 times each second using VPM software (Bolls et al., 2001; Potter & Bolls, 2012). A Beckman standard Ag/AgCl electrode was also placed on the forearm as the ground to filter out noise. The Corrugator activation during each of the experimental tasks was computed from the sampled signal using software designed for this task (VPM Analog), which aggregated the EMG data for each quarter second of the stimuli (Bradley & Lang, 2000; Cook, 1999). We calculated change scores for each task by subtracting the Corrugator measure from a one-second baseline measure taken prior to each task. A change in Corrugator activation in microvolts is caused by a negative emotional response; larger numbers signifying

---

1. An alternative method of assessing emotional response is measuring the Zygomaticus major muscle, or "smile muscle," using facial EMG [58]. We measured both the Corrugator supercilii and Zygomaticus major using facial EMG in a pilot study and found the signal for Zygomaticus muscle activation to be so strongly affected by motion artifact during voicemail usage that it was not useable for analysis. The Corrugator supercilii activation did not suffer from this issue. As a result, we did not include the Zygomaticus major muscle for this study.

greater Corrugator activation which indicates *negative* valence, and negative numbers representing Corrugator deactivation, which indicates *positive* valence.

The arousal of emotional response was measured by skin conductance level (Bolls et al., 2001). This psychophysiological change is triggered by the sympathetic nervous system, which controls flight or fight responses (Cacioppo, Tassinary, & Berntson, 2007). When people experience emotion, one side effect of the sympathetic nervous system response is an increase in sweat on the hands and on the feet. This increases the electrical conductivity of the skin at those locations and is a simple, effective means to measure emotional arousal (Bolls et al., 2001). In this study, we measured skin conductance level on the left foot so that the electrode placement did not interfere with the participant typing.

Skin conductance was collected by passing .5 V across two Beckman standard Ag/AgCl electrodes placed on the plantar surface of the participant's left foot. The electrodes were filled with electrically neutral gel to help adhesion. The analog signal from these electrodes was passed through a Coulbourn skin conductance coupler and sampled 20 times per second using the VPM software (Boucsein, 2012; Potter & Bolls, 2012). The skin conductance level during each of the experimental tasks was computed using VPM Analog which aggregated the data for each quarter second (Bradley & Lang, 2000; Cook, 1999). We then calculated change scores for each task by subtracting the skin conductance measure from a one-second baseline measure taken prior to each task (Cuthbert et al., 2003; Potter & Bolls, 2012). The data represents changes in the conductivity measured in microSiemens with higher conductivity an indicator of higher emotional arousal.

The facial EMG and skin conductance data was collected, post-processed, and analyzed according to established guidelines in the psychophysiological literature including the analysis of transformed physiological data (Boucsein, 2012; Cacioppo et al., 2007; Potter & Bolls, 2012).

To assess whether the physical act of speaking or typing affected the dependent variables, each participant separately typed and spoke aloud a passage of text after the electrodes were placed. We found no significant differences in arousal or valence between typing and speaking, so we conclude there are no differences due to the physical act of speaking versus typing.

The emotional content of the composed messages was analyzed using content analysis to determine the valence and arousal of the email text and transcribed voicemail messages. We computed valence and arousal scores by comparing textual content against the largest library of normed affective words (Warriner, Kuperman, & Brysbaert, 2013). For accurate comparison, all text was corrected for spelling errors prior to analysis and the scores were adjusted for message length. Emoticons were converted into text prior to analysis; for example) was converted to "smile". We followed standard procedures for computing valence and arousal scores (Hancock et al., 2007; Warriner et al., 2013).

3.4. Controlling emotional mood

Emotional responses relate to an individual's mood, but the constructs are distinct (Schwarz & Clore, 2003). Emotional responses are brief, while mood states can persist for several minutes or more (Schwarz & Clore, 2003). We did not want the participants' existing moods to influence the emotional responses caused by media and task type, so we induced a positive mood in all participants. Participants were shown two humorous videos, one before the first two tasks and one before the last two tasks. We carefully selected clips from the comedian Brian Regan without swearing, violence, or stereotyping. Similar inductions are widely used for inducing positive and negative mood (Schaefer, Nils, Sanchez, & Philippot, 2010).

3.5. Procedure

After receiving consent, the experimenter explained the psychophysiological measures and set up the electrodes. Participants completed a demographic questionnaire, which included their sexual orientation and the name of their romantic partner or someone they would like as a romantic communication partner. A mood induction video was shown and the participants then composed two messages using email and voicemail. Participants then watched a second mood induction video, composed two additional communication messages, and were debriefed.

4. Results

After the data were collected, we post-processed the physiology data and combined it with the behavioral data. We used multivariate repeated measures GLM using SPSS to analyze the data because it allowed us to examine the psychophysiological and task data with repetition across participants and allows us to assess interaction effects among the independent variables. This type of analysis is typical in psychophysiological studies like this one (Faulk & Bartholomew, 2012; Kordik, Eska, & Schultheiss, 2012; Moya-Albiol et al., 2013; Ottaviani et al., 2014; Potter & Bolls, 2012; Werner, Kerschreiter, Kindermann, & Duschek, 2013). The means and results of the statistical analysis are presented in Tables 1 and 2.

Table 1. Means of dependent variables.

Measure	Utilitarian		Romantic	
	Email	Voicemail	Email	Voicemail
Corrugator	.220	.013	.063	−.002
Skin conductance	.313	−.436	.119	−.415
Message valence	5.995	6.143	6.278	5.513
Message arousal	3.894	3.886	4.161	3.589

Gender was not found to be a significant factor (F = .193, p = .941) and is omitted in the final analysis. We examined if the individuals were already in a romantic relationship or whether the messages were to someone they were interested in courting. This factor was non-significant (F = .155, p = .960), and all participants were used in the analysis. Only one participant self-reported a same-sex gender preference and we do not have the statistical power to examine if the results differ by this factor, so it is omitted from the analyses.

Email was hypothesized to cause greater negative physiological responses in message senders than voicemail. To test this, we examined changes in the Corrugator response during message composition. The increase in Corrugator activation approached significance but did not meet the α = .05 threshold (F = 3.92, p = .052). As hypothesized, email messages (M = .075) elicited higher levels of Corrugator activation compared with voicemail (M = −.017), but this difference is not statistically significant. Thus H1a is not supported. As an aside, we note that utilitarian tasks triggered significantly more corrugator activation than romantic tasks, indicating greater negative emotional valence.

We hypothesized that email would elicit less emotional arousal in senders during message composition than voicemail. This hypothesis was tested by examining changes in the sender's skin conductance. Media had a significant effect on the emotional arousal experienced by the sender (F = 54.800, p < .001); however, this relationship is in the opposite direction to what was hypothesized. Email was significantly more arousing (M = .199) than voicemail (M = −.418) (see Fig. 2). H1b is not supported because it is significant in the opposite direction.

We tested H2a that email messages will have less positive content than voicemail messages by examining the valence scores for each message. Higher valence scores indicate that the message contained a more positive valence words than messages with low scores. We found a significant relationship between media and the valence of message content (F = 11.199, p = .001). Senders created email messages that were more positive (M = 6.159) than voicemail messages (M = 5.893). This result does not support H2a; however, there exists a significant interaction between task and media on message valence that limits interpretability of this result.

Table 2. Statistical results (p-values).

Source	Emotional valence (corrugator)	Emotional arousal (skin conductance)	Message valence	Message arousal
Media	.052	.001***	.001***	.001***
Task	.013*	.490	.100	.018*
Media × Task	.215	.145	.001**	.002**

*p < .05; **p < .01; ***p < .001.

We argued that email messages will contain less arousing content than voicemail messages. Higher arousal scores indicate the use of stronger, more arousing language. We found a significant relationship between media and message content arousal, but in the opposite direction of what was hypothesized (F = 41.684, p < .001). Senders created more arousing email messages (M = 4.109) than voicemail messages (M = 3.787). This result does not support H2b, but as with H2a there is a significant interaction effect which supersedes this result.

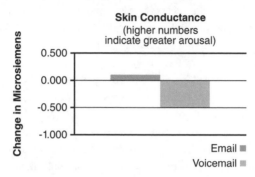

Figure 2. Change in skin conductance by media.

We hypothesized that the communication task type would moderate the relationship between media and physiological emotional response. We expected the composition of romantic voicemails to be more positive and arousing and utilitarian emails to be more negative and less arousing. The media by communication task interaction on Corrugator was not significant (F = 1.566, p = .215). There is also no evidence of a media by communication task interaction on skin conductance (F = 1.960, p = .145). We find no support for H3a and H3b.

Communication task type was hypothesized to moderate the relationship between media and message content valence. We expected participants to compensate for the limitations of email by including more positive content in their romantic communication. The data show a significant interaction between media and communication task on message content valence (F = 11.823, p = .001) (see Fig. 3). As expected, emails composed for romantic communication tasks (M = 6.278) contained more positive language than romantic voicemails (M = 5.513). The opposite was true for utilitarian communication tasks: voicemails (M = 6.143) were more positive than emails (M = 5.995). H4a is supported.

We expected communication task type to moderate the relationship between media and message content arousal such that romantic emails would contain the most arousing content. The data support this interaction (F = 10.043, p = .004) and romantic emails contained significantly more arousing language (M = 4.161) than romantic voicemails (M = 3.589). We found utilitarian emails (M = 3.894) and utilitarian voicemails (M = 3.886) to be very similar in arousing content. H4b is supported (see Fig. 4).

5. Discussion

We believe that this study makes three important contributions. First, the use of media induced different emotional responses in the sender compared to the use of voicemail, whether they were aware of it or not. Contrary to our hypothesis, the use of email induced more arousing psychophysiological responses than voicemail. This effect was consistent across task, regardless of whether the message was utilitarian or romantic. Therefore, this study finds no support for the proposition of MNT that more natural media cause greater arousal.

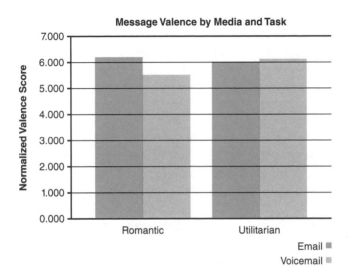

Figure 3. Message valence by media and communication task.

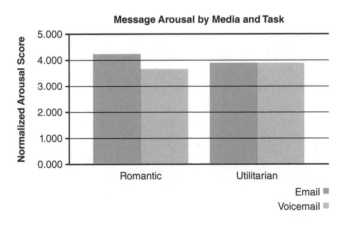

Figure 4. Message arousal by media and communication task.

This could have been caused by a negative emotion when using email, such as frustration from adapting to a less natural media. However, we did not find differences in corrugator activation, so this is unlikely. A key difference between email and voicemail is rehearsability, the ability for senders to edit a message during composition (Dennis et al., 2008). Email enables senders to modify the content as messages are composed to ensure they are crafted to the needs of the situation. Voicemail lacks this feature; a sender records a voicemail in a single take, and it can be sent or discarded and re-recorded, but not edited. Thus senders engage with email messages longer and may think about the task more deeply than when leaving voicemails. This extra processing may increase arousal.

The second contribution of this study is showing that the medium shapes message content. What you choose to say depends upon the medium you use. We theorized that media and task would jointly influence emotional content in the messages and found support for these hypotheses. Senders of utilitarian messages sent less positive emails than voicemails for the same communication task. In contrast, when composing romantic messages, senders included the most positive and most arousing emotional content in emails and the least positive and least arousing content in voicemails. When writing romantic emails, senders consciously or subconsciously added more positive content to their messages, perhaps to compensate for the medium's inability to convey vocal tone. Our participants naturally adapted to the limitations of the media and compensated for the lack of cues. This supports the compensatory adaptation proposition of MNT, which suggests that individuals can overcome the limitations of unnatural media.

We expected that using email for romantic communication would be more frustrating than using voicemail, but our data do not show this. There was neither greater emotional arousal nor greater negative emotional valence when using email for romantic tasks versus utilitarian tasks. Task type did not moderate the sender's physiological emotional response. Email and other less natural media may not suffer from some of the drawbacks suggested by prior research. Senders using email are capable of communicating emotional content; they simply adapt to the capabilities and limitations of the medium to communicate the message they want to send.

Third, these results taken together suggest that "the medium is the message" (McLuhan, 1964) in a more fundamental way than we have previously understood. McLuhan argued that the medium changed how the recipient processed messages. Our results show that the medium changes how message senders feel and what they say. Use of communication media influences senders physiologically and alters what they choose to communicate.

5.1. Implications for research

We looked at how media use changed the fundamental emotions of the message sender and the emotional content of the message sent. Using email made the sender feel more emotionally aroused compared to using voicemail which is surprising as prior research (and MNT) suggests email should be less arousing. Ours is the first research to show that email leads to greater arousal. Why did this occur? What characteristics of this medium trigger stronger emotional responses? We theorized that there might be a poor fit between the task and the medium, but this was not the case; email triggered greater emotional arousal for all tasks. We need more basic research into how media use affects the emotions of senders—and receivers which we did not investigate.

Email is widely and regularly used. We did not find a significant media main effect on emotional valence, but the means approached significance. Do senders feel more negative when composing emails for other task types or during different time periods? We measured the emotional impact over a short period of time. It is unknown how the strength of emotional response might change as composition time increases. Would an hour spent working on email make the user even more likely to feel stronger negative emotions, even if the email is not emotional in its own right? This emotional response may influence subsequent tasks. Similarly, if writing an email causes emotional arousal, what does this mean for receiving an email after writing one? The emotion that sending email evokes may make individuals receiving email perceive the messages as more emotional in content.

We studied two ubiquitous media, email and voicemail. It is unknown to what extent these findings apply to other media. According to MNT, synchronous text chat should be more natural than email. Would use of synchronous text chat induce the same negative emotions email induced? Our participants were young and media savvy; they grew up using email and voicemail, and are regular users of both. To them, these media may be more "natural" than they are to an older generation. Would the negative emotional impacts of email be stronger for an older generation that did not grow up using it? We need more research on the emotional effects of using other media and by less experienced users.

We found that romantic email messages contained the most positive emotional content followed by utilitarian voicemails. Interestingly, romantic voicemails contained the least positive emotional content. Walther (1996) found lean, unnatural media to work for building relationships, so perhaps people do use these media very differently. We need more research on the use of putatively lean media for non-utilitarian tasks such as romantic tasks. If we fail to study the effect of various technologies on non-work activities, we are missing an important part of people's lives. Without a broader, interdisciplinary scope for our research, our theories may be narrow and limited in scope (Walsham, 2012). We may not find the boundary conditions to our work and overgeneralize.

We need to further examine the effects of the increased emotional content in the messages sent using unnatural media. Does increased emotional content adequately compensate for the lack of vocal cues in the transmission of emotion? The explicit statements of emotion using words may have a stronger or weaker effect on the receiver than the tone, but this is unknown. This effect may also differ by the receiver's emotional intelligence—his or her ability to perceive and present emotions (Goleman, 1995). When emotional content is communicated explicitly using words, those with lower emotional intelligence may be better able to understand than when it is communicated using more subtle cues such as vocal tone (Goleman, 1995). We need more research to better understand whether users with different emotional intelligence have different emotional reactions to messages sent using different media.

Finally, the psychophysiological methods used in this study have the potential to offer a new lens into the behaviors surrounding media use. We believe we need more research using these physiological methods, as they offer a unique view into individual and team behavior.

5.2. Implications for practice

Media and task influenced the emotions of senders and the emotional content of the messages they sent. The first implication from this is that senders must choose their medium carefully and be aware of how that choice subtly induces emotional responses and influences what is communicated. When you compose an email, you feel greater emotional arousal than if you send the same message using a voicemail, even if you are not consciously aware of it. Email composed for utilitarian tasks is likely to contain more emotional content than a voicemail for the same task and romantic emails are likely to contain the highest level of emotional content.

We often respond to messages in the same medium we receive them. Receiving an email usually induces the message recipient to respond with an email, and receiving voicemail usually induces a phone call (or a voicemail). The choice to send an email likely triggers an emotional reaction in the sender, but also the message recipient as he or she composes a response. Flaming in email (Polites & Karahanna, 2013) may not only be caused by poor message content, but also by the emotions that composing email induces which may spill over into the message content.

Finally, the explicit emotional content of the message differed depending upon the medium used. It is important to think about the explicit emotional content of the message you compose, even for utilitarian tasks. In email, we get right to the point in a utilitarian message; it contains less positive emotion. The implication for practice is to understand this and how it affects the message recipient. We encourage email users to pause to consider the impact of receiving a utilitarian email message with less emotion on the message recipient. Perhaps it would be better to add some explicit emotional content into utilitarian emails.

While we believe this study makes important contributions, it does have some limitations. Our participants were a fairly homogenous sample of undergraduate students and may not be representative of the population as a whole. The tasks were designed to be appropriate for this population; however, care should be taken in generalizing the results to other populations. Additional research should examine these phenomena in other populations, particularly those less experienced in the use of these media. Similarly, our participants composed messages to complete tasks that were given them and were instructed that their emails and voicemails were being recorded, both of which may have influenced their behavior. Portable psychophysiological recording apparatus may allow researchers to examine how individuals compose email and voicemail messages during the course of work and personal life, which could provide greater understanding of how the task and technology influence senders and the messages they compose. Another limitation is that our participants only composed four messages in this study—two utilitarian and two romantic—which limits our ability to evaluate the effects over a larger number of messages. Further research is needed to determine the psychophysiological impacts of task and technology over time.

6. Conclusion

We tested a theoretical model based on MNT to examine the impact of media and communication task type on the emotional responses of senders and their communication behavior. We have shown that we may not fully understand how some of the most widely used communication technologies subtly impact the physiology of the users and the messages they compose. Email causes greater physiological arousal and senders compensated for the limitations of email when sending romantic messages. Email and voicemail may both be suitable for all types of communication tasks as long as senders understand how they are influenced by the media and how their messages are subtly modified during composition.

References

Adelaar, T., Chang, S., Lancendorfer, K. M., Lee, B., & Morimoto, M. (2003). Effects of media formats on emotions and impulse buying intent. *Journal of Information Technology, 18*(4), 247–266.

Bolls, P. D., Lang, A., & Potter, R. F. (2001). The effects of message valence and listener arousal on attention, memory, and facial muscular responses to radio advertisements. *Communication Research, 28*(5), 627–651.

Boucsein, W. (2012). *Electrodermal activity* (2nd ed.). New York: Springer.

Bradley, M. M., & Lang, P. J. (2000). Affective reactions to acoustic stimuli. *Psychophysiology, 37*(2), 204–215.

Bradley, M. M., Lang, P. J., & Cuthbert, B. N. (1993). Emotion, novelty, and the startle reflex: habituation in humans. *Behavioral Neuroscience, 107*(6), 970–980.

Byron, K. (2008). Carrying too heavy a load? The communication and miscommunication of emotion by email. *Academy of Management Review, 33*(2), 309–327.

Cacioppo, J. T., Petty, R. E., Losch, M. E., & Kim, H. S. (1986). Electromyographic activity over facial muscle regions can differentiate the valence and intensity of affective reactions. *Journal of Personality and Social Psychology, 50*(2), 260–268.

Cacioppo, J. T., Tassinary, L. G., & Berntson, G. (2007). *Handbook of psychophysiology*. Cambridge, Massachusetts: Cambridge University Press.

Carlson, J. R., & Zmud, R. W. (1999). Channel expansion theory and the experiential nature of media richness perceptions. *Academy of Management Journal, 42*(2), 153–170.

Clore, G. L., & Ketelaar, T. (1997). Minding our emotions: on the role of automatic, unconscious affect. In R. S. Wyer, Jr. (Ed.), *The automaticity of everyday life* (pp. 105–120). Mahwah, New Jersey: Lawrence Erlbaum Associates.

Cook, E. W. (1999). *VPM analog*. Birmingham: Alabama.

Critchley, H. D., Rotshtein, P., Nagai, Y., O'Doherty, J., Mathias, C. J., & Dolan, R. J. (2005). Activity in the human brain predicting differential heart rate responses to emotional facial expressions. *NeuroImage, 24*(3), 751–762.

Cuthbert, B. N., Lang, P. J., Strauss, C., Drobes, D., Patrick, C. J., & Bradley, M. M. (2003). The psychophysiology of anxiety disorder: fear memory imagery. *Psychophysiology, 40*(3), 407–422.

Daft, R. L., Lengel, R. H., & Trevino, L. K. (1987). Message equivocality, media selection, and manager performance: implications for information systems. *MIS Quarterly, 11*(3), 355–366.

Dennis, A. R., Fuller, R. M., & Valacich, J. S. (2008). Media, tasks, and communication processes: a theory of media synchronicity. *MIS Quarterly, 32*(3), 575–600.

Dennis, A. R., Minas, R. K., & Bhagwatwar, A. P. (2013). Sparking creativity: improving electronic brainstorming with individual cognitive priming. *Journal of Management Information Systems, 29*(4), 195–216.

Derks, D., Fischer, A. H., & Bos, A. E. R. (2008). The role of emotion in computer-mediated communication: a review. *Computers in Human Behavior, 24*(3), 766–785.

Egland, K. L., Spitzberg, B. H., & Zormeier, M. M. (1996). Flirtation and conversational competence in cross-sex platonic and romantic relationships. *Communication Reports, 9*(2), 105–117.

Faulk, K. E., & Bartholomew, J. B. (2012). The moderating effect of physical activity on cardiovascular reactivity following single fat feedings. *Psychophysiology, 49*(1), 145–149.

Goleman, D. (1995). *Emotional intelligence.* New York: Bantam Dell.

Hancock, J. T., Landrigan, C., & Silver, C. (2007). Expressing emotion in text-based communication. In *Proceedings of the SIGCHI conference on human factors in computing systems* (p. 932).

Hazlett, R., & Benedek, J. (2007). Measuring emotional valence to understand the user's experience of software. *International Journal of Human-Computer Studies, 65*(4), 306–314.

Hian, L. B., Chuan, S. L., Trevor, T. M. K., & Detenber, B. H. (2004). Getting to know you: exploring the development of relational intimacy in computer-mediated communication. *Journal of Computer-Mediated Communication, 9*(3).

Hudlicka, E. (2003). To feel or not to feel: the role of affect in human–computer interaction. *International Journal of Human-Computer Studies, 59*(1–2), 1–32.

Johnson, A. J., Haigh, M. M., Becker, J. A. H., Craig, E. A., & Wigley, S. (2008). College students' use of relational management strategies in email in long-distance and geographically close relationships. *Journal of Computer-Mediated Communication, 13*, 381–404.

Kiesler, S., Zubrow, D., Moses, A. M., & Geller, V. (1985). Affect in computer-mediated communication: an experiment in synchronous terminal-to-terminal discussion. *Human-Computer Interaction, 1*(1), 77–104.

Kock, N. (2004). The psychobiological model: towards a new theory of computer-mediated communication based on Darwinian evolution. *Organization Science, 15*(3), 327–348.

Kock, N. (2005a). Compensatory adaptation to media obstacles: an experimental study of process redesign dyads. *Information Resources Management Journal, 18*(2), 41–67.

Kock, N. (2005b). Media richness or media naturalness? The evolution of our biological communication apparatus and its influence on our behavior toward e-communication tools. *IEEE Transactions on Professional Communication, 48*(2), 117–130.

Kock, N. (2007). Media naturalness and compensatory encoding: the burden of electronic media obstacles is on senders. *Decision Support Systems, 44*(1), 175–187.

Kock, N. (2009). Information systems theorizing based on evolutionary psychology: an interdisciplinary review and theory integration framework. *MIS Quarterly, 33*(2), 395–418.

Kordik, A., Eska, K., & Schultheiss, O. C. (2012). Implicit need for affiliation is associated with increased corrugator activity in a non-positive, but not in a positive social interaction. *Journal of Research in Personality, 46*(5), 604–608.

Kruger, J., Epley, N., Parker, J., & Ng, Z. (2005). Egocentrism over e-mail: can we communicate as well as we think? *Journal of Personality and Social Psychology, 89*(6), 925.

Lang, P. J., & Bradley, M. M. (2010). Emotion and the motivational brain. *Biological Psychology, 84*(3), 437–450.

McLuhan, M. (1964). *Understanding media: The extensions of man*. New York: McGraw-Hill.

Miller-Ott, A. E., Kelly, L., & Duran, R. L. (2012). The effects of cell phone usage rules on satisfaction in romantic relationships. *Communication Quarterly, 60*(1), 17–34.

Moya-Albiol, L., De Andrés-García, S., Sanchis-Calatayud, M. V., Sariñana- Gonzàlez, P., Ruiz-Robledillo, N., Romero-Martínez, A., et al. (2013). Psycho-physiological responses to cooperation: the role of outcome and gender. *International Journal of Psychology, 48*(4), 542–550.

Ottaviani, C., Borlimi, R., Brighetti, G., Caselli, G., Favaretto, E., Giardini, I., et al. (2014). Worry as an adaptive avoidance strategy in healthy controls but not in pathological worriers. *International Journal of Psychophysiology, 93*(3), 349–355.

Pizzagalli, D. A. (2007). Electroencephalography and high-density electrophysiological source localization. In J. T. Cacioppo, L. G. Tassinary, & G. G. Berntson (Eds.), *Handbook of psychophysiology* (pp. 56–84). New York: Cambridge University Press.

Polites, G. L., & Karahanna, E. (2013). The embeddedness of information systems habits in organizational and individual level routines: development and disruption. *MIS Quarterly, 37*(1), 221–246.

Potter, R. F., & Bolls, P. (2012). *Psychophysiological measurement and meaning: Cognitive and emotional processing of media*. New York: Routledge.

Riedl, R., Banker, R. D., Benbasat, I., Davis, F. D., Dennis, A. R., Dimoka, A., et al. (2010). On the foundations of neuroIS: reflections on the Gmunden retreat 2009. *Communications of the AIS, 27*.

Schaefer, A., Nils, F., Sanchez, X., & Philippot, P. (2010). Assessing the effectiveness of a large database of emotion-eliciting films: a new tool for emotion researchers. *Cognition & Emotion, 24*(7), 1153–1172.

Schwarz, N., & Clore, G. L. (2003). Mood as information: 20 years later. *Psychological Inquiry, 14*(3), 296–303.

Short, J., Williams, E., & Christie, B. (1976). *The social psychology of telecommunications*. London: Wiley.

Skovholt, K., Grønning, A., & Kankaanranta, A. (2014). The communicative functions of emoticons in workplace e-mails: :-). *Journal of Computer-Mediated Communication, 19*(4), 780–797.

Stieglitz, S., & Dang-Xuan, L. (2013). Emotions and information diffusion in social media—sentiment of microblogs and sharing behavior. *Journal of Management Information Systems, 29*(4), 217–248.

Straub, D., & Karahanna, E. (1998). Knowledge worker communications and recipient availability: toward a task closure explanation of media choice. *Organization Science, 9*(2), 160–175.

Sussman, S. W., & Sproull, L. (1999). Straight talk: delivering bad news through electronic communication. *Information Systems Research, 10*(2), 150–166.

Valenzuela, S., Park, N., & Kee, K. F. (2009). Is there social capital in a social network site?: Facebook use and college students' life satisfaction, trust, and participation. *Journal of Computer-Mediated Communication, 14*(4), 875–901.

Venkatesh, V. (2000). Determinants of perceived ease of use: integrating control, intrinsic motivation, and emotion into the technology acceptance model. *Information Systems Research, 11*(4), 342–365.

Vlahovic, T. A., Roberts, S., & Dunbar, R. (2012). Effects of duration and laughter on subjective happiness within different modes of communication. *Journal of Computer-Mediated Communication, 17*(4), 436–450.

Walsham, G. (2012). Are we making a better world with ICTs? Reflections on a future agenda for the IS field. *Journal of Information Technology, 27*(2), 87–93.

Walther, J. B. (1996). Computer-mediated communication: impersonal, interpersonal, and hyperpersonal interaction. *Communication Research, 23*(1), 3–43.

Warriner, A. B., Kuperman, V., & Brysbaert, M. (2013). Norms of valence, arousal, and dominance for 13,915 English lemmas. *Behavior Research Methods, 45*(4), 1191–1207.

Werner, N. S., Kerschreiter, R., Kindermann, N. K., & Duschek, S. (2013). Interoceptive awareness as a moderator of affective responses to social exclusion. *Journal of Psychophysiology, 27*(1), 39–50.

vanOyen Witvliet, C., & Vrana, S. R. (1995). Psychophysiological responses as indices of affective dimensions. *Psychophysiology, 32*(5), 436–443.

Yin, D., Bond, S., & Zhang, H. (2014). Anxious or angry? Effects of discrete emotions on the perceived helpfulness of online reviews. *MIS Quarterly, 38*(2), 539–560.

Zhang, S. (2009). Senderrecipient perspectives of honest but hurtful evaluative messages in romantic relationships. *Communication Reports, 22*(2), 89–101.

Gender and Sexuality

Petra Doan is a Professor of urban and regional planning at Florida State University. She is the co-founder of the first transgender support group in Tallahassee.

The Tyranny of Gendered Spaces: Reflections from Beyond the Gender Dichotomy
Petra Doan

Tyranny refers to the exercise of power which is cruelly or harshly administered; it usually involves some form of oppression by those wielding power over the less powerful. John Stuart Mill (1869) warned about the tyranny of the majority since the sheer weight of numbers can never be sufficient to make an unjust act any more just. History gets written by those who claim victory, and the winners wield the economic power and social influence that enable them to establish the standards for acceptable political and social behaviors. When these histories and standards routinely exclude minority groups, tyranny flourishes.

In this article I argue that transgendered and gender variant people experience the gendered division of space as a special kind of tyranny—the tyranny of gender—that arises when people dare to challenge the hegemonic expectations for appropriately gendered behavior in western society. These gendered expectations are an artifact of the patriarchal dichotomization of gender and have profound and painful consequences for many individuals. For the gender variant, the tyranny of gender intrudes on every aspect of the spaces in which we live and constrains the behaviors that we display....

The term *transgender* is a collective term that refers to people assigned to one gender who do "not perform or identify as that gender, and ha[ve] taken some steps—temporary or permanent—to present in another gender" (D. Valentine 2003, 27–28). Most often included in this category are transsexuals, transvestites, crossdressers, drag queens, drag kings, tranny bois and other gender queer individuals who defy easy categorization. The edges of the category are less clear—i.e. not all intersexed people consider themselves transgendered, though some do (Chase 1998; Kessler 1998; Turner 1999). Even more individuals may identify as their birth sex, but present in such an ambiguous way that their gender is often mistaken (Browne 2004; Lucal 1999). For this entire spectrum of individuals I use the term *gender variant* (Doan 2007), of which the transgendered are one subset....

Coming to Terms with My Transgendered Self

As a child I was powerfully aware that I did not fit into the box marked boy, though I struggled for many years to fit into the gender assigned to me by society....As a young person I understood that I was born in a boy's body, but I also felt a conflict between the inward sense of my gender and the outward expectations for my behavior as a boy. I asked a therapist many years later whether my acquiescence to these gendered rules undermined my authenticity as a transgendered person. He told me that in 1959 gender variance was seen as a severe form of mental illness and if I had told my parents I wanted to be a girl, I might have received electroshock and aversion therapy as a cure. At that time, my understanding of the gender rules enabled my self-preservation, by opting for self-suppression.

Accordingly, I buried my gender deep in my bodily core and struggled mightily to maintain a bearded façade, the increasingly brittle outer shell designed to project masculinity. After many years of struggle, the lack of authenticity was causing many sleepless nights and much introspection about whether or not I could continue to live my life as the man I was seen to be. At some point the depression became so intense that I experienced a kind of dark night of the soul. After much reflective searching I realized that to keep living, I had to face the world as my "true self" (Brown and Rounsley 1996). Making this change was one of the most difficult experiences of my life. At the age of 42, I "came out" to my family[1] and to my department colleagues, explaining that integrity required that I no longer silence the gender I knew myself to be.

My transition was facilitated by my therapist (a psychiatrist) who eschewed gate-keeping and encouraged me to explore the multi-dimensional and non-dichotomous identity that I was experiencing as gender. However, his questions helped me understand the consequences of displaying my differently gendered identity to the rest of the world. Although I wanted desperately to be a girl since I was young, I came to realize that I could never be "just a girl"; I will always be something more and something less. In most public settings I present as and am read as a woman, though often a rather gender variant woman. Because the patriarchal social structure does not tolerate intermediate genders, rejecting the

---

1. I had hoped that getting married and fathering two children would silence my gender questioning and anchor my identity as a man, but that is not the way that gender identity works. Though my marriage ended, I remain in close contact with my children and am now in a committed same-sex relationship.

male label meant I had to embrace the label female. Accordingly, I underwent reassignment surgery so that my driver's license and passport indicate that I am female. But I refuse to retreat into that post-operative closet and live in fear that I will be outed as once having had an M on my passport. I choose to live as a visibly queer transgendered person and refuse to re-enter the closet of some post-operative transsexuals who live in fear they will be "outed" as once having lived as some other gender.

My employment as a tenured professor provided me with a relatively "safe" location within which to transform the public presentation of my gender. It also enabled me to begin to shift my research agenda during a one semester sabbatical in which I "discovered" the field of feminist and queer geography. Previously I had researched transgender and transsexual identities, but until I came out as transsexual I was afraid to integrate these insights into my academic work for fear of being marginalized for writing about such a controversial topic. When I encountered the rich research on spatial aspects of queer identity on my sabbatical, it was like finding a vein of unexpected gold.

Part of my intellectual journey has involved coming to grips with the way that the spaces in which I live, work and play are inherently gendered. For many years I literally only expressed the gender of my true self in the most secret spaces within the privacy of my own home—in the very real confines of a large walk-in closet. The closet is both a literary metaphor for gay and lesbian oppression in the US (Sedgwick 1990) and a form of material reality within diverse spatial contexts (Brown 2000). However, for transgendered people it is an essential space in which we live and at times hide the clothing and accoutrements of our identities. I think my fascination with the public or private nature of space is based on this highly personal understanding that for me coming out meant that I had to move from the protective shelter of the closet, to the slightly more risky privacy of my bedroom, to the semi-private space of my living room in the evening with the shades tightly drawn, to the bright glare of daylight where I would be in public view of the neighbors and all the world....

My own experience of meeting other transgendered people suggests that there is a wide diversity in our understanding of what gender is and how it should be displayed. Gender is not a dichotomy but a splendid array of diverse experiences and performances. I resonate with Bondi's (2004, 12) argument that "the binary construct of gender... [is] a superfluous and unnecessary distraction from the reality of the human condition." ...

I recognize that my identity is "contingent and constructed in relation to temporal factors of generation, transitional time span, and social and cultural understandings and practices" (Hines 2006, 64). However, a critical component of that contingency is an awareness of the ways that expressions of non-dichotomous gender are still resisted by the dominant social structure. I understand clearly that gender variant identities challenge gender norms at a significant social cost, namely the "trade-offs in terms of such things as social power, social approval and material benefits" (Mehta and Bondi 1999, 70). The tyranny of gender oppresses those whose behavior, presentation and expression fundamentally challenge socially accepted gender categories. Gendered bodies are subjected to a regulatory regime (Foucault 1978) that enforces the boundaries of properly gendered behaviors. Browne (2004) has called this gender policing "genderism" and argues that the "active contestations of other people's policing of sexed norms draws attention to the attempt to expel that which de-stabilizes self-other dichotomies" (Browne 2006, 122). This disciplining takes place within ourselves, but also in external spaces that permit others to pass judgment on people who transgress the gender dichotomy. From my own experiences I can attest that individuals who persist in violating gender norms are marginalized in both queer and other public spaces (K. Namaste 1996; Doan 2001, 2006, 2007). This article explores some of the mechanisms of that gendered policing in different spatial contexts.

My Transgendered Experience of Gendered Spaces

In the following sections I present my experiences as a transgendered woman across the continuum of spaces ranging from more public to more private locations. I am cognizant that my experiences, difficult as they may have been, are grounded in a complex web of privilege including: my tenured faculty position, my white racial identity and my upper middle class upbringing. I consider myself lucky that I have never been gender-bashed (K. Namaste 1996), though I have certainly experienced blatant genderism (Hill 2003; Browne 2004) and violent trans-phobia (Feinberg 1996) triggered by my gender status. Some transgendered people respond to this tyranny with rage (Stryker 1994), and that anger can lead to a manifesto for change (Stone 1991) and increased gender activism.

> We are entitled to our anger in response to this oppression: our anger is a message to ourselves that we need to get active and change something in order to survive. So we resist the oppression, the violence—we resist the tendency of the culture to see us as a joke. (Bornstein 1994, 81)

In my case I have tried to channel my anger along a different path that avoids what Viviane Namaste (2000) has called the powerful silencing of transgendered individuals, rendering them invisible for the most part to North American society. Gender transitions are almost never private affairs; by design they occur in public space and provide a different lens with which to view the gendering of public spaces. The following examples illustrate some of my own experiences with public spaces as a person whose gender does not easily fit into a dichotomous box.

In public spaces the tyranny of gender operates when certain individuals feel empowered to act as heteronormatively constructed gender enforcers in public spaces. These policing behaviors are sometimes exaggerated by the presence of other silent but supportive watchers. At the same time gender variant performance in public spaces that is supported by a wider community can be a powerful statement against the dichotomy.

Public Transit

Public spaces such as streets, transportation facilities and elevators contain structural elements that enable the operation of gender tyranny. Gardner (1995) describes the public harassment of women by men as endemic in our society, but it is a more serious problem for those whose expression of gender varies from the heteronormative, as the following experiences illustrate. After my first overseas trip using my new passport with F for a sex designator, I passed through US Customs at JFK airport without so much as a raised eyebrow. Outside the secure area I had a pre-arranged meeting with an airport limo driver. The arrival area was jammed with people and I followed the driver outside to the equally crowded sidewalk to the parking area. When the limo driver asked about my trip, I responded without thinking in my deep bass voice. I was happy to be back in the US and must have relaxed my usual vigilance because I paid no attention to the crowd of people around us. Shortly thereafter I stopped abruptly before crossing an exit for an underground parking garage, causing the man who was right behind me to bump into me. This man immediately began screaming at me and I realized his anger was not because of the bodily collision that had prevented us from being hit by an oncoming car, but because he realized that I was trans. He must have heard me speaking earlier and my sudden stop had ignited his smouldering anger. He started yelling, "I know what you are! You can't fool me! You are disgusting!" I refused to be cowed and asked him point blank what he thought I was. He, in turn, became so agitated that I thought he was going to throw a punch. If the limo driver had not quietly stepped up next to me as a supportive presence, I would have been assaulted on the spot. My gender expression in that public space offended his sense of appropriate public behavior and he acted to sanction that violation in as public a fashion as possible.

Vulnerability in an Elevator

Crowding in public spaces brings people into closer proximity than usual and increases gendered vulnerability in such spaces. Several years ago I experienced this gendering in an up-front and personal way. One evening on a business trip I entered the ground floor entrance of a hotel and entered a reasonably full elevator car. I stood next to a youngish woman and across from an older man who appeared to be her companion for the evening. He was clearly inebriated, and as soon as I entered the space, he began staring at me, obviously disturbed by something about my presentation of gender. Just before we reached the next floor, he stepped up very close to me, and giving a lecherous wink said "Well, look what we have here!" I tried simply staring him down, but as the doors opened, he reached up and grabbed both of my breasts and squeezed, apparently expecting to find the falsies used by drag queens. I was stunned by this unexpected sexual assault and stood there in a speechless state of shock as he turned and walked away. By squeezing my breasts he was objectifying and assaulting what Young (1998) calls the most visible sign of a woman's femininity. In my case he assumed he was attacking my false femininity to expose me for an imposter. Unfortunately his discovery of his error did little to lessen the indignity of the assault ....

The Workplace

Coming out at a public university provided many unique experiences of gendered spaces. My first day on the job as a woman was especially memorable. As I entered the building I felt I was entering the eye of a hurricane, at the calm center of a turbulent storm of gendered expectations. As I walked down the hall I could hear conversation in front of me suddenly stop as all eyes turned to look at the latest "freak show." As I passed each office there was a moment of eerie quiet, followed by an uproar as the occupants began commenting on my appearance. Some people just stared, a few others told me how brave I was and one person told me that I looked "just like a woman." Another gave me a taste of what it means to be objectified by telling me proudly that I was his very first transsexual. These events helped me to realize that my presentation of gender was not just a personal statement, but a co-constructed event. I presented myself, and the academic world watched and passed judgment. I am grateful for the presence of my colleagues and students whose support deflected some of this turbulence.

Classrooms

... In my new mode of presentation as a woman, I noticed an undermining of the implicit assumption of my academic competency. When the world perceived me as a man, I found it quite easy to step to the front of a lecture hall and assume the role of a knowledgeable professor. I never had difficulty in keeping or maintaining the attention of any class. After transition, however, this experience changed quite markedly. On the first day of class my students accepted me as an openly transgendered woman, but it slowly dawned on me that I was also no longer automatically perceived as an expert in my field.[2] I perceived a distinct "prove it" attitude on the part of the students. Since my transition I have to work much harder to establish my credentials and maintain control of the classroom than I did when I was perceived as a straight man.

At my university all classes with more than 10 students are required to provide a standardized student evaluation form. Although my overall student evaluations are high, in almost every class there are some who resent being taught by an openly transgendered professor. The mandated evaluation survey includes the following open-ended questions: *What did you like most about the course? What could be improved?* One undergraduate student in my World Cities class responded, "Nothing. Input a new teacher. S/he's a man dressed like

---

2. I cannot be certain whether it was my womanhood that caused the issue or my gender variance, but I am sure it was vastly different from the response I received when I was perceived as a man.

a female! It's gross!" In this comment the student critiques my teaching, refutes my gender and expresses disgust typical of trans-phobic comments. A second open-ended question asks: *What did you like best about the instructor?* Another undergraduate respondent answered, "How could a university hire a person who pretends to be female? It's horrible! I recently explained to my parents that one of my professors is a man that had a sex change and she about lost it." This comment refutes my gender as well as the possibility of sex change itself and then implies some administrator may get an irate phone call from a parent. These comments are attempts to regulate my behavior or at least to strike back at my gender non-conformance.

These examples from two separate student evaluations do not represent the vast majority of my students, but they do illustrate the vitriol lurking in the back of the classroom ....

Only once have I ever felt physically threatened from students who were not known to me. I was proctoring a final exam for my graduate Growth of Cities class when there was suddenly a lot of loud talking just outside the classroom. Since several of my students seemed disturbed by the interruptions, I opened the door and asked the disruptive students to be quiet since I was giving an exam. Several minutes later someone in the hall kicked open the door with a loud bang and yelled at the top of his lungs, "Shemale!" Although this person did not dare show his face, the uproarious laughter suggested that his feelings were widely shared. I was upset and felt very vulnerable after this violation of my classroom space. I stifled the rage that told me to charge into the hall and confront the disruptive students and sat in silence, unsure how to proceed. Eventually, a student loaned me her cell phone to call campus security. When the campus police arrived five minutes later, they cleared the students from the hallway and escorted me back to the safety and privacy of my office. Although I was grateful for the support of my student and the assistance of the police, I was deeply shaken at the public humiliation and sense of violation created by this hate speech ....

Public Restrooms

One of the scariest spaces for a person in the midst of a gender transition is a public restroom. The biological urge forces a regular choice between one of two doors with different labels (men/women, gents/ladies, guys/gals, buoys/gulls, etc.). Each excursion for me into the most private of public gendered spaces risked discovery and a potential confrontation with others outraged by my perceived transgression. Browne (2004) has called this "the bathroom problem" and suggests that masculine appearing women regularly experience harassment and difficulties in such places ....

At work I had to face the gendered restroom question directly. When I first transitioned, I became temporarily "disabled" since the administration's interim solution was that I use the single access handicapped restroom on a different floor of my building. One day not long after I began using this facility, I was mortified to discover the bathroom had no locking mechanism. I was using the facility when the door opened unexpectedly, exposing me for a moment to some students in the hallway just outside. My gender difference provided a new-found awareness that I too was "not anywhere near the project" (Chouinard and Grant 1996), that I and others like me had fallen between the cracks of a dichotomous world....

The Mall

Shopping malls are enclosed spaces that use private security to provide the appearance of a safer experience than a public street. Some geographers have argued that malls create "a setting for free personal expression and association, for collective cultural expression and transgression, and for unencumbered human interaction and material transaction" (Goss 1993, 25). The transgendered rite of passage known as mall-walking puts this to the test. Frequently novice trans women have not yet grasped that the mundane act of shopping is a highly gendered experience, especially for women whose size (bodily bigness) does not fit normative expectations of attractiveness (Colls 2006). As a transgendered person inhabiting a tall and broad-shouldered body, I was unsure how well I would pass as a woman and so postponed my first mall-walking experience until I was out of town. I was determined to explore my emerging sense that I was a woman by performing that gender in public. In preparation for the excursion, I donned my favorite dress, put on two pair of hose to cover my not yet shaven legs and took extra care with my make-up (to cover evidence of my male beard).

As I entered the mall, it slowly dawned on me that performing gender at home in front of a mirror was nothing like the dance that is gender in a public place. I felt that everyone was staring at me. In hindsight I realize that I was feeling the panoptic (Foucault 1977) nature of shopping malls, both because of the omnipresent but often hidden security guards (Ainley 1998) and also because of the power of the hetero-normative gaze (Pérez 2003; Doan 2007). I experienced an odd sense of "being watched" that was partly a result of my own anxiety about "passing" and partly my rather over-dressed attire for a mall on a Saturday afternoon. I could feel the stares boring into my back as I passed, and decided to skip the shopping and just walk from one end to the other....The gaze of each person I passed was part of the overall "policing practices" that questioned my gender and undermined the tenuousness of the category (Browne 2006).

At Home

The home is often considered a space of safety in which individuals escape the constant surveillance of identity (Saunders 1989), but for lesbians the home does not always deter heteronormativity that may infiltrate via neighbors and family (Johnston and Valentine 1995). For many in the LGBT community, "evocations of home are embedded in the struggles to create and maintain spaces of belonging and comfort in the face of adversity without (or within) the lesbian and gay community" (Fortier 2001, 412). Although the home is usually considered a heteronormative habitation, it can be queered through private interactions with same-sex partners or by supportive family members (Gorman-Murray 2007, 2008). In my case, after being subjected to the ever present tyranny of gender across the continuum of public…spaces, my home is a necessary place of refuge, but one that is not uncontested. The tyranny of gender intrudes via modern communication systems which allow the home to become "a 'phantasmagoric' place, to the extent that electronic media of various kinds allow the intrusion of distant events into the space of domesticity" (Morley 2001, 428).

The telephone constitutes the most significant invasion of my private space. Though I have put my phone number on a Do Not Call list for telemarketers, I still receive a large number of unsolicited calls. I do not allow trans-phobic people in my home, but I generally answer the phone when it rings. Callers who do not know me invariably hear my voice and assume that I am male. Part of my witness related to integrity involves telling them patiently that they are speaking to a woman. However, many callers refuse to disbelieve their ears and continue this pronoun abuse by calling me Mister and Sir. After a few attempts to persuade them otherwise I often simply hang up in frustration at this intrusion of the tyranny of gendered pronouns into my own space. Many people do not understand the power of these little words and how painful the persistent use of inappropriate pronouns can be. After a long day of being out in heteronormatively defined spaces (and getting my share of confused looks and the occasional, yes sir), it feels like a violation to be subjected to such indignity at home. As a result I find that I am less likely to answer the phone (no doubt skewing all those public opinion survey calls). When I need to make a new contact with someone, I am much less likely to call on the phone and will use either a face to face meeting or an exchange of email. I do not mind being visible and even speaking in public spaces as a differently gendered person, but I need a home-place where I can simply be myself without being subject to the insults of the tyranny of gender.

Conclusions

…Different types of gendered spaces have varying potential for confrontation and transformation. There are places in which I never raise my voice above a whisper, such as public restrooms. In addition, when I use public transportation in unfamiliar locations or when I travel the back roads through unfamiliar terrain, I rarely engage those around me in idle conversation until I am able to get a reading on how invested they might be in the dichotomy of gender. I am not shy, just careful. I recognize that my gender performance is simultaneously modulated by the observers of my gender as well as the spaces in which we interact. These modulations do not shift my own sense of gender, but they do shape the visibility and impact of my gender performance. Sometimes I can choose when to perform my gender in ways that might expand the boundaries of the gender dichotomy and sometimes I cannot. I recognize the privilege contained within my subject position as a white middle class transsexual woman and resonate deeply with what Green (2004, 183–4) has written about becoming a visible trans man.

> By claiming our identity as men or women who are also transpeople, by asserting that our bodies are just as normal for us as anyone else's is for them, by insisting on our right to express our own gender, to modify our bodies and shape our identities, is as inalienable as our right to know our true religion, we claim our humanity and our right to be treated fairly under the law and within the purviews of morality and culture. To do that we must educate—if we have the ability and emotional energy to do so. That is what visibility is all about.

As more victims of gender tyranny step into the light and become visible, the need to re-conceptualize the relationship between gender and space will also become more evident. In the introduction to the special "Trans" issue of *Women's Studies Quarterly*, Stryker, Currah, and Moore (2008, 12) suggest that

> we understand genders as potentially porous and permeable spatial territories (arguably numbering more than two), each capable of supporting rich and rapidly proliferating ecologies of embodied difference.... Any gender-defined space is not only populated with diverse forms of gendered embodiment, but striated and crosshatched by the boundaries of significant forms of difference other than gender, within all of which gender is necessarily implicated.

Consequently, a number of questions arise from this work at the intersection of gender and spatial theory. Feminist and queer geographers might usefully explore the parameters of the tyranny of gender as it constrains behavior in a spectrum of spaces and localities. Are there social and spatial contexts that empower the performance of non-binary genders and how do they operate? How does non-normative gender performance influence others' perception of space and the action they take as a result? How does the spatiality of non-conforming gender performance serve to strengthen or weaken the gender dichotomy?

The time has come to expand our understanding of gender beyond its social construction and include a distinct spatiality within which a range of gendered and other differences can be performed. Gender variance exists throughout the human and natural world and has real consequences for people in their daily lives. Gender strongly influences the ways that spaces are perceived and the kinds of activities that are possible, acceptable, or even safe within them. The tyranny of the gender dichotomy is an artifact of the patriarchal structuring of gendered space and it is time to lay it aside, not just for trans people, but for us all.

Acknowledgments

The author gratefully acknowledges the substantive contributions of Kath Browne, Sally Hines and Catherine Nash whose encouragement and careful critiques helped to hone this article. The article also benefitted from the thoughtful comments and suggestions of the anonymous referees. Finally, the author also wishes to acknowledge the helpful comments of Lori Reid and Margeaux Mutz and the indefatigable support of Elizabeth Kamphausen in sustaining this project.

References

Ainley, Rosa. 1998. Watching the detectors: Control and the panopticon. In *New frontiers of space, bodies, and gender*, ed. Rosa Ainley, 88–100. London: Routledge.

Bondi, Liz. 2004. Tenth anniversary address: For a feminist geography of ambivalence. *Gender, Place and Culture* 11, no. 1: 3–15.

Bornstein, Kate. 1994. *Gender outlaw: On women, men, and the rest of us*. New York: Routledge.

Brown, Michael. 2000. *Closet space: Geographies of metaphor from the body to the globe*. London: Routledge.

Brown, Mildred, and Chloe Ann Rounsley. 1996. *True selves: Understanding transsexualism—for families, friends, coworkers, and helping professionals*. San Francisco: Jossey-Bass.

Browne, Kath. Genderism and the bathroom problem: (Re)materializing sexed sites, (re)creating sexed bodies. *Gender, Place and Culture* 11: 331–46.

———. 2006. "A right geezer bird (man-woman)": The sites and sounds of female embodiment. *ACME: An International E-Journal for Critical Geographies* 5, no. 2: 121–43.

Chase, Cheryl. 1998. Hermaphrodites with attitude: Mapping the emergence of intersex political activism. *GLQ: A Journal of Lesbian and Gay Studies* 4, no. 2: 189–211.

Chouinard, Vera, and Ali Grant. 1996. On being not anywhere near the project: Ways of putting ourselves in the project. In *Body space: Destabilizing geographies of gender and sexuality*, ed. Nancy Duncan, 170–93. New York: Routledge.

Colls, Rachel. 2006. Outsize/outside: Bodily bignesses and the emotional experiences of British women shopping for clothes. *Gender, Place and Culture* 13, no. 5: 529–45.

Doan, Petra. 2001. Are the transgendered the mine shaft canaries of urban areas? *Progressive Planning: Special Issue on Queers and Planning*. New York: Planners Network. http://www.plannersnetwork.org/2001/03/are-the-transgendered-the-mine-shaft-canaries-of-urban-areas/.

———. 2006. Violence and transgendered people. *Progressive Planning: Special Issue on Gender and Violence*. New York: Planners Network. http://www.planners network.org/publications/mag20062spring.html

———. 2007. Queers in the American city: Transgendered perceptions of urban spaces. *Gender, Place and Culture* 14: 57–74.

Feinberg, Leslie. 1996. *Transgendered warriors: From Joan of Arc to Dennis Rodman*. Boston: Beacon Press.

Fortier, Anne-Marie. 2001. "Coming home": Queer migrations and multiple evocations of home. *European Journal of Cultural Studies* 4: 405–24.

Foucault, Michel. 1977. *Discipline and punish: The birth of the prison*. Trans. A. Sheridan. New York: Pantheon.

———. 1978. *The history of sexuality, Volume 1: An introduction*. Trans. R. Hurley. New York: Random House.

Gardner, Carol Brooks. 1995. *Passing by: Gender and public harassment*. Berkeley: University of California Press.

Gorman-Murray, Andrew. 2007. Contesting domestic ideals: Queering the Australian home. *Australian Geographer* 38, no. 2: 195–213.

———. 2008. Queering the family home: Narratives from gay, lesbian and bisexual youth coming out in supportive family homes in Australia. *Gender, Place and Culture* 15, no. 1: 31–44.

Goss, Jon. 1993. The magic of the mall. *Annals of the Association of American Geographers* 83: 18–47.

Green, Jamison. 2004. *Becoming a visible man.* Nashville: Vanderbilt University Press.

Hill, Darryl. 2003. Genderism, transphobia, and gender-bashing: A framework for interpreting anti-transgender violence. In *Understanding and dealing with violence: A multicultural approach*, ed. Barbara Wallace and Robert Carter, 113–36. Thousand Oaks, CA: Sage Publications.

Hines, Sally. 2006. What's the difference? Bringing particularity to queer studies of transgender. *Journal of Gender Studies* 15, no. 1: 49–66.

Johnston, Lynda, and Gill Valentine. 1995. Wherever I lay my girlfriend that's my home: The performance and surveillance of lesbian identities in domestic environments. In *Mapping desire: Geographies of sexualities*, ed. David Bell and Gill Valentine, 99–113. London: Routledge.

Kessler, Suzanne. 1998. *Lessons from the intersexed.* New Brunswick, NJ: Rutgers University Press.

Lucal, Betsy. 1999. What it means to be gendered me: Life on the boundaries of a dichotomous gender system. *Gender and Society* 13, no. 6: 781–97.

Mehta, A., and L. Bondi. 1999. Embodied discourse: On gender and fear of violence. *Gender, Place, and Culture* 16: 67–84.

Mill, John Stuart. 1869. *On liberty.* 4th ed. London: Longman, Roberts and Green.

Morley, David. 2001. Belongings: Place, space and identity in a mediated world. *European Journal of Cultural Studies* 4: 425–48.

Namaste, Ki. 1996. Gender bashing: Sexuality, gender, and the regulation of public space. *Environment and Planning D: Society and Self* 14, no. 2: 221–40.

Namaste, Viviane K. 2000. *Invisible lives: The erasure of transsexual and transgendered people.* Chicago: University of Chicago Press.

Pérez, Emma. 2003. Queering the borderlands: The challenges of excavating the invisible and unheard. *Frontiers* 24: 122–31.

Saunders, Peter. 1989. The meaning of home in contemporary English culture. *Housing Studies* 4: 177–92.

Sedgwick, Eve Kosofsky. 1990. *The epistemology of the closet.* Berkeley: University of California Press.

Stone, Sandy. 1991. The "empire" strikes back: A posttranssexual manifesto. In *Bodyguards: The cultural politics of gender ambiguity*, ed. Katrina Straub and Julia Epstein, 280–304. New York: Routledge.

Stryker, Susan. 1994. My words to Victor Frankenstein above the village of Chamounix: Performing transgender rage. *GLQ: A Journal of Gay and Lesbian Studies* 1: 237–54.

Stryker, Susan, Paisley Currah, and Lise Jean Moore. 2008. Introduction: Trans-, trans, or transgender? *Women's Studies Quarterly* 36, no. 3/4: 11–22.

Turner, Stephanie. 1999. Intersex identities: Locating new intersections of sex and gender. *Gender and Society* 13, no. 4: 457–79.

Valentine, David. 2003. "The calculus of pain": Violence, anthropological ethics, and the category transgender. *Ethnos* 68, no. 1: 27–48.

Young, Iris Marion. 1998. Breasted experience: The look and the feeling. In *The politics of women's bodies: Sexuality, appearance, and behavior*, ed. Rose Weltz, 125–36. Oxford: Oxford University Press.

Cordelia Fine is a psychologist and author of two books on neuroscience. She is also a Professor at Melbourne Business School in Australia.

The "Seductive Allure" of Neuroscience
Cordelia Fine

I once bought a toy drum that promised to stimulate my child's auditory nerve. I took this to mean that it made noise. Clearly, the genius minds behind the marketing had stumbled on the discovery that information sounds far more impressive when couched in the grand language of neuroscience. (By the way, have I mentioned yet that these words of mine you're reading are stimulating your occipital lobe, as well as refining the neural circuitry of your anterior cingulate gyrus and dorsolateral prefrontal cortex? This isn't just a book—it's a neurological workout.) There's something special about neuroscientific information. It sounds so unassailable, so very…well, *scientific*, that we privilege it over boring, old-fashioned behavioral evidence. It brings a satisfying feel to empty scientific explanations. And it seems to tell us who we really are.

After Lawrence Summers's controversial suggestion that women might be inherently less capable of high-level science, Steven Pinker and Simon Baron-Cohen were not the only ones to talk brain differences. So did Leonard Sax. Refreshingly, Sax did not argue that brain research hints at an innate female inferiority, on average, in science and math. Instead, he argued that the problem lies in an educational system that teaches boys and girls the same things at the same time. This is a mistake because, as he explained in the *Los Angeles Times*, "while the areas of the brain involved in language and fine motor skills (such as handwriting) mature about six years earlier in girls, the areas involved in math and geometry mature about four years earlier in boys."[1] Sax argues that teaching should be sensitive to sex differences in the timing of development of the various regions of the brain because "[a] curriculum which ignores those differences will produce boys who can't write and girls who think they're 'dumb at math.'"[2]

Now, I'm all behind Sax's goal of improving educational outcomes for boys and girls. There might be good reasons for single-sex schooling. But what are we to make of his claim that, as he put it to *CBS News*, "[b]oth boys and girls are being shortchanged as a result of the neglect of hard-wired gender differences"?[3]

By now, you will probably be uneasy about the idea that complex psychological skills like language, math, and geometry can be pinpointed to a single part of the brain. It's simply not the case that people use one particular lobe, or a circumscribed area of the brain, to read a novel, or write an essay, or solve an equation, or calculate the angle of a triangle. And, unfortunately, neuroscience has yet to reach the stage at which it can peer into the brain and determine capacity for solving simultaneous equations or readiness to learn calculus. I can understand why this relatively subtle point didn't set off alarm bells in Sax or the editors or journalists who brought comments like this to the public eye. But why did no one query the relevance of Sax's statement on the grounds that boys are clearly *not*, in fact, four years ahead of girls in math—they are not ahead of them at all, as it happens.[4] Nor, of course, is the language ability of a twelve-year-old boy comparable to that of a six-year-old girl. Even if we are happy to relate one part of the brain to complex cognition, clearly, this concept of neural maturation is a very poor index of actual ability—a far worse measure than, say, a math test. So why does this kind of neurononsense get column inches?

One reason may be that neuroscience easily outranks psychology in the implicit hierarchy of "scientificness."[5] Neuroscience, after all, involves expensive, complex machinery. It generates smart-looking three-dimensional images of the brain. The technicians almost certainly wear white coats. It involves quantum mechanics, for goodness' sake! I ask you, what kind of a match for this is a simple piece of paper on which a six-year-old girl has successfully added 7 and 9? Bioethicist Eric Racine and colleagues coined the term "neuro-realism" to describe how fMRI coverage can make psychological phenomena somehow seem more real or objective than evidence collected in a more ordinary fashion. They describe now, for example, brain activation in the reward centers of the brain while people ate unhealthy food was provided as evidence that "[f]at really does bring pleasure."[6] If patterns of firing in the brain can be seen as better proof of someone feeling pleasure than them selecting the box on the questionnaire marked "Yes, I really enjoyed eating that doughnut," then it's not surprising that children's actual academic skills can be so easily overlooked when brain research is enjoying the spotlight.

I also suspect that because the brain is such a biological organ, with its axons and fat and neurochemicals and electrical impulses, there is the temptation to chalk up whatever sex differences we see in the brain to differences in male and female nature, as Michael Gurian and Kathy Stevens do in *The Minds of Boys*:

> The social thinkers of the 1950s, 1960s, and 1970s did not have PET scans, MRIs, SPECT scans, and other biological research tools available to them ....Because they could not look inside the heads of human beings to see the differences in the brains of males and females, they had to lean away from nature-based theory toward social trends theory. They had to overemphasize the power of nurture in gender studies because they didn't have a way to study the actual nature of male and female.[7]

Gurian and Stevens seem to equate "actual nature" with "brain." But really, when you think about it, where else but in the brain would we see the effects of socialization or experience? As Mark Liberman puts it, "how else would socially constructed cognitive differences manifest themselves? In flows of pure spiritual energy, with no effect on neuronal activity, cerebral blood flow, and functional brain imaging techniques?"[8] The "neuro-curmudgeons" from the James

S. McDonnell Foundation have picked up on this "brain = innate" tendency, too. In response to an article in the *New York Times* that claimed from an fMRI study that "a mother's impulse to love and protect her child appears to be hard-wired into her brain" one neuro-curmudgeon put out a plea to "take experience and learning seriously. Just because you see a response [in the brain]—you don't get to claim it's hard-wired."[9]

Another draw of neurononsense is what Yale researchers have referred to as "the seductive allure of neuroscience explanations." Deena Skolnick Weisberg and her colleagues found that people are pretty good at spotting bad explanations of psychological phenomena. Suppose, for example, you read about a study in which researchers found that men performed better than women on spatial reasoning tasks. Would you be satisfied by the circular explanation that "women's poor performance relative to men's explains the gender difference in spatial reasoning abilities"? Probably not. The researchers aren't explaining their result, they're redescribing it: *women are worse at spatial reasoning because women are worse at spatial reasoning*. But simply add neuroscience and the same non-explanations suddenly seem much more satisfying:

> Brain scans of the right premotor area, known to be involved in spatial relational tasks, indicate that **women's poor performance relative to men's** causes different types of brain responses. This **explains the gender difference in spatial reasoning abilities**.

In bold text is the circular explanation that people found unsatisfying. The extra neuroscience bit tells us that spatial reasoning recruits a part of the brain, which should hardly surprise us. But it doesn't tell us *why* women performed worse than men. The explanation is still circular. But the neuroscience disguises this, even for students enrolled in an introductory cognitive science class, Weisberg and colleagues found.[10] Although it's not yet clear what it is, exactly, about neuroscience that is so persuasive, it's been found that people find scientific arguments more compelling when accompanied by an image showing brain activation rather than, say, a bar graph showing the same information.[11]

All of which should make us very concerned that this talk of brain differences might influence opinion and policy far more than it should. As Weisberg suggests, the seductive nature of neuroscience creates "a dangerous situation in which it may not be the best research that wins debates in the public sphere."[12]

The effects of neuroscience may be personal as well as political. Gender stereotypes are legitimated by these pseudo-scientific explanations. Suddenly, one is being modern and scientific, rather than old-fashioned and sexist. Do you want to claim, in a book for teachers and parents, that "the world of the abstract…is explored more by the male brain than the female," thus explaining males' dominance in physics?[13] Why then, go right ahead! So long as the magic word *brain* is there, no further information required. But we have to wonder about the effect of this kind of information as it feeds back into society. As we saw in the first part of this book, the activation of gender stereotypes, even by means as subtle as our suspicion that they have found a home in the minds of others, can have measurable effects on our attitudes, identity, and performance.

Neurosexism may also effect such changes directly. We can currently only speculate on the enervating effect of popular gender-science books on male patterns of leaving the milk to be bought by someone else. But there is evidence that media reports of gender that emphasize biological factors leave us more inclined to agree with gender stereotypes, to self-stereotype ourselves, and even for our performance to fall in line with those stereotypes.[14] For example, one study found that women given a journal article to read that claimed that men are better at math because of innate, biological, and genetic differences performed worse on a GRE-like math test than women shown an essay saying that men's greater effort underlies their superior performance. Likewise, women who had just read an essay arguing that there are genetically caused sex differences in mathematical ability performed substantially worse on a GRE-like test, compared with women who read that experiential factors explain sex differences in math ability, psychologists Ilan Dar-Nimrod and Steven Heine found. (Being told this information by the experimenter had the same effect.) This damaging effect of the genetic account, the researchers suggest, may stem from people's assumption that genetically based differences are more profound and immutable than differences that arise from social factors. "[M]erely considering the role of genes in math performance can have some deleterious consequences," they conclude. "These findings raise discomforting questions regarding the effects that scientific theories can have on those who learn about them and the obligation that scientists have to be mindful of how their work is interpreted."[15]

"Caveat lector" is Weisberg's advice. Neuroscientists who work in this area have some responsibility for how their findings of sex differences in the brain are interpreted and communicated. When this is done carelessly, it may have a real and significant impact on people's lives. Many neuroscientists do appear to be aware of this. They are appropriately cautious about interpreting sex differences in the brain, and many also take the time to remind journalists of just how far we are from mapping sex differences in the brain onto the mind. (And of course they may find their work being misrepresented, regardless.) Others, however, as we have seen, are more cavalier.

Not everyone would agree that the topic of sex differences in the brain requires a particular sensitivity. For example, sex-difference researcher Doreen Kimura has argued that "[w]e can't allow ourselves to get into a situation in which we say . . . 'This is a finding that won't upset anyone, so I'm willing to generalize from it, but this other finding may be unpopular, so I need more evidence to support it before reporting it.'"[16] I am not inclined to agree that the content of the research makes no difference to the degree of care scientists should take in generalizing a result, or their concern in how it is popularized by others. I have, for example, heard neuroscientists who work in the area of drug dependency talk about the efforts they go to to prevent simplification or distortion of their findings by the media. This is not because they are worried about "upsetting" people, but because it is a sensitive area, and "brain facts" about dependency can change people's attitudes and feelings about a particular social group. These neuroscientists didn't seem to consider it unreasonable to work under a heavier burden of caution—a burden that I suggest it is also appropriate to place on those who comment on sex differences in the brain.[17]

Finally, there's an urgent need for editors, journalists, and schools to develop far more skeptical attitudes toward claims made about sex differences in the brain. It is appalling to me that one can, apparently, say whatever drivel one likes about the male and female brain, and enjoy the pleasure of seeing it published in a reputable newspaper, changing a school's educational policy, or becoming a best seller. Scientists can help here (as many already are). Weisberg suggests (in relation to the interpretation of imaging studies in general) that we "take a more active stance as scientists, medical practitioners, and researchers." She advocates that researchers become "vocal critics" of misleading articles, put more pressure on "newspaper and magazine writers to cover scientific issues with more depth and nuance," and, to this end, offer their expertise to members of the media.[18]

Neurosexism promotes damaging, limiting, potentially self-fulfilling stereotypes. Three years ago, I discovered my son's kindergarten teacher reading a book that claimed that his brain was incapable of forging the connection between emotion and language. And so I decided to write this book.[19] To make this kind of confident claim about hardwired psychological differences between males and females is to overlook the likelihood of spurious findings, the teething problems of new technology, the obscurity of the relationship between brain structure and psychological function, and the difficulty of inferring psychological states from neuroimaging data. Dazzled by the seductive scientificness of neuroscience, commentators become blind to low-tech behavioral evidence of gender similarity, or flexibility in response to the social context. And, as we'll explore more in the next chapter, the very concept of hardwiring needs some updating.

Endnotes

1. (Sax, 2005), para. 8. In fairness to Sax, he is following the lead of the authors of the research paper on which this claim is made. They found different patterns of EEG waves (synchrony versus asynchrony) in children at rest, related these EEG patterns to complex psychological processes like language, mathematics, and social cognition (which, recall, the children were not engaged in), and then suggested that their results "have implications for gender differences in 'readiness-to-learn'"—even though they report no gender differences in any of the cognitive abilities their EEG data were supposedly tapping (Hanlon, Thatcher, & Cline, 1999), p. 503.

2. From Sax's Web site: http://www.whygendermatters.com, accessed on December 9, 2009. More recently, the NASSPE Web site (see http://www.singlesexschools.org/research-brain. htm) has drawn on a structural imaging study (Lenroot et. al., 2007) to further bolster this argument. This study found sex differences in the trajectory of volume changes in the brain across time, although many of these differences did not survive correction for total brain volume, which is greater in boys. In any case, the psychological implications of these findings are unknown. As the researchers put it: "Differences in brain size between males and females should not be interpreted as implying any sort of functional advantage or disadvantage" (p. 1072).

3. Quoted in (Dakss 2005), para. 29.

4. (Hyde et al., 2008).

5. (Kemper, 1990), p. 13.

6. (Racine, Bar-Ilan, & Illes, 2005), p. 160.

7. (Gurian & Stevens, 2005), p. 42.

8. http://itre.cis.upenn.edu/~myl/languagelog/archives/003246.html, accessed on October 5, 2009.

9. http://www.jsmf.org/neuromill/chaff.htm#bn64, accessed on October 5, 2009.

10. (Weisberg et al., 2008). A similar favoring of findings attained from neuroscientific methods was found by (Morton et al., 2006).

11. (McCabe & Castel, 2008).

12. (Weisberg, 2008), p. 54.

13. (Gurian, Henley & Trueman, 2001), p. 45 and see p. 53.

14. (Brescoll & LaFrance, 2004; Coleman & Hong, 2008; Dar-Nimrod & Heine, 2006; Thoman et al. 2008).

15. (Dar-Nimrod & Heine, 2006), p. 435.

16. (Kimura, 1999), p. 8.

17. See also arguments made by Bleier with regard to scientists' responsibility for the presentation of data in their writing (Bleier, 1986) and also (Bishop & Wahlsten, 1997).

18. (Weisberg, 2008), p. 55.

19. Hats off to the bloggers who regularly discuss these issues, in particular the tireless Mark Liberman.

Katrina Karkazis is a medical anthropologist and bioethicist at Stanford Center for Biomedical Ethics. She is interested in intersex issues and how they relate to medical policies.

Taxonomies of Intersexuality to the 1950s
Katrina Karkazis

Until the middle of the twentieth century medical intervention in hermaphroditism (later known as intersexuality) remained relatively uncommon, in part because the technological capacity to intervene, especially at birth, was limited. Unable to change the hermaphroditic body, medical investigations both informed and were informed by legal and social understandings of sex, the biological features generally used to define femaleness or maleness, in the West.

Over the past several centuries, a binary model of sex as unequivocally male or female has remained the almost universal axiom, despite evidence from human and animal biology calling this distinction into question. Over time, the biological markers of male and female have shifted, yet not the notion of sex as binary and discrete. This belief in two distinct sexes is an example of a concept so patently obvious and "natural" to most people that pointing to its historicity, and thus to its inherent unnaturalness, proves confounding, even incomprehensible to many. Yet the history of understandings of and approaches to hermaphroditism repeatedly points to attempt to use the phenomenon to reinforce the binary model, rather than to question it, from what have been called the Hippocratic and Aristotelian attitudes of the early modern period to the long-standing gonadal diagnostic principles of the nineteenth-century German pathologist Theodor Klebs (Daston and Park 1995; Dreger 1998a).

During the first half of the twentieth century, medical approaches to intersexuality moved further away from observation and classification and more toward intervention. Advancements in surgical techniques, the discovery of "sex" hormones, new understandings of sex differentiation in embryology, and the ability to test for sex chromosomes—as well as the consolidation of medical and scientific authority—not only shaped how somatic sexual difference was understood but also how intersexuality could be treated by suggesting sites and modes of intervention. Such intervention was—and largely remains—aimed at enabling the individual to fit, more or less superficially, into the binary model of sex.

The labeling of certain bodies as intersex is intimately and inextricably tied to understandings of supposedly normal male and female bodily characteristics.[1] To call a boy hermaphroditic, one must already have some idea of what normal male and female bodies look like, what traits they possess, and of the parameters of acceptable behavior for men and women. In this vein, medical practitioners have used knowledge, instruments, and technologies to read bodies, ascribe them a sex, and, when one is not evident, apply a sex in practice. In the case of intersexuality, sex is not merely conceived but enacted, thereby producing and reproducing the category sex and our understanding of what males and females are. Here I trace some of the earlier historical understandings of human reproduction, sexual difference, and hermaphroditism. While not meant to be exhaustive, this history serves as a background to later debates and shows that understandings of hermaphroditism, like much else, are subject to the constraints of time and place.

It might be tempting to dismiss earlier classificatory schemes for hermaphroditism (and for men and women) as quaint and inconsequential. Indeed, it is important to caution against drawing linear connections among conceptualizations of hermaphroditism in different historical epochs (Daston and Park 1995). Yet earlier strains of thought are echoed in current conceptualizations of intersexuality, including in tensions over what intersexuality is and how it should be treated.

A central point of concern and debate has been whether those classified as hermaphrodites are both male and female, neither, or some unique combination thereof. The range and intensity with which hermaphroditism has been an object of interest and speculation has fluctuated; however, over the past century, the cause, classification, and social status of hermaphroditism have proven an enduring medical and social interest. Heightened anxiety over hermaphroditism and the urgency of addressing it are linked to societal changes in gender roles and the corresponding associations between hermaphroditism and other moral and social concerns. Accompanying the intense fascination with and anxiety concerning hermaphroditism has been a with and the anxiety concerning hermaphroditism has been a need to classify gender-atypical bodies and normalize them—often relying on clinical medicine—to mitigate the threat they pose to the binary model of gender: in other words, the need to give them a single sex. Another issue is the enduring debate over what features should mark and individual's "true" sex, and who should make that determination. Since the late nineteenth century, medical discourses have exercised hegemony over political, legal, and even literary discourses, but this was not always the case. Finally, over several centuries of contemplating and addressing intersexuality in the West, theories for understanding and dealing with intersexuality have shifted considerably.

The Early Modern Period

Hermaphroditism has provoked curiosity for centuries because of its implications for the binary model of sex. Historians have demonstrated that understandings of sex differences before the modern period differed markedly from contemporary ones. Laqueur has argued that during premodern times, a one-sex model prevailed, in which understandings of sex focused more on similarity than on difference, and that "sex was a sociological, not an ontological category" (1990: 8).[2]

Other historians have sought to complicate the binary periodization of sex into modern and premodern by turning an eye to the heterogeneity of conceptualizations within early modern accounts of hermaphroditism (Daston and Park

1995). Instead of a one-sex model, Lorraine Daston and Katherine Park propose two competing views of hermaphroditism, which they characterize as Hippocratic and Aristotelian because of their roots in the respective authors' early works on human generation, arguing that these were widely debated in early modern times. The Hippocratic view held that hermaphrodites were an intermediate sex exactly between male and female. By contrast, Aristotelians viewed male and female as opposite poles, with no possible intermediate points. For them, hermaphroditism was a condition primary of the genitals, and thus hermaphrodites did not have an indeterminate sex, but rather doubled or redundant genitalia. In the Aristotelian view, an individual's true sex was always either male or female and thus never truly ambiguous. Not only was the genesis of hermaphroditism subject to debate within medicine but, Daston and Park assert, medical understandings and discussions of hermaphroditism did not dominate legal and political discussions. It was only in sixteenth-century France that hermaphroditism because strongly associated with sexual ambiguity (1995).

Intersexuality has attracted much recent attention because it calls into question a series of intractable dichotomies—nature versus culture, and male versus female, to name two—but according to Daston and Park these dichotomies were not relevant in the early modern period. After 1550, however, a frenzy of interest in hermaphroditism and a newly urgent association with morally charged sexual behavior and sexuality—such as sodomy, transvestitism, and even pornography—explicitly sexualized those labeled hermaphrodites. This intense concern and sexual association led to a resurgence of Hippocratic explanations of generation and sex difference. Hermaphroditism because "emblematic of all kinds of sexual ambiguity and associated with all practices that appeared to blur or erase the lines between the sexes" (Daston and Park 1995: 424).

From the sixteenth to the eighteenth century legal understandings of hermaphroditism in France and England were not always in accord with medical understandings of the time (Epstein 1990). Legal definitions of biological sex (and thus of hermaphroditism) were rigid, assuming two sexes, male and female. In contrast, medical understandings of biological sex as revealed in medical were more varied, complex, and contradictory, recognizing a spectrum of sex rather than the mutually exclusive categories of male and female. Legal sex identity was important because of its implications for marriage, property ownership, and civic status. Once a person was assigned a sex, even if prevailing notion held that it was the dominant rather than the "true" sex, the person was treated as a member of that sex for all legal purposes.

A significant question, of course, was who determined a person's sex. In the sixteenth-century, jurists relied on outside testimony from medical experts to determine a person's sex, rather than allowing adults in such cases to make determinations about their own sex. In contrast to Michel Foucault (1980) and Laqueur, who both argue that so-called hermaphrodites could freely choose their sex in the early modern period, Daston and Park contend that the decision was not without conflicts, in part because hermaphroditism, newly associated with sexual ambiguity, sexual deceit, and fraud, was seen as challenging the model of binary sex (1995: 426).

In the eighteenth century views shifted, leading to an emphasis on biological difference, not similarity, between men and women (Schiebinger 1989). Medicine extended sex differences to every part of the body from bones to brains, and these differences were codified by language: male and female sex organs, which had previously shared the same names, were now distinguished by separate terms. According to Lacquer (1990), this shift marks the emergence of the two-sex model of the human body.

The new emphasis on sex differences was not prompted by scientific developments. Indeed, scientific work provided numerous examples of discoveries that could have strengthened the one-sex model: for example, the budding field of embryology claimed that reproductive organs begin from the same embryonic structure. But the political, economic, and cultural transformations of the eighteenth century created the context in which identifying racial differences between the sexes became culturally imperative. Incommensurable sex difference was created despite, not because of, new scientific discoveries (Laqueur 1990: 169).

The Nineteenth Century

Despite their differences of opinion on understandings of sex difference in the early modern period, historians agree that scientific and medical interest in hermaphroditism increased markedly in the nineteenth century. In *Hermaphrodites and the Medical Invention of Sex*, the historian of science Alice Dreger describes how if a person designated a hermaphrodite visited a doctor, it was usually to receive a diagnosis, to relieve discomfort or pain, or for sex determination or revision; in some instances, the patient sought to marry or avoid conscription in to the army.[3] By the middle of the nineteenth century, there were two predominant classification systems for hermaphroditism, proposed by the French anatomist Isidore Geoffroy Saint-Hilaire and the British obstetrician James Young Simpson, with each system dominant in its author's respective country. By the mid-nineteenth century, the wide-spread expansion of hospitals enabled clinicians to see a greater number of individuals with rare conditions such as hermaphroditism, but except for a handful of the most notable clinicians, most saw very few.

In 1833, Saint-Hilaire presented his system for sex determination on the basis of the body's sexual organs and on whether or not they were concordant within an individual. He divided the sexual organs into six segments that he deemed the essential markers of sex. In this system of classification, one was truly male or female if all six segments were wholly male or female; any combination of male and female segments indicated hermaphroditism. Echoing earlier views, Saint-Hilaire argued that hermaphroditism was rooted both in excesses and arrests of otherwise normal sex development. Consequently he categorized individuals according to those segments in which they had excess and those in which they were lacking. Operating from an understanding of normal sex development, Saint-Hillaire believed, would enable an understanding of abnormal sex development. In turn, the study of abnormal variations could allow greater insight into normal sex development. As with many of today's investigations, his attempts to define the abnormal derived from the explicit desire to identify normal sex difference.

The long-standing British classificatory system emerged in the late 1830s when Simpson divided hermaphroditism into "spurious" and "true," categories that persisted through much of the century. Spurious hermaphrodites possessed genitals that were "approximate in appearance" to those of the opposite sex, whereas true hermaphrodites had a mixture of male and female organs. Characteristics of spurious hermaphroditism in the female could include a prolapsed uterus or enlarged clitoris. In the male, spurious hermaphroditism included adhesion of the penis to the scrotum, hypospadias (an abnormal position of the meatus, the opening from which urine passes), and an extroversion of the urinary bladder (an abnormality in which the bladder protrudes outside the abdomen), because the latter were thought characteristic of the female sex. Examples of true hermaphroditism included the combination of an ovary and a testis, conflicting external and internal sexual organs, and a combination of male and female internal sexual organs.

Nevertheless, scientists and doctors did not agree on which traits conclusively determined sex, in part because few traits were sex exclusive. For example, ejaculate was an unreliable indicator because some men did not emit it, while some women did. Similarly, some women menstruated, but others did not. Cases of doubtful or even "mistaken" sex, where clinicians believed an individual was living as the "wrong" sex, elicited negotiation and disagreement among scientists and clinicians about which traits or body parts were masculine or feminine and thus about whether an individual should be considered male or female. Consequently, medical professionals relied on culturally derived and gendered notions about anatomy for sex determination. Clinicians, however, also made determinations about an individual's true sex with an eye toward the person's gendered behavior and sexual desire.

In the second half of the nineteenth century, doctors sought to build a broader consensus on true markers of sex. In 1876, the German pathologist Klebs was the first to suggest a taxonomy based exclusively on the analysis of gonadal tissue and on whether an individual had ovaries or testes. Klebs distinguished between pseudo- and true hermaphroditism, a classification system that remained until a 2006 call for a change in nomenclature. Those who had both ovarian and testicular tissue were called true hermaphrodites. Those who had a "doubling of the external genitalia with a single kind of sexual gland," that is, either ovarian or testicular tissue, were labeled pseudohermaphrodites (following Simpson's definition for spurious hermaphroditism) (Dreger 1998a: 145). Pseudohermaphrodites were individuals who were "really" male or female, as indicated by their gonads, but whose mixed external anatomy, especially their genitals, obscured their sex. The category of pseudohermaphroditism was further divided into masculine (testes present with female genitalia) and feminine (ovaries present with male genitalia).

Under Kleb's system, someone with a typically female body type and feminine external genitalia who also had testes would be classified as a male. Klebs codified an already widely accepted notion, namely, that gonads alone indicated an individual's true sex. If clinicians could find conclusive evidence of either ovaries or testes, the problem of sex determination was ostensibly solved.

Practically, gonadal sex determination proved difficult. Because surgical intervention on living patients was not common until the beginning of the twentieth century, the only way nineteenth-century doctors could assess the gonadal tissue of an individual was by palpation in living patients or by autopsy after death. In part because of the inability to assess gonadal tissue in living patients, many individuals were classified as hermaphroditic after death. In part because of the inability to assess gonadal tissue in living patients, many individuals were classified as hermaphroditic after death. Even autopsy did not always reveal an individual's gonadal type, as gonads could be ambiguous or malformed. Moreover, Kleb's model did not account for individuals found to have both ovarian and testicular tissue.

By the end of the nineteenth century, several important medical and scientific shifts began taking place. Clinicians could use microscopic analysis to positively identify the structure of the gonad, though more often for deceased than for living individuals. By the early 1900s, however, improved techniques of anesthesia and asepsis permitted exploratory surgery in living patients. As doctors began to perform more of these procedures, they increasingly and glaringly faced the limits of the classificatory system for hermaphroditism. They confirmed that some women had testes but phenotypically were completely feminine. Should these feminine-appearing individuals be classified as males because of their testes? Moreover, if an individual was diagnosed as a true hermaphrodite, was that person supposed to live neither as a male nor a female? Socially, this stance seemed absurd and untenable.

Dreger (1998a) has argued that the appeal of a gonadal definition of true sex lay in its ability to preserve a clear distinction between males and females, not simply in theory but in practice. As social changes increasingly shifted and blurred the boundaries or masculine and feminine behavior, rooting gender in biology began to seem increasingly important. The period witnessed increasing attention to concern with homosexuality, another phenomenon that disturbed conventional binary notions of sex and gender. Suffragists also began challenging the boundaries of gender-appropriate social roles and behaviors. Because the definitions of hermaphroditism necessarily touched on the supposedly true nature of male and female, managing hermaphroditic bodies would help maintain the social body (Matta 2005, Reis 2005).

The medical and technological developments of the late 1800s and early 1900s enabled the assessment and diagnosis of certain types of hermaphroditism in subsequent decades. Still some cases of hermaphroditism went undiagnosed and without intervention until adolescence, when secondary sex characteristics sometimes appeared that were incongruous with the individual's social sex. Although medical evaluation and intervention aimed to simplify the diagnosis and treatment of hermaphroditism, assigning a single true sex—a social necessity required to prevent inappropriate marriages and other social dilemmas—in fact became more complex in the early twentieth century, as the markers of and methods of determining this true sex became multiple diverse, conflicting, and negotiable. Rather than simply displacing previous markers, each new discovery added to the complexity of sex determination.

The Early Twentieth Century

Developments in science and medicine during the first half of the twentieth century—such as advancements in surgical techniques, the medicalization of the birth process, new understandings of sex differentiation in the burgeoning field of embryology, the discovery of sex hormones, and the understanding of and ability to test for sex chromosomes—as well as the consolidation of medical and scientific authority not only shaped how somatic sexual difference, and thus hermaphroditism (or intersexuality), was understood but also how it could be treated by suggesting sites and modes of intervention. In the era before modern surgical techniques and hormone treatments, however, medicine's power and ability to intervene in hermaphroditism was largely restricted to observation, diagnosis, classification, and attempts at explanation and sex determination (Dreger 1998a). The study of hermaphroditic individuals proved, moreover, somewhat a matter of chance. Until the early twentieth century, the prevalence of traditional, woman-centered home birth meant that most newborns were not seen by a doctor. As male doctors gradually replaced midwives, and as women and their physicians believed that increased medicalization would make giving birth safer and more comfortable, childbirth shifted to the hospital (Leavitt 1986). This change gave physicians a larger role in the birth process. Still, some people classed as hermaphrodites never came to the attention of the medical profession because they had no visible anomalies in their external sex characteristics. Individuals without outward signs of their condition were assigned a sex at birth based on the configuration of the genitals. If contradictions arose when the individual reached puberty, patients could seek clinical help on a case-by-case basis. Although some individuals designated hermaphrodite later chose to visit a doctor about their condition, others never sought medical attention; some even independently chose the gender in which they lived (Dreger 1998a). Indeed, some individuals may not have perceived anything unusual about their development.

The turn of the century brought new possibilities of medical treatment, albeit crude ones, consisting mainly of rudimentary surgery to remove organs deemed incongruous with the true (i.e., gonadal) or social sex of the patient. Yet such possible treatments were accompanied by questions about the best course of action. A medical controversy erupted when case histories published in medical journals revealed that clinicians did not always assign sex according to the gonadal composition, and in some instances had not ascertained the individual's gonadal makeup before making judgments about that person's sex and "treatment options" (Mak 2005). Some clinicians, rather than ascertaining an individual's true sex, were increasingly preoccupied with erasing external, visible signs of sexual ambiguity, thus giving the patient one sex.

In 1902, for example, a Dutch gynecologist argued that when determining sex, the external genitalia and their suitability for copulation, as well as the "inner life" of the individual, were more important than gonadal composition (Mak 2005: 67). The physician was highly critical of the "inhumane" clinical practice of forcing people to live in a particular sex. Another case from 1904 sparked intense controversy when a professor in gynecology in New York performed genital surgery according to the patient's wishes, having paid scant attention to her "true" sex (Mak 2005: 67). The tacit exceptions which doctors made to the strict clinical diagnosis to accommodate social realities were, over time, explicitly incorporated into their protocols.

These case histories reveal a shift from the nineteenth-century model of gonadal sex to the mid-twentieth-century model of determining a "best sex" based on an assessment of one's likely gender identity (Mak 2005: 68).[4] The interest in this concept may have surfaced because of surgical advancements and the many cases in which assigning a sex to an individual based on his or her gonads would have proven socially impossible. During this period, psychiatric interest in cases of "sexual inversion," which at the time referred to both same-sex desire and having a gender consciousness at odds with one's sex of rearing, was also growing (Mak 2005: 85–86). The diagnostic techniques, explanations, and categorizations developed in the study of sexual inversion and sex-gender consciousness began to influence medical interests, observations, and the treatment for hermaphroditism, resulting in a growing interest in the latter's gender consciousness (Mak 2005: 86).

In the early 1910s, the British surgeon William Blair Bell, recognizing the possible incongruity between an individual's gonads and his or her phenotype, challenged the gonadal definition of true sex. Bell understood that an individual's gonads did not determine the development of that individual's physical and psychological traits: he thus pointed out that none of the biological markers of sex, whether gonads or genitals, acted as its sole determinants. To address the conundrum, Bell proposed a commonsensical model of sex determinations: sex should be determined by the majority of the physical characteristics, with an emphasis on secondary sex characteristics (Dreger 1998a: 164). According to this model, if a woman came to see Bell and she looked "womanly," Bell declared her a woman, even if she had testes. Despite these innovations, Bell's model was, like those of his predecessors, aimed at eliminating physical ambiguity: as explained by his contemporaries Théodore Tuffier and André Lapointe, with whom he agreed, "The possession of a [single] sex is a necessity of our social order, for hermaphrodites as well as for normal subjects" (qtd. in Dreger 1998a: 161).

Increasing Awareness of Sexual Ambiguity

Hermaphroditism became an increasingly medical issue precisely at a period of heightened concern with and anxiety about the relationship among bodies, gender, and desire. As males and females came to be thought of as utterly distinct, hermaphrodites and homosexuals came to be understood as troubling these distinctions. Historically, heightened concerns about hermaphroditism and homosexuality coincided with and can be traced to nineteenth- and twentieth-century medical and evolutionary discourses on deviance (Katz 1995). The terms *homosexual* and *heterosexual* arose in the late nineteenth century—though with different meanings in their current usage—coinciding with an intense interest in hermaphroditism. In its earliest usage, *heterosexuality* actually referred to those who had sexual desire for both sexes, not the opposite sex only, and thus it was applied primarily of those who deviated from gender, erotic, and procreative norms, whereas homosexuals were those whose "mental state" was that of the opposite sex. Thus heterosexuality, what today we would call bisexuality, was associated with a condition called "physical hermaphroditism" (Katz 1995: 20). Homosexuality and hermaphroditism overlapped in part because the hermaphrodite posed a threat to the moral order as someone who could practice nonprocreative sex. This, not the gender of the individual's partner, made for the predominant concern at the turn of the century (Matta 2005).

Although some sought social and psychological explanations for phenomena such as effeminacy in men, tomboyishness in women, and same-sex desire, others proposed biological explanations. Based on the observation that the human embryo in its early physical development does not have an apparent sex, sexual differentiation, they suggested, may be only partial. This view provided an early theory of bisexuality in which all bodies have aspects of both male and female and thus masculine and feminine traits.

In the late nineteenth century and the early twentieth, the life sciences were focused on the interconnected problems of heredity, development, evolution and reproduction, which served as the basis for the emergence and realignment of the newly bounded disciplines of genetics, developmental embryology, and the reproductive sciences (Clarke 1998: 66–67). Researchers in a variety of disciplines sought to tackle the question of the inheritance of acquired characteristics. A series of discoveries between 1880 and 1910 suggested that chromosomes carried heredity information and that sex determination was tied to a so-called sex chromosome. These findings ushered in the notion of a chromosomal basis for sex.

Endocrinology in particular stirred considerable interest in the early twentieth century because it seemed to promise unambiguous medical explanations for sexual ambiguity. By 1910, endocrinologists had discovered that ovaries and testes secrete chemicals and thus are glands, not simply producers of gametes (reproductive cells).[5] As scientists began to isolate and identify various hormones, they located the source of sexual differentiation not in the gonads themselves but in their secretions. Investigators belied the secretions of the testes and ovaries to be sex-specific hormones that functioned as the chemical messengers of masculinity and femininity (Oudshoorn 1994). These hormones, they believed, shaped not only the physical body but also the human psyche and behavior (Hausman 1995: 23).

Early endocrinologists believed they could identify bodies as female or male simply by the hormones present in them: females had estrogen and males testosterone. It was not until 1921 that researchers found the same hormones in both males and females (Oudshoorn 1994). Frank R. Lilllie, a zoologist who conducted research on freemartin cows (sterile female calves whose genitalia appear to be masculinized), first suggested a hormonal basis for hermaphroditism in 1916 (Lillie 1916, 1917). Lillie felt that an investigation of the embryology of the intersex freemartin calf would not only uncover the explanation for this phenomenon but might also shed light on the normal processes of sexual differentiation (Carpel and Coveney 2004). He was the first to link the early stages of sexual development with the adult phenotype.

Freemartins occur when the affected female cow is one of a pair of twins, the other twin being male. Breeders were very familiar with the freemartin cow and knew that their infertility resulted from their atypical reproduction anatomy: female external genitalia and some degree of phenotypically male internal organs. Using the then prevalent gonadal criterion of true sex, many assumed that freemartins were insufficiently masculinized genetic males because of their more male typical internal organs. Lillie hypothesized that freemartins actually were genetic females that had been modified by their male twin during gestation; this masculinization resulted from male hormones traveling through placental blood from the male fetus into the female one.[6] Lillie's careful assessment of freemartin cases revealed that the morphological features of sexual development were not uniformly affected: freemartins' female traits were derived from their chromosomes, but their male traits came from the fetal environment (i.e., from the hormonal milieu).

This study affected a shift away from understanding the gonads as the sole locus of true sex. If the influence of hormones in utero could result in a substantial mix of sex attributes, then true sex must be regarded as more than simply the function of the gonads. The development of endocrinology also raised the possibility of using endocrine therapies to correct an individual's sexual ambiguity. Moreover, it undermined the concept of a true sex by demonstrating that the hormonal environment in utero could derail typical sexual development.

An alternative view was offered by Richard Goldschmidt, an unorthodox German geneticist and biologist who conducted research on the role of genetics in sex determination. While performing experiments on breeding gypsy moths, which are typically sexually dimorphic (possessing distinct primary sex characteristics), Goldshmidt found he could produce a sexual continuum in moths, which he called "intersex" (Dietrich 2003). In a 1917 article, he proposed a "time law of intersexuality," by which each individual contained the "factors" required to become both male and female. Intersexes were produced, he argued, according to the amount of time the individual spent developing as one sex before reaching a turning point at which they began to develop into the opposite sex (Dietrich 2003). Extending this theory to vertebrates, he proposed an intersexuality grounded in both genetic difference and hormonal action, what he called zygotic intersexuality and hormonal intersexuality. Intersexuality in invertebrates was grounded in genetic differences present in the zygote, whereas intersexuality in vertebrates included sexual differentiation later in life mediated by hormones and controlled by hormone-producing tissues (Dietrich 2003: 69). Not long thereafter clinicians adopted the term *intersex* and began extending it to humans.

Early Twentieth-Century Interventions

As biology revealed numerous conflicting and contradictory signifiers of sex, the clinicians of the 1920s and the 1940s expressed uncertainty and some anxiety about assigning sex to intersex individuals (Hausman 1995: 79). Treatment for intersexuality was thus highly contested. Even so, improved techniques of anesthesia and asepsis led to the increasing use of surgery to correct perceived genital anomalies. Hugh Hampton Young, one of the first to offer such surgical treatments in the United States, at times sought to reconcile an individual's biology with his or her identity as male or female.

Young, who became the head of genitourinary surgery as Johns Hopkins in 1897, began publishing on hermaphroditism in 1921. As early as 1915, Young began developing surgical techniques for genitourinary diseases at Johns Hopkins, and in 1916 he established the Brady Urological Institute within the medical school, making Johns Hopkins a primary center for cases of so-called indeterminate sex. His classic 1926 urology textbook, *Young's Practice of Urology*, coauthored with David M. Davis, was based on his experience treating the urological conditions of 12,500 patients and represented an early effort to provide comprehensive coverage of the burgeoning field of urology (Young and Davis 1926).

Early in his career, Young's interest in surgical challenges led him to develop surgical techniques to aid hermaphroditic patients. At the time, surgical intervention in hermaphroditism was uncommon. As a result, his expertise garnered referrals from physicians across the country of "interesting" or "unusual" cases (Kenan 1998). By 1937, when he published *Genital Abnormalities, Hermaphroditism, and Related Adrenal Diseases*, Young had seen an impressive number of patients (Young 1937). This book, the first American treatise on the types of human hermaphroditism, provides detailed case histories for fifty-five patients. It also includes more than five hundred step-by-step, intricate illustrations of the highly specialized surgical techniques Young developed for the treatment of hermaphroditism, many of which became the basis for future surgical techniques.[7] In the mid-1930s, for example, Young pioneered genital reconstructive procedures, including clitoral and vaginal plastic surgery on children. During the same period, before clinicians understood the pathophysiology of congenital adrenal hyperplasia (CAH) or employed steroid replacement therapy, Young devised a technique to slow the progressive virilization of female patients by surgically "debulking" the enlarged adrenal glands (Meldrum, Mathews, and Gearhart 2001).

Young's work revealed not only unusual surgical dexterity but also the complexities inherent in determining whether a person was male or female (Kenen 1998). He would often determine a patient's sex by assessing the gonadal tissue. However, Young considered the presence of ovaries or testes alone insufficient for sex determination: he implicitly required evidence of their normal hormonal function, which he determined by assessing nonphysical attributes such as personality traits and sexual desire (Kenan 1998). Without perhaps intending to, Young deployed flexible definitions of sex. Nevertheless, his therapeutic goal was to fit his patient into one of two sexes.

The practices of these early medical pioneers demonstrate the variability in the diagnosis and treatment of hermaphroditism in the nineteenth century and the early twentieth. During this period, medical understandings of what should count as true sex shifted. Moreover, the determination of an individual's true sex was based on each individual observer's interpretation of a wealth of somatic data. Different clinicians using the same classificatory scheme might very well arrived at an opposite determination of sex for the same individual.

One publication from this period was unique in its criticism of Kleb's gonadal model of classification. Alexander P. Cawadias, an English physician and the author of *Hermaphroditos: The Human Intersex*, viewed intersex as a constitutional disturbance involving multiple systems of the body. He argued against Kleb's category of the true hermaphrodite, which he claimed was "repeated parrot-like in all our textbooks," calling it the "non-existent third sex." He argued vigorously for seeing intersexuality as an exaggeration of a normal process: "Intersexuality is a normal phenomenon. There is no absolute male nor absolute female. Every male possesses latent female features, and vice versa. Thus the so-called 'normal' male and female represent the lowest degree of intersexuality, which is thus a physiological phenomenon" (Cawadias 1943: 3, 5). Although this characterization of all humans as intersex represented his attempt to complicate our understanding of sex, his views did not gain any traction. It would be another ten years before John Money would attempt to bring this disparate knowledge into a more nuanced and systematic understanding of gender development.

While theoretically gonadal sex was understood to indicate true sex well into the 1930s and even the 1940s, pragmatically, clinicians often turned to the sex of rearing when determining sex for adolescent or adult patients (Redick 2004; Mak 2005). Concerns centered not around whether intersex individuals should be assigned as male or female, but precisely how clinicians should arrive at the decision. By the early 1940s, the strict reliance on gonadal sex determination provoked anxiety: an intersex individual's direction of libido often conflicted with the gonadal sex (Redick 2004). Although clinicians were concerned with an individual's libido early as the 1920s, it was regarded predominantly as an indicator of gonadal function. (The concern that sex-assignment decisions might result in individuals' feeling desire for members of their own assigned sex—might, in essence, create homosexuals—emerged only in the 1940s, coinciding with a more widespread societal concern.)

Later refinements in medical technology allowed for more systematic ways of understanding and categorizing bodies. In 1948 Murray Barr discovered a microscopic chromatin mass (now known as the Barr body), which is present in female but not in male mammalian cells, allowing for an investigation of the "genetic sex" of individuals with ambiguous external genitalia. Tissues from so-called true hermaphrodites and pseudohermaphrodites were examined and gave reliable results; but these results, while clinically useful, did not necessarily simplify sex determination. By the 1950s, scientists had developed reliable tests that used chromatins in skin samples to determine chromosomal sex (Moore, Graham, and Barr 1953; Moore and Barr 1955).[8]

By the late 1940s, physicians began to revisit the role of psychological factors in making decisions about surgery for intersex patients (Ingersoll and Finesinger 1947), and psychological sex began to compete with and even displace the gonads as the indicator of true sex (Redick 2004). Still, no unifying theory, principles, or method existed for the gender assignment for intersex persons; treatment practices could vary widely, with even the most seasoned practitioners expressing uncertainty about how to reconcile biology and psychosocial outlook. Advances in science and medicine complicated rather than clarified gender. The midcentury saw not only vigorous scientific debate over the extent to which hormonal or genetic processes determined sex attributes and the extent to which the psyche should be determined sex attributes and the extent to which the psyche should be considered in treatment decisions; but clinical specialists, primarily urologists and endocrinologists, also found themselves at odds over how best to treat intersex patients. Urologists were inclined to resolve contractions of sex such as ambiguous genitalia through corrective surgery. Endocrinologists, by contrast, tried to apply theories of hormone secretions to treat intersexuality with the administrations of hormones (Redick 2004: 47). Endocrinologists' understandings of hormonal complexity undermined the notion of discrete binary sex, but this revelation did not undermine their belief "that two sexes existed, or that every person must belong to one of the two sexes" (Redick 2004: 47). Now that greater degrees of medical intervention were possible, the central issue became how best to intervene. These disagreements foreshadowed modern debates over medical treatment for intersex diagnoses as history takes us from ideas of true sex to those of one sex to, finally, those of best sex.

Despite several centuries of speculation and investigation, then, no coherent or unifying theory has emerged for understanding and dealing with intersexuality in the West, either socially or medically. The following chapter looks at the most ambitious attempt of the twentieth century to establish such a model, one that served as the basis for the treatment of intersexuality for the better part of fifty years and is still influential today.

Endnotes

1. Far from being natural or inherent, concepts of the psychologically or physiologically normal or abnormal have been crafted since the mid-1800s, when the British scientist Francis Galton put forth his eugenic principles and the term *normal*, which had previously meant "perpendicular," began to be applied widely to the human body and psyche.

2. Londa Schiebinger observes that sixteenth-century anatomists were interested in similarities rather than differences between males and females: Vesalius did not differentiate the nonreproductive parts of the male and female body. In his view, all other organs were interchangeable between the sexes (Shiebinger 1989: 184).

3. Throughout this section, my account of nineteenth-century understandings of hermaphroditism is drawn from Dreger 1998a.

4. Mak's revelation that European clinicians at the turn of the century began to consider the "sex-gender consciousness" or a subjective sense of oneself as male or female stands in contrast to arguments by Dreger (1998a) and Hausman (1995) that medical opinion about objective sex dominated until the 1920s.

5. The term *hormone* was coined in 1905. Estrin was isolated in 1923, progesterone in 1929, and testosterone in 1935 (Oudshoorn 1994).

6. It was still unclear why male embryos subverted the development of the female twin, but females did not affect their male twin. To explain this, "Lillie pointed to evidence for the earlier appearance of steroidogenic cells in males, and concluded that differentiation of males occurs early enough to influence female development whereas development of females occurs too late to affect development of the male co-twin. He also made the important suggestion that the extent of transformation of the female twin depended on the stage at which extensive anastomoses exposed her to circulating male hormones" (Capel and Coveney 2004: 854–55).

7. William Didusch, a medical illustrator trained at Johns Hopkins, made the drawings for this book while observing Young performing surgeries in the operating theater.

8. Around 1960, scientists determined that the Y chromosome was the determinant rather than the marker of maleness (Kevles 1986: 241–45). Thus chromosomes governed sex determination, and hormones dictated sex differentiation.

Michael Kimmel is a SUNY Distinguished Professor of Sociology and Gender Studies at Stony Brook University where he founded the Center for the Study of Men and Masculinities.

"Bros Before Hos": The Guy Code
Michael Kimmel

Whenever I ask young women what they think it means to be a woman, they look at me puzzled, and say, basically, "Whatever I want." "It doesn't mean anything at all to me," says Nicole, a junior at Colby College in Maine. "I can be Mia Hamm, I can be Britney Spears, I can be Madame Curie or Madonna. Nobody can tell me what it means to be a woman anymore."

For men, the question is still meaningful—and powerful. In countless workshops on college campuses and in high-school assemblies, I've asked young men what it means to be a man. I've asked guys from every state in the nation, as well as about fifteen other countries, what sorts of phrases and words come to mind when they hear someone say, "Be a man!"[1]

The responses are rather predictable. The first thing someone usually says is "Don't cry," then other similar phrases and ideas—never show your feelings, never ask for directions, never give up, never give in, be strong, be aggressive, show no fear, show no mercy, get rich, get even, get laid, win—follow easily after that.

Here's what guys say, summarized into a set of current epigrams. Think of it as a "Real Guy's Top Ten List."

1. "Boys Don't Cry"

2. "It's Better to Be Mad Than Sad"

3. "Don't Get Mad—Get Even"

4. "Take It Like a Man"

5. "He Who Has the Most Toys When He Dies, Wins"

6. "Just Do It," or "Ride or Die"

7. "Size Matters"

8. "I Don't Stop to Ask for Directions"

9. "Nice Guys Finish Last"

10. "It's All Good"

The unifying emotional subtext of all these aphorisms involves never showing emotions or admitting to weakness. The face you must show to the world insists that everything is going just fine, that everything is under control, that there's nothing to be concerned about (a contemporary version of Alfred E. Neuman of

---

1. This workshop idea was developed by Paul Kivel of the Oakland Men's Project. I am grateful to Paul for demonstrating it to my classes. [All notes are Kimmel's.]

MAD magazine's "What, me worry?"). Winning is crucial, especially when the victory is over other men who have less amazing or smaller toys. Kindness is not an option, nor is compassion. Those sentiments are taboo.

This is "The Guy Code," the collection of attitudes, values, and traits that together composes what it means to be a man. These are the rules that govern behavior in Guyland, the criteria that will be used to evaluate whether any particular guy measures up. The Guy Code revisits what psychologist William Pollack called "the boy code" in his bestselling book *Real Boys*[2]—just a couple of years older and with a lot more at stake. And just as Pollack and others have explored the dynamics of boyhood so well, we now need to extend the reach of that analysis to include late adolescence and young adulthood.

In 1976, social psychologist Robert Brannon summarized the four basic rules of masculinity:[3]

1. "No Sissy Stuff!" Being a man means not being a sissy, not being perceived as weak, effeminate, or gay. Masculinity is the relentless repudiation of the feminine.

2. "Be a Big Wheel." This rule refers to the centrality of success and power in the definition of masculinity. Masculinity is measured more by wealth, power, and status than by any particular body part.

3. "Be a Sturdy Oak." What makes a man is that he is reliable in a crisis. And what makes him so reliable in a crisis is not that he is able to respond fully and appropriately to the situation at hand, but rather that he resembles an inanimate object. A rock, a pillar, a species of tree.

4. "Give 'em Hell." Exude an aura of daring and aggression. Live life out on the edge. Take risks. Go for it. Pay no attention to what others think.

Amazingly, these four rules have changed very little among successive generations of high-school and college-age men. James O'Neil, a developmental psychologist at the University of Connecticut, and Joseph Pleck, a social psychologist at the University of Illinois, have each been conducting studies of this normative definition of masculinity for decades. "One of the most surprising findings," O'Neil told me, "is how little these rules have changed."

---

2. See William Pollack, *Real Boys: Rescuing Our Sons from the Myths of Boyhood* (New York: Henry Holt, 1998).

3. See Robert Brannon and Deborah David, "Introduction" to *The Forty-Nine Per Cent Majority* (Reading, MA: Addison-Wesley, 1976).

Masculinity: A Legend in Your Own Mind. THINK AGAIN (S.A. Bachman + David John Attyah).

Being a Man Among Men

Where do young men get these ideas? "Oh, definitely, my dad," says Mike, a twenty-year-old sophomore at Wake Forest. "He was always riding my ass, telling me I had to be tough and strong to make it in this world."

"My older brothers were always on my case," says Drew, a twenty-four-year-old University of Massachusetts grad. "They were like, always ragging on me, calling me a pussy, if I didn't want to play football or wrestle. If I just wanted to hang out and like play my Xbox, they were constantly in my face."

"It was subtle, sometimes," says Warren, a twenty-one-year-old at Towson, "and other times really out front. In school, it was the male teachers, saying stuff about how explorers or scientists were so courageous and braving the elements and all that. Then, other times, it was phys-ed class, and everyone was all over everyone else talking about 'He's so gay' and 'He's a wuss.'"

"The first thing I think of is my coach," says Don, a twenty-six-year-old former football player at Lehigh. "Any fatigue, any weakness, any sign that being hit actually hurt and he was like 'Waah! [fake crying] Widdle Donny got a boo boo. Should we kiss it guys?' He'd completely humiliate us for showing anything but complete toughness. I'm sure he thought he was building up our strength and ability to play, but it wore me out trying to pretend all the time, to suck it up and just take it."

The response was consistent: Guys hear the voices of the men in their lives—fathers, coaches, brothers, grandfathers, uncles, priests—to inform their ideas of masculinity.

This is no longer surprising to me. One of the more startling things I found when I researched the history of the idea of masculinity in America for a previous book was that men subscribe to these ideals not because they want to impress women, let alone any inner drive or desire to test themselves against some abstract standards. They do it because they want to be positively evaluated by other men. American men want to be a "man among men," an Arnold Schwarzenegger-like "man's man," not a Fabio-like "ladies' man." Masculinity is largely a "homo social" experience: performed for, and judged by, other men.

Noted playwright David Mamet explains why women don't even enter the mix. "Women have, in men's minds, such a low place on the social ladder of this country that it's useless to define yourself in terms of a woman. What men need is men's approval." While women often become a kind of currency by which men negotiate their status with other men, women are for possessing, not for emulating.

The Gender Police

Other guys constantly watch how well we perform. Our peers are a kind of "gender police," always waiting for us to screw up so they can give us a ticket for crossing the well-drawn boundaries of manhood. As young men, we become relentless cowboys, riding the fences, checking the boundary line between masculinity and femininity, making sure that nothing slips over. The possibilities of being unmasked are everywhere. Even the most seemingly insignificant misstep can pose a threat or activate that haunting terror that we will be found out.

On the day the students in my class "Sociology of Masculinity" were scheduled to discuss homophobia, one student provided an honest and revealing anecdote. Noting that it was a beautiful day, the first day of spring after a particularly brutal Northeast winter, he decided to wear shorts to class. "I had this really nice pair of new Madras shorts," he recounted. "But then I thought to myself, these shorts have lavender and pink in them. Today's class topic is homophobia. Maybe today is not the best day to wear these shorts." Nods all around.

Our efforts to maintain a manly front cover everything we do. What we wear. How we talk. How we walk. What we eat (like the recent flap over "manwiches"— those artery-clogging massive burgers, dripping with extras). Every mannerism, every movement contains a coded gender language. What happens if you refuse or resist? What happens if you step outside the definition of masculinity? Consider the words that would be used to describe you. In workshops it generally takes less than a minute to get a list of about twenty terms that are at the tip of everyone's tongues: wimp, faggot, dork, pussy, loser, wuss, nerd, queer, homo, girl, gay, skirt, Mama's boy, pussy-whipped. This list is so effortlessly generated, so consistent, that it composes a national well from which to draw epithets and put-downs.

Ask any teenager in America what is the most common put-down in middle school or high school? The answer: "That's so gay." It's said about anything and everything—their clothes, their books, the music or TV shows they like, the sports figures they admire. "That's so gay" has become a free-floating put-down, meaning bad, dumb, stupid, wrong. It's the generic bad thing.

Listen to one of America's most observant analysts of masculinity, Eminem. Asked in an MTV interview in 2001 why he constantly used "faggot" in every one of his raps to put down other guys, Eminem told the interviewer, Kurt Loder,

> The lowest degrading thing you can say to a man when you're battling him is to call him a faggot and try to take away his manhood. Call him a sissy, call him a punk. "Faggot" to me doesn't necessarily mean gay people. "Faggot" to me just means taking away your manhood.[4]

But does it mean homosexuality? Does it really suggest that you suspect the object of the epithet might actually be attracted to another guy? Think, for example, of how you would answer this question: If you see a man walking down the street, or meet him at a party, how do you "know" if he is homosexual? (Assume that he is not wearing a T-shirt with a big pink triangle on it, and that he's not already holding hands with another man.)

When I ask this question in classes or workshops, respondents invariably provide a standard list of stereotypically effeminate behaviors. He walks a certain way, talks a certain way, acts a certain way. He's well dressed, sensitive, and emotionally expressive. He has certain tastes in art and music—indeed, he has *any* taste in art and music! Men tend to focus on the physical attributes, women on the emotional. Women say they "suspect" a man might be gay if he's interested in what she's talking about, knows something about what she's talking about, or is sensitive and a good listener. One recently said, "I suspect he might be gay if he's looking at my eyes, and not down my blouse." Another said she suspects

---

4. Richard Kim, "A Bad Rap?" in *The Nation*, March 5, 2001, p. 5.

he might be gay if he shows no sexual interest in her, if he doesn't immediately come on to her.

Once I've established what makes a guy "suspect," I ask the men in the room if any of them would want to be thought of as gay. Rarely does a hand go up—despite the fact that this list of attributes is actually far preferable to the restrictive one that stands in the "Be a Man" box. So, what do straight men do to make sure that no one gets the wrong idea about them?

Everything that is perceived as gay goes into what we might call the Negative Playbook of Guyland. Avoid everything in it and you'll be all right. Just make sure that you walk, talk, and act in a different way from the gay stereotype; dress terribly; show no taste in art or music; show no emotions at all. Never listen to a thing a woman is saying, but express immediate and unquenchable sexual interest. Presto, you're a real man, back in the "Be a Man" box. Homophobia—the fear that people might *misperceive* you as gay—is the animating fear of American guys' masculinity. It's what lies underneath the crazy risk-taking behaviors practiced by boys of all ages, what drives the fear that other guys will see you as weak, unmanly, frightened. The single cardinal rule of manhood, the one from which all the other characteristics—wealth, power, status, strength, physicality—are derived is to offer constant proof that you are not gay.

Homophobia is even deeper than this. It's the fear *of* other men—that other men will perceive you as a failure, as a fraud. It's a fear that others will see you as weak, unmanly, frightened. This is how John Steinbeck put it in his novel *Of Mice and Men*:

> "Funny thing," [Curley's wife] said. "If I catch any one man, and he's alone, I get along fine with him. But just let two of the guys get together an' you won't talk. Jus' nothin' but mad." She dropped her fingers and put her hands on her hips. "You're all scared of each other, that's what. Ever'one of you's scared the rest is goin' to get something on you."[5]

In that sense, homosexuality becomes a kind of shorthand for "unmanliness"—and the homophobia that defines and animates the daily conversations of Guyland is at least as much about masculinity as it is about sexuality.

But what would happen to a young man if he were to refuse such limiting parameters on who he is and how he's permitted to act? "It's not like I want to stay in that box," says Jeff, a first-year Cornell student at my workshop. "But as soon as you step outside it, even for a second, all the other guys are like, 'What are you, dude, a fag?' It's not very safe out there on your own. I suppose as I get older, I'll get more secure, and feel like I couldn't care less what other guys say. But now, in my fraternity, on this campus, man, I'd lose everything."

The consistency of responses is as arresting as the list is disturbing: "I would lose my friends." "Get beat up." "I'd be ostracized." "Lose my self-esteem." Some

---

5. John Steinbeck, *Of Mice and Men* (New York: Scribner's, 1937), p. 57.

say they'd take drugs or drink. Become withdrawn, sullen, a loner, depressed. "Kill myself," says one guy. "Kill them," responds another. Everyone laughs, nervously. Some say they'd get mad. And some say they'd get even. "I dunno," replied Mike, a sophomore at Portland State University. "I'd probably pull a Columbine. I'd show them that they couldn't get away with calling me that shit."

Guys know that they risk everything—their friendships, their sense of self, maybe even their lives—if they fail to conform. Since the stakes are so enormous, young men take huge chances to prove their manhood, exposing themselves to health risks, workplace hazards, and stress-related illnesses. Here's a revealing factoid. Men ages nineteen to twenty-nine are three times less likely to wear seat belts than women the same age. Before they turn nineteen though, young men are actually *more* likely to wear seat belts. It's as if they suddenly get the idea that as long as they're driving the car, they're completely in control, and therefore safe.[6] Ninety percent of all driving offenses, excluding parking violations, are committed by men, and 93 percent of road ragers are male.[7] Safety is emasculating! So they drink too much, drive too fast, and play chicken in a multitude of dangerous venues.

The comments above provide a telling riposte to all those theories of biology that claim that this definition of masculinity is "hard-wired," the result of millennia of evolutionary adaptation or the behavioral response to waves of aggression-producing testosterone, and therefore inevitable. What these theories fail to account for is the way that masculinity is coerced and policed relentlessly by other guys. If it were biological, it would be as natural as breathing or blinking. In truth, the Guy Code fits as comfortably as a straightjacket.

Boys' Psychological Development: Where the Guy Code Begins

Masculinity is a constant test—always up for grabs, always needing to be proved. And the testing starts early. Recently, I was speaking with a young black mother, a social worker, who was concerned about a conversation she had had with her husband a few nights earlier. It seems that her husband had taken their son to the barber, which, she explained to me, is a central social institution in the African American community. As the barber prepared the boy's hair for treatment, using, apparently some heat and some painful burning chemicals, the boy began to cry. The barber turned to the boy's father and pronounced, "This boy is a wimp!" He went on, "This boy has been spending too much time with his mama! Man, you need to put your foot down. You have got to get this boy away from his mother!"

That evening the father came home, visibly shaken by the episode, and announced to his wife that from that moment on the boy would not be spending

---

6. Eric Nagourney, "Young Men with No Attachments" in *New York Times*, January 4, 2005.

7. Mary Blume, "The Feminist Future of the Automobile" in *International Herald Tribune*, October 8, 2004, p. 11.

as much time with her, but instead would do more sports and other activities with him, "to make sure he doesn't become a sissy."

After telling me this story, the mother asked what I thought she should do. "Gee," I said, "I understand the pressures that dads feel to 'toughen up' their sons. But how old is your boy, anyway?"

"Three and a half," she said.

I tried to remind her, of course, that crying is the natural human response to pain, and that her son was behaving appropriately. But her story reminded me of how early this pressure starts to affect an emotionally impervious manly stoicism.

Ever since Freud, we've believed that the key to boys' development is separation, that the boy must switch his identification from mother to father in order to "become" a man. He achieves his masculinity by repudiation, dissociation, and then identification. It is a perilous path, but a necessary one, even though there is nothing inevitable about it—and nothing biological either. Throw in an overdominant mother, or an absent father, and we start worrying that the boy will not succeed in his masculine quest.

Boys learn that their connection to mother will emasculate them, turn them into Mama's Boys. And so they learn to act *as if* they have made that leap by pushing away from their mothers. Along the way they suppress all the feelings they associate with the maternal—compassion, nurturance, vulnerability, dependency. This suppression and repudiation is the origin of the Boy Code. It's what turns those happy, energetic, playful, and emotionally expressive five-year-olds into sullen, withdrawn, and despondent nine-year-olds. In the recent spate of bestselling books about boys' development, psychologists like William Pollack, James Garbarino, Michael Thompson, Dan Kindlon, and others, argue that from an early age boys are taught to refrain from crying, to suppress their emotions, never to display vulnerability. As a result, boys feel effeminate not only if they *express* their emotions, but even if they *feel* them. In their bestseller, *Raising Cain*, Kindlon and Thompson describe a "culture of cruelty" in which peers force other boys to deny their emotional needs and disguise their feelings. It's no wonder that so many boys end up feeling emotionally isolated.

These books about boys map the inner despair that comes from such emotional numbness and fear of vulnerability. Pollack calls it the "mask of masculinity," the fake front of impervious, unemotional independence, a swaggering posture that boys believe will help them to present a stoic front. "Ruffled in a manly pose," the great Irish poet William Butler Yeats put it in his poem "Coole Park" (1929), "For all his timid heart."

The ruffling starts often by age four or five, when he enters kindergarten, and it gets a second jolt when he hits adolescence. Think of the messages boys get: Stand on your own two feet! Don't cry! Don't be a sissy! As one boy in Pollack's book summarizes it: "Shut up and take it, or you'll be sorry." When I asked my nine-year-old son, Zachary, what he thought of when I said "be a man" he said that one of his friends said something about "taking it like a man. So," he explained, "I think it means acting tougher than you actually are."

Recently a colleague told me about a problem he was having. It seems his seven-year-old son, James, was being bullied by another boy on his way home from school. His wife, the boy's mother, strategized with her son about how to handle such situations in the future. She suggested he find an alternate route home, tell a teacher, or perhaps even tell the boy's parents. And she offered the standard "use your words, not your fists" conflict-reducer. "How can I get my wife to stop treating James like a baby?" my colleague asked. "How will he ever learn to stand up for himself if she turns him into a wimp?"

The Boy Code leaves boys disconnected from a wide range of emotions and prohibited from sharing those feelings with others. As they grow older, they feel disconnected from adults, as well, unable to experience the guidance towards maturity that adults can bring. When they turn to anger and violence it is because these, they believe, perhaps rightly, are the only acceptable forms of emotional expression allowed them. Just as the Boy Code shuts boys down, the Guy Code reinforces those messages, suppressing what was left of boyhood exuberance and turning it into sullen indifference.

No wonder boys are more prone to depression, suicidal behavior, and various other forms of out-of-control or out-of-touch behaviors than girls are. No wonder boys drop out of school and are diagnosed as emotionally disturbed four times more often as girls, get into fights twice as often, and are six times more likely than girls to be diagnosed with Attention Deficit and Hyperactivity Disorder (ADHD).[8]

---

8. See, for example, Brad Knickerbocker, "Young and Male in America: It's Hard Being a Boy" in *Christian Science Monitor*, April 29, 1999.

Ariel Levy is a writer for *The New Yorker* and author of *Female Chauvinist Pigs: Women and the Rise of Raunch Culture.*

Either/Or: Sports, Sex, and the Case of Caster Semenya
Ariel Levy

When people in South Africa say "Limpopo," they mean the middle of no-where. They are referring to the northernmost province of the country, along the border with Botswana, Zimbabwe, and Mozambique, where few people have cars or running water or opportunities for greatness. The members of the Moletjie Athletics Club, who live throughout the area in villages of small brick houses and mud-and-dung huts, have high hopes nonetheless.

One day in late September, twenty teen-age athletes gathered for practice on a dirt road in front of Rametlwana Lower Primary School, after walking half an hour through yellow cornfields from their homes, to meet their coach, Jeremiah Mokaba. The school's track is not graded, and donkeys and goats kept walking across it to graze on the new grass that was sprouting as the South African winter gave way to spring. "During the rainy season, we can't train," said Mokaba, a short man wearing a brown corduroy jacket with a golden Zion Christian Church pin on the lapel. "We have nowhere to go inside."

For cross-country, Mokaba and his co-coach, Phineas Sako, train their run-ners in the miles of bush that spread out behind the track, toward the mountains in the distance. The land is webbed with brambles, and the thorns are a serious problem for the athletes, who train barefoot. "They run on loose stones, scrap-ing them, making a wound, making a scar," Sako, a tall, bald man with rheumy eyes and a big gap between his two front teeth, said. "We can't stop and say we don't have running shoes, because we don't have money. The parents don't have money. So what must we do? We just go on."

The athletes and their coaches apologized for not having a clubhouse in which to serve tea. They didn't like talking out in the wind and the dust. There was music playing down the road at a brick-front bar, and chickens squawking in people's front yards, where they are kept in enclosures made out of tree branches. "The most disadvantaged rural area," Sako said, laughing a little and stretching his arms out wide. "That is where you are."

The fastest runner in the club now is a seventeen-year-old named Andrew who recently became the district champion in the fifteen-hundred-metre event. The average monthly income for black Africans in Limpopo—more than ninety-seven per cent of the local population—is less than a thousand rand per month, roughly a hundred and thirty-five dollars. (For white residents, who make up two per cent of the population, it is more than four times that amount.) "I think I will go to the Olympics," Andrew said, with conviction.

Joyce, a tiny girl in a pink sweater who is eighteen but looked much younger, was similarly optimistic. "I want to be the world champion," she said, her voice so soft it was almost a whisper. "I *will* be the world champion. I want to participate in athletics and have a scholarship. Caster is making me proud. She won. She put our club on the map."

Caster Semenya, the current world champion in the eight hundred metres, was a member of the Moletjie Athletics Club until a year ago. She was born in Ga-Masehlong, a village about fifteen miles from the track, and she was, Coach Sako said, "a natural." Even before Semenya left Limpopo for college, in Pretoria, she had won a gold medal in her event at the 2008 Commonwealth Youth Games, in Pune, India, with a time of 2:04, eleven seconds behind the senior world record set by the Czech runner Jarmila Kratochvílová in 1983. "I used to tell Caster that she must try her level best," Sako said. "By performing the best, maybe good guys with big stomachs full of money will see her and then help her with schooling and the likes. That is the motivation." He added, "And she always tried her level best." Semenya won another gold medal in July, in Mauritius, at the African Junior Athletics Championships, lowering her time by a remarkable seven and a half seconds, to come in at 1:56.72. This beat the South African record for that event, held by Zola Budd, and qualified Semenya for her first senior competition, the 2009 World Championships, in Berlin.

Semenya won the eight-hundred-metre title by nearly two and a half seconds, finishing in 1:55.45. After the first lap of the race, she cruised past her competitors like a machine. She has a powerful stride and remarkable efficiency of movement: in footage of the World Championships, you can see the other runners thrashing behind her, but her trunk stays still, even as she is pumping her muscle-bound arms up and down. Her win looks effortless, inevitable. "Even when we were training, I used to pair her with the males," Sako told me. "I feel like she was too powerful for ladies." It was a stunning victory for Semenya, for the Moletjie Athletics Club, and for South Africa.

After the race, Semenya told reporters, "Oh, man, I don't know what to say. It's pretty good to win a gold medal and bring it home." (Her voice is surprising. As Semenya's father, Jacob, has put it, "If you speak to her on the telephone, you might mistake her for a man.") She continued, "I didn't know I could win that race, but for the first time in my life the experience, the World Championships…" She broke into a grin. "I couldn't believe it, man."

Since the day Semenya broke Zola Budd's record, people in South Africa had been talking about her. Semenya does not look like most female athletes. People questioned whether she was really a woman. Some even e-mailed the International Association of Athletics Federations, the worldwide governing body for track and field, with their doubts. Before Semenya was awarded her gold medal in Berlin, on August 20th, a reporter asked about a story that had been circulating at the Championships, that Semenya's sex was unclear and that she had been required to undergo gender-verification testing before the race. The I.A.A.F. confirmed the rumor, arguably in violation of its confidentiality policies. ("The choice is that you lie, which we don't like to do," Nick Davies, the communications director, told the *New York Times*.) The story ripped around the world. Several of Semenya's competitors in the race were incensed that she had been allowed to participate. "These kind of people should not run with us," Elisa Cusma, of Italy, who came in sixth, said. "For me, she is not a woman. She is a man."

"Just look at her," Mariya Savinova, of Russia, who finished fifth, said.

Semenya is breathtakingly butch. Her torso is like the chest plate on a suit of armor. She has a strong jawline, and a build that slides straight from her ribs to her hips. "What I knew is that wherever we go, whenever she made her first appearance, people were somehow gossiping, saying, 'No, no, she is not a girl,'" Phineas Sako said, rubbing the gray stubble on his chin. "'It looks like a boy'—that's the right words—they used to say, 'It looks like a boy.' Some even asked me as a coach, and I would confirm: it's a girl. At times, she'd get upset. But, eventually, she was just used to such things." Semenya became accustomed to visiting the bathroom with a member of a competing team so that they could look at her private parts and then get on with the race. "They are doubting me," she would explain to her coaches, as she headed off the field toward the lavatory.

South Africa has eleven official languages. The majority of people in Limpopo speak the Pedi language, and many also speak English and Afrikaans, which schoolchildren were required to learn under apartheid. Sako's English was fluent but rough, and he frequently referred to Semenya as "he." "Caster was very free when he is in the male company," Sako said. "I remember one day I asked her, 'Why are you always in the company of men?' He said, 'No, man, I don't have something to say to girls, they talks nonsense. They are always out of order.'"

On September 11th, Australia's *Daily Telegraph*, a tabloid owned by Rupert Murdoch, reported that Semenya's test results had been leaked, and that they showed that Semenya, though she was brought up as a girl and had external female genitalia, did not have ovaries or a uterus. Semenya was born with undescended testes, the report said, which provided her with three times the amount of testosterone present in an average female—and so a potential advantage over competitors.

"I know what Caster has got," her aunt Johanna Lamola told the *Times*. "I've changed her nappies." Semenya's father said, "I don't even know how they do this gender testing. I don't know what a chromosome is. This is all very painful for us—we live by simple rules." Semenya did not cheat. She has not been evasive. It is very common for élite female athletes, who exert themselves to their physical limits as a matter of course, not to menstruate. There's no reason that Semenya or her coaches would have been alarmed if she were amenorrheic. "Maybe it's because we come from a disadvantaged area," Jeremiah Mokaba said. "They couldn't believe in us."

The I.A.A.F. has yet to inform Semenya whether she can continue running in international female competitions. I asked Sako what he thought would happen. "Caster," he said firmly, "will remain Caster."

Sports have played an important role in modern South African history. A crucial part of the African National Congress's strategy to end apartheid during "the struggle," as everyone calls it, was to secure international condemnation of South Africa's government through boycotts and the banning of South African athletes from all international competitions. Conversely, during the 1995 rugby World Cup Nelson Mandela managed to unite the entire country behind the Springboks, the South African team, which had been a hated symbol of Afrikaner white supremacism. It was pivotal to his success in avoiding civil war and in establishing a new sense of national solidarity. Sports are "more powerful than governments in breaking down racial barriers," Mandela said. "Sport has the power to change the world. It has the power to inspire, the power to unite people that little else has." Sometimes it can unite people against other people. The South African Minister of Sport and Recreation, Makhenkesi Stofile, has warned, "If the I.A.A.F. expels or excludes Semenya from competition or withdraws the medal, I think it would be the Third World War."

In August, when Semenya returned from Germany, thousands of cheering supporters waited to welcome her at O. R. Tambo Airport, outside Johannesburg. President Jacob Zuma met with her to offer his congratulations, as did Nelson Mandela.

Phat Joe, one of the most famous radio d.j.s in the country, was fired by Kaya FM for suggesting on his show that Semenya might have testicles. Lolly Jackson, the owner of a chain of strip clubs called Teazers, put up an enormous billboard in a suburb of Johannesburg picturing a naked woman lying flat on her back above the words "No Need for Gender Testing!" Jackson subsequently claimed that the billboard had nothing to do with Semenya, but he sent her lawyers, at the firm of Dewey & LeBoeuf, a check for twenty thousand rand.

"I think it is the responsibility of South Africa to rally behind this child and tell the rest of the world she remains the hero she is and no one will take that away from her," Winnie Madikizela-Mandela, an ex-wife of Mandela's and a recently elected Member of Parliament, was quoted as saying in the London *Telegraph*. "There is nothing wrong with being a hermaphrodite. It is God's creation. She is God's child." By contrast, the African National Congress Youth League, a division of the African National Congress, issued a statement saying that it "will never accept the categorization of Caster Semenya as a hermaphrodite, because in South Africa and the entire world of sanity, such does not exist."

The African National Congress is part of the Tripartite Alliance, with the South African Communist Party and the Congress of South African Trade Unions. This year's meeting of the Congress happened to coincide with Heritage Day, and many of the hundreds of delegates who assembled at a conference center outside Johannesburg were in traditional tribal dress. Winnie Madikizela-Mandela wore a Xhosa turban and cape. A representative from the police and prison workers' union, wearing nothing but a loincloth made from springbok pelts and a Swazi necklace of red pompoms, mingled with fellow union members at the back of an enormous auditorium, where delegates were debating the items of the day: whether to support the legalization of prostitution in time for the soccer World Cup, which South Africa will host in 2010, and whether to pass a resolution in support of Caster Semenya.

The sessions are meant to evoke the African tradition of villagers gathering to share opinions on local matters. Everyone gets to speak, though men speak much more than women. The prostitution question was examined from every angle: some were concerned about "the downgrading of our women by capitalism"; others felt that every source of income was desperately needed and that sex workers, like everybody else, deserved the protection of a union. After several hours, the delegates decided that what was needed was more discussion.

The South African Minister of Women, Children, and Persons with Disabilities, Noluthando Mayende-Sibiya, went to the lectern dressed in red Xhosa regalia to speak about "the issue of our young star, Caster Semenya." Everyone applauded. "She is our own," Mayende-Sibiya said. "She comes from the working class." The crowd blew horns in support, and some people ululated. "You cannot be silent! The human rights of Caster have been violated," she concluded. The resolution passed with unusual alacrity.

South Africans have been appalled by the idea of a person who thinks she is one thing suddenly being told that she is something else. The classification and reclassification of human beings has a haunted history in this country. Starting with the Population Registration Act of 1950, teams of white people were engaged as census-takers. They usually had no training, but they had the power to decide a person's race, and race determined where and with whom you could live, whether you could get a decent education, whether you had political representation, whether you were even free to walk in certain areas at certain hours. The categories were fickle. In 1985, according to the census, more than a thousand people somehow changed race: nineteen whites turned Colored (as South Africans call people of mixed heritage); seven hundred and two Coloreds turned white, fifty Indians turned Colored, eleven Colored turned Chinese, and so on. (No blacks turned white, or vice versa.)

Taxonomy is an acutely sensitive subject, and its history is probably one of the reasons that South Africans—particularly black South Africans—have rallied behind their runner with such fervor. The government has decreed that Semenya can continue running with women in her own country, regardless of what the I.A.A.F. decides.

South Africans have compared the worldwide fascination with Semenya's gender to the dubious fame of another South African woman whose body captivated Europeans: Saartjie Baartman, the Hottentot Venus. Baartman, an orphan born on the rural Eastern Cape, was the servant of Dutch farmers near Cape Town. In 1810, they sent her to Europe to be exhibited in front of painters, naturalists, and oglers, who were fascinated by her unusually large buttocks and had heard rumors of her long labia. She supposedly became a prostitute and an alcoholic, and she died in France in her mid-twenties. Until 1974, her skeleton and preserved genitals were displayed at the Musée de l'Homme, in Paris. Many South Africans feel that white foreigners are yet again scrutinizing a black female body as though it did not contain a human being.

Mayende-Sibiya has asked that the United Nations get involved in Semenya's case, and I asked her what she thought it could do. "I would like to see it getting more information from the I.A.A.F.," she said over lunch at the Congress. "We wrote to the I.A.A.F. to ask a number of questions, including what precedents informed the action that it took on Caster. Why pick up on her? What were the reasons? The I.A.A.F. has not responded, and that to me raises questions on how it conducts business." Mayende-Sibiya is a big, warm woman, a grandmother and a former nurse, who hugs everyone she meets. She sighed. "There is a lot that has gone wrong in this process."

The I.A.A.F. has behaved erratically on the issue. On November 19th, the South African Ministry of Sport and Recreation announced that the I.A.A.F. had said that Semenya could keep her medal, but the I.A.A.F. refused to confirm this. Its president, Lamine Diack, was scheduled to visit South Africa several weeks ago to talk to Semenya and to representatives of the government, but he cancelled his trip at the last minute. In late October, I got in touch with the I.A.A.F., with questions about Semenya, and received a form-letter reply (dated September 11th) that it would not comment on the case until after its council meeting, at the end of November. Then, a few hours later, Nick Davies, the director of communications, wrote back by e-mail:

> Two things triggered the investigation. Firstly, the incredible improvement in this athlete's performance . . . and more bluntly, the fact that SOUTH AFRICAN sport Web sites were alleging that she was a hermaphrodite athlete. One such blog (from sport24.co.za) stated, "Caster Semenya is an interesting revelation because the 18 year old was born a hermaphrodite and, through a series of tests, has been classified as female." With this blatant allegation, and bearing in mind the almost supernatural improvement, the I.A.A.F. believed that it was sensible to make sure, with help of A.S.A., that the athlete was negative in terms of doping test results, and also that there was no gender ambiguity which may have allowed her to have the benefits of male hormone levels, whilst competing against other women.

A.S.A. is the abbreviation for Athletics South Africa, the national governing body in charge of track and field. The group's president, Leonard Chuene, who was also on the board of the I.A.A.F., and had been in Berlin for the Championships, told reporters when he returned, "We are not going to allow Europeans to define and describe our children." South Africa would have no part in tests conducted by "some stupid university somewhere," Chuene, who also happens to be from Limpopo, said. "The only scientists I believe in are the parents of this child." He claimed to be shocked by the way that the I.A.A.F. had treated Semenya, and he resigned from the board in protest before he left Berlin. (A week later, Chuene wrote the I.A.A.F. a letter saying that his resignation had been hasty, and asked to be reinstated.)

In fact, Chuene was not only aware of the Berlin tests; he had authorized them, and, at the urging of the I.A.A.F., he had also had Semenya tested before she left Pretoria. On August 3rd, the I.A.A.F.'s anti-doping administrator, Dr. Gabriel Dollé, had sent an e-mail to Harold Adams, A.S.A.'s team doctor, citing the Website posting that Nick Davies mentioned to me, which alleged that Semenya is a "hermaphrodite . . . classified as female." Dollé asked Adams if sex verification had been conducted—or ought to be. (Debora Patta, the host of a South African investigative program called "3rd Degree," obtained the e-mail exchange and forwarded it to me.) Adams then sent the following e-mail to Leonard Chuene and A.S.A.'s general manager, Molatelo Malehopo:

> After thinking about the current confidential matter I would suggest we make the following decisions.
>
> 1. We get a gynae opinion and take it to Berlin.
>
> 2. We do nothing and I will handle these issues if they come up in Berlin.
>
> Please think and get back to me A.S.A.P.

Malehopo replied the same day, agreeing to the exam. Semenya was taken to the Medforum Medi-Clinic, in Pretoria, for tests by a gynecologist.

"They did not even consult us as parents," Semenya's mother, Dorcus, told the *Star*, a South African daily. "They acted like thieves. They did whatever they wanted to do with our child without informing us."

On August 8th, Adams and Semenya flew to Germany to join the rest of the South African team and the A.S.A. staff at the training camp. Adams, who is also one of President Zuma's personal physicians, told Chuene that the Pretoria test results were "not good." He recommended that they withdraw Semenya from the competition, rather than subject her to further testing.

"The reason for my advice was that the tests might prove too traumatic for Ms. Semenya to handle, especially without the necessary support of family and friends around her," Harold Adams wrote in a subsequent report to Parliament. "The other reason was that being tested at the World Championships would not give her enough time to consult extensively and perhaps arrive at a decision to refuse the testing."

Leonard Chuene did not take Adams's advice. Instead, Semenya ran in a qualifying heat on August 16th and then in the semifinals, the next day. After her success in the semifinals, a television reporter outside the stadium blurted out, "With that comes rumors. I heard one that you were born a man?" The video is very hard to watch. As the reporter speaks, Semenya's breathing quickens, and she appears to be on the verge of panic. Then she looks at the ground and says, "I have no idea about that thing....I don't give a damn about it," and walks away from the cameras. August 18th was supposed to be a rest day before the finals. Semenya spent it undergoing a second round of tests. The next day, after two weeks of confusion and scrutiny, Semenya won the gold medal.

In September, the Johannesburg weekly *Mail & Guardian* exposed Chuene's dishonesty about authorizing the tests in Pretoria and Berlin. Chuene contends that he was simply following I.A.A.F. procedure, and that his deceit was a well-intentioned attempt to maintain confidentiality. After the story broke, he held a press conference to apologize for lying to the nation, but the apology was not unconditional. "Tell me someone," he said, "who has not lied to protect a child."

Semenya is back at the University of Pretoria now, training with her coach, Michael Seme. I asked Seme how he thought she was doing. "Sometimes you can look at somebody thinking he is O.K.," Seme said. "But you find out in his heart, maybe it is complaining. I can't see what's happening in her heart."

At a meeting of the British Gynaecological Society on April 25, 1888, Dr. Fancourt Barnes declared that he had "in the next room a living specimen of a hermaphrodite." The person was nineteen years old, and had always believed that she was female. Barnes thought otherwise. He cited "1) the appearance of the head, 2) the *timbre* of the voice, 3) the non-development of the breasts," and "the utter absence of anything like a uterus or ovaries," as evidence of the subject's insufficient femininity.

Other members of the society who examined the patient disagreed. Dr. James Aveling asserted that "the face was feminine, the throat was decidedly that of a woman." Dr. Charles Henry Felix Routh argued that Barnes's diagnosis was "guess work," and claimed that "the mere fact" that this patient might not have a uterus was "no argument against its being a woman." (Routh was not entirely convinced that the patient lacked a uterus and suggested that unless Barnes tried to "pass his entire hand into her rectum" they could not be sure.) Dr. Heywood Smith finally "suggested that the Society should divide on the question of sex," and so it did. Before the doctors sent their patient home with her mother, they took a photograph. In the foreground, a "medical man" holds the "living specimen" 's genitals with his thumb and forefinger for the camera, between her spread legs. In the background is the blurred image of the subject's head, not quite obscured by the blanket that covers her torso. The subject's face is grainy, but it is set in an unmistakable expression of powerless panic.

The society's inability to reach consensus was due, in part, to its failure to locate either testicles or ovaries in the patient. Until 1915, that was the generally accepted determining factor for sex. In "Hermaphrodites and the Medical Invention of Sex," Alice Domurat Dreger calls the period from 1870 to 1915 "the Age of Gonads."

The way doctors, scientists, and sports officials have determined sex has changed radically over the years. Before 1968, the International Olympic Committee verified the sex of female athletes by looking between their legs. Athletes complained about these humiliating inspections—which weren't always conclusive—and, for the 1968 Olympics, in Mexico City, the I.O.C. decided to implement chromosomal testing. (There were rumors that some men from Eastern Bloc nations had plans to masquerade as women.) These assessments proved problematic, too.

In normal human development, when a zygote has XY, or male, chromosomes, the SRY—sex-determining region Y—gene on the Y chromosome "instructs" the zygote's protogonads to develop as testes, rather than as ovaries. The testes then produce testosterone, which issues a second set of developmental instructions: for a scrotal sac to develop and for the testes to descend into it, for a penis to grow, and so on. But the process can get derailed. A person can be born with one ovary and one testicle. The SRY gene can end up on an X chromosome. A person with a penis who thinks he is male can one day find out that he has a uterus and ovaries. "Then, there is chromosomal variability that is invisible," Anne Fausto-Sterling, the author of "Sexing the Body," told me. "You could go your whole life and never know."

All sorts of things can happen, and do. An embryo that is chromosomally male but suffers from an enzyme deficiency that partially prevents it from "reading" testosterone can develop into a baby who appears female. Then, at puberty, the person's testes will produce a rush of hormones and this time the body won't need the enzyme (called 5-alpha-reductase) to successfully read the testosterone. The little girl will start to become hairier and more muscular. Her voice may deepen, and her testes may descend into what she thought were her labia. Her clitoris will grow into something like a penis. Is she still a girl? Was she ever?

If a chromosomally male embryo has androgen-insensitivity syndrome, or A.I.S., the cells' receptors for testosterone, an androgen, are deaf to the testosterone's instructions, and will thus develop the default external sexual characteristics of a female. An individual with androgen-insensitivity syndrome has XY chromosomes, a vagina, and undescended testes, but her body develops without the ability to respond to the testosterone it produces. In fact, people with complete A.I.S. are less able to process testosterone than average women. Consequently, they tend to have exceptionally "smooth-skinned bodies with rounded hips and breasts and long limbs," Dreger writes in "Hermaphrodites."

People with incomplete A.I.S., on the other hand, could end up looking and sounding like Caster Semenya. Their bodies hear *some* of the instructions that the testosterone inside them is issuing. But that does not necessarily mean that they would have an athletic advantage.

For example, the Spanish hurdler Maria Patiño, who had A.I.S., went to the World University Games in Kobe, Japan, in 1985, and forgot to bring a letter from her doctor verifying that she was female. Until 1999, gender verification was compulsory for all female athletes. Officials scraped some cells from the inside of her cheek for chromatin testing. If visual inspection had still been the standard, Patiño's gender never would have been questioned. Her genitals, and the rest of her, looked female, but according to the test she was male. The story got out, and she was stripped of her past titles. Her boyfriend left her. Her scholarship was revoked, and she was evicted from the national athletic residence.

In 1991, the International Association of Athletics Federations abandoned this method as unreliable, and, nine years later, so did the International Olympic Committee. Patiño was requalified in 1988, when she was able to prove that her body could not make use of its testosterone, and that she had developed as a woman. "I knew I was a woman," Patiño said, "in the eyes of medicine, God, and most of all in my own eyes."

The approach that the I.A.A.F. appears to be taking in its review of Semenya's test results from Berlin is not unlike the British Gynaecological Society's muddled attempt to determine the sex of its living specimen. The I.A.A.F.'s gender policy states that an athlete "can be asked to attend a medical evaluation before a panel comprising gynecologist, endocrinologist, psychologist, internal medicine specialist, expert on gender/transgender issues." It has not come up with a single litmus test for sex; its goal, like that of the I.O.C. in such situations, is to reach consensus. The federation does not define the criteria that its group of experts must use to reach their determination, however. "It seems to be working with a kind of 'I know it when I see it' policy," Dreger, a professor of clinical medical humanities and bioethics at Northwestern University's Feinberg School of Medicine, told me. The policy does not indicate who should be tested and on what grounds. An athlete will be examined if "there is any 'suspicion'" or if there is a 'challenge'" to her sex. Evidently, a blog post qualifies as a challenge.

In conjunction with other sports bodies, the I.A.A.F. will hold a special conference, in January, 2010, to review the policy. On November 18th, it sent out a press release stating that there would be "no discussion of Caster Semenya's case" at the November council meeting, despite its earlier promise to resolve the issue there.

Unfortunately for I.A.A.F. officials, they are faced with a question that no one has ever been able to answer: what is the ultimate difference between a man and a woman? "This is not a solvable problem," Alice Dreger said. "People always press me: 'Isn't there one marker we can use?' No. We couldn't then and we can't now, and science is making it more difficult and not less, because it ends up showing us how much blending there is and how many nuances, and it becomes impossible to point to one thing, or even a set of things, and say that's what it means to be male.

In 2000, Anne Fausto-Sterling, a professor of biology at Brown University, conducted what remains the study of record on the frequency of intersexuality, and concluded that 1.7 per cent of the population develops in a way that deviates from the standard definition of male or female. (Some scholars have argued that Fausto-Sterling's categories are too broad, because they include individuals who show no noticeable expression of their chromosomal irregularity.) Based on this figure, intersexuality is much more common than Down syndrome or albinism, though it can be harder to keep track of: every baby born in the United States is registered as "male" or "female."

The word "hermaphrodite" is as outdated and offensive to the people it once described as the word "mulatto." In one Greek myth, Hermes, the son of Zeus, and Aphrodite, the goddess of love, have a child endowed with all the attributes of both of them. "Hermaphrodite" implies a double-sexed creature, fully male and fully female, which is a physical impossibility for human beings. (You can be half and half, but you can't be all and all.)

In the nineteen-nineties, a movement spearheaded by an activist who used to call herself Cheryl Chase, and now goes by the name Bo Laurent, insisted that what was needed was a new identity. Chase founded the Intersex Society of North America (now defunct) to draw attention to the frequently tragic consequences of doctors' performing irreversible surgery on newborns to enforce a sex—one that the baby might just as easily as not grow up to reject. The society advocated assigning intersex children a gender at birth but leaving their bodies intact, so that upon adulthood they could make their own choices about whether they wished to undergo surgical modification.

Then something unexpected happened. "The intersex identity started getting inhabited by people who weren't really intersex," Dreger said. "The people who accumulated around the intersex identity tended to be queer and out and comfortable with this identity outside the gender binary." They felt that refraining from interfering with infants' ambiguous genitalia was the first step on a desirable path to dissolving gender altogether. To them, this idea was "as politically inspiring as it is utterly disconnected from the actual experience of intersex people or the heart-wrenching decisions their parents have to make when an intersex child is born," as Vernon A. Rosario, a professor of psychiatry at U.C.L.A., put it in a recent issue of *The Gay and Lesbian Review*.

Semenya, whether she wants to be or not, has become a hero to many people who "don't fit the sex and gender boxes," as Jarvis, from Winnipeg, posted on the Web site casterrunsforme.com. A person named Megan Ewart wrote, "I'll bet you've got a lot more transgendered allies than just me that are feeling your pain."

Now there is an even newer term of art for people born with ambiguously sexed bodies who do not wish to be connected with the "L.G.B.T.Q.I."—lesbian, gay, bisexual, transgender, queer, intersex—camp: "disorders of sex development," or D.S.D. By naming the condition a medical "disorder," advocates of the D.S.D. label hope to make the people it describes seem less aberrant. "Oddly enough, it does normalize it in a certain way," Fausto-Sterling said. "It's putting it on the same plane as other anomalous development—like congenital anomalies of the heart." Advocates of the D.S.D. label are not seeking to create a third sex. Rather, they want disorders of sex development to be treated like any other physical abnormality: something for doctors to monitor but not to operate on, unless the patient is in physical discomfort or danger.

In science and medicine, categories are imperative, but they are also inflected by social concerns. "Mammals," for example, were so named by Linnaeus, in the eighteenth century, because their females produce milk to suckle their young. Was it irrelevant that scientists like Linnaeus sought to encourage mothers to breast-feed their own children, and to do away with the "unnatural" custom of wet-nursing? "There are philosophers of science who argue that when scientists make categories in the natural world—shapes, species—they are simply making a list of things that exist: natural kinds," Fausto-Sterling said. "It's scientist as discoverer. The phrase that people use is 'cutting nature at its joint.' There are other people, myself included, who think that, almost always, what we're doing in biology is creating categories that work pretty well for certain things that we want to do with them. But there is no joint."

If sex is not precisely definable, how else might sports be organized? Theoretically, athletes could be categorized by size, as they are in wrestling and boxing. But then women would usually lose to men. Or athletes could be categorized by skill level. Almost always, this would mean that the strongest élite female athletes would compete against the weakest élite male athletes, which would be pretty demoralizing all the way around.

Another option would be to divide athletes biochemically. Testosterone is, for an athlete, truly important stuff. Developmentally, testosterone spurs linear bone growth in adolescents. Fully grown people use testosterone in doping because it helps create muscle mass and increases red-blood-cell production, which, in turn, increases cellular oxygen-carrying capacity. The more oxygen an athlete has in her cells, the more efficiently her muscles operate and the longer it takes for her body to start producing lactic acid, the substance that causes cramps and pain. Testosterone makes a faster, better athlete, and enables a body to recover more quickly from exhaustion. Hypothetically, according to Eric Vilain, a professor of human genetics and pediatrics at U.C.L.A., those with a certain level of functional testosterone (testosterone that the body can actually make use of) could be in one group, and those below it could be in another. Although the first group would be almost all male and the second group would be almost all female, the division would be determined not by gender but by actual physical advantages that gender supposedly, yet unreliably, supplies.

But, setting aside the issue of gender, there is still no such thing as a level playing field in sports. Different bodies have physical attributes, even abnormalities, that may provide a distinct advantage in one sport or another. The N.B.A., for instance, has had several players with acromegaly—the overproduction of growth hormone. Michael Phelps, who has won fourteen Olympic gold medals, has unusually long arms and is said to have double-jointed elbows, knees, and ankles. Is Caster Semenya's alleged extra testosterone really so different?

There is much more at stake in organizing sports by gender than just making things fair. If we were to admit that at some level we don't know the difference between men and women, we might start to wonder about the way we've organized our entire world. Who gets to use what bathroom? Who is allowed to get married? (Currently, the United States government recognizes the marriage of a woman to a female-to-male transsexual who has had a double mastectomy and takes testosterone tablets but still has a vagina, but not to a woman who hasn't done those things.) We depend on gender to make sense of sexuality, society, and ourselves. We do not wish to see it dissolve.

What the I.A.A.F. concludes about Caster Semenya could have ramifications for sports in general and for South Africa in particular. This is true not only because it is Semenya's place of origin. South Africa has an unusually high level of intersex births. Nobody knows why.

During apartheid, for every white town there was a black township. Only the white towns appeared on maps, though the townships were nearly always more populous. John Carlin, in his account of the 1995 rugby World Cup, "Playing the Enemy: Nelson Mandela and the Game That Made a Nation," describes townships as "the black shadows of the towns." Khayelitsha is the black shadow of Cape Town. According to the most recent census, half a million people live there, but in reality the number is probably much higher. Many of their parents and grandparents settled in the Cape Flats, outside of Cape Town, after the Group Areas Acts of the nineteen-fifties made it illegal for them to live in the city. "Khayelitsha" is Xhosa for "New Home." Shacks made of corrugated tin, cardboard, and scrap wood, many without electricity or running water, sprawl for miles along mostly unmarked dirt roads, punctuated by beauty parlors and fruit stands in structures no bigger than British telephone booths.

By Khayelitsha standards, Funeka Soldaat's small home, with its solid brick walls and tiled floor, is very fine. Soldaat is an L.G.B.Q.T.I. activist. Both she and a cousin—whom Soldaat, following local custom, referred to as her sister—were born with anomalous genitalia, and both underwent "corrective" partial clitoridectomies when they were young, which they now regret. This is the standard "treatment" for babies born with a clitoris longer than one centimetre but smaller than 2.5 centimetres, at which point it becomes a medically acceptable penis. The scar tissue that forms after such a procedure can impede sensation for the rest of a person's life.

"My sister, she look just like Caster," Soldaat said, smiling. "She don't have the breasts. She never get a period. Everybody thinks she's a guy, just like Caster. We call them, in Xhosa, *italasi*. It is not a new thing—everybody has a word for it." That there is a name for intersex does not mean it is a condition that is ever spoken about. "One thing that is so difficult for African people: there's no way that you can discuss about something that's happened below the belt," Soldaat said. "All the time you don't know what's happening in your body, and there's nobody that try to explain to you. *Then* it becomes a problem. If my mom would know that I'm intersex and there's nothing wrong about it, then there was nothing going to make me panic."

Particularly in remote areas, where babies tend to be born in the presence of a mother, a grandmother, and maybe a midwife, it is easy to keep a baby's genitalia a secret. People want to insulate their children from the shame of being different, so they simply pretend that they are not. "Limpopo and Eastern Cape are the high incidence of intersex people," Soldaat said. "And when you grow up in the rural areas it's a mess, because people don't even go to doctors." The determination of gender is made very simply. "It depends what they do when they go to the loo," Soldaat said. "That's what makes their children to be women. If they go to the loo and they sit, that's it."

On her coffee table, Soldaat had a photocopy of the South African magazine *You*, which featured a photo spread showing Caster Semenya dressed in high heels and a short skirt, her hair fluffed out and her face made up. Her expression was painfully uncomfortable, and the pictures were garish.

"My sister was crying when she saw this whole thing on paper," Soldaat said, flipping through the pages. "It's a disaster. She look like a drag queen! I can just imagine her at night when she's alone, looking at these pictures."

Soldaat tossed the papers on the floor. "When we are really, really poor sometimes, and we really, really want to protect ourselves, people take an advantage," she said. "That's why it was easy for people to force her to do this, for A.S.A. to do this." Athletics South Africa received a payment from *You* in exchange for Semenya's appearance in its pages. "To say that she enjoyed doing this, that's a lie! There is no way. There is no way!"

Soldaat has a shaved head and was wearing big jeans and a baseball cap with the words "Mama Cash," the name of a Dutch women's-rights organization, on it. She is a lesbian, and she said that she suspected Semenya is, too.

"Everyone! Everyone who is like this likes women," Soldaat said, laughing. "Everyone!" ("Caster has never cared about men other than as friends," her father told a reporter. "Her sisters were always after boys in the way that I, too, was always after girls when I was younger. But Caster has never been interested in any of that.") If Soldaat is right, then Semenya's life may well get more difficult. Soldaat was going to court later that day to listen to the proceedings against several men accused of raping and murdering a lesbian in Khayelitsha. "They are raping lesbians to correct them," she said. "In order they can be a proper woman."

Soldaat said that Semenya should run with women. "It will never be like intersex women have their own Olympic Games—that's ridiculous!" she said. Soldaat has a big, raucous laugh, and the idea of that imaginary competition absolutely killed her. Soldaat was a runner herself when she was young. "If she can't run in the Olympics, Caster has to continue running with other girls in South Africa. Because, really, that's what she wants, that's what she is, that's what keeps her alive: that's running."

The only thing more slippery than the science in the Semenya case is the agendas of the men who have involved themselves in it. There is a bounty of political gain for whoever spins the story most successfully.

Julius Malema, the president of the A.N.C. Youth League, has said that he does not believe in the existence of intersex people, and has tried to frame the concept as a suspect and unwelcome import from abroad. "Hermaphrodite, what is that?" Malema asked at a press conference in October. "Somebody tell me, what is 'hermaphrodite' in Pedi? There's no such thing. So don't impose your hermaphrodite concepts on us." (The word is *tarasi*, according to a professor of South African languages at Yale.) The Youth League issued a press release decrying a "racist attack on Semenya" orchestrated by the media in "Australia, which is the most lucrative destination for South Africa's racists and fascists who refused to live under a black democratic government."

Julius Malema is not known for being levelheaded. He won the presidency of the Youth League in a highly contested election in 2008. Just a few months later, while Jacob Zuma was fending off charges of racketeering and fraud (the charges have since been dropped), Malema became notorious for vowing, "We are prepared to die for Zuma. Not only that, we are prepared to take up arms and kill for Zuma." (Zuma also beat a rape charge, in 2006.) Zuma has called Malema "a leader in the making," worthy of "inheriting the A.N.C." one day. Malema has demonstrated an ability to mobilize people and an almost reckless willingness to use charges of racism to do so. He has been Leonard Chuene's most steadfast defender.

Chuene has, since the revelation of his deceit, become almost as controversial a figure in South Africa as Caster Semenya. Countless editorials have accused Chuene of sacrificing her in his quest for a gold medal and have demanded his ouster. In Dr. Harold Adams's report to Parliament, he calls Chuene's decision "short-sighted and grossly irresponsible." Though Chuene received a vote of confidence from Athletics South Africa's board after his admission, the A.N.C.

asked him to apologize; its rival party, the Democratic Alliance, demanded his resignation, and the Deputy Minister of Sport called him a liar. Minister Mayende-Sibiya told me that Chuene's behavior was "totally unacceptable."

Julius Malema has continued to paint any criticism of Chuene as racist. In early October, one of A.S.A.'s biggest sponsors, Nedbank, announced that it would withdraw its support pending a change in A.S.A.'s leadership. Malema retaliated by calling for a boycott of the bank. "We will teach them a lesson about the power of the masses," Malema said. "They may have money, but we can defeat them because we have the masses."

On three occasions, Leonard Chuene's personal assistant made an appointment for me to interview "the president," as she calls her boss. She always called or e-mailed at the last minute to cancel. We had several calls scheduled, but Chuene never picked up his phone at the appointed time. Then, one day, I got on an airplane going to Polokwane, a small northern city. Sitting in an empty row, in a navy blazer and pressed jeans, was Leonard Chuene.

Chuene wanted to know how I recognized him. Only minutes before, I had been looking at his photograph in a newspaper, alongside a story about Nedbank's withdrawal of funds from A.S.A. and A.S.A.'s failing finances. "I have become more famous than Caster," he said, and chuckled. Chuene has a shiny bald head and a little gut. He was once a serious runner and has completed more than a hundred marathons, he told me. He said he had no choice but to get Semenya tested. "You cannot just argue like a fool and say no. This is not the law of the jungle!" He speaks very quickly. He explained why he had not heeded Adams's advice to withdraw Semenya from the race.

"I don't have the results in my hand!" he said. "How did you expect me to take an informed decision?"

Indeed, Adams had had word from the Pretoria clinic but no actual documentation of the test results. "Where is the evidence?" Chuene said. "Now I come back home and they will say, 'When this black child from the rural be No. 1, why do you deprive her?' "

Chuene shrugged. "They say I lied. That's what they are saying. I said no. There is confidentiality! I.A.A.F. is in trouble for breaching that. Who was going to be Leonard to say that?" The engines started roaring as the small plane took off. "It was 22-Catch situation!" Chuene shouted over the noise. "If I will do this, it's 'Why did you withdraw her?' If I did not, 'Why did you allow her to run?' Whatever way you look at it, I'm judged. I'm judged!"

There were around twenty people on the plane. We were airborne, and the engines quieted. Chuene did not. "The stupid leader is the one who says, 'I'm not sure; I don't know.' I had to take a decision! She must run. If Chuene didn't allow her, it meant she was going to stay in South Africa. This thing has given her more opportunity! Everybody knows her. The world is out there to say, 'Your problems are our problems.' Imagine if I had not let her win!" As we touched down in Polokwane, he said, "If there is to be help, it is because of the opportunity created by Leonard Chuene."

Recently, Semenya told the *Guardian*, "It's not so easy. The university is O.K. but there is not many other places I can go. People want to stare at me now. They want to touch me. I'm supposed to be famous." She added, "I don't think I like it so much."

The law firm Dewey & LeBoeuf announced in September that it was taking on Caster Semenya as a client. It is still sorting through what happened and deciding whom to sue. One afternoon, I drove with Benedict Phiri, an associate in the firm's Johannesburg office, across the Blood River from Polokwane to Ga-Masehlong to meet Semenya's mother. Ga-Masehlong is a small village dotted with jacaranda trees; goats graze on the garbage and the grass on the roadsides. The houses have tin roofs, and people put rocks on top of them to keep them from blowing away. There are satellite dishes in several yards, but most people have dug their own wells and collect firewood from the bush for cooking. Everyone knows everyone else in Ga-Masehlong, and it was easy to get directions to the house of the champion.

At the Semenya home, there was a flyer tacked to the front door promoting a lecture that Julius Malema was giving at the local elementary school. Phiri knocked. We heard shuffling and then the sound of locks turning and bolts sliding. Phiri called out that he was Caster's lawyer, but nobody came to the door.

A few minutes later, a pretty girl wearing an orange fleece jacket walked into the yard and introduced herself as Maphela. She said she was fourteen. "Do you want my story?" she asked in English. "I am Caster's sister! But I am not like her. I am different from Caster." I asked her what she meant, and Maphela replied emphatically, "I am not that way."

Maphela looked toward the window where her mother, Dorcus, was hiding her face behind the curtain and motioning vigorously for her daughter to stop speaking with us. We asked Maphela if she would tell her mother that Phiri was Caster's lawyer. Maphela ran off toward the back door.

We sat on the stoop of a cooking hut in the Semenyas' front yard, and waited with the chickens and the goats. An elderly neighbor named Ike came into the yard. "Caster has done a wonderful thing," he said. "This has brought to mind when the Philistines were persecuting the Israelites." Ike told us that he just wanted to check on the family and see how their visit from Julius Malema the previous evening had gone. This made Phiri nervous.

After a few minutes, Maphela returned. She told us that her mother would not meet with Phiri, because she did not agree that Caster should have a lawyer.

As we drove away through the bush, Phiri called his boss in Johannesburg, a white former rugby player named Greg Nott. I could hear Nott yelling through the phone. "We knew this would happen all along," Phiri said, trying to calm him. "Julius Malema is Chuene's ally, and Julius is giving Caster money."

On the occasion of the A.N.C. Youth League's sixty-fifth anniversary, in October, Julius Malema presented Caster Semenya with a hundred and twenty thousand rand (about sixteen thousand dollars) at a gala dinner in Johannesburg. "I can even see it," Phiri said on the phone. "They probably told the mom, 'People will come and say they're her lawyer. Don't believe it.' " Phiri was afraid that Malema would step in and persuade the family to side with Chuene, who comes from the same region, and whose interests might not be served by lawyers poking around. One of the first things that Dewey & LeBoeuf did when the firm took the case was to ask both A.S.A. and the I.A.A.F. to provide documentation of the tests and any other pertinent paperwork; neither organization has fully complied.

The firm is representing Semenya pro bono, so good publicity will be its only reward. "And that," Phiri said, "could blow up in our faces."

Nobody wants Chuene out of office more than an old friend and colleague named Wilfred Daniels, who started at A.S.A. with him, sixteen years ago. "From day one we connected, in the struggle days, you know?" Daniels said. "We were like, we *belong* together." Both Daniels, fifty-eight, and Chuene, fifty-seven, grew up as promising athletes who could never compete internationally because of apartheid. They understood each other then, but not anymore.

Daniels—whom everyone calls Wilfie—is the unofficial mayor of Stellenbosch, a leafy college town in the wine country. He likes to hold court at the Jan Cats restaurant, in front of the elegant Stellenbosch Hotel. As he sat at his street-front table on a sunny afternoon in a green Izod jacket and track pants, drinking a bottle of Chenin blanc, every other person who passed by stopped to pay his respects, or at least waved at him driving by. Daniels was a famous athlete in his youth, and he is even more famous now. In early September, he resigned from A.S.A. in protest over its handling of Caster Semenya, and had since been in the papers constantly. "We allowed it," he said. "If we as management were on our game, we would've objected. We accompanied her to the slaughter. And that is my dilemma."

Daniels was not directly involved in the testing or the coverup. During the first training session in Berlin, "while she was warming up and stretching, putting on her spikes, she told me they had done tests on her. I said, 'What tests?'" Semenya told him that she didn't know what they were for, but she described what had happened. "They put her feet in straps and 'they work down there,' she said. They told her it was dope tests." Semenya had undergone routine doping tests many times before. She knew that this was something very different.

"If you and me who come from the big cities, if we find it repulsive, I mean, what about a rural girl," Daniels said. "She doesn't know what's happening around her. She's seven, eight months in the city now, in Pretoria, a new life altogether, and nobody takes the time to explain to her?" He shook his head in disgust. "It was unprovoked talk, and she's not somebody who talks, normally. And she spoke to me as a Colored guy, as a man, about intimate, female things. That to me was like a cry for help."

The sins of A.S.A., as Daniels sees it, are, first, not giving Semenya adequate information about the Pretoria tests—including her right to refuse them—and, second, not pulling her out of the competition in Berlin.

"It's the day before the championships," Daniels said. "Eighteen years old, your first World Championships, the greatest race of your life. You can't focus, because you have to go for gender testing. And you come back and you have to watch on TV: they are explaining the possibilities. I found her in her room, sitting in front of the TV like this," Daniels put his hand up to his face to show how close she was to the screen. "And they're talking about her and she's trying to understand what they're saying. Because nobody has spoken to her, to tell her, Look, this is what these tests might mean. I felt so ashamed."

Daniels has worked in various capacities at A.S.A. over the years, first in management, then as a coach, and, most recently, as A.S.A.'s coördinator with the High Performance Centre, the program at the University of Pretoria where Semenya is now. Daniels does not agree with the I.A.A.F.'s assessment that Semenya's seven-and-a-half-second improvement was "supernatural." She went from training on the dirt roads of Limpopo to a world-class facility. She is also an extraordinarily hard worker. "Understand: Maria Mutola is her hero," Daniels said. "So she had wonderful goals and ideals for herself; she was really trying to emulate her hero one day." Maria Mutola is a runner from Mozambique whose event, like Semenya's, was the eight hundred metres. Mutola also happened to have a strikingly masculine appearance.

Daniels believes that the best that can happen for Semenya at this point is to have a career like his. He has travelled the world and met many of his heroes. He has a cellar with more than two thousand bottles of red wine. He eats his grilled springbok at Jan Cats and clearly enjoys being a local eminence. But it is probably not the life he would have led if apartheid hadn't prevented him from competing internationally; and it is not the life that was in front of Caster Semenya before she went to Germany. "I understand that her running days are over," Daniels said.

There's another scenario, in which Semenya's story could become one of against-all-odds victory. The I.A.A.F. could apologize and decree Semenya female. Kobus van der Walt, the director of sport at the High Performance Centre, pointed out that though Semenya has beaten the South African record for her event, she hasn't come anywhere near Kratochvílová's world record, which means that there are plenty of women with a chance of besting Semenya. Conceivably, one day we will see Caster Semenya at the Olympics with a medal hanging from her neck. She could be the poster child for triumphant transgression.

But that is not what Daniels thinks will happen. "Now her life is over," he said. "Not only as an athlete but as a human being. Even if the I.A.A.F. says there's nothing wrong with her, people will always look at her twice. There should be hell to pay for those responsible." He pounded his fist on the table. "I've got a daughter. If that was my daughter, what would I have done as a father? Somebody might have been dead by now."

On November 5th, Chuene and the entire board of A.S.A. were suspended by the South African Sports Confederation and Olympic Committee, pending an investigation into how they handled Caster Semenya.

One afternoon at the High Performance Centre, I sat up in the bleachers, killing time before a meeting with Kobus Van der Walt. I was surrounded by a spread of neatly partitioned fields, like a Brueghel painting: there are twenty-four cricket nets, six rugby fields, twenty-two outdoor tennis courts, nine soccer fields, seven squash courts, and a track surrounded by a three-thousand-seat stadium, all kept in impeccable condition. Runners in little packs zoomed around the fields and into the distance. Spring sunlight flicked along the blue of the swimming pool.

A figure in a black sweatshirt with the hood up walked along the path about thirty yards in front of me. There was something about this person's build and movements that drew my attention. I got up and followed along the path, until I caught up to the person where he or she was stopped behind the cafeteria, talking to a waiter and a cook, both of whom were much shorter than she was. It was Caster Semenya.

She wore sandals and track pants and kept her hood up. When she shook my hand, I noticed that she had long nails. She didn't look like an eighteen-year-old girl, or an eighteen-year-old boy. She looked like something else, something magnificent.

I told her I had come from New York City to write about her, and she asked me why.

"Because you're the champion," I said.

She snorted and said, "You make me laugh."

I asked her if she would talk to me, not about the tests or Chuene but about her evolution as an athlete, her progression from Limpopo to the world stage. She shook her head vigorously. "No," she said. "I can't talk to you. I can't talk to anyone. I can't say to anyone how I feel or what's in my mind."

I said I thought that must suck.

"No," she said, very firmly. Her voice was strong and low. "That doesn't suck. It sucks when I was running and they were writing those things. That sucked. That is when it sucks. Now I just have to walk away. That's all I can do." She smiled a small, bemused smile. "Walk away from all of this, maybe forever. Now I just walk away." Then she took a few steps backward, turned around, and did.

Ruth Padawer is a contributing writer for *The New York Times Magazine* and an Adjunct Faculty at Columbia Journalism School.

When Women Become Men at Wellesley
Ruth Padawer

Hundreds of young women streamed into Wellesley College on the last Monday of August, many of them trailed by parents lugging suitcases and bins filled with folded towels, decorative pillows and Costco-size jugs of laundry detergent. The banner by the campus entranceway welcoming the Class of 2018 waved in the breeze, as if beckoning the newcomers to discover all that awaited them. All around the campus stood buildings named after women: the Margaret Clapp library, the Betsy Wood Knapp media and technology center, dorms, labs, academic halls, even the parking garage. The message that anything is possible for women was also evident at a fenced-in work site, which bore the sign "Elaine Construction," after a firm named for one woman and run by another.

It was the first day of orientation, and along the picturesque paths there were cheerful upper-class student leaders providing directions and encouragement. They wore pink T-shirts stamped with this year's orientation theme: "Free to Explore"—an enticement that could be interpreted myriad ways, perhaps far more than the college intended. One of those T-shirted helpers was a junior named Timothy Boatwright. Like every other matriculating student at Wellesley, which is just west of Boston, Timothy was raised a girl and checked "female" when he applied. Though he had told his high-school friends that he was transgender, he did not reveal that on his application, in part because his mother helped him with it, and he didn't want her to know. Besides, he told me, "it seemed awkward to write an application essay for a women's college on why you were not a woman." Like many trans students, he chose a women's college because it seemed safer physically and psychologically.

From the start, Timothy introduced himself as "masculine-of-center genderqueer." He asked everyone at Wellesley to use male pronouns and the name Timothy, which he'd chosen for himself.

For the most part, everyone respected his request. After all, he wasn't the only trans student on campus. Some two dozen other matriculating students at Wellesley don't identify as women. Of those, a half-dozen or so were trans men, people born female who identified as men, some of whom had begun taking testosterone to change their bodies. The rest said they were transgender or genderqueer, rejecting the idea of gender entirely or identifying somewhere between female and male; many, like Timothy, called themselves transmasculine. Though his gender identity differed from that of most of his classmates, he generally felt comfortable at his new school.

Last spring, as a sophomore, Timothy decided to run for a seat on the student-government cabinet, the highest position that an openly trans student had ever sought at Wellesley. The post he sought was multicultural affairs coordinator, or "MAC," responsible for promoting "a culture of diversity" among students and staff and faculty members. Along with Timothy, three women of color indicated their intent to run for the seat. But when they dropped out for various unrelated reasons before the race really began, he was alone on the ballot. An anonymous lobbying effort began on Facebook, pushing students to vote "abstain." Enough "abstains" would deny Timothy the minimum number of votes Wellesley required, forcing a new election for the seat and providing an opportunity for other candidates to come forward. The "Campaign to Abstain" argument was simple: Of all the people at a multiethnic women's college who could hold the school's "diversity" seat, the least fitting one was a w*hite man.*

"It wasn't about Timothy," the student behind the Abstain campaign told me. "I thought he'd do a perfectly fine job, but it just felt inappropriate to have a white man there. It's not just about that position either. Having men in elected leadership positions undermines the idea of this being a place where women are the leaders."

I asked Timothy what he thought about that argument, as we sat on a bench overlooking the tranquil lake on campus during orientation. He pointed out that he has important contributions to make to the MAC position. After all, at Wellesley, masculine-of-center students *are* cultural minorities; by numbers alone, they're about as minor as a minority can be. And yet Timothy said he felt conflicted about taking a leadership spot. "The patriarchy is alive and well," he said. "I don't want to perpetuate it."

In the 19th century, only men were admitted to most colleges and universities, so proponents of higher education for women had to build their own. The missions at these new schools both defied and reinforced the gender norms of the day. By offering women access to an education they'd previously been denied, the schools' very existence was radical, but most were nevertheless premised on traditional notions: College-educated women were considered more likely to be engaging wives and better mothers, who would raise informed citizens. Over time, of course, women's colleges became more committed to preparing students for careers, but even in the early 1960s, Wellesley, for example, taught students how to get groceries into the back of a station wagon without exposing their thighs.

By the late 1960s, however, gender norms were under scrutiny. Amid the growing awareness of civil rights and women's liberation, academic separation based on gender, as with race, seemed increasingly outdated. As a vast majority of women opted for coed schools, enrollment at women's colleges tumbled. The number of women's colleges dropped to fewer than 50 today from nearly 300.

Credit: William Ryerson/The Boston Globe, via Getty Images

Figure 1. The 1968 Wellesley hoop-rolling contest. This year, the contest
was won by a trans man.

In response to shifting ideas about gender, many of the remaining women's colleges redefined themselves as an antidote to the sexism that feminists were increasingly identifying in society. Women's colleges argued that they offered a unique environment where every student leader was a woman, where female role models were abundant, where professors were far more likely to be women and where the message of women's empowerment pervaded academic and campus life. All that seemed to foster students' confidence. Women's colleges say their undergrads are more likely to major in fields traditionally dominated by men. Wellesley alumnae in particular are awarded more science and engineering doctorates than female graduates of any other liberal-arts college in the nation, according to government data. Its alums have become two secretaries of state; a groundbreaking string theorist; a NASA astronaut; and Korea's first female ambassador.

As women's colleges challenged the conventions of womanhood, they drew a disproportionate number of students who identified as lesbian or bisexual. Today a small but increasing number of students at those schools do not identify as women, raising the question of what it means to be a "women's college." Trans students are pushing their schools to play down the women-centric message. At Wellesley, Smith, Mount Holyoke and others, they and their many supporters have successfully lobbied to scrub all female references in student government constitutions, replacing them with gender-neutral language. At Wellesley, they have pressed administrators and fellow students to excise talk of sisterhood, arguing that that rhetoric, rather than being uplifting, excludes other gender minorities. At many schools, they have also taken leadership positions long filled by women: resident advisers on dorm floors, heads of student groups and members of college government. At Wellesley, one transmasculine student was a dorm president. At Mills College, a women's school in California, even the president of student government identifies as male.

What's a women's college to do? Trans students point out that they're doing exactly what these schools encourage: breaking gender barriers, fulfilling their deepest yearnings and forging ahead even when society tries to hold them back. But yielding to their request to dilute the focus on women would undercut the identity of a women's college. While women in coed schools generally outpace men in enrollment and performance, the equation shifts after college: Recent female graduates working full time earn far less than their male counterparts, and more experienced women are often still shut out of corporate and political leadership—all of which prompts women's-college advocates to conclude that a four-year, confidence-building workshop still has its place.

"Sisterhood is why I chose to go to Wellesley," said a physics major who graduated recently and asked not to be identified for fear she'd be denounced for her opinion. "A women's college is a place to celebrate being a woman, surrounded by women. I felt empowered by that every day. You come here thinking that every single leadership position will be held by a woman: every member of the student government, every newspaper editor, every head of the Economics Council, every head of the Society of Physics. That's an incredible thing! This is what they advertise to students. But it's no longer true. And if all that is no longer true, the intrinsic value of a women's college no longer holds."

A few schools have formulated responses to this dilemma, albeit very different ones. Hollins University, a small women's college in Virginia, established a policy several years ago stating it would confer diplomas to only women. It also said that students who have surgery or begin hormone therapy to become men—or who legally take male names—will be "helped to transfer to another institution." Mount Holyoke and Mills College, on the other hand, recently decided they will not only continue to welcome students who become trans men while at school but will also admit those who identify on their applications as trans men, noting that welcoming the former and not the latter seemed unjustifiably arbitrary.

But most women's colleges, including Wellesley, consider only female applicants. Once individuals have enrolled and announced that they are trans, the schools, more or less, leave it to the students to work out how trans classmates fit into a women's college. Two of those students hashed it out last fall after Kaden Mohamed, then a Wellesley senior who had been taking testosterone for seven months, watched a news program on WGBH-TV about the plummeting number of women's colleges. One guest was Laura Bruno, another Wellesley senior. The other guest was the president of Regis College, a women's school that went coed in 2007 to reverse its tanking enrollment. The interviewer asked Laura to describe her experience at an "all-female school" and to explain how that might be diminished "by having men there." Laura answered, "We look around and we see only women, only people like us, leading every organization on campus, contributing to every class discussion."

Kaden, a manager of the campus student cafe who knew Laura casually, was upset by her words. He emailed Laura and said her response was "extremely disrespectful." He continued: "I am not a woman. I am a trans man who is part of your graduating class, and you literally ignored my existence in your interview....You had an opportunity to show people that Wellesley is a place that is complicating the meaning of being an 'all women's school,' and you chose instead to displace a bunch of your current and past Wellesley siblings."

Laura apologized, saying she hadn't meant to marginalize anyone and had actually vowed beforehand not to imply that all Wellesley students were women. But she said that under pressure, she found herself in a difficult spot: How could she maintain that women's colleges would lose something precious by including men, but at the same time argue that women's colleges should accommodate students who identify as men?

Although it may seem paradoxical, Jesse Austin said he chose to attend Wellesley because being female never felt right to him. "I figured if I was any kind of woman, I'd find it there. I knew Wellesley would have strong women. They produce a ton of strong women, strong in all sorts of ways."

When Jesse arrived on campus in the fall of 2009, his name was Sara. Eighteen years old, Sara wore form-fitting shirts and snug women's jeans, because growing up in a small, conservative town in Georgia, she learned that that's what girls were supposed to do—even though she never felt like a girl. As a child, Sara had always chosen to be male characters in pretend plays, and all her friends were boys. In middle school, those boys abandoned her because she was a social liability: not feminine enough to flirt with and not masculine enough to really be one of the guys. In high school, at the urging of well-intentioned female classmates, she started wearing her hair down instead of pulled back and began dressing like they did, even though people kept pointing out that she still acted and carried herself like a boy. "I had no idea that gender was something you could change," Jesse told me recently. "I just thought I needed to make myself fit into these fixed places: There are boys, and there are girls. I knew I didn't fit; I just didn't know what was wrong with me."

Around the middle of Sara's first year at Wellesley, she attended a presentation by trans alums, including one who was in the process of transitioning. As Sara listened, the gender dysphoria she'd always felt suddenly made sense. "It was all so clear to me," Jesse told me. "All I needed were the words." Sara spent the next two weeks scouring the Internet for videos and information on becoming a man. She learned that unlike previous generations, today's trans young adults don't consider physical transformation a prerequisite for identity. Some use hormones; some have their breasts removed in "top" surgery; some reject medical interventions altogether, as unnecessary invasions and expense. She discovered that sexual orientation is independent of gender: Some trans men are attracted to women, some to men, some to both. And she learned that trans men aren't necessarily determined to hide the fact they were raised as girls, or that they once attended a women's college.

Soon after, Sara cut her hair short and bought her first pair of men's jeans. Sara told friends she was a man. By second semester, he was using male pronouns and calling himself Jesse, the other name his mother had considered for her daughter. He also joined a tiny campus group for students who knew or suspected they were trans men. It was called Brothers, a counterweight to the otherwise ubiquitous message of sisterhood.

That summer, Jesse saw a gender therapist, and early in his sophomore year, he began injecting testosterone into his thigh every two weeks, making him one of the first students to medically transform into a man while at Wellesley. He became the administrator of Brothers. Though he felt supported, he also felt alone; all the other trans men on campus had graduated, and the other students in Brothers were not even sure they identified as men. Outside Brothers, everything at Wellesley was still sisterhood and female empowerment. Nevertheless, he said, "I thought of Wellesley as my home, my community. I felt fine there, like I totally belonged."

Jesse decided he wanted to have top surgery over winter break, and his parents agreed to pay for it. He returned for spring semester but only briefly, taking a sudden leave of absence to go home and help care for his ill father. When Jesse re-enrolled at Wellesley a year and a half later, in fall 2012, much had changed in Jesse and at school. Having been on testosterone for two years at that point, Jesse no longer looked like a woman trying to pass as a man. His voice was deep. His facial hair was thick, though he kept it trimmed to a stubble. His shoulders had become broad and muscular, his hips narrow, his arms and chest more defined.

Wellesley was different, too. By then, a whole crowd of people identified as trans—enough for two trans groups. Brothers had officially become Siblings and welcomed anyone anywhere on the gender spectrum except those who identified as women. Meanwhile, Jesse and some transmasculine students continued to meet unofficially as Brothers, though Jesse was the only one on testosterone.

Trans students point out that they're doing exactly what women's colleges encourage: breaking gender barriers, fulfilling their deepest yearnings and forging ahead even when society tries to hold them back.

Over all, campus life had a stronger trans presence than ever. At least four of the school's 70 R.A.s did not identify as women. Student organizations increasingly began meetings by asking everyone to state preferred names and pronouns. Around campus, more and more students were replacing "sisterhood" with "siblinghood" in conversation. Even the school's oldest tradition, Flower

Sunday—the 138-year-old ceremony that paired each incoming student with an upper-class Big Sister to support her—had become trans-inclusive. Though the school website still describes Flower Sunday as "a day of sisterhood," the department that runs the event yielded to trans students' request and started referring to each participant as a Big or Little "Sister/Sibling"—or simply as Bigs and Littles.

And yet even with the increased visibility of trans students on campus, Jesse stood out. When he swiped his Wellesley ID card to get into friends' dorms, the groundskeepers would stop him and say, "You can't go in there without a woman to escort you." Residential directors who spotted him in the dorm stairwells told him the same thing. In his own dorm, parents who were visiting their daughters would stop him to ask why he was there. Because bathrooms in the dorms are not labeled "women" or "men" but rather "Wellesley only" and "non-Wellesley," students who didn't know Jesse would call him out for using the "Wellesley only" bathroom instead of the one for visitors. When he tried to explain he *was* a Wellesley student, people sometimes thought he was lying.

"Everything felt very different than it had before," he said of that semester. "I felt so distinctly male, and I felt extremely awkward. I felt like an outsider. My voice was jarring—a male voice, which is so distinct in a classroom of women—so I felt weird saying much in class. I felt much more aware of Wellesley as a women's place, even though the college was starting to change."

Once spring semester ended, Jesse withdrew. "I still think of Wellesley as a women's place, and I still think that's a wonderful idea," he said. "It just didn't encompass me anymore. I felt it was a space I shouldn't tread in."

Some female students, meanwhile, said Wellesley wasn't female enough. They complained among themselves and to the administration that sisterhood had been hijacked. "Siblinghood," they argued, lacked the warm, pro-women connotation of "sisterhood," as well as its historic resonance. Others were upset that even at a women's college, women were still expected to accommodate men, ceding attention and leadership opportunities intended for women. Still others feared the changes were a step toward coeducation. Despite all that, many were uneasy: As a marginalized group fighting for respect and clout, how could women justify marginalizing others?

"I felt for the first time that something so stable about our school was about to change, and it made me scared," said Beth, a junior that year, who asked to be identified by only her middle name because she was afraid of offending people she knew. "Changing 'sister' to 'sibling' didn't feel like it was including more people; it felt like it was taking something away from sisterhood, transforming our safe space for the sake of someone else. At the same time, I felt guilty feeling that way." Beth went to Kris Niendorf, the director of residential life, who listened sympathetically and then asked: Why does "sibling" take away from your experience? After thinking about it, Beth concluded that she was connected to her classmates not because of gender but because of their shared experiences at Wellesley. "That year was an epiphany for me. I realized that if we excluded trans students, we'd be fighting on the wrong team. We'd be on the wrong side of history."

Exactly how Wellesley will resolve the trans question is still unclear. Trans students say that aside from making sure every academic building on campus has a unisex bathroom, Wellesley has not addressed what gender fluidity means for Wellesley's identity. Last spring, Alex Poon won Wellesley's 131-year-old hoop-rolling race, an annual spirit-building competition among seniors. Alex's mother was the hoop-rolling champion of the Class of '82 and had long ago taught her daughters the ways of the hoop, on the assumption that they would one day attend her alma mater. (One of Alex's older sisters was Wellesley Class of '11; another went to Bryn Mawr.) Alex was a former Girl Scout who attended an all-girls high school. But unknown to his mother, he was using Google to search for an explanation for his confusing feelings. By the time Alex applied to Wellesley, he secretly knew he was trans but was nonetheless certain Wellesley was a good fit. For one thing, going there was a family tradition; for another, it was a place where gender could be reimagined. In his sophomore year at Wellesley, he went public with his transgender status.

On hoop-rolling day, Alex—wearing a cap backward on his buzz-cut hair—broke through the finish-line streamer. President H. Kim Bottomly took a selfie with him, each with a wide smile. A small local newspaper covered the event, noting that for the first time in the school's history, the winner was a man. And yet the page on Wellesley's website devoted to school traditions continues to describe the race as if it involves only women. "Back in the day, it was proclaimed that whoever won the Hoop Roll would be the first to get married. In the status-seeking 1980s, she was the first to be C.E.O. Now we just say that the winner will be the first to achieve happiness and success, whatever that means to her." But Alex isn't a her, and he told me that his happiness and success includes being recognized for what he is: a man.

That page is not the only place on the site where Wellesley markets itself as a school of only female students. Elsewhere, it crows that "all the most courageous, most provocative, most accomplished people on campus are women." The student body, it says, is "2,300 smart, singular women feeling the power of 2,300 smart, singular women together" on a campus where "our common identity, spirit and pride as Wellesley women" are celebrated. Those sorts of messages, trans students say, make them feel invisible.

"I just wish the administration would at least acknowledge our existence," said Eli Cohen, a Wellesley senior who has been taking testosterone for nearly a year. "I'd be more O.K. with 'We're not going to cater to you, because men are catered to everywhere else in life,' rather than just pretending we don't exist."

Some staff and faculty members, however, are acknowledging the trans presence. Women-and-gender-studies professors, and a handful of others, typically begin each semester asking students to indicate the names and pronouns they prefer for themselves. Kris Niendorf, director of campus and residential life, recruits trans students who want to be R.A.s., as she does with all minorities. Niendorf also initiated informational panels with trans students and alums. And before this school year began, at the urging of trans students, Niendorf required all 200 student leaders to attend a trans-sensitivity workshop focused on how to "create a more inclusive Wellesley College." For the last few years, orientation organizers have also included a trans student as one of the half-dozen upper-class students who stand before the incoming first-years and recount how they overcame a difficult personal challenge.

And yet many trans students feel that more needs to be done. They complain that too many professors assume all their students are women. Students provided numerous examples in courses across subject areas where they've been asked their viewpoint "as a woman." In a course on westerns two years ago, an essay assignment noted that western films and novels were aimed at male audiences and focused on masculinity. The professors asked students for their perspective "as a female reader or watcher"—wording that offended the three trans students in class. When a classmate pointed out the problematic wording to the professors, the instructors asked everyone instead "to explore how your own gender identity changes how you approach westerns."

At times, professors find themselves walking a fine line. Thomas Cushman, who has taught sociology at Wellesley for the last 25 years, first found out about Wellesley's trans population five years ago, after a student in one of his courses showed up at Cushman's office and introduced himself as a trans male. The student pointed out that every example Cushman gave in class referred to women, and every generic pronoun he used was female, as in "Ask your classmate if she...." He told Cushman that Wellesley could no longer call itself a "women's college," given the presence of trans men, and he asked Cushman to use male pronouns and male examples more often, so trans students didn't feel excluded. Cushman said he would abide by whatever pronoun individual students requested for themselves, but he drew the line at changing his emphasis on women.

"All my life here," Cushman told me, "I've been compelled to use the female pronoun more generously to get away from the sexist 'he.' I think it's important to evoke the idea that women are part of humanity. That should be affirmed, especially after being denied for so long. Look, I teach at a women's college, so whenever I can make women's identity central to that experience, I try to do that. Being asked to change that is a bit ironic. I don't agree that this is a 'historically' women's college. It is still a *women's* college."

On the second day of orientation this fall, Eli Cohen arrived on campus in a muscle T and men's shorts, with a carabiner full of keys hanging from his belt loop. He was elated to be back to the place that felt most like home. It was the first time in four years that Eli had not been part of orientation—first as a newcomer and then two years as an R.A. We hung out in the Lulu Chow Wang Campus Center, known affectionately as Lulu, and watched the excited first-years flutter by, clutching their orientation schedules and their newly purchased Wellesley wear.

Just 12 days earlier, Eli underwent top surgery, which he said gave him a newfound self-assurance in his projection of manhood. It had been nine months since he started testosterone, and the effects had become particularly noticeable over the three-month summer break. His jaw line had begun to square, his limbs to thicken and the hair on his arms and legs to darken. And of course now his chest was a flat wall. As his friends caught sight of him for the first time in months, they hugged him and gushed, "You look sooo good!"

Though Eli secretly suspected in high school that he was a boy, it wasn't until after he arrived at Wellesley that he could imagine he might one day declare himself a man. By his second year, he had buzz-cut his hair and started wearing men's clothes. He asked his friends to call him Beckett, which is similar to his female birth name, which he asked me not to mention. His parents live only 14 miles away and dropped by for short visits. He left his girl nameplate on his dorm door. His friends understood that whenever his parents arrived, everyone was to revert to his female name and its attendant pronouns. He was an R.A. at the time and decided not to reveal his male name to his first-year students, figuring it was too complicated to explain which name to use when.

Given how guarded he had to be, being Beckett was exhausting and anxiety-inducing. Demoralized, he eventually told his pals to just use his birth name. The summer after his sophomore year, he got an internship at a Boston health center serving the L.G.B.T. community, and many of his co-workers were trans. Their confidence gave him confidence. When the Wellesley office that coordinates internships sent out an email to all interns that began, "Good morning, ladies…," he emailed back to say he did not identify as a woman. The coordinator apologized and explained that all the names on her paperwork from Wellesley were female.

By summer's end, he began introducing himself as Eli, a name utterly unlike his birth name. Eli mustered the courage to tell his parents. It took a little while for his mother to accept that her only daughter was actually a son, but she came around.

When I asked Eli if trans men belonged at Wellesley, he said he felt torn. "I don't necessarily think we have a right to women's spaces. But I'm not going to transfer, because this is a place I love, a community I love. I realize that may be a little selfish. It may be a lot selfish." Where, he wondered, should Wellesley draw a line, if a line should even be drawn? At trans men? At transmasculine students? What about students who are simply questioning their gender? Shouldn't students be "free to explore" without fearing their decision will make them unwelcome?

Other trans students have struggled with these questions, too. Last December, a transmasculine Wellesley student wrote an anonymous blog post that shook the school's trans community. The student wrote to apologize for "acting in the interest of preserving a hurtful system of privileging masculinity." He continued: "My feelings have changed: I do not think that trans men belong at Wellesley.... This doesn't mean that I think that all trans men should be kicked out of Wellesley or necessarily denied admission." He acknowledged he didn't know how Wellesley could best address the trans question, but urged fellow transmasculine classmates to "start talking, and thinking critically, about the space that we are given and occupying, and the space that we are taking from women."

The reactions were swift and strong. "A lot of trans people on campus felt emotionally unsafe," recalled Timothy, a sophomore that year. "A place that seemed welcoming suddenly wasn't. The difficulty was that because it was a trans person saying it, people who don't have enough of an understanding to appreciate the nuance of this can say, 'Well, even a trans person says there shouldn't be trans people at Wellesley, so it's O.K. for me to think the same thing, too.' "

Students and alums—queer and straight, trans and not—weighed in, sometimes in agreement but other times in anger. Some accused the blogger of speaking on behalf of women as if they were unable to speak for themselves. Others accused him of betraying transmasculine students. (He declined to comment for this article.) But other students, including several transmasculine ones, were glad he had the courage to start a public discussion about Wellesley's deeply conflicted identity. "It's a very important conversation to have," Eli said. "Why can't we have this conversation without feeling hurt or hated?"

In some ways, students are already having that conversation, though perhaps indirectly. Timothy ended up easily winning his seat on the student government last spring, capturing two-thirds of the votes. Given that 85 percent of the student body cast ballots in that race, his victory suggests most students think that transmasculine students—and transmasculine leaders—belong at Wellesley.

Another difficult conversation about trans students touches on the disproportionate attention they receive on campus. "The female-identified students somehow place more value on those students," said Rose Layton, a lesbian who said she views trans students as competitors in the campus dating scene. "They flirt with them, hook up with them. And it's not just the hetero women, but even people in the queer community. The trans men are always getting this extra bit of acknowledgment. Even though we're in a women's college, the fact is men and masculinity get more attention and more value in this social dynamic than women do."

Jesse Austin noticed the paradox when he returned to campus with a man's build and full swath of beard stubble after nearly two years on testosterone. "That was the first time in my life I was popular! People were clamoring to date me."

Trans bodies are seen as an in-between option, Timothy said. "So no matter your sexuality, a trans person becomes safe to flirt with, to explore with. But it's not really the person you're interested in, it's the novelty. For lesbians, there's the safety of 'I may be attracted to this person, but they're "really" a woman, so I'm not actually bi or straight.' And for straight people, it's 'I may be attracted to a woman's body, but he's a male, so I'm not really lesbian or bi.'"

Kaden Mohamed said he felt downright objectified when he returned from summer break last year, after five months of testosterone had lowered his voice, defined his arm muscles and reshaped his torso. It was attention that he had never experienced before he transitioned. But as his body changed, students he didn't even know would run their hands over his biceps. Once at the school pub, an intoxicated Wellesley woman even grabbed his crotch and that of another trans man.

"It's this very bizarre reversal of what happens in the real world," Kaden said. "In the real world, it's women who get fetishized, catcalled, sexually harassed, grabbed. At Wellesley, it's trans men who do. If I were to go up to someone I just met and touch her body, I'd get grief from the entire Wellesley community, because they'd say it's assault—and it is. But for some reason, when it's done to trans men here, it doesn't get read the same way. It's like a free pass, that suddenly it's O.K. to talk about or touch someone's body as long as they're not a woman."

While trans men are allowed at most women's colleges if they identify as female when applying, trans women—people raised male who go on to identify as women—have found it nearly impossible to get through the campus gates. Arguably, a trans woman's identity is more compatible with a women's college than a trans man's is. But most women's colleges require that all of an applicant's documentation indicate the candidate is female. That's a high bar for a 17- or 18-year-old born and raised male, given that so few come out as trans in high school. (Admissions policies at private undergraduate schools are exempt from Title IX, which bans gender discrimination at schools receiving federal funds.) Two years ago, Calliope Wong, a high-school trans woman from Connecticut, applied to Smith College, but her application was returned because her federal aid form indicated she was male. She posted the rejection letter online, catalyzing a storm on the Internet and student rallies at Smith. Smith eventually agreed to require that the applicant be referred to as female only in the transcript and recommendation letters, but not on financial-aid documents; by then, however, Wong had decided to attend the University of Connecticut.

For its part, Wellesley has never admitted a trans woman, at least not knowingly. Many Wellesley students, including some who are uncomfortable having trans men on campus, say that academically eligible trans women should be admitted, regardless of the gender on their application documents.

Others are wary of opening Wellesley's doors too quickly—including one of Wellesley's trans men, who asked not to be named because he knew how unpopular his stance would be. He said that Wellesley should accept only trans women who have begun sex-changing medical treatment or have legally changed their names or sex on their driver's licenses or birth certificates. "I know that's a lot to ask of an 18-year-old just applying to college," he said, "but at the same time, Wellesley needs to maintain its integrity as a safe space for women. What if someone who is male-bodied comes here genuinely identified as female, and then decides after a year or two that they identify as male—and wants to stay at Wellesley? How's that different from admitting a biological male who identifies as a man? Trans men are a different case; we were raised female, we know what it's like to be treated as females and we have been discriminated against as females. We get what life has been like for women."

In May, Mills College became the first women's college to broaden its admissions policy to include self-identified trans women, even those who haven't legally or medically transitioned and even if their transcripts or recommendation letters refer to them as male. The new policy, which begins by affirming Mills's commitment to remaining a women's college, also welcomes biological females who identify anywhere on the gender spectrum, as long as they haven't become legally male. The change grew out of two years of study by a committee of faculty and staff, which noted that Mills has always fought gender-based oppression and concluded, "Trans inclusiveness represents not an erasure but an updating of this mission."

Mills also aims to educate students, staff and faculty members to be more trans inclusive, said Brian O'Rourke, who oversees enrollment at the college and was the president's liaison to the committee. I asked O'Rourke if that included reducing the focus on women in the classroom. "I honestly don't know," he said. "We had a national speaker on trans issues join us on campus about a year ago, and one of the things she suggested is that we stop referring to Mills as a women's college, because that concept is exclusionary. In the auditorium, there was an audible gasp. We've had a lot of conversations about how to stress women's leadership and women's empowerment and at the same time, include people who may not identify as women. The answer is: We don't know yet."

Last month, Mount Holyoke College announced a more far-reaching policy: It would admit all academically qualified students regardless of their anatomy or self-proclaimed gender, except for those biologically male at birth who still identify as male. In a list that reflects just how much traditional notions of gender have been upended, Mount Holyoke said eligible candidates now include anyone born biologically female, whether identified as woman, man, neither or "other" and anyone born biologically male who identifies as a woman or "other." The school president, Lynn Pasquerella, said she and her officers made the decision after concluding it was an issue of civil rights.

But Pasquerella said accommodations for trans students will not include changing the school's mission. "We're first and foremost committed to being a women's college," she told me. "I'm not going to stop using the language of sisterhood." She mentioned she taught a class in critical race theory two years ago and told her students, "When I use the term 'sisterhood,' I'm using it in a way that acknowledges the fact that not everybody here identifies as a woman. It is a rhetorical device ..., but it is not intended to exclude anybody."

I said her explanation seemed like the one for using "he" as a generic pronoun for a male or female. She offered a different analogy, noting the parallel between women's colleges and historically black colleges and universities. "Isn't it still legitimate to speak of being a community of color even if you have half a dozen students who aren't individuals of color?" she asked. "The same might be said about women's colleges. Our mission was built upon education for women, and while we recognize that not everyone identifies this way, this is who we are and how we talk about things."

Meanwhile, Wellesley continues to struggle with its own identity. In August, Debra DeMeis, the dean of students, told me the administration had not yet worked out how to be a women's college at a time when gender is no longer considered binary. President H. Kim Bottomly and Jennifer C. Desjarlais, the dean of admissions, declined to talk to me. But a few days after Mount Holyoke's announcement, Bottomly released a statement saying that Wellesley would begin to think about how to address the trans question.

On the last Friday in May, some 5,000 parents, alumnae and soon-to-be graduates streamed onto the rolling field near Severance Hall, named after Elisabeth Severance, a generous 1887 alumna. It was a gorgeous, temperate morning for Wellesley's 136th annual commencement, and once the last baccalaureate degree was conferred, the audience was asked to stand. As is the school's tradition, two graduates led an uplifting rendition of "America, the Beautiful." The lyrics, for those who needed them, were printed in the commencement program, including the chorus: "And crown thy good, with brotherhood, from sea to shining sea!"

Those words were penned by Katharine Lee Bates, an 1880 graduate of Wellesley who defied the expectations of her gender, and not just by becoming a professor, published author and famous poet. A pastor's daughter, she never married, living instead for 25 years with Katharine Coman, founder of Wellesley's economics department, with whom she was deeply in love. When a colleague described "free-flying spinsters" as a "fringe on the garment of life," Bates, then 53, answered: "I always thought the fringe had the best of it."

As parents, professors and graduates joined in the singing of Bates's most famous poem, many felt an intense pride in their connection to the graduates and this remarkable college, which has sent forth so many women who leave impressive marks on the world. As the hundreds of voices rounded the curve on "And crown thy good with ...," the unknowing parents continued to "brotherhood," the word that was always supposed to stand in for women too, but never really did. Wellesley women long ago learned that words matter, and for decades, this has been the point in the song when their harmonious choral singing abruptly becomes a bellow as they belt out "sisterhood," drowning out the word that long excluded them and replacing it with a demand for recognition. It's one of the most powerful moments of commencement, followed every year by cheers, applause and tears, evoked by the rush of solidarity with women throughout time, and the thrill of claiming in one of the nation's most famous songs that women matter—even if the world they're about to enter doesn't always agree.

In the last few years, a handful of graduates have changed that word once again, having decided that "sisterhood," no matter how well intended, is exclusionary, and so they instead call out "siblinghood." A few trans men find even that insufficient, and in that instant, they roar the word that represents them best: "brotherhood," not as a sexist stand-in for all humankind, but as an appeal from a tiny minority struggling to be acknowledged.

In truth, it's difficult to distinguish in the cacophony each of the words shouted atop one another. What is clear is that whatever word each person is hollering is immensely significant as a proclamation of existence, even if it's hard to make out what anyone else is saying.

Jesse J. Prinz is a Distinguished Professor of Philosophy at City University of New York and a Research Professor at the Philosophy Department of the University of North Carolina at Chapel Hill. His research focuses on cognitive science, philosophy of psychology, philosophy of language, moral psychology, and aesthetics.

Gender and Geometry
Jesse J. Prinz

When we think about cultural differences, we tend to think about groups who live in different places, speak different languages, and worship different gods. But cultural differences can be very local, as when urban subcultures live side by side in the same town. The most local cultural divide of all, however, is the gender divide. Men and women work the same fields, worship in the same churches, and sleep in the same beds, but they reside in different cultures. Men and women are treated differently, they often do different things with their leisure time, and they are subject to very different cultural expectations. Of course, men and women are also biologically different. And this raises a puzzle for science. If men and women perform differently on tests of intellectual ability, should the difference be pinned on nature or nurture or both?

Difference and Discrimination

The Summers Debacle

On 14 January 2005, Lawrence Summers, the president of Harvard University, sparked a media frenzy by suggesting that innate cognitive differences are a leading cause of the fact that women are underrepresented in the science and engineering faculties of elite universities. He voiced this opinion while speaking at a private conference at the National Bureau of Economic Research, but soon his assessment was being reported by newspapers across the globe. Critics argue that Summers's remarks were uninformed and irresponsible. In his speech, Summers claimed that discrimination and socialization play little role in gender inequity within the academy. There is a considerable body of research to the contrary. Summers also implied that women are biologically inferior to men, in that they are genetically less likely to attain the levels of aptitude demanded by prestigious programmes in science, maths, and engineering. This, we will see, is also at odds with the evidence. Biology may make some contribution to cognitive differences between men and women, but differences in academic achievement may owe more to socialization.

The same people who presume that the cognitive differences between men and women are primarily biological also tend to conclude that these differences are inalterable. If this conclusion is combined with the view that women are cognitively inferior to men, then the inevitable upshot is that they are incapable of achieving the same standards. This is exactly what Summers implied, and that is why his speech was offensive to so many. The offense was compounded by the fact that Harvard has had a depressingly bad record when it comes to hiring women. During Summers's reign as president, only 12 percent of the new tenured faculty appointments went to women. Summers was not in charge of selecting new faculty—departments do that—but he participated in tenure decisions, and he could have encouraged departments to recruit women more actively. Instead, female appointments declined appreciably during his time at the helm. When Summers raised the spectre of biological differences, his detractors inferred that he might be guilty of gender bias, falsely believing that men are more likely than women to be naturally brilliant.

Before presenting the evidence against this conjecture, we should note that it is nothing new. In 1873, a respected Harvard medical professor named Edward Clarke published a book called *Sex in Education, or a Fair Chance for the Girls*, in which he warns that women who attend college risk becoming infertile and hysterical. He conjectured that when women tried to use their underdeveloped cognitive capacities to learn, blood would be diverted to the brain from the uterus, which would then atrophy. In 1889, C.C. Coleman, an American physician, issued a similar warning:

Women beware. You are on the brink of destruction: You have hitherto been engaged in crushing your waists; now you are attempting to cultivate your mind ... you are exerting your understanding to learn Greek, and solve propositions in Euclid. Beware!! Science pronounces that the woman who studies is lost.

The French psychologist Gustave Le Bon went even further:

[T]here are a large number of women whose brains are closer in size to gorillas' than to the most developed male brains. This inferiority is so obvious that no one can contest it for a moment ...[Women] represent the most inferior forms of human evolution and ... they are closer to children and savages than to an adult, civilized man ...A desire to give them the same education, and, as a consequence, to propose the same goals for them, is a dangerous chimera.

Such attitudes were not esoteric or anachronistic. Clarke's book went through seventeen printings, and the scientific community widely believed Le Bon's contention that women are no smarter than children. The fact that women have more youthful proportions than men was taken as incontrovertible physiological evidence for the conclusion that their intellectual development did not advance beyond childhood. The prevailing view throughout the nineteenth century was that women are intellectually inferior to men.

This prejudice had a measurable impact. Most obviously, women were not allowed to vote. Women's suffrage came to Great Britain and Germany in 1918, to the United States in 1920 and to France in 1944. Women were also excluded from many professions. At one time, women were deemed incapable of working as stenographers or secretaries, two fields they came to dominate. The presumption of inequality seriously delimited women's access to education. Women were generally excluded from college education until the nineteenth century. In 1837, Oberlin College in Ohio became the first college to admit female students, but they were assigned a special curriculum, which included cooking and cleaning rather than Latin and Greek. Even the feminist reformers of this period were happy to admit that women could never equal men. In 1823, Harriet Martineau argued that women should be given access to higher education in England, so that they could become "companions to men, instead of playthings or servants."[1] This may sound like a plea for equality, but Martineau was also quick to concede that "the acquirements of women can seldom equal those of men, and it is not desirable that they should." Accordingly, women were often educated in separate schools, and they were discouraged or prevented from pursuing graduate degrees, especially in maths and science. Sofia Kovalevskaya was the first woman to earn a mathematics doctorate in Europe, in 1874. In 1895, Caroline Baldwin Morrison became the first woman in the United States to receive a doctorate in science. The first European woman to receive a doctorate in science was Marie Curie, in 1902; she went on to win two Nobel Prizes. For the majority of women, graduate education was not an option, and, though almost half of all college students were women in the early twentieth century, many went to women's schools that were not always equal to their male counterparts. Widespread coeducation is a recent development. Princeton and Yale opened their doors to women in 1969. Harvard beat them to the punch by conferring degrees to women in 1964, but those women had to be enrolled in Radcliffe Women's College, which did not officially merge with Harvard until 1999.

Summers struck a nerve against this background. His remarks were especially wounding to women in academia who have extensive first-hand knowledge of inequitable treatment. Women are routinely ignored, talked down to, and hit on by male college professors. They are often not encouraged in their academic pursuits and not believed in. Women in academia also know that the struggle for equal treatment is a slow one. Most had many more professional opportunities than their mothers, and it seems implausible that bias would simply evaporate in the space of a single generation.

The Science of Difference

By the 1970s, few people would openly suggest that women are less intelligent than men, but the same period saw an increase in scientific testing of gender difference. Flagrant claims of male superiority were replaced by the rhetoric of separate but equal. Scientists began broadcasting evidence that women think differently, and, more often than not, they assumed these differences were biologically based.

---

1. Martineau, H. (1823). On female education. *Monthly Repository*, 18, 77–81.

There is now a considerable body of evidence showing that men perform better on some tasks, while women perform better on others. The male advantage shows up most frequently in two areas: spatial reasoning and maths. In spatial reasoning, men are on average better at imaging geometrical objects at different orientations ("mental rotation"), finding an object that has been embedded in a complex picture, and orienting a rod so that it is perpendicular with the floor of a room. When it comes to spatial navigation, men are more likely than women to use their sense of compass directions and geometrical information. In maths, male scores on standardized tests tend to be higher. In 2004, male high school students scored 7 percent higher on the maths portion of the Scholastic Assessment Test (SAT), and, in earlier years, those numbers have been as high as 15 percent. Moreover, 78 percent of the students who got perfect scores on the maths SAT were male.

Women's strengths tend to lie elsewhere. They outperform men on certain verbal tasks and on tasks that involve recognition of fine details and contextual information. In terms of language, women do better than men at coming up with words that begin with a particular letter, and they are better at recalling words from lists; they also use considerably more words than men in the course of a day. In visual memory tasks, women also have some advantages over men. They are better at recalling where an object was located in an array. Unlike men, women tend to navigate using landmarks rather than compass directions. Where a man might recall that the bank is three blocks north, a woman might recall that the bank is just past the post office.

Women tend to be less efficient than men when it comes to spatial tasks that involve understanding three-dimensional configurations of objects or object parts. Some of the largest gender differences have been reported in studies of mental rotation. In mental rotation tasks, subjects are presented with a picture of two objects at different orientations, and they are asked whether the two objects are the same. To answer, subjects must mentally rotate one object to see if it aligns with the other. Women make more errors than men, and there is some evidence that they tend to use a different strategy. One way to see how a person solves a problem is by giving them two tasks at the same time and seeing if one interferes with the other. Men do badly at mental rotation tasks if they are doing another spatial task at the same time, such as keeping an arrangement of dots in their minds. Women are not impaired at mental rotation while they are memorizing arrangements of dots, but they are impaired if they are trying to hold a list of words in their minds. This suggests that women may be relying on their language skills when they mentally rotate objects. Perhaps they are labelling each part of the object and reasoning about how it would change when rotated.

Some naturists have advanced evolutionary explanations of gender differences. Differences in maths and language are difficult to explain in evolutionary terms, because sophisticated maths and language skills appear recently in human evolution, and it's far from obvious why either sex would have greater use for capacities than the other. Are women with greater vocabulary and men who excel in algebra really more likely to procreate? Most evolutionary speculation has centered around spatial skills. According to one popular view, men are better at spatial cognition because male ancestors were hunters, and hunting requires a high degree of spatial precision. This hypothesis is not really plausible, however. First of all, it's not clear what specific skills such as mental rotation have to do with hunting. Second, some spatial skills, such as finding embedded objects in a complex scene, are equally useful for both hunting and gathering, which is believed to have been dominated by women. Third, the male advantage in spatial cognition has been reported in species that don't hunt, such as rats, who are scavengers by nature. If gender differences in cognition are at all based in biology, we have no good explanation of why they evolved. It is possible that such differences are just a freak by product of how male and female brains happen to be wired.

The differences between men and women are often small, and some people perform in ways that are atypical for their sex. But, however small, the differences do show up reliably on a variety of tests, and they often ring true anecdotally. For example, it's something of a cliché that men have a better sense of direction, and women have a better eye for details. Men refuse to ask for directions because they feel confident about where they are going. Women may be more likely to remember where the car keys are, and they may be more likely to notice an interesting building or odd looking person as they drive along the road.

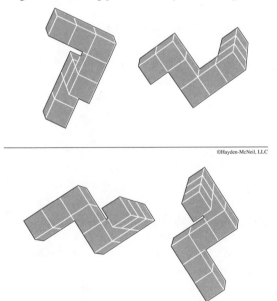

©Hayden-McNeil, LLC

Figure 1. Mental rotation task. Which pairs are the same?[2]

2. Based on Shepard, R. N., and Metzler, J. (1971). Mental rotation of three-dimensional objects. *Science*, 171, 701–3.

Gendered Jobs?

In his speech, Summers suggested that gender differences in thinking might be used to explain why women are underrepresented in certain university departments. In particular, it might explain why there are comparatively few women in maths, engineering, and scientific fields that are highly quantitative, such as physics. Summers also implied that the cognitive differences are biologically determined. Both of these conjectures are misguided. Biology contributes to cognitive differences between men and women, but there are important cultural factors as well, and cultural factors may be the primary cause of academic hiring inequity.

The underrepresentation of women in university departments may owe something to cognitive differences, but it owes much more to discrimination. The disproportion of men to women in the academy is far greater than the extent of the alleged cognitive differences. Based on data from 2001, the National Science Foundation reports that, in American maths and physics departments, male full professors outnumber female full professors by a ratio of 10 to 1. In engineering departments, the ratio is about 36 to 1. If faculty employment ratios were driven entirely by statistical differences in thinking styles, we might expect women to outnumber men in fields that rely heavily on language skill, such as English and philosophy. This is not the case. In Harvard's English department, twenty of fifty-three faculty members are women, and in the philosophy department, five of eighteen are women. For all the rhetoric about women being better than men in some cognitive domains, there is little evidence that their superior aptitude ever affords greater opportunities for women than for men. Up until very recently, men have dominated in all areas of the academy. We mustn't forget that, one hundred years ago, there were virtually no women teaching in universities. It would have been absurd to think this was due to differences in cognitive style. Women just weren't given the opportunity. The current numbers suggest that there has been exponential progress in women's educational equity, but they also suggest that discrimination remains a serious problem.

In fact, there is direct evidence for discrimination against women in hiring. Rhea Steinpreis and her colleagues at the University of Wisconsin in Milwaukee sent out a CV to a large number of psychology professors and asked them to assess whether the person named on the CV was worthy of hiring.[3] Each professor received a CV with exactly the same content, but in half the cases, the name on the CV was Brian Miller, and in the other half it was Karen Miller. Despite the fact that the imaginary job applicants were equally qualified, those who received the male applicant's CV were about 50 percent more likely to say that he should be hired than those who received the female applicant's CV. The majority of professors evaluating the female applicant said she should not be hired, and the overwhelming majority of professors evaluating the male applicant said that he

---

3. Steinpreis, R., Anders, K. A., and Ritzke, D. (1999). The impact of gender on the review of the curricula vitae of job applicants and tenure candidates: A national empirical study. *Sex Roles*, 41, 509–28.

should be hired. It must be noted that all the professors who participated in this study probably believe that it is wrong to show preferential treatment to a man, yet that is exactly what they did unwittingly. Female professors were as likely as male professors to show this form of bias. This is direct and powerful evidence for the existence of discrimination in academic hiring. Similar studies have shown that the very same paper is rated as superior if it has a male author's name on it rather than a female name. There is also evidence showing that female professors receive less mentoring than their male counterparts when they are starting out, they are given lower salaries, and they are regarded more negatively when they are assertive. Each of these factors can negatively impact prospects for women in academia.

Given the evidence for discrimination, it is possible that employment inequity has very little to do with cognitive differences. If graduate admissions committees, hiring committees, and tenure committees are unconsciously biased against women, then we have a perfectly good explanation of why men outnumber women in the academy. The fact that inequity is greater in some fields than in others may be the result of residual stereotypes about women's capabilities. There used to be very few women in law and medicine, and now women are catching up with men rapidly. Our conception of what women can do is continually shifting. Given this history, and evidence for continued biases in hiring, there is no reason to think that cognitive differences are a major factor in the current distribution of university jobs.

Explaining Gender Differences

In blaming academic employment inequity on discrimination, I don't mean to deny that there are cognitive differences between men and women. There may be. As we have seen, men and women tend to perform differently on certain tests. Men do better with maths, mental rotation, and embedded pictures, and women do better with verbal memory and fluency and with recalling where objects were located. These differences need to be explained. There are three possibilities. One possibility is that men and women are equally good at the skills in question, but they just perform differently on tests. Another possibility is that there are biological differences that have an impact on cognition. A third possibility is that cultural variables lead men and women to think somewhat differently. It turns out that each of these variables is partially right.

Testing Troubles

Let's begin with the possibility that gender differences in thinking are, in part, an illusion generated by misleading performance, on tests. There is some strong evidence for the suggestion that differences between male and female math scores can be partially explained this way. The primary evidence for male superiority in maths comes from the fact that men do better on the maths portion of standardized tests, such as the SAT and the Graduate Record Exam

(GRE). But these results actually conflict with records of classroom performance. In American high schools, girls take about the same number of mathematics classes as boys, and they get better grades. Women also comprise almost half of the maths majors in American colleges, and they do just as well as men. These indicators suggest that women and men have comparable aptitude for mathematics. "Why, then, do men do better on standardized tests? One possibility is that women underperform because they believe that they are less capable than men. In a simple experiment Claude Steele and his colleagues gave a maths test to a group of male and female college students, after telling them in advance that men tend to do better than women.[4] Lo and behold, the women did worse. Then the experimenters gave the same test to another group of male and female college students without saying anything in advance, and their scores came out the same. This phenomenon, which has been replicated many times, is called stereotype threat; if you make a negative stereotype salient to people, they will inadvertently conform to it. These effects are widespread. If you tell people of color that they do not generally perform as well on a test as whites, their scores will drop, and if you tell white men that their scores are usually lower than Asians', there will also be a significant decline in performance.

A negative stereotype can become salient without even mentioning it. To demonstrate this, Michael Inzlicht and Talia Ben-Zeev gave female college students maths portions from the GRE.[5] The women took the test in a room with other women, with men, or with a combination of men and women. When women were placed in a room with men, their performance declined, and the extent of the decline was proportionate to the number of men in the room. Male performance was not affected by the presence of women. Apparently, when women take standardized tests in the presence of men, they unconsciously recall the stereotype that men are better at maths, and their performance drops off. If the presence of men adversely affects female performance in maths, one might wonder why women do as well as men in their maths courses. One possible explanation is that a male presence has an adverse affect only when women are taking standardized tests. Unlike the ordinary tests that students take for their maths courses, standardized tests are overtly comparative. Everyone knows that the SAT and GRE are used to make college and university admissions decisions, and scores are given as a percentile in comparison to other students. With ordinary classroom tests, students are less likely to see themselves as competing with other students, so stereotypes pertaining to comparative performance (women are worse than men) are less likely to come to mind.

---

4. Spencer, S. J., Steele, C. M., and Quinn, D. M. (1999). Stereotype threat and women's math performance. *Journal of Experimental Social Psychology*, 35, 4–28.

5. Inzlicht, M., and Ben-Zeev, T. (2000). A threatening intellectual environment: Why females are susceptible to experiencing problem-solving deficits in the presence of males. *Psychological Science*, 11, 365–71.

This research suggests that the cognitive differences between men and women may be exaggerated. Some of the variation in test performance may result from the unconscious fulfilment of negative stereotypes. But this probably isn't the whole story. First, it's not clear that there are negative gender stereotypes associated with every cognitive test that shows gender differences. Why, for example, are women better at verbal memory and recalling how objects are arranged? Why are women worse than men at embedded picture tasks? Second, there is a nagging question of where the stereotypes come from. Many stereotypes have no basis in reality; they are merely used to denigrate. We can instill fear by saying that Jews are greedy, and we can justify economic disparity by saying that blacks are lazy. The claim that women are worse than men at mental rotation is potentially insulting, in that it implies that men are more intelligent, but it's hard to see how this particular claim would have been deliberately devised to hold women back. Third, there is evidence that biology has a role in the cognitive differences between men and women.

Biological Factors

The evidence for a link between biology and cognitive differences comes from several sources. First, there is evidence from neuroscience. Compared with women, men seem to have more grey matter, the pinkish grey tissue comprised of cell bodies covering the surface of the brain. But women have more white matter, the connective tissue just below the surface that allows cells to communicate. Male brains are larger overall, but women have faster brains, and some studies suggest that women's brains have more cells and larger areas dedicated to language. There are also differences in how male and female brains function. For men, IQ scores correlate best with activity in the frontal cortex and parietal cortex. In women, IQ scores are correlated with different areas of the frontal cortex, including language areas, and there is little correlation with the parietal cortex.[6] Differences in brain function could explain male and female performance on spatial tasks. For both men and women, mentally rotating an object involves many of the same brain areas, but in women there is greater activity in areas associated with object recognition, and in men there is greater activity in areas associated with motor control. One possibility is that women try to mentally rotate an object by visually analyzing its parts, whereas men are more likely to imagine physically moving the object around.

These findings are intriguing, but difficult to interpret. We often don't know the significant brain differences; for example, we have a very limited understanding of the link between brain size and brain function. Moreover, different labs report different results, and some alleged contrasts between male and female brains have been called into question. For example, it was widely reported that female brains are more symmetrical than male brains, with certain language

---

6. Haier, R. J., Jung, R. E., Yeo, R. A., Head, K., and Alkire, M. T. (2005). The neuroanatomy of general intelligence: Sex matters. *Neurolmage*, 25, 320–27.

functions actively involving both hemispheres rather than being predominantly located in the left. But a recent analysis of multiple brain scanning studies suggests that this isn't the case; both male and female brains seem to be equally asymmetrical. Studies of the brain also raise a difficult chicken and egg problem. If male and female brains function differently, those differences could result from differences in socialization. Differences in how the sexes are educated could affect brain function. We know, for example, that trained musicians, mathematicians, and taxi drivers have brains that function somewhat differently from those of the rest of us.

Even if we take current findings from brain science as tentative, there is some reliable evidence for the conjecture that biology contributes to gender differences in cognition. For one thing, gender differences show up in other creatures. Male rhesus monkeys outperform females on a spatial memory task, in which they have to find a food reward that changes locations on each round. The male spatial advantage can even be found in rodents. In rats, mice, and meadow voles, males often out-perform females when learning the location of food in mazes. In rats, the pattern changes when the food can be located by memorizing landmarks; females do better than males at using such information. These findings are intriguing, because they confirm the pattern we see in humans: Males in many mammalian species are more adept than females at spatial tasks.

Research on animals suggests that some of the cognitive differences between men and women may be deeply rooted in biology, but there are reasons to exercise caution when drawing this conclusion. First, gender differences have not been found in all animals. Male meadow voles are maze masters, but male prairie voles are not. Second, when gender differences are found, they are often ephemeral. In some species, the gender differences disappear with age, training, or at different stages in the reproductive cycle. Third, in some species, the gender differences we find in animals may actually contrast with the human case on closer analysis. As I mentioned, male rhesus monkeys outperform females in remembering the location of objects, but in human beings spatial memory is often better in women. Finally, there is also some risk in drawing inferences from one species to another, because each has its own evolutionary history. Consider an analogous case. Members of polygynous societies might find comfort in knowing that male gorillas keep a harem of females, but it would be a mistake to infer from this comparison that polygyny is the natural arrangement for human beings; a wide range of sexual arrangements can be observed in the animal kingdom.

The best evidence for an interaction between biology, gender, and thought comes from hormone studies. Consider testosterone, the principal male hormone. It turns out that fluctuations in testosterone correlate with fluctuations in cognitive performance. As men age, testosterone levels drop, and, when those levels drop, there are correlative drops in performance in maths and spatial skills. Hormone replacement therapy can improve performance. Similar effects have also been observed in women. Women naturally produce some testosterone, but only about a seventh of the amount that men produce. Studies have shown women with comparatively high testosterone levels outperform women with low testosterone levels on spatial tasks and maths tasks. Giving women a single dose of testosterone improves their performance on mental rotation tasks. That doesn't mean we should all take megadoses of testosterone. Optimal performance is associated with moderate levels of the hormone. Women with high testosterone levels and men with low levels perform better than people with too much or too little.

Cognitive effects have also been associated with the principal female hormone, estrogen. In particular, estrogen is positively correlated with verbal memory and verbal fluency, two skills that tend to be better in women than in men. Two to three weeks after menstruation, when estrogen levels are high, women score better on verbal tests. When estrogen levels decline in menopause, there are correlated drops in verbal skills. When men with prostate cancer take estrogen, their verbal memory improves.

These findings suggest that cognitive differences between men and women are influenced by hormonal differences. Testosterone and estrogen can change the way we think. But we should not get too carried away. For one thing, the correlations between hormone levels and cognitive abilities are ceiling high. A maths wiz can have low testosterone, and a verbal savant can have low estrogen. In fact, there is little reason to think that individuals who make great achievements in these domains have impressive levels of the corresponding hormones. For example, it was recently discovered that people working in the hard sciences tend to have low testosterone levels, or at least levels that were low during crucial periods of early development. This underscores the point that women are not being excluded from science because of inadequate biology.

A second reason to doubt the importance of hormones comes from the fact that gender gaps are closing. A few decades ago, the performance gap between men and women was twice as large, but the hormonal differences were, we can presume, just as great as they are today. If hormones were the primary source of cognitive differences between the sexes, we should see greater stability over time.

A third reason for caution is that hormone differences may have social causes. Suppose that hormone levels were perfectly correlated with cognitive skills. It still would not follow that hormones are the *ultimate* cause of gender differences, because variation in hormone levels can be affected by environmental factors including socialization. For example, depression causes testosterone levels to drop. It also happens to be the case that women are twice as likely to be depressed as men. Why? Perhaps it is because women are socialized into feeling inadequate, subordinate, or limited in their opportunities. Thus, socialization can cause depression, depression lowers testosterone, and low testosterone levels in women diminish performance on maths and spatial tasks. Perhaps women do worse than men statistically because societal factors make women more depressed. Hormone levels might be the proximate cause of sex differences, and not the ultimate causes.

Finally, hormones cannot explain all the data on cognitive differences, because there are demonstrable interactions between hormone levels and environmental factors. Here's a case in point. As we have seen, women are more likely to do badly on maths tests when they are reminded of the stereotype that women are less numerically competent than men. It turns out that the effects of stereotype threat are magnified for women who have high levels of testosterone. Remember, these are the women who are ordinarily likely to do best on maths tests. When women who are talented in maths are reminded of negative stereotypes, their performance plummets. Women with low testosterone do not show the same effect. Consequently, when stereotypes are primed, naturally talented women actually perform worse than women who have not had a helping hand from biology.

Learned Limitations

The impact of stereotypes on cognitive performance suggests that social environment plays a role in the cognitive differences between men and women. If drawing attention to a negative stereotype can affect a woman's performance while she is taking a test, imagine what a lifetime of exposure to negative stereotypes can do. There is overwhelming evidence that women are treated differently from men, and these differences begin from the earliest days of life. In the face of such obvious and overt differences in socialization, it is remarkable that researchers ever looked to biology as the primary source of differences in cognition. In the nineteenth century, scientists thought that women's childlike appearance, such as their lack of facial hair, explained the fact that women were more ignorant than men. The more obvious explanation was that women were prevented from having equal education, employment opportunity, government involvement, and personal autonomy. If women were less informed than the men who controlled their lives in the nineteenth century, it was a consequence of the fact that women were treated like children. With 20/20 hindsight we know that biological differences are too small and too ephemeral to explain the gross inequality that existed at that time.

History teaches a sobering lesson. Our contemporary attempt to explain gender differences by appeal to biology alone may look preposterous fifty years from now, when women have had more time to prove themselves in every branch of the academy. Biological differences exist, but they can be swamped, exaggerated, and shaped by culture. In response, a well-intentioned naturist might argue that men and women now enjoy equal education and equal opportunity. In the nineteenth century, women were denied equal access to higher education, but now they are not. So, the naturist will say, any residual cognitive differences must be due to biology. This line of argument is sheer folly. Women and men may attend the same schools, but they are not treated the same way. Attending the same classes does not entail having the same education.

Studies have shown a pervasive and systematic pattern of unequal treatment in contemporary classrooms. Dedicated and well-intentioned teachers fall prey to societal gender bias and treat female students inequitably. Here are some unsettling facts. Male students are given more praise and criticism than female students; teachers call on male students more often; male students are given more time to answer questions when called on; male students are asked harder questions; female students are more frequently asked to report matters of fact, rather than matters of opinion or analysis; teachers generally give male students more feedback; in that feedback, teachers are more likely to give male students advice that helps them arrive at correct answers the next time around rather than just telling them the correct response. This pattern of preferential treatment starts early and has an impact. By the time women are in college, their style of academic engagement differs markedly from their male classmates. Where men make assertions in the classroom, thereby advertising their intelligence, women are much more likely to ask questions, advertising their ignorance. In fact, women who make assertions in classrooms tend to make them with the same intonation as a question, inadvertently playing dumb when they know the answer.[7] Men speak four times as often and shout out answers eight times as often.[8] Teachers are more receptive to these male interruptions, they direct more questions at men, are more likely to develop remarks made by men, and they offer men more encouragement.

A die-hard naturist or an unrepentant sexist might argue that all these classroom differences are the result of biological differences and not the other way around. Perhaps teachers treat males as more intelligent because they are more intelligent. The problem with that explanation is that female performance on aptitude tests suggests that they are as capable as men in most areas, and better than men in some areas. Women's aptitude for science is comparable to men's during teenage years, but social factors are working against them. A recent study shows that teenage boys and girls have comparable interest in, and aptitude for, science, but parents systematically report that their daughters have less interest and talent.[9] In the same study, fathers were shown to be significantly more demanding when helping their sons with science projects. The biases at

7. Tannen, D. (1994). *Talking from 9 to 5*. New York: William Morrow.

8. Swarm, J. (1988). Talk control: An illustration from die classroom of problems in analyzing male dominance of conversation. In J. Coates and D. Cameron (eds.), *Women in their speech communities*. London: Longman.

9. Tenenbaum, H. R., and Leaper, C. (2003). Parent-child conversations about science: The socialization of gender inequities? *Developmental Psychology*, 39, 34–47. See also: Simpkins, S. D., Davis-Kean, P. E., and Eccles, J. S. (2006). Math and science motivation: A longitudinal examination of the links between choices and belief. *Developmental Psychology*, 42, 70–83; Jacobs, J. E., Davis-Kean, P., Bleeker, M., Eccles, J. S. and Malanchuk, O. (2005). I can, but I don't want to: The impact of parents, interests, and activities on gender differences in math. In A. Gallagher and J. Kaufman (eds.), *Gender differences in mathematics*. Cambridge: Cambridge University Press.

home reinforce the pattern at school. Ultimately, girls lose confidence in their ability to become good scientists. There is some evidence that these deleterious effects can be mitigated by sending girls to single-sex schools. Girls who graduate from single-sex schools have higher educational aspirations than their coed counterparts, they are more likely to attend top universities, and they are more likely to pursue graduate degrees. These girls are also more confident, and they are considerably less likely to fall into the stereotypically female pattern of turning assertions into questions when they contribute to classroom discussion. Girls in single-sex schools are also more likely to profess an interest in maths.[10] These girls are not biologically different from those who attend coed schools; they have just been socialized differently. With boys around, girls become second-class citizens.

Socialization is not restricted to educational settings. Children are exposed to an endless barrage of images showing men and women playing gender-specific sex roles. In movies, television shows, magazines, and pop music, kids learn gender-specific attitudes and behaviors. These differences even show up in sources of entertainment designed for young people. In children's books, male characters are five times more likely than female characters to be portrayed as aggressive, and more than three times as likely to be portrayed as competitive. Girls are more than twice as likely to be portrayed as emotionally expressive, and almost four times as likely to be portrayed as passive.[11]

Gender socialization begins at birth. Girls and boys are named differently, dressed differently, and put in differently decorated rooms. These overt differences cue caregivers into different patterns of socialization. This has been nicely demonstrated by a series of studies in which adults are presented with a baby wearing either pink clothes and bearing a female name or wearing blue clothes and bearing a male name.[12] In these studies, the same baby is used, but some adults think it's a boy and others think it's a girl, and that makes all the difference. For example, when a six-month-old baby is labelled "Beth," adults described "her" as soft, nice and delicate. When the same baby is introduced as "Adam," adults describe "him" as strong, active, and intelligent. If adults see a video clip of a baby reacting to a jack-in-the-box, they will describe that baby as frightened if they think it's a girl and as angry if they think it's a boy. Adults will also play different games with male and female babies. If several toys are present, adults will hand "Beth" a doll. If they think the same baby is named "Adam," they will hand over a toy hammer or truck. Adults also give positive feedback to babies when they pick up toys that fit the gender stereotype. This is not just fun and games.

10. Lee, V. E., and Bryk, A. S. (1986). Effects of single sex secondary schools on student achievement and attitudes. *Journal of Educational Psychology*, 78, 381–95.

11. Evans, L., and Davies, K. (2000). No sissy boys here: A content analysis of the representation of masculinity in elementary school reading textbooks. *Sex Roles*, 42, 255–70.

12. Will, J. A., Self, P. A., and Dantan, N. (1976). Maternal behavior and perceived sex of infant. *American Journal of Orthopsychiatry*, 46,135–9; Vogel, D. A., Lake, M. A., Evans, S., and Karraker, K. H. (1991). Children's and adults' sexstereotyped perception of infants. *Sex Roles*, 24, 605–16.

Studies suggest that, regardless of sex, children who play more with stereotypically three-dimensional toys, such as construction sets, do better on maths tests than children who play with dolls. Socialization encourages girls to be less active than boys, more timid and more preoccupied with beauty than brains or brawn. Such socialization could easily affect thinking styles. A typical boy may spend hours making models and building go-carts, and a typical girl may spend hours imagining dialogues between Barbie dolls. The boy gets extensive training in spatial reasoning, and the girl becomes a master of language. Later, when they are given tests as teenagers, the boy will do better at mental rotation, and the girl will show greater verbal fluency....

If there are biological differences between men and women, those differences probably get magnified through socialization. But it need not work that way. If we stop assuming that one sex is inherently better at certain cognitive tasks than the other, we can encourage both sexes to master the same range of important skills. Training would allow men to improve verbal skills and increase their sensitivity to contextual information, such as landmarks, and training would allow women to rival men in maths and spatial skills. If we design curricula to maximize the capacities of both boys and girls, sex differences in cognitive abilities may shrink away. Rather than blaming biology for inequality, we should blame ourselves for not taking steps to even the playing field.

Pepper Schwartz is a Professor of Sociology at the University of Washington in Seattle. She often writes for public audiences and serves as AARP's Love and Relationship Ambassador.

The Social Construction of Heterosexuality
Pepper Schwartz

Much of modern sex research has grown from the social constructionist viewpoint articulated by Simon and Gagnon in *Sexual Conduct*, the pathbreaking book that encouraged a generation of young scholars to look beyond the collection of data points and into the cultural construction of sexual norms, values, perceptions, and behaviors. Way ahead of their time, Simon and Gagnon made all things problematic and asked us to at least understand the cultural lens we used to interpret behavior and gender. . . .

I would not be surprised to get a ho-hum reaction to this enterprise. We tend to explain the exotic and problematize the exception. If most people are five foot ten, we try to explain under five feet or over seven. If something is common and normative, we think we understand it, and we certainly feel no need to explain it. But, in fact, that tendency merely constructs a black box, a familiar shape that fools us into thinking we can explain something merely because we come in contact with it every day. This acceptance of the common obfuscates in two ways: we create post hoc justifications about why what exists is supposed to exist (and mistake that for wisdom), and by accepting a "natural order of things" we hide all the nuances of "fact" by inhibiting further investigation or critique. As a result, we have neglected the social construction of heterosexuality as if it was unproblematic—as if we are born, and poof! we are totally and adequately heterosexual, a mere outcome of some natural selection with an invariant program that creates heterosexuality as a uniform product, with no other markers or interesting differences within until other shades of sexual orientation are introduced.

In fact, "doing heterosexuality" is no less problematic than homosexuality—though its punishments are more for failure than for accomplishment—and the norm is enforced and sanctioned differently from exceptional behavior. Reactions to failures of heterosexual enactment are less violently corrected than portrayals of homosexual identity—except, of course, when a failure of adequate enactment causes an attribution of homosexuality, and psychic or physical violence follows in order to preserve normative heterosexual roleplaying along narrowly constructed and strongly idealized stereotypes.

Just what are those stereotypes and idealistic portrayals of heterosexuality? They vary by region of the world, country, and subculture, but they share a common body of work, and those normative expectations are fed to us at the same time we are being breast-fed. Countless research papers have shown that even infants are programmed into adult sexual niches: we are socially constructed as heterosexual as soon as we are propelled out into the world. Hospitals still paste blue or pink bows on babies' heads, and oohs and ahs about the "little man" and baby girl usually quickly include comments on chests, legs, and genitals, creating expectations for the man or woman to be. Baby boys are held less and cooed at less, says the research, not because they are loved less (there is certainly some evidence that they may be loved more in some families) but because they are being handled in a way that preserves their manliness—their heterosexuality— right from the start. Little girls are dressed in brighter colors and frillier outfits because they are supposed to be supremely adorable as part of their core equip- ment right from the beginning.

Heterosexuality has its grave expectations. They are not articulated all at once—some are never openly articulated—but we all know that a lack of articulation of norms doesn't mean they don't exist. Briefly, I would like to men- tion some of the presumptions and social scripts that guide our management of heterosexuality, and comment on some of the consequences of our peculiar rules and regulations.

There are several overarching requirements of heterosexuality that I believe organize the major script of being heterosexual in American society. First of all, heterosexuality is confabulated with gender performance. Whatever the cul- ture, its norms about masculinity and femininity are supposed to co-vary with heterosexual enactment, and gender itself is expected to be unambiguous and performed according to the cultural outlines of the moment. Even today, after the sexual and gender revolutions of the late 1960s and 70s, heterosexual dress codes, mannerisms, and body language are still strictly mandated. Although our culture has antiheroes who disdain these conventions (most notably located in the worlds of rock and roll, grunge, heavy metal and other communities of art and counterculture), the majority culture creates cultural icons in its magazines, TV shows, [and] movies, featuring models that tell us what exact gender displays portray heterosexual correctness.

Fashion designers and media stars are quite important. They become the cultural trend setters for the young. No one who has observed the fashion impact of Britney Spears, Lindsay Lohan, and other teen idols can deny with a straight face (as it were) that popular culture creates gender norms. And, I should add, it is not just children or teens who use movie stars and band members as guides to sexual correctness: the Academy Awards telecast is watched by millions of avid viewers with one of the central agendas of the entire evening being the observation of who wears what, who appears with whom, and how all of this translates into sexiness. Just about every sitcom and drama is a commentary on who is a man's man, who is a man's woman, and how do characters carry off their evocation of male and female sexual power. Even as we note characters as caricatures, they serve as sexual ideals. The fan magazines exist and prosper because millions of Americans want to follow the stars' lives, copy their wedding dress, gossip about their love affairs, and resemble them as much as possible. This goes way beyond casual ogling; stars are the new royals and their lifestyle choices—such as turning to plastic surgery—begin national trends, in this case creating a new acceptance of plastic surgery so that standards of attractiveness in middle-aged women are changing (helped, of course, by television shows making the process as well as the product fascinating. *The Swan* and several other programs actually show operations or stages of recovery, touting the self-determination of the patient while minimizing the pain and possibility of complications. Of course, in the very act of setting standards based on stars, gender roles become more problematic, since it is hard to measure up against the fantasy embodiment of masculinity and femininity). It is fair to assume that for many who mimic the style and look of a sex god or goddess, the gap between their idol and themselves serves to erode the individual's confidence in competent heterosexual performance. Who can ever be as "male" and macho as Bruce Willis, wisecracking as he incinerates a building full of bad guys, saves his buddy, and beds the astoundingly beautiful women who populate action films? Who can be as charming as Cameron Diaz—perfectly proportioned and the object of everyone's desire? Who can be as winsome and pure of heart as Julia Roberts, a woman leggier than most runway models, in the storybook romances in which she stars? In drama after drama, she offers the eternal portrayal of female heterosexuality: seeking Prince Charming, losing Prince Charming, regaining Prince Charming. The themes of romantic acquisition and loss may be recast within the frame of a professional woman's life, but this reframing pales next to the strong outline of normative female heterosexuality: that is, for a woman, the central and most important theme in her life will be love. Love is the question, love is the answer, and whatever it takes to get it, keep it, maintain it, and cherish it is what the movie is really about.

We venerate and create fantasy masculinity and femininity—often, ironically enough, portrayed through the exquisite acting of gay or lesbian actors—but the truth really doesn't matter. The James Bonds, the lone wolves, and the cynical detectives and cops tell us what male sexuality in America is supposed to look like. The young lovelies and studmuffins of the movies and TV sitcoms tell us what adequate heterosexuality is supposed to look like. The unspoken subclause is that the rest of us who could not fit well in the ensemble casts of *Friends*, *CSI*, or *Grey's Anatomy* have a sexuality that is unfinished, inadequate, and somehow unworthy. This is a disastrous recognition for those who have already experienced self-doubt about their masculinity or femininity within their peer group. Most young girls and women are insecure about whether they are attractive, articulate or desirable. Even without comparison to mythic media icons, they struggle mightily to feel sexually worthy. Women turn themselves into wraiths trying to be thin enough, and put themselves in physical jeopardy by paying surgeons to sculpt their bodies so that they can have thighs, abdomens, and breasts that fit the sexual profile of what they believe men want. Women, and increasingly men, spend thousands of scarce discretionary dollars to change their faces and physiques to fit prevailing standards of beauty so that they will be able to compete in the heterosexual mating market or retain spouses who might otherwise stray to better models of masculinity and femininity.

One can't help but reflect on this: while noblemen of the eighteenth century might have had to work at being dandies, twenty-first century men are spared these indignities. Just being male used to be enough to be granted provisional heterosexual status. However, increasingly, in some sort of cosmic justice, men seem to be following suit: commercial interests have finally realized that having both sexes terminally insecure is better for business than just having one sex feel inadequate, so now men are in the mix of creating better bodies, more hair (on their head; now many men feel required to get electrolysis for the stuff on their back!), and stiffer erections to make sure that they look and act like the cultural cut-outs they believe will ensure their sexual selection by women. The medical establishment is only too happy to oblige these neuroses.

The past decade has seen the collusion of pharmaceutical research with the medical establishment to create a cultural crisis about potency. The new standard of genital adequacy is to have penises that could compete with the fantasy penises in purple passages in X-rated books and movies. Now "rock hard penises" and "hot throbbing members" will actually exist in life as they do on porn stars. The vision of what a penis ought to look and act like can come true by using Viagra, Levitra, or Cialis, even if few men naturally match the size or performance of these porno-penises unaided by a drug. Viagra, so the media and doctors on lease from Pfizer have said, can give you the erection you've always dreamed of, and as a result, a new baseline standard of erections and performance gets created. Penis performance, always a potential problem for men, now invokes new fears: readiness throughout the lifestyle becomes standard. The natural aging of the organ becomes deviant as we try to create genitals that conform to standards created by chemists rather than nature. Male heterosexuality requires a stiff erection unto death. In order to make male heterosexuality unambiguous, we create a new version of what constitutes achievement of competent sexuality.

There is, of course, a female equivalent. Far before Viagra became a global brand, women's and fashion magazines created yearly standards for the year's "look," which often meant a new kind of body. The mass media would launch cover stories announcing "breasts are back" (I'm not kidding—this was a real cover in 2005) or "the six secrets to making him go crazy all night." Women's magazines, and increasingly men's magazines, do not have stories on sex—the magazines are almost *entirely* about mating and dating—and even the products are advertised to help live the good life of a popular sexual being. If we stand back for a moment, it becomes clear that the entire message of advertising is that heterosexuality is *not* natural: it is not easy—and, indeed, it will take everything they can sell you for you to even hope to sustain a decent sexual presentation and the possibility of creating a successful seduction, engagement, and marriage.

Being successful—as a body—as an actor—as a heterosexual—is certainly not seen as a fact of nature. No—*it is seen as an act of will.*

Which leads us to the obvious conclusion that, far from being normal, heterosexual identity is fragile. Very fragile. Easily polluted. Given all the possible paths leading to failure of sexual competence, we are warned that we must be very careful in our construction of it.

This ability to fail publicly brings us to our second proposition: that our performance of heterosexuality is supposed to be accepted and applauded by others. All of this dressing up and strutting out is not just to attract the opposite sex—it is supposed to fend off criticism and attribution as a homosexual. Homosexuality and heterosexuality are like twins: no matter how different they become, they are part of the same piece, the same drama. Homosexuality exists in its own right—but if it did not, it would be invented to enforce compliance to proper gender enactment.

Straight men dress in ways to announce their sexuality, much the way the homosexual men often mimic it to announce their own: exaggerating the costumes of masculinity into mating signals for men with men. The two sexualities, considered so polar, actually butt up next to each other, trying to accomplish different things with the same cultural and physical equipment.

But that is the point, is it not? Heterosexual men and homosexual men have the same socialization, as do heterosexual women and homosexual women, so it takes some work to distinguish our sexual presentation from one another. No wonder then that we have "fey" gay men and "butch" lesbians. Gay men and women need to work hard to create territory that is unambiguously in revolt against heterosexuality because heterosexuality itself is much more subtle and problematic than we pretend it to be. Hence, exaggerated performances exist among both heterosexuals and homosexuals as each group tries to demonstrate who they are to like others and elicit appropriate reactions. Still, no matter how broad a sexual display is, the audience may not react to even the most counternormative gender role if sexuality is not seen as problematic in that area. For example, there are some locales where people seem almost naïvely unconscious. One sees, for example, environments where women present themselves as "butch" and may even have the build and demeanor of a man, and men who are as fey as anyone who ever cross-dressed in a San Francisco gay rights parade are benignly unconscious of the thin line they walk in the gender role enactment wars. Part of this innocence is one of place: residents of small towns that cannot imagine that anyone in their town could be gay and so integrate their friend's and neighbor's generally non-normative gender display into some other social construct ("weird," "eccentric," "not vain," etc.) rather than gayness. Even though the butch farmer's wife may be secretly hankering after the farmer's wife next door, "audiences" may attribute the non-normative gender or sexual display to asexuality rather than homosexuality. As long as the person in question does not claim an alternate sexuality, they may be spared approbation. On the other hand, this is not always the case. The young who resemble disapproved-of, nonheterosexual attributes can justly quake in school halls, worrying that they will be attacked emotionally or physically—or just disdained.

This brings up a third specification: we are supposed to have certain kinds of bodies that reveal our heterosexuality. For all the jokes about "Pat" on *Saturday Night Live* (the person we could not figure out as male or female, who would confuse us by tempting us with a clue as to her "real" gender and then add another clue that would cancel out the first lead), the truth is that the real joke on us was how much anxiety it caused the viewer to watch a character without a gender and/or sexual identity we could identify. In general, we *hate* the idea that someone is not firmly assigned to a body type and look that telegraphs both gender and sexuality. In fact, it occurs to me that this intolerance of gender ambiguity may be one of the reasons our society hates fat people. Fat pads out physical differences between the sexes; the roundness we associate with women covers both men and women who are fat: breasts and chests look alike, genitals shrink in reference to the greater bulk of the body, and facial contours become more similar. It is another kind of androgyny, and most people are extremely uncomfortable with it when it is so extreme that they cannot distinguish biological sex. Extreme androgyny like Pat is seen as sexual failure—and therefore sexual identity may be imputed as homosexual even though homosexuality really has nothing to do with body type. Still, all kinds of gender ambiguity or cross-referencing the other gender (especially using the other gender's costumes or customs) has been historically grounds for severe punishment (including death, in some countries and during certain periods of history) or humiliation (open season as a target for humor or bullying). Interestingly, temporary trespass of gender/sexual confabulation is allowable for certain kinds of ritual celebrations such as fraternity costume parties, English music hall performances or Halloween. Anyone who wants to continue the joke too long, however, is quickly labeled deviant, and—to show how strong our feelings are—subjected to violence or contempt. Our culture does not want to lose the hard edges of gender, precisely because people depend on the standards of gender enactment to help them delineate heterosexuality from homosexuality. Imprecise as that may be, it is the tool most people use for a quick assessment of sexual identity.

This brings me to a fourth point about heterosexuality, which has to do not with the body, but the psyche: In order to be considered heterosexual, individuals are presumed to be singularly and unproblematically aroused [by] the opposite sex and the opposite sex only.

Within sexual identity, the heterosexual package includes the idea that heterosexuality is unitary—all or nothing. We are not supposed to have to learn heterosexuality; it is supposed to come with our genitals and gender behavior. Any indication of flexibility (a continuum of arousal and attraction that may be greatest toward people of the opposite sex but has some arousal to same-sex persons) is, even among the most sophisticated of people, seen as discrediting heterosexuality. In some American Indian cultures, bisexuality is acknowledged as having a place in the sexual pantheon and can be seen as a gift; heterosexuality can co-exist with homosexuality in the same person without putting either into question. In most Western societies, however, and in many non-Western societies, same-sex arousal immediately incurs identity reassignment; we do not want to think of our sexuality as polymorphous. Indeed, the Freudian phrase would be "polymorphous perverse": a disordered drive rather than merely a lusty or extensive one. In our society, sexual identity as a heterosexual allows for no trespass of this central vision of unadulterated heterosexuality.

Interestingly, though, we have developed a pragmatic out for some people who can satisfy the gender norms of heterosexuality so satisfactorily that if they choose the right explanation for same-sex behavior we will not discredit them. While, in most cases, we disallow any behavior but heterosexual conduct, we do have a vision of male and female sexuality that allows a "loophole"—if you will, an apt phrase for the conundrum. Indeed, there are men who so satisfy the norms of masculinity that they can get away with nonheterosexual behavior, at least for a time, and not be reassigned a gay identity. These are the men who are so hypermasculine we believe their accounts of a sexuality so brutish that, when they say any hole will do, we believe them! Rock stars who are outrageous in every other respect are often allowed to have both male and female partners and continue to maintain their dominant sexual status as heterosexual. Another common example are men in prisons, men who have a scarcity of females, or men from cultures where maleness is considered so sexually powerful that they can just enforce their definition of the situation on anything as long as they take in certain cultural scripts that protect heterosexual identity. As an example, I once interviewed a Greek man named Spiro who was sexually adept with both men and women. He seemed to have no trouble having both male and female partners without having either leave him because of his bisexual activity. When I asked him how he could have sex with both men and women without being labeled as gay, he replied, "It is no problem. You see we have four types of men in Greece: men who fuck men, men who fuck men and women, men who fuck women, and queers." I was somewhat flummoxed since I knew he had sex with both men and women and would not consider himself "queer." So I asked him, "Who are the people you consider 'queer'?" "Oh," he said. "The queers are the ones who *get* fucked." Or, put another way, Spiro had a culture that created a vision of men as voracious sexual creatures who naturally will have what they can—as long as they are not degraded by taking the female role, a humiliation from which, apparently, one is denied reentry into the club of heterosexual men. If you are a man who wants to have sex with men in Greece, yet do not want to be thought of as homosexual, you can accomplish this goal, as long as you do not blunder into the "female" sexual role. How this translates intrapsychically may be more difficult, except if you are, like Spiro, from a culture where sexually available women are scarce and sex, any way you can get it, is approved of by your friends.

The allowances for women are different, though not entirely. There are some women whose heterosexual credentials are so impeccable that they evoke increased erotic interest in men rather than relabeling when they take on a same-sex lover. Madonna, for example, gave a well-publicized passionate kiss on the lips to Britney Spears, which, while it got headlines, did not hurt Madonna's draw as a performer or her perception by fans as an outrageous heterosexual woman. In some parts of the United States there are those who would give erotic points to women who have sex with women even if they are not superstars . . . as long as the sexual encounter is done for the pleasure of men. Women can have sex with women as performers—or as the hors d'oeuvre in a meal that will be consummated in heterosexual intercourse. Simply put, in our contemporary urban culture, situational bisexuality is sexy, but real lesbianism is an affront.

One exemption from that reaction is lesbianism as a heterosexual porno fantasy. Women who look like *Playboy* bunnies, who are voracious sexual creatures—wild enough to do anything—are asked to do the inevitable porno three-way, and doing so does not endanger their heterosexual status. As long as female performers in porno eventually show that they are sexually available to men, their homosexual sex is seen as kinky rather than as deviant. These women never take on a lesbian identity; their job is to be warm-up artists, create sexual titillation, and make sure that the male viewer simply sees them as an erotic surrogate until he "finishes" the "job." The women in porno movies who make love to one another create a drama of female ecstasy that excites the male viewer rather than threatens him. These actresses do not leave the folds of heterosexuality even in fantasy (although, in reality, many of them are stalwartly lesbian). For our purposes, however, what is interesting is that there are these temporary havens for homosexuality—but sexual identity is preserved because of the belief that beautiful, sexy women will be steadfastly immune to female charms when men are available. Furthermore, if the women who have had sex with each other follow convention and don't try to also take on male prerogatives (such as male dress or demeanor), same-sex appetite is seen as an erotic augmentation rather than a substitution. It is an odd erotic peccadillo of male sexuality that almost all female sexual behavior is catalogued as a dress rehearsal for male sexual enjoyment. Only when the male is truly convinced that the woman has absolutely no desire for the male voyeur does the wrath of homophobia come to rest at lesbian destinations. Lesbians to most men are bisexuals, and bisexuals are heterosexuals-in-waiting; however, this fluid assignment is often not so gently experienced by the women who must decide if there is a sexual central self that is not really performing for men, but instead seeks a way to justify erotic and/or emotional desire for other women.

This relates to the fifth point: that heterosexual arousal is supposed to be strong and unambiguous. This is a very interesting requirement, and it flies in the face of almost every fact we know about sexual performance. More correctly, sexual arousal is always problematic some of the time: there when you don't want it, absent when you are hoping it will overwhelm you. Arousal is highly sensitive to other emotions—fear of rejection, tension, performance anxieties, distraction, and fatigue; in other words, numerous states of mind and body. Additionally, we are affected by subtle cues in the environment or in the other person's behavior that may consciously or unconsciously affect our behavior: the wrong words, the wrong look and suddenly we are deflated; a serious performance problem for men, especially if it happens often and becomes habitual. Many men, reflecting back on their boyhood, have talked about how disorienting it was not to have an erection under conditions one was supposed to (or to have it when one was not supposed to) and the doubts and fears and dysfunction that followed. Because an erection is supposed to be "natural"—both a perk and prerequisite of heterosexuality—its absence, or the presence of ambivalence, is supposed to be instructive of malfunction, or, in the eyes of society, potential deviance. In other words, your status as a heterosexual goes up or down with your penis.

Women have a variation of this theme, albeit not such a publicly noticeable one. For example, in a sexual interaction, women may be quite worried about the presence or absence of lubrication. Some women's vaginas lubricate quite copiously when aroused; other women remain quite dry no matter how aroused they are, or become less lubricated as they age and approach perimenopause or menopause. Women, like men, vary in the way their body reacts to stimulation. However, in the Book of Heterosexuality, aroused women are supposed to lubricate, and the lack thereof has been known to cause women—and their partners—some worry that the body is the truer source of information than the mind, and that not lubricating indicates lesser sexual interest or excitement. Lubrication, while easily fixable by modern waterbased or silicone products, is perceived to be telling the woman (and her partner) something elemental. A standard of competent heterosexuality is unmet. Women have been let off this hook somewhat by being defined as having a mostly reactive sexuality (i.e., "you do not have to be the first to be sexually aroused," "as a woman you are entitled to be only mildly interested until you are aggressively aroused by a man"). In this scenario, if you are *not* aroused, it is not that you are not heterosexual, it is just that this is the wrong person, you are not in love enough, or that your lover is not man enough to arouse you. In general, however, women's heterosexuality is perceived to be awakened by love. Love is supposed to be the motor of women's sexual emotions. In fact, female sexuality is supposed to be so relational that even inappropriate (i.e., homosexual) arousal can sometimes happen without necessarily impacting heterosexual identity. In this perspective, women are turned on because they are in love, and love is the motivating sexual force. Same-sex behavior, rather than exhibiting an essential part of a woman's true nature, is merely another act of true womanhood—female sexuality created by the power of love. Many women who have had extended lesbian relationships in their biography but do not wish to identify as a lesbian may, post hoc, define their same-sex love affair as primarily a love relationship with a sexual component that could only last for the length of that relationship. This vision of self-limiting sexuality (over when the love relationship is over) is not sustained by our culture when it concerns men. One moment of adult non-heterosexual arousal—no matter how passing the moment—is likely to be seen as definitive evidence of a core homosexual set of desires.

Sixth: the appropriate [sex]—that is to say, the opposite sex—is supposed to be attracted to us. Sexual identity can be so shaky that it can also be changed by other people's attention to us rather than our own feelings about ourselves. In the movie *In and Out*, actor Kevin Kline is woefully out of touch with his sexual psyche. He is in his early forties and has gone with his girlfriend for years and years without any genital contact. When one of his famous students assumes he is gay—because of inappropriate gender behavior (including, if you will, that he is neat!) and "outs" him, it is the first time he is forced to confront himself. The gay news reporter who is sent to cover the story immediately sees the Kline character as a "closet case." Not one really sexual moment happens that shows Kline demonstrating sexual desire for another man, but the beginning of his uncloseting is not proved by whom he is attracted to (or not attracted to, as the case may be) but also by how others see him and by *who* wants him.

Thus, every heterosexual who is not claimed by the opposite sex as a heart-throb in their youth has doubts—and not only because of being ignored or feeling invisible, but also because of sexual aspirations lofted his or her way by other people with insecure sexual identities. Teenagers, young men and women, and women and men with sexually mixed biographies are all unsure of who they are and who they want, and so they all are more likely to project their own lack of ease onto another person.

Straw Dogs, a subtly homophobic film released several decades ago, insinuates that the central figure Dustin Hoffman is emasculated because he cannot control his flirtatious, wayward wife. This does not mean an immediate homosexual label, but it does mean that his character is not adequately heterosexual because he isn't macho enough to make the men fear him when they ogle and sexually harass her. Written to be a "ball buster" by nature, she is humiliated when the men verbally insult her and he does nothing. In turn, the "virile" workmen have nothing but contempt for a man who will not get physically aggressive when other men decline to respect his woman and ogle her without retribution. The local men hate him for his effeteness and his social class (he has been pilloried by the working-class men fixing his house as being a "poof") and it becomes a war to the death when the working men get more and more contemptuous of him and turn into sexually salivating males who plan to lay claim to the wife. They study Hoffman and decide that he is a putz because they can see his wife is running around on him, and they are pretty sure he knows that she is. Whether or not he knows or does not know, in their minds he *should* know, and do something about it. They decide to do with her as they will since he is obviously not a manly man who deserves to have his female property respected. In the end, however, in order to protect his home, woman, and life, Hoffman "gets it" and resorts to primordial battle to retrieve his wife and his self-respect. They attack him and he triumphs over them, but in order to do so, it is necessary for him to kill every one of these men. At the end of the film, in the eyes of his wife, himself and the director, the Hoffman character becomes a true man in the deepest sense of heterosexual glory.

For women, the archetypal story is the transformation story—that of a woman not sufficiently self-discovered enough to take on the accoutrements of femininity and win her man. Pure evocations of this theme can be found in the musical *Annie Get Your Gun* when the Annie Oakley character cleans up to try to get her man, or when the Rancher's Daughter in *Rodeo* puts on a dress to go to the dance. The high point of claiming heterosexuality is claiming one's birthright of loveliness and recognizing one's longing for a man. Women do not necessarily get assigned a lesbian identity if they do not put men in as the obvious center of their life, but they may be seen as desexed if they are not adequately heterosexually active.

Being desexed is not an easy place to be sent to, however. Let a woman tell you what it feels like to be invisible—that is, not sexually attractive enough to be noticed as they walk by, enter a room, or try to engage in interactions with men. Women see other women drawing male attention but feel too old, too heavy, too short, too tall, too awkward, too bright—too *something* to get some of that attention themselves. When a woman feels this way, her sexuality is irrelevant and therefore denied her. If she is not desired, she does not exist. Many teenage as well as older women feel consigned to this purgatory where nature or nurture has somehow failed to give them the talents they need to feel fully sexual.

Given how hard all of this is to accomplish, my seventh point is both ironic and laughable: once our sexuality is enacted, it is supposed to be stable and un-conflicted. Heterosexuality is supposed to be a rock. Once established, it is not supposed to turn into anything else, which is a comfort to young men and women who may feel that once heterosexuality is initially established, they can relax *if* they become satisfied with the way they look, turn on to people, get turned on to, match the norms of the present gender culture, and so on.

My own research tells me that that reassessment of one's sexual self can occur, and when it does, it is most likely to come through relationships—that indeed our sexuality *is* relational, especially (but not only) for women. The annals of research on sexual identity are full of stories of women who had never had even a same-sex fantasy who unexpectedly became besotted with a specific person and found their sexuality bending towards the bright light of that love. For example, I have interviewed a woman who was having an affair with another woman while her husband, dreadfully ill, was incapacitated for half a year. They met at work and it was love at first sight. They stayed together for years without the husband finding out and the revelation to one of the partners of the extent of her sexual interest was deeply unsettling to her. She could not deny the fact of her love and attraction—and she was 60 years old when she received this new information about herself! Whether the revision of self-identity occurs because of a special partnership or because one is just totally furious with men because of a series of bad intentions or behaviors, it is shocking to most people to realize they have a flexible sexual self. I have interviewed many women who became homosexual not through lust, but through disgust with the men who had disappointed and abused them. Heterosexual identity may not always unravel when a person shuts down because of a disastrous relationship or a love affair that seems to transcend gender, but most people would not be surprised that it had to change.

The fact is that change is shocking to participants. Heterosexual identity—all sexual identity—is considered immutable by most lay people, except insofar as someone's "true" sexuality may be repressed, suppressed, or denied. The cultural prejudice and presumption is that the presence of any homosexual feeling is a dead giveaway of one's sexual essence because homosexual behavior is somehow more a truth of the body than heterosexuality. (The reasoning seems to be that any homosexual behavior demonstrates a true core sexual predilection, since no person would take on the stigma of homosexuality if it were not compulsively necessary.) Both homosexuals and heterosexuals have displayed incredulity and downright rejection of an applicant for a new sexual identity or claim when the claim is from a heretofore homosexual male who is now in love with a woman and believes that his sexuality is oriented in a new way. Our culture doesn't even want to believe such a male really feels what he says he feels. Heterosexuality, in this instance, is so weak that it is easily eclipsed and overpowered by homosexuality. In cases of homosexual exploration, even minimal acts are coded maximally, but in cases of heterosexual exploration by gay men, new sexual experience with women is considered trivial and even psychologically distressed. Despite this reaction, from the lay and scientific community alike, there is still some scientific evidence and certainly adequate anecdotal evidence that both men and women can regroup sexual identity in adulthood when a single important emotional relationship refocuses their sexual energy.

Finally, my eighth and last point about heterosexuality is that intercourse is the heterosexual lingua franca and all else is tangential embroidery. Men and women are not just catalogued because of the gender eroticized but how we eroticize our partner of any gender. Our acts define us, not just our psychology. Key among these acts is the central act of heterosexuality, intercourse. Competent and complete heterosexuals are supposed to prefer intercourse to all other acts. Heterosexuals should have intercourse more frequently than other acts; it should be the main location for our ejaculations and orgasms; and, in general, it should be played as the main event in lovemaking, even if there is a very full program of other kinds of sexual behaviors. Indeed, we seem to need to check in with various kinds of studies, to be checked against the facts and figures of normalcy. While the famous Kinsey studies tried to make it clear that, in their opinion, one pattern of "outlets" was as good as another, those famous studies showed means and medians for sexual acts that made the mean not only average but prescriptive.

This presumption continues in modern texts on human sexuality. Questionnaires, which get at only a rough estimate of sexual habits, are given credence way beyond what their crafters ever believed in, and these ballpark figures now not only define heterosexuality, they define "healthy" or "inhibited" heterosexuality, thereby giving heterosexuals new ways to feel insufficient or suspect. A gigantic field of sexual therapy has arisen since the late 1960s (when Masters and Johnson first published their books on actual sexual behavior), and the public has become quite aware of all the ways there are to fail sexual "competency."

In sum, while heterosexuality is seen as natural, naturally organized around intercourse, strongly held, invariant once achieved, and wholly captivating by those who own it, we know, inside our hearts, and in the light of evidence, that none of these suppositions are entirely true. The question I would pose now is, does this obvious social construction of heterosexuality really matter? Does it matter if heterosexuality is much less unitary, stable or scripted than we thought it was?

That's Not Clear . . .

We are far more a work in progress—a tender rather than solid template— than most of us are comfortable with. However, our intolerance of ambiguity makes it likely that we wish to overdefine our sexual identity, to not code our homosexual attractions or fantasies if at all possible, and to try like hell to accomplish heterosexuality as best we can. Except for the bravest and culturally independent among us, we want sexual categories, not open-ended choices or a continuum of desire and identity. Because heterosexuality is so hard to achieve and so fragile to sustain, we seem to need to continue to ignore the gradations of sexual reality and construct a sexual persona that gives us peace of mind in the present, if not necessarily for the future.

As for we social scientists, we continue to ignore such discordant data about sexual identification, desire, or fantasy, or believe it only defines a small number of heterosexually functioning men and women. We know that many heterosexuals have occasional same-sex fantasies or dreams of same-sex behavior, but we do not include it to reshape our definition of heterosexuality and its potential plasticity.

This is why the Kinsey scale has remained an academic rather than a popular concept. The scale, which goes from 0 to 6, with 0 being totally heterosexual, 6 being totally homosexual, and 3 being you don't care what comes through the door, was revolutionary in the late 1940s and early 50s, when the study was initially done, but arguably could be just as revolutionary today. If we believe, as we might, that heterosexuality is a continuum of sexual desire rather than a bipolar construction, heterosexuality would be more truly described as often coexisting with homosexual desire, fantasy, love, or attraction. But we have intense resistance to trying to know how heterosexuality is actually practiced rather than socially constructed, and this has rather grave costs for everyone:

First, the stereotypes of invariant heterosexuality help us all fail being heterosexual enough, and this causes among many people low self-esteem, miscategorization of their sexuality, and fear of being "deviant." If our sexuality were less prescribed as a central identity and more as a behavior—one open to a multitude of expressions—we would be less immobilized by fear if we thought or did something less common. Indeed, in today's society, there is movement toward a less static vision of heterosexuality. The young, perhaps more with bravado than anything else, are more comfortable with various combinations of ambisexuality and more often than not, unapologetic for their choices.

Second, this same fear encourages some people in our society to discourage extending civil liberties to gays because we are fearful of compromising our heterosexuality. This school wants all the rewards in society to bolster heterosexuality, thereby keeping us more protected from, I guess, ourselves. There are movements to keep gay people from having legal marriage. Could it be that restrictions of same-sex couples originate because we are so unsure about the steadiness of our heterosexuality that we feel extending heterosexual institutions to same-sex couples will endanger heterosexuality itself? This casts heterosexuality as a strangely unpowerful identity, one so weak that if its institutions are shared that marriage will unravel—but there is really no evidence at all that this will happen.

The third and maybe most important response to the perspective I have offered about our present vision of heterosexuality is that of the intrapsychic costs—of the present exaggerated naturalness of heterosexuality. The unannounced and unspoken contradictions of a pure heterosexuality cause great emotional difficulty to many people—especially at tender ages when self-confidence is low. With little reality to lean on, men and women experience extreme discomfort as they must face their fantasies or discordant early behavior. Surely much of our sexual dysfunction, insecurity, and panic comes from these early years of contradictions and high expectations.

My fourth and final point: even if many individuals concretize their heterosexual identity without much suffering or feelings of insufficiency, do we not incur sexual or psychic costs because we see heterosexuality as incongruent with certain kinds of acts or fantasies? For example, can a heterosexual man enjoy (without guilt or fears of sexual deviance) the experience of anal sex or have sex, happily, without intromission? Can a heterosexual woman enjoy a man who is less than traditionally masculine or prefer sexuality without intercourse as the centerpiece of her heterosexual life without feeling that she has betrayed "normal" heterosexuality? Intercourse itself is so central to the proof of heterosexuality that men and women who might enjoy oral sex more might never feel free to downgrade intercourse as the way they generally have the most pleasure. Why shouldn't sexuality be more varied if it is about pleasure and not demonstration of heterosexual membership?

In conclusion, I think it is clear that if heterosexuality were indelible, easy to achieve, and easy to keep, we wouldn't make all this fuss over it. The liberation of all sexualities is the liberation of each one. While political activism may be organized around the integration of homosexuality and homosexuals into the mainstream, it is not clear that there is a mainstream to be integrated into. Rather, there are many people trying to find a sexual identity that integrates their desires, experiences, and fantasies, however diverse they may be. Opening up the definition of heterosexuality will not endanger our welfare. We need to be able to do life as it evolves, creating sexualities that are unique rather than scripted from the one-size-fits-no-one-very-well tradition.

Christina Hoff Sommers is a Resident Scholar at the American Enterprise Institute where she studies the relationship between gender, sexuality, and politics.

The Boys at the Back
Christina Hoff Sommers

Boys score as well as or better than girls on most standardized tests, yet they are far less likely to get good grades, take advanced classes or attend college. Why? A study coming out this week in *The Journal of Human Resources* gives an important answer. Teachers of classes as early as kindergarten factor good behavior into grades—and girls, as a rule, comport themselves far better than boys.

The study's authors analyzed data from more than 5,800 students from kindergarten through fifth grade and found that boys across all racial groups and in all major subject areas received lower grades than their test scores would have predicted.

The scholars attributed this "misalignment" to differences in "noncognitive skills": attentiveness, persistence, eagerness to learn, the ability to sit still and work independently. As most parents know, girls tend to develop these skills earlier and more naturally than boys.

No previous study, to my knowledge, has demonstrated that the well-known gender gap in school grades begins so early and is almost entirely attributable to differences in behavior. The researchers found that teachers rated boys as less proficient even when the boys did just as well as the girls on tests of reading, math and science. (The teachers did not know the test scores in advance.) If the teachers had not accounted for classroom behavior, the boys' grades, like the girls', would have matched their test scores.

That boys struggle with school is hardly news. Think of Shakespeare's "whining schoolboy with his satchel and shining morning face, creeping like snail unwillingly to school." Over all, it's likely that girls have long behaved better than boys at school (and earned better grades as a result), but their early academic success was not enough to overcome significant subsequent disadvantages: families' favoring sons over daughters in allocating scarce resources for schooling; cultural norms that de-emphasized girls' education, particularly past high school; an industrial economy that did not require a college degree to earn a living wage; and persistent discrimination toward women in the workplace.

Those disadvantages have lessened since about the 1970s. Parents, especially those of education and means, began to value their daughters' human capital as much as their sons'. Universities that had been dominated by affluent white men embraced meritocratic values and diversity of gender, race and class. The shift from a labor-intensive, manufacturing-reliant economy to a knowledge-based service economy significantly increased the relative value of college and postgraduate degrees. And while workplace inequities persisted, changing attitudes, legislation and litigation began to level the occupational playing field.

As these shifts were occurring, girls began their advance in education. In 1985, boys and girls took Advanced Placement exams at nearly the same rate. Around 1990, girls moved ahead of boys, and have never looked back. Women now account for roughly 60 percent of associate's, bachelor's and master's degrees and have begun to outpace men in obtaining Ph.D.'s.

There are some who say, well, too bad for the boys. If they are inattentive, obstreperous and distracting to their teachers and peers, that's their problem. After all, the ability to regulate one's impulses, delay gratification, sit still and pay close attention are the cornerstones of success in school and in the work force. It's long past time for women to claim their rightful share of the economic rewards that redound to those who do well in school.

As one critic told me recently, the classroom is no more rigged against boys than workplaces are rigged against lazy and unfocused workers. But unproductive workers are adults—not 5-year-olds. If boys are restless and unfocused, why not look for ways to help them do better? As a nation, can we afford not to?

A few decades ago, when we realized that girls languished behind boys in math and science, we mounted a concerted effort to give them more support, with significant success. Shouldn't we do the same for boys?

When I made this argument in my book "The War Against Boys," almost no one was talking about boys' academic, social and vocational problems. Now, 12 years later, the press, books and academic journals are teeming with such accounts. Witness the crop of books in recent years: Leonard Sax's "Boys Adrift," Liza Mundy's "The Richer Sex," Hanna Rosin's "The End of Men."

For a revised version of the book, due out this summer, I've changed the subtitle—to "How Misguided Policies Are Harming Our Young Men" from "How Misguided Feminism Is Harming Our Young Men"—and moved away from criticizing feminism; instead I emphasized boy-averse trends like the decline of recess, zero-tolerance disciplinary policies, the tendency to criminalize minor juvenile misconduct and the turn away from single-sex schooling. As our schools have become more feelings-centered, risk-averse, collaboration-oriented and sedentary, they have moved further and further from boys' characteristic sensibilities. Concerns about boys arose during a time of tech bubble prosperity; now, more than a decade later, there are major policy reasons—besides the stale "culture wars" of the 1990s—to focus on boys' schooling.

One is the heightened attention to school achievement as the cornerstone of lifelong success. Grades determine entry into advanced classes, enrichment programs and honor societies. They open—or close—doors to higher education. "If grade disparities emerge this early on, it's not surprising that by the time these children are ready to go to college, girls will be better positioned," says Christopher M. Cornwell, an economist at the University of Georgia and an author of the new study, along with his colleague David B. Mustard and Jessica Van Parys of Columbia University.

A second reason is globalization. Richard Whitmire, an education writer, and William Brozo, a literacy expert, write that "the global economic race we read so much about—the marathon to produce the most educated work force, and therefore the most prosperous nation—really comes down to a calculation: whichever nation solves these 'boy troubles' wins the race." That's probably an overstatement, but we do know that the large-scale entry of women into the work force paid large economic dividends. It stands to reason that raising male academic achievement is essential to raising labor productivity and, ultimately, living standards.

A third reason: improving the performance of black, Latino and lower-income kids requires particular attention to boys. Black women are nearly twice as likely to earn a college degree as black men. At some historically black colleges, the gap is astounding: Fisk is now 64 female; Howard, 67 percent; Clark Atlanta, 75 percent. The economist Andrew M. Sum and his colleagues at the Center for Labor Market Studies at Northeastern University examined the Boston Public Schools and found that for the graduating class of 2007, there were 191 black girls for every 100 boys going on to attend a four-year college or university. Among Hispanics, the ratio was 175 girls for every 100 boys; among whites, 153 for every 100.

Young men from middle-class or more comfortable backgrounds aren't lagging quite as far behind, but the gender gap exists there, too. Judith Kleinfeld, a psychology professor at the University of Alaska, Fairbanks, analyzed the reading skills of white males from college-educated families. She showed that at the end of high school, 23 percent of the these boys scored "below basic," compared with 7 percent of their female counterparts. "This means that almost one in four boys who have college-educated parents cannot read a newspaper with understanding," she wrote.

WHAT might we do to help boys improve? For one thing, we can follow the example of the British, the Canadians and the Australians. They have openly addressed the problem of male underachievement. They are not indulging boys' tendency to be inattentive. Instead, they are experimenting with programs to help them become more organized, focused and engaged. These include more boy-friendly reading assignments (science fiction, fantasy, sports, espionage, battles); more recess (where boys can engage in rough-and-tumble as a respite from classroom routine); campaigns to encourage male literacy; more single-sex classes; and more male teachers (and female teachers interested in the pedagogical challenges boys pose).

These efforts should start early, but even high school isn't too late. Consider Aviation High School in New York City. A faded orange brick building with green aluminum trim, it fits comfortably with its gritty neighbors—a steelyard, a tool-supply outlet and a 24-hour gas station and convenience store—in Long Island City, Queens.

On a visit to Aviation I observed a classroom of 14- and 15-year-olds focused on constructing miniaturized, electrically wired airplane wings from mostly raw materials. In another class, students worked in teams—with a student foreman and crew chief—to take apart and then rebuild a small jet engine in just 20 days. In addition to pursuing a standard high school curriculum, Aviation students spend half of the day in hands-on classes on airframes, hydraulics and electrical systems. They put up with demanding English and history classes because unless they do well in them, they cannot spend their afternoons tinkering with the engine of a Cessna 411.

The school's 2,200 pupils—mostly students of color, from low-income households—have a 95 percent attendance rate and a 90 percent graduation rate, with 80 percent going on to college. The school is coed; although girls make up only 16 percent of the student population, they appear to be flourishing. The New York City Department of Education has repeatedly awarded Aviation an "A" on its annual school progress reports. U.S. News & World Report has cited it as one of the best high schools in the nation.

"The school is all about structure," an assistant principal, Ralph Santiago, told me. The faculty emphasizes organization, precision, workmanship and attention to detail. The students are kept so busy and are so fascinated with what they are doing that they have neither the time nor the desire for antics.

Not everyone of either sex is interested in airplanes. But vocational high schools with serious academic requirements are an important part of the solution to male disengagement from school.

I can sympathize with those who roll their eyes at the relatively recent alarm over boys' achievement. Where was the indignation when men dominated higher education, decade after decade? Isn't it time for women and girls to enjoy the advantages? The impulse is understandable but misguided. I became a feminist in the 1970s because I did not appreciate male chauvinism. I still don't. But the proper corrective to chauvinism is not to reverse it and practice it against males, but rather basic fairness. And fairness today requires us to address the serious educational deficits of boys and young men. The rise of women, however long overdue, does not require the fall of men.

Bryan Wuest is a Ph.D. Candidate at the Cinema and Media Studies Program at University of California Los Angeles; his research focuses on expressions of sexuality in media.

Stories like Mine: Coming Out Videos and Queer Identities on YouTube
Bryan Wuest

In a YouTube 'coming out' video, an eager young video maker tells us:

I decided to make this YouTube to find other people like me, people who are coming out, they're in the process, people who have already came out and kind of have a story like mine, so that I can help them and they can help me.—jacobtubification, in 'My First Video!/Coming Out' (YouTube 2010)

Demonstrating cautious optimism about his sexual identity and his future, this video, similar to those discussed throughout this chapter, offers a marked contrast to the troubling position of queer youth within recent news reports. Billy Lucas, Cody Barker, Seth Walsh, Tyler Clementi, Asher Brown and Raymond Chase—these six young people committed suicide during September 2010 as a result of anti-queer bullying.[1] Their schoolmates harassed these six teens to the point that they decided to take their own lives. Many young people who identify as queer, or are perceived as queer, are similarly at risk: the Trevor Project, an organization with the goal of preventing queer youth suicide, reports that gay, lesbian and bisexual youth are four times more likely than straight youth to attempt suicide, and that nearly 50% of transgender Youths seriously consider suicide with 25% actually attempting it (Trevor Project 2013).

Responding to these statistics and September's increase in suicides, gay Journalist and political figure Dan Savage created the It Gets Better Project (IGBP). This online repository of videos mainly produced by queer adults share stories of bullying, homophobia and survival in high school while framing queer identity affirmation as the ability to overcome oppression. This project exceeded Savage's expectations, getting widespread media coverage on outlets like the *New York Times*, the *L.A. Times* and CNN, and inspiring thousands of individuals and groups to make their own videos. This included many who did not identify as queer, but presented themselves as supports for queer youth. Notably in October 2010, President Barack Obama even recorded and uploaded his own It Gets Better video on the White House YouTube site, indicating the project's place in mainstream liberal politics.

However, the popularity of the IGBP as a portal of online media is not without precedent; young queer people had already been using YouTube for years to post and watch thousands of coming out stories, learn about queer culture and in general connect with other queer people throughout the country and around the world. Videos from as early as 2007 include Chris Crocker's humorous 'Why I'm Gay' (YouTube 2013c) and Matthew Lush's serious 'Coming Out' (YouTube 2013b), which have both received over a million views. These are only two examples of many pre-IGBP videos that have received hundreds of thousand or over a million views. These are only two examples of the many pre-IGBP videos that have received hundreds of thousands or over a million views, suggesting the importance of examining these videos' place within queer youth culture and experience.

This is unsurprising because, as Suzanne Walters (2001) explains in her study of queer visibility in the United States, 'we [as queers] are largely born to and raised by those different from us, are not birthed into a ready-made identity, and must actively seek out and construct a community and identity whose existence is predicated on that seeking....' (pp. 28–29). In the same vein, Joseph Goodwin (1989) argues in his study of gay acculturation that

> [b]ecause of its covert nature, the gay community lacks the formal institutions that usually assist in enculturation. The family, churches, schools, and social organizations all take part in teaching people how to operate in the straight culture.... Without comparable sources of instruction and support, gay people must rely primarily upon each other to learn how to function effectively within the gay world. (p. xiv)

When young people, most likely born to straight parents, begin to understand themselves as queer, they have no built-in support or education structure and may not have other visible queer people in their lives to act as examples or models. Additionally, a heterocentric culture that devalues queerness and deviation from societal gender norms has the effect of implicitly and sometimes explicitly discouraging youth from expressing their newfound self-understanding, either in words or actions.

I see queer youth using YouTube to overcome these obstacles and facilitate their own identity development through two important methods: visibility and acculturation. By 'acculturation', I mean queer youth receiving information about a shared culture and experience in order to better equip themselves to both interact within the queer community and to survive in mainstream culture. I mean 'visibility' in two ways: both viewers seeing varied representations of queerness, and vloggers deliberately making themselves visible and 'real'. In another study of coming out videos, Jonathan Alexander and Elizabeth Losh argue that

> in many coming out videos the performative quality of the speech act also reminds the viewer that an actual change of state takes place through the speaker's rhetoric ... the digital replication of this revelation [of sexual orientation] not only marks a life-changing rhetorical occasion but may actually constitute it. (2010, p. 39)

Simply put, these videos may be recounting the occasion of the vlogger's coming out process, or the vlogger may be first coming out *in this video*, performing this rhetorical act for the first time.

These rhetorical acts are important for their establishment of public and personal identity, a significant process for queer youth. Writing about identities, Jeffrey Weeks comments that 'we search for them, claim them, assert and affirm them....They provide a bedrock for our most fundamental being and most prized social belongings" (2007, p. 43). Joshua Gamson connects this importance to gains in the lesbian, gay, bisexual and transgender civil rights movement in recent decades by pointing out that the formation of a 'public collective identity' and 'quasi-ethnicity' has been an exceedingly efficient strategy (1995, p. 391). But he emphasizes that this is indeed a *strategy*, one that he calls an ethnic/essentialist politic.' While acknowledging it significance, Weeks also comments on the overall fiction of sexual identity as conceived today:

> it is only over the past century or so ... that distinctive homosexual
> 'forms of existence', with sexualized identities, communities and sexual
> political movements, have emerged .... Movements such as these are
> not simply expressing a pre-existing essence of social being. Identities
> and belongings are being constructed in the very process of organiza-
> tion itself. (2000, pp. 184–185)

Consequently, when talking about identity this essay does not claim the concept as something essential that young viewers are able to uncover in the core of themselves by watching these videos; rather, I recognize the significance of the concept in current popular understandings of queerness in culture and society. Although it is a simplifying, essentializing discursive strategy, identity is important in practice, especially for social groups that require coherence and solidarity in order to work against institutional oppression. When writing about autobiographical videomaking on the internet and elsewhere, documentary scholar Michael Renov describes the self-representational non-fiction work by members of marginalized groups as 'almost always affirmational of a self culturally specific and publicly defined. Public declarations of private selves have come to be defining acts of contemporary life, often imbued with great urgency' (2004, p. xvii). In this essay I take this urgency seriously, temporarily putting aside critiques of identity politics in favour of analysing how these videos are valued by queer youth.

As I'll discuss below, queer youth often highly value representations of queer people as they provide a framework whereby to understand and organize their burgeoning desires and feelings of difference. Visibility has of course long been held as a central aspect of the struggle for queer equality and queer identities have begun to find much more media expression in the past two decades. Even in 2001, Walters describes television as the 'most conspicuous and visible marker for this new era of lesbian and gay visibility [one that has] beamed gay life (or a television version of it) into millions of homes across this country and abroad' (2001, p. 59).

Yet regardless of this need for queer youth to simply see evidence that other queers exist, both Walters and Mary Gray (in her 2009 study of queer visibility in rural America) argue that an increase in the number of queer representations does not necessarily correlate with viewers, queer or straight, gaining a better understanding of the experience of being queer. In Gray's study of young rural queers, she observed that the subjects often reported finding more substantive or 'authentic' representations of queer identifies in online forums such as PlanetOut.com and Gay.com (both now subsidiaries of Here Media, a large queer media conglomeration). On these sites, the youth she studied were able to read and post coming out stories on message boards and connect with other queer youth. Gray argues her subjects valued this venue for visibility over film and television because of the latter's focus on queers in urban areas where 'a critical mass of LGBT visibility is taken for granted' (2009, p. 124). Through this online forum, with users from across the globe, queer youth were able to find people and stories that reflected their own specific situation more accurately than, for example, the characters of *Will & Grace*, *Queer as Folk* or *The L Word*.

As part of my methodology, in order to find what the creators making videos outside the context of the IGBP would say about their work, I created a YouTube account and contacted about two dozen vloggers, whom I selected by searching for coming out videos with the highest view counts. I also filmed and uploaded a video of myself explaining the project, and sought volunteers willing to answer questions about their coming out videos (YouTube 2014a). Contacting the vloggers of highly viewed videos created some dominant tendencies in my sample set; demographically the vloggers tended to be young (about 18–26 years old) white cismen who at the time of making the video were already out and were speaking from a place of authority and knowledge about the coming out experience.[2] Such a presence demands further research to question this phenomenon, involving examinations of vloggers who present lower view counts and who may be considered less 'out'. Within my research several vloggers generously agreed to respond to my email survey; their videos all represent the higher range of popularity, and the surveys that I sent them were partly based on a general template and partly customized to their videos and situations. With these interviews[3] and my own analysis of some case examples as well as the medium of YouTube itself, I examine how the creators and consumers of these videos use these texts for the purposes of visibility and acculturation as they explore queer identities.

Visibility and Acculturation

The videos I watched before I came out myself helped me realize there were people who were like me out there. In my town there were no support groups or gay hang out places, and I had no gay friends, so I felt alone, and YouTube opened a world to me.

These comments by interviewee D.B. (see Note 3) emphasize how coming out videos operate as a site of visibility and representation for queer youth. D.B. made his own coming out video in response to requests from people who had viewed his other videos where he'd made reference to being gay without actually disclosing his coming out story; although he first resisted making a coming out video, feeling it was 'cliché', he eventually relented almost out of a feeling of obligation, affirming: 'Since I used YouTube to find comfort myself, the least I could do was…contribute to something that I took advantage of in my time of need.'

As mentioned above, Gray notes that some queer youth find online resources to be a venue for more personally meaningful instances of queer representation, especially when their own circumstances do not match what they see in film and television's queer characters. With increasing media literacy and continuing technological development, the ability and means to record and upload videos are more accessible, evident in laptops that often have built-in webcams and simple video editing software, alongside the fact that many youth have spent enough time consuming media to understand the basics of producing their own. YouTube's usability and accessibility for users regardless of geography increases the volume and specificity of the representations available for consumption.

YouTube's titles and tags can enable this specificity of representation and consumption, by more precisely communicating a video's topic or intentions. Vloggers often choose generic titles and tags that are common to a majority of these videos: titles like 'Coming Out', 'Coming Out Gay', 'Coming Out Story', 'My Coming Out Story' and 'Coming Out of the Closet' represent but a fraction of the slight variations on the theme; tags like 'gay', 'LGBT', 'GLBT', 'homosexual' and 'queer' appear on many of the videos as well. However, some users build on this template by adding titles and tags reflecting specific religious affiliations, locations or other details that locate the video's story in a particular situation. Titles of this variety include 'Out in West Texas', 'Coming Out as a GAY TEEN', 'Coming Out to my Parents Story', 'Coming Out and Christian', 'Coming Out to my parents their denial', 'coming out as a gay mormon', while sample tags include 'closeted', 'mormon', 'acceptance', 'boy scout', 'teen', 'advice' and 'help'. A viewer could search 'coming out texas' and see the video 'Out in West Texas', which could reflect the viewer's own experience and context more accurately than a video about coming out in West Hollywood, California, or a viewer could search for 'coming out advice' and find videos tagged with 'advice' that offers specific tips on coming out instead of more general personal narratives. While one goal of coming out videos seems to be establishing a shared, universal rite of passage among young queers, these vloggers use titles and tags to situate their videos in much more specific contexts, suggesting that their location, age or situation adds a unique aspect to their coming out experience. These specificities allow viewers to more narrowly search for certain types of videos (e.g. a YouTube search for 'help coming out to parents' returns pages of videos specifically about that) without eliminating the videos from more general searches. This works to help viewers find exactly what they are looking for (and in turn garners the vlogger more hits). In the manner that Jeffrey Weeks states that people 'search for [identities], claim them, assert and affirm them' (2007, p. 43), this directly relates the use of a personal identity, or relationship to wider social identities, to 'make sense of individual experiences' (p. 49). This may be connected to the particular value of the 'narrow' searching option within online media; where during their searching and claiming, youth whose individual experiences do not match the queer representations that they may see in film and television can use YouTube to actively seek out representations that potentially relate to their developing understanding of themselves. I argue that the opportunity for youth to be able to match their own experiences to those of others offers affirmation to video viewers and suggests an idea of a shared identity, which queer youth can employ to resist both internal and external negativity about their otherness.

If viewers are still unable to find satisfactory representations of their own experiences even after searching YouTube, they may choose to create and upload their own video. Interviewee Rob (see Note 3), who lives in Australia, 'found that the representation of young intelligent gay Australians was lacking on YouTube'. The queer Australian vloggers that Rob observed were more likely talk about topics he saw as frivolous, such as shopping and style, rather than gay politics. Rob had made offline acquaintances with other queers in Sydney and felt that the online representations were not reflecting him or the community he had come to know, so he began vlogging.

D.B. and Rob demonstrate two different (though not exclusive) motives for vlogging/uploading coming out videos. While D.B. framed his video as a way to support other queer youth in need, Rob talks about his own video as a corrective measure to the representations he saw. He demonstrates another aspect of visibility, through creating a (relatively) permanent account of a certain aspect of his community. This motive does not preclude his hope that the video would also aid others struggling to come out; in fact, he mentions becoming 'part of a picture' of coming out stories for the next generation of queers. But he also seems driven by a desire to write and preserve a history of queer Australian that reflects his experience and values. It is not a surprising or unique impulse for a member of an oppressed group to want to manage the group image to pre-empt criticism from unsupportive outsiders.

After observing out, confident vloggers explaining their successful journeys towards queer identities, viewers may desire the knowledge of how to reach that state themselves, and develop familiarity with this culture that they have observed. Goodwin (1989) proposes a five-step process of acculturation for gay men:

1. gay self-identification

2. decision to associate with 'other gays' (however vaguely defined that term)

3. association with gay subculture

4. development of subcultural competency

5. assumption of the role of teacher of guide for subcultural neophytes. (p. 3)

Goodwin's model is focused on the move from the outside of the gay community to the inside, and his idea of competency is limited to knowledge of the rarefied inner workings of the subculture and communication between its members. I would like to adapt this model to frame the discussion of acculturation via YouTube. In this context, the first three steps are the same: self-identifying (at least as sexually curious or unsure), watching coming out videos (which is a way of associating with other queers, though in a potentially very unilateral way) and deciding to research one's sexuality and what it means to be gay, via YouTube. At this point, in the specific context of YouTube this model splits in two directions. First, viewers are discovering how to navigate the queer YouTube community by becoming familiar with the 'genre' of coming out video, learning the most prominent vloggers, commenting on videos and communicating with other members. But at the same time, they are also receiving important information and advice on coming out and being out in their offline lives. This splits their movement into two paths. They are simultaneously becoming more integrated into the queer YouTube community *and* developing the skills to safely navigate outside of it: they harvest the information they need and apply it to offline social situations in less supportive environments. Hence, interviewee Dan (see Note 3) reports coming to YouTube for that explicit purpose. When he was considering coming out and felt the need for advice or help, he realized the dearth of support structures in his local area. He turned to the internet with the hope of finding (written) coming out stories to act as examples or models for his own, but found YouTube's collection of coming out videos. Interviewee Mary (see Note 3) was at the other end of this situation as the provider of advice when her coming out video was featured on the front page of YouTube for Coming Out Day 2007 (which was organized by the Human Rights Campaign to encourage the production of more coming out videos). Her video has received over 500,000 views, and she says she received 'hundreds of direct messages…from closeted gay youth across the country, inspired by the video, but scared to death and seeking help, advice and resources for their own coming out. Most of them in rural areas where there is not much out there for them.'

This use of YouTube both for visibility and acculturation bears striking similarities to the results drawn by Gilbert Herdt (1989) in his study of queer youth:

It can be argued that social and technological changes have made media and periodical images of the gay world available to many adolescents, even those in rural areas. Gay groups, especially supportive homophile self-help groups, today serve essentially as…cohorts and contexts for coming out. (pp. 22–23)

Herdt writing in 1989 before the advent of YouTube, anticipates a cultural and social world that may be aided by online technology and social networking as evident in YouTube. In this way Herdt demonstrates the conditions and needs for such a technology, serving the needs of minority social groups, in our contemporary world, offering visibility and articulation.

Two very different videos will demonstrate the varying kinds of positioning vloggers perform and the ways that visibility and acculturation can function in these videos. 'My First Video!/Coming Out', dated June 8, 2010 and showing just over 2,000 views, is the first video uploaded by vlogger jacobtubification.[4] He offers personal details about his age and location, then after a moment's hesitation adds 'and, uh, I'm gay'. He explains that he is still in the closet, and that his videos will be his first steps to coming out and becoming comfortable with 'saying it out loud'. Interestingly, he also describes his YouTube account as a way to establish accountability, announcing his plan to come out to at least three people (offline) in the next year, at the same time hoping that having committed to this on YouTube will encourage his resolve. His video also makes an appeal to people with comparable experiences:

Maybe other people are like me and they're uncomfortable with coming out and being gay, you know, this can be support for them, and be support for me. Because I know there are other people out there like me. And if people have advice, and they've gone through this, and they had good experience or bad experience, I'd love to hear back from them too.

His hope of both supporting and being supported by 'other people…like me' is an implicit appeal for connection/community with similar individuals, whether through comments, response videos, or private messages. Later in the video, after explaining his own personal closet narrative, he makes this appeal more explicit, stating his goal of finding 'other people like me, people who are coming out, they're in the process, people who have already came [sic] out and kind of have a story like mine….' He ends the video by mentioning being cut off from 'the community' and 'any [knowledge] about LGBT issues', and requesting that viewers 'stick around for my journey'. All of this demonstrates his interest in visibility and acculturation: besides making himself visible as a gay man, purportedly for the first time he mentions the value of seeing other people in similar situations; additionally, he desires advice from other people who have undergone the coming out process, specifically people like him with similar stories.

In strong contrast, the video 'Coming Out', uploaded on August 17, 2007 by user GayGod (YouTube 2013a, 2013b), shows over 1.2 million views (with almost 10,000 comments) and is by a vlogger that has built himself into something of a YouTube celebrity. The opening of this video has motion graphics showing the URLs of his personal site and his MySpace. His personal site links to his online store where one can buy shirts, bracelets and other items branded with text reflecting peace, love, equality, gay rights and his name, Matthew Lush. He is one example of an assortment of gay vloggers who have built a sort of brand around themselves and establish fame (or notoriety) on YouTube; other vloggers sometimes mention Lush or his videos by name, and his almost 200 videos have been viewed a total or more than 37 million times.[5]

Considering his online presence and celebrity, it is unsurprising that his video takes a much more personal didactic approach. He is clearly not seeking support or advice: he begins the video by saying, "I want to talk to you all about coming out. Coming out is different for everyone; it all depends on where you live, religion, and other key factors. Hopefully this video will help you with any of your coming out problems.' After his introduction, the video is divided into several sections, answering questions that appear as intertitles ('When is the best time to come out?' 'Who do I come out to first?' 'How do I come out?' 'Good or bad experience?') He answers these with general advice, but also connects the advice to his personal coming out story, citing it to illustrate a particular point.

While for the most part this is not a 'standard' coming out video that discloses a personal narrative, I see it operating within the acculturation function of these videos. Already having gone through the coming out process, both online and offline, Lush anticipates that viewers will be searching for advice on performing this process themselves. In fact, he directs viewers to offer the video as aid to their other queer or questioning friends; in a mix of support and self-promotion, Lush's written description of the video reads: 'I really hope this helps. Please post this in a bulletin to help your friends!' His video 'My COMING OUT Story' (uploaded on April 21, 2010, with over 128,000 views) actually tells his coming out narrative, a harrowing story of abuse and abandonment. Even in this video, Lush dispenses advice based on what he sees as the mistakes he made in his coming out process, and emphasizes that regardless of his missteps, the process as a whole was vital to the formation of his character. He ends with 'I hope you enjoyed this story, and I hope it helps in any way.'

These two videos have very different goals and approaches, illustrating the range of content in coming out videos on YouTube. Videos' content can be plotted along a number of spectrums: closetedness vs. outness, asking for help vs. offering help and narrative vs. advice (simply recounting personal events vs. delivering bulleted lists of general coming out strategies). But certain features appear again and again: when vloggers first understood themselves as queer (common answers are 'from birth' or later in life after general feelings of difference throughout pre-adolescence), exact locations and contexts (often in granular detail) of their first coming out, technology's role in their process and the reactions of friends and especially parents. What is perhaps most noteworthy about content, though, is how often the comment sections of these videos are filled with viewers expressing support and remarking on how similar the video's reported events are to their own experiences.

Conclusion

This essay has analysed one part of a complex phenomenon. The videos I watched, mostly highly viewed ones, represent only a small segment of the potential texts and users, evident in the diversity of video content potentially available within YouTube, relative to ranges of viewership, potentially available within YouTube, relative to ranges of viewership, and varying generic forms. Within this limitation, many questions and varying generic forms. Within this limitation, many questions remain about vloggers of colour, or female vloggers, or transgender/genderqueer vloggers, or older vloggers or simply less-viewed vloggers. While for the most part they are absent or underrepresented in the higher levels of viewer popularity on YouTube, these users have equal claim to the online space and comparable cultural needs that YouTube is fulfilling, at least in part, for popular vloggers. We can expand our scope even more if we consider the incredible viewcounts on so many of these videos, which make it clear there are huge numbers of viewers consuming these videos without actually participating in the vlogging process themselves. What are these users' experiences? How do the benefits they draw from this phenomenon differ from those who participate more actively?

However, it is important to note that writing about the use of these texts by queer youth does risk exaggerating the positive impact of coming out videos on YouTube. The September suicides that inspired the IGBP occurred in spite of the years of coming out videos this essay analyses, and even since the institutionalization of IGBP young people have continued to take their own lives as a result of anti-queer bullying. In an especially striking case, 14-year-old Jamie Rodemeyer of Buffalo, New York created an IGBP video in May 2011 before committing suicide the following September. Another topic that requires further research is the multivalent effects of this work of producing representations. Besides noting the limited impact that these videos have on those who they are meant to reach, as gravely demonstrated by continuing recognition of queer youth suicides, we might also ask how creating these visible records as signposts for young queer viewers constrains the range of identities they might develop and explore. As mentioned above, space does not allow for fuller analysis of identity politics in relations to these videos, but it is nonetheless important to ask in what ways the coming out videos on YouTube establish certain possibilities for identification and foreclose on others by representing and naturalizing certain configurations of sexual identity over others. This kind of representational critique is more often employed in the case of institutions creating images of marginalized groups (the powerful producing knowledge about the 'other'), but cases in which members of a marginalized group present images of themselves for consumption need more investigation.

That said, the use of YouTube for coming out videos remains significant in its reflection of wider issues of queer youth's place in the mainstream, through understanding the support structures that queer youth build for themselves in a community of like-minded peers can help make clear what potential there is in mainstream culture, and specific need to be addressed within this. Analysing this online activity can also reframe our understanding of queer youth agency; while discrimination and devaluation of queerness certainly remains a central aspect of the contemporary queer experience, this YouTube activity rewrites at least in part the story of queer youth's oppression by societal structures. In his column responding to Billy Lucas' suicide, Dan Savage (2013) justifies the IGBP in this way:

> Gay adults aren't allowed to talk to these kids. Schools and churches don't bring us in to talk to teenagers who are being bullied. Many of these kids have homophobic parents who believe that they can prevent their gay children from growing up to be gay … by depriving them of information, resources, and positive role models. Why are we waiting for permission to talk to these kids? We have the ability to talk directly to them right now. We don't have to wait for permission to let them know that it gets better.

Savage's statement here about gay adults omits an important point: *queer youth themselves* also decided not to wait for permission to talk to other queer youth, their peers, and have already been finding their way onto the computer screens in teens' bedrooms in order to offer these resources, information and role models. Beyond simply reassuring these teens that things improve if they can just make it through high school in the style of It Gets Better, the coming out videos discussed in this chapter can help to equip queer youth, or help them to equip themselves, with models in media production and identity formation, involving self-recognition and know-how, useful in navigating the sometimes adverse terrain of a heterocentric society.

Notes

1. These September 6, 2010 suicides took place all across the United States. These were: Billy Lucas, who died aged 15 on September 9, from Greensburg, Indiana; Cody Barker, who died aged 17 on September 13, from Shiocton Wisconsin; Tyler Clementi, who died aged 18 on September 22, from Piscataway, New Jersey; Asher Brown, who died aged 13 on September 23, from Houston Texas; Seth Walsh, who died aged 13 on September 28 (and was on life support from September 19), from Tehachapi, California; Raymond Chase, who died aged 19 on September 29, from Providence, Rhode Island.

2. The prefix *cis-* means that the person is not transgender/genderqueer, but rather identifies with the way they were gendered at birth by doctors/parents. The term is useful to denaturalize cis-gender identity and avoid the inherent 'othering' of talking about, for

example, 'men' and 'transmen'; the *cis-* prefix avoids making non-trans identity a norm from which trans identity deviates.

3. The Interviews took place in 2011, and were with: D.B.—Gay cisman, 19-year-old student, Alberta, Canada; Rob—Gay cisman, 23-year-old office worker, Sydney, Australia; Dan—Gay cisman, 18-year-old student, Philadelphia, Pennsylvania; Mary—Lesbian ciswoman, 37-year-old filmmaker, Brooklyn, New York.

4. This number reflects when I analysed the video in December 2011; Jacob has since removed his videos from the site.

5. This number is accurate as of December 2013; Lush continues to make videos and his viewcount continues to rise.

References

Alexander, J. and Losh, E. 2010. 'A YouTube of One's Own?': 'Coming Out' Videos as Rhetorical Action. In C. Pullen and M. Cooper, eds. *LGBT Identity and Online New Media*. New York: Routledge, pp. 37–50.

Gamson, J. 1995. Must Identity Movements Self-Destruct? A Queer Dilemma. *Social Problems*, 42(3), pp. 390–407.

Goodwin, J.P. 1989. *More Man than You'll Ever be: Gay Folklore and Acculturation in Middle America*. Bloomington: Indiana University Press.

Gray, M.L. 2009. *Out in the Country: Youth, Media, and Queer Visibility in Rural America*. New York: New York University Press.

Herdt, G. 1989. Introduction: Gay and Lesbian Youth Emergent Identities, and Cultural Scenes at Homes and Abroad. *Journal of Homosexuality*, 17(1/2), pp. 1–42.

Renov, M. 2004. *The Subject of Documentary*. Minneapolis: University of Minnesota Press.

Savage, D. 2013. Give 'Em Hope'. *The Stranger*, September 23, 2010. http://www.thestranger.com/seattle/SavageLove?oid=4940874 [Accessed July 27, 2013].

The Trevor Project. 2013. *Suicidal Signs and Facts*. West Hollywood: The Trevor Project. http://www.thetrevorproject.org/suicide-prevention/facts-about-suicide [Accessed July 25, 2013].

YouTube. 2010. jacobtubification. 2010. My First Video!/Coming Out. URL unavailable [Accessed December 2, 2010; video has since been deleted].

YouTube. 2013a. GayGod—Coming Out. http://www.youtube.com/watch?v=WkkRbVZ-5RE [Accessed August 24, 2013].

YouTube. 2013b. GayGod—My COMING OUT Story. http://www.youtube.com/watch?v=NOXUe0jmnDE [Accessed August 24, 2013].

YouTube. 2013c. Chris Crocker—Why I'm Gay . . . . http://www.youtube.com/watch?v=J1VB3oNEEHI [Accessed December 12, 2013].

YouTube 2014a. http://www.youtube.com/watch?v=FEfmX2jHOU8 [Accessed February 11, 2014].

Walters, S. 2001. *All the Rate: The Story of Gay Visibility in America*. Chicago: University of Chicago Press.

Weeks, J. 2000. *Making Sexual History*. Cambridge: Polity Press.

Weeks, J. 2007. Necessary Fictions: Sexual Identities and the Politics of Diversity. In K.E. Lovaas and M.M. Jenkins, eds. *Sexualities and Communication in Everyday Life*. Thousand Oaks, California: Sage Publications, pp. 41–53.

Food

Donald L. Barlett is an American investigative journalist who often collaborates with **James B. Steele.** The team has won numerous journalism awards including a Pulitzer Prize for National Reporting.

Monsanto's Harvest of Fear
Donald L. Barlett and James B. Steele

Gary Rinehart clearly remembers the summer day in 2002 when the stranger walked in and issued his threat. Rinehart was behind the counter of the Square Deal, his "old-time country store," as he calls it, on the fading town square of Eagleville, Missouri, a tiny farm community 100 miles north of Kansas City.

The Square Deal is a fixture in Eagleville, a place where farmers and towns-people can go for lightbulbs, greeting cards, hunting gear, ice cream, aspirin, and dozens of other small items without having to drive to a big-box store in Bethany, the county seat, 15 miles down Interstate 35.

Everyone knows Rinehart, who was born and raised in the area and runs one of Eagleville's few surviving businesses. The stranger came up to the counter and asked for him by name.

"Well, that's me," said Rinehart.

As Rinehart would recall, the man began verbally attacking him, saying he had proof that Rinehart had planted Monsanto's genetically modified (G.M.) soybeans in violation of the company's patent. Better come clean and settle with Monsanto, Rinehart says the man told him—or face the consequences.

Rinehart was incredulous, listening to the words as puzzled customers and employees looked on. Like many others in rural America, Rinehart knew of Monsanto's fierce reputation for enforcing its patents and suing anyone who allegedly violated them. But Rinehart wasn't a farmer. He wasn't a seed dealer. He hadn't planted any seeds or sold any seeds. He owned a small—a *really* small—country store in a town of 350 people. He was angry that somebody could just barge into the store and embarrass him in front of everyone. "It made me and my business look bad," he says. Rinehart says he told the intruder, "You got the wrong guy."

When the stranger persisted, Rinehart showed him the door. On the way out the man kept making threats. Rinehart says he can't remember the exact words, but they were to the effect of: "Monsanto is big. You can't win. We will get you. You will pay."

Scenes like this are playing out in many parts of rural America these days as Monsanto goes after farmers, farmers' co-ops, seed dealers—anyone it suspects may have infringed its patents of genetically modified seeds. As interviews and reams of court documents reveal, Monsanto relies on a shadowy army of private investigators and agents in the American heartland to strike fear into farm country. They fan out into fields and farm towns, where they secretly videotape and photograph farmers, store owners, and co-ops; infiltrate community meetings; and gather information from informants about farming activities. Farmers say that some Monsanto agents pretend to be surveyors. Others confront farmers on their land and try to pressure them to sign papers giving Monsanto access to their private records. Farmers call them the "seed police" and use words such as "Gestapo" and "Mafia" to describe their tactics.

When asked about these practices, Monsanto declined to comment specifically, other than to say that the company is simply protecting its patents. "Monsanto spends more than $2 million a day in research to identify, test, develop and bring to market innovative new seeds and technologies that benefit farmers," Monsanto spokesman Darren Wallis wrote in an e-mailed letter to *Vanity Fair*. "One tool in protecting this investment is patenting our discoveries and, if necessary, legally defending those patents against those who might choose to infringe upon them." Wallis said that, while the vast majority of farmers and seed dealers follow the licensing agreements, "a tiny fraction" do not, and that Monsanto is obligated to those who do abide by its rules to enforce its patent rights on those who "reap the benefits of the technology without paying for its use." He said only a small number of cases ever go to trial.

Some compare Monsanto's hard-line approach to Microsoft's zealous efforts to protect its software from pirates. At least with Microsoft the buyer of a program can use it over and over again. But farmers who buy Monsanto's seeds can't even do that.

The Control of Nature

For centuries—millennia—farmers have saved seeds from season to season: they planted in the spring, harvested in the fall, then reclaimed and cleaned the seeds over the winter for re-planting the next spring. Monsanto has turned this ancient practice on its head.

Monsanto developed G.M. seeds that would resist its own herbicide, Roundup, offering farmers a convenient way to spray fields with weed killer without affecting crops. Monsanto then patented the seeds. For nearly all of its history the United States Patent and Trademark Office had refused to grant patents on seeds, viewing them as life-forms with too many variables to be patented. "It's not like describing a widget," says Joseph Mendelson III, the legal director of the Center for Food Safety, which has tracked Monsanto's activities in rural America for years.

Indeed not. But in 1980 the U.S. Supreme Court, in a five-to-four decision, turned seeds into widgets, laying the groundwork for a handful of corporations to begin taking control of the world's food supply. In its decision, the court extended patent law to cover "a live human-made microorganism." In this case, the organism wasn't even a seed. Rather, it was a *Pseudomonas* bacterium developed by a General Electric scientist to clean up oil spills. But the precedent was set, and Monsanto took advantage of it. Since the 1980s, Monsanto has become the world leader in genetic modification of seeds and has won 674 biotechnology patents, more than any other company, according to U.S. Department of Agriculture data.

Farmers who buy Monsanto's patented Roundup Ready seeds are required to sign an agreement promising not to save the seed produced after each harvest for re-planting, or to sell the seed to other farmers. This means that farmers must buy new seed every year. Those increased sales, coupled with ballooning sales of its Roundup weed killer, have been a bonanza for Monsanto.

This radical departure from age-old practice has created turmoil in farm country. Some farmers don't fully understand that they aren't supposed to save Monsanto's seeds for next year's planting. Others do, but ignore the stipulation rather than throw away a perfectly usable product. Still others say that they don't use Monsanto's genetically modified seeds, but seeds have been blown into their fields by wind or deposited by birds. It's certainly easy for G.M. seeds to get mixed in with traditional varieties when seeds are cleaned by commercial dealers for re-planting. The seeds look identical; only a laboratory analysis can show the difference. Even if a farmer doesn't buy G.M. seeds and doesn't want them on his land, it's a safe bet he'll get a visit from Monsanto's seed police if crops grown from G.M. seeds are discovered in his fields.

Most Americans know Monsanto because of what it sells to put on our lawns—the ubiquitous weed killer Roundup. What they may not know is that the company now profoundly influences—and one day may virtually control—what we put on our tables. For most of its history Monsanto was a chemical giant, producing some of the most toxic substances ever created, residues from which have left us with some of the most polluted sites on earth. Yet in a little more than a decade, the company has sought to shed its polluted past and morph into something much different and more far-reaching—an "agricultural company" dedicated to making the world "a better place for future generations." Still, more than one Web log claims to see similarities between Monsanto and the fictional company "U-North" in the movie *Michael Clayton,* an agribusiness giant accused in a multibillion-dollar lawsuit of selling an herbicide that causes cancer.

Monsanto's genetically modified seeds have transformed the company and are radically altering global agriculture. So far, the company has produced G.M. seeds for soybeans, corn, canola, and cotton. Many more products have been developed or are in the pipeline, including seeds for sugar beets and alfalfa. The company is also seeking to extend its reach into milk production by marketing an artificial growth hormone for cows that increases their output, and it is taking aggressive steps to put those who don't want to use growth hormone at a commercial disadvantage.

Even as the company is pushing its G.M. agenda, Monsanto is buying up conventional-seed companies. In 2005, Monsanto paid $1.4 billion for Seminis, which controlled 40 percent of the U.S. market for lettuce, tomatoes, and other vegetable and fruit seeds. Two weeks later it announced the acquisition of the country's third-largest cottonseed company, Emergent Genetics, for $300 million. It's estimated that Monsanto seeds now account for 90 percent of the U.S. production of soybeans, which are used in food products beyond counting. Monsanto's acquisitions have fueled explosive growth, transforming the St. Louis–based corporation into the largest seed company in the world.

In Iraq, the groundwork has been laid to protect the patents of Monsanto and other G.M.-seed companies. One of L. Paul Bremer's last acts as head of the Coalition Provisional Authority was an order stipulating that "farmers shall be prohibited from re-using seeds of protected varieties." Monsanto has said that it has no interest in doing business in Iraq, but should the company change its mind, the American-style law is in place.

To be sure, more and more agricultural corporations and individual farmers are using Monsanto's G.M. seeds. As recently as 1980, no genetically modified crops were grown in the U.S. In 2007, the total was 142 million acres planted. Worldwide, the figure was 282 million acres. Many farmers believe that G.M. seeds increase crop yields and save money. Another reason for their attraction is convenience. By using Roundup Ready soybean seeds, a farmer can spend less time tending to his fields. With Monsanto seeds, a farmer plants his crop, then treats it later with Roundup to kill weeds. That takes the place of labor-intensive weed control and plowing.

Monsanto portrays its move into G.M. seeds as a giant leap for mankind. But out in the American countryside, Monsanto's no-holds-barred tactics have made it feared and loathed. Like it or not, farmers say, they have fewer and fewer choices in buying seeds.

And controlling the seeds is not some abstraction. Whoever provides the world's seeds controls the world's food supply.

Under Surveillance

After Monsanto's investigator confronted Gary Rinehart, Monsanto filed a federal lawsuit alleging that Rinehart "knowingly, intentionally, and willfully" planted seeds "in violation of Monsanto's patent rights." The company's complaint made it sound as if Monsanto had Rinehart dead to rights:

During the 2002 growing season, Investigator Jeffery Moore, through surveillance of Mr. Rinehart's farm facility and farming operations, observed Defendant planting brown bag soybean seed. Mr. Moore observed the Defendant take the brown bag soybeans to a field, which was subsequently loaded into a grain drill and planted. Mr. Moore located two empty bags in the ditch in the public road right-of-way beside one of the fields planted by Rinehart, which contained some soybeans. Mr. Moore collected a small amount of soybeans left in the bags which Defendant had tossed into the public right-of way. These samples tested positive for Monsanto's Roundup Ready technology.

Faced with a federal lawsuit, Rinehart had to hire a lawyer. Monsanto eventually realized that "Investigator Jeffery Moore" had targeted the wrong man, and dropped the suit. Rinehart later learned that the company had been secretly investigating farmers in his area. Rinehart never heard from Monsanto again: no letter of apology, no public concession that the company had made a terrible mistake, no offer to pay his attorney's fees. "I don't know how they get away with it," he says. "If I tried to do something like that it would be bad news. I felt like I was in another country."

Gary Rinehart is actually one of Monsanto's luckier targets. Ever since commercial introduction of its G.M. seeds, in 1996, Monsanto has launched thousands of investigations and filed lawsuits against hundreds of farmers and seed dealers. In a 2007 report, the Center for Food Safety, in Washington, D.C., documented 112 such lawsuits, in 27 states.

Even more significant, in the Center's opinion, are the numbers of farmers who settle because they don't have the money or the time to fight Monsanto. "The number of cases filed is only the tip of the iceberg," says Bill Freese, the Center's science-policy analyst. Freese says he has been told of many cases in which Monsanto investigators showed up at a farmer's house or confronted him in his fields, claiming he had violated the technology agreement and demanding to see his records. According to Freese, investigators will say, "Monsanto knows that you are saving Roundup Ready seeds, and if you don't sign these information-release forms, Monsanto is going to come after you and take your farm or take you for all you're worth." Investigators will sometimes show a farmer a photo of himself coming out of a store, to let him know he is being followed.

Lawyers who have represented farmers sued by Monsanto say that intimidating actions like these are commonplace. Most give in and pay Monsanto some amount in damages; those who resist face the full force of Monsanto's legal wrath.

Scorched-Earth Tactics

Pilot Grove, Missouri, population 750, sits in rolling farmland 150 miles west of St. Louis. The town has a grocery store, a bank, a bar, a nursing home, a funeral parlor, and a few other small businesses. There are no stoplights, but the town doesn't need any. The little traffic it has comes from trucks on their way to and from the grain elevator on the edge of town. The elevator is owned by a local co-op, the Pilot Grove Cooperative Elevator, which buys soybeans and corn from farmers in the fall, then ships out the grain over the winter. The co-op has seven full-time employees and four computers.

In the fall of 2006, Monsanto trained its legal guns on Pilot Grove; ever since, its farmers have been drawn into a costly, disruptive legal battle against an opponent with limitless resources. Neither Pilot Grove nor Monsanto will discuss the case, but it is possible to piece together much of the story from documents filed as part of the litigation.

Monsanto began investigating soybean farmers in and around Pilot Grove several years ago. There is no indication as to what sparked the probe, but Monsanto periodically investigates farmers in soybean-growing regions such as this one in central Missouri. The company has a staff devoted to enforcing patents and litigating against farmers. To gather leads, the company maintains an 800 number and encourages farmers to inform on other farmers they think may be engaging in "seed piracy."

Once Pilot Grove had been targeted, Monsanto sent private investigators into the area. Over a period of months, Monsanto's investigators surreptitiously followed the co-op's employees and customers and videotaped them in fields and going about other activities. At least 17 such surveillance videos were made, according to court records. The investigative work was outsourced to a St. Louis agency, McDowell & Associates. It was a McDowell investigator who erroneously fingered Gary Rinehart. In Pilot Grove, at least 11 McDowell investigators have worked the case, and Monsanto makes no bones about the extent of this effort: "Surveillance was conducted throughout the year by various investigators in the field," according to court records. McDowell, like Monsanto, will not comment on the case.

Not long after investigators showed up in Pilot Grove, Monsanto subpoenaed the co-op's records concerning seed and herbicide purchases and seed-cleaning operations. The co-op provided more than 800 pages of documents pertaining to dozens of farmers. Monsanto sued two farmers and negotiated settlements with more than 25 others it accused of seed piracy. But Monsanto's legal assault had only begun. Although the co-op had provided voluminous records, Monsanto then sued it in federal court for patent infringement. Monsanto contended that by cleaning seeds—a service which it had provided for decades—the co-op was inducing farmers to violate Monsanto's patents. In effect, Monsanto wanted the co-op to police its own customers.

In the majority of cases where Monsanto sues, or threatens to sue, farmers settle before going to trial. The cost and stress of litigating against a global corporation are just too great. But Pilot Grove wouldn't cave—and ever since, Monsanto has been turning up the heat. The more the co-op has resisted, the more legal firepower Monsanto has aimed at it. Pilot Grove's lawyer, Steven H. Schwartz, described Monsanto in a court filing as pursuing a "scorched earth tactic," intent on "trying to drive the co-op into the ground."

Even after Pilot Grove turned over thousands more pages of sales records going back five years, and covering virtually every one of its farmer customers, Monsanto wanted more—the right to inspect the co-op's hard drives. When the co-op offered to provide an electronic version of any record, Monsanto demanded hands-on access to Pilot Grove's in-house computers.

Monsanto next petitioned to make potential damages punitive—tripling the amount that Pilot Grove might have to pay if found guilty. After a judge denied that request, Monsanto expanded the scope of the pre-trial investigation by seeking to quadruple the number of depositions. "Monsanto is doing its best to make this case so expensive to defend that the Co-op will have no choice but to relent," Pilot Grove's lawyer said in a court filing.

With Pilot Grove still holding out for a trial, Monsanto now subpoenaed the records of more than 100 of the co-op's customers. In a "You are Commanded ..." notice, the farmers were ordered to gather up five years of invoices, receipts, and all other papers relating to their soybean and herbicide purchases, and to have the documents delivered to a law office in St. Louis. Monsanto gave them two weeks to comply.

Whether Pilot Grove can continue to wage its legal battle remains to be seen. Whatever the outcome, the case shows why Monsanto is so detested in farm country, even by those who buy its products. "I don't know of a company that chooses to sue its own customer base," says Joseph Mendelson, of the Center for Food Safety. "It's a very bizarre business strategy." But it's one that Monsanto manages to get away with, because increasingly it's the dominant vendor in town.

Chemicals? What Chemicals?

The Monsanto Company has never been one of America's friendliest corporate citizens. Given Monsanto's current dominance in the field of bioengineering, it's worth looking at the company's own DNA. The future of the company may lie in seeds, but the seeds of the company lie in chemicals. Communities around the world are still reaping the environmental consequences of Monsanto's origins.

Monsanto was founded in 1901 by John Francis Queeny, a tough, cigar-smoking Irishman with a sixth-grade education. A buyer for a wholesale drug company, Queeny had an idea. But like a lot of employees with ideas, he found that his boss wouldn't listen to him. So he went into business for himself on the side. Queeny was convinced there was money to be made manufacturing a substance called saccharin, an artificial sweetener then imported from Germany. He took $1,500 of his savings, borrowed another $3,500, and set up shop in a dingy warehouse near the St. Louis waterfront. With borrowed equipment and secondhand machines, he began producing saccharin for the U.S. market. He called the company the Monsanto Chemical Works, Monsanto being his wife's maiden name.

The German cartel that controlled the market for saccharin wasn't pleased, and cut the price from $4.50 to $1 a pound to try to force Queeny out of business. The young company faced other challenges. Questions arose about the safety of saccharin, and the U.S. Department of Agriculture even tried to ban it. Fortunately for Queeny, he wasn't up against opponents as aggressive and litigious as the Monsanto of today. His persistence and the loyalty of one steady customer kept the company afloat. That steady customer was a new company in Georgia named Coca-Cola.

Monsanto added more and more products—vanillin, caffeine, and drugs used as sedatives and laxatives. In 1917, Monsanto began making aspirin, and soon became the largest maker worldwide. During World War I, cut off from imported European chemicals, Monsanto was forced to manufacture its own, and its position as a leading force in the chemical industry was assured.

After Queeny was diagnosed with cancer, in the late 1920s, his only son, Edgar, became president. Where the father had been a classic entrepreneur, Edgar Monsanto Queeny was an empire builder with a grand vision. It was Edgar—shrewd, daring, and intuitive ("He can see around the next corner," his secretary once said)—who built Monsanto into a global powerhouse. Under Edgar Queeny and his successors, Monsanto extended its reach into a phenomenal number of products: plastics, resins, rubber goods, fuel additives, artificial caffeine, industrial fluids, vinyl siding, dishwasher detergent, anti-freeze, fertilizers, herbicides, pesticides. Its safety glass protects the U.S. Constitution and the *Mona Lisa*. Its synthetic fibers are the basis of Astroturf.

During the 1970s, the company shifted more and more resources into biotechnology. In 1981 it created a molecular-biology group for research in plant genetics. The next year, Monsanto scientists hit gold: they became the first to genetically modify a plant cell. "It will now be possible to introduce virtually any gene into plant cells with the ultimate goal of improving crop productivity," said Ernest Jaworski, director of Monsanto's Biological Sciences Program.

Over the next few years, scientists working mainly in the company's vast new Life Sciences Research Center, 25 miles west of St. Louis, developed one genetically modified product after another—cotton, soybeans, corn, canola. From the start, G.M. seeds were controversial with the public as well as with some farmers and European consumers. Monsanto has sought to portray G.M. seeds as a panacea, a way to alleviate poverty and feed the hungry. Robert Shapiro, Monsanto's president during the 1990s, once called G.M. seeds "the single most successful introduction of technology in the history of agriculture, including the plow."

By the late 1990s, Monsanto, having rebranded itself into a "life sciences" company, had spun off its chemical and fibers operations into a new company called Solutia. After an additional reorganization, Monsanto re-incorporated in 2002 and officially declared itself an "agricultural company."

In its company literature, Monsanto now refers to itself disingenuously as a "relatively new company" whose primary goal is helping "farmers around the world in their mission to feed, clothe, and fuel" a growing planet. In its list of corporate milestones, all but a handful are from the recent era. As for the company's early history, the decades when it grew into an industrial powerhouse now held potentially responsible for more than 50 Environmental Protection Agency Superfund sites—none of that is mentioned. It's as though the original Monsanto, the company that long had the word "chemical" as part of its name, never existed. One of the benefits of doing this, as the company does not point out, was to channel the bulk of the growing backlog of chemical lawsuits and liabilities onto Solutia, keeping the Monsanto brand pure.

But Monsanto's past, especially its environmental legacy, is very much with us. For many years Monsanto produced two of the most toxic substances ever known—polychlorinated biphenyls, better known as PCBs, and dioxin. Monsanto no longer produces either, but the places where it did are still struggling with the aftermath, and probably always will be.

"Systemic Intoxication"

Twelve miles downriver from Charleston, West Virginia, is the town of Nitro, where Monsanto operated a chemical plant from 1929 to 1995. In 1948 the plant began to make a powerful herbicide known as 2,4,5-T, called "weed bug" by the workers. A by-product of the process was the creation of a chemical that would later be known as dioxin.

The name dioxin refers to a group of highly toxic chemicals that have been linked to heart disease, liver disease, human reproductive disorders, and developmental problems. Even in small amounts, dioxin persists in the environment and accumulates in the body. In 1997 the International Agency for Research on Cancer, a branch of the World Health Organization, classified the most powerful form of dioxin as a substance that causes cancer in humans. In 2001 the U.S. government listed the chemical as a "known human carcinogen."

On March 8, 1949, a massive explosion rocked Monsanto's Nitro plant when a pressure valve blew on a container cooking up a batch of herbicide. The noise from the release was a scream so loud that it drowned out the emergency steam whistle for five minutes. A plume of vapor and white smoke drifted across the plant and out over town.Residue from the explosion coated the interior of the building and those inside with what workers described as "a fine black powder." Many felt their skin prickle and were told to scrub down.

Within days, workers experienced skin eruptions. Many were soon diagnosed with chloracne, a condition similar to common acne but more severe, longer lasting, and potentially disfiguring. Others felt intense pains in their legs, chest, and trunk. A confidential medical report at the time said the explosion "caused a systemic intoxication in the workers involving most major organ systems." Doctors who examined four of the most seriously injured men detected a strong odor coming from them when they were all together in a closed room. "We believe these men are excreting a foreign chemical through their skins," the confidential report to Monsanto noted. Court records indicate that 226 plant workers became ill.

According to court documents that have surfaced in a West Virginia court case, Monsanto downplayed the impact, stating that the contaminant affecting workers was "fairly slow acting" and caused "only an irritation of the skin."

In the meantime, the Nitro plant continued to produce herbicides, rubber products, and other chemicals. In the 1960s, the factory manufactured Agent Orange, the powerful herbicide which the U.S. military used to defoliate jungles during the Vietnam War, and which later was the focus of lawsuits by veterans contending that they had been harmed by exposure. As with Monsanto's older herbicides, the manufacturing of Agent Orange created dioxin as a by-product.

As for the Nitro plant's waste, some was burned in incinerators, some dumped in landfills or storm drains, some allowed to run into streams. As Stuart Calwell, a lawyer who has represented both workers and residents in Nitro, put it, "Dioxin went wherever the product went, down the sewer, shipped in bags, and when the waste was burned, out in the air."

In 1981 several former Nitro employees filed lawsuits in federal court, charging that Monsanto had knowingly exposed them to chemicals that caused long-term health problems, including cancer and heart disease. They alleged that Monsanto knew that many chemicals used at Nitro were potentially harmful, but had kept that information from them. On the eve of a trial, in 1988, Monsanto agreed to settle most of the cases by making a single lump payment of $1.5 million. Monsanto also agreed to drop its claim to collect $305,000 in court costs from six retired Monsanto workers who had unsuccessfully charged in another lawsuit that Monsanto had recklessly exposed them to dioxin. Monsanto had attached liens to the retirees' homes to guarantee collection of the debt.

Monsanto stopped producing dioxin in Nitro in 1969, but the toxic chemical can still be found well beyond the Nitro plant site. Repeated studies have found elevated levels of dioxin in nearby rivers, streams, and fish. Residents have sued to seek damages from Monsanto and Solutia. Earlier this year, a West Virginia judge merged those lawsuits into a class-action suit. A Monsanto spokesman said, "We believe the allegations are without merit and we'll defend ourselves vigorously." The suit will no doubt take years to play out. Time is one thing that Monsanto always has, and that the plaintiffs usually don't.

Poisoned Lawns

Five hundred miles to the south, the people of Anniston, Alabama, know all about what the people of Nitro are going through. They've been there. In fact, you could say, they're still there.

From 1929 to 1971, Monsanto's Anniston works produced PCBs as industrial coolants and insulating fluids for transformers and other electrical equipment. One of the wonder chemicals of the 20th century, PCBs were exceptionally versatile and fire-resistant, and became central to many American industries as lubricants, hydraulic fluids, and sealants. But PCBs are toxic. A member of a family of chemicals that mimic hormones, PCBs have been linked to damage in the liver and in the neurological, immune, endocrine, and reproductive systems. The Environmental Protection Agency (E.P.A.) and the Agency for Toxic Substances and Disease Registry, part of the Department of Health and Human Services, now classify PCBs as "probable carcinogens."

Today, 37 years after PCB production ceased in Anniston, and after tons of contaminated soil have been removed to try to reclaim the site, the area around the old Monsanto plant remains one of the most polluted spots in the U.S.

People in Anniston find themselves in this fix today largely because of the way Monsanto disposed of PCB waste for decades. Excess PCBs were dumped in a nearby open-pit landfill or allowed to flow off the property with storm water. Some waste was poured directly into Snow Creek, which runs alongside the plant and empties into a larger stream, Choccolocco Creek. PCBs also turned up in private lawns after the company invited Anniston residents to use soil from the plant for their lawns, according to *The Anniston Star.*

So for decades the people of Anniston breathed air, planted gardens, drank from wells, fished in rivers, and swam in creeks contaminated with PCBs—without knowing anything about the danger. It wasn't until the 1990s—20 years after Monsanto stopped making PCBs in Anniston—that widespread public awareness of the problem there took hold.

Studies by health authorities consistently found elevated levels of PCBs in houses, yards, streams, fields, fish, and other wildlife—and in people. In 2003, Monsanto and Solutia entered into a consent decree with the E.P.A. to clean up Anniston. Scores of houses and small businesses were to be razed, tons of contaminated soil dug up and carted off, and streambeds scooped of toxic residue. The cleanup is under way, and it will take years, but some doubt it will ever be completed—the job is massive. To settle residents' claims, Monsanto has also paid $550 million to 21,000 Anniston residents exposed to PCBs, but many of them continue to live with PCBs in their bodies. Once PCB is absorbed into human tissue, there it forever remains.

Monsanto shut down PCB production in Anniston in 1971, and the company ended all its American PCB operations in 1977. Also in 1977, Monsanto closed a PCB plant in Wales. In recent years, residents near the village of Groesfaen, in southern Wales, have noticed vile odors emanating from an old quarry outside the village. As it turns out, Monsanto had dumped thousands of tons of waste from its nearby PCB plant into the quarry. British authorities are struggling to decide what to do with what they have now identified as among the most contaminated places in Britain.

"No Cause for Public Alarm"

What had Monsanto known—or what should it have known—about the potential dangers of the chemicals it was manufacturing? There's considerable documentation lurking in court records from many lawsuits indicating that Monsanto knew quite a lot. Let's look just at the example of PCBs.

The evidence that Monsanto refused to face questions about their toxicity is quite clear. In 1956 the company tried to sell the navy a hydraulic fluid for its submarines called Pydraul 150, which contained PCBs. Monsanto supplied the navy with test results for the product. But the navy decided to run its own tests. Afterward, navy officials informed Monsanto that they wouldn't be buying the product. "Applications of Pydraul 150 caused death in all of the rabbits tested" and indicated "definite liver damage," navy officials told Monsanto, according to an internal Monsanto memo divulged in the course of a court proceeding. "No matter how we discussed the situation," complained Monsanto's medical director, R. Emmet Kelly, "it was impossible to change their thinking that Pydraul 150 is just too toxic for use in submarines."

Ten years later, a biologist conducting studies for Monsanto in streams near the Anniston plant got quick results when he submerged his test fish. As he reported to Monsanto, according to *The Washington Post*, "All 25 fish lost equilibrium and turned on their sides in 10 seconds and all were dead in 3½ minutes."

When the Food and Drug Administration (F.D.A.) turned up high levels of PCBs in fish near the Anniston plant in 1970, the company swung into action to limit the P.R. damage. An internal memo entitled "confidential—f.y.i. and destroy" from Monsanto official Paul B. Hodges reviewed steps under way to limit disclosure of the information. One element of the strategy was to get public officials to fight Monsanto's battle: "Joe Crockett, Secretary of the Alabama Water Improvement Commission, will try to handle the problem quietly without release of the information to the public at this time," according to the memo.

Despite Monsanto's efforts, the information did get out, but the company was able to blunt its impact. Monsanto's Anniston plant manager "convinced" a reporter for *The Anniston Star* that there was really nothing to worry about, and an internal memo from Monsanto's headquarters in St. Louis summarized the story that subsequently appeared in the newspaper: "Quoting both plant management and the Alabama Water Improvement Commission, the feature emphasized the PCB problem was relatively new, was being solved by Monsanto and, at this point, was no cause for public alarm."

In truth, there was enormous cause for public alarm. But that harm was done by the "Original Monsanto Company," not "Today's Monsanto Company" (the words and the distinction are Monsanto's). The Monsanto of today says that it can be trusted—that its biotech crops are "as wholesome, nutritious and safe as conventional crops," and that milk from cows injected with its artificial growth hormone is the same as, and as safe as, milk from any other cow.

The Milk Wars

Jeff Kleinpeter takes very good care of his dairy cows. In the winter he turns on heaters to warm their barns. In the summer, fans blow gentle breezes to cool them, and on especially hot days, a fine mist floats down to take the edge off Louisiana's heat. The dairy has gone "to the ultimate end of the earth for cow comfort," says Kleinpeter, a fourth-generation dairy farmer in Baton Rouge. He says visitors marvel at what he does: "I've had many of them say, 'When I die, I want to come back as a Kleinpeter cow.'"

Monsanto would like to change the way Jeff Kleinpeter and his family do business. Specifically, Monsanto doesn't like the label on Kleinpeter Dairy's milk cartons: "From Cows *Not* Treated with rBGH." To consumers, that means the milk comes from cows that were not given artificial bovine growth hormone, a supplement developed by Monsanto that can be injected into dairy cows to increase their milk output.

No one knows what effect, if any, the hormone has on milk or the people who drink it. Studies have not detected any difference in the quality of milk produced by cows that receive rBGH, or rBST, a term by which it is also known. But Jeff Kleinpeter—like millions of consumers—wants no part of rBGH. Whatever its effect on humans, if any, Kleinpeter feels certain it's harmful to cows because it speeds up their metabolism and increases the chances that they'll contract a painful illness that can shorten their lives. "It's like putting a Volkswagen car in with the Indianapolis 500 racers," he says. "You gotta keep the pedal to the metal the whole way through, and pretty soon that poor little Volkswagen engine's going to burn up."

Kleinpeter Dairy has never used Monsanto's artificial hormone, and the dairy requires other dairy farmers from whom it buys milk to attest that they don't use it, either. At the suggestion of a marketing consultant, the dairy began advertising its milk as coming from rBGH-free cows in 2005, and the label began appearing on Kleinpeter milk cartons and in company literature, including a new Web site of Kleinpeter products that proclaims, "We treat our cows with love…not rBGH."

The dairy's sales soared. For Kleinpeter, it was simply a matter of giving consumers more information about their product.

But giving consumers that information has stirred the ire of Monsanto. The company contends that advertising by Kleinpeter and other dairies touting their "no rBGH" milk reflects adversely on Monsanto's product. In a letter to the Federal Trade Commission in February 2007, Monsanto said that, notwithstanding the overwhelming evidence that there is no difference in the milk from cows treated with its product, "milk processors persist in claiming on their labels and in advertisements that the use of rBST is somehow harmful, either to cows or to the people who consume milk from rBST-supplemented cows."

Monsanto called on the commission to investigate what it called the "deceptive advertising and labeling practices" of milk processors such as Kleinpeter, accusing them of misleading consumers "by falsely claiming that there are health and safety risks associated with milk from rBST-supplemented cows." As noted, Kleinpeter does not make any such claims—he simply states that his milk comes from cows not injected with rBGH.

Monsanto's attempt to get the F.T.C. to force dairies to change their advertising was just one more step in the corporation's efforts to extend its reach into agriculture. After years of scientific debate and public controversy, the F.D.A. in 1993 approved commercial use of rBST, basing its decision in part on studies submitted by Monsanto. That decision allowed the company to market the artificial hormone. The effect of the hormone is to increase milk production, not exactly something the nation needed then—or needs now. The U.S. was actually awash in milk, with the government buying up the surplus to prevent a collapse in prices.

Monsanto began selling the supplement in 1994 under the name Posilac. Monsanto acknowledges that the possible side effects of rBST for cows include lameness, disorders of the uterus, increased body temperature, digestive problems, and birthing difficulties. Veterinary drug reports note that "cows injected with Posilac are at an increased risk for mastitis," an udder infection in which bacteria and pus may be pumped out with the milk. What's the effect on humans? The F.D.A. has consistently said that the milk produced by cows that receive rBGH is the same as milk from cows that aren't injected: "The public can be confident that milk and meat from BST-treated cows is safe to consume." Nevertheless, some scientists are concerned by the lack of long-term studies to test the additive's impact, especially on children. A Wisconsin geneticist, William von Meyer, observed that when rBGH was approved the longest study on which the F.D.A.'s approval was based covered only a 90-day laboratory test with small animals. "But people drink milk for a lifetime," he noted. Canada and the European Union have never approved the commercial sale of the artificial hormone. Today, nearly 15 years after the F.D.A. approved rBGH, there have still been no long-term studies "to determine the safety of milk from cows that receive artificial growth hormone," says Michael Hansen, senior staff scientist for Consumers Union. Not only have there been no studies, he adds, but the data that does exist all comes from Monsanto. "There is no scientific consensus about the safety," he says.

However F.D.A. approval came about, Monsanto has long been wired into Washington. Michael R. Taylor was a staff attorney and executive assistant to the F.D.A. commissioner before joining a law firm in Washington in 1981, where he worked to secure F.D.A. approval of Monsanto's artificial growth hormone before returning to the F.D.A. as deputy commissioner in 1991. Dr. Michael A. Friedman, formerly the F.D.A.'s deputy commissioner for operations, joined Monsanto in 1999 as a senior vice president. Linda J. Fisher was an assistant administrator at the E.P.A. when she left the agency in 1993. She became a vice president of

Monsanto, from 1995 to 2000, only to return to the E.P.A. as deputy administrator the next year. William D. Ruckelshaus, former E.P.A. administrator, and Mickey Kantor, former U.S. trade representative, each served on Monsanto's board after leaving government. Supreme Court justice Clarence Thomas was an attorney in Monsanto's corporate-law department in the 1970s. He wrote the Supreme Court opinion in a crucial G.M.-seed patent-rights case in 2001 that benefited Monsanto and all G.M.-seed companies. Donald Rumsfeld never served on the board or held any office at Monsanto, but Monsanto must occupy a soft spot in the heart of the former defense secretary. Rumsfeld was chairman and C.E.O. of the pharmaceutical maker G. D. Searle & Co. when Monsanto acquired Searle in 1985, after Searle had experienced difficulty in finding a buyer. Rumsfeld's stock and options in Searle were valued at $12 million at the time of the sale.

From the beginning some consumers have consistently been hesitant to drink milk from cows treated with artificial hormones. This is one reason Monsanto has waged so many battles with dairies and regulators over the wording of labels on milk cartons. It has sued at least two dairies and one co-op over labeling.

Critics of the artificial hormone have pushed for mandatory labeling on all milk products, but the F.D.A. has resisted and even taken action against some dairies that labeled their milk "BST-free." Since BST is a natural hormone found in all cows, including those not injected with Monsanto's artificial version, the F.D.A. argued that no dairy could claim that its milk is BST-free. The F.D.A. later issued guidelines allowing dairies to use labels saying their milk comes from "non-supplemented cows," as long as the carton has a disclaimer saying that the artificial supplement does not in any way change the milk. So the milk cartons from Kleinpeter Dairy, for example, carry a label on the front stating that the milk is from cows not treated with rBGH, and the rear panel says, "Government studies have shown no significant difference between milk derived from rBGH-treated and non-rBGH-treated cows." That's not good enough for Monsanto.

The Next Battleground

As more and more dairies have chosen to advertise their milk as "No rBGH," Monsanto has gone on the offensive. Its attempt to force the F.T.C. to look into what Monsanto called "deceptive practices" by dairies trying to distance themselves from the company's artificial hormone was the most recent national salvo. But after reviewing Monsanto's claims, the F.T.C.'s Division of Advertising Practices decided in August 2007 that a "formal investigation and enforcement action is not warranted at this time." The agency found some instances where dairies had made "unfounded health and safety claims," but these were mostly on Web sites, not on milk cartons. And the F.T.C. determined that the dairies Monsanto had singled out all carried disclaimers that the F.D.A. had found no significant differences in milk from cows treated with the artificial hormone.

Blocked at the federal level, Monsanto is pushing for action by the states. In the fall of 2007, Pennsylvania's agriculture secretary, Dennis Wolff, issued an edict prohibiting dairies from stamping milk containers with labels stating their products were made without the use of the artificial hormone. Wolff said such a label implies that competitors' milk is not safe, and noted that non-supplemented milk comes at an unjustified higher price, arguments that Monsanto has frequently made. The ban was to take effect February 1, 2008.

Wolff's action created a firestorm in Pennsylvania (and beyond) from angry consumers. So intense was the outpouring of e-mails, letters, and calls that Pennsylvania governor Edward Rendell stepped in and reversed his agriculture secretary, saying, "The public has a right to complete information about how the milk they buy is produced."

On this issue, the tide may be shifting against Monsanto. Organic dairy products, which don't involve rBGH, are soaring in popularity. Supermarket chains such as Kroger, Publix, and Safeway are embracing them. Some other companies have turned away from rBGH products, including Starbucks, which has banned all milk products from cows treated with rBGH. Although Monsanto once claimed that an estimated 30 percent of the nation's dairy cows were injected with rBST, it's widely believed that today the number is much lower.

But don't count Monsanto out. Efforts similar to the one in Pennsylvania have been launched in other states, including New Jersey, Ohio, Indiana, Kansas, Utah, and Missouri. A Monsanto-backed group called afact—American Farmers for the Advancement and Conservation of Technology—has been spearheading efforts in many of these states. afact describes itself as a "producer organization" that decries "questionable labeling tactics and activism" by marketers who have convinced some consumers to "shy away from foods using new technology." afact reportedly uses the same St. Louis public-relations firm, Osborn & Barr, employed by Monsanto. An Osborn & Barr spokesman told *The Kansas City Star* that the company was doing work for afact on a pro bono basis.

Even if Monsanto's efforts to secure across-the-board labeling changes should fall short, there's nothing to stop state agriculture departments from restricting labeling on a dairy-by-dairy basis. Beyond that, Monsanto also has allies whose foot soldiers will almost certainly keep up the pressure on dairies that don't use Monsanto's artificial hormone. Jeff Kleinpeter knows about them, too.

He got a call one day from the man who prints the labels for his milk cartons, asking if he had seen the attack on Kleinpeter Dairy that had been posted on the Internet. Kleinpeter went online to a site called StopLabelingLies, which claims to "help consumers by publicizing examples of false and misleading food and other product labels." There, sure enough, Kleinpeter and other dairies that didn't use Monsanto's product were being accused of making misleading claims to sell their milk.

There was no address or phone number on the Web site, only a list of groups that apparently contribute to the site and whose issues range from disparaging organic farming to downplaying the impact of global warming. "They were criticizing people like me for doing what we had a right to do, had gone through a government agency to do," says Kleinpeter. "We never could get to the bottom of that Web site to get that corrected."

As it turns out, the Web site counts among its contributors Steven Milloy, the "junk science" commentator for FoxNews.com and operator of junkscience.com, which claims to debunk "faulty scientific data and analysis." It may come as no surprise that earlier in his career, Milloy, who calls himself the "junkman," was a registered lobbyist for Monsanto.

Jennifer Cockrall-King is a food culture writer and speaker. Each year she coordinates and produces The Okanagan Food & Wine Writers Workshop, a professional development event for food and beverage writers.

Chicago: The Vertical Farm
Jennifer Cockrall-King

The line of the buildings stood clear-cut and black against the sky; here and there out of the mass rose the great chimneys, with the river of smoke streaming away to the end of the world.

—*Upton Sinclair*, The Jungle *(1906)*

Dickson Despommier's *The Vertical Farm: Feeding the World in the 21st Century* arrived in late 2010 to as much promotion and anticipation as a book gets these days.[1] Well before the book's publication, Despommier appeared as a guest on the *Colbert Report*, the culturally influential satirical news program on U.S. specialty channel Comedy Central. Musician and activist Sting blurbed the book's cover. Majora Carter, a MacArthur "genius" fellow, contributed the foreword. And the *Economist* appointed Despommier "the father of vertical farming" in its magazine pages. Articles about vertical farming were seemingly everywhere at once. According to the media, the year 2010 was the year of the vertical farm—essentially a skyscraper layered with pigs, fish, arugula, tomatoes, and lettuce. There was just one problem. No one had yet built one.

Sure, there were a number of architectural renderings on paper just waiting for a visionary developer or a wealthy billionaire looking for a legacy project. Despommier's book features images of the 30-story verdant spiraling staircase that American architect Blake Kurasek envisioned as his 2008 graduate thesis project at the University of Illinois at Urbana-Champaign.[2] It also includes the drawing for the Dragonfly vertical farm concept, an elaborate 132-floor wing-shaped "metabolic farm for urban agriculture" designed for the New York City skyline by Belgian architect Vincent Callebaut.[3] These visions were (and still are) undeniably intellectually interesting and aesthetically impressive, as are those of Despommier and fellow professor Eric Ellingsen's own glass pyramidal farm.[4] Ellingsen's work was designed with Abu Dhabi in mind, as it is likely the only city with the money to build such structures for food production. These vertical farms, however, would likely come with a $100 million price tag or more—perhaps just one of the reasons they remain more science fiction than food-growing reality.

A few years ago, not many outside academia had heard the term "vertical farm," but the concept has been around since the Hanging Gardens of Babylon, with its mythical living walls of cascading greenery. With traditional farming being so land-, water-, labor-, and fuel-intensive, it was a logical leap to transform the two-dimensional nature of farming by shrinking its footprint radically and adding a third dimension: height. A farm built as a high-rise, with different crops or livestock layered on every floor, could conceivably allow large-scale food production right into the middle of any space-starved urban setting.

The vertical farming school of thought has led to some provocative designs. MVRDV, a Dutch design firm, proposed Pig City in 2001, an open-air 40-story farm that would house 15 million pigs and produce enough organic pork for half a million people and endless amounts of manure for biogas.[5] It earned the vertical farm an early nickname of "sky-scraper." Other open-air vertical-farming concepts emerged soon after on architects' drawing boards in Toronto, Vancouver, Paris, and Chicago, but none were actually built.

The most recent wave of vertical-farming ideas is especially focused on "closed-loop systems." (Think a traditional mixed farm, sliced into layers, stacked vertically, and hermetically sealed under glass.) Livestock waste is intensively recycled as plant fertilizer; freshwater fish grow in tanks and produce nutrient-rich water for salad crops; water loss due to evaporation is minimized; and the whims of Mother Nature no longer interrupt the 24/7, 365-day-a-year indoor growing system. Hungry deer, grasshoppers, and other pests wouldn't devastate crops. Climate wouldn't matter—nor would climate change, droughts, or mid-crop hailstorms.

For some, this will be the only way to feed our growing cities in scenarios of nine billion people living in the megacities of the very near future. For others, it's putting the cart before the horse. Vertical-farm designers and architects talk about aeroponics (soilless growing where roots are merely misted with nutrient-dense water), hydroponics (growing plants in nutrient-rich water but without the need for soil), and aquaponics (indoor fish farming tied in with hydroponic techniques to form a self-cleansing and self-fertilizing water-recycling loop) as if we've perfected these techniques. We've been experimenting with them on rather small scales, but large-scale farming is another matter. The technology isn't there yet. Then again, Leonardo da Vinci drew models for helicopters in the fifteenth century.

What will push the technology forward? Maybe a combination of factors that are currently upon us: Climate change, rapid urbanization, the rise in fuel costs of conventional farming and transportation, and population growth may finally stretch our current food resources to the limits.

Time will tell if these models, or versions of them, will become viable as the technology catches up to the visions of the future of urban farming. For that to happen, however, a lot of ground will have to be covered. Specifically, there will have to be a significant leap in construction and indoor growing technology, especially for the fanciful vertical-farm skyscrapers in Despommier's book to leap from page into being.

Just when I thought the vertical farm was decades away from becoming a reality and that we'd continue to imagine elaborate futuristic scenarios that seemed to completely ignore that agriculture is a marginal business, I learned of Chicago industrial developer John Edel and the new urban reuse project he's calling The Plant. It lacked the ego-driven designs of the other vertical farms that were languishing on paper, and its modesty and practicality made the idea of an indoor multistory farm seem feasible. It was enough to make me want to take a look for myself. After all, if Edel could accomplish even a modest version of a vertical farm, it would be urban-agriculture history in the making. I made plans to visit Chicago to see The Plant in its early stages of becoming the world's first, albeit four-story, vertical farm.[6]

The Plant, Chicago

As Blake Davis took off his dust mask and slapped puffs of concrete off his hands, he joked, "Clearly, as you can see, I'm a college professor."[7] Davis, a burly Chicagoan with a crew cut and a constant grin, teaches urban agriculture at the Illinois Institute of Technology. The day I met him, however, he was putting some skills to use from his preprofessorial days. His worn Carhartt work jacket and overalls were covered in fine concrete dust from jackhammering concrete floors rotten with moisture. By afternoon, he'd be wielding a plasma torch—like a welding torch, but it cuts through stainless steel, slicing panels of it out of meat smokers for food-safe countertops and other novel reuses. Chicago had "literally, millions of square feet" of vacant, often abandoned, industrial space "right in the city," Davis said. "It costs too much to tear down."

Davis was just one of several members of Edel's team of highly skilled, sustainability-minded volunteers determined to strip the former 1925-built, 93,500-square-foot (8,700-square-meter) meatpacking plant back to its outer red-brick shell and put as much of the recycled materials back into use to create a working model for a vertical farm.

While other entrepreneurs might be tight-lipped about their prototype projects—vertical farms are the current holy grail of urban agriculture, and there will likely be significant amounts of money for those who can deliver workable models—Edel instead cleared a few hours to show me around his "fixer-upper." He let me roam at will to chat with people like Davis, Alex Poltorak (another volunteer with engineering credentials), and Audrey Thibault (an industrial designer who, as her jobs kept leaving for China, figured that she "just wanted to be part of something awesome" like The Plant).[8]

It's an experiment in motion with two rather ambitious purposes. If Edel and his team can figure out the right models and mix of elements that actually work synergistically,[1] they will have built a viable physical and economic model for a vertical farm. Edel also intends that The Plant will serve as an open-source laboratory and catalyst for industrial reuse in a city that has no shortage of ready-built shells just waiting for a reason to remain standing.

---

1. synergistically: In a cooperative, mutually beneficial way.

Chicago's Stockyards

In 1878, Gustavus Swift built the first refrigerated railcar, which quickly allowed the meatpacking industry to concentrate in Chicago, scale up to incredible efficiencies, and go on to dominate the national market. By the turn of the 1900s, the Union Stockyards covered 435 acres (176 hectares) and became known as "the hog butcher to the world." If that was a slight exaggeration, it was at least the butcher that fed America. Eighty-two percent of the meat consumed in the United States at the time came from the Union Stockyards. It achieved huge efficiencies of scale that had never been attempted in livestock agriculture before. Historic photos show aerial views of the 40 acres (16 hectares) of cattle and hog pens; what would now be referred to as a Concentrated Animal Feedlot Operation (CAFO).

The industrialized meat trade came with significant hidden costs then as it does now. The poverty, squalor, and brutal working (and living) conditions experienced by workers in the meatpacking industry were immortalized in Upton Sinclair's 1906 novel *The Jungle*. Waves of cheap, nonunionized immigrant and "underclass" labor allowed for the innovation of assembly-line slaughtering, butchering, and processing of the carcasses.[9]

The Back of the Yards neighborhood came to life as a bedroom community, if you will, for the waves of immigrants who cut and packed meat, and for the various businesses—tanneries, soap manufacturers, and instrument-string makers, for example—that surrounded the meatpacking industry on the south and west boundary of the Union Stockyards. By the 1950s, however, meatpacking was headed west, closer to the herds and where land was cheaper. The stockyards officially closed in 1971, and the only relic from that era is a giant limestone entrance arch. Back of the Yards transitioned somewhat into an industrial park. But over the years, the massive infrastructure had a dwindling reason to exist. And when industry leaves, as it did in this part of Chicago, infrastructure is left to crumble and decay. The scale of the surplus in Chicago has generally led to blight.

Much of what I saw as I left Chicago's vibrant skyscrapers and downtown core known as the Loop and made my way to the city's historic stockyards and Back of the Yards' district was heading in the direction of decay and blight. There were too many gaps in the residential streets where houses should otherwise be standing together. There were too many rusted padlocks on gates and chain-link fences encircling trucking depots, warehouses, and factories of indeterminate purposes. The businesses that remained were the signposts of a neighborhood in decline: fast-food joints, liquor stores, and convenience stores with bars on the windows.

The red-brick Peer Foods building, built in 1925 and added to over the years, was a holdout; the family-owned specialty smoked-and-cured-meat company had stayed in business in the Back of the Yards until 2007.

At the time, Edel was in negotiations with the city to buy a six-hundred-thousand-square-foot World War I armory turned vacant Chicago Board of Education building. Faced with a $12 million demolition price tag, the city seemed prepared to sell it for $1.[10]

Edel already had a bit of local reputation for industrial building rehab. He had left a lucrative broadcast television design job that involved too much computer-assisted drawing and modeling to instead scratch an itch for preserving historic buildings by finding low-cost creative uses for them and reusing the materials that were simply lying around inside most of them.

In 2002, he bought a 1910 paint factory that had been officially unoccupied since the 1960s and had since become a derelict, bike-gang-ridden building with shot-out windows. (The building, in Edel's words, had been colonized by "lots of tough guys" with names like Googs, Mack, Santa Claus, the Boob, and Cowboy. There were "lots of guns, lots of knives," involved in the "informal economy" that had taken over the building.) Edel completely reformed the 24,000-square-foot (2,230-square-meter) building, putting his industrial design training, a tremendous amount of personal and volunteer sweat equity, and innate scavenger mentality into play. Useful industrial machines, like a giant, old air compressor that was left behind, were put back into service to run the air chisels used to poke holes in brick walls and the jackhammer used to remove unwanted concrete. Scrap sheet metal was refashioned to create such items as a new entrance awning, and former machine-tool parts and pipes found lying around became an art-school-esque stairway banister. Edel planted a living green roof with thousands of heat-and-drought-tolerant sedum (a succulent plant that needs little irrigation) to mitigate storm water runoff and installed cisterns to catch rainwater for reuse in the building. (Seen from above, or on Google Earth, the thousands of sedum create a red-and-green pattern of Edel's daughter's smiling face.)

Edel did it all on a shoestring budget, and 95 percent of the existing derelict structure was repurposed. The building is now home to Bubbly Dynamics, though its official name is the Chicago Sustainable Manufacturing Center.[11] Bubbly Dynamics now runs at 100 percent occupancy and is a magnet for the niche boutique manufacturing and sustainable technologies entrepreneurs in Chicago. It is home to 35 permanent salaried jobs, which include a co-op of five custom-bicycle-frame builders, a fabric-print-screening outfit, and a tutoring program for at-risk children. It's full and extremely efficient, and it turns a profit for Edel, the landlord. It was all the proof he needed to confirm his gut feeling that no building is so derelict that it can't be saved and made profitable.

After the success of Bubbly Dynamics, Edel's next idea was to turn another hopeless case of a building into a zero-waste organic food-producing building in Chicago. He thought he'd found it with the Board of Education building. Edel wanted to create a net-zero building that combined some select food-manufacturing processes with the growing of food.

"Everybody in city government, except one alderman, was in support of it. Instead, he wanted to tear down the 'orange-rated' historical building we were trying to acquire and have a Walmart. That was *his* dream," Edel recounted.[12] (Orange-rated is a Chicago urban-planning term that means that the building was one step below landmark protection status.)

One alderman's Walmart dream was enough to stall the process for two years, but during that time, Edel continued to plan an ambitious new life for the 600,000-square-foot (55,741-square-meter) space, using his team and networks of like-minded, hands-on experts who had gravitated to Edel and Bubbly Dynamics. That's when and how Davis fell into Edel's orbit. Davis was looking for urban-agriculture projects for his students, and Edel's business models included lots of volunteer hours and "open-source expertise." While Edel worked on acquiring space, Davis and his students began working on a symbiotic aquaponics/hydroponics system integrating fish production with a plant-growing system in the basement of Bubbly Dynamics.

Though the one-dollar price tag of the Board of Education building was attractive, the negotiations with the city were dragging on. Edel decided that ultimately it wasn't worth the wait, given all the existing inventory of available buildings in Chicago. He found a former meat slaughtering, smoking, and processing plant that was in relatively good shape. It had been built in 1925 but over the years had been upgraded and expanded. And it had sat empty for only four years, so there hadn't been time for too much to deteriorate. Most importantly, it was built for food production, which would save Edel an enormous amount of time and money because it was already up to code for many food-related commercial purposes.

Edel closed on the old Peer Foods Building on July 1, 2010, for $5.50 per square foot. What sounds like a real estate bargain, however, amounted to a $525,000 purchase that would test even Edel's resourcefulness. But Edel seems just as capable of attracting paying tenants as he is overqualified volunteers. There's already a list of entrepreneurs who have signed up for space at The Plant, which will move businesses in as its space is completed.

Touring The Plant

I wasn't prepared for how shockingly cold (and dark) it would be inside The Plant on the early January day I had arranged to visit.[13] It certainly wasn't the natural-light-flooded ethereal skyscraper that the academic vertical-farming camp was known for; it wasn't even the conventional greenhouse structure one associates with a covered growing space. There were high ceilings, which on that particular day actually seemed to trap the chill, making it a few degrees cooler on the inside than it was outdoors.

I had somewhat naively assumed that Edel would have to "work around" the lack of natural light, that it was a problem to be solved. Instead, Edel explained that the thick brick walls and lack of windows was a major benefit of The Plant.

What currently functioned as windows—antique glass block—would, however, have to be replaced. ("Glass block neither lets light in, nor does it keep heat in or out," said Edel. As windows, they were useless.) One of the few outside purchases that the building would get was some new windows with high-efficiency glass.

However, high-efficiency glass is very limiting as well, explained Edel, holding up a sample of a high-efficiency window product he had been considering. "See how dark the glass is?" It was a smoky-gray color. High-efficiency glass, by its very nature, blocks those parts of the light spectrum that plants need for growing. And clear glass, which lets more of the light spectrum pass through, allows too much heat transfer. Edel then explained the problem of light units in northern latitudes during the Chicago winter. "In the upper Midwest on a day like today," he snorted, "you'll get no usable light. In an ideal [summer] day, you might get light penetration of about 15 feet.

"That means you'll be growing under artificial lights anyway. And the last thing you want is huge amounts of glass for that heat energy to escape through." Any gains made by electrical savings on using natural light would be negated or completely irrelevant compared to the heating costs escaping out through glass. Besides, a well-insulated brick building such as The Plant will be very effective at trapping heat inside in the winter (the heat from the lights can go a long way toward heating a building if it's well enough insulated, Edel believes) and keeping it cooler in the summer. Heat, as I would learn that day, is as valuable an asset in an ultra-efficient vertical farm in a cold climate as anything else.

But the great advantage, Edel explained, to the cavernous nature of the building is that "you can control the time of day." This gives Edel the ability to "grow at night" when electricity costs are a fraction of what they are during the day when the demand is high. And plants need a period of darkness just like they need a period of light, so you can create night during the day, when energy costs are high. Edel figures he can cut the energy expenses in half by growing during nonpeak hours.

The other advantage, continued Edel, is that "you can create different time zones in various parts of the indoor system. You can flatten your nominal load so that you don't have demand spikes." Electrical utility companies like to charge you at the rate when you are at your peak daily energy consumption rate. By "moving the time of day around" between a few growing zones, again, you can achieve a "flatter," more consistent pattern of consumption and therefore save on utilities. Flattening the demand for electrical consumption will play a huge role in regulating the metabolism of the building as the building starts to produce its own electrical power and heating when the anaerobic digester is built and takes over the energy needs of the tenants and the food-growing spaces.

The one concession Edel has made to a tiny bit of inefficiency will be the "growing lobby." Large windows along the front of the building will let in lots of natural light. "We'll have things like hops and lavender, and probably the finishing tanks for the tilapia where the water is really clean and the fish look pretty."

Heat and light were not the only valuable commodities in the building's equation; oxygen and carbon dioxide also needed to be considered. Nathan Wyse, a fresh-faced twenty-something, came by The Plant that day to talk to Edel. Wyse was a potential tenant who was looking to take his Thrive label of kombucha—a fermented medicinal tea hitting the lucrative mainstream specialty-beverage market these days—to the next business level.

The yeasts used to ferment the sugars in kombucha require oxygen and produce excess carbon dioxide in the fermentation process. Growing plants, handily, love carbon dioxide. According to Edel, plants "do quite well on six times the normal atmospheric carbon dioxide." Wyse asked if Edel could think about how these two gases could be exchanged efficiently between the brewing space and the growing spaces at The Plant.[14] If they could be exchanged, Wyse's aeration of his batches of kombucha would be greatly enhanced. Edel suggested that they could likely pipe excess carbon dioxide into growing areas, while drawing oxygen out (one being a heavier gas than the other) to recirculate it between the kombucha fermentation beds and the growing beds.

"So you've already thought about this?" Wyse asked.

"I just did," said Edel, matter-of-factly.

"OK, well, I'd gladly exchange carbon dioxide for oxygen for better fermentation."

I felt like I'd stepped into the future, where resources like oxygen and carbon dioxide are valued on an open-market trading system. Clearly, a closed-loop system, such as a vertical farm, as Edel conceived it, was so much more than providing artificial light to a few plants and recycling fish waste as plant fertilizer. It was about striking a delicate balance in the building to create a zero-waste ecosystem where "the only thing that will go out is food."

As we climbed the stairs to the second floor, the unmistakable greasy aroma of bacon wrapped itself around me. "The smokers were in use twenty-four-seven right up until the day Peer Foods moved out," confirmed Edel.

Some of the smokers were new: huge stainless steel tanks with what looked like ships' portholes at about five feet high. The stainless steel was valuable, and Edel and crew had already started to hack it into panels for food-grade countertops and tables. Other panels would become the new bathroom stalls.

There were also older cavernous smokers that smelled like they had been used continuously for a century, which was likely not far off. Smoke stains had left huge black licks up the beautiful 1920s glazed-tile walls. I remarked that it was a shame to think that buildings like this were decaying and being torn down due to a lack of knowledge of how to resuscitate existing construction. And yet, city aldermen had dreams of demolition and replacement with Walmarts.

"Building a new building is a really inefficient thing to do!" Edel fired back. "Plants don't care about columns, or taking a freight elevator to get out to a market. Really an existing structure is the best possible situation."[15]

The stainless steel smoke tanks were in the area designated to be the bakery, one of the food-based business incubator areas. Start-ups will be able to rent the space by the hour and still be in a completely 2,000-square-foot (185-square-meter) food-grade shared commercial kitchen, a major economic hurdle for most people getting into the food-production business, given the overhead on commercial space. Tenants can also rent garden plots on the rooftop garden and source other items, like mushrooms, that will be grown in other parts of the building. "There'll be a wood-fired oven in here," enthused Edel. The heat from the bakery will be important to heat the other parts of the building. Because of the original function of the building as a food facility, the floors undulate every few feet where floor drains exist. "How expensive would that have been to put in?"

"All of these rooms were great forests of electrical wires, pipes, and everything else. There was meat-cutting equipment everywhere. We are keeping bits of it and reusing almost everything. The oldest wiring is only 15 years old, fortunately." There was even a beauty to the age-blackened iron rails formerly used to move the carcasses along from one worker to the next. Edel was planning to keep them suspended from the timber supports as a historical memento of the building's past.

"This is the one mess I'm going to keep because it's so out of control," he laughed, pointing toward one particularly absurd tangle of meters, pipes, wiring, gauges, and switches. Edel quipped that this is where his art school education will come into play. A floor-to-ceiling glass wall will be installed and dramatic lighting will be focused on the "industrial found art"—a ready-made point of interest that will be a central art piece on the third floor, visible from the conference room and the incubator office space that will be rented out to small businesses that will use The Plant's commercial baking, brewing, and food-preparation facilities.

The New Chicago Brewing Company has signed on to be a major keystone tenant, and there will even be a homebrew co-op that operates out of The Plant. Not only will brewing produce a lot of heat; it will supply vast amounts of spent brewing mash to compost for the gardens and green house or for the biodigester.

We descended into a dark, cavernous basement for the grand finale. We cautiously picked our way around scrap metal, spools of wiring, and over curbs that were scheduled to be sledge-hammered like we were climbing through the innards of a submarine. Edel pointed out rooms that would soon be filled with mushroom beds. He had secured a former military fighter jet engine that would be put into use for electrical generation once the biodigester was built.

Edel yanked on a solid steel door, and we passed from the submarine scenario into a laboratory-white immense room bathed in a fuchsia light on one side, with gurgling vats of tilapia-filled water on the other. The Plant Vertical Farm wasn't just demolition and future scenarios; there was actual food growing in test systems in this basement room.

"This is Growing System Number One," said Edel as we walked toward the four square plastic 275-gallon (1,000-liter) tubs that were the fish tanks. This was the project that Davis's students were working on, tweaking and perfecting, so that it could be implemented on a larger scale when The Plant ramped up its food ecosystem.

Slivers of fingerling tilapia flashed around the tank, and as soon as they saw us looming over, they made for the surface. "They would eat twenty-four hours a day," said Edel, as the fish poked at the water's surface. There were two more tanks attached to this chain of plastic vats and white plastic PVC pipes, and the nearby pump was noisily forcing water around through the tanks. Sixty market-weight tilapia swirled in the final tank. "You want to control how much you feed them or they'll get too big, too fast. And you also have to balance the amount of food with the amount of plants you are growing." Edel explained that the fish were "on a diet" until they got more plants into the system.

The water from the fish pens flowed into another water-filled tank with run-of-the-mill hardware-store black plastic garden netting for filtering. Edel explained that the netting caused "the richer stuff" to fall to the bottom of the filter tank. When The Plant's biodigester is ready, this solid fish waste will be used to produce methane gas, which will be turned back into heat and electrical energy.

The next tank after the netting had a black plastic honeycomb-like panel—"a $400 mistake," whined Edel. The tank is simply a place to harbor the bacteria that turns the ammonia of the fish waste into the nitrites and nitrates (the nitrogen compounds) that make fantastic plant fertilizer. Instead of the special, expensive plastic comb, Edel proposed that "rocks or old chopped-up plastic bottles" would do just as good a job for a fraction of the price.

The pump then sent the water from the filters into shallow pans where foam rafts studded with tiny plant plugs floated on clear but nitrogen-rich water. Each hole in the raft contained a small plastic basket filled with coconut husk to stabilize the roots of each little seedling of arugula, red lettuce, or whatever the team wants to grow. The coconut husk fiber is nearly indestructible yet is porous enough to not restrict the rooting systems that dangle through the gaps in the baskets and into the water. As the plants take up the nitrogen, they effectively clean the water—as they do in ecosystems in nature—allowing the water to be recycled back into the fish tanks for the waste-fertilizer loop to begin again.

The plants looked very happy and healthy bathed in the fuchsia light of the state-of-the-art LED grow lights. "Plants can't see green," Edel explained, so you only need the red and blue lights. Edel, Davis, and students are testing the LED lights, as they are relative newcomers to the market; but if they work, they'll be much more efficient than other grow lights commonly used. A computer engineer is working out the open-source software and hardware that will move the lights along a variable-height track suspended above the seedlings. The lights move slowly from one end of the beds to the other "so they don't end up growing like this," explained Edel, listing sharply to one side.

I finally asked the big question that seems to be a sticking point where new ideas tend to hit the proverbial brick wall of city bylaws.

"And you're allowed to do all of this?"

Overall, the city has just let Edel and company continue without too much concern. The brewing permit was a hassle, but they got it. "The only other resistance we'd had is from the zoning department that didn't like the idea of fish and aquaculture," said Edel. "Not for any *good* reason, because under the same zoning, you can crush cars, smelt iron, and slaughter cattle. But raising organic fish for some reason is bad. Go figure."

The fish were not yet a particular concern anyhow, as they were part of Davis's students' course work. They were working out the details of this aquaponics-agricultural loop as part of the student curriculum, which involved the micro-greens, sprouts, and mushrooms that would soon be tested out at The Plant.

Part of this course work also included marketing plans and economic feasibility studies by students at the Illinois Institute of Technology. When I asked Davis how strong the demand was in Chicago for locally grown food, he replied that even drawing from a radius of 500 miles around the city, there aren't enough farms for the markets and the demand that already exists. And being right in the city will be a huge advantage for restaurants willing to pay a premium for ultra-fresh product. "We're about the only people who can say, 'We'll pick this for you at nine a.m., have it to you by ten, and you can serve it for lunch.' "[16]

The other factor that favors the viability of vertical farming in the city, according to Davis, is that Chicago's public school system now sets aside 20 percent of its school lunch budget for local foods. "Even keeping in mind that they don't actually go to school in the summer when most of the food is produced, it still creates opportunity for us."

Food wholesale produce suppliers have also told Davis that they'll take everything The Plant can produce. So whether it is Chicago's sustainable and premium restaurants willing to pay top dollar for The Plant's fresh, local, organic food, or local produce wholesalers, or the Chicago Public School System (though clearly the school board wouldn't be able to out-compete the other two on price), finding markets for the food will be the easy part.

In Davis's opinion, however, Edel's plan of having manufacturing tenants subsidize the food-growing spaces was a key element to turning The Plant into reality while the other more ambitious "food-only" skyscrapers are lingering on paper at this point. "We've been to almost every other urban agriculture site within 500 miles, and we noticed that almost all of them are being run on job-training grants from foundations. We thought that this was probably not a good way to run this. That's why I really jumped on to this project. It's technically interesting, but it has a commitment to creating a business model that can be replicated. The problem with social services and 40-story urban farms is that you train a bunch of people, but there are no businesses out there to hire them."[17]

When I remarked that it's somewhat surprising that the world's first vertical farm won't be nestled in among skyscrapers in uptown Manhattan, or in the anything-is-possible cities like Shanghai and Dubai; that it will happen on a very modest scale, on a very modest budget, in Chicago, Davis just smiled. "That's kind of the tension between New York and the Midwest. All the actual urban agriculture is happening within 500 miles of Chicago, and all the press is about these 40-story buildings."

"When Sam Walton [founder of Walmart] started, he didn't try to build a 400,000-square-foot superstore. He took an old Kresge's and said, 'I'm going to figure out this business model in this relatively small space. If it's successful, I'll make another one.' And at some point, you can afford to build a single-purpose building for a Walmart. I think if you get good at urban agriculture, and have a few technological breakthroughs, at some point you'll need an architect to design an 80-story urban farm. Maybe your business model will be sound to do that. It's just a bit premature right now."

I asked if the city was therefore giving The Plant any breaks or help in any way. "They're not subsidizing it," answered Davis. "But the most important thing in Chicago is that they're letting us do it."

Edel's concept of industrial reuse seems like a reasonable solution to the very sticky wicket that has so far kept urban vertical farms confined to academic presentations and scrolls of architectural plans. And, as Edel put it, "You've got to sell a lot of rutabagas to pay for a $100 million building." Edel's ability to reinvigorate unwanted commercial space, make it beautiful, and, perhaps most importantly, make it productive and profitable once again, might just be a catalyst that will serve post-industrial Chicago well. And it might be vertical farming's Sputnik moment, launching a vertical-farm race, so to speak, that will leave those ego-driven skyscrapers on the drawing board for the time being.

Notes

1. Dickson Despommier, *The Vertical Farm: Feeding the World in the 21st Century* (New York: Thomas Dunne Books, 2010).

2. Blake Kurasek's Living Skyscraper can be viewed at http://blakekurasek.com/theliving-skyscraper.html.

3. Vincent Callebaut's Dragonfly vertical farm can be viewed at http://vincent.callebaut.org/page1-img-dragonfly.html.

4. Despommier and Ellingsen's pyramidal vertical farm can be viewed at http://www.verticalfarm.com/designs?folder=b9aa20a4-9c6a-4983-b3ad-390c4f1fa562.

5. MVRDV's website is at http://www.mvrdv.nl.

6. The Plant's website is at http://www.plantchicago.com/.

7. Blake Davis (adjunct professor of urban agriculture at Illinois Institute of Technology), personal interview with the author, The Plant, Chicago, Illinois, January 29, 2011.

8. Personal interviews were conducted on-site at The Plant with John Edel (owner/developer/director, The Plant), Blake Davis (adjunct professor of urban agriculture, IIT), Alex Poltorak (volunteer, The Plant), and Audrey Thibault (volunteer, The Plant), Chicago, Illinois, January 29, 2011.

9. I found several sources that reference the influence of the Chicago Stockyard's "disassembly line" on Henry Ford's idea for the automobile assembly line. He saw the efficiencies gained by giving one worker one specific task and then moving the carcasses on to the next worker. Ford reversed the process to put cars together, but the idea of worker specialization was born on the blood-soaked floors of stockyard slaughterhouses. One source, among many online, that states this is http://www.pbs.org/wgbh/amex/chicago/peopleevents/p_armour.html.

10. The backstory of how John Edel came to purchase the Peer Foods building and information on The Plant came from a personal interview with John Edel, January 29, 2011.

11. Bubbly Dynamics draws its nickname from nearby Bubbly Creek, a waterway named during the days of the stockyards and the attendant business that sprung up around the century-long livestock and slaughter industry in Chicago, where boiled waste and decaying matter made the creek appear to bubble.

12. John Edel, personal interview with the author, The Plant, Chicago, Illinois, January 29, 2011.

13. Ibid.

14. John Edel and Nathan Wyse in conversation with the author, The Plant, Chicago, Illinois, January 29, 2011.

15. John Edel, personal interview with the author, The Plant, Chicago, Illinois, January 29, 2011.

16. Blake Davis, in-person interview with the author, The Plant, Chicago, Illinois, January 29, 2011.

17. Ibid.

Blake Hurst is a third-generation farmer from Atchison County, Missouri and the president of the Missouri Farm Bureau. His work is featured in a wide variety of publications including *The Federalist, The National Review*, The American Enterprise Institute, and *The New York Times.*

The Omnivore's Delusion: Against the Agri-intellectuals
Blake Hurst

I'm dozing, as I often do on airplanes, but the guy behind me has been broadcasting nonstop for nearly three hours. I finally admit defeat and start some serious eavesdropping. He's talking about food, damning farming, particularly livestock farming, compensating for his lack of knowledge with volume.

I'm so tired of people who wouldn't visit a doctor who used a stethoscope instead of an MRI demanding that farmers like me use 1930s technology to raise food. Farming has always been messy and painful, and bloody and dirty. It still is.

But now we have to listen to self-appointed experts on airplanes frightening their seatmates about the profession I have practiced for more than 30 years. I'd had enough. I turned around and politely told the lecturer that he ought not believe everything he reads. He quieted and asked me what kind of farming I do. I told him, and when he asked if I used organic farming, I said no, and left it at that. I didn't answer with the first thought that came to mind, which is simply this: I deal in the real world, not superstitions, and unless the consumer absolutely forces my hand, I am about as likely to adopt organic methods as the Wall Street Journal is to publish their next edition by setting the type by hand.

He was a businessman, and I'm sure spends his days with spreadsheets, projections, and marketing studies. He hasn't used a slide rule in his career and wouldn't make projections with tea leaves or soothsayers. He does not blame witchcraft for a bad quarter, or expect the factory that makes his product to use steam power instead of electricity, or horses and wagons to deliver his products instead of trucks and trains. But he expects me to farm like my grandfather, and not incidentally, I suppose, to live like him as well. He thinks farmers are too stupid to farm sustainably, too cruel to treat their animals well, and too careless to worry about their communities, their health, and their families. I would not presume to criticize his car, or the size of his house, or the way he runs his business. But he is an expert about me, on the strength of one book, and is sharing that expertise with captive audiences every time he gets the chance. Enough, enough, enough.

Industrial Farming and Its Critics

Critics of "industrial farming" spend most of their time concerned with the processes by which food is raised. This is because the results of organic production are so, well, troublesome. With the subtraction of every "unnatural" additive, molds, fungus, and bugs increase. Since it is difficult to sell a religion with so many readily quantifiable bad results, the trusty family farmer has to be thrown into the breach, saving the whole organic movement by his saintly presence, chewing on his straw, plodding along, at one with his environment, his community, his neighborhood. Except that some of the largest farms in the country are organic—and are giant organizations dependent upon lots of hired stoop labor doing the most backbreaking of tasks in order to save the sensitive conscience of my fellow passenger the merest whiff of pesticide contamination. They do not spend much time talking about that at the Whole Foods store.

The most delicious irony is this: the parts of farming that are the most "industrial" are the most likely to be owned by the kind of family farmers that elicit such a positive response from the consumer. Corn farms are almost all owned and managed by small family farmers. But corn farmers salivate at the thought of one more biotech breakthrough, use vast amounts of energy to increase production, and raise large quantities of an indistinguishable commodity to sell to huge corporations that turn that corn into thousands of industrial products.

Most livestock is produced by family farms, and even the poultry industry, with its contracts and vertical integration, relies on family farms to contract for the production of the birds. Despite the obvious change in scale over time, family farms, like ours, still meet around the kitchen table, send their kids to the same small schools, sit in the same church pew, and belong to the same civic organizations our parents and grandparents did. We may be industrial by some definition, but not our own. Reality is messier than it appears in the book my tormentor was reading, and farming more complicated than a simple morality play.

On the desk in front of me are a dozen books, all hugely critical of present-day farming. Farmers are often given a pass in these books, painted as either naïve tools of corporate greed, or economic nullities forced into their present circumstances by the unrelenting forces of the twin grindstones of corporate greed and unfeeling markets. To the farmer on the ground, though, a farmer blessed with free choice and hard won experience, the moral choices aren't quite so easy. Biotech crops actually cut the use of chemicals, and increase food safety. Are people who refuse to use them my moral superiors? Herbicides cut the need for tillage, which decreases soil erosion by millions of tons. The biggest environmental harm I have done as a farmer is the topsoil (and nutrients) I used to send down the Missouri River to the Gulf of Mexico before we began to practice no-till farming, made possible only by the use of herbicides. The combination of herbicides and genetically modified seed has made my farm more sustainable, not less, and actually reduces the pollution I send down the river.

Finally, consumers benefit from cheap food. If you think they don't, just remember the headlines after food prices began increasing in 2007 and 2008, including the study by the Food and Agriculture Organization of the United Nations announcing that 50 million additional people are now hungry because of increasing food prices. Only "industrial farming" can possibly meet the demands of an increasing population and increased demand for food as a result of growing incomes.

So the stakes in this argument are even higher. Farmers can raise food in different ways if that is what the market wants. It is important, though, that even people riding in airplanes know that there are environmental and food safety costs to whatever kind of farming we choose.

Pigs in a Pen

In his book *Dominion*, author Mathew Scully calls "factory farming" an "obvious moral evil so sickening and horrendous it would leave us ashen." Scully, a speechwriter for the second President Bush, can hardly be called a man of the left. Just to make sure the point is not lost, he quotes the conservative historian Paul Johnson a page later:

> The rise of factory farming, whereby food producers cannot remain competitive except by subjecting animals to unspeakable deprivation, has hastened this process. The human spirit revolts at what we have been doing.

Arizona and Florida have outlawed pig gestation crates, and California recently passed, overwhelmingly, a ballot initiative doing the same. There is no doubt that Scully and Johnson have the wind at their backs, and confinement raising of livestock may well be outlawed everywhere. And only a person so callous as to have a spirit that cannot be revolted, or so hardened to any kind of morality that he could countenance an obvious moral evil, could say a word in defense of caging animals during their production. In the quote above, Paul Johnson is forecasting a move toward vegetarianism. But if we assume, at least for the present, that most of us will continue to eat meat, let me dive in where most fear to tread.

Lynn Niemann was a neighbor of my family's, a farmer with a vision. He began raising turkeys on a field near his house around 1956. They were, I suppose, what we would now call "free range" turkeys. Turkeys raised in a natural manner, with no roof over their heads, just gamboling around in the pasture, as God surely intended. Free to eat grasshoppers, and grass, and scratch for grubs and worms. And also free to serve as prey for weasels, who kill turkeys by slitting their necks and practicing exsanguination. Weasels were a problem, but not as much a threat as one of our typically violent early summer thunderstorms. It seems that turkeys, at least young ones, are not smart enough to come in out of the rain, and will stand outside in a downpour, with beaks open and eyes skyward, until they drown. One night Niemann lost 4,000 turkeys to drowning, along with his dream, and his farm.

Now, turkeys are raised in large open sheds. Chickens and turkeys raised for meat are not grown in cages. As the critics of "industrial farming" like to point out, the sheds get quite crowded by the time Thanksgiving rolls around and the turkeys are fully grown. And yes, the birds are bedded in sawdust, so the turkeys do walk around in their own waste. Although the turkeys don't seem to mind, this quite clearly disgusts the various authors I've read whom have actually visited a turkey farm. But none of those authors, whose descriptions of the horrors of modern poultry production have a certain sameness, were there when Neimann picked up those 4,000 dead turkeys. Sheds are expensive, and it was easier to raise turkeys in open, inexpensive pastures. But that type of production really was hard on the turkeys. Protected from the weather and predators, today's turkeys may not be aware that they are a part of a morally reprehensible system.

Like most young people in my part of the world, I was a 4-H member. Raising cattle and hogs, showing them at the county fair, and then sending to slaughter those animals that we had spent the summer feeding, washing, and training. We would then tour the packing house, where our friend was hung on a rail, with his loin eye measured and his carcass evaluated. We farm kids got an early start on dulling our moral sensibilities. I'm still proud of my win in the Atchison County Carcass competition of 1969, as it is the only trophy I have ever received. We raised the hogs in a shed, or farrowing (birthing) house. On one side were eight crates of the kind that the good citizens of California have outlawed. On the other were the kind of wooden pens that our critics would have us use, where the sow could turn around, lie down, and presumably act in a natural way. Which included lying down on my 4-H project, killing several piglets, and forcing me to clean up the mess when I did my chores before school. The crates protect the piglets from their mothers. Farmers do not cage their hogs because of sadism, but because dead pigs are a drag on the profit margin, and because being crushed by your mother really is an awful way to go. As is being eaten by your mother, which I've seen sows do to newborn pigs as well.

I warned you that farming is still dirty and bloody, and I wasn't kidding. So let's talk about manure. It is an article of faith amongst the agri-intellectuals that we no longer use manure as fertilizer. To quote Dr. Michael Fox in his book *Eating with a Conscience,* "The animal waste is not going back to the land from which the animal feed originated." Or Bill McKibben, in his book *Deep Economy*, writing about modern livestock production: "But this concentrates the waste in one place, where instead of being useful fertilizer to spread on crop fields it becomes a toxic threat."

In my inbox is an email from our farm's neighbor, who raises thousands of hogs in close proximity to our farm, and several of my family member's houses as well. The email outlines the amount and chemical analysis of the manure that will be spread on our fields this fall, manure that will replace dozens of tons of commercial fertilizer. The manure is captured underneath the hog houses in cement pits, and is knifed into the soil after the crops are harvested. At no time is it exposed to erosion, and it is an extremely valuable resource, one which farmers use to its fullest extent, just as they have since agriculture began.

In the southern part of Missouri, there is an extensive poultry industry in areas of the state where the soil is poor. The farmers there spread the poultry litter on pasture, and the advent of poultry barns made cattle production possible in areas that used to be waste ground. The "industrial" poultry houses are owned by family farmers, who have then used the byproducts to produce beef in areas where cattle couldn't survive before. McKibben is certain that the contracts these farmers sign with companies like Tyson are unfair, and the farmers might agree. But they like those cows, so there is a waiting list for new chicken barns. In some areas, there is indeed more manure than available cropland. But the trend in the industry, thankfully, is toward a dispersion of animals and manure, as the value of the manure increases, and the cost of transporting the manure becomes prohibitive.

We Can't Change Nature

The largest producer of pigs in the United States has promised to gradually end the use of hog crates. The Humane Society promises to take their initiative drive to outlaw farrowing crates and poultry cages to more states. Many of the counties in my own state of Missouri have chosen to outlaw the the building of confinement facilities. Barack Obama has been harshly critical of animal agriculture. We are clearly in the process of deciding that we will not continue to raise animals the way we do now. Because other countries may not share our sensibilities, we'll have to withdraw or amend free trade agreements to keep any semblance of a livestock industry.

We can do that, and we may be a better society for it, but we can't change nature. Pigs will be allowed to "return to their mire," as Kipling had it, but they'll also be crushed and eaten by their mothers. Chickens will provide lunch to any number of predators, and some number of chickens will die as flocks establish their pecking order.

In recent years, the cost of producing pork dropped as farmers increased feed efficiency (the amount of feed needed to produce a pound of pork) by 20 percent. Free-range chickens and pigs will increase the price of food, using more energy and water to produce the extra grain required for the same amount of meat, and some people will go hungry. It is also instructive that the first company to move away from farrowing crates is the largest producer of pigs. Changing the way we raise animals will not necessarily change the scale of the companies involved in the industry. If we are about to require more expensive ways of producing food, the largest and most well-capitalized farms will have the least trouble adapting.

The Omnivores' Delusions

Michael Pollan, in an 8,000-word essay in the New York Times Magazine, took the expected swipes at animal agriculture. But his truly radical prescriptions had to do with raising of crops. Pollan, who seemed to be aware of the nitrogen problem in his book *The Omnivore's Dilemma*, left nuance behind, as well as the laws of chemistry, in his recommendations. The nitrogen problem is this: without nitrogen, we do not have life. Until we learned to produce nitrogen from natural gas early in the last century, the only way to get nitrogen was through nitrogen produced by plants called legumes, or from small amounts of nitrogen that are produced by lightning strikes. The amount of life the earth could support was limited by the amount of nitrogen available for crop production.

In his book, Pollan quotes geographer Vaclav Smil to the effect that 40 percent of the people alive today would not be alive without the ability to artificially synthesize nitrogen. But in his directive on food policy, Pollan damns agriculture's dependence on fossil fuels, and urges the president to encourage agriculture to move away from expensive and declining supplies of natural gas toward the unlimited sunshine that supported life, and agriculture, as recently as the 1940s. Now, why didn't I think of that?

Well, I did. I've raised clover and alfalfa for the nitrogen they produce, and half the time my land is planted to soybeans, another nitrogen producing legume. Pollan writes as if all of his ideas are new, but my father tells of agriculture extension meetings in the late 1950s entitled "Clover and Corn, the Road to Profitability." Farmers know that organic farming was the default position of agriculture for thousands of years, years when hunger was just around the corner for even advanced societies. I use all the animal manure available to me, and do everything I can to reduce the amount of commercial fertilizers I use. When corn genetically modified to use nitrogen more efficiently enters the market, as it soon will, I will use it as well. But none of those things will completely replace commercial fertilizer.

Norman Borlaug, founder of the green revolution, estimates that the amount of nitrogen available naturally would only support a worldwide population of 4 billion souls or so. He further remarks that we would need another 5 billion cows to produce enough manure to fertilize our present crops with "natural" fertilizer. That would play havoc with global warming. And cows do not produce nitrogen from the air, but only from the forages they eat, so to produce more manure we will have to plant more forages. Most of the critics of industrial farming maintain the contradictory positions that we should increase the use of manure as a fertilizer, and decrease our consumption of meat. Pollan would solve the problem with cover crops, planted after the corn crop is harvested, and with mandatory composting. Pollan should talk to some actual farmers before he presumes to advise a president.

Pollan tells of flying over the upper Midwest in the winter, and seeing the black, fallow soil. I suppose one sees what one wants to see, but we have not had the kind of tillage implement on our farm that would produce black soil in nearly 20 years. Pollan would provide our nitrogen by planting those black fields to nitrogen-producing cover crops after the cash crops are harvested. This is a fine plan, one that farmers have known about for generations. And sometimes it would even work. But not last year, as we finished harvest in November in a freezing rain. It is hard to think of a legume that would have done its thing between then and corn planting time. Plants do not grow very well in freezing weather, a fact that would evidently surprise Pollan.

And even if we could have gotten a legume established last fall, it would not have fixed any nitrogen before planting time. We used to plant corn in late May, plowing down our green manure and killing the first flush of weeds. But that meant the corn would enter its crucial growing period during the hottest, driest parts of the summer, and that soil erosion would be increased because the land was bare during drenching spring rains. Now we plant in early April, best utilizing our spring rains, and ensuring that pollination occurs before the dog days of August.

A few other problems come to mind. The last time I planted a cover crop, the clover provided a perfect habitat in early spring for bugs, bugs that I had to kill with an insecticide. We do not normally apply insecticides, but we did that year. Of course, you can provide nitrogen with legumes by using a longer crop rotation, growing clover one year and corn the next. But that uses twice as much water to produce a corn crop, and takes twice as much land to produce the same number of bushels. We are producing twice the food we did in 1960 on less land, and commercial nitrogen is one of the main reasons why. It may be that we decide we would rather spend land and water than energy, but Pollan never mentions that we are faced with that choice.

His other grand idea is mandatory household composting, with the compost delivered to farmers free of charge. Why not? Compost is a valuable soil amendment, and if somebody else is paying to deliver it to my farm, then bring it on. But it will not do much to solve the nitrogen problem. Household compost has somewhere between 1 and 5 percent nitrogen, and not all that nitrogen is available to crops the first year. Presently, we are applying about 150 pounds of nitrogen per acre to corn, and crediting about 40 pounds per acre from the preceding years soybean crop. Let's assume a 5 percent nitrogen rate, or about 100 pounds of nitrogen per ton of compost. That would require 3,000 pounds of compost per acre. Or about 150,000 tons for the corn raised in our county. The average truck carries about 20 tons. Picture 7,500 trucks traveling from New York City to our small county here in the Midwest, delivering compost. Five million truckloads to fertilize the country's corn crop. Now, that would be a carbon footprint!

Pollan thinks farmers use commercial fertilizer because it is easier, and because it is cheap. Pollan is right. But those are perfectly defensible reasons. Nitrogen quadrupled in price over the last several years, and farmers are still using it, albeit more cautiously. We are using GPS monitors on all of our equipment to ensure that we do not use too much, and our production of corn per pound of nitrogen is rapidly increasing. On our farm, we have increased yields about 50 percent during my career, while applying about the same amount of nitrogen we did when I began farming. That fortunate trend will increase even faster with the advent of new GMO hybrids. But as much as Pollan might desire it, even President Obama cannot reshuffle the chemical deck that nature has dealt. Energy may well get much more expensive, and peak oil production may have been reached. But food production will have a claim on fossil fuels long after we have learned how to use renewables and nuclear power to handle many of our other energy needs.

Farming and Connectedness

Much of farming is more "industrial," more technical, and more complex than it used to be. Farmers farm more acres, and are less close to the ground and their animals than they were in the past. Almost all critics of industrial agriculture bemoan this loss of closeness, this "connectedness," to use author Rod Dreher's term. It is a given in most of the writing about agriculture that the knowledge and experience of the organic farmer is what makes him so unique and so important. The "industrial farmer," on the other hand, is a mere pawn of Cargill, backed into his ignorant way of life by forces too large, too far from the farm, and too powerful to resist. Concern about this alienation, both between farmers and the land, and between consumers and their food supply, is what drives much of the literature about agriculture.

The distance between the farmer and what he grows has certainly increased, but, believe me, if we weren't closely connected, we wouldn't still be farming. It's important to our critics that they emphasize this alienation, because they have to ignore the "industrial" farmer's experience and knowledge to say the things they do about farming.

But farmers have reasons for their actions, and society should listen to them as we embark upon this reappraisal of our agricultural system. I use chemicals and diesel fuel to accomplish the tasks my grandfather used to do with sweat, and I use a computer instead of a lined notebook and a pencil, but I'm still farming the same land he did 80 years ago, and the fund of knowledge that our family has accumulated about our small part of Missouri is valuable. And everything I know and I have learned tells me this: we have to farm "industrially" to feed the world, and by using those "industrial" tools sensibly, we can accomplish that task and leave my grandchildren a prosperous and productive farm, while protecting the land, water, and air around us.

Michael Idov is a staff writer for *New York Magazine*. He is best known for his stint as the editor-in-chief for *GQ Russia* and his novel *Ground Up*.

When Did Young People Start Spending 25% of Their Paychecks on Pickled Lamb's Tongues?

Michael Idov

On the Tuesday before we meet, Diane Chang sends me a list of places where she wants to eat in the coming week. Here it is, in alphabetical order: ABC Kitchen, Abistro, Bhojan, Bianca, Cafe Katja, Char No. 4, Coppelia, Cotan, Diner, Eisenberg's, Han Joo Chik BBQ, Henan Feng Wei, Marlow & Sons, Schnitzi, St. Anselm, Sun in Bloom, Tanoreen, Upstate Craft Beer & Oyster Bar, Vinegar Hill House, and Wondee Siam. For our dinner, she eventually settles on Wondee Siam II, on Ninth and 54th (but emphatically not the original Wondee Siam, on Ninth and 53rd).

Chang arrives at the tiny Thai place with her friends Jasmine, a stylist, and Marcos, a graphic designer. They, too, have their food bona fides: Marcos snaps quick photos of each dish as it is placed on the table; Jasmine's phone holds carefully curated favorite-restaurant lists for New York and L.A. Both are a little older—30-plus to Chang's 27—but Chang is clearly the group's leader. She has picked the place, orders for everyone (shrimp salad, deep-fried catfish, and crispy pork off the restaurant's "secret menu"), and generally steers the conversation toward the plates in front of us.

Petite and stylish, with a self-consciously goofy smile, Chang works in online and social-media marketing. She is, in culinary parlance, a civilian—her job has nothing to do with New York's sprawling food industry or with the chattering class that's gathered around it. Her leisure time and modest discretionary income, however, are devoted almost entirely to food and restaurants.

"I'm not a foodie, I just like what I like," she says. "Yes, I know, it's just like hipsters saying, 'I'm not a hipster.'" (The cliché cracks her up.) "But it's like when my boss says, 'Oh, you're such a foodie.' I'm like, *Oh God.* When I hear the word *foodie*, I think of Yelp. I don't want to be lumped in with Yelp." Just then, her iPhone goes off, and I glimpse her screen saver. It's a close-up photo of a pile of gnarly, gristly pig's feet, skin singed and torn, half-rendered fat and pearlescent cartilage beaming back the flash. The dish is from a tiny food stall in Taipei, she tells me. "It's braised in a soy-based sauce, and they serve it on rice with pickled mustard greens."

There have, of course, always been people in this town for whom food is a serious cultural pursuit. Traditionally, they have been older, white, and affluent. Knowing the newest and finest restaurants to frequent and where to find the very best things to eat have long been essential New York status markers. One of the main hallmarks of twentysomething life, on the other hand, has typically been to not give a shit what and where you eat. As recently as the late nineties, a steady diet of burritos and takeout Chinese, with an ironic-but-not-really TV dinner thrown in now and then, was part of the Generation X ethic. An abiding interest in food was something for old people or snobs, like golf or opera. The notion of idolizing chefs, filling notebooks with restaurant "life lists," or talking about candied foie gras on a date was out-and-out bizarre.

Lately, however, food has become a defining obsession among a wide swath of the young and urbane. It is not golf or opera. It's more like indie rock. Just like the music of, say, Drag City bands on a nineties campus, food is now viewed as a legitimate option for a hobby, a topic of endless discussion, a playground for one-upmanship, and a measuring stick of cool. "It's a badge of honor," says Chang. "Bragging rights." She says she disliked M.Wells, last year's consensus "It" restaurant, partly because of "the fact that everybody loves it, and I just don't want to believe the hype." The quest for ever greater obscurity, a central principle of the movement, reaches a kind of event horizon in Chang's friend James Casey, the publisher of an idiosyncratic annual food magazine called *Swallow*. Lately, Casey has been championing the theory that mediocre food is better than good, the equivalent of a jaded indie kid extolling the virtues of Barry Manilow.

Food's transformation from a fusty hobby to a youth-culture phenomenon has happened remarkably fast. The simultaneous rise of social networks and camera phones deserves part of the credit (eating, like sex, is among the most easily chronicled of pursuits), but none of this would have happened without the grassroots revolution in fine dining. "You can now eat just as quality food with a great environment without the fuss and the feeling of sitting at the grown-up table," says Chang's friend Amy, who is, incidentally, a cook at the very grown-up Jean Georges.

The timeline looks roughly like this: In 1998, Mario Batali gutted the space that was once home to the stodgy Coach House and replaced it with the loud and brilliant Babbo. The *Times* later cited Babbo's "Led Zeppelin soundtrack" as "one of the dividing lines between a restaurant with three stars, which it unequivocally deserves, and one with the highest rating of four." That missed the point. The whole *idea* was to fuse fine dining and rock and roll. Anthony Bourdain's 2000 *Kitchen Confidential* destroyed the archetype of the foofy French chef in a toque and replaced it with an image of cooks as young tattooed badasses. Then, in 2004, a young neurotic chef named David Chang (no relation to Diane) opened Momofuku Noodle Bar, serving what Bourdain has called the kind of food that chefs themselves like to eat after-hours—that is, simple, ingredient-driven food, often global, that is unfailingly delicious but not necessarily expensive or stuffy. Somewhere along the line, young people even began to view cooking as a form of artistic expression. The idea of eating well wasn't just democratized. It was now, improbably enough, edgy.

Diane Chang is a prime specimen of the new breed of restaurant-goer. The species is obsessive and omnivorous. Although they lean toward cheap ethnic food and revile pretension, they do not ultimately discriminate by price point or cuisine. They might hit a vegan joint like Sun in Bloom one day, its neighbor Bark Hot Dogs the next, then subsist on ramen for a week before blowing a paycheck on a sixteen-course lunch at Ko. They are not especially concerned with locavorism or sustainability or foraging. Sometimes nirvana simply takes the form of an authentic, ice-cold Mexican Coke. They abhor restaurant clichés (Carnegie Deli, Peter Luger) and studiously avoid chains (Olive Garden, McDonald's) but are not above the occasional ironic trip to either. They consume food media—blogs, books, *Top Chef* and other "quality" TV shows but definitely not Food Network—like so many veal sweetbreads. *Lucky Peach*, Chang's quarterly journal, is required reading. They talk about food and restaurants incessantly, and their social lives are organized around them. Some are serious home cooks who seek to duplicate the feats of their chef-heroes in their own kitchens; others barely use a stove. Above all, they are avowed culinary agnostics whose central motivation is simply to hunt down and enjoy the next most delicious meal, all the better if no one else has yet heard of it. Dish snapshots and social-network check-ins are a given.

As Chang and her friends plow through the menu at Wondee Siam, I feel no need to raise the subject of food. Discounting Marcos's recent singlehood, which quickly turns into a discussion of his "Single Man diet," the topic is virtually the only one on the table. A conversational pattern recurs: a restaurant name-drop, a quick Zagat-style assessment, next topic. The amazing Chinese New Year dinner at a Vietnamese place on Orchard ("You have to know the chef"). Lone Star barbecue ("So. Delicious"). A server at Roberta's ("stuck-up"). Red Rooster ("My girlfriend is really good friends with the chef," but "it's just a scene"). This leads to a sidebar on "scene" restaurants—Miss Lily's, La Esquina, the Smile—with the conclusion that the food is always disappointing.

At one point, Chang turns to me. "So what's your favorite restaurant in New York?" she asks. Without thinking, I give my standby answer, which hasn't changed in the past four years or so: Eleven Madison Park. I feel the air whoosh out of the room. "Ah." There falls a pause while I savor, perhaps for the first time, at age 35, the full extent of feeling old and out of touch. It's not that the group doesn't respect chef Daniel Humm. It's that my answer is so pathetically predictable. I should have said Torrisi, I think. No, Parm. They are probably way over Torrisi already. On the food-as-indie-rock matrix, I have just accidentally confessed to loving the Dave Matthews Band. Chang gives me a forgiving look and reaches for more crispy pork.

Diane Chang was born in a predominantly Chinese community in San Gabriel Valley, near Los Angeles. Her early life was steeped in the tastes and aromas of Sichuan cuisine. Chang's China-born grandmother, "an amazing, amazing cook," taught her traditional dishes. As for the local options, "We had

Sizzler," she deadpans. She hadn't tried American food until grade school, when the one-two punch of sugar and salt predictably floored her. "Like, Lunchables? So much better than the fish my grandmother just spent two hours on," she says, laughing. "Then you get older and you wise up." But not before gaining fifteen pounds on UCLA cafeteria food. At the dorm, Chang had an all-day unlimited cafeteria pass, "like a MetroCard for food," so she ended up popping in for a snack every couple of hours. Trying to right her ways, she developed an eating disorder, and gave up carbs. "Bread is her greatest frenemy," says her friend Katherine, a former food-magazine staffer. "Who is she kidding? She loves food too much to deny herself anything."

In 2006, after moving out of the dorm, Chang grew more serious about food as a hobby. She cycled through several identities, from going vegetarian to joining a group called the Burger Club, which was exactly what it sounds like—friends and strangers comparison-eating their way through the L.A. hamburger scene. She began to hit progressively more-obscure places, spurred on by blogs and trying to one-up friends. Chang's college years coincided with the first explosion of websites like Chowhound—"The ones that were super bare-bones," she says, "just people talking about food. The food blogs are still big, but they really had their moment in the early aughts. And I think that's why food became such a thing." She ate at obscure L.A. haunts, and began frequenting a nameless pop-up Burmese restaurant that operated on weekends out of someone's garage. After one visit, she got food poisoning. She later reasoned that by Sunday evening, when she had eaten it, the chicken was no longer fresh. So she stopped going—on Sundays.

This was also the time where her trips to New York began, for job interviews and, of course, food. On one such sojourn, Chang managed to get into Momofuku Ko in the first months of its existence, despite the furious loading and reloading of the restaurant's website at precisely 10 a.m. that landing a reservation requires. She impulsively booked a party of four—the maximum number Ko's arcane rules allow—and then realized she had no idea whom to invite along. "I was just out of college at the time, so nobody had money," she remembers. "I was super-poor. It's like, which one of my friends will shell out 160 bucks for a lunch?" The impasse lasted until Chang's then-boyfriend found a way to expense half of the outing as client entertainment. The lunch took up three hours, involved sixteen courses, and left Chang, the would-be un-foodie, unimpressed. "Remember when he just made burritos?" she asks, sighing, the culinary equivalent of claiming R.E.M. sold out after *Chronic Town*.

Besotted with New York, she landed a job and moved here in January 2010. "I was about to be paid close to nothing, but I decided that the pay cut was worth it to live in one of the most exhilarating cities in the world." She bunked with an old friend in an apartment on the corner of Allen and Broome. It was a perfect young food lover's destination: one foot in Chinatown, one on the LES. The first thing she did on her first day as a New Yorker was get coffee from 88 Orchard, then banana bread from Babycakes, dumplings from Vanessa's, and finally a litchi martini at Congee Village. Her first real New York restaurant experience, however, was Blue Hill, with the same ex-boyfriend who footed the bill for Ko. "Since food was a major part of our relationship, we knew we had to pick somewhere delicious for dinner," Chang remembers. "I was a big fan of Dan Barber." She had acorn-squash pasta that she didn't like: too stringy. "Honestly, I don't remember too much about the meal," she says, a statement directly contradicted by the previous one, "but the whole experience resonates to this day because I felt kind of out of place among a lot of older, more affluent people. But, oddly enough, wondering how the cost of the meal will affect my budget made me feel more of a New Yorker."

Chang earns about $70,000 a year; her rent in Park Slope, where she lives now ("the worst food destination ever"), runs $1,100 a month. As for the rest, "I spend it all on food," she says flatly. During the one week I asked Chang to keep tabs on her restaurant-going and market purchases, she ate at fourteen restaurants, pizza joints, and cafés, and spent $350. The largest single bill she racked up was $58, although Han Joo, a Korean barbecue spot in Flushing famous for its slanted grills that pour rendered pork fat onto kimchee, required a $38 cab ride. Chang also made a few dishes at home, including potatoes with crème fraîche and smoked paprika (a re-creation of a brunch favorite from Vinegar Hill House), pozole, chile verde, a red-lentil soup with pistou, and a fennel salad, the last two from New York *Times* recipes. When it comes to grocery shopping, Chang hits the nearby Grand Army Plaza farmers' market every Saturday and buys the rest of her provisions in precision-targeted outings: meat at the Park Slope outpost of the cult upstate butcher Fleisher's, spices at Sahadi's. During the week she recorded her purchases, there was only one backslide into the mainstream. After the $20 organic chicken she saw at the farmers' market proved a little too expensive, she grabbed a couple of shrink-wrapped chicken breasts at Key Food.

About two months after we first meet, I am having dinner with Chang at Williamsburg's St. Anselm, one of the few places she has yet to cross off her original list. We order butcher's steak, grilled artichoke hearts ("Don't you always feel so humbled eating an artichoke?"), a patty melt, and a couple of other dishes I strain to remember two days later; Chang will probably be able to recall them, in succession, two years from now. She photographs each, and shares them on Instagram. Chang keeps a blog, of course. It's called Beets N' Jamz (she pairs meals she's eaten recently, i.e., a breakfast taco from Brooklyn Taco, with songs, i.e., Fleetwood Mac's "Hypnotized," and refers to herself as D.J. Panko). It replaces her two previous bread-focused blogs called Lotta Loaf and Baguettaboutit. But these days Chang is much more interested in throwing real-life parties. "Diane is very good about bringing people together," says her friend Katherine, "and it will always involve food." Her first year in New York, Chang organized an Oktoberfest picnic for a dozen people in Brooklyn Bridge Park. She made pretzels, pigs in a blanket, and curried ketchup, all from scratch. Chang's birthdays are equally elaborate culinary group outings: In 2010, she went to Spicy & Tasty, a cult Sichuan eatery in Flushing. Last year, she considered Tanoreen, a Middle Eastern restaurant in Bay Ridge, but decided instead on Tulcingo del Valle, an unassuming Mexican place in Hell's Kitchen. She also tried to start a Barbecue Club on the model of her Burger Club in L.A., but found the scene too limited. "You've got Fatty 'Cue, Fette Sau, Rub, you have Hill Country, Dinosaur . . . but then it's like, where are you going to go, Dallas BBQ? Burgers are so much easier in New York. I'm kind of sick of burgers a little bit, though." Which doesn't prevent her from sampling my patty melt.

Aside from Robert Sietsema and Jonathan Gold, with their tight focus on rustic and ethnic food, Chang doesn't trust food critics. She used to simply go on friends' recommendations, but the blogs changed the game. Now the choice of a place for dinner turns into an oft-tortuous multistep process. When someone recommends a place, Chang goes online. Despite her distrust of Yelp and sites like it, she still reads them compulsively, at least to look at the photos. "It doesn't matter if it's good or bad," she says. "I just want to know." Last night, she had three options, she tells me. "And I was just stressing out and stressing out about it. The reason I ended up choosing Neptune was, like, 'Okay, I mean, that's the one from way out of left field, no one ever talks about it, maybe I'll stumble across a gem.' But it's like, I also realize, there's not a single restaurant no one has ever talked about any more."

Sometimes, of course, this approach misfires. Neptune, an obscure Polish restaurant on First Avenue, proved the biggest disappointment of the fourteen places where Chang ate that week. The idea belonged to Chang's then-boyfriend, another card-carrying food fanatic. (For the couple's first date, they had gone to a festival called "Egg Rolls and Egg Creams.") Telling me about the Neptune debacle, Chang sounds depressed, apologetic even. "We happened to be in Union Square, which always throws us off in our food choices," she says. She had suggested ABC Kitchen for her favorite cumin-carrot salad and a glass of wine. Maybe Cotan for Japanese? Or Zabb Elee for Thai? But no, the boyfriend insisted on Neptune. He felt really bad, she says. "It was the first time he's ever struck out picking a restaurant." They broke up not long afterward.

Barbara Kingsolver is a prolific American novelist, essayist, and poet. Her work often focuses on the relationships between people, their communities, and the broader environments in which they live.

You Can't Run Away on Harvest Day
Barbara Kingsolver

The Saturday of Labor Day weekend dawned with a sweet, translucent bite, like a Golden Delicious apple. I always seem to harbor a childlike hope through the berry-stained months of June and July that summer will be for keeps. But then a day comes in early fall to remind me why it should end, after all. In September the quality of daylight shifts toward flirtation. The green berries on the spicebush shrubs along our lane begin to blink red, first one and then another, like faltering but resolute holiday lights. The woods fill with the restless singing of migrant birds warming up to the proposition of flying south. The cool air makes us restless too: jeans and sweater weather, perfect for a hike. Steven and I rose early that morning, looked out the window, looked at each other, and started in on the time-honored marital grumble: Was this *your* idea?

We weren't going on a hike today. Nor would we have the postsummer Saturday luxury of sitting on the porch with a cup of coffee and watching the farm wake up. On the docket instead was a hard day of work we could not postpone. The previous morning we'd sequestered half a dozen roosters and as many torn turkeys in a room of the barn we call "death row." We hold poultry there, clean and comfortable with water but no food, for a twenty-four-hour fast prior to harvest. It makes the processing cleaner and seems to calm the animals also. I could tell you it gives them time to get their emotional affairs in order, if that helps. But they have limited emotional affairs, and no idea what's coming.

We had a lot more of both. Our plan for this gorgeous day was the removal of some of our animals from the world of the living into the realm of food. At five months of age our roosters had put on a good harvest weight, and had lately opened rounds of cockfighting, venting their rising hormonal angst against any moving target, including us. When a rooster flies up at you with his spurs, he leaves marks. Lily now had to arm herself with a length of pipe in order to gather the eggs. Our barnyard wasn't big enough for this much machismo. We would certainly take no pleasure in the chore, but it was high time for the testosterone-reduction program. We sighed at the lovely weather and pulled out our old, bloody sneakers for harvest day.

There was probably a time when I thought it euphemistic to speak of "harvesting" animals. Now I don't. We calculate "months to harvest" when planning for the right time to start poultry. We invite friends to "harvest parties," whether we'll be gleaning[1] vegetable or animal. A harvest implies planning, respect, and

---

1. *gleaning*: Gathering, collecting.

effort. With animals, both the planning and physical effort are often greater, and respect for the enterprise is substantially more complex. It's a lot less fun than spending an autumn day picking apples off trees, but it's a similar operation on principle and the same word.

Killing is a culturally loaded term, for most of us inextricably tied up with some version of a command that begins, "Thou shalt not." Every faith has it. And for all but perhaps the Jainists of India, that command is absolutely conditional. We know it does not refer to mosquitoes. Who among us has never killed living creatures on purpose? When a child is sick with an infection we rush for the medicine spoon, committing an eager and purposeful streptococcus massacre. We sprinkle boric acid or grab a spray can to rid our kitchens of cockroaches. What we mean by "killing" is to take a life cruelly, as in murder—or else more accidentally, as in "Oops, looks like I killed my African violet." Though the results are incomparable, what these different "killings" have in common is needless waste and some presumed measure of regret.

Most of us, if we know even a little about where our food comes from, understand that every bite put into our mouths since infancy (barring the odd rock or marble) was formerly alive. The blunt biological truth is that we animals can only remain alive by eating other life. Plants are inherently more blameless, having been born with the talent of whipping up their own food, peacefully and without noise, out of sunshine, water, and the odd mineral ingredient sucked up through their toes. Strangely enough, it's the animals to which we've assigned some rights, while the saintly plants we maim and behead with moral impunity. Who thinks to beg forgiveness while mowing the lawn?

The moral rules of destroying our fellow biota[2] get even more tangled, the deeper we go. If we draw the okay-to-kill line between "animal" and "plant," and thus exclude meat, fowl, and fish from our diet on moral grounds, we still must live with the fact that every sack of flour and every soybean-based block of tofu came from a field where countless winged and furry lives were extinguished in the plowing, cultivating, and harvest. An estimated 67 million birds die each year from pesticide exposure on U.S. farms. Butterflies, too, are universally killed on contact in larval form by the genetically modified pollen contained in most U.S. corn. Foxes, rabbits, and bobolinks are starved out of their homes or dismembered by the sickle mower. Insects are "controlled" even by organic pesticides; earthworms are cut in half by the plow. Contrary to lore, they won't grow into two; both halves die.

To believe we can live without taking life is delusional. Humans may only cultivate nonviolence in our diets by degree. I've heard a Buddhist monk suggest the *number* of food-caused deaths is minimized in steak dinners, which share one death over many meals, whereas the equation is reversed for a bowl of clams. Others of us have lost heart for eating any steak dinner that's been shoved

2. *biota*: Living things, both plant and animal.

through the assembly line of feedlot life—however broadly we might share that responsibility. I take my gospel from Wendell Berry, who writes in *What Are People For*, "I dislike the thought that some animal has been made miserable in order to feed me. If I am going to eat meat, I want it to be from an animal that has lived a pleasant, uncrowded life outdoors, on bountiful pasture, with good water nearby and trees for shade. And I am getting almost as fussy about food plants."

I find myself fundamentally allied with a vegetarian position in every way except one: however selectively, I eat meat. I'm unimpressed by arguments that condemn animal harvest while ignoring, wholesale, the animal killing that underwrites vegetal foods. Uncountable deaths by pesticide and habitat removal—the beetles and bunnies that die collaterally for our bread and veggie-burgers—are lives plumb wasted. Animal harvest is at least not gratuitous, as part of a plan involving labor and recompense. We raise these creatures for a reason. Such premeditation may be presumed unkind, but without it our gentle domestic beasts in their picturesque shapes, colors, and finely tuned purposes would never have had the distinction of existing. To envision a vegan version of civilization, start by erasing from all time the Three Little Pigs, the boy who cried wolf, *Charlotte's Web*, the golden calf, *Tess of the d'Urbervilles*. Next, erase civilization, brought to you by the people who learned to domesticate animals. Finally, rewrite our evolutionary history, since *Homo sapiens* became the species we are by means of regular binges of carnivory.

Most confounding of all, in the vegan revision, are the chapters addressing the future. If farm animals have civil rights, what aspect of their bondage to humans shall they overcome? Most wouldn't last two days without it. Recently while I was cooking eggs, my kids sat at the kitchen table entertaining me with readings from a magazine profile of a famous, rather young vegan movie star. Her dream was to create a safe-haven ranch where the cows and chickens could live free, happy lives and die natural deaths. "Wait till those cows start bawling to be milked," I warned. Having nursed and weaned my own young, I can tell you there is no pain to compare with an overfilled udder. We wondered what the starlet might do for those bursting Jerseys, not to mention the eggs the chickens would keep dropping everywhere. What a life's work for that poor gal: traipsing about the farm in her strappy heels, weaving among the cow flops, bending gracefully to pick up eggs and stick them in an incubator where they would maddeningly *hatch*, and grow up bent on laying *more* eggs. It's dirty work, trying to save an endless chain of uneaten lives. Realistically, my kids observed, she'd hire somebody.

Forgive us. We know she meant well, and as fantasies of the superrich go, it's more inspired than most. It's just the high-mindedness that rankles; when moral superiority combines with billowing ignorance, they fill up a hot-air balloon that's awfully hard not to poke. The farm-liberation fantasy simply reflects a modern cultural confusion about farm animals. They're human property, not just legally but biologically. Over the millennia of our clever history, we created from wild progenitors[3] whole new classes of beasts whose sole purpose was to feed us. If turned loose in the wild, they would haplessly starve, succumb to predation, and destroy the habitats and lives of most or all natural things. If housed at the public expense they would pose a more immense civic burden than our public schools and prisons combined. No thoughtful person really wants those things to happen. But living at a remove from the actual workings of a farm, most humans no longer learn appropriate modes of thinking about animal harvest. Knowing that our family raises meat animals, many friends have told us—not judgmentally, just confessionally—"I don't think I could kill an animal myself." I find myself explaining: It's not what you think. It's nothing like putting down your dog.

Most nonfarmers are intimate with animal life in only three categories: people; pets (i.e., junior people); and wildlife (as seen on nature shows, presumed beautiful and rare). Purposely beheading any of the above is unthinkable, for obvious reasons. No other categories present themselves at close range for consideration. So I understand why it's hard to think about harvest, a categorical act that includes cutting the heads off living lettuces, extended to crops that blink their beady eyes. On our farm we don't especially enjoy processing our animals, but we do value it, as an important ritual for ourselves and any friends adventurous enough to come and help, because of what we learn from it. We reconnect with the purpose for which these animals were bred. We dispense with all delusions about who put the *live* in livestock, and who must take it away.

A friend from whom we buy pasture-grazed lamb and poultry has concurred with us on this point. Kirsty Zahnke grew up in the U.K., and observes that American attitudes toward life and death probably add to the misgivings. "People in this country do everything to cheat death, it seems. Instead of being happy with each moment, they worry so much about what comes next. I think this gets transposed to animals—the preoccupation with 'taking a life.' My animals have all had a good life, with death as its natural end. It's not without thought and gratitude that I slaughter my animals, it is a hard thing to do. It's taken me time to be able to eat my own lambs that I had played with. But I always think of Kahlil Gibran's words:

When you kill a beast, say to him in your heart:

By the same power that slays you, I too am slain, and I too shall be consumed.

For the law that delivers you into my hand shall deliver me into a mightier hand.

Your blood and my blood is naught but the sap that feeds the tree of heaven."

---

3. *progenitor*: Ancestor.

Kirsty works with a local environmental organization and frequently hosts its out-of-town volunteers, who camp at her farm while working in the area. Many of these activists had not eaten meat for many years before arriving on the Zahnkes' meat farm—a formula not for disaster, she notes, but for education. "If one gets to know the mantras of the farm owners, it can change one's viewpoint. I would venture to say that seventy-five percent of the vegans and vegetarians who stayed at least a week here began to eat our meat or animal products, simply because they see what I am doing as right—for the animals, for the environment, for humans."

I respect every diner who makes morally motivated choices about consumption. And I stand with nonviolence, as one of those extremist moms who doesn't let kids at her house pretend to shoot each other, *ever*, or make any game out of human murder. But I've come to different conclusions about livestock. The ve-vangelical pamphlets showing jam-packed chickens and sick downer-cows usually declare, as their first principle, that all meat is factory-farmed. That is false, and an affront to those of us who work to raise animals humanely, or who support such practices with our buying power. I don't want to cause any creature misery, so I won't knowingly eat anything that has stood belly deep in its own poop wishing it was dead until *bam*, one day it was. (In restaurants I go for the fish, or the vegetarian option.)

But meat, poultry, and eggs from animals raised on open pasture are the traditional winter fare of my grandparents, and they serve us well here in the months when it would cost a lot of fossil fuels to keep us in tofu. Should I overlook the suffering of victims of hurricanes, famines, and wars brought on this world by profligate fuel consumption? Bananas that cost a rain forest, refrigerator-trucked soy milk, and prewashed spinach shipped two thousand miles in plastic containers do not seem cruelty- free, in this context. A hundred different paths may lighten the world's load of suffering. Giving up meat is one path; giving up bananas is another. The more we know about our food system, the more we are called into complex choices. It seems facile to declare one single forbidden fruit, when humans live under so many different kinds of trees.

To breed fewer meat animals in the future is possible; phasing out those types destined for confinement lots is a plan I'm assisting myself, by raising heirloom breeds. Most humans could well consume more vegetable foods, and less meat. But globally speaking, the vegetarian option is a luxury. The oft-cited energetic argument for vegetarianism, that it takes ten times as much land to make a pound of meat as a pound of grain, only applies to the kind of land where rain falls abundantly on rich topsoil. Many of the world's poor live in marginal lands that can't support plant-based agriculture. Those not blessed with the fruited plain and amber waves of grain must make do with woody tree pods, tough-leaved shrubs, or sparse grasses. Camels, reindeer, sheep, goats, cattle, and other ruminants are uniquely adapted to transform all those types of indigestible cellulose into edible milk and meat. The fringes of desert, tundra, and marginal grasslands on every continent—coastal Peru, the southwestern United States, the Kalahari, the Gobi, the Australian outback, northern Scandinavia—are inhabited by herders. The Navajo, Mongols, Lapps, Masai, and countless other resourceful tribes would starve without their animals....

After many meatless years it felt strange to us to break the taboo, but over time our family has come back to carnivory. I like listening to a roasting bird in the oven on a Sunday afternoon, following Julia Child's advice to "regulate the chicken so it makes quiet cooking noises" as its schmaltzy aroma fills the house. When a friend began raising beef cattle entirely on pasture (rather than sending them to a CAFO[4] as six-month-olds, as most cattle farmers do), we were born again to the idea of hamburger. We can go visit his animals if we need to be reassured of the merciful cowness of their lives.

As meat farmers ourselves we are learning as we go, raising heritage breeds: the thrifty antiques that know how to stand in the sunshine, gaze upon a meadow, and munch. (Even mate without help!) We're grateful these old breeds weren't consigned to extinction during the past century, though it nearly did happen. Were it not for these animals that can thrive outdoors, and the healthy farms that maintain them, I would have stuck with tofu-burgers indefinitely. That wasn't a bad life, but we're also enjoying this one.

Believing in the righteousness of a piece of work, alas, is not what gets it done. On harvest day we pulled on our stained shoes, sharpened our knives, lit a fire under the big kettle, and set ourselves to the whole show: mud, blood, and lots of little feathers. There are some things about a chicken harvest that are irrepressibly funny, and one of them is the feathers; in your hair, on the backs of your hands, dangling behind your left shoe the way toilet paper does in slapstick movies. Feathery little white tags end up stuck all over the chopping block and the butchering table like Post-it notes from the chicken hereafter. Sometimes we get through the awful parts on the strength of black comedy, joking about the feathers or our barn's death row and the "dead roosters walking."

But today was not one of those times. Some friends had come over to help us, including a family that had recently lost their teenage son in a drowning accident. Their surviving younger children, Abby and Eli, were among Lily's closest friends. The kids were understandably solemn and the adults measured all our words under the immense weight of grief as we set to work. Lily and Abby went to get the first rooster from the barn while I laid out the knives and spread plastic sheets over our butchering table on the back patio. The guys stoked a fire under our 50-gallon kettle, an antique brass instrument Steven and I scored at a farm auction.

The girls returned carrying Rooster #1 upside down, by the legs. Inversion has the immediate effect of lulling a chicken to sleep, or something near to it.

---

4. *CAFO*: Concentrated Animal Feed Operation.

What comes next is quick and final. We set the rooster gently across our big chopping block (a legendary fixture of our backyard, whose bloodstains hold visiting children in thrall), and down comes the ax. All sensation ends with that quick stroke. He must then be held by the legs over a large plastic bucket until all the blood has run out. Farmers who regularly process poultry have more equipment, including banks of "killing cones" or inverted funnels that contain the birds while the processor pierces each neck with a sharp knife, cutting two major arteries and ending brain function. We're not pros, so we have a more rudimentary setup. By lulling and swiftly decapitating my animal, I can make sure my relatively unpracticed handling won't draw out the procedure or cause pain.

What you've heard is true: the rooster will flap his wings hard during this part. If you drop him he'll thrash right across the yard, unpleasantly spewing blood all around, though the body doesn't *run*—it's nothing that well coordinated. His newly detached head silently opens and closes its mouth, down in the bottom of the gut bucket, a world apart from the ruckus. The cause of all these actions is an explosion of massively firing neurons without a brain to supervise them. Most people who claim to be running around like a chicken with its head cut off, really, are not even close. The nearest thing might be the final convulsive seconds of an All-Star wrestling match.

For Rooster #1 it was over, and into the big kettle for a quick scald. After a one-minute immersion in 145-degree water, the muscle tissue releases the feathers so they're easier to pluck. "Easier" is relative—every last feather still has to be pulled, carefully enough to avoid tearing the skin. The downy breast feathers come out by handfuls, while the long wing and tail feathers sometimes must be removed individually with pliers. If we were pros we would have an electric scalder and automatic plucker, a fascinating bucket full of rotating rubber fingers that does the job in no time flat. For future harvests we might borrow a friend's equipment, but for today we had a pulley on a tree limb so we could hoist the scalded carcass to shoulder level, suspending it there from a rope so several of us could pluck at once. Lily, Abby, and Eli pulled neck and breast feathers, making necessary observations such as "Gag, look where his head came off," and "Wonder which one of these tube thingies was his windpipe." Most kids need only about ninety seconds to get from *eeew gross* to solid science. A few weeks later Abby would give an award-winning, fully illustrated 4-H presentation entitled "You Can't Run Away on Harvest Day."

Laura and Becky and I answered the kids' questions, and also talked about Mom things while working on back and wing feathers. (Our husbands were on to the next beheading.) Laura and I compared notes on our teenage daughters—relatively new drivers on the narrow country roads between their jobs, friends, and home—and the worries that come with that territory. I was painfully conscious of Becky's quiet, her ache for a teenage son who never even got to acquire a driver's license. The accident that killed Larry could not have been avoided through any amount of worry. We all cultivate illusions of safety that could fall away in the knife edge of one second.

I wondered how we would get through this afternoon, how *she* would get through months and years of living with impossible loss. I wondered if I'd been tactless, inviting these dear friends to an afternoon of ending lives. And then felt stupid for that thought. People who are grieving walk with death, every waking moment. When the rest of us dread that we'll somehow remind them of death's existence, we are missing their reality. Harvesting turkeys—which this family would soon do on their own farm—was just another kind of work. A rendezvous with death, for them, was waking up each morning without their brother and son.

By early afternoon six roosters had lost their heads, feathers, and viscera, and were chilling on ice. We had six turkeys to go, the hardest piece of our work simply because the animals are larger and heavier. Some of these birds were close to twenty pounds. They would take center stage on our holiday table and those of some of our friends. At least one would be charcuterie—in the garden I had sage, rosemary, garlic, onions, everything we needed for turkey sausage. And the first two roosters we'd harvested would be going on the rotisserie later that afternoon.

We allowed ourselves a break before the challenge of hoisting, plucking, and dressing the turkeys. While Lily and her friends constructed feather crowns and ran for the poultry house to check in with the living, the adults cracked open beers and stretched out in lawn chairs in the September sun.

Our conversation turned quickly to the national preoccupation of that autumn: Katrina, the hurricane that had just hit southern Louisiana and Mississippi. We were horrified by the news that was beginning to filter out of that flooded darkness, the children stranded on rooftops, the bereaved and bewildered families slogging through streets waist-deep in water, breaking plate glass windows to get bottles of water. People drowning and dying of thirst at the same time.

It was already clear this would be an epic disaster. New Orleans and countless other towns across southern Louisiana and Mississippi were being evacuated and left for dead. The news cameras had focused solely on urban losses, sending images of flooded streets, people on rooftops, broken storefronts, and the desperate crises of people in the city with no resources for relocating or evacuating. I had not seen one photograph from the countryside—a wrecked golf course was the closest thing to it. I wondered about the farmers whose year of work still lay in the fields, just weeks or days away from harvest, when the flood took it all. I still can't say whether the rural victims of Katrina found their support systems more resilient, or if their hardships simply went unreported.

The disaster reached into the rest of the country with unexpected tentacles. Our town and schools were already taking in people who had lost everything. The office where I'd just sent my passport for renewal was now underwater. Gasoline had passed $3 a gallon, here and elsewhere, leaving our nation in sticker shock. U.S. citizens were making outlandish declarations about staying home. Climate scientists were saying, "If you warm up the globe, you eventually pay for it." Economists were eyeing our budget deficits and predicting collapse, mayhem, infrastructure breakdown. In so many ways, disaster makes us take stock. For me it had inspired powerful cravings about living within our means. I wasn't thinking so much of my household budget or the national one but the *big* budget, the one that involves consuming approximately the same things we produce. Taking a symbolic cue from my presumed-soggy passport, I suddenly felt like sticking very close to home, with a hand on my family's production, even when it wasn't all that easy or fun—like today.

Analysts of current events were mostly looking to blame administrators. Fair enough, but there were also, it seemed, obvious vulnerabilities here—whole populations, depending on everyday, long-distance lifelines, supplies of food and water and fuel and everything else that are acutely centralized. That's what we consider normal life. Now nature had written a hugely abnormal question across the bottom of our map. I wondered what our answers might be . . . .

Bill McKibben is an American environmentalist, author, and journalist who has written extensively on the impact of global warming.

The Only Way to Have a Cow
Bill McKibben

May I say—somewhat defensively—that I haven't cooked red meat in many years? That I haven't visited a McDonald's since college? That if you asked me how I like my steak, I'd say I don't really remember? I'm not a moral abstainer—I'll eat meat when poor people in distant places offer it to me, especially when they're proud to do so and I'd be an ass to say no. But in everyday life, for a series of reasons that began with the dietary scruples of the woman I chose to marry, hamburgers just don't come into play.

I begin this way because I plan to wade into one of the most impassioned fracases now underway on the planet—to meat or not to meat—and I want to establish that I Do Not Have A Cow In This Fight. In recent years vegetarians and vegans have upped their attack on the consumption of animal flesh, pointing out not only that it's disgusting (read Jonathan Safran Foer's new book) but also a major cause of climate change. The numbers range from 18 percent of the world's greenhouse gas emissions to—in one recent study that was quickly discredited—51 percent. Whatever the exact figure, suffice it to say it's high: there's the carbon that comes from cutting down the forest to start the farm, and from the fertilizer and diesel fuel it takes to grow the corn, there's the truck exhaust from shipping cows hither and yon, and most of all the methane that emanates from the cows themselves (95 percent of it from the front end, not the hind, and these millions of feedlot cows would prefer if you used the word *eructate* in place of *belch*). This news has led to an almost endless series of statistical calculations: going vegan is 50 percent more effective in reducing greenhouse gas emissions than switching to a hybrid car, according to a University of Chicago study; the UN Food and Agriculture Organization finds that a half pound of ground beef has the same effect on climate change as driving an SUV ten miles. It has led to a lot of political statements: the British health secretary last fall called on Englishmen to cut their beefeating by dropping at least a sausage a week from their diets, and Paul McCartney has declared that "the biggest change anyone could make in their own lifestyle to help the environment would be to become vegetarian." It has even led to the marketing of a men's flip-flop called the Stop Global Warming Toepeeka that's made along entirely vegan lines.

Industrial livestock production is essentially indefensible—ethically, ecologically, and otherwise. We now use an enormous percentage of our arable land to grow corn that we feed to cows who stand in feedlots and eructate until they are slaughtered in a variety of gross ways and lodge in our ever-larger abdomens. And the fact that the product of this exercise "tastes good" sounds pretty lame as an excuse. There are technofixes—engineering the corn feed so it produces less methane, or giving the cows shots so they eructate less violently. But this type of tailpipe fix only works around the edges, and with the planet warming fast that's not enough. We should simply stop eating factory-farmed meat, and the effects on climate change would be but one of the many benefits.

Still, even once you've made that commitment, there's a nagging ecological question that's just now being raised. It goes like this: long before humans had figured out the whole cow thing, nature had its own herds of hoofed ungulates. Big herds of big animals—perhaps 60 million bison ranging across North America, and maybe 100 million antelope. That's considerably more than the number of cows now resident in these United States. These were noble creatures, but un-couth—*eructate* hadn't been coined yet. They really did just belch. So why weren't they filling the atmosphere with methane? Why wasn't their manure giving off great quantities of atmosphere-altering gas?

The answer, so far as we can tell, is both interesting and potentially radical in its implications. These old-school ungulates weren't all that different in their plumbing—they were methane factories with legs too. But they used those legs for something. They didn't stand still in feedlots waiting for corn, and they didn't stand still in big western federal allotments overgrazing the same tender grass. They didn't stand still at all. Maybe they would have enjoyed stationary life, but like teenagers in a small town, they were continually moved along by their own version of the police: wolves. And big cats. And eventually Indians. By predators.

As they moved, they kept eating grass and dropping manure. Or, as soil scientists would put it, they grazed the same perennials once or twice a year to "convert aboveground biomass to dung and urine." Then dung beetles buried the results in the soil, nurturing the grass to grow back. These grasslands covered places that don't get much rain—the Southwest and the Plains, Australia, Africa, much of Asia. And all that grass-land sequestered stupendous amounts of carbon and methane from out of the atmosphere—recent preliminary research indicates that methane-loving bacteria in healthy soils will sequester more of the gas in a day than cows supported by the same area will emit in a year.

We're flat out of predators in most parts of the world, and it's hard to imagine, in the short time that we have to deal with climate change, ending the eating of meat and returning the herds of buffalo and packs of wolves to all the necessary spots. It's marginally easier to imagine mimicking those systems with cows. The key technology here is the single-strand electric fence—you move your herd or your flock once or twice a day from one small pasture to the next, forcing them to eat everything that's growing there but moving them along before they graze all the good stuff down to bare ground. Now their manure isn't a problem that fills a cesspool, but a key part of making the system work. Done right, some studies suggest, this method of raising cattle could put much of the atmosphere's oversupply of greenhouse gases back in the soil inside half a century. That means shifting from feedlot farming to rotational grazing is one of the few changes we could make that's on the same scale as the problem of global warming. It won't do away with the need for radically cutting emissions, but it could help get the car exhaust you emitted back in high school out of the atmosphere.

Oh, and grass-fed beef is apparently much better for you—full of Omega 3s, like sardines that moo. Better yet, it's going to be more expensive, because you can't automate the process the same way you can feedlot agriculture. You need the guy to move the fence every afternoon. (That's why about a billion of our fellow humans currently make their livings as herders of one kind or another—some of them use slingshots, or dogs, or shepherd's crooks, or horses instead of electric fence, but the principle is the same.) More expensive, in this case, as in many others, is good; we'd end up eating meat the way most of the world does—as a condiment, a flavor, an ingredient, not an entrée.

I doubt McDonald's will be in favor. I doubt Paul McCartney will be in favor. It doesn't get rid of the essential dilemma of killing something and then putting it in your mouth. But it's possible that the atmosphere would be in favor, and that's worth putting down your fork and thinking about.

Marion Nestle is the Paulette Goddard Professor of Nutrition, Food Studies, and Public Health at New York University, a Professor of Sociology at New York University, and a Visiting Professor of Nutritional Sciences at Cornell.

Eating Made Simple
Marion Nestle

As a nutrition professor, I am constantly asked why nutrition advice seems to change so much and why experts so often disagree. Whose information, people ask, can we trust? I'm tempted to say, "Mine, of course," but I understand the problem. Yes, nutrition advice seems endlessly mired in scientific argument, the self-interest of food companies and compromises by government regulators. Nevertheless, basic dietary principles are not in dispute: eat less; move more; eat fruits, vegetables and whole grains; and avoid too much junk food.

"Eat less" means consume fewer calories, which translates into eating smaller portions and steering clear of frequent between-meal snacks. "Move more" refers to the need to balance calorie intake with physical activity. Eating fruits, vegetables and whole grains provides nutrients unavailable from other foods. Avoiding junk food means to shun "foods of minimal nutritional value"—highly processed sweets and snacks laden with salt, sugars and artificial additives. Soft drinks are the prototypical junk food; they contain sweeteners but few or no nutrients.

If you follow these precepts, other aspects of the diet matter much less. Ironically, this advice has not changed in years. The noted cardiologist Ancel Keys (who died in 2004 at the age of 100) and his wife, Margaret, suggested similar principles for preventing coronary heart disease nearly 50 years ago.

But I can see why dietary advice seems like a moving target. Nutrition research is so difficult to conduct that it seldom produces unambiguous results. Ambiguity requires interpretation. And interpretation is influenced by the individual's point of view, which can become thoroughly entangled with the science.

Nutrition Science Challenges

This scientific uncertainty is not overly surprising given that humans eat so many different foods. For any individual, the health effects of diets are modulated by genetics but also by education and income levels, job satisfaction, physical fitness, and the use of cigarettes or alcohol. To simplify this situation, researchers typically examine the effects of single dietary components one by one.

Studies focusing on one nutrient in isolation have worked splendidly to explain symptoms caused by deficiencies of vitamins or minerals. But this approach is less useful for chronic conditions such as coronary heart disease and diabetes that are caused by the interaction of dietary, genetic, behavioral and social factors. If nutrition science seems puzzling, it is because researchers typically examine single nutrients detached from food itself, foods separate from diets, and risk factors apart from other behaviors. This kind of research is "reductive" in that it attributes health effects to the consumption of one nutrient or food when it is the overall dietary pattern that really counts most.

For chronic diseases, single nutrients usually alter risk by amounts too small to measure except through large, costly population studies. As seen recently in the Women's Health Initiative, a clinical trial that examined the effects of low-fat diets on heart disease and cancer, participants were unable to stick with the restrictive dietary protocols. Because humans cannot be caged and fed measured formulas, the diets of experimental and control study groups tend to converge, making differences indistinguishable over the long run—even with fancy statistics.

It's the Calories

Food companies prefer studies of single nutrients because they can use the results to sell products. Add vitamins to candies, and you can market them as health foods. Health claims on the labels of junk foods distract consumers from their caloric content. This practice matters because when it comes to obesity—which dominates nutrition problems even in some of the poorest countries of the world—it is the calories that count. Obesity arises when people consume significantly more calories than they expend in physical activity.

America's obesity rates began to rise sharply in the early 1980s. Sociologists often attribute the "calories in" side of this trend to the demands of an overworked population for convenience foods—prepared, packaged products and restaurant meals that usually contain more calories than home-cooked meals.

But other social forces also promoted the calorie imbalance. The arrival of the Reagan administration in 1980 increased the pace of industry deregulation, removing controls on agricultural production and encouraging farmers to grow more food. Calories available per capita in the national food supply (that produced by American farmers, plus imports, less exports) rose from 3,200 a day in 1980 to 3,900 a day two decades later.

The early 1980s also marked the advent of the "shareholder value movement" on Wall Street. Stockholder demands for higher short-term returns on investments forced food companies to expand sales in a marketplace that already contained excessive calories. Food companies responded by seeking new sales and marketing opportunities. They encouraged formerly shunned practices that eventually changed social norms, such as frequent between-meal snacking, eating in book and clothing stores, and serving larger portions. The industry continued to sponsor organizations and journals that focus on nutrition-related subjects and intensified its efforts to lobby government for favorable dietary advice. Then and now food lobbies have promoted positive interpretations of scientific studies, sponsored research that can be used as a basis for health claims, and attacked critics, myself among them, as proponents of "junk science." If anything, such activities only add to public confusion.

Supermarkets as "Ground Zero"

No matter whom I speak to, I hear pleas for help in dealing with supermarkets, considered by shoppers as "ground zero" for distinguishing health claims from scientific advice. So I spent a year visiting supermarkets to help people think more clearly about food choices. The result was my book *What to Eat.*

Supermarkets provide a vital public service but are not social services agencies. Their job is to sell as much food as possible. Every aspect of store design—from shelf position to background music—is based on marketing research. Because this research shows that the more products customers see, the more they buy, a store's objective is to expose shoppers to the maximum number of products they will tolerate viewing.

If consumers are confused about which foods to buy, it is surely because the choices require knowledge of issues that are not easily resolved by science and are strongly swayed by social and economic considerations. Such decisions play out every day in every store aisle.

Are Organics Healthier?

Organic foods are the fastest-growing segment of the industry, in part because people are willing to pay more for foods that they believe are healthier and more nutritious. The U.S. Department of Agriculture forbids producers of "Certified Organic" fruits and vegetables from using synthetic pesticides, herbicides, fertilizers, genetically modified seeds, irradiation or fertilizer derived from sewage sludge. It licenses inspectors to ensure that producers follow those rules. Although the USDA is responsible for organics, its principal mandate is to promote conventional agriculture, which explains why the department asserts that it "makes no claims that organically produced food is safer or more nutritious than conventionally produced food. Organic food differs from conventionally grown food in the way it is grown, handled and processed."

This statement implies that such differences are unimportant. Critics of organic foods would agree; they question the reliability of organic certification and the productivity, safety and health benefits of organic production methods.

Meanwhile the organic food industry longs for research to address such criticisms, but studies are expensive and difficult to conduct. Nevertheless, existing research in this area has established that organic farms are nearly as productive as conventional farms, use less energy and leave soils in better condition. People who eat foods grown without synthetic pesticides ought to have fewer such chemicals in their bodies, and they do. Because the organic rules require pretreatment of manure and other steps to reduce the amount of pathogens in soil treatments, organic foods should be just as safe—or safer—than conventional foods.

Similarly, organic foods ought to be at least as nutritious as conventional foods. And proving organics to be more nutritious could help justify their higher prices. For minerals, this task is not difficult. The mineral content of plants depends on the amounts present in the soil in which they are grown. Organic foods are cultivated in richer soils, so their mineral content is higher.

But differences are harder to demonstrate for vitamins or antioxidants (plant substances that reduce tissue damage induced by free radicals); higher levels of these nutrients relate more to a food plant's genetic strain or protection from unfavorable conditions after harvesting than to production methods. Still, preliminary studies show benefits: organic peaches and pears contain greater quantities of vitamins C and E, and organic berries and corn contain more antioxidants.

Further research will likely confirm that organic foods contain higher nutrient levels, but it is unclear whether these nutrients would make a measurable improvement in health. All fruits and vegetables contain useful nutrients, albeit in different combinations and concentrations. Eating a variety of food plants is surely more important to health than small differences in the nutrient content of any one food. Organics may be somewhat healthier to eat, but they are far less likely to damage the environment, and that is reason enough to choose them at the supermarket.

Dairy and Calcium

Scientists cannot easily resolve questions about the health effects of dairy foods. Milk has many components, and the health of people who consume milk or dairy foods is influenced by everything else they eat and do. But this area of research is especially controversial because it affects an industry that vigorously promotes dairy products as beneficial and opposes suggestions to the contrary.

Dairy foods contribute about 70 percent of the calcium in American diets. This necessary mineral is a principal constituent of bones, which constantly lose and regain calcium during normal metabolism. Diets must contain enough calcium to replace losses, or else bones become prone to fracture. Experts advise consumption of at least one gram of calcium a day to replace everyday losses. Only dairy foods provide this much calcium without supplementation.

But bones are not just made of calcium; they require the full complement of essential nutrients to maintain strength. Bones are stronger in people who are physically active and who do not smoke cigarettes or drink much alcohol. Studies examining the effects of single nutrients in dairy foods show that some nutritional factors—magnesium, potassium, vitamin D and lactose, for example—promote calcium retention in bones. Others, such as protein, phosphorus and sodium, foster calcium excretion. So bone strength depends more on overall patterns of diet and behavior than simply on calcium intake.

Populations that do not typically consume dairy products appear to exhibit lower rates of bone fracture despite consuming far less calcium than recommended. Why this is so is unclear. Perhaps their diets contain less protein from meat and dairy foods, less sodium from processed foods and less phosphorus from soft drinks, so they retain calcium more effectively. The fact that calcium balance depends on multiple factors could explain why rates of osteoporosis (bone density loss) are highest in countries where people eat the most dairy foods. Further research may clarify such counterintuitive observations.

In the meantime, dairy foods are fine to eat if you like them, but they are not a nutritional requirement. Think of cows: they do not drink milk after weaning, but their bones support bodies weighing 800 pounds or more. Cows feed on grass, and grass contains calcium in small amounts—but those amounts add up. If you eat plenty of fruits, vegetables and whole grains, you can have healthy bones without having to consume dairy foods.

A Meaty Debate

Critics point to meat as the culprit responsible for elevating blood cholesterol, along with raising risks for heart disease, cancer and other conditions. Supporters cite the lack of compelling science to justify such allegations; they emphasize the nutritional benefits of meat protein, vitamins and minerals. Indeed, studies in developing countries demonstrate health improvements when growing children are fed even small amounts of meat.

But because bacteria in a cow's rumen attach hydrogen atoms to unsaturated fatty acids, beef fat is highly saturated—the kind of fat that increases the risk of coronary heart disease. All fats and oils contain some saturated fatty acids, but animal fats, especially those from beef, have more saturated fatty acids than vegetable fats. Nutritionists recommend eating no more than a heaping tablespoon (20 grams) of saturated fatty acids a day. Beef eaters easily meet or exceed this limit. The smallest McDonald's cheeseburger contains 6 grams of saturated fatty acids, but a Hardee's Monster Thickburger has 45 grams.

Why meat might boost cancer risks, however, is a matter of speculation. Scientists began to link meat to cancer in the 1970s, but even after decades of subsequent research they remain unsure if the relevant factor might be fat, saturated fat, protein, carcinogens or something else related to meat. By the late 1990s experts could conclude only that eating beef probably increases the risk of colon and rectal cancers and possibly enhances the odds of acquiring breast, prostate and perhaps other cancers. Faced with this uncertainty, the American Cancer Society suggests selecting leaner cuts, smaller portions and alternatives such as chicken, fish or beans—steps consistent with today's basic advice about what to eat.

Fish and Heart Disease

Fatty fish are the most important sources of long-chain omega-3 fatty acids. In the early 1970s Danish investigators observed surprisingly low frequencies of heart disease among indigenous populations in Greenland that typically ate fatty fish, seals and whales. The researchers attributed the protective effect to the foods' content of omega-3 fatty acids. Some subsequent studies—but by no means all—confirm this idea.

Because large, fatty fish are likely to have accumulated methylmercury and other toxins through predation, however, eating them raises questions about the balance between benefits and risks. Understandably, the fish industry is eager to prove that the health benefits of omega-3s outweigh any risks from eating fish. Even independent studies on omega-3 fats can be interpreted differently. In 2004 the National Oceanic and Atmospheric Administration—for fish, the agency equivalent to the USDA—asked the Institute of Medicine (IOM) to review studies of the benefits and risks of consuming seafood. The ensuing review of the research on heart disease risk illustrates the challenge such work poses for interpretation.

The IOM's October 2006 report concluded that eating seafood reduces the risk of heart disease but judged the studies too inconsistent to decide if omega-3 fats were responsible. In contrast, investigators from the Harvard School of Public Health published a much more positive report in the *Journal of the American Medical Association* that same month. Even modest consumption of fish omega-3s, they stated, would cut coronary deaths by 36 percent and total mortality by 17 percent, meaning that not eating fish would constitute a health risk.

Differences in interpretation explain how distinguished scientists could arrive at such different conclusions after considering the same studies. The two groups, for example, had conflicting views of earlier work published in March 2006 in the British Medical Journal. That study found no overall effect of omega-3s on heart disease risk or mortality, although a subset of the original studies displayed a 14 percent reduction in total mortality that did not reach statistical significance. The IOM team interpreted the "nonsignificant" result as evidence for the need for caution, whereas the Harvard group saw the data as consistent with studies reporting the benefits of omega-3s. When studies present inconsistent results, both interpretations are plausible. I favor caution in such situations, but not everyone agrees.

Because findings are inconsistent, so is dietary advice about eating fish. The American Heart Association recommends that adults eat fatty fish at least twice a week, but U.S. dietary guidelines say: "Limited evidence suggests an association between consumption of fatty acids in fish and reduced risks of mortality from cardiovascular disease for the general population ... however, more research is needed." Whether or not fish uniquely protects against heart disease, seafood is a delicious source of many nutrients, and two small servings per week of the less predatory classes of fish are unlikely to cause harm.

Sodas and Obesity

Sugars and corn sweeteners account for a large fraction of the calories in many supermarket foods, and virtually all the calories in drinks—soft, sports and juice—come from added sugars.

In a trend that correlates closely with rising rates of obesity, daily per capita consumption of sweetened beverages has grown by about 200 calories since the early 1980s. Although common sense suggests that this increase might have something to do with weight gain, beverage makers argue that studies cannot prove that sugary drinks alone—independent of calories or other foods in the diet—boost the risk of obesity. The evidence, they say correctly, is circumstantial. But pediatricians often see obese children in their practices who consume more than 1,000 calories a day from sweetened drinks alone, and several studies indicate that children who habitually consume sugary beverages take in more calories and weigh more than those who do not.

Nevertheless, the effects of sweetened drinks on obesity continue to be subject to interpretation. In 2006, for example, a systematic review funded by independent sources found sweetened drinks to promote obesity in both children and adults. But a review that same year sponsored in part by a beverage trade association concluded that soft drinks have no special role in obesity. The industry-funded researchers criticized existing studies as being short-term and inconclusive, and pointed to studies finding that people lose weight when they substitute sweetened drinks for their usual meals.

These differences imply the need to scrutinize food industry sponsorship of research itself. Although many researchers are offended by suggestions that funding support might affect the way they design or interpret studies, systematic analyses say otherwise. In 2007 investigators classified studies of the effects of sweetened and other beverages on health according to who had sponsored them. Industry-supported studies were more likely to yield results favorable to the sponsor than those funded by independent sources. Even though scientists may not be able to prove that sweetened drinks cause obesity, it makes sense for anyone interested in losing weight to consume less of them.

The examples I have discussed illustrate why nutrition science seems so controversial. Without improved methods to ensure compliance with dietary regimens, research debates are likely to rage unabated. Opposing points of view and the focus of studies and food advertising on single nutrients rather than on dietary patterns continue to fuel these disputes. While we wait for investigators to find better ways to study nutrition and health, my approach—eat less, move more, eat a largely plant-based diet, and avoid eating too much junk food—makes sense and leaves you plenty of opportunity to enjoy your dinner.

Robert Paarlberg is a Professor at Wellesley College and Associate at the Weatherhead Center for International Affairs at Harvard University. He researches food and agricultural policy with a focus on farming technologies and poverty in the developing world.

Attention Whole Foods Shoppers
Robert Paarlberg

From Whole Foods recyclable cloth bags to Michelle Obama's organic White House garden, modern eco-foodies are full of good intentions. We want to save the planet. Help local farmers. Fight climate change—and childhood obesity, too. But though it's certainly a good thing to be thinking about global welfare while chopping our certified organic onions, the hope that we can help others by changing our shopping and eating habits is being wildly oversold to Western consumers. Food has become an elite preoccupation in the West, ironically, just as the most effective ways to address hunger in poor countries have fallen out of fashion.

Helping the world's poor feed themselves is no longer the rallying cry it once was. Food may be today's cause célèbre, but in the pampered West, that means trendy causes like making food "sustainable"—in other words, organic, local, and slow. Appealing as that might sound, it is the wrong recipe for helping those who need it the most. Even our understanding of the global food problem is wrong these days, driven too much by the single issue of international prices. In April 2008, when the cost of rice for export had tripled in just six months and wheat reached its highest price in 28 years, a New York Times editorial branded this a "World Food Crisis." World Bank President Robert Zoellick warned that high food prices would be particularly damaging in poor countries, where "there is no margin for survival." Now that international rice prices are down 40 percent from their peak and wheat prices have fallen by more than half, we too quickly conclude that the crisis is over. Yet 850 million people in poor countries were chronically undernourished before the 2008 price spike, and the number is even larger now, thanks in part to last year's global recession. This is the real food crisis we face.

It turns out that food prices on the world market tell us very little about global hunger. International markets for food, like most other international markets, are used most heavily by the well-to-do, who are far from hungry. The majority of truly undernourished people—62 percent, according to the U.N. Food and Agriculture Organization—live in either Africa or South Asia, and most are small farmers or rural landless laborers living in the countryside of Africa and South Asia. They are significantly shielded from global price fluctuations both by the trade policies of their own governments and by poor roads and infrastructure. In Africa, more than 70 percent of rural households are cut off from the closest urban markets because, for instance, they live more than a 30-minute walk from the nearest all-weather road.

Poverty—caused by the low income productivity of farmers' labor—is the primary source of hunger in Africa, and the problem is only getting worse. The number of "food insecure" people in Africa (those consuming less than 2,100 calories a day) will increase 30 percent over the next decade without significant reforms, to 645 million, the U.S. Agriculture Department projects.

What's so tragic about this is that we know from experience how to fix the problem. Wherever the rural poor have gained access to improved roads, modern seeds, less expensive fertilizer, electrical power, and better schools and clinics, their productivity and their income have increased. But recent efforts to deliver such essentials have been undercut by deeply misguided (if sometimes well-meaning) advocacy against agricultural modernization and foreign aid.

In Europe and the United States, a new line of thinking has emerged in elite circles that opposes bringing improved seeds and fertilizers to traditional farmers and opposes linking those farmers more closely to international markets. Influential food writers, advocates, and celebrity restaurant owners are repeating the mantra that "sustainable food" in the future must be organic, local, and slow. But guess what: Rural Africa already has such a system, and it doesn't work. Few smallholder farmers in Africa use any synthetic chemicals, so their food is de facto organic. High transportation costs force them to purchase and sell almost all of their food locally. And food preparation is painfully slow. The result is nothing to celebrate: average income levels of only $1 a day and a one-in-three chance of being malnourished.

If we are going to get serious about solving global hunger, we need to de-romanticize our view of preindustrial food and farming. And that means learning to appreciate the modern, science-intensive, and highly capitalized agricultural system we've developed in the West. Without it, our food would be more expensive and less safe. In other words, a lot like the hunger-plagued rest of the world.

Original Sins

Thirty years ago, had someone asserted in a prominent journal or newspaper that the Green Revolution was a failure, he or she would have been quickly dismissed. Today the charge is surprisingly common. Celebrity author and eco-activist Vandana Shiva claims the Green Revolution has brought nothing to India except "indebted and discontented farmers." A 2002 meeting in Rome of 500 prominent international NGOs, including Friends of the Earth and Greenpeace, even blamed the Green Revolution for the rise in world hunger. Let's set the record straight.

The development and introduction of high-yielding wheat and rice seeds into poor countries, led by American scientist Norman Borlaug and others in the 1960s and 70s, paid huge dividends. In Asia these new seeds lifted tens of millions of small farmers out of desperate poverty and finally ended the threat of periodic famine. India, for instance, doubled its wheat production between 1964 and 1970 and was able to terminate all dependence on international food aid by

1975. As for indebted and discontented farmers, India's rural poverty rate fell from 60 percent to just 27 percent today. Dismissing these great achievements as a "myth" (the official view of Food First, a California-based organization that campaigns globally against agricultural modernization) is just silly.

It's true that the story of the Green Revolution is not everywhere a happy one. When powerful new farming technologies are introduced into deeply unjust rural social systems, the poor tend to lose out. In Latin America, where access to good agricultural land and credit has been narrowly controlled by traditional elites, the improved seeds made available by the Green Revolution *increased* income gaps. Absentee landlords in Central America, who previously allowed peasants to plant subsistence crops on underutilized land, pushed them off to sell or rent the land to commercial growers who could turn a profit using the new seeds. Many of the displaced rural poor became slum dwellers. Yet even in Latin America, the prevalence of hunger declined more than 50 percent between 1980 and 2005.

In Asia, the Green Revolution seeds performed just as well on small non-mechanized farms as on larger farms. Wherever small farmers had sufficient access to credit, they took up the new technology just as quickly as big farmers, which led to dramatic income gains and no increase in inequality or social friction. Even poor landless laborers gained, because more abundant crops meant more work at harvest time, increasing rural wages. In Asia, the Green Revolution was good for both agriculture and social justice.

And Africa? Africa has a relatively equitable and secure distribution of land, making it more like Asia than Latin America and increasing the chances that improvements in farm technology will help the poor. If Africa were to put greater resources into farm technology, irrigation, and rural roads, small farmers would benefit.

Organic Myths

There are other common objections to doing what is necessary to solve the real hunger crisis. Most revolve around caveats that purist critics raise regarding food systems in the United States and Western Europe. Yet such concerns, though well-intentioned, are often misinformed and counterproductive—especially when applied to the developing world.

Take industrial food systems, the current bugaboo of American food writers. Yes, they have many unappealing aspects, but without them food would be not only less abundant but also less safe. Traditional food systems lacking in reliable refrigeration and sanitary packaging are dangerous vectors for diseases. Surveys over the past several decades by the Centers for Disease Control and Prevention have found that the U.S. food supply became steadily safer over time, thanks in part to the introduction of industrial-scale technical improvements. Since 2000, the incidence of *E. coli* contamination in beef has fallen 45 percent. Today in the United States, most hospitalizations and fatalities from unsafe food come not from sales of contaminated products at supermarkets, but from the mishandling or improper preparation of food inside the home. Illness outbreaks from contaminated foods sold in stores still occur, but the fatalities are typically quite limited. A nationwide scare over unsafe spinach in 2006 triggered the virtual suspension of all fresh and bagged spinach sales, but only three known deaths were recorded. Incidents such as these command attention in part because they are now so rare. Food Inc. should be criticized for filling our plates with too many foods that are unhealthy, but not foods that are unsafe.

Where industrial-scale food technologies have not yet reached into the developing world, contaminated food remains a major risk. In Africa, where many foods are still purchased in open-air markets (often uninspected, unpackaged, unlabeled, unrefrigerated, unpasteurized, and unwashed), an estimated 700,000 people die every year from food- and water-borne diseases, compared with an estimated 5,000 in the United States.

Food grown organically—that is, without any synthetic nitrogen fertilizers or pesticides—is not an answer to the health and safety issues. The *American Journal of Clinical Nutrition* last year published a study of 162 scientific papers from the past 50 years on the health benefits of organically grown foods and found no nutritional advantage over conventionally grown foods. According to the Mayo Clinic, "No conclusive evidence shows that organic food is more nutritious than is conventionally grown food."

Health professionals also reject the claim that organic food is safer to eat due to lower pesticide residues. Food and Drug Administration surveys have revealed that the highest dietary exposures to pesticide residues on foods in the United States are so trivial (less than one one-thousandth of a level that would cause toxicity) that the safety gains from buying organic are insignificant. Pesticide exposures remain a serious problem in the developing world, where farm chemical use is not as well regulated, yet even there they are more an occupational risk for unprotected farmworkers than a residue risk for food consumers.

When it comes to protecting the environment, assessments of organic farming become more complex. Excess nitrogen fertilizer use on conventional farms in the United States has polluted rivers and created a "dead zone" in the Gulf of Mexico, but halting synthetic nitrogen fertilizer use entirely (as farmers must do in the United States to get organic certification from the Agriculture Department) would cause environmental problems far worse.

Here's why: Less than 1 percent of American cropland is under certified organic production. If the other 99 percent were to switch to organic and had to fertilize crops without any synthetic nitrogen fertilizer, that would require a lot more composted animal manure. To supply enough organic fertilizer, the U.S. cattle population would have to increase roughly fivefold. And because those animals would have to be raised organically on forage crops, much of the land in the lower 48 states would need to be converted to pasture. Organic field crops also have lower yields per hectare. If Europe tried to feed itself organically, it would need an additional 28 million hectares of cropland, equal to all of the remaining forest cover in France, Germany, Britain, and Denmark combined.

Mass deforestation probably isn't what organic advocates intend. The smart way to protect against nitrogen runoff is to reduce synthetic fertilizer applications with taxes, regulations, and cuts in farm subsidies, but not try to go all the way to zero as required by the official organic standard. Scaling up registered organic farming would be on balance harmful, not helpful, to the natural environment.

Not only is organic farming less friendly to the environment than assumed, but modern conventional farming is becoming significantly more sustainable. High-tech farming in rich countries today is far safer for the environment, per bushel of production, than it was in the 1960s, when Rachel Carson criticized the indiscriminate farm use of DDT in her environmental classic, *Silent Spring*. Thanks in part to Carson's devastating critique, that era's most damaging insecticides were banned and replaced by chemicals that could be applied in lower volume and were less persistent in the environment. Chemical use in American agriculture peaked soon thereafter, in 1973. This was a major victory for environmental advocacy.

And it was just the beginning of what has continued as a significant greening of modern farming in the United States. Soil erosion on farms dropped sharply in the 1970s with the introduction of "no-till" seed planting, an innovation that also reduced dependence on diesel fuel because fields no longer had to be plowed every spring. Farmers then began conserving water by moving to drip irrigation and by leveling their fields with lasers to minimize wasteful runoff. In the 1990s, GPS equipment was added to tractors, autosteering the machines in straighter paths and telling farmers exactly where they were in the field to within one square meter, allowing precise adjustments in chemical use. Infrared sensors were brought in to detect the greenness of the crop, telling a farmer exactly how much more (or less) nitrogen might be needed as the growing season went forward. To reduce wasteful nitrogen use, equipment was developed that can insert fertilizers into the ground at exactly the depth needed and in perfect rows, only where it will be taken up by the plant roots.

These "precision farming" techniques have significantly reduced the environmental footprint of modern agriculture relative to the quantity of food being produced. In 2008, the Organization for Economic Cooperation and Development published a review of the "environmental performance of agriculture" in the world's 30 most advanced industrial countries—those with the most highly capitalized and science-intensive farming systems. The results showed that between 1990 and 2004, food production in these countries continued to increase (by 5 percent in volume), yet adverse environmental impacts were reduced in every category. The land area taken up by farming declined 4 percent, soil erosion from both wind and water fell, gross greenhouse gas emissions from farming declined 3 percent, and excessive nitrogen fertilizer use fell 17 percent.

Biodiversity also improved, as increased numbers of crop varieties and livestock breeds came into use.

Seeding the Future

Africa faces a food crisis, but it's not because the continent's population is growing faster than its potential to produce food, as vintage Malthusians such as environmental advocate Lester Brown and advocacy organizations such as Population Action International would have it. Food production in Africa is vastly less than the region's known potential, and that is why so many millions are going hungry there. African farmers still use almost no fertilizer; only 4 percent of cropland has been improved with irrigation; and most of the continent's cropped area is not planted with seeds improved through scientific plant breeding, so cereal yields are only a fraction of what they could be. Africa is failing to keep up with population growth not because it has exhausted its potential, but instead because too little has been invested in reaching that potential.

One reason for this failure has been sharply diminished assistance from international donors. When agricultural modernization went out of fashion among elites in the developed world beginning in the 1980s, development assistance to farming in poor countries collapsed. Per capita food production in Africa was declining during the 1980s and 1990s and the number of hungry people on the continent was doubling, but the U.S. response was to withdraw development assistance and simply ship more food aid to Africa. Food aid doesn't help farmers become more productive—and it can create long-term dependency. But in recent years, the dollar value of U.S. food aid to Africa has reached 20 times the dollar value of agricultural development assistance.

The alternative is right in front of us. Foreign assistance to support agricultural improvements has a strong record of success, when undertaken with purpose. In the 1960s, international assistance from the Rockefeller Foundation, the Ford Foundation, and donor governments led by the United States made Asia's original Green Revolution possible. U.S. assistance to India provided critical help in improving agricultural education, launching a successful agricultural extension service, and funding advanced degrees for Indian agricultural specialists at universities in the United States. The U.S. Agency for International Development, with the World Bank, helped finance fertilizer plants and infrastructure projects, including rural roads and irrigation. India could not have done this on its own—the country was on the brink of famine at the time and dangerously dependent on food aid. But instead of suffering a famine in 1975, as some naysayers had predicted, India that year celebrated a final and permanent end to its need for food aid.

Foreign assistance to farming has been a high-payoff investment everywhere, including Africa. The World Bank has documented average rates of return on investments in agricultural research in Africa of 35 percent a year, accompanied by significant reductions in poverty. Some research investments in African agriculture have brought rates of return estimated at 68 percent. Blind to these realities, the United States cut its assistance to agricultural research in Africa 77 percent between 1980 and 2006.

When it comes to Africa's growing hunger, governments in rich countries face a stark choice: They can decide to support a steady new infusion of financial and technical assistance to help local governments and farmers become more productive, or they can take a "worry later" approach and be forced to address hunger problems with increasingly expensive shipments of food aid. Development skeptics and farm modernization critics keep pushing us toward this unappealing second path. It's time for leaders with vision and political courage to push back.

HRH the Prince of Wales is the eldest child and heir apparent of Queen Elizabeth II. He is the president of The Prince's Charity, which is the largest multi-cause charitable enterprise in the United Kingdom. His philanthropic interests include environmental sustainability, architecture preservation, education, youth opportunity, the built environment, and responsible business practices.

On the Future of Food
HRH the Prince of Wales

Over the past 30 years I have been venturing into extremely dangerous territory by speaking about the future of food. I have all the scars to prove it...! Questioning the conventional world view is a risky business. And the only reason I have done so is for the sake of your generation and for the integrity of Nature herself. It is your future that concerns me and that of your grandchildren, and theirs too. That is how far we should be looking ahead. I have no intention of being confronted by my grandchildren, demanding to know why on Earth we didn't do something about the many problems that existed, when we knew what was going wrong. The threat of that question, the responsibility of it, is precisely why I have gone on challenging the assumptions of our day. And I would urge you to do the same, because we need to face up to asking whether how we produce our food is actually fit for purpose in the very challenging circumstances of the twenty-first century. We simply cannot ignore that question any longer.

Very nearly 30 years ago I began by talking about the issue, but I realized in the end I had to go further. I had to put my concern into action, to demonstrate how else we might do things so that we secure food production for the future, but also, crucially, to take care of the Earth that sustains us. Because if we don't do that, if we do not work within Nature's system, then Nature will fail to be the durable, continuously sustaining force she has always been. Only by safeguarding Nature's resilience can we hope to have a resilient form of food production and ensure food security in the long term.

This is the challenge facing us. We have to maintain a supply of healthy food at affordable prices when there is mounting pressure on nearly every element affecting the process. In some cases we are pushing Nature's life-support systems so far, they are struggling to cope with what we ask of them. Soils are being depleted, demand for water is growing ever more voracious, and the entire system is at the mercy of an increasingly fluctuating price of oil.

Remember that when we talk about agriculture and food production, we are talking about a complex and interrelated system and it is simply not possible to single out just one objective, like maximizing production, without also ensuring that the system which delivers those increased yields meets society's other needs. As Eric[1] has highlighted, these should include the maintenance of public health,

---

1. **Eric:** Eric Schlosser also spoke at the conference, http://www.georgetown.edu/story/futureoffoodgallery.html.

the safe-guarding of rural employment, the protection of the environment, and contributing to overall quality of life.

So I trust that this conference will not shy away from the big questions. Chiefly, how can we create a more sustainable approach to agriculture while recognizing those wider and important social and economic parameters—an approach that is capable of feeding the world with a global population rapidly heading for nine billion? And can we do so amid so many competing demands on land, in an increasingly volatile climate, and when levels of the planet's bio-diversity are under such threat or in serious decline?

As I see it, these pressures mean we haven't much choice in the matter. We are going to have to take some very brave steps. We will have to develop much more sustainable, or durable forms of food production because the way we have done things up to now are no longer as viable as they once appeared to be. The more I talk with people about this issue, the more I realize how vague the general picture remains of the perilous state we are in. So, just to be absolutely clear, I feel I should offer you a quick pen sketch of just some of the evidence that this is so.

Certainly, internationally, food insecurity is a growing problem. There are also many now who consider that global food systems are well on the way to being in crisis. Yield increases for staple food crops are declining. They have dropped from 3 percent in the 1960s to 1 percent today—and that is really worrying be-cause, for the first time, that rate is less than the rate of population growth. And all of this, of course, has to be set against the ravages caused by climate change. Already yields are suffering in Africa and India where crops are failing to cope with ever-increasing temperatures and fluctuating rainfall. We all remember the failure of last year's wheat harvest in Russia and droughts in China. They have caused the cost of food to rocket and, with it, inflation around the world, stoking social discontent in many countries, notably in the Middle East. It is a situation I fear will only become more volatile as we suffer yet more natural disasters....

Set against these threats to yields is the ever-growing demand for food. The United Nations Food and Agriculture Organization estimates that the demand will rise by 70 percent between now and 2050. The curve is quite astonishing. The world somehow has to find the means of feeding a staggering 219,000 new mouths every day. That's about 450 since I started talking! What is more, with incomes rising in places like China and India, there will also be more people wealthy enough to consume more, so the demand for meat and dairy products may well increase yet further. And all that extra livestock will compete for feed more and more with an energy sector that has massively expanded its demand for biofuels. Here in the U.S., I am told, four out of every ten bushels of corn are now grown to fuel motor vehicles.

This is the context we find ourselves in and it is set against the backdrop of a system heavily dependent upon fossil fuels and other forms of diminish-ing natural capital—mineral fertilizers and so on. Most forms of industrialized agriculture now have an umbilical dependency on oil, natural gas, and other non-renewable resources. One study I have read estimates that a person today on a typical Western diet is, in effect, consuming nearly a U.S. gallon of diesel every day! And when you consider that in the past decade the cost of artificial nitrogen fertilizers has gone up fourfold and the cost of potash three times, you start to see how uncomfortable the future could become if we do not wean ourselves off our dependency. And that's not even counting the impact of higher fuel prices on the other costs of production—transport and processing—all of which are passed on to the consumer. It is indeed a vicious circle.

Then add the supply of land into the equation—where do we grow all of the extra plants or graze all that extra stock when urban expansion is such a pressure? Here in the United States I am told that one acre is lost to development every minute of every day—which means that since 1982 an area the size of Indiana has been built over—though that is small fry compared with what is happening in places like India where, somehow, they have to find a way of housing another 300 million people in the next 30 years. But on top of this is the very real problem of soil erosion.

Again, in the U.S., soil is being washed away 10 times faster than the Earth can replenish it, and it is happening 40 times faster in China and India. Twenty-two thousand square miles of arable land is turning into desert every year and, all told, it appears a quarter of the world's farmland, two billion acres, is degraded.

Given these pressures, it seems likely we will have to grow plants in more difficult terrain. But the only sustainable way to do that will be by increasing the long-term fertility of the soil, because, as I say, achieving increased production using imported, non-renewable in-puts is simply not sustainable.

There are many other pressures on the way we produce our food, but I just need to highlight one more, if I may, before I move on to the possible solutions, because it is so important. It is that magical substance we have taken for granted for so long—water.

In a country like the United States a fifth of all your grain production is dependent upon irrigation. For every pound of beef produced in the industrial system, it takes 2,000 gallons of water. That is a lot of water and there is plenty of evidence that the Earth cannot keep up with the demand. The Ogallala Aquifer on the Great Plains, for instance, is depleting by 1.3 trillion gallons faster than rainfall can replenish it. And when you consider that of all the water in the world, only 5 percent of it is fresh and a quarter of that sits in Lake Baikal in Siberia, there is not a lot left. Of the remaining 4 percent, nearly three quarters of it is used in agriculture, but 30 percent of that water is wasted. If you set that figure against future predictions, then the picture gets even worse. By 2030 it is estimated that the world's farmers will need 45 percent more water than today. And yet already, because of irrigation, many of the world's largest rivers no longer reach the sea for part of the year—including, I am afraid, the Colorado and Rio Grande.

Forgive me for laboring these points, but the impact of all of this has already been immense. Over a billion people—one-seventh of the world's population—are hungry and another billion suffer from what is called "hidden hunger," which is the lack of essential vitamins and nutrients in their diets. And on the reverse side of the coin, let us not forget the other tragic fact—that over a billion people in the world are now considered overweight or obese. It is an increasingly insane picture. In one way or another, half the world finds itself on the wrong side of the food equation.

You can see, I hope, that in a global ecosystem that is, to say the least, under stress, our apparently unbridled demands for energy, land, and water put overwhelming pressure on our food systems. I am not alone in thinking that the current model is simply not durable in the long term. It is not "keeping everything going continuously" and it is, therefore, not sustainable.

So what is a "sustainable food production" system? We should be very clear about it, or else we will end up with the same system that we have now, but dipped in "green wash." For me, it has to be a form of agriculture that does not exceed the carrying capacity of its local ecosystem and which recognizes that the soil is the planet's most vital renewable resource. Topsoil is the cornerstone of the prosperity of nations. It acts as a buffer against drought and as a carbon sink and it is the primary source of the health of all animals, plants, and people. If we degrade it, as we are doing, then Nature's capital will lose its innate resilience and it won't be very long, believe you me, before our human economic capital and economic systems also begin to lose their resilience.

Let's, then, try and look for a moment at what very probably is not a genuinely sustainable form of agriculture—for the long term, and by that I mean generations as yet unborn. In my own view it is surely not dependent upon the use of chemical pesticides, fungicides, and insecticides; nor, for that matter, upon artificial fertilizers and growth-promoters or G.M. You would have perhaps thought it unlikely to create vast monocultures and to treat animals like machines by using industrial rearing systems. Nor would you expect it to drink the Earth dry, deplete the soil, clog streams with nutrient-rich run-off and create, out of sight and out of mind, enormous dead zones in the oceans. You would also think, wouldn't you, that it might not lead to the destruction of whole cultures or the removal of many of the remaining small farmers around the world? Nor, presumably, would it destroy biodiversity at the same time as cultural and social diversity.

On the contrary, genuinely sustainable farming maintains the resilience of the entire ecosystem by encouraging a rich level of biodiversity in the soil, in its water supply, and in the wildlife—the birds, insects, and bees that maintain the health of the whole system. Sustainable farming also recognizes the importance to the soil of planting trees; of protecting and enhancing water-catchment systems; of mitigating, rather than adding to, climate change. To do this it must be a mixed approach. One where animal waste is recycled and organic waste is composted to build the soil's fertility. One where antibiotics are only used on animals to treat illnesses, not deployed in prophylactic doses to prevent them; and where those animals are fed on grass-based regimes as Nature intended.

You may think this an idealized definition—that it isn't possible in "the real world"—but if you consider this the gold standard, then for food production to become more "sustainable" it has to reduce the use of those substances that are dangerous and harmful not only to human health, but also to the health of those natural systems, such as the oceans, forests, and wetlands, that provide us with the services essential to life on this planet—but which we rashly take for granted. At the same time, it has to minimize the use of non-renewable external inputs. Fertilizers that do not come from renewable sources do not enable a sustainable approach which, ultimately, comes down to giving back to Nature as much as it takes out and recognizing that there are necessary limits to what the Earth can do. Equally, it includes the need for producers to receive a reasonable price for their labors above the price of production. And that, ladies and gentlemen, leads me to the nub of what I would like you to consider.

Having myself tried to farm as sustainably as possible for some 26 years in England, which is not as long as other people here I know, I certainly know of plenty of current evidence that adopting an approach which mirrors the miraculous ingenuity of Nature can produce surprisingly high yields of a wide range of vegetables, arable crops, beef, lamb, and milk. And yet we are told ceaselessly that sustainable or organic agriculture cannot feed the world. I find this claim very hard to understand. Especially when you consider the findings of an impeccably well-researched International Assessment of Agricultural Knowledge, Science and Technology for Development, conducted in 2008 by the U.N. I am very pleased, by the way, to see that the co-chair of that report, Professor Hans Herren, will be taking part in the International Panel discussion towards the end of the conference. His report drew on evidence from more than 400 scientists worldwide and concluded that small-scale, family-based farming systems, adopting so-called agro-ecological approaches, were among the most productive systems in developing countries. This was a major study and a very explicit statement. And yet, for some strange reason, the conclusions of this exhaustive report seem to have vanished without trace.

This is the heart of the problem, it seems to me—why it is that an industrialized system, deeply dependent on fossil fuels and chemical treatments, is promoted as viable, while a much less damaging one is rubbished and condemned as unfit for purpose. The reasons lie in the anomalies that exist behind the scenes.

I would certainly urge you, first, to look at the slack in the system. Under the current, inherently unsustainable system, in the developed world we actually throw away approximately 40 percent of the food we have bought.

Food is now much cheaper than it was and one of the unexpected consequences of this is, perhaps, that we do not value it as once we did. I cannot help feeling some of this problem could be avoided with better food education. You only have to consider the progress your First Lady, Mrs. Obama, has achieved lately by launching her "Let's Move" campaign—a wonderful initiative, if I may say so. With manufacturers making their "Healthy Weight Commitment" and pledging to cut 1.5 trillion calories a year from their products; with Walmart promising to sell products with less sugar, salt, and trans-fats, and to reduce their prices on healthy items like fresh fruits and vegetables; and with the first lady's big drive to improve healthy eating in schools and the excellent thought of urging doctors to write out prescriptions for exercise; these are marvellous ideas that I am sure will make a major difference.

Alas, in developing countries approximately 40 percent of food is lost between farm and market. Could that be remedied too, this time by better on-farm storage? And we should also remember that many, if not most, of the farmers in the developing world are achieving a fraction of the yields they might do if the soil was nurtured more with an eye to organic matter content and improved water management.

However, the really big issue we need to consider is how conventional, agri-industrial techniques are able to achieve the success they do, and how we measure that success. And here I come to the aspect of food production that troubles me most.

The well-known commentator in this country on food matters, Michael Pollan, pointed out recently that, so far, the combined market for local and organic food, both in the U.S. and Europe, has only reached around 2 or 3 percent of total sales. And the reason, he says, is quite simple. It is the difficulty in making sustainable farming more profitable for producers and sustainable food more affordable for consumers. With so much growing concern about this, my International Sustainability Unit carried out a study into why sustainable food production systems struggle to make a profit, and how it is that intensively produced food costs less. The answer to that last question may seem obvious, but my I.S.U. study reveals a less apparent reason.

It looked at five case studies and discovered two things: firstly, that the system of farm subsidies is geared in such a way that it favors overwhelmingly those kinds of agricultural techniques that are responsible for the many problems I have just outlined. And secondly, that the cost of that damage is not factored into the price of food production. Consider, for example, what happens when pesticides get into the water supply. At the moment, the water has to be cleaned up at enormous cost to consumer water bills; the primary polluter is not charged. Or take the emissions from the manufacture and application of nitrogen fertilizer, which are potent green house gases. They, too, are not costed at source into the equation.

This has led to a situation where farmers are better off using intensive methods and where consumers who would prefer to buy sustainably produced food are unable to do so because of the price. There are many producers and consumers who want to do the right thing but, as things stand, "doing the right thing" is penalized. And so this raises an admittedly difficult question—has the time arrived when a long, hard look is needed at the way public subsidies are generally geared? And should the recalibration of that gearing be considered so that it helps healthier approaches and "techniques"? Could there be benefits if public finance were redirected so that subsidies are linked specifically to farming practices that are more sustainable, less polluting, and of wide benefit to the public interest, rather than what many environmental experts have called the curiously "perverse" economic incentive system that too frequently directs food production?

The point, surely, is to achieve a situation where the production of healthier food is rewarded and becomes more affordable and that the Earth's capital is not so eroded. Nobody wants food prices to go up, but if it is the case that the present low price of intensively produced food in developed countries is actually an illusion, only made possible by transferring the costs of cleaning up pollution or dealing with human health problems onto other agencies, then could correcting these anomalies result in a more beneficial arena where nobody is actually worse off in net terms? It would simply be a more honest form of accounting that may make it more desirable for producers to operate more sustainably—particularly if subsidies were redirected to benefit sustainable systems of production. It is a question worth considering, and I only ask it because my concern is simply that we seek to produce the healthiest food possible from the healthiest environment possible—for the long term—and to ensure that it is affordable for ordinary consumers . . . .

I am a historian, not an economist, but what I am hinting at here is that it is surely time to grasp one of the biggest nettles of all and re-assess what has become a fundamental aspect of our entire economic model. As far as I can see, responding to the problems we have with a "business as usual" approach towards the way in which we measure G.D.P. offers us only short-term relief. It does not promise a long-term cure. Why? Because we cannot possibly maintain the approach in the long term if we continue to consume our planet as rapaciously as we are doing. Capitalism depends upon capital, but our capital ultimately depends upon the health of Nature's capital. Whether we like it or not, the two are in fact inseparable.

There are alternative ways to growing our food which, if used with new technology—things like precision irrigation, for instance—would go a very long way to resolving some of the problems we face. If they are underpinned by smarter financial ways of supporting them, they could strengthen the resilience of our agriculture, marine, and energy systems. We could ensure a means of supply that is capable of withstanding the sorts of sudden fluctuations on international markets which are bound to come our way, as the price of oil goes up and the impact of our accelerating disruption of entire natural systems becomes greater.

In essence what I am suggesting here is something very simple. We need to include in the bottom line the true costs of food production—the true financial costs and the true costs to the Earth. It is what I suppose you could call "Accounting for Sustainability," a name I gave to a project I set up six years ago, initially to encourage businesses to expand their accounting process so that it incorporates the interconnected impact of financial, environmental, and social elements on their long-term performance. What if Accounting for Sustainability was applied to the agricultural sector? This was certainly the implicit suggestion in a recent and very important study by the U.N. The Economics of Ecosystems and Biodiversity, or T.E.E.B., assessed the multi-trillion-dollar importance to the world's economy of the natural world and concluded that the present system of national accounts needs to be upgraded rapidly so they include the health of natural capital, and thereby accurately reflect how the services offered by natural ecosystems are performing—let alone are paid for. Incidentally, to create a genuine market for such services—in the same way as a carbon market has been created—could conceivably make a substantial contribution to reducing poverty in the developing world.

This is very important. If we hope to redress the market failure that will otherwise blight the lives of future generations, we have to see that there is a direct relationship between the resilience of the planet's ecosystems and the resilience of our national economies . . . .

It is, I feel, our apparent reluctance to recognize the interrelated nature of the problems and therefore the solutions, that lies at the heart of our predicament and certainly of our ability to determine the future of food. How we deal with this systemic failure in our thinking will define us as a civilization and determine our survival. Ladies and gentlemen, let me end by reminding you of the words of one of your own founding fathers and visionaries. It was George Washington who entreated your forebears to "Raise a standard to which the wise and honest can repair; the rest is in the hands of God"—and, indeed, as so often in the past, in the hands of your great country, the United States of America.

Nicola Twilley is a writer and the co-director of Studio-X NYC—Columbia University Graduate School of Architecture, Planning, and Preservation's think tank/event space/gallery dedicated to fostering thought and collaboration around the future of cities. **Cynthia Graber** is a print and radio journalist who, along with Twilley, created the podcast *Gastropod*. You can listen to the audio that accompanies this piece by going to https://mosaicscience.com/story/why-calorie-broken.

Why the Calorie Is Broken
Nicola Twilley and Cynthia Graber

"For me, a calorie is a unit of measurement that's a real pain in the rear."

Bo Nash is 38. He lives in Arlington, Texas, where he's a technology director for a textbook publisher. And he's 5'10" and 245 lbs—which means he is classed as obese.

In an effort to lose weight, Nash uses an app to record the calories he consumes and a Fitbit band to track the energy he expends. These tools bring an apparent precision: Nash can quantify the calories in each cracker crunched and stair climbed. But when it comes to weight gain, he finds that not all calories are equal. How much weight he gains or loses seems to depend less on the total number of calories, and more on where the calories come from and how he consumes them. The unit, he says, has a "nebulous quality to it."

Tara Haelle is also obese. She had her second son on St Patrick's Day in 2014, and hasn't been able to lose the 70 lbs she gained during pregnancy. Haelle is a freelance science journalist, based in Illinois. She understands the science of weight loss, but, like Nash, doesn't see it translate into practice. "It makes sense from a mathematical and scientific and even visceral level that what you put in and what you take out, measured in the discrete unit of the calorie, should balance," says Haelle. "But it doesn't seem to work that way."

Nash and Haelle are in good company: more than two-thirds of American adults are overweight or obese. For many of them, the cure is diet: one in three are attempting to lose weight in this way at any given moment. Yet there is ample evidence that diets rarely lead to sustained weight loss. These are expensive failures. This inability to curb the extraordinary prevalence of obesity costs the United States more than $147 billion in healthcare, as well as $4.3 billion in job absenteeism and yet more in lost productivity.

At the heart of this issue is a single unit of measurement—the calorie—and some seemingly straightforward arithmetic. "To lose weight, you must use up more calories than you take in," according to the Centers for Disease Control and Prevention. Dieters like Nash and Haelle could eat all their meals at McDonald's and still lose weight, provided they burn enough calories, says Marion Nestle, professor of nutrition, food studies and public health at New York University. "Really, that's all it takes."

But Nash and Haelle do not find weight control so simple. And part of the problem goes way beyond individual self-control. The numbers logged in Nash's Fitbit, or printed on the food labels that Haelle reads religiously, are at best good guesses. Worse yet, as scientists are increasingly finding, some of those calorie counts are flat-out wrong—off by more than enough, for instance, to wipe out the calories Haelle burns by running an extra mile on a treadmill. A calorie isn't just a calorie. And our mistaken faith in the power of this seemingly simple measurement may be hindering the fight against obesity.

§

The process of counting calories begins in an anonymous office block in Maryland. The building is home to the Beltsville Human Nutrition Research Center, a facility run by the US Department of Agriculture. When we visit, the kitchen staff are preparing dinner for people enrolled in a study. Plastic dinner trays are laid out with meatloaf, mashed potatoes, corn, brown bread, a chocolate-chip scone, vanilla yoghurt and a can of tomato juice. The staff weigh and bag each item, sometimes adding an extra two-centimetre sliver of bread to ensure a tray's contents add up to the exact calorie requirements of each participant. "We actually get compliments about the food," says David Baer, a supervisory research physiologist with the Department.

The work that Baer and colleagues do draws on centuries-old techniques. Nestle traces modern attempts to understand food and energy back to a French aristocrat and chemist named Antoine Lavoisier. In the early 1780s, Lavoisier developed a triple-walled metal canister large enough to house a guinea pig. Inside the walls was a layer of ice. Lavoisier knew how much energy was required to melt ice, so he could estimate the heat the animal emitted by measuring the amount of water that dripped from the canister. What Lavoisier didn't realise—and never had time to find out; he was put to the guillotine during the Revolution—was that measuring the heat emitted by his guinea pigs was a way to estimate the amount of energy they had extracted from the food they were digesting.

Until recently, the scientists at Beltsville used what was essentially a scaled-up version of Lavoisier's canister to estimate the energy used by humans: a small room in which a person could sleep, eat, excrete, and walk on a treadmill, while temperature sensors embedded in the walls measured the heat given off and thus the calories burned. (We now measure this energy in calories. Roughly speaking, one calorie is the heat required to raise the temperature of one kilogram of water by one degree Celsius.) Today, those 'direct-heat' calorimeters have largely been replaced by 'indirect-heat' systems, in which sensors measure oxygen intake and carbon dioxide exhalations. Scientists know how much energy is used during the metabolic processes that create the carbon dioxide we breathe out, so they can work backwards to deduce that, for example, a human who has exhaled 15 litres of carbon dioxide must have used 94 calories of energy.

The facility's three indirect calorimeters are down the halls from the research kitchen. "They're basically nothing more than walk-in coolers, modified to allow people to live in here," physiologist William Rumpler explains as he shows us around. Inside each white room, a single bed is folded up against the wall, alongside a toilet, sink, a small desk and chair, and a short treadmill. A couple of airlocks allow food, urine, faeces and blood samples to be passed back and forth. Apart from these reminders of the room's purpose, the vinyl-floored, fluorescent-lit units resemble a 1970s dorm room. Rumpler explains that subjects typically spend 24 to 48 hours inside the calorimeter, following a highly structured schedule. A notice pinned to the door outlines the protocol for the latest study:

6:00 to 6:45pm—Dinner,
11:00pm—Latest bedtime, mandatory lights out,
11:00pm to 6:30am—Sleep, remain in bed even if not sleeping.

In between meals, blood tests and bowel movements, calorimeter residents are asked to walk on the treadmill at 3 miles per hour for 30 minutes. They fill the rest of the day with what Rumpler calls "low activity." "We encourage people to bring knitting or books to read," he says. "If you give people free hand, you'll be surprised by what they'll do inside the chamber." He tells us that one of his less cooperative subjects smuggled in a bag of M&Ms, and then gave himself away by dropping them on the floor.

Using a bank of screens just outside the rooms, Rumpler can monitor exactly how many calories each subject is burning at any moment. Over the years, he and his colleagues have aggregated these individual results to arrive at numbers for general use: how many calories a 120-lb woman burns while running at 4.0 miles an hour, say, or the calories a sedentary man in his 60s needs to consume every day. It's the averages derived from thousands of extremely precise measurements that provide the numbers in Bo Nash's movement tracker and help Tara Haelle set a daily calorie intake target that is based on her height and weight.

Measuring the calories in food itself relies on another modification of Lavoisier's device. In 1848, an Irish chemist called Thomas Andrews realised that he could estimate calorie content by setting food on fire in a chamber and measuring the temperature change in the surrounding water. (Burning food is chemically similar to the ways in which our bodies break food down, despite being much faster and less controlled.) Versions of Andrews's "bomb calorimeter" are used to measure the calories in food today. At the Beltsville centre, samples of the meatloaf, mashed potatoes and tomato juice have been incinerated in the lab's bomb calorimeter. "We freeze-dry it, crush into a powder, and fire it," says Baer.

Humans are not bomb calorimeters, of course, and we don't extract every calorie from the food we eat. This problem was addressed at the end of the 19th century, in one of the more epic experiments in the history of nutrition science. Wilbur Atwater, a Department of Agriculture scientist, began by measuring the calories contained in more than 4,000 foods. Then he fed those foods to volunteers and collected their faeces, which he incinerated in a bomb calorimeter. After subtracting the energy measured in the faeces from that in the food, he arrived at the Atwater values, numbers that represent the available energy in each gram of protein, carbohydrate and fat. These century-old figures remain the basis for today's standards. When Baer wants to know the calories per gram figure for that night's meatloaf, he corrects the bomb calorimeter results using Atwater values.

§

This entire enterprise, from the Beltsville facility to the numbers on the packets of the food we buy, creates an aura of scientific precision around the business of counting calories. That precision is illusory.

The trouble begins at source, with the lists compiled by Atwater and others. Companies are allowed to incinerate freeze-dried pellets of product in a bomb calorimeter to arrive at calorie counts, though most avoid that hassle, says Marion Nestle. Some use the data developed by Atwater in the late 1800s. But the Food and Drug Administration (FDA) also allows companies to use a modified set of values, published by the Department of Agriculture in 1955, that take into account our ability to digest different foods in different ways.

Atwater's numbers say that Tara Haelle can extract 8.9 calories per gram of fat in a plate of her favourite Tex-Mex refried beans; the modified table shows that, thanks to the indigestibility of some of the plant fibres in legumes, she only gets 8.3 calories per gram. Depending on the calorie-measuring method that a company chooses—the FDA allows two more variations on the theme, for a total of five—a given serving of spaghetti can contain from 200 to 210 calories. These uncertainties can add up. Haelle and Bo Nash might deny themselves a snack or sweat out another few floors on the StairMaster to make sure they don't go 100 calories over their daily limit. If the data in their calorie counts is wrong, they can go over regardless.

There's also the issue of serving size. After visiting over 40 US chain restaurants, including Olive Garden, Outback Steak House and PF Chang's China Bistro, Susan Roberts of Tufts University's nutrition research centre and colleagues discovered that a dish listed as having, say, 500 calories could contain 800 instead. The difference could easily have been caused, says Roberts, by local chefs heaping on extra french fries or pouring a dollop more sauce. It would be almost impossible for a calorie-counting dieter to accurately estimate their intake given this kind of variation.

Even if the calorie counts themselves were accurate, dieters like Haelle and Nash would have to contend with the significant variations between the total calories in the food and the amount our bodies extract. These variations, which scientists have only recently started to understand, go beyond the inaccuracies in the numbers on the back of food packaging. In fact, the new research calls into question the validity of nutrition science's core belief that a calorie is a calorie.

Using the Beltsville facilities, for instance, Baer and his colleagues found that our bodies sometimes extract fewer calories than the number listed on the label. Participants in their studies absorbed around a third fewer calories from almonds than the modified Atwater values suggest. For walnuts, the difference was 21 per cent. This is good news for someone who is counting calories and likes to snack on almonds or walnuts: he or she is absorbing far fewer calories than expected. The difference, Baer suspects, is due to the nuts' particular structure: "All the nutrients—the fat and the protein and things like that—they're inside this plant cell wall." Unless those walls are broken down—by processing, chewing or cooking—some of the calories remain off-limits to the body, and thus are excreted rather than absorbed.

Another striking insight came from an attempt to eat like a chimp. In the early 1970s, Richard Wrangham, an anthropologist at Harvard University and author of the book *Catching Fire: How cooking made us human*, observed wild chimps in Africa. Wrangham attempted to follow the entirely raw diet he saw the animals eating, snacking only on fruit, seeds, leaves, and insects such as termites and army ants. "I discovered that it left me incredibly hungry," he says. "And then I realised that every human eats their food cooked."

Wrangham and his colleagues have since shown that cooking unlaces microscopic structures that bind energy in foods, reducing the work our gut would otherwise have to do. It effectively outsources digestion to ovens and frying pans. Wrangham found that mice fed raw peanuts, for instance, lost significantly more weight than mice fed the equivalent amount of roasted peanut butter. The same effect holds true for meat: there are many more usable calories in a burger than in steak tartare. Different cooking methods matter, too. In 2015, Sri Lankan scientists discovered that they could more than halve the available calories in rice by adding coconut oil during cooking and then cooling the rice in the refrigerator.

Wrangham's findings have significant consequences for dieters. If Nash likes his porterhouse steak bloody, for example, he will likely be consuming several hundred calories less than if he has it well-done. Yet the FDA's methods for creating a nutrition label do not for the most part account for the differences between raw and cooked food, or pureed versus whole, let alone the structure of plant versus animal cells. A steak is a steak, as far as the FDA is concerned.

Industrial food processing, which subjects foods to extremely high temperatures and pressures, might be freeing up even more calories. The food industry, says Wrangham, has been "increasingly turning our food to mush, to the maximum calories you can get out of it. Which, of course, is all very ironic, because in the West there's tremendous pressure to reduce the number of calories you're getting out of your food." He expects to find examples of structural differences that affect caloric availability in many more foods. "I think there is work here for hundreds and probably thousands of nutritionists for years," he says.

There's also the problem that no two people are identical. Differences in height, body fat, liver size, levels of the stress hormone cortisol, and other factors influence the energy required to maintain the body's basic functions. Between two people of the same sex, weight and age, this number may differ by up to 600 calories a day—over a quarter of the recommended intake for a moderately active woman. Even something as seemingly insignificant as the time at which we eat may affect how we process energy. In one recent study, researchers found that mice fed a high-fat diet between 9am and 5pm gained 28 per cent less weight than mice fed the exact same food across a 24-hour period. The researchers suggested that irregular feedings affect the circadian cycle of the liver and the way it metabolises food, thus influencing overall energy balance. Such differences would not emerge under the feeding schedules in the Beltsville experiments.

Until recently, the idea that genetics plays a significant role in obesity had some traction: researchers hypothesised that evolutionary pressures may have favoured genes that predisposed some people to hold on to more calories in the form of added fat. Today, however, most scientists believe we can't blame DNA for making us overweight. "The prevalence of obesity started to rise quite sharply in the 1980s," says Nestle. "Genetics did not change in that ten- or twenty-year period. So genetics can only account for part of it."

Instead, researchers are beginning to attribute much of the variation to the trillions of tiny creatures that line the coiled tubes inside our midriffs. The microbes in our intestines digest some of the tough or fibrous matter that our stomachs cannot break down, releasing a flow of additional calories in the process. But different species and strains of microbes vary in how effective they are at releasing those extra calories, as well as how generously they share them with their host human.

In 2013, researchers in Jeffrey Gordon's lab at Washington University tracked down pairs of twins of whom one was obese and one lean. He took gut microbes from each, and inserted them into the intestines of microbe-free mice. Mice that got microbes from an obese twin gained weight; the others remained lean, despite eating the exact same diet. "That was really striking," said Peter Turnbaugh, who used to work with Gordon and now heads his own lab at the University of California, San Francisco. "It suggested for the first time that these microbes might actually be contributing to the energy that we gain from our diet."

The diversity of microbes that each of us hosts is as individual as a fingerprint and yet easily transformed by diet and our environment. And though it is poorly understood, new findings about how our gut microbes affect our overall energy balance are emerging almost daily. For example, it seems that medications that are known to cause weight gain might be doing so by modifying the populations of microbes in our gut. In November 2015, researchers showed that risperidone, an antipsychotic drug, altered the gut microbes of mice who received it. The microbial changes slowed the animals' resting metabolisms, causing them to increase their body mass by 10 per cent in two months. The authors liken the effects to a 30-lb weight gain over one year for an average human, which they say would be the equivalent of an extra cheeseburger every day.

Other evidence suggests that gut microbes might affect weight gain in humans as they do in lab animals. Take the case of the woman who gained more than 40 lbs after receiving a transplant of gut microbes from her overweight teenage daughter. The transplant successfully treated the mother's intestinal infection of *Clostridium difficile*, which had resisted antibiotics. But, as of the study's publication last year, she hadn't been able to shed the excess weight through diet or exercise. The only aspect of her physiology that had changed was her gut microbes.

All of these factors introduce a disturbingly large margin of error for an individual who is trying, like Nash, Haelle and millions of others, to count calories. The discrepancies between the number on the label and the calories that are actually available in our food, combined with individual variations in how we metabolise that food, can add up to much more than the 200 calories a day that nutritionists often advise cutting in order to lose weight. Nash and Haelle can do everything right and still not lose weight.

None of this means that the calorie is a useless concept. Inaccurate as they are, calorie counts remain a helpful guide to relative energy values: standing burns more calories than sitting; cookies contain more calories than spinach. But the calorie is broken in many ways, and there's a strong case to be made for moving our food accounting system away from that one particular number. It's time to take a more holistic look at what we eat.

§

Wilbur Atwater worked in a world with different problems. At the beginning of the 20th century, nutritionists wanted to ensure people were well fed. The calorie was a useful way to quantify a person's needs. Today, excess weight affects more people than hunger; 1.9 billion adults around the world are considered overweight, 600 million of them obese. Obesity brings with it a higher risk of diabetes, heart disease and cancer. This is a new challenge, and it is likely to require a new metric.

One option is to focus on something other than energy intake. Like satiety, for instance. Picture a 300-calorie slice of cheesecake: it is going to be small. "So you're going to feel very dissatisfied with that meal," says Susan Roberts. If you eat 300 calories of a chicken salad instead, with nuts, olive oil and roasted vegetables, "you've got a lot of different nutrients that are hitting all the signals quite nicely," she says. "So you're going to feel full after you've eaten it. That fullness is going to last for several hours."

As a result of her research, Roberts has created a weight-loss plan that focuses on satiety rather than a straight calorie count. The idea is that foods that help people feel satisfied and full for longer should prevent them from overeating at lunch or searching for a snack soon after cleaning the table. Whole apples, white fish and Greek yoghurt are on her list of the best foods for keeping hunger at bay.

There's evidence to back up this idea: in one study, Roberts and colleagues found that people lost three times more weight by following her satiety plan compared with a traditional calorie-based one—and kept it off. Harvard nutritionist David Ludwig, who also proposes evaluating food on the basis of satiety instead of calories, has shown that teens given instant oats for breakfast consumed 650 more calories at lunch than their peers who were given the same number of breakfast calories in the form of a more satisfying omelette and fruit. Meanwhile, Adam Drewnowski, a epidemiologist at the University of Washington, has his own calorie upgrade: a nutrient density score. This system ranks food in terms of nutrition per calorie, rather than simply overall caloric value. Dark green vegetables and legumes score highly. Though the details of their approaches differ, all three agree: changing how we measure our food can transform our relationship with it for the better.

Individual consumers could start using these ideas now. But persuading the food industry and its watchdogs, such as the FDA, to adopt an entirely new labelling system based on one of these alternative measures is much more of a challenge. Consumers are unlikely to see the calorie replaced by Roberts's or Drewnowski's units on their labels any time soon; nonetheless, this work is an important reminder that there are other ways to measure food, ones that might be more useful for both weight loss and overall health.

Down the line, another approach might eventually prove even more useful: personalised nutrition. Since 2005, David Wishart of the University of Alberta has been cataloguing the hundreds of thousands of chemical compounds in our bodies, which make up what's known as the human metabolome. There are now 42,000 chemicals on his list, and many of them help digest the food we eat. His food metabolome database is a more recent effort: it contains about 30,000 chemicals derived directly from food. Wishart estimates that both databases may end up listing more than a million compounds. "Humans eat an incredible variety of foods," he says. "Then those are all transformed by our body. And they're turned into all kinds of other compounds." We have no idea what they all are, he adds—or what they do.

According to Wishart, these chemicals and their interactions affect energy balance. He points to research demonstrating that high-fructose corn syrup and other forms of added fructose (as opposed to fructose found in fruit) can trigger the creation of compounds that lead us to form an excess of fat cells, unrelated to additional calorie consumption. "If we cut back on some of these things," he says, "it seems to revert our body back to more appropriate, arguably less efficient metabolism, so that we aren't accumulating fat cells in our body."

It increasingly seems that there are significant variations in the way each one of us metabolises food, based on the tens of thousands—perhaps millions—of chemicals that make up each of our metabolomes. This, in combination with the individuality of each person's gut microbiome, could lead to the development of personalised dietary recommendations. Wishart imagines a future where you could hold up your smartphone, snap a picture of a dish, and receive a verdict on how that food will affect you as well as how many calories you'll extract from it. Your partner might receive completely different information from the same dish.

Or maybe the focus will shift to tweaking your microbial community: if you're trying to lose weight, perhaps you will curate your gut microbiome so as to extract fewer calories without harming your overall health. Peter Turnbaugh cautions that the science is not yet able to recommend a particular set of microbes, let alone how best to get them inside your gut, but he takes comfort from the fact that our microbial populations are "very plastic and very malleable"—we already know that they change when we take antibiotics, when we travel and when we eat different foods. "If we're able to figure this out," he says, "there is the chance that someday you might be able to tailor your microbiome" to get the outcomes you want.

None of these alternatives is ready to replace the calorie tomorrow. Yet the need for a new system of food accounting is clear. Just ask Haelle. "I'm kind of pissed at the scientific community for not coming up with something better for us," she confesses, recalling a recent meltdown at TGI Friday's as she navigated a confusing datasheet to find a low-calorie dish she could eat. There should be a better metric for people like her and Nash—people who know the health risks that come with being overweight and work hard to counter them. And it's likely there will be. Science has already shown that the calorie is broken. Now it has to find a replacement.

Race, Ethnicity, and Heritage

Mahzarin R. Banaji is the Richard Clarke Cabot Professor of Social Ethics in the Department of Psychology at Harvard University and the George A. and Helen Dunham Cowan Chair in Human Dynamics at the Santa Fe Institute. Her research focuses on how unconscious thinking and feeling unfold in social contexts. **Anthony G. Greenwald** is a Professor of Psychology at Washington University; his recent research focuses on implicit and unconscious cognition, especially applied to phenomena of stereotyping, prejudice, and the mental processing of subliminal stimuli.

On Stereotypes
Mahzarin R. Banaji and Anthony G. Greenwald

Categories

The recognized starting point for modern scientific understanding of stereotypes is Gordon Allport's 1954 book *The Nature of Prejudice*. Allport wrote: "The human mind must think with the aid of categories.... Once formed, categories are the basis for normal prejudgment. We cannot possibly avoid this process. Orderly living depends on it."[3]

The term *Homo categoricus* acknowledges the scientific impact of Allport's view of the importance of mental categories. A category is a collection of things having enough in common so that it is convenient to treat them as kin. The similarity among category members does not need to be great. The category of *car* includes things as different as toy cars, cable cars, and railroad cars. But the use of categories has a powerful effect on our behavior—as a quick look at a situation involving some subordinate categories within the *car* category will make clear: If you are driving on a highway and closing rapidly on a fast-moving car in front of you, your own speed in the next few seconds will be drastically different if you categorize that speeding vehicle as *police car* rather than as *sports car.* Another example: You will act very differently toward small white crystals that you categorize as *sugar* than toward ones you categorize as *salt*, even though you can't visibly tell one from the other in a spoon.

The categories that we use for people also affect our behavior in very clear ways. For example:

■ In a department store to make a purchase, you readily surrender your credit card to a total stranger whom you categorize as a *salesclerk.* You trust this stranger to be a typical member of the salesclerk category—that is, someone who will not surreptitiously record your account information and then sell it to an identity thief.

■ Entering a medical clinic, you assume the obedient role of *patient* (another category). Even though you may never have seen any of the medical staff before, you unquestioningly follow the instructions of people who are dressed in ways that lead you to categorize them as *doctor* or *nurse.* Having so categorized them, you then proceed to trust them with your life—not to mention your willingness to strip naked in their presence.

■ Driving on highways, you stay in your proper lane, you obey the traffic lights, and (a remarkably high percentage of the time) you stop at the stop signs. Without giving it a moment's thought, you behave as a member of the category *driver* and trust that others whom you categorize as drivers will be good members of that category and will act likewise.

Consider the alternatives. You might request a criminal-record check for all salesclerks. You might ask for the diplomas and current certifications of all the medical personnel you encounter. And you might refuse to venture out driving, for fear of being crushed under the wheels of other vehicles. If you did actually behave in so cautious a fashion, however, you yourself might be classified as paranoid or agoraphobic (two more categories), as a consequence of which you would experience inconveniences far greater than those you risk just by trusting others to be good members of their categories. Yes, there are tales of salesclerks who engage in identity theft, stories of medical impostors, and news reports of accidents caused by inebriated, incompetent, and sleepy drivers. It is remarkable that, for almost all of us, knowing that these possibilities exist does not stop us from shopping, getting medical help, or driving. Categories are not only extremely convenient—they are essential in permitting us to get about the business of our lives.

A Mind Built to Use Categories

To show how, as Allport put it, "orderly living" depends on the use of categories, we shall describe four of the many feats that our minds perform with the aid of categories. Each of these is carried out so effortlessly that, even while doing them, we remain entirely unaware of the mental virtuosity that they draw upon.

Feat 1: Multidimensional Categories—A Snap!

Can you make sense of this string of sixteen words?

1991 Subaru Legacy 4-door sedan with 4-cylinder engine, front-wheel drive, and automatic transmission.

Possibly you understood it in no more than the few seconds it took to read it. Next question: Would you have known that the string identified something quite different if it included "station wagon with standard transmission" in place of "sedan with automatic transmission"? If you can answer yes to both questions, you can regard yourself as the proud owner of a seven-dimensional category structure for automobiles. The seven dimensions are the seven columns of Table 1.

The sixteen-word Subaru description is one of thousands of distinct automobile categories that can be formed by stringing together identifiers from the seven columns of the table. The ability to conjure up pictures of a great many distinct automobile categories is one of two important characteristics of Feat 1. The second is the ease and automaticity with which your mind regularly makes use of this seven-dimensional structure.

Because some people are not so familiar with automobiles, not everyone can rapidly decode the sixteen words that describe the 1991 Subaru. If the Subaru example did not work for you, hold on for a moment—the much larger number of groups categorized in Feat 2 should establish the point.

Table 1. Seven-Dimensional Automobile Category Generator

Model	Year	Body Type	Engine Size	Power Source	Transmission	Drive
Ford Taurus	1990	Hatchback	4-cylinder	Diesel	Manual 4-speed	Front wheel
Cadillac Seville	1991	Station wagon	6-cylinder	Electric	Manual 5-speed	Rear wheel
VW Jetta	1992	Convertible	8-cylinder	Hybrid	Automatic	4-wheel
. . .	. . .	SUV		Gasoline		
Subaru Legacy	2007	Pickup				
Audi Turbo	2008	2-door sedan				
Toyota Camry	2009	4-door sedan				
Mercedes 550SL	2010	Van				

Feat 2: Millions of Person Categories Creatable on the Fly

Table 2 shows a small part of a six-dimensional structure that generates distinct categories of people by stringing together terms from its six columns. Some of the categories identified by these six-label strings encompass a relatively large number of people. For example, there are many middle-aged, White, male, Christian, Detroit factory workers. At the same time, if you don't live in Detroit, there is a good chance that you may never have met even one such person. Nevertheless, few Americans will have difficulty in forming an immediate mental conception of that factory worker on reading or hearing the six-label description. You may think that you can form an immediate impression of the Detroit factory worker because you've seen or heard or read about people like him in news media (talking about the closing of factories or being on strike, perhaps), in fiction, through friends, and so on.

But in fact, your facility with the six dimensions of Table 2 cannot be explained that simply. Your category-forming capacity is actually great enough to allow you to instantly conceive even a person described by an entirely unfamiliar combination of the six dimensions. For example, try thinking about a Black, Muslim, sixtyish, French, lesbian professor. Most readers of this book are unlikely to know even one person who could be identified by any four of those six identifiers. (Try it!) But that doesn't make it difficult to imagine one. It's almost a certainty that you will easily be able to form a picture in your mind of a person quite unlike anyone you have ever met: A Black, Muslim, sixtyish, French, lesbian professor.

For people who recognize the four sexuality/gender categories in the table, along with five race groups (add Native American to the four shown), plus approximately fifty nationalities or regions, about ten religions, eight age groups, and perhaps fifty occupations, Table 2 will produce a staggeringly large number of person categories—four million. The rapidity with which we can use the six identifiers to arrive at a picture of a category of person, however large (the Detroit factory worker) or small (the French professor) the category, confirms the brain's agility as a maker and user of categories.

Table 2. Six-Dimensional Person Category Generator

Race	Religion	Age	Nationality/ Region	Sex/Gender	Occupation
White	Christian	Young	French	Male	Professor
Asian	Muslim	Middle-aged	Detroit	Female	Homemaker
Black	Jewish	Sixtyish	Australian	Gay	Flight attendant
Hispanic	Zoroastrian	Elderly	American	Lesbian	Factory Worker

Feat 3: Leaping beyond the Available Information[4]

How does your brain deal with learning that a person is "American"—for example, "My English professor is American" or "An American passenger was held for questioning" or "The American lottery winner remained anonymous"? Before reading the next paragraph, please humor us by forming a mental image of one of these—say, the anonymous American lottery winner. Try to visualize that person in the process of making a phone call to claim the winnings.

What characteristics does your imagined person have in addition to being American? We suspect that your imagined person is very likely also White, male, and adult. And if your imagined American did have those three added characteristics, very likely they entered your mind without your having to consciously place them there. You can't form a mental image of a person without attributing a male or female gender to that person, and usually a race and an age too. That said, you could—in theory—have imagined a female Hispanic American teenager making the call to collect the lottery winnings. But there's a much higher likelihood that your mind generated the image of a White male adult. The characteristics that you added can be thought of as your default values for the race, gender, and age of a typical American. Why might White, male, and adult be the default characteristics for an otherwise undescribed "American"? Likely it's because those are the characteristics of Americans whom you see, hear, and read about in newspapers, radio, television, and conversation most frequently, no matter whether they are the characteristics of those you meet and talk with most often as you go about your day.

If you are at all skeptical about the idea that in forming these mental pictures we use default characteristics to flesh out and go far beyond the basic information we've been given, then think about it this way: The default attributes that we add are so taken for granted and so automatic that, without thinking about why we do this, we are usually careful to specify a *different* set of attributes when the default ones don't apply. Thus you simply say "American" when you are referring to a White American. But if you're talking about another kind of American, you may instead say "Asian American" or "African American." Similarly, when you refer to a "taxi driver" you are almost certainly referring to a male taxi driver. If not, you may say "lady cab driver."

You can now understand something that might have been puzzling when we described the 1933 Princeton stereotype study .... The students were asked to describe typical characteristics of nationality or race categories that were identified by single words, such as *Americans, Germans, Chinese,* and *Italians.* The Princeton students almost certainly assumed, without giving it any thought, that when they were asked to choose characteristics typical of Americans, they were expected to provide traits characteristic of White, male, adult Americans. The two traits that they most often selected for Americans, *materialistic* and *ambitious,* are very unlikely to be characteristics that the students would have chosen if they had been asked to describe American women or children.[5]

Feat 4: Cooperative Categorization

People often actively send signals about the categories to which they themselves belong. Thus, on first meeting, we can often read these signals to help us identify a person's occupation. At the service station, we know that the person wearing coveralls is a mechanic, not a customer. In the hospital, the person in the white coat is a nurse or doctor, not a patient. The use of clothing to identify different occupations is just one of many ways in which people routinely help others to easily place them into appropriate categories.

Probably the most common, and arguably the most important, of these cooperative categorization strategies are those that help others to categorize us as male or female. If you are puzzled by this statement, wondering, "Who needs help in classifying people as male or female?" your puzzlement indicates only how unthinkingly—and routinely—almost everyone provides this help.

Although it is not difficult to distinguish male from female using natural body shape and facial features, we nevertheless use a wide variety of additional aids to help the process along. Women typically wear their hair longer than men. Most men and women wear sex-typical clothes that serve to accentuate body shape differences between male and female. Many people wear styles of collars, sleeves, belts, and shoes that are distinctively masculine or feminine. Cosmetics, manicures, jewelry, and gestures add still more markings that advertise—perhaps *flaunt* is the better word—maleness or femaleness. It could be an interesting exercise in economics to calculate the fraction of American wealth spent on clothing, cosmetics, and other accessories that ease the work of categorizing one another as male or female.

Race is another feature that can usually be identified fairly rapidly without help, but it too is a category that people often choose to make, more identifiable by their choice of hairstyle, clothing, speech, gesture, and other signifiers.

Of course, such signifiers can be co-opted by other groups—witness the phenomenon of White suburban teenagers dressing "ghetto" to make a particular impression. This brings us to recognize that the cooperative categorization phenomenon also has its uncooperative variant form, in which we send visual signals for the explicit purpose of *mis*representing a category to which we belong.

The most common form of uncooperative categorization is the effort that many put into projecting the appearance of an age group younger than their own. A great deal of money is made supplying elders with cosmetics, hair dyes, surgery, and drugs designed to erase wrinkles, shore up sagging body parts, disguise hair that is turning gray or white, and replace hair that has disappeared. Given the traits stereotypically associated with old age—being slow, forgetful, hard of hearing, feeble, and so on—it is easy enough to see why elderly people might want to make it appear that they belong to a younger age group!

Less often disguised than age are religion and ethnicity, but they too are the object of uncooperative categorization under certain circumstances. A well-known strategy is to replace an ethnically identifiable name, such as Winona Horowitz, Issur Demsky, Anna Maria Louisa Italiano, or Jacob Cohen, with something less ethnically identifiable—like the names Winona Ryder, Kirk Douglas, Anne Bancroft, and Rodney Dangerfield (as these people are better known). A more recent cultural invention of the uncooperative categorization variety is the "whitening" of résumés submitted by African Americans in applying for jobs. This involves removing mentions of memberships and positions in obviously African American organizations and altering or omitting names of traditionally Black colleges or universities.

Notwithstanding the relative ease of engaging in uncooperative categorization, many members of often-stigmatized ethnic, racial, or sexual orientation categories not only avoid misrepresenting their categories but choose to do quite the opposite, making it easy for others to place them in their often-stigmatized categories. This suggests that the advantages of signaling those identities may often outweigh the disadvantages.

Think, for example, of gays and lesbians. Although they remain stigmatized and disadvantaged in many settings in modern America, many have decided to make their sexual orientation known—at least to other members of their category, and sometimes to the world at large. Such assists to "gaydar" (the ability to assess another's sexual orientation from a distance) make it much easier for gays to identify one another, and—if the signals are not of the secret-handshake type—often for non-gays to do so as well, helping avoid potential embarrassment on both sides.

Of the four feats, cooperative categorization stands apart from the others, being the only one that directly shows the everyday working of stereotypes. When cooperative categorization comes into play, a stereotype operates, interestingly, exactly opposite to the fashion usually expected. Instead of knowing a person's category (for example, female) and expecting a stereotypic trait (for example, long hair), we observe the long hair and infer that the person is female. Another paradox of cooperative categorization is that deliberately displaying a stereotyped characteristic (for example, the male professor's pipe and elbow-patched jacket) can have the possibly unwanted effect of strengthening observers' conception of the stereotype's validity.

The remainder of this chapter will make use of the mental virtuosity of Feats 1, 2, and 3 to decribe further how stereotypes function in our daily lives. We reach a conclusion that should be a surprise to those familiar with existing scientific understanding of stereotypes.

How We Use Stereotypes

Most of us think that the statement *Ducks lay eggs* is quite reasonable. But "Ducks lay eggs" is actually false for a substantial majority of the world's ducks, and not for one but two reasons. First, because fewer female than male ducklings survive the hatching process, more than half the world's ducks are non-egg-laying males.[6] Second, among female ducks, many are too young to be egg layers. Without doubt, egg-laying ducks are a distinct minority. We anticipate your reaction: "In agreeing that 'Ducks lay eggs' was reasonable, I meant only that I knew that *some* ducks lay eggs, not that *all* ducks lay eggs."

Fair enough. But suppose that the statement had been *Dogs wear clothes.* This is certainly true of *some* dogs. Would you have classified that statement as reasonable? Not likely. In our understanding, "Ducks lay eggs" seems more reasonable than "Dogs wear clothes" because most people have a strong *duck = egg layer* association. And unless you have been greatly influenced by William Wegman's photos of Man Ray, Fay Ray, and their successors, you probably do not have a *dog = clothes wearer* association.

The "Ducks lay eggs" example gives a clue to how stereotypes influence our thinking. Just as we may incorrectly assume that a duck seen swimming in a nearby pond can lay eggs, we may—equally unthinkingly—assume that an elderly person we have just met has poor memory. The *old = forgetful* stereotype is valid only to the extent that a greater proportion of elderly than young people have poor memory. Nevertheless, that stereotype may influence your reactions to *all* elderly people, including ones whose memories may be far better than your own.[7]

Here is another illustration of the tendency to think in stereotypes. For each of the five traits listed on the left below, do you see that trait as a better description of the first of the two groups named to the right, or the second?

Table 3.

Trait	Groups
Leadership	Men more than women?
Musical talent	African Americans more than Native Americans?
Legal Expertise	Jews more than Christians?
Math ability	Asians more than Whites?
Criminality	Italians more than Dutch?

Any yes answer suggests that you possess a stereotype that, undoubtedly, many others also have. It's true that possessing these stereotypes doesn't make it inevitable that you will use them when you are making judgments about individual people, or that you will make important decisions based on them. For example, a corporate manager may believe that the *leader = male* stereotype is generally valid but may still be able to recognize that a specific woman who has shown outstanding leadership potential would be a good candidate for an executive position. At the same time, the bar she would have to clear might be higher than for men competing for the same position. Similarly, a teacher with a *math = male* stereotype may encourage an obviously gifted girl to pursue her studies in math. But this same teacher may also underestimate the math abilities of many other girls, all the while being more ready to recognize the potential of boys and to single them out for extra help and attention.

Does Stereotyping Have a Useful Purpose?

While we may concede Gordon Allport's point that "the human mind must think with the aid of categories," and that, as he said, orderly living is not possible without using categories, we also have to wonder about the ultimate consequences of our category-making and category-using activities. For, as Allport also told us, "Once formed, categories are the basis for normal prejudgment." Another way of saying this is that the categories that our brains form so easily give rise to stereotypes. Thus we associate certain categories with certain prejudged attributes—Africans with having rhythm, Asians with being good at math, women with being inattentive drivers, and so forth.

Indeed, stereotyping by social category is so widely practiced as to deserve recognition as a universal human trait—as implied by the term *Homo categoricus*, which we used as the title for this chapter. Scientists understand universal traits in terms of the idea of adaptiveness or usefulness. Universal traits are generally assumed either to be presently adaptive or to be unfortunate by-products of other presently adaptive characteristics, or perhaps to be troublesome vestiges of previously (but no longer) adaptive characteristics.

The currently dominant explanation for the pervasiveness of stereotyping is of the "unfortunate by-product" type—stereotyping is an unfortunate by-product of the otherwise immensely useful human ability to conceive the world in terms of categories. Many social psychologists see this explanation as plausible, and we are among them.

There is also a theory of the "presently adaptive" type. This theory supposes that many people derive a useful self-esteem boost because stereotypes allow them to see their own group as superior to other groups. Having unfavorable stereotypes of many other groups makes this fairly easy to do. But this theory is less than compelling, in part because humans have so many other ways to boost self-esteem, and in part because it leads to an expectation that is most likely untrue—that those occupying the higher- status roles in their society or possessing the society's default characteristics should engage in more stereotyping than those lower in the hierarchy.

We offer here a new (and admittedly speculative) theory of the benefits of stereotyping that is also of the "presently adaptive" variety: Stereotyping achieves the desirable effect of allowing us to rapidly perceive total strangers as distinctive individuals.

We hope you read that last sentence at least twice, trying to find words that you thought you must have missed on first reading. The assertion "Stereotyping allows us to perceive strangers as distinctive individuals" may seem incomprehensible, even ludicrous, to anyone who thinks of stereotypes as the one-size-fits-all mental boxes into which we force all members of a group, no matter how different from one another they may be. Recall the inspiration for Walter Lippmann's coinage in 1922—the printer's metal plate that produced many identical copies. If stereotypes cause us to view all _____ (you name the group: Cheerleaders, Italians, Muslims, rocket scientists, whatever) as being alike, then it would seem to follow that stereotypes must undermine, rather than facilitate, our ability to perceive strangers as distinct individuals.

We come to our seemingly absurd theory courtesy of the second mental feat of which *Homo categoricus* is capable: The ability to simultaneously use six (possibly more) person identifiers to produce mental images of many distinct categories of people. Applying the stereotypes associated with these six or so identifiers simultaneously produces a result very different from Lippmann's "identical copies."

This will be a good time to recall the Black, Muslim, sixtyish, French, lesbian professor we used to illustrate Feat 2. Each of her six identifiers carries its own set of stereotypic traits. Using one identifier at a time would mean seeing her only with the Black stereotype, or only the Muslim stereotype, or only the stereotype for one of her other four category labels. But processing her six identifiers together, all at once, lets us conceive of a person who is distinctly different from anyone else we know. Maybe they didn't quite break the mold when they made her, but she'll be seen as a distinct individual, someone whom we will not readily confuse with anyone else we know.

To make our paradoxical explanation convincing, it may help if we make clear how easy it is to grasp half a dozen or so person identifiers within a fraction of a second. We do this all the time. Imagine a person who walks past you while you wait to board an airplane. Five identifiers will almost always be immediately available—sex, age, race, height, and weight. Clothing may permit us to add multiple other identifiers, perhaps including income, social class, religion, ethnicity, and occupation. Each of these identifiers has stereotypical traits associated with it. When our minds automatically activate all these stereotypes at once, we get a rich, complex perception of the person, even though the passerby we are contemplating is a total stranger. After no more than a brief glance we should be able to distinguish this passerby from just about everyone else in sight, and quite possibly from everyone else in the airport. This is why we conclude that the mental virtuosity described in Feat 2 allows us to use stereotypes to *perceive strangers as distinctive individuals.*

Who Uses Stereotypes? Who Gets Stereotyped?

It is not possible to be human and to avoid making use of stereotypes. Stereotypes make up a submerged but significant portion of the meaning that we read into words such as *old, female, Asian,* and *Muslim.* These submerged, automatically activated meanings go well beyond dictionary definitions. For example, nowhere in any dictionary of the English language will you find *old* defined as "slow," "forgetful," "hard of hearing," or "feeble," but these are all parts of the stereotype that the category *old* is packaged with. Not having stereotypes to provide meaning to our person categories would be like knowing the words of a language without knowing what they mean. In other words, *everyone uses stereotypes.*

The answer to "Who gets stereotyped?" is less simple. Stereotypes are not distributed equally. If you can be described by the default attributes of your society—the attributes that don't need to be mentioned because they are assumed unless explicitly stated otherwise (see Feat 3)—you will be subject to less stereotyping than others. You won't be stereotyped by the members of your in-group—those who share the default characteristics that you have—and you may be stereotyped little by others. In Japan, young Japanese men are unlikely to be stereotyped. However, in the United States, they are likely to be stereotyped. This is perhaps why those who belong to their society's "default" categories may see stereotyping as less of a problem than others do—they are much less likely to be its victims.

On the other hand, those who lack their society's default characteristics are likely to be stereotyped, and not just by others but by themselves—which can be to their disadvantage. This conclusion has only recently been established in research, and it may be the unkindest cut of all. The stereotypes applied to a group are sometimes self-applied by members of the group to themselves, and in that case the stereotypes may act as self-undermining and self-fulfilling prophecies.

Self-fulfilling prophecies can be beneficial. An own-group stereotype might guide African Americans toward becoming better track athletes, basketball players, or jazz musicians. Asian stereotypes may prompt Asian Americans to work hard in school, win scholarships, and launch themselves into high-paying careers in science, medicine, and engineering.

But when stereotypes are unfavorable, as many are, the forces that cause people to act in ways that conform to the stereotype applied to their own group can have damaging effects. Elders who internalize stereotypes of the elderly are at greater risk of declining health; women who internalize gender stereotypes are at risk of underperforming in math and science; African Americans who internalize stereotypes of their own group are at risk of not living up to their academic potential. It doesn't take the (stereotypical) rocket scientist to understand the potential for harm in stereotypes.[8]

Notes

3. Allport's statement about the importance of categories appears in his *Nature of Prejudice* (Allport, 1954). A collection of modern perspectives on Allport's contributions to understanding stereotypes and prejudice was published in a fiftieth-anniversary celebration of the book (Dovidio, Glick, & Rudman, 2005). A contemporary overview of scientific work on stereotypes is available in a comprehensive text by David Schneider (2004).

4. The label for Feat 3—"leaping beyond the available information"—is borrowed from an influential essay by cognitive psychologist Jerome Bruner, "Going beyond the information given" (Bruner, 1957).

5. The supposition that stereotypes captured by the methods of the 1933 Princeton study consist of traits characteristic of men (not women) of the various national groups was later tested and confirmed in research by social psychologists Alice Eagly and Mary Kite (1987).

6. Many sources report that sex ratios in ducks, estimated by a variety of methods, show that males are in the majority (e.g., Brown, 1982).

7. The use of "Ducks lay eggs" to illustrate the extent to which a statement that properly applies to "some" (ducks in this case) may be inappropriately applied to "most" is borrowed from illustrations used by cognitive psychologist Sam Glucksberg (Khemlani, Glucksberg, & Rubio Fernandez, 2007).

8. The self-fulfilling prophecy aspect of stereotypes about the elderly has been described by Levy (2009). The self-fulfilling aspect of female and African American stereotypes has received attention in a large body of recent research on stereotype threat, especially by Claude Steele and his colleagues (Steele, Spencer, & Aronson, 2002).

References

Allport, G. W. (1954). *The nature of prejudice.* Cambridge, MA: Perseus.

Brown, D. E. (1982). Sex ratios, sexual selection and sexual dimorphism in waterfowl. *American Birds, 36,* 259–260.

Bruner, J. S. (1957). Going beyond the information given. In H. Gruber et al. (eds.), *Contemporary approaches to cognition* (pp. 41–69). Cambridge, MA: Harvard University Press.

Dovidio, J. F., Glick, P., & Rudman, L. A. (eds.) (2005). *On the nature of prejudice: Fifty years after Allport.* Malden, MA: Blackwell.

Eagly, A. H., & Kite, M. E. (1987). Are stereotypes of nationalities applied to both women and men? *Journal of Personality and Social Psychology, 53,* 451–462.

Katz, D., & Braly, K. (1933). Racial stereotypes of one hundred college students. *Journal of Abnormal and Social Psychology, 28,* 280–290.

Khemlani, S., Glucksberg, S., & Rubio Fernandez, P. (2007). Do ducks lay eggs? How people interpret generic assertions. In D. S. McNamara & J. G. Trafton (eds.), *Proceedings of the 29th Annual Cognitive Science Society,* 64–70. Austin, TX: Cognitive Science Society.

Levy, B. (2009). Stereotype embodiment: A psycho-social approach to aging. *Current Directions in Psychological Science, 18,* 332–336.

Lippmann, W. (1922). *Public opinion.* New York: Harcourt, Brace.

Madon, S., et al. (2001). Ethnic and national stereotypes: The Princeton trilogy revisited and revised. *Personality and Social Psychology Bulletin, 27,* 996–1010.

Rice, S. A, (1926). "Stereotypes": A source of error in judging human character. *Journal of Personnel Research, 5,* 267–276.

Schneider, D. J. (2004). *The psychology of stereotypes.* New York: Guilford.

Steele, C. M., Spencer, S. J., & Aronson, J. (2002). Contending with group image: The psychology of stereotype and social identity threat. In M. P. Zanna (ed.), *Advances in experimental social psychology,* vol. 34 (pp. 379–440). San Diego, CA: Academic Press.

Naomi Gerstel is a Distinguished Professor in the Department of Sociology at the University of Massachusetts Amherst. **Natalia Sarkisian** is an Associate Professor in the Sociology Department at Boston College. Both of them conduct research on the relationships between race, gender, class, and work.

The Color of Family Ties: Race, Class, Gender, and Extended Family Involvement
Naomi Gerstel and Natalia Sarkisian

When talking about family obligations and solidarities, politicians and social commentators typically focus on the ties between married couples and their children. We often hear that Black and Latino/a, especially Puerto Rican, families are more disorganized than White families, and that their family ties are weaker, because rates of non-marriage and single parenthood are higher among these minority groups. But this focus on the nuclear family ignores extended family solidarities and caregiving activities. Here we examine these often overlooked extended kinship ties.[1]

Taking this broader perspective on family relations refutes the myth that Blacks and Latinos/as lack strong families. Minority individuals are more likely to live in extended family homes than Whites and in many ways more likely to help out their aging parents, grandparents, adult children, brothers, sisters, cousins, aunts, uncles, and other kin.

According to our research using the second wave of the National Survey of Families and Households, as Figures 1 and 2 show, Blacks and Latinos/as, both women and men, are much more likely than Whites to share a home with extended kin: 42 percent of Blacks and 37 percent of Latinos/ as, but only 20 percent of Whites, live with relatives. Similar patterns exist for living near relatives: 54 percent of Blacks and 51 percent of Latinos/as, but only 37 percent of Whites, live within two miles of kin. Blacks and Latinos/as are also more likely than Whites to frequently visit kin. For example, 76 percent of Blacks, 71 percent of Latinos/ as, but just 63 percent of Whites see their relatives once a week or more.

---

1. For the extensive analysis underlying this discussion, see: (1) Natalia Sarkisian, Mariana Gerena, and Naomi Gerstel, "Extended Family Integration Among Mexican and Euro Americans: Ethnicity, Gender, and Class," *Journal of Marriage and Family*, 69 (2007), 1 (February), 40–54. (2) Natalia Sarkisian, Mariana Gerena, and Naomi Gerstel, "Extended Family Ties Among Mexicans, Puerto Ricans and Whites: Superintegration or Disintegration?," *Family Relations*, 55 (2006), 3 (July), 331–344. (3) Natalia Sarkisian and Naomi Gerstel, "Kin Support Among Blacks and Whites: Race and Family Organization," *American Sociological Review*, 69 (2004), 4 (December), 812–837. (4) Amy Armenia and Naomi Gerstel, "Family Leaves, The FMLA, and Gender Neutrality: The Intersection of Race and Gender," *Social Science Research*, 35 (2006), 871–891. (5) Naomi Gerstel and Natalia Sarkisian, "A Sociological Perspective on Families and Work: The Import of Gender, Class, and Race," in Marcie Pitt Catsouphes, Ellen Kossek, and Steven Sweet (eds.), *The Work and Family Handbook: Multi-disciplinary Perspectives, Methods, and Approaches* (Mahwah, NJ: Lawrence Erlbaum, 2006), pp. 237–266. (6) Naomi Gerstel and Natalia Sarkisian, "Marriage: The Good, the Bad, and the Greedy," *Contexts*, 5 (2006) 4 (November), 16–21. (7) Naomi Gerstel and Natalia Sarkisian, "Intergenerational Care and the Greediness of Adult Children's Marriages," in J. Suitor and T. Owens (eds.), *Interpersonal Relations Across the Life Course. Advances in the Life Course Research*, Volume 12 (Greenwich, CT: Elsevier / JAI Press, 2007). [Gerstel and Sarkisian's note.]

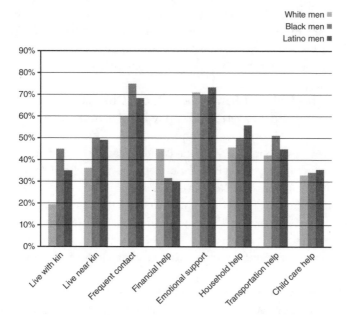

Figure 1. Ethnicity and extended kin involvement among men. Data from National Survey of Families and Households, 1992–1994.

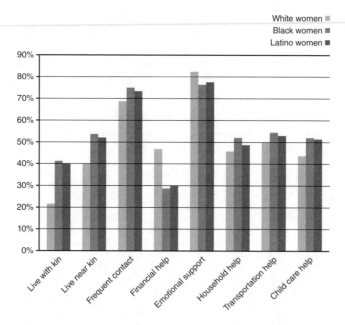

Figure 2. Ethnicity and extended kin involvement among women. Data from National Survey of Families and Households, 1992–1994.

Even if they don't live together, Blacks and Latinos/as are as likely as Whites—and in some ways more likely—to be supportive family members. But there are important racial and ethnic differences in the type of support family members give each other. Whites are more likely than ethnic minorities to give and receive large sums of money, and White women are more likely than minority women to give and receive emotional support, such as discussing personal problems and giving each other advice. When it comes to help with practical tasks, however, we find that Black and Latino/a relatives are more likely than Whites to be supportive: they are more likely to give each other help with household work and child care, as well as with providing rides and running errands. These differences are especially pronounced among women.

This is not to say that Black and Latino men are not involved with kin, as is implied in popular images of minority men hanging out on street corners rather than attending to family ties. In fact, Black and Latino men are more likely than White men to live near relatives and to stay in touch with them. White men, however, are more likely to give and receive large-scale financial help. Moreover, the three groups of men are very similar when it comes to giving and getting practical help and emotional support.

These data suggest that if we only consider married couples or parents and their young children, we are missing much of what families in general and families of color in particular do for each other. A focus on nuclear families in discussions of race differences in family life creates a biased portrait of families of color.

Explaining Race Differences: Is It Culture or Class?

When discussing differences in family experiences of various racial and ethnic groups, commentators often assume that these differences can be traced to cultural differences or competing "family values." Sometimes these are expressed in a positive way, as in the stereotype that Latino families have more extended ties because of their historical traditions and religious values. Other times these are expressed in a negative way, as when Blacks are said to lack family values because of the cultural legacy of slavery and subsequent years of oppression. Either way, differences in family behaviors are often explained by differences in cultural heritage.

In contrast, in our research, we find that social class rather than culture is the key to understanding the differences in extended family ties and behaviors between Whites and ethnic minorities. To be sure, differences in cultural values do exist. Blacks and Latinos/as are more likely than Whites to say they believe that extended family is important; both groups are also more likely to attend religious services. Blacks tend to hold more egalitarian beliefs about gender than Whites, while Latinos/as, especially Mexican Americans, tend to hold more "traditional" views. But these differences in values do not explain racial differences in actual involvement with relatives. It is, instead, social class that matters most in explaining these differences.

Table 1. Education, Income, and Poverty Rates by Race

	Whites	Blacks	Latinos/as
Median household income	$50,784	$30,858	$35,967
Percentage below poverty line	8.4%	24.7%	22.0%
Education:			
Less than high school	14.5%	27.6%	47.6%
High school graduate	58.5%	58.1%	42.0%
Bachelor's degree or higher	27.0%	14.3%	10.4%

Data from U.S. Census Bureau, 2005.

It is widely known (and confirmed by U.S. Census data presented in Table 1) that Blacks and Latinos/as tend to have far less income and education than Whites. Families of color are also much more likely than White families to be below the official poverty line. In our research, we find that the differences in extended family ties and behaviors between Whites and ethnic minorities are primarily the result of these social class disparities.

Simply put, White, Black, and Latino/a individuals with the same amount of income and education have similar patterns of involvement with their extended families. Just like poor minorities, impoverished Whites are more likely to exchange practical aid and visit with extended kin than are their wealthier counterparts. Just like middle-class Whites, middle-class Blacks and Latinos/as are more likely to talk about their personal concerns or share money with relatives than are their poorer counterparts.

More specifically, it is because Whites tend to have more income than Blacks and Latinos/as that they are more likely to give money to their relatives or get it from them. And the higher levels of emotional support among White women can be at least in part traced to their higher levels of education, perhaps because schooling encourages women to talk out their problems and makes them more likely to give (and get) advice.

Conversely, we find that the relative economic deprivation of racial/ethnic minorities leads in many ways to higher levels of extended family involvement. Individuals' lack of economic resources increases their need for help from kin and boosts their willingness to give help in return. Because Blacks and Latinos/as typically have less income and education than Whites, they come to rely more on their relatives for daily needs such as child care, household tasks, or rides. The tendency of Blacks and Latinos/as to live with or near kin may also reflect their greater need for kin cooperation, as well as their decreased opportunities and pressures to move away, including moving for college.

Social Class and Familial Trade-Offs

How do our findings on race, social class, and familial involvement challenge common understandings of minority families? They show that poor minority families do not necessarily lead lives of social isolation or lack strong family solidarities. The lower rates of marriage among impoverished groups may reflect not a rejection of family values but a realistic assessment of how little a woman (and her children) may be able to depend upon marriage. Sociologists Kathryn Edin and Maria Kefalas (2007) recently found that because disadvantaged men are often unable to offer women the kind of economic security that advantaged men provide, poor women are less likely to marry. Instead, these women create support networks beyond the nuclear family, regularly turning to extended kin for practical support.

Reliance on extended kin and lack of marital ties are linked. In another analysis of the National Survey of Families and Households, we found that, contrary to much rhetoric about marriage as a key source of adult social ties, marriage actually diminishes ties to kin. Married people—women as well as men—are less involved with their parents and siblings than those never married or previously married. These findings indicate a trade-off between commitments to nuclear and extended family ties. Marriage, we have found, is a "greedy" institution: it has a tendency to consume the bulk of people's energies and emotions and to dilute their commitments beyond the nuclear family.

On the one hand, then, support given to spouses and intimate partners sometimes comes at the expense of broader kin and community ties. Indeed, married adult children take care of elderly parents less often than their unmarried siblings. Marriage can also cut people off from networks of mutual aid. Married mothers, for example, whether Black, Latina, or White, are often unable to obtain help from kin in the way that their single counterparts can. Although the "greedy" nature of marriage may pose a problem across social class, it is especially problematic for those less well off economically, as these individuals most need to cultivate wider circles of obligation, mutual aid, and reciprocity.

On the other hand, support to relatives sometimes comes at the expense of care for partners, and can interfere with nuclear family formation or stability. Indeed, individuals who are deeply immersed in relationships with extended families may be less likely to get married or, if they marry, may be less likely to put the marital ties first in their loyalties. Several decades ago in her observations of a poor Black community, anthropologist Carol Stack (1974) found that the reciprocal patterns of sharing with kin and "fictive kin" forged in order to survive hardship often made it difficult for poor Blacks either to move up economically or to marry. To prevent the dilution of their social support networks, some extended families may even discourage their members from getting married, or unconsciously sabotage relationships that threaten to pull someone out of the family orbit. As sociologists Domínguez and Watkins (2003) argue, the ties of mutual aid that help impoverished individuals survive on a day-to-day basis may also prevent them from saying "no" to requests that sap their ability to get ahead or pursue individual opportunities.

MORE NONTRADITIONAL FAMILY UNITS

Guy, Chair, Three-Way Lamp

A Woman, Her Daughter, Forty-four
My Little Ponies

The Troy Triplets and Their
Personal Trainer

Two Guys, Two Gals, Two Phones,
a Fax, and a Blender

R. Chast

Roz Chast / The New Yorker Collection / www.cartoonbank.com

Overall, we should avoid either denigrating or glorifying the survival strate-gies of the poor. Although social class disparities are key to understanding racial and ethnic variation in familial involvement, it is too simple to say that class differences create "more" involvement with relatives in one group and "less" in another. In some ways economic deprivation increases ties to kin (e.g., in terms of living nearby or exchanging practical help) and in other ways it reduces them (e.g., in terms of financial help or emotional support). These findings remind us that love and family connections are expressed both through talk and action. Equally important, focusing solely on the positive or on the negative aspects of either minority or White families is problematic. Instead, we need to think in terms of trade-offs—among different kinds of care and between the bonds of kinship and the bonds of marriage. Both tradeoffs are linked to social class.

Why Do These Differences in Family Life Matter?

Commentators often emphasize the disorganization and dysfunction of Black and Latino/a family life. They suggest that if we could "fix" family values in minority communities and get them to form married-couple households, all their problems would be solved. This argument misunderstands causal connections by focusing on the family as the source of problems. Specifically, it ignores the link between race and class and attributes racial or ethnic differences to cultural values. Instead, we argue, it is important to understand that family strategies and behaviors often emerge in response to the challenges of living in economic deprivation or constant economic insecurity. Therefore, social policies should not focus on changing family behaviors, but rather aim to support a range of existing family arrangements and improve economic conditions for the poor.

Social policies that overlook extended family obligations may introduce, re-produce, or even increase ethnic inequalities. For example, the relatives of Blacks and Latinos/as are more likely than those of Whites to provide various kinds of support that policymakers tend to assume is only provided by husbands and wives. Such relatives may need the rights and support systems that we usually reserve for spouses. For instance, the Family and Medical Leave Act is an important social policy, but it only guarantees unpaid leave from jobs to provide care to spouses, children, or elderly parents requiring medical attention. Our findings suggest that, if we really want to support families, such policies must be broadened to include adult children, needy grown-up brothers and sisters, cousins, aunts and uncles. Similarly, Medicaid regulations that only pay for non-familial care of ill, injured, or disabled individuals implicitly discriminate against Blacks and Latinos/as who provide significant amounts of care to extended kin. "Pro-marriage" policies that give special incentives to impoverished women for getting married may penal-ize other women who turn down marriage to a risky mate and rely instead on grandparents or other relatives to help raise their children.

Extended family obligations should be recognized and accommodated where possible. But they should not be counted on as a substitute for antipoverty mea-sures, nor should marriage promotion be used in this way. Policymakers must recognize that support from family—whether extended or nuclear—cannot fully compensate for the disadvantages of being poor, or minority, or both. Neither marital ties nor extended family ties can substitute for educational opportunities, jobs with decent wages, health insurance, and affordable child care. Instead of hoping that poor families pull themselves out of poverty by their own bootstraps, social policy should explicitly aim to rectify economic disadvantages. In turn, improvements in economic opportunities and resources will likely shape families.

References

Domínguez, Silvia, and Celeste Watkins. "Creating Networks for Survival and Mobility: Examin-ing Social Capital Amongst Low-Income African-American and Latin-American Mothers." *Social Problems*, 50 (2003), 1 (February), 111–135.

Edin, Kathryn, and Maria Kefalas. *Promises I Can Keep: Why Poor Women Put Motherhood Before Marriage* (Berkeley, CA : University of California Press, 2007).

Stack, Carol B. *All Our Kin: Strategies for Survival in a Black Community* (New York: Harper and Row, 1974).

Diane Goldstein is a 21-year veteran of law enforcement who retired as the first female lieutenant for the Redondo Beach Police Department in California. She is currently a columnist, commentator, and Executive Board Member for Law Enforcement Against Prohibition—an organization of law enforcement officials opposed to the current war on drugs.

I'm a Cop and I Support Black Lives Matter: How Can We Heal These Wounds?
Diane Goldstein

On Friday morning, I woke up and deactivated my Facebook account, frustrated by the highly charged, divisive rhetoric appearing in my stream from friends and activists on opposing sides of the Black Lives Matter versus Blue Lives Matter argument. Over the weekend, in the wake of the Dallas shootings, I've watched along with the rest of the country as renewed protests and hundreds of arrests took place. The stark exposure of our national fault lines is distressing, and while there is hope, you have to search hard to find it.

I'm a retired police professional, a 20-year-veteran of California law enforcement. I'm also a criminal justice reform activist, a board member of Law Enforcement Against Prohibition. So the diversity of my social media friends reflects my values—values which now appear to be at war with each other.

I greatly fear that the violence of this past week will further exacerbate the deep divides in our society. The loss of five police officers protecting Black Lives Matter protesters in Dallas can now be added to the losses of the scores of people of color, including Alton Sterling in Baton Rouge and Philando Castile in Minnesota, who have recently fallen victim to the troubling state of police-community relations in America—and yes, in too many cases, to enforcement strategies based on structural racism. Every one of these deaths is not only tragic in itself, but also further poisons relations and entrenches opinions.

By now, I'm emotionally drained from continually trying to explain to friends, allies, opponents and interviewers how I can be both pro-law enforcement *and* pro-Black Lives Matter.

I'm exhausted from continually having to explain why it's not President Obama's fault that officers lost their lives; that there is no statistical basis for a so-called war on the police; that Black Lives Matter doesn't mean that police lives *don't* matter; that most police officers are not racist or bad.

Not that I'm looking for sympathy; I chose this fight through my work at LEAP. The deep divisions in our country that make such explanations necessary have resulted from many issues, including both overt and structural racism. Post-Ferguson in 2014 I wrote about how the War on Drugs has poisoned community policing and shifted us away from policing by consent. I largely blame our inability to admit to our policing failures, to accept that whether or not we *intended* to damage or marginalize communities of color, that *is* what has occurred.

The formation of Black Lives Matter is a direct outcome of our poorly designed criminal justice and economic policies. One of my graduate school professors, Elliott Currie, wrote in his book *Crime and Punishment in America* (2013) that our over-emphasis on punishment, above all else, is just "an attempt to sweep the problem of America's poorest communities under the rug."

In addition to the undoubted failings of law enforcement itself, it's clear that the police have also been given an insurmountable challenge, a task which, like Sisyphus with his boulder, we will never be able to complete. That's because law enforcement cannot change the many socioeconomic issues that contribute to crime.

We put pressure on law enforcement agencies to produce lower crime rates, something we take as an indicator of a healthy community. Yet we ignore the fact that law enforcement budgets compete with funding for other badly needed programs, such as education, mental health services, community after-school programs, and the creation of jobs and infrastructure. Together, these programs have been shown to prevent crime and to make a community safer far more effectively than an emphasis on law enforcement alone.

For example, according to a report by the organization Fight Crime: Invest in Kids,[1] researchers estimated that three out of 10 high school students drop out of high school, or to fail to graduate on time. By increasing that high-school graduation rate by 10 percent nationally, the researchers predicted we could prevent over 3,000 murders and nearly 175,000 aggravated assaults in the United States annually.

Recognizing that public safety is a multifaceted challenge, the responsibility of not just the police but a whole range of agencies and services, will require a significant shift in police culture and management. If we truly understood that our role should simply be to limit negative community interventions, improve community interactions and be accountable to our constituents, we could reduce the violence that impacts both communities of color and the police.

The war of words about whose lives matter more serves no useful purpose. Yet that doesn't mean that initial responsibility for putting things right should fall equally on everyone. Instead, I believe it's down to *us*, the members of the law enforcement profession, to start the reconciliation process—because we are the ones in the position of power.

In the current climate, it may be surprising to hear that many of us have already taken steps to do so, embracing reform rather than rejecting it. In a cruel irony, Dallas Police Chief David Brown, who has worked hard and effectively around civil rights, community relations, violence reduction and transparency, is an example of what professional policing can aspire to be. His leadership has seen a dramatic reduction in excessive force complaints, and the publication of

---

1. Christeson, B., Lee, B., Schaefer, S., Kass, D., & Messner-Zidell, S. (2008). School or the Streets: Crime and America's Dropout Crisis. Fight Crime: Invest in Kids, 1–12

information about (increasingly rare) officer-involved shootings in Dallas—the kind of openness that can help re-establish trust.

"Police officers are guardians of this great democracy," he said during a news conference on Friday morning. "The freedom to protest, the freedom of speech, the freedom of expression—all freedoms we fight for, with our lives. It's what makes us who we are as Americans. And so we risk our lives for those rights. So we won't militarize our policing standards, but we will do it in a much safer way every time, like we chose to do it this time."

"We ought to think that we are one of the leaves of a tree, and the tree is all humanity," Pablo Casals, the Spanish musician, once wrote. "We cannot live without the others, without the tree."

Reflecting on these words after the tragic events of last week, I tried to focus on potential solutions, rather than the divisive language and anger—understandable though much of it is.

I found hope in some sane, unifying voices. For example, in this article by Seth Stoughton, a law professor at the University of South Carolina, he stated that "despite their very different perspectives, participants in both movements [Black Lives Matter and Blue Lives Matter] have essentially the same concerns."

And Van Jones, the activist, attorney and author, explained in this video that both law enforcement and Black Lives Matter share many of the same feelings, that it's open season on them.

The entertainer Trevor Noah made a similar point:

"If you're pro-Black Lives Matter, you're assumed to be anti-police, and if you're pro-police, then you surely hate black people, when in reality, *you can be pro-cop and pro-black,* which is what we should *all* be."

These voices of moderation and understanding are right. We as law enforcement professionals have an opportunity—as well as the responsibility—to find the common ground necessary to reconcile, to listen and to change policing for the better. It won't be easy, but we *have* to do this to heal our country's wounds and save lives.

Linda Holtzman is Professor Emeritus at Webster University. Her work focuses on diversity, activism, media misinformation, stereotypes, and human rights. **Leon Sharpe** is Adjunct Faculty at the Webster University School of Communications and principal of The Praxis Group—a strategic consulting firm that specializes in building organizational capacity, developing effective leaders, training high-performance teams, leveraging workforce diversity, and managing institutional change.

Theories and Constructs of Race
Linda Holtzman and Leon Sharpe

Key Terms

assimilation: Assimilation is the process through which newcomers (children entering a new school, families moving to a new neighborhood, and immigrants arriving in the United States) adjust to a situation by deciding how much of their old culture and habits they want to give up and how much of their new culture they want to absorb. In the context of immigration to the United States, this process includes surface and deep culture: anything from clothing, food, and language to child-rearing, dating and marriage practices, and treatment of elders in the community. Throughout U.S. history, there have been diverse waves of voluntary immigrants and refugees. Other groups have involuntarily become part of the United States through the violent conquest of their land (Mexicans, American Indians) or violent enslavement (African Americans). In order to be considered true Americans, these newcomers were expected to assimilate. The unspoken rules of assimilation were that the closer the immigrants were to existing U.S. citizens of European heritage in terms of skin color and ability to blend in, the more likely they were able to make active choices about the degree to which they wanted to reject their former culture in favor of their new culture. The more they assimilated, and the more their skin color allowed them to assimilate, the more they were entitled to the same privileges as the Europeans who came before them. Most immigrant groups of color, including Africans, Asians, and American Indians, were not entitled to citizenship until decades—sometimes a century—after newer European immigrants because the color of their skin was not considered sufficiently white. Because of this and due to the nature of racial separation in the United States, assimilation was available unequally to whites and people of color, depending on the time of their arrival to the United States.

critical race theory (CRT): An academic discipline that analyzes race in the United States through the lens of power and law. CRT is based on several core tenets, including the permanence of racism, critique of liberalism, whiteness as property, interest convergence, intersection of racism with other forms of oppression, centrality of personal experience, and use of the counternarrative as an explanatory and analytical tool.

internalized racism: The process by which people of color take in negative messages of overt and covert racism, superiority, and inferiority, and apply those messages to themselves and others in ways that are self-destructive rather than self-affirming. Internalized racism, which is always involuntary, is the direct by-product of historical and ongoing racial targeting.

internalized white supremacy: This term has begun to be used more frequently since the late twentieth century. Antiracist activists and scholars have a few different, but highly compatible concepts defining to whom the term is applicable. In general, internalized white supremacy is the assumption of white superiority in intelligence, in achievement, and in the centrality in U.S. culture by individuals who are often unaware of its powerful existence. People who internalize this dimension of white supremacy are not generally the same people whose outright racial hatred counts them among the members of the Ku Klux Klan and other racial hate groups. In fact, these people are often shocked and alarmed as they investigate this phenomenon and discover that they have been operating on the assumptions that the tenets of white superiority are "the truth." These messages strongly presume the centrality of European Americans to the individual achievement and success in the United States and to worldwide recognition in literature, science, world peace, and other fields.

meta-narrative: A comprehensive "story" of history and knowledge that unifies and simplifies the culture and value of a group or nation. When meta-narratives are applied to nations, they frequently are used to explain and justify the existing power structure.

racial discrimination: An individual act or an institutional pattern that results in the unequal treatment of members of a targeted racial group. Racial discrimination is an *action* or *behavior* that may result from conscious or unconscious *beliefs* (stereotypes) about a racial group or from predetermined *feelings* (prejudices) toward that group.

racialize: To see or describe something from a racial perspective; to emphasize race or to make something seem racial. For example, in the early twentieth century; Jews were racialized in Europe, Russia, and most of the United States. Today, in much of the United States, Judaism is regarded as a religion rather than a race. Another example occurred in the aftermath of the 9/11 terrorist attacks with the widespread racialization of Muslims and people of Middle Eastern descent.

racism: A system of institutionalized power that operates through overt or covert policies that favor white people and are biased against people of color. Racism continues to exist today in the hiring practices of some private businesses, government agencies, hospitals, universities, and so on, even where there are policies that clearly state they will not discriminate. Despite such policies, these institutions often devise strategies and engage in practices that result in the virtual elimination of people of color from their pools of potential candidates. Another commonly used approach to understanding racism is based on the comparative analysis of levels of social access—to quality education, jobs, promotions, and other opportunities—between white people and people of color.

schema: A mental model or pattern of thinking that influences the way we organize and simplify our knowledge of the world around us.

white privilege: A set of unearned advantages and opportunities created by racism that are often far more visible to people of color than they are to whites. Despite the pervasiveness of racism in the history and current structures of the United States, many white people believe that racism was eradicated by the late twentieth century and that individual achievement and success are based solely on individual intelligence, motivation, and hard work. As a result of this type of misinformation and socialization, many whites believe that all of their successes are built exclusively on their own talent, skills, merit, and hard work. In fact, in many small and large ways, whites have access to different opportunities and are treated differently than people of color, giving them an often invisible boost to this success to which people of color do not have the same access. For example, white parents rarely need to think about the danger present for their sons at a mall or on the street if they are stopped by a police officer. Ample research and statistics indicate that young African American or Latino men are far more likely to be harassed, abused, and/or arrested by police than young white men. The privilege here is that white parents generally only need to think about this danger if their son will be in an area in which there is high crime. But the danger there is potential criminals, not the police. Whites are rarely asked to speak on behalf of their whole race or justify the criminal activity or failure of other whites, while people of color are frequently asked to do all of these things. White privilege allows whites the luxury and advantage of living in a world where their personal worth, rightness, and personhood are continually validated in ways that do not apply for people of color (Olson, n.d).

white supremacy: White supremacy is typically thought of as the extremist views and actions of hate groups such as the Ku Klux Klan, White Citizens Council, and Aryan Brotherhood. This definition of white supremacy is the categorical belief and the actions based on the belief that, in every way, whites are superior to people of color. Often Jews and sometimes Catholics are also included in the category of so-called inferior people. Many of these hate groups are responsible for what we call "hate crimes," in which these "inferior" people are subjected to violence, torture, murder, and destruction of property, which are seen as justified by white supremacist individuals and organizations that believe that these "inferior" groups will destroy America if not eliminated.

There is another type of white supremacy that is more subtle, yet equally insidious in the way it pervades the minds of individuals and permeates the culture. This type assumes the dominance and superiority of white culture as reflected in the academic curricula of U.S. history and literature and science, in which the contributions of white people are more visible and valued more greatly than the contributions of people of color. In this scenario, hate and hate crimes are not central; however, white people are seen as at the center of U.S. culture. "And so you see that white centrality, especially in the way that the culture, the dominant white culture, fights for the right to tell the story, not only of America, but of the world in ways that leave white people at the center and are based on assumptions of the superiority of white people—even if as a culture we've renounced overt segregation and discrimination" (Wells 2013). By this definition, white supremacy is not always based on intent or on individual or even institutional racial hate or bigotry. However, if we look at the demographics of wealth and poverty, educational achievement and level of attainment, and job status, to name a few, we will be able to predict who is most likely to be at the top and who is most likely to be at the bottom, with race as the central factor of these predictions. Then we know that the system is infested with structural racism and the messages involve white supremacy.

Theories and Constructs of Race

The shifting meaning of race throughout U.S. history provides important clues to its definition. It is not biological, nor is it based primarily on skin color. It is not necessarily based on ethnicity nor is it based on country of origin. Rather, race is constructed socially, culturally, politically, and economically. "Various racial categories have been created or changed to meet the emerging economic and social needs of white United States culture. Racial categories artificially emphasize the relatively small external physical differences among people and leave room for the creation of false notions of mental, emotional, and intellectual differences as well" (Adams, Bell, and Griffin 1997, 83).

While race itself is fiction, the consequences of racism are a historical and contemporary fact of American life. "Racism is based on the concept of whiteness—an identity concept invented and enforced by power and violence. Whiteness is a constantly shifting boundary separating those who are entitled to have certain privileges from those whose exploitation and vulnerability to violence is justified by their not being white" (Kivel 1996, 17). The historical mutability of race is significant because of how it has been used as a marker of group identity and a means of access to privilege in this country and elsewhere. The possession of whiteness represents a valued status that confers upon its owners a set of exclusive citizenship rights (Lipsitz 1998).

The centrality of race in our society is one of the core tenets of **critical race theory (CRT)**. CRT emerged originally in the 1980s as an outgrowth of critical legal studies (Crenshaw et al. 1995; Delgado and Stefancic 2001; Taylor, Gillborn, and Ladson-Billings 2009). Over the years, CRT has expanded to other disciplines such as education. Its ideas and methodologies have also been applied in other areas of focus such as LatCrit, AsianCrit, TribalCrit, FemCrit, and QueerCrit. One of the key concepts of critical race theory is that racism is a core component of the systems and structures of power in our nation. Racial inequity is so deeply embedded in our institutional practices, so integral to our interpersonal relationships and individual attitudes, so inextricably woven into the warp and woof of everyday life, that it has become a permanent feature of the American experience. Therefore, racism, in all its manifestations, must be continuously critiqued and challenged.

Not surprisingly, foundational elements of racial inequity often go unexamined, underanalyzed, or misrepresented by the mainstream media: "Specific media frames select out limited aspects of an issue in order to make it salient for mass communication, a selectivity usually promoting a narrow reading of that issue.... A particular frame structures the thinking process and shapes what people see or do not see, in important societal settings" (Feagin 2009, 27). A 2007 study of print media coverage of racial disparities in health care, education, early child development, and employment determined that because racism is framed, for the most part, as being rooted in interpersonal relationships between individuals or among groups of individuals, the systemic nature of race-based power dynamics is rarely reported. In examining the explanatory frames of 140 news articles published by major outlets in eight metropolitan areas nationwide, the study found that articles

> provided clear and unambiguous accounts of how racism can exist in
> a number of institutions and were easy for a wide audience to identify
> as racist. However, the dominance of such stories reinforces the notion
> that racism is primarily about individual actions rather than embedded
> in social structures. Furthermore, overt and blatant acts of racism were
> framed as aberrant occurrences that were unfortunate, but did not
> effectively challenge the perception that the United States has largely
> transcended its racial past. (O'Neil 2009)

The mischaracterization of contemporary racial oppression as interpersonal and episodic gets in the way of our ability to come to grips with its fundamental nature, which is structural and systemic. Young people today have grown up and come of age during an era when *legally sanctioned* racial segregation of public facilities appears to be a thing of the past. Overt acts of racial violence, although they still occur, are less common than they were prior to the civil rights era. Youth of color and their white counterparts form friendships and interact socially across racial lines more freely today than at any other time in America's past. Yet despite the popular notion that we now live in a "postracial" society, racial injustice continues to thrive in the United States. Glaring racial disparities continue to exist in education, employment, healthcare, housing, bank lending policies, the criminal justice and penal system, household income, household net worth, and a host of other areas. Thus, what has been referred to as America's "pathology of denial" about race (Leary 2006) impedes our ability to develop systemic solutions that will lead to the dismantling of the **racialized** institutional foundations of our country. It prevents us from devising strategies that are structurally transformative.

The Social and Psychological Impact of Race

The continuous racial targeting of people of color and the privileging of whites, along with misinformation about race passed along from one generation to the next and reinforced through the media, has imbued people of all races with a distorted sense of personal and group identity. Not surprisingly, given the centuries of racial stereotyping and negative messaging directed at people of color, research indicates that a majority of white Americans continue to have strong feelings of racial bias (Banaji and Greenwald 2013, 169–188; Greenwald and Krieger 2006). Many white people in the United States are socialized to regard their race as representing not only the majority group but also the societal norm—the cultural standard and benchmark for what it means to be American. According to one writer, "For many white people, the idea that we have racial identities is difficult to come to terms with. We usually see ourselves simply as people. Whiteness, by virtue of its status as the dominant social position, is unmarked. It is relatively easy for white persons to go through life never thinking about their own racial identity. Whiteness functions as the normative ideal against which other people are categorized and judged" (Kaufman 2001).

This illusory standard of a white societal norm reinforces the notion that people of color are not merely different but also deficient. Studies indicate that, despite a decline in overt expressions of racial bigotry, a large percentage of white Americans continue to consciously or unconsciously regard white identity as positive and black identity as negative (Schmidt and Nosek 2010). The unconscious belief among whites in the superiority of their own racial group relative to blacks and other people of color is a form of *implicit bias*—learned social stereotypes that are some times triggered automatically in individuals without their awareness (Greenwald and Banaji 1995). There is evidence to indicate that implicit racial bias exists in children as young as six years old and endures through adulthood (Baron and Banaji 2006). Implicit bias has the capacity to influence people's judgments in regard to how they think about and treat individuals who are racially different from them even when they openly express non-prejudicial views; "to characterize the nature of an individual's prejudice correctly, one must consider both explicit racial attitudes as well as implicit, automatic biases" (Son Hing et al. 2008).

The espousing of racial openness and egalitarianism while simultaneously harboring negative racial attitudes is prevalent in contemporary society. The acting out of biased beliefs through jokes, slurs, and other racial actions and commentary is less likely to occur openly in what sociologist Joe R. Feagin refers to as the *frontstage* of public, professional, and mixed-race gatherings where a diverse range of people is present. Yet such behaviors occur quite frequently in *backstage* settings among friends and close acquaintances where whites with negative feelings toward people of color can comfortably express their beliefs without fear of being judged or marginalized socially (Feagin 2009, 184). A study analyzing more than 600 personal journals from college students throughout the nation revealed thousands of instances of racially bigoted behavior such as name-calling, inappropriate racial humor, and references to stereotypes. Although often characterized as innocent fun, such actions reinforce racial polarization and antagonism (Feagin 2009, 185–190).

In addition, the toleration of duplicitous frontstage/backstage behavior contributes to the perpetuation of an American societal norm that enables schools, employers, public service providers, real estate brokers, law enforcement agencies, and a host of other institutions to publicly embrace equal opportunity policies while privately engaging in practices that deny equal access and fair treatment to members of racially targeted groups. While many white individuals are overtly racist, millions of others benefit from institutionally sanctioned racial privilege in ways that are often invisible to them. When Linda [Holtzman] wrote earlier of her personal story, she discussed the anti-Semitism her grandparents faced in Russia and as new immigrants to the United States. But because they and their descendants would ultimately be considered white, they were allowed to find work and housing and education from which African Americans and Japanese Americans were prohibited. Without ever initiating or participating in one overtly hateful act, they benefited from racism.

Misinformation about race and identity also contributes adversely to the socialization of people of color in the United States. The myth of racial inferiority and superiority has been upheld not only by physical violence and discriminatory policies but also by the psychological violence conveyed through the stereotyping and racist messaging to which people of color, beginning early in childhood, are continuously exposed. In the interest of dominant-group hegemony, false notions of a race-based hierarchy are promulgated relentlessly through virtually every mainstream institution in our society. "Oppressed people come to embody in their very being the negations imposed on them and thus, in the reproduction of their lives, harbor a tendency to contribute to the perpetuation of their own oppression" (Outlaw 2005, 14).

People of color in America have always had to wage a battle against **internalized racism**, a condition that can cause an individual to assume self-deprecating attitudes and engage in self-destructive behaviors that reflect the traumatizing effects of racial targeting. When people are regularly subjected to the physical and psychological abuse of overt and covert racial oppression, they sometimes respond by re-enacting that abuse on themselves and other members of their racial group. When Leon [Sharpe] wrote earlier about the stories he heard his adult family members telling with such vividness and ironic humor, he was speaking of the unremitting conversations of self-empowerment and cultural affirmation that many African Americans draw upon as a source of healing strength and collective power to counteract the insidious impact of internalized racism. Such stories have been as much a part of the black resistance movement in American history as any civil rights march, economic boycott, or slave uprising.

Internalized racism, which is always involuntary, is a direct by-product of historical and ongoing racial targeting. It works in many ways. For instance, social psychologist Claude M. Steele has advanced the theory of *stereotype threat* to explain the extent to which a person's performance can be detrimentally affected by the psychological triggering of negative stereotypes assigned to one's social group identity (Steele and Aronson 1995; Steele 1997; Steele 2010). Laura Padilla has written about the manner in which many Latinos accept the negative stereotypes directed at their own group and thus question the qualifications of other Latinos who are successful. She refers to this phenomenon as *envidia* or intragroup jealousy and regards it as a clear example of how behaviors resulting from internalized racism can sabotage communities of color (Padilla 2001). Social researcher Dr. Joy DeGruy (formerly Leary) posits the concept of intergenerational trauma resulting from what she has termed *post-traumatic slave syndrome*, a consequence of multigenerational oppression of Africans and their descendants resulting from centuries of chattel slavery followed by decades of institutionalized racism that continues to inflict emotional injury (Leary 2006). In a similar vein, social worker Maria Yellow Horse Brave Heart, through her research and clinical work examining manifestations of intergenerational trauma among Native Americans, has focused on diagnosing and treating what she identifies as *historical unresolved grief* (Brave Heart 2000). Internalized racism among people of color and implicit racial bias among whites are unhealthy psychosocial reactions to the toxic power of racial targeting. Because of their detrimental effects, they must be actively addressed and rigorously interrupted whenever possible. Nevertheless, the injury they cause can only be fully healed as racism in our society is eliminated.

The Science and Pseudoscience of Race

Is race a scientifically verifiable concept? Does racial difference actually exist among human beings? According to biologists, a race is a distinct evolutionary lineage within a species that is sharply defined by measurable genetic differences. Genetic differences between populations are necessary but not sufficient to define race (Templeton 2002). Obviously, differences exist between populations within the human species. Members of what we regard as different racial groups have visibly diverse physical characteristics (skin color, hair texture, facial features). Thus, the question becomes, do diverse human populations exhibit sufficient differences at the genetic level to constitute a scientific basis for establishing the existence of separate races within our species?

A segment of the 2003 documentary *Race: The Power of Illusion* depicts a multiethnic group of students meeting with a DNA expert. They compare their skin colors, submit blood and DNA samples, and then discuss their thoughts as to which of their classmates share the closest genetic similarity with them. Most, if not all, of them assume that the students within their own "racial" group will be the closest to them genetically. When their DNA is analyzed, the students are surprised to learn that their assumptions are wrong. The white students do not share the same genetic traits with one another, nor do the African American, Latino, or Asian students. In fact, what they all discover is that, according to the scientific evidence upon which the film is based, there is just as much genetic variation among people of the same so-called "race" as there is among people across racial populations (Gould 1981, 323; Lewontin 1970; Templeton 2002). Differences indeed exist among humans, but they are not racial.

Skin color, the most common visual cue that most of us use as a determinant of race, does not reflect extreme genetic difference, nor does it reflect a distinct evolutionary history. Diversity of skin color merely indicates the geographical adaptation of various populations as they migrated out of equatorial Africa and moved further north to regions where ultraviolet rays from the sun were less concentrated. Overexposure to certain UV rays can destroy folic acid in the body, thus having a detrimental effect on reproduction. In tropical regions, humans evolved with darker skin and large stores of melanin, which protects the body from the harmful effects of solar radiation. On the other hand, insufficient exposure to UV rays can impede the body's ability to produce vitamin D, thus preventing the absorption of calcium by the intestines. As some human populations migrated north and south into the temperate regions, their bodies gradually adapted by developing lighter skin complexions and the ability to tan so as to make optimum use of the available ultraviolet light. Difference in skin color among humans is nothing more than an indicator of the areas of the world to which one's ancestors migrated (Jablonski and Chaplin 2000; 2003). In short, there are no available data to support racial classifications or any form of social hierarchy based on racial or ethnic group membership (Cartmill 1998, 653).

So does that completely answer our question? Is race merely an optical illusion—a trick of the sun? No, it is much more complex than that. Lani Guinier writes, "If we think in categories and think about race only in one category, we conflate many different spheres of racial meaning. We fail to specify if we mean biological race, political race, historical race, or cultural race. We simplify race as a fixed category from which many people want to escape" (Guinier and Torres 2002, 4). Despite the scientific refutation of racial taxonomy as a legitimate means for biologically differentiating and categorizing diverse populations within the human species, it continues to endure as a reality in the social realm. "That race is a social construct rather than a biological fact does not minimize its impact on our lives ... racial distinctions have powerful social meaning with profound real-world consequences" (Croteau and Hoynes 1997, 138). Most people in our society have a sense of themselves as possessing a racial identity and belonging to a racial group. Various official forms and surveys continue to have checkboxes for designating one's race. Most people harbor conscious and unconscious stereotypes and biases about other racial groups in comparison with their own. People still laugh at racial humor, people still spout racial slurs, and those racial slurs still have the capacity to sting and enrage. People still live in racially segregated communities. People are still denied jobs and promotions because of race. People are still discriminated against economically, incarcerated disproportionately, and educated less effectively because of race. People still attack and kill people because of race.

Stories and Counterstories: Decoding the Master Script

The identity and relationship dynamics of race are so pervasive in our lives today that it feels as though current notions of race have existed since the beginning of historical time. Yet that is far from true. Prior to the fifteenth century, the idea of racial divisions among humans was of minimal significance and had little impact on people's interactions with one another (Vaughan 1995). The early European aggression and hostility toward the indigenous people of Africa, Asia, and the Americas was driven by economic interests and justified primarily by a belief in the right of Christian nations such as Spain, Portugal, Great Britain, and the Netherlands to conquer any civilization and claim any land that was not under the sovereign domain of Christians.

Erecting a social construct with the epic staying power, counterrational robustness, and destructive force that has been exhibited by "race" over the centuries was not a brief or simple process. Our present-day concept of race is based on false ideas, myths, and fabrications that accumulated over the centuries to form a grand, sweeping story or **meta-narrative** to justify the exploitation of entire populations of human beings and the appropriation of their labor, land, natural resources, cultural artifacts, and intellectual property. The social construction of the American meta-narrative—the master script on race and racial hierarchy—has been formulated and upheld through an elaborate system of dehumanizing **schemas**. These racial schemas are mental models created through the telling and retelling of stories that reinforce the idea of a racial hierarchy with the white race at the top, other races beneath, and the black race at the very bottom. Such stories have been utilized to frame our history from a perspective that upholds the language, logic, and worldview of the dominant group and suppresses the language, logic, and worldviews of those who have been targeted for racial oppression.

Throughout our history, there have been an untold number of assaults on the humanness of people of color in the interest of white hegemony. These assaults prime, activate, and reinforce racial schemas and uphold the meta-narrative. They range from the creation of stereotypes and the passage of oppressive laws to the wholesale enslavement, colonization, and genocide of entire populations. In addition to attacks on life, land, and liberty, Africans, Asians, Latinos, Native Americans, and Pacific Islanders have been subject to relentless assaults on their linguistic and cultural traditions, their communal and kinship bonds, their ancestral ties, and their spiritual beliefs.

We have learned that many of the stories we have been told about race are demonstrably false. Yet if those stories go uncontested, we will accept them as truth because of the way we have been socialized. One of the strategies for challenging these stories is through the development of counterstories that refute the assumptions upon which the original stories are based. A counterstory (also referred to as a counternarrative) is a tool utilized by critical race theorists as a means of contesting the race meta-narrative. Counterstories reframe the dehumanizing schemas by revealing additional facts, examining the same facts from different perspectives, personalizing the experiences of the targeted, humanizing the voices of the oppressed, and critically analyzing the misinformation that the dominant group has heretofore represented as unimpeachable.

Let us turn our attention now to an example of how a critical counternarrative can be used to challenge a dehumanizing schema. One of the prevailing beliefs about America's past is that the indigenous people of the Western Hemisphere were primitive, uncivilized, and underdeveloped, with little or no understanding of science and technology prior to the arrival of Europeans from more sophisticated and advanced civilizations. This is a schema—a pattern of thinking that influences the way we organize and simplify our knowledge of the world around us. Let us call it the "primitive people" schema. This schema about American Indians has been repeated in various versions so often over the years that many people accept it as historical fact even though it is just a story—a story told by one group about another. The false beliefs based on this schema can be activated in our minds by a variety of stereotypical words or images, such as "redskins" or "tomahawks," which have become embedded in our popular culture. The schema is dehumanizing because it perpetuates the myth that American Indians were simple people of inferior culture and intelligence. Moreover, this "primitive people" schema contributes to the global meta-narrative of racial hierarchy by implying that, despite the brutality suffered at the hands of whites, the Indians were better off because they had the opportunity to be exposed to more "civilized" people with superior science and technology.

In reality, the notion of Native American technology as limited is grounded in Eurocentric cultural assumptions and misconceptions. If we can acknowledge that simple fact, then we can begin to craft a counternarrative that gets us closer to the truth. Native American science and technology appear to have been highly developed within the context of the Native American social, cultural, and ecological worldview. Conversely, given what we know of the adverse environmental impact that some European technology has had on the North American continent and the rest of the planet, it seems neither appropriate nor accurate to regard European technology as particularly advanced or superior. From the vantage point of twenty-first-century hindsight, the early encounters between the people of the Americas and the people of Europe could more accurately be described as the interrupted development of the technologies of one civilization in service to the overdevelopment of the technologies of another. In other words, it was a missed opportunity for mutually constructive technological synergy. Had the prevailing paradigm of the time been one of cultural reciprocity rather than cultural conquest, it is conceivable that, today, earth-dwellers of all cultures—and all species, for that matter—might be the grateful beneficiaries of the best of both technological frameworks....

Summary

Students in elementary school and high school in the United States receive limited and often distorted information about our country's racial history. Most of us learned primarily about the immigrant experiences of Europeans in the New World and only bits and pieces about the enslavement of Africans and the conquest of American Indians and Mexicans. We have rarely learned about the immigration experiences of Puerto Ricans, Cubans, Vietnamese, Chinese, or Japanese. Often the information that we get is limited or glossed over to eliminate elements of racial cruelty, violence, or suppression. Sometimes the information that we get is taught to us as African American history or Asian American history—as if it is something completely separate from American history. At best, perhaps we have been taught that while there are unfortunate aspects of racism (slavery) and conquest (American Indians) in our history, there have been many efforts to right these wrongs so that racially the United States now has a level playing field in which people of all races have equal life chances. Rarely is there any analysis of the connection between individual acts of racial hatred and the institutional or structural racism in laws or private businesses that discriminate in housing, health care, education, and employment. And seldom is there any mention of the individuals, groups, and movements that have worked to undo the policies and effects of racism.

There are hard facts in U.S. history. There have been times when dehumanizing a whole group of people has merged with individual acts of hatred and with laws and policies that promote violence and oppression, causing many, many people to die because of racism. While the omission or revision of this part of our history may be intended to keep children from learning such painful parts of our past, the consequences of the distortion of U.S. racial history are far-reaching. "Education as socialization influences students simply to accept the rightness of our society. American history textbooks overtly tell us to be proud of America. The more schooling, the more socialization, and the more likely the individual will conclude that America is good" (Loewen 1995, 307). Education that does not lie is not equivalent to socializing students to believe that America is "bad" rather than "good." Rather it calls for teaching students about the complexities of our stories and how to make inquiries and draw conclusions that allow for critical thinking and autonomous decision making.

The combination of our personal experiences, our formal education, and our exposure to entertainment media constitutes our socialization about race. If this socialization tells us that all is well racially and that everyone has equal life chances regardless of race or ethnicity, we are likely to see any racial problem or failure as strictly the fault of an individual. If we believe that there are no racial barriers to employment, then we will see unemployment among people of color as lazy or slovenly. If we believe that education is equitable for everyone, we will not be open to discuss or vote for remedies to address defects in the educational system that have an adverse impact on students of color. The lump sum of these distortions can be dehumanizing for everyone.

...Acclaimed writer and activist Audre Lorde wrote, "In our work and in our living, we must recognize that difference is a reason for celebration and growth, rather than a reason for destruction." While our history regarding race may be painful, we must learn it in much the same way that Germans must learn about the Holocaust: to understand our part in it, to understand its impact on the present, to learn how to act on its contemporary implications, and to ensure that it will never happen again. Past history cannot be changed. It can only be rediscovered, reexamined, and revealed. Presenting counternarratives is an essential stage of that revelatory process. But it is only the beginning. We not only have to tell the counterstories, we have to live them. It is only through the liberatory cycle of continuous collective action, personal reflection, honest dialogue, and more action that we can transform our society, purge the toxic racist strains from the American meta-narrative, and put a process in motion that will enable future generations to write it anew.

Bibliography

Adams, Maurianne, Lee Anne Bell, and Pat Griffin, eds. 1997. *Teaching for Diversity and Social Justice: A Sourcebook.* New York: Routledge.

Banaji, Mahzarin R., and Anthony G. Greenwald. 2013. *Blindspot: Hidden Biases of Good People.* New York: Delacorte Press.

Baron, Andrew S., and Mahzarin Banaji. 2006. "The Development of Implicit Attitudes: Evidence of Race Evaluations from Ages 6 and 10 and Adulthood." *Psychological Science* 17, no. 1: 53–58.

Brave Heart, MariaYellow Horse. 2000. "Wakiksuyapi: Carrying the Historical Trauma of the Lakota." *Tulane Studies in Social Welfare* 21–22: 245–266.

Cartmill, Matt. 1998. "The Status of Race Concept in Physical Anthropology." *American Anthropologist* (New Series) 100, no. 3: 651–660.

Crenshaw, Kimberle, Neil T. Gotanda, Gary Peller, and Kendall Thomas, eds. 1995. *Critical Race Theory: The Key Writings That Formed the Movement.* New York: The New Press.

Croteau, David, and William Hoynes. 1997. *Media/Society: Industries, Images, and Audiences.* Thousand Oaks, CA: Pine Forge Press.

Delgado, Richard, and Jean Stefancic. 2001. *Critical Race Theory: An Introduction.* New York: New York University Press.

Feagin. Joe R. 2009. *The White Racial Frame: Centuries of Racial Framing and Counter-Framing.* New York: Routledge.

Gould, Stephen Jay. 1981. *The Mismeasure of Man.* New York: W. W. Norton.

Greenwald, Anthony G., and Linda H. Krieger. 2006. "Implicit Bias: Scientific Foundations." *California Law Review* 94, no. 4.

Greenwald, Anthony G., and Mahzarin Banaji. 1995. "Implicit Social Cognition: Attitudes, Self-Esteem, and Stereotypes." *Psychological Review* 1: 4–27.

Guinier, Lani, and Gerald Torres. 2002. *The Miner's Canary: Enlisting Race, Resisting Power, Transforming Democracy.* Cambridge, MA: Harvard University Press.

Jablonski, Nina G., and George Chaplin. 2000. "The Evolution of Human Skin Colorization." *Journal of Human Evolution* 39(1): 57–106.

———. 2003. "Skin Deep." *Scientific American,* 13, no. 2 (August): 72–79.

Kaufman, Cynthia. 2001. "A User's Guide to White Privilege." *Radical Philosophy Review* 4, no. 1/2: 30–38.

Kivel, Paul. 1996. *Uprooting Racism: How White People Can Work for Racial Justice.* Gabriola Island. BC: New Society.

Leary, Joy DeGruy. 2006. *Post-Traumatic Slave Syndrome: America's Legacy of Enduring Injury and Healing.* Milwaukie, OR: Uptone Press.

Lewontin, Richard C. 1970. "Further Remarks on Race and the Genetics of Intelligence." *Bulletin of the Atomic Scientists* 26(5): 23–25.

Lipsitz, George, ed. 1998. *The Possessive Investment in Whiteness: How White People Profit from Identity Politics.* Philadelphia: Temple University Press.

Loewen, James W. 1995. *Lies My Teachers Told Me: Everything Your American History Textbook Got Wrong.* New York: Touchstone.

Olson, Joan. (n.d.) "The Four Faces of Racism." Unpublished handout adapted from Cultural Bridges Training. Posted in the compilation *We're All In It Together* by North American Students of Co-operation (NASCO). http://kalamazoo.coop/sites/default/filesWe're%20all%20in%20it%20together.pdf.

O'Neil, Moira. 2009. *Invisible Structures of Opportunity: How Media Depictions of Race Trivialize Issues of Diversity and Disparity.* Washington, DC: FrameWorks Institute.

Outlaw, Lucius T. 2005. *Critical Social Theory in the Interests of Black Folks.* Lanham, MD: Rowman & Littlefield.

Padilla, Laura M. 2001. "But You're Not a Dirty Mexican": Internalized Oppression, Latinos & Law. *Texas Hispanic Journal of Law & Policy* 7: 1.

Schmidt, Kathleen, and Brian A. Nosek. 2010. "Implicit (and Explicit) Racial Attitudes Barely Changed During the Campaign and Early Presidency of Barack Obama." *Journal of Experimental Social Psychology* 46: 308–314.

Son Hing, Leanne S., Greg A. Chun-Yang, Leah K. Hamilton, and Mark P. Zanna. 2008. "A Two-Dimensional Model That Employs Explicit and Implicit Attitudes to Characterize Prejudice." *Journal of Personality and Social Psychology* 94(6): 971–987.

Steele, Claude M. 1997. "A Threat in the Air: How Stereotypes Shape Intellectual Identity and Performance." *American Psychologist* 52: 613–629.

———. 2010. *Whistling Vivaldi: And Other Clues to How Stereotypes Affect Us.* New York: W. W. Norton.

Steele, Claude M., and Joshua Aronson. 1995. "Stereotype Threat and the Intellectual Test Performance of African Americans." *Journal of Personality and Social Psychology* 69(5): 797–811.

Taylor, Edward, David Gilborn, and Gloria Ladson-Billings, eds. 2009. *Foundations of Critical Race Theory in Education.* New York: Routledge.

Templeton, Alan R. 2002. "Out of Africa Again and Again." *Nature* 416: 45–51.

Vaughan, Alden T. 1995. *Roots of American Racism: Essays on the Colonial Experience.* New York: Oxford University Press.

Wells, Kathleen. 2013. "Prof. Robert Jensen Discusses Racism, White Supremacy and White Privilege (Part 2)." *The Blog/HuffPost Black Voices.* www.huffington post.com/kathleen-wells/prof-robert-jensen-discus_b_2500184.html.

Haiming Liu is a Professor of Asian American studies in the Ethnic and Women's Studies Department of California State Polytechnic University, Pomona. His most recent book focuses on the relationship between Chinese culture, American culture, and food. Lianlian Lin is a Professor of Management and Human Resources at the College of Business Administration at California State Polytechnic University, Pomona whose research focuses on the intersection of culture and business.

Food, Culinary Identity, and Transnational Culture: Chinese Restaurant Business in Southern California
Haiming Liu and Lianlian Lin

On a Thursday afternoon in November 1985, General Lee's, the oldest restaurant in Los Angeles Chinatown, was permanently closed. Originally called Man Jen Low (Ten Thousand Treasure House), the restaurant dated back to 1878 and had hosted many Hollywood celebrities and California dignities in its peak days.[1] The closure of this landmark restaurant marked significant changes in Chinese American communities that have occurred since the 1965 immigration reform. When a new wave of Chinese immigrants arrived, they brought in new tastes, created new businesses, and built new communities. Suburban Chinese neighborhoods emerged in Monterey Park and a host of San Gabriel Valley cities where thousands of Chinese restaurants have now congregated. Authentic Chinese food has replaced Americanized dishes as the mainstream in Los Angeles Chinatown and in these new suburbs.[2] Cookery and the menus of many contemporary Chinese restaurants now closely follow the culinary trends of Asia. Riding on the immigrant boom, the Southern California Chinese restaurant business began a new chapter in Chinese American history.

Food is a meaningful aspect of Chinese American experience. This article explores how the restaurant business reflects the social background, lifestyle, and ethnic identity of the post-1965 Chinese immigrants. In food and restaurant experience, we see how transnational culture is deeply ingrained in the contemporary Chinese American community. Instead of wholesale assimilation, post-1965 Chinese immigrants have selectively maintained some of their native cultural traditions such as food. With restaurants, grocery stores, and ethnic strip malls visibly congregated and rooted in the San Gabriel Valley, the transnational and multicultural identity of Chinese Americans is no longer an abstract idea but a solid and tangible reality. Food culture of contemporary Chinese Americans brings out a seemingly paradoxical outcome of immigrant adaptation. It is not only possible but also increasingly preferred for many immigrants to maintain their Chinese ethnicity while becoming American. Furthermore, the significance of the Chinese restaurant business goes beyond Chinese American experience. It shows how American food history is a story of new immigrants bringing in new tastes and new diets, adding and enriching American culinary culture rather than a melting-pot tale of different ethnic groups assimilating into one dominant culture. Multiculturalism has made food choices continually expand in this nation of immigrants.

Chinese Restaurants before 1965

Restaurant entrepreneurs and cooks were part of the early Chinese migration flow. Canton Restaurant in San Francisco, the first Chinese restaurant in America, was established as early as 1849. By 1856, a San Francisco business directory listed five restaurants and thirty-eight grocery stores among eighty-eight Chinese businesses.[3] In 1900, there only were two or three Chinese restaurants in Los Angeles, frequented almost exclusively by Chinese. By 1910, however, there were at least fifteen Chinese restaurants. Many white American customers "discovered that Chinese food was quite good and not at all poisonous as some had imagined." Several of these Chinese restaurants were outside Chinatown, and a few were in downtown Los Angeles.[4] Restaurant business was one of the earliest economic enterprises pursued by pioneer Chinese immigrants. More important, during the Exclusion period (1882–1943), when the racial environment forced many early Chinese immigrants out of their skilled occupations and channeled them into menial service jobs, restaurant occupations became one of the few available and limited employment opportunities. Living under the shadow of Chinese exclusion laws, Chinese immigrants could also form partnerships to start restaurant businesses with relatively little start-up money and claim merchant status, as those laws permitted only merchant immigrants to enter. Though operating restaurants required long hours and hard labor, it did not pose a direct competition to white laborers. Chinese immigrants recognized the potential of the restaurant business in a racially stratified society.

When Chinese cuisine established a niche in the American food market, restaurant businesses began to provide important hiring opportunities for the Chinese. The 1920 census indicates that of the 45,614 Chinese employed in the United States, 26,488 of them worked in restaurants and laundries.[5] In the 1930s, 6 percent of the Chinese adult males in California and 20 to 25 percent of Chinese adult males in East Coast cities worked in the restaurant business.[6] According to a 1938 report by the Oriental Division of the U.S. Employment Service in San Francisco, 90 percent of Chinese youth were service workers, mainly in the culinary trades. While the defense industry was in great need of professional employees, Chinese college graduates were passed by. In 1941, 5,000 young Chinese in San Francisco had no future worthy of their education but seemed destined to wash dishes, carry trays, cut meat, and dry fish in Chinatown.[7] In Chinese American experience, the restaurant job is not only an ethnic label but also an American-made and self-employed occupation. By the late 1940s, there were about 4,300 Chinese restaurants in the continental Untied States. Seven percent of the American population frequented Chinese restaurants. Ten years later the number of Chinese restaurants had increased to 4,500, with over 20 percent of Americans frequenting Chinese restaurants. In 1959, New York City alone had about 750 Chinese restaurants.[8] By then, Chinese restaurant food had become thoroughly Americanized. Neither the customers nor the restaurant operators cared if the food was genuinely Chinese or not. Chop suey was a familiar name when Americans ate out. The expectation of the clientele was that Chinese restaurants would provide fast and cheap Americanized food like chop suey, chow mein, or egg flower soup. More sophisticated Chinese menus would include more expensive dishes like *wu dip har* (butterfly shrimp) or *tim suen yu* (sweet and sour fish).[9] From the late nineteenth century to the 1970s, Chinatowns in the metropolitan cities always attracted tourists and visitors who were interested in Chinese food. While antique stores, furniture houses, and gift shops also attracted tourists, restaurants with Americanized Chinese food were the anchor businesses. Relying on tourist business, Chinatowns looked like ethnic "theme parks" in the eyes of many Americans.

Chinatown Turning Chinese

When the Immigration and Nationality Act of 1965 ended the former U.S. immigration policy based on race and nationalities and provided 20,000 immigration quotas to every country annually, Chinese immigrants quickly took advantage of the new policy. Similar to the old immigrants, post-1965 Chinese immigrants followed a chain migration pattern. Husband or wife, or both, arrived first and then sponsored their children, parents, and siblings. Soon family networks expanded as relatives, in-laws, and friends followed. Since the new immigration act favored family reunification, the Chinese population grew rapidly. Between 1965 and 1984, an estimated 419,373 Chinese entered the United States—almost as many as the 426,000 Chinese who had come here between 1849 and 1930.[10] Under the new immigration act, Chinese family networks and social relationship rebounded.

Post-1965 Chinese immigrants were far more diverse in their class and cultural background than the earlier immigrants had been. Many were educated professionals, engineers, technicians, or exchange students. Between 1950 and 1993, Taiwan sent 120,000 students to the United States, and fewer than 27,000 of them returned home after graduation.[11] From 1979 to 1989, mainland China sent about 80,000 graduate students and their spouses and children to the United States, and a majority of them stayed after graduation.[12] Whether they were from mainland China, Taiwan, or Hong Kong, post-1965 Chinese immigrants preferred residence destinations in metropolitan cities like New York, Los Angeles, or San Francisco, where they could find a Chinatown. Homesick immigrants probably missed Chinese food most among the many familiar commodities available in Chinatowns. To the new immigrants, Chinatown was not only a symbol of Chinese ethnicity but also a place that touched their cultural sensibilities. It gave them a sense of home.

Chinatown, as sociologist Min Zhou points out, also developed a structure of opportunities that would help channel immigrants into the larger American society.[13] Many newly arrived immigrants found temporary or stable jobs in Chinatown, especially in the restaurant business. Although the racial environment in American society was considerably improved in the 1960s, language barriers and lack of a U.S. college diploma or a professional license were still major obstacles to career success for some entrepreneurial and professional immigrants. The restaurant business continued to be one of the major economic enterprises available to the Chinese. Many new immigrants turned to the restaurant business for careers and job opportunities. According to Henry Tsai, "Chinese restaurants have gained a slight increase in the percentage of Chinese work force. The 0.8 percent increase between 1960 and 1970 was due mainly to the influx of new immigrants from Hong Kong, who were unable to find employment commensurate with their education, experience, or qualifications."[14] In the late 1960s, there were about 10,000 Chinese restaurants in the continental United States.[15] As a result, restaurant jobs are often the first work experience for many post-1965 Chinese immigrants.

Following the 1965 immigration reform, Chinatowns in San Francisco, Los Angeles, and New York experienced a heavy influx of new immigrants. In 1966, only one-fifth of the 42,000 Chinese residents in San Francisco actually lived in Chinatown. Thoroughly Americanized fourth-, third-, and second-generation Chinese Americans had dispersed to other sections or suburbs of the city. In contrast, an estimated 7,400 of the annual 20,000 newly arriving Chinese immigrants were expected to settle in San Francisco Chinatown.[16] The same was true of Los Angeles Chinatown. In 1959, only a few hundred of the 22,000 Chinese residents in the Los Angeles area lived in Chinatown. The majority had moved to the suburbs.[17] Ten years later, there were 15,000 Chinese residents in Los Angeles Chinatown. Many were new immigrants who did not speak English.[18] Following the influx of the new immigrants, rent and real estate prices quickly went up, especially after wealthy Chinese merchants from Hong Kong or Taiwan began to invest and purchase housing properties in Los Angeles Chinatown. When Chinatown was too crowded or too expensive to accommodate the needs of the growing new immigrant community, as in the situation in the Los Angeles area, Chinese immigrants began to move out of Chinatown into nearby cities, like Monterey Park. However, Chinatown remained an important cultural base for the Chinese. Post-1965 immigrants were often consumers of their own enclave economy. Whenever they wanted to see an herbalist doctor for a minor disease, consult a Fengshui master before purchasing a house, or watch the lion dance parade during the Lunar New Year, they would visit Chinatown. Shopping in a Chinese grocery store and having a family meal in a favorite restaurant in Chinatown was weekend routine for many Chinese families. With banks, grocery markets, book or video stores, and especially Chinese restaurants, Chinatown continued to serve as a magnet for the Chinese.

After the arrival of the new immigrants, Chinese visitors in Los Angeles Chinatown gradually outnumbered non-Chinese tourists. In 1977, a business-man in Chinatown observed: "Five years ago, you won't find many Chinese dur-ing the weekends. Now 80–90% are Chinese."[19] The new immigrants brought not only new business but also new tastes to Chinatown. Instead of chop suey or paper-wrapped chicken, they preferred genuine Chinese cuisine. President Richard Nixon's visit to China in 1972 aroused a great interest in Chinese food within American society, too. Peking duck emerged as a well-known dish, while chop suey lost its historical appeal. Food and menus in Los Angeles Chinatown's restaurants began to change. Americanized dishes gradually gave away to genuine Chinese food. "At the Golden Palace, non-Chinese were ushered to one side of the restaurant, decorated with plush black banquettes and dim lights, and Chi-nese to the other side, which has a more authentic décor, full lighting and simple square tables and chairs."[20] Catering to the new immigrants, the Golden Palace stayed open all night and became the only restaurant for a long time that could accommodate large banquets. Following the restaurant style in Hong Kong, the Golden Palace was also one of the pioneer restaurants in Los Angeles to serve dim sum food by waitresses pushing carts between tables.[21] As the number of Chinese clients was rapidly growing, Chinese restaurants in Chinatown began to make necessary adjustments in their recipes and cookery. Good Chinese chefs were in great demand.

In the early 1970s, there was actually a shortage of qualified Chinese chefs. Chinese restaurants in Los Angeles Chinatown competed with each other in offering higher wages in order to get a good chef. While a beginning cook made about $550 a month, a first-rate chef could earn as much as $1,200. Chinese res-taurant owners also worked with the federal Department of Labor's Manpower Training Program to produce more professionally trained chefs. Each paid half of the salary of the intern cooks during the training period.[22] Cantonese cuisine was no longer the dominant food as restaurants featuring Shanghai, Sichuan, or Hunan flavor also appeared in Chinatown. Andrew Cherng, founder of the Panda Express, opened the Plum Tree Inn in Los Angeles Chinatown in partnership with his father, Ming Tsai Cherng, and Mark Ting, while operating their Panda Inn restaurant in Pasadena.[23] Both the elder Cherng and Mark Ting were experienced chefs from Shanghai. Not far away from the Plum Tree Inn was the All Lucky, a much less elegant and more down-to-earth restaurant owned by P. C. Lee, a professional chef who specialized in Sichuan cuisine. Though only large enough for twenty-four seats, this authentic, spicy Sichuan beef noodle joint used seventy to eighty pounds of noodles every day.[24] Beginning in the 1980s, the arrival of refugee ethnic Chinese immigrants from Vietnam also promoted Chaozhou (Chiu Chow) cuisine, another food tradition in Guangdong Province. By 1997, there were an estimated forty-seven restaurants in Los Angeles Chinatown.[25] The immigrant boom not only rejuvenated Chinatown but also helped it transition from an ethnic theme park for tourists to a cultural resource center for its own people. When Chinatown was not big enough for the new immigrants, they began to move into Monterey Park, a city a few miles away east of downtown Los Angeles.

Monterey Park as a New Home

Post-1965 Chinese immigrants chose Monterey Park because it was close to Los Angeles Chinatown. The new immigrants could conveniently fulfill their needs for food and groceries. This city also had convenient access to Interstate 10 to the north, Interstate 710 to the west, and Interstate 60 to the south. Moreover, the city was one of the most affordable and diverse suburban communities at that time.[26] All these qualities attracted the Chinese. In the late 1970s and early 1980s, dramatic changes were taking place in Monterey Park as Chinese immigrants and their families moved there in increasing numbers. Soon the city was dubbed "Little Taipei" or "New Suburb Chinatown." In 1960, there were only 346 Chinese in Monterey Park.[27] Ten years later the number had increased to 2,202. Between 1980 and 1990, the Chinese population grew from 8,082 to 21,971, representing a change from 14.9 to 36.2 percent of Monterey Park's total population.[28]

Following the immigrant flow, Chinese restaurants, grocery stores, and other businesses quickly developed. As the immigrants transformed Monterey Park from a predominately white American city to a Chinese suburban community, "the first thing Monterey Park residents noticed were the Chinese restaurants that popped up." Then there were "three Chinese shopping centers, Chinese banks, and a theatre that only showed Hong Kong movies."[29] Before 1965, there was only one Chinese restaurant in Monterey Park. By 1983, there were more than forty.[30] Chinese restaurant business quickly generated a chain of changes. Chinese real estate and loan offices, gift shops, salons, video and book stores, herbal medicine and acupuncture services, minisupermarkets, and more restaurants appeared block by block, up and down the north-south Atlantic Boulevard and the west-east Garvey Avenue, the city's two main thoroughfares. In 1978–79, the city issued 2,700 business licenses. By the mid-1990s, the number had almost doubled to 5,000. The Chinese owned from two-thirds to three-fourths of the city's business enterprises.[31] Vacant lots, unoccupied office buildings, and desolate shopping plazas in Monterey Park were revitalized with a stream of Chinese retail and service businesses. The changes were so fast and so overwhelming that the longtime white, Latino, and native-born Asian residents became confused and estranged. Grocery markets, food, and the restaurant business were probably more controversial than any other Chinese commercial activities. Many of the old residents were shocked to discover that "Safeway and Alpha Beta, once anchors for the Anglo and Latino communities, have been replaced with the Hung Hoa supermarket and a two-story Pagoda-roofed Chinese shopping center that stands as the most dominant architectural structure in the city."[32] Jen

Shen Wu, an immigrant from Taiwan, opened the first Chinese supermarket in Monterey Park in 1978. Soon Wu's Diho Market became a chain of stores with 400 employees and $30 million in annual sales.[33] Diho was followed by the Hong Kong Supermarket, the Ai Hoa Supermarket, and others.[34]

Restaurant business became the most visible ethnic enterprise by post-1965 Chinese immigrants. As more Chinese moved into Monterey Park, the number of Chinese restaurants was growing at an amazing speed. By 1987, the city had over sixty Chinese restaurants, representing 75 percent of the dining business in the city.[35] Similar to the pre-1965 restaurant business, most Chinese restaurants in Monterey Park were also family-owned small businesses. Harbor Village and Ocean Star, located on Atlantic Boulevard, became two of the largest city revenue generators in Monterey Park.[36] Ocean Star, owned by Robert Y. Lee, had 800 seats and was one of the largest Chinese restaurants in San Gabriel Valley.[37] Embedded in the rapid growth of food and restaurant business was the vision of post-1965 Chinese immigrants about their life in America. While willing to settle down and embrace American culture, many new immigrants were reluctant to abandon some of their own cultural traditions, especially their food habits. With their modest prices, genuine flavor, and great variety, Chinese restaurants in Monterey Park made Chinese residents feel comfortably at home and their adaptation process in America a lot less painful. Familiar food helped immigrants settle down in their newly adopted country.

Food is one of the most tangible cultural forms representing an ethnic group. The restaurant business in Monterey Park not only helped new immigrants maintain their food habits but also represented who they were. According to historian Huping Ling's cultural community theory, concentrated Chinese restaurants in Monterey Park was a phenomenon that reflected cultural congregation for ethnic identity.[38] A 1995 *Los Angeles Times* article observed that "in Monterey Park, there are now so many Chinese restaurants that you could eat Chinese every weekend for more than a year and never hit the same place twice."[39] But the significance of the Chinese restaurant business in Monterey Park is not just their number. Different from their counterparts earlier and elsewhere that catered mainly to white clients, no Chinese restaurant in Monterey Park would serve chop suey or egg foo yung because no clients would order it. Targeting new immigrants and serving genuine Chinese food, Chinese restaurants in Monterey Park set off a new trend and began a new chapter in Chinese culinary history. Genuine Chinese food would become the mainstream dishes on the menu. The Chinese restaurant business would feature different Chinese regional cuisines. Recipes, ingredients, and cookery in the post-1965 Chinese restaurant businesses in America would follow closely their counterparts in Asia. The Chinese community remains transnational and multiregional in its food culture.

In 1987, a *Los Angeles Times* restaurant review listed the top ten Chinese restaurants in Monterey Park and Alhambra. Wonder Seafood Restaurant was one of them. Dishes on its menu included abalone and duck hot pot, crystal shrimp with sweetened walnuts, and ground pigeon topped with plum sauce. But according to Ricky Wu, coowner of the restaurant, his true culinary masterpiece was a three-snake soup, made from cobra, rattler, and a third snake for which Wu said there is no English name. "This legendary dish is considered a wintertime delicacy for its unique warming effect and mythical powers as an aphrodisiac." Wu confessed that it really should be five-snake soup, but it was difficult to get all the snakes in America.[40] Wu's masterpiece represents more than an exotic dish. Rather, it demonstrates how Chinese restaurants tried to serve authentic food to their Chinese clients. Another famous dish at Wu's restaurant was "Fo Tiao Qiang," which means "Buddha jumped over the wall" because "he smelled the soup, and it smelled so delicious." However, this is only one of three versions about the origin of this expensive entrée, the most famous dish in Fujian cuisine. In content, "this stew that serves 10 contains abalone, conch, soft-shell turtle and a host of other ingredients."[41] Using a variety of different nutritious ingredients and slow fire to cook are keys to its cookery.

As an authentic Chinese dish in Wonder Seafood Restaurant, "Fo Tiao Qiang" illustrates how food follows human migration and travels from one place to another. In Chinese society, most of the famous dishes in metropolitan cities like Beijing, Shanghai, or Guangzhou actually originated from smaller towns. When "Fo Tiao Qiang," a dish that originated in a small town in Fujian Province, spread to Guangzhou in the mid-1960s and to Hong Kong in the 1980s, the dish became renowned and began to appear on the menu of government banquets for foreign heads of state, business executives, and film celebrities. Soon upper-scale overseas Chinese restaurants across the world, especially in Southeast Asia, learned the recipe and served the dish to homesick merchant immigrants. Many post-1965 immigrants in the Monterey Park area were immigrants from Taiwan who spoke the same dialect and shared similar cultural traditions with the people in Fujian Province. Due to their transnational business networks, merchant immigrants from Taiwan also frequently traveled to Guangzhou and Hong Kong. Many tasted this famous dish there with business friends. Now back home in Monterey Park, they could also enjoy it at the Wonder Seafood Restaurant.

San Gabriel Valley as a Chinese Food Capital

Monterey Park was only the beginning of much deeper and wider changes that would be brought about by Chinese immigrants in the San Gabriel Valley, a vast suburbia to the east of the city of Los Angeles. Some immigrant entrepreneurs foresaw such changes early. Fred Hsie, whose Mandarin Realty played an instrumental role in advertising Monterey Park in Hong Kong and Taiwan as a Chinese Beverly Hills, invited twenty prominent white residents of Monterey Park to dinner in 1977 and told them that "Monterey Park was going to be [the] next Chinatown and that changes were inevitable."[42] On another occasion, Hsie predicted that in five years Monterey Park would be comparable to Los Angeles

Chinatown and then surpass it. Another Chinese merchant echoed his prediction by saying that in ten years the whole San Gabriel Valley would be like Monterey Park as the Chinese purchased real estate properties heavily in Alhambra, Montebello, Rosemead, and El Monte.[43] Less than a decade later, their vision was fully realized. Atlantic Boulevard does not end in Monterey Park but reaches northward to where Alhambra, San Marino, and South Pasadena intersect. Garvey Avenue goes eastward from Monterey Park through Rosemead and El Monte. Chinese restaurants and strip malls naturally expanded into these neighboring cities. Using Monterey Park as a model or an entry port, post-1965 Chinese immigrants quickly spread into many cities in the San Gabriel Valley.

Since the 1965 immigration reform, the Chinese population in the area has soared. According to a 1987 *Los Angeles Times* article, an estimated 100,000 Chinese and other Asians had moved into the western San Gabriel Valley area since 1980 and more than doubled the number of Asians living in the twenty-seven cities and unincorporated areas of the San Gabriel Valley to an estimated 180,000 people. For every entering Asian, there would be a departing white. Of the region's 327,000 residents, the white population dropped from 78 percent in 1970 to 56 percent in 1980 to an estimated 36 percent in 1987.[44] By 1990, the Chinese population in Southern California rose to 324,274, making it the largest Chinese community in the nation. By 2000, Southern California had become the home of 523,597 Chinese residents.[45] About 50 percent of this population concentrated in the San Gabriel Valley area and spread into cities like Alhambra, Rosemead, San Marino, South Pasadena, San Gabriel, and Arcadia, and all the way east to West Covina, Hacienda Heights, Rowland Heights, Diamond Bar, and Walnut. In some cities, the Chinese population has reached over 30 to 40 percent. While Monterey Park's Chinese population constitutes, for example, about 44.3 percent, San Marino has 43.4 percent; Arcadia, 36.3 percent; San Gabriel, 36.3 percent; Alhambra, 35.9 percent; Rosemead, 32.5 percent; and Rowland Heights, 31.5 percent (see Table 1). All the above cities have Asians as the largest population group.[46] The Chinese and Asian presence in the region significantly boosted the sagging real estate market in the early 1990s. For example, nearly one of five home buyers in Los Angeles County in 1992 had a Chinese last name.[47] The demographic change has made not only Monterey Park but also the San Gabriel Valley home to the largest concentration of Chinese Americans in the nation. Many non-Asian residents in this region had to learn how to live as a minority in America and tasted a life that they had probably not experienced before.

While the Chinese population was spreading into the San Gabriel Valley, Monterey Park, the "first suburban Chinatown," gradually lost its leading status as the Chinese dining center. Many other cities in the region began to look like Monterey Park. Chinese minimalls, shopping plazas, financial and real estates services, and other retail businesses proliferated. Chinese restaurants took the lead in such business expansion and often clustered on the major streets in those cities. In many cases, wealthy merchants from Hong Kong, Taiwan, or Southeast Asia purchased commercial blocks, let go the old business tenants, remodeled the buildings, and then leased them out to Chinese restaurant proprietors and other retail or service business owners. "There's a Chinese restaurant in Rosemead where the Builder's Emporium used to be, a Chinese restaurant in Alhambra in what once was the Chowder House. The Edwards Drive-In in San Gabriel is now an enormous stucco mall. It has fifteen restaurants in it, all Chinese."[48] Following this pattern, post-1965 Chinese immigrants have transformed the social landscape in the San Gabriel Valley. At the same time, backlash by other residents against the Chinese eventually slowed down the uncontrolled growth of the restaurant business in Monterey Park. City officials and many residents, including the Chinese, wanted to induce more high-end mainstream retail businesses to the city.

Table 1. The Chinese Restaurants and Ratio to Chinese Population at Nine San Gabriel Valley City/Areas

| City/Areas | Restaurant Number | | | Total Population in 2000 | Chinese Population and Percent in 2000 | | Ratio of Chinese Restaurants & Chinese Population* |
	1988	1997	2007				
Alhambra	28	49	57	85804	30836	35.9%	1: 540
Arcadia	5	11	35	53054	19274	36.3%	1: 550
Chinatown	58	43	44	15000*	n.a.	n.a.	1: 340
Hacienda Heights	7	15	28	53122	13090	24.6%	1: 467
Monterey Park	48	57	72	60051	26582	44.3%	1: 369
Rosemead	4	26	27	53505	17372	32.5%	1: 643
Rowland Heights	1	37	65	48553	15273	31.5%	1: 234
San Gabriel	13	55	96	39804	14460	36.3%	1: 150
San Marino	1	1	2	12945	5616	43.4%	1: 2808
Total	165	294	426				1: 677

* The ratio compares the number of Chinese restaurants in 2007 with the Chinese population in the city/area based on 2000 census data. The ratio in Chinatown compares the number of Chinese restaurants with total population.

Sources: The Chinese restaurant number was based on *Chinese Yellow Pages* 1988, 1997, and 2007; *Chinese Consumer Yellow Pages* 1997 and 2007. Chinese population information is from www.census.gov, accessed July 20, 2007. Chinatown population information is from "Selling the Taste of Chinatown," *Los Angeles Times*, June 14, 2004, and the number of Chinatown restaurants is identified based on their street locations.

But Monterey Park still has more Chinese restaurants than many other cities. As Table 1 indicates, the city had seventy-two Chinese restaurants in 2007, while its closest neighboring city, Alhambra, had fifty-seven (see Table 1). However, the city of San Gabriel has surpassed Monterey Park with the highest number of Chinese restaurants (ninety-six) due to the booming Chinese business on Valley Boulevard. When Arcadia became another city well liked by many middle-class and wealthy Taiwanese residents, the number of Chinese restaurants rose to thirty-five there. As the Chinese have continuously moved toward the east, Rowland Heights has become another important Chinese dining area. While it listed sixty-five Chinese restaurants in 2007, clustering on a few major streets, its neighboring city Hacienda Heights had twenty-eight. Though Table 1 includes both dessert shops and formal dining restaurants, the area still has a considerable number of Chinese restaurants.

A pattern in the Chinese restaurant business in the San Gabriel Valley is that each city with concentrated Chinese residents has a few famous Chinese restaurants as a major attraction. Monterey Park has the Ocean Star and Harbor Village. Arcadia has the celebrated Din Tai Fung dumpling house. San Gabriel has the high-end restaurant Mission 261. Rowland Heights has the Sea Harbor Seafood Restaurant and Sam Woo Restaurant, or Sam Woo B.B.Q. Big. Famous Chinese restaurants follow wherever the immigrants have congregated. Sam Woo, for example, also has branch operations in Monterey Park, San Gabriel, and Irvine, which is not in the San Gabriel Valley but has a large Chinese population. Another pattern is that Chinese restaurants cluster on certain streets rather than spreading out evenly in most of these San Gabriel Valley cities. "Rosemead has 50 restaurants jammed into five square miles. Rowland Heights has 30, give or take one or two."[49] Main Street in Alhambra, Valley Boulevard in San Gabriel, the cross streets of Baldwin and Duarte Road in Arcadia, and Colima Street in Rowland Heights have become what Atlantic Boulevard is in Monterey Park. Concentrated restaurants have formed a dining destination in each city. In a few decades, Chinese strip malls or shopping centers, often with a restaurant as the anchor business, have been sprawling across the entire stretch of the San Gabriel Valley, from Monterey Park in the west to Diamond Bar in the east. Fred Hsie's vision has become a reality.

The most visible dining destination, however, is not a single city but Valley Boulevard, which goes through Alhambra, San Gabriel, and Rosemead. "The boulevard—a bustling swath of Asian supermarkets, about 100 Asian restaurants and scores of small shops selling products as varied as woodsilk towels and chrysanthemum tea—is not only a regional shopping district, but also has put San Gabriel on the international destination map."[50] Its only counterpart is probably Main Street in Flushing, New York. Most of 100 Chinese restaurants have crammed together on a two-mile "golden stretch" in the city of San Gabriel and a couple of blocks of Alhambra. In 1982, land on Valley Boulevard in Alhambra was sold for $20 a square foot. Five years later, the price had doubled or tripled. "One local banker said a customer paid $8 million for property on Valley Boulevard in 1985 and sold it a year later for $12 million."[51] Numerous Chinese restaurants border each other on both sides of the street, while many others are crowded inside a dozen strip malls on the boulevard. Together, they draw huge crowds of customers during the lunch and dinner hours, especially on the weekends and holidays. In order to survive the competition, each restaurant claims its regional tradition or special flavor, maintains its own cuisine style, develops its own unique dishes, and offers its own special deals. Business relationships among the Chinese restaurants on the Valley Boulevard are a subtle interaction. While competing with each other for clientele, the businesses bond together to create a visible Chinese cuisine hub.

Food and Identity

Food is an expression of ethnic resilience. The different flavors in Chinese restaurant business reflect the diverse cultural backgrounds of the post-1965 Chinese immigrants, who are very different from early Cantonese immigrants. Coming from Guangdong Province, early Chinese immigrants had similar dietary habits. Chinese restaurants operated by those immigrants and their descendants served mainly Cantonese food. At the turn of the twentieth century, Cantonese immigrants invented dishes like chop suey and generated a stream of American-ized Chinese dishes like chow mein, General Tso's chicken, egg foo yung, and paper-wrapped chicken. When hundreds of chop suey houses expanded into the American food market, Chinese restaurant food became thoroughly Ameri-canized Chinese cuisine. The dynamic interaction between Chinese food and American customers was an interesting process of cultural negotiation. While Chinese restaurant business helped shape the American diet, Chinese food was simultaneously being shaped, transformed, and sometimes altered by Ameri-can popular tastes. At the same time, Chinese restaurants diverged from their counterparts in China in both operation and cookery. Tea was offered as a free soft drink; soup was served at the beginning rather than the end of the meal; and the fortune cookie was invented as a free dessert delivered with the bill. Though Americanized Chinese dishes appeared less and less Chinese in their form and flavor, they became more and more rooted in their adopted country. Ironically, chop suey houses and restaurant businesses became a conspicuous ethnic label for Chinese Americans before 1965.

Post-1965 Chinese restaurants followed some of the operational traditions of chop suey houses. They also provided tea as a free drink and fortune cookies as part of the meal. Both Chinese and non-Chinese customers took these two features for granted when eating at a Chinese restaurant. However, menus in Chinese restaurants in the San Gabriel Valley are very different from chop suey houses, as they represent a variety of different regional food traditions in China. The Chinese American community is probably the most diverse ethnic group in the United States. According to a 1993 Los Angeles Times article, Chinese Ameri-cans in Southern California have diverse cultural roots. One in four was born in the United States, while a similar proportion was born in China and immigrated here—either directly or, more likely, by way of Taiwan or Hong Kong. China: 25%, United States: 24%, Taiwan: 22%, Vietnam: 11%, Hong Kong: 8%, Other, Asia: 7%, Other, World: 3%.[52] This diversity, first of all, reflects the history of China in the late nineteenth century and the first half of the twentieth century, when foreign invasion and civil wars drove large numbers of Chinese overseas. After the Opium War in 1839–42, a huge number of Chinese went to Southeast Asia, North and South America, Europe, and Africa. Some became contract laborers; many were free immigrants. The Japanese invasion of China in the 1930s also pushed away many Chinese from South China to Vietnam, Laos, and Cambodia. The civil war between the Nationalists and Communists caused further outflow migration to Hong Kong and Taiwan. When the Communist government defeated the Nationalist government in 1949, one to two million officials, employees, and other followers of the Nationalist government escaped to Taiwan.[53] Chinese diaspora communities are now located all over the world.

China is not only a nation-state but also a cultural entity with many subcultural groups. Like regional dialects, food culture reflects Chinese immigrants as a group of diverse subcultures. In Chinese food culture, northerners prefer steamed bread or noodles as a staple food, while southerners like rice. Geographic ecology, farming tradition, and regional culture have shaped local taste. Food habits are therefore different from region to region. In general, Chinese society has eight cuisine traditions based on geographic locations. Each cuisine tradition has a few famous dishes that have become nationally well known—for example, Peking duck, Shanghai steamed dumplings, and Yangzhou meatballs. A Mandarin-speaking guest in a Cantonese dim sum restaurant often needs to order and get service in English as Cantonese-speaking cart waitresses do not speak Mandarin. Instead of engaging in two mutually incomprehensible dialects, it is a lot easier for them to communicate in English. Due to different food traditions and taste preferences, the restaurants along Valley Boulevard feature all kinds of Chinese regional cuisines. "From the pot stickers and succulent dumplings of the northern provinces to the peppery Sichuan dishes of the west to the rich, sweetened Shanghai specialties of the east to the steamed and quickly stir-fried seafood of the south, virtually every form of Chinese regional cooking is represented in the restaurants of Monterey Park, Alhambra and San Gabriel."[54] The diverse cultural roots and the diaspora background of Chinese immigrants have made the Chinese restaurant business a colorful world.

Monterey Park or Valley Boulevard as contemporary suburban Chinese community looks physically different from a traditional Chinatown. There are no red lanterns, dragon banners, or fake Chinese architecture. Chinese restaurants and other businesses in San Gabriel Valley are not meant for sightseeing tourists but for the local Chinese residents. Post-1965 Chinese immigrants did not create isolated ethnic enclaves here but have changed and enriched the local community with new cultures and new economic activities. The famous restaurant Yu Zhen Lou in the city of San Gabriel has simply used its street address, Mission 261, as its English restaurant name. The restaurant occupies a mission-style historic building, under a 150-year-old grapevine, on the 100-year site of the town's city hall. The historic architecture remains unchanged. The previous tenant of the building was a famous Mexican restaurant named Panchito's Mexican Kitchen. Its owner, Frank Ramirez, had run it for forty years. When the historic site failed to attract enough tourists and prosper after the city spent about $2.6 million state and local funds to renovate it in the early 1990s, Panchito's eventually closed.[55] Three Chinese immigrant brothers—Harvey, Lewis, and York Ng—noticed the growing Chinese population in the area, sought the opportunity, and switched from their real estate business to restaurant careers. Today Mission 261 is ranked as one of the best dim sum and full-service sit-down Chinese restaurants in Southern California. The most famous dishes include "the ones shaped like small animals: 'ducklings' of fried taro, 'bees' of minced shrimp molded around bits of salted egg (with 'stripes' of finely sliced seaweed), seafood dumplings shaped like baby carp, custard-filled dumplings molded like inquisitive little rabbits."[56] In Mission 261, we see continuities and discontinuities in California history. Its Chinese name, Yu Zhen Lou (Royal Treasure House), reminds us of the name Man Jen Low, the oldest Chinese restaurant in Chinatown. Its English name embodies the legacy of the Mission San Gabriel Archangel built in 1771. The building bears the memory of the landmark Panchito's restaurant and its famous margaritas. But the food illustrates how the San Gabriel Valley has emerged as an Asian cultural hub since the 1980s. New immigrants have arrived, brought a new culture, and become part of the local American history.

Chinese communities in the San Gabriel Valley are not isolated ethnic ghettos like traditional Chinatown. They are integrated American neighborhoods with Asians as the majority population. Many post-1965 Chinese immigrants have maintained their Asian lifestyle and ethnic identity while working and living in the United States. They do not see this preference as conflicting with their American life. At work, they speak English, crack jokes with their colleagues, and comfortably behave as typical Americans. At home, however, they speak Mandarin, Cantonese, Fujianese, or another Chinese dialect. About 49.6 percent of the Chinese speak their native language at home when their English is not fluent. But another 35.8 percent, with fluent English ability, still use Chinese at home. Only 14.5 percent speak just English at home.[57] They also eat Chinese food, listen to Chinese-language radio stations, watch Chinese-language television channels, and/or read Chinese-language newspapers.[58] These media outlets typically keep the Chinese American community attuned to developments in all home areas—Hong Kong, Taiwan, and China. The Chinese media also inform the community about events related to the Chinese community in Canada, Australia, Europe, South America, and Southeast Asia, as many contemporary Chinese have relatives and friends in those places. Compared with a homogeneous American neighborhood, these San Gabriel Valley cities are probably more sensitive to cultural diversity issues, more informed about international events, and more dynamic in economic activities.

Problems of Congested Business and Hygiene Standards

Congested businesses and sanitary conditions are two major issues confronting the Chinese restaurant world today. As Table 1 indicates, the ratio between Chinese residents and Chinese restaurants is about 540 or 550 to 1 in cities like Alhambra or Arcadia. In the city of San Gabriel, the ratio between the Chinese population and the restaurants is 150 to 1; in Monterey Park, 369 to 1; and Rowland Heights, 234 to 1 (see Table 1). By 2004, as home to over 240,000 Chinese residents, the San Gabriel Valley had more than 2,000 Chinese restaurants. In comparison, Los Angeles Chinatown, according to a *Los Angeles Times* article, has about 80 Chinese restaurants for 15,000 residents.[59] It is still an attractive Chinese food destination. A few big Hong Kong seafood restaurants like the Empress Pavilion opened there in the 1980s, while some of the old restaurants continued to serve Americanized dishes such as chop suey. However, cities like Monterey Park, San Gabriel, and Rowland Heights have overshadowed Los Angeles Chinatown as the new Chinese food centers. The rapid growth of Chinese restaurants in the San Gabriel Valley has skewed the ratio between Chinese population and Chinese restaurants.

Obviously, Chinese restaurants do not serve just the Chinese or the residents within the valley region. But the ratio between Chinese restaurants and their Chinese clients is still conspicuously unbalanced. The skewed ratio has made the competition among Chinese restaurants extremely intensive. Offering a bonus dish over a certain amount of spending or a free dessert during the weekend is a common strategy in this competition. Some Chinese restaurants spy on each other's menus and recipes or undercut each other's prices. Fierce competition has made change of ownership a frequent phenomenon and driven some of the restaurants bankrupt. A concentrated Chinese population is not the only factor that determines the number of Chinese restaurants. How a city government has responded and negotiated with Chinese restaurant businesses, whether the local residents welcomed the restaurant, and whether the city already had a strong commercial sector are all relevant factors. San Marino, one of the wealthiest neighborhoods in Southern California, has a 43.4 percent Chinese population with a Chinese American mayor, Matthew Lin. But the city has only two Chinese restaurants, one of which, Lollicup, is a kind of drink/snack-type establishment. Two other restaurants seem to have Chinese owners, though neither is a Chinese restaurant. According to the city directory, there are fourteen restaurants in San Marino in total.[60] The wealthy white and Chinese residents are obviously not interested in seeing many restaurants in their million-dollar-house neighborhood. San Marino's geographic proximity to other West San Gabriel Valley cities allows its residents to meet their culinary needs in neighboring cities. Pasadena is another West San Gabriel Valley city with about fourteen Chinese restaurants out of ninety-five restaurants that were rated. Its prosperous "Old Town" food and retail district does not need new establishments to replace them.

Chinese restaurant operators have frequently argued that food preparation is complicated in Chinese cookery; they have to deal with many more ingredients and equipment than their non-Chinese counterparts, and they are committed to following a thousand years of tradition in Chinese cooking. In Chinese food culture, authenticity and flavor are far more important than the hygiene issue. Chinese clients often judge a restaurant according to the flavor of the food rather than the sanitary condition of its kitchen. Many Chinese restaurants have paid inadequate attention to hygiene standards, especially when most of their clients are Chinese. The Los Angeles County Department of Health Services regularly sends health inspectors to score restaurants on a 100-point scale. Inspectors will check everything from inadequate cooling or heating of food to the chef's personal hygiene, the use of leftovers, or unclean equipment. An A grade is granted when a restaurant scores between 90 and 100 points, a B for 80 to 89 points, and a C for 70 to 79 points. Below 70, a restaurant will be ordered to close.[61] Though the county's restaurant ratings do not differentiate types of restaurants according to their ethnic background, we were able to distinguish and verify Chinese restaurants based on their names in the *Chinese Yellow Pages*. Our study reveals that in eight cities/areas of Los Angeles County, 80.9 percent of the non-Chinese restaurants get an A, while Chinese restaurants fall far behind, with only 33.6 percent of them rated as A and 60.5 percent rated as B. In comparison, only 18 percent of non-Chinese restaurants get a B (see Table 2). Hygiene standards are a gripping issue for Chinese restaurant businesses.

But the hygiene issue is not impossible to solve. Hygiene standards, for example, remain consistently high for those Chinese restaurants that serve mainly non-Chinese clients. Table 2 provides a comparison of ratings by Los Angeles County among five groups of restaurants: (1) all restaurants in eight Chinese-concentrated cities/areas; (2) Chinese restaurants in Los Angeles Chinatown that serve many tourists; (3) Panda Express chain restaurants, which provide more Americanized Chinese fast food; (4) P. F. Chang's China Bistro chain restaurants, which target mainly middle-class non-Chinese clients; and (5) Chinese restaurants in Pasadena, a predominantly white community. The difference is telling. Panda Express had 106 stores inspected in 2007, and their rating was all A. Seven stores of P. F. Chang's in West Los Angeles were all ranked A.[62] Much higher than the San Gabriel Valley area, Chinatown also has 48 percent of its Chinese restaurants ranked as A. Outside of the San Gabriel Valley, some sit-down Chinese restaurants, whether operated by Chinese or non-Chinese owners, have consistently received an A in their ranking. In Pasadena, 78 percent of the Chinese restaurants were ranked as A, which is the highest percentage in the area. In comparison, as Table 2 indicates, Monterey Park only had 23 percent of its Chinese restaurants ranked as A, while Rosemead had 26 percent. The hygiene issue is mainly a problem for Chinese restaurants in Chinese-concentrated communities. Obviously neither the Chinese proprietors nor the Chinese clients have taken the hygiene issue seriously. In an increasingly competitive Chinese restaurant market, however, hygiene standards are not a small issue. They directly relate to the customers' health and will certainly impact the foot traffic of a restaurant. Furthermore, the county government will order closure of those restaurants that fall below a C level. In food culture, the hygiene issue also embodies a culinary image of Chinese restaurant business collectively. Chinese restaurant operators need to drastically improve their sanitary ranking if they want to further expand their business into the American food market.

Table 2. Los Angeles County Restaurant Ratings in Selected San Gabriel Valley City/Areas (2006–2007)

Restaurant	Number	A	B	C	D	Total
Chinese Restaurants in Eight Cities/Areas:						
Alhambra	54	37%	57%	6%	0	100%
Arcadia	44	36%	62%	2%	0	100%
Hacienda Heights	24	42%	58%	0	0	100%
Monterey Park	74	23%	69%	8%	0	100%
Rosemead	43	26%	60%	12%	2%	100%
Rowland Heights	87	31%	60%	8%	1%	100%
San Gabriel	113	42%	57%	1%	0	100%
San Marino	2	0	50%	50%	0	100%
Total Chinese Restaurant in the Eight Cities/Areas	441	33.6%	60.5%	5.4%	0.5%	100%
Non-Chinese Restaurant in the Eight Cities/Areas	857	80.9%	18%	1.1%	0	100%
All Restaurants in the Eight Cities/Areas	1298	64.8%	32.4%	2.6%	0.2%	100%
Chinese Restaurant in LA Chinatown*	69	48%	51%	1%	0	100%
Panda Express Chinese Fast Food in Los Angeles County	106	100%	0	0	0	100%
P.F. Chang's China Bistro In Los Angeles County	7	100%	0	0	0	100%
Pasadena	14	78.6%	21.4%	0	0	100%

Rating Criteria: A, 90–100; B, 80–89; C, 70–79

*Chinatown data is identified by zip code (90012) and location.

Sources: Rating information are restaurants inspected and rated by the Los Angeles County Public Health Department during 2006–7 with a few inspected in 2005, from Web site: www.lapublichealth. org, accessed July 2007; Chinese restaurants are identified based on compiled information from *Chinese Consumer Yellow Pages* 2007; *Chinese Yellow Pages* 2007; *California Yellow Pages* 2007–2008; *Chinese E-Search Yellow Pages* 2006–2007; Citywide Dining List from the City of Alhambra Web site, www.cityofalhambra.org; Dining in Arcadia from the City of Arcadia Web site, www.ci.arcadia. ca.us; Pasadena rating data is from the City of Pasadena Web site, www.cityofpasadena.net, all accessed July 20, 2007.

Conclusion

The emergence of numerous Chinese restaurants has changed the social landscape of Southern California and made Chinese Americans a visible ethnic community. From a bunch of chop suey eateries in the 1960s, the Chinese restaurant business here has evolved into a food capital of Chinese cuisine. As authentic Chinese food has replaced Americanized Chinese dishes, the booming restaurant business becomes a concrete example to show how transnationalism is deeply embedded in Chinese American life. While becoming Americans, post-1965 Chinese immigrants have maintained certain aspects of their ethnicity, such as food. Different Chinese cuisine styles and restaurant operations also illustrate the diverse social origins and the diaspora background of the new immigrants. In the Chinese restaurant world, we see how the San Gabriel Valley in Southern California has become a new American community.

Chinese food is not only popular in Southern California but across the nation. Due to its long and historical presence in American society, Chinese cuisine has become one of the most popular ethnic foods in the United States. There are more than 40,000 Chinese restaurants across the nation—a number much larger than the combined total number of McDonald's in the United States (13,774), Wendy's in the United States (6,300), and Burger Kings (7,482) in the United States and Canada.[63] Unlike in the San Gabriel Valley in Southern California, non-Chinese customers constitute the majority of the clientele for Chinese restaurant businesses outside of Chinatowns or suburban neighborhoods with concentrated Chinese residents. According to a 2000 report by the National Restaurant Association in the United States, Italian, Mexican, and Chinese cuisines have already joined the mainstream. "Those three cuisines have become so ingrained in American culture that they are no longer foreign to the American palate." More than nine out of ten consumers are familiar with and have tried these foods, and about half report eating them frequently. Hunan, Mandarin, and Szechwan variations of Chinese cuisines, like some European cuisines, are known to between 70 and 80 percent of consumers.[64] Serving a non-Chinese clientele is different from serving Chinese customers, as the former are more familiar with Americanized dishes. However, most of the Chinese restaurants for non-Chinese clients have also changed as they began to serve Hunan, Shanghai, or Sichuan food. Americanized Chinese food like chop suey is no longer a hit dish. In such a situation, the culinary trend in the San Gabriel Valley may very well be influencing the menu and cookery of Chinese restaurants in other areas of the United States.

Notes

ACKNOWLEDGMENTS: We are deeply thankful for the two anonymous reviewers' comments and editor Huping Ling's encouragement and suggestions on this article.

1. For the closure and history of General Lee's, see David Holley, "General Lee's Bows to Change after Century of Service," *Los Angeles Times*, October 11, 1985. However, according

to another article, "From Chop Suey to Chiu Chow," by Charles Perry, *Los Angeles Times*, February 21, 2007, the menu of this restaurant in the 1950s gave its founding date as 1890. By 1900, there were but two or three Chinese restaurants, frequented mostly by Chinese, in Los Angeles Chinatown. Man Jen Low must be one of them. The restaurant became known as General Lee's since the 1950s as the owner was a World War II veteran (but not a general) and was the grandson of the founder. The original Man Jen Low was first located outside Chinatown, then moved to a three-story building in the old Chinatown; it moved to New (that is, present-day) Chinatown after old Chinatown was torn down in 1933 to make way for the Union Station. New Chinatown was built in 1938.

2. Chop suey, General Tso's chicken, and egg foo yung are popular dishes in Americanized Chinese restaurants. Though some Chinese restaurants still serve chop suey, authentic food now predominates.

3. "Chinese Directory" listed in *Oriental*, February 8, 1856. This was a bilingual weekly published from 1855 to 1857. The directory is listed in the English section.

4. William Mason, "The Chinese in Los Angeles," Los Angeles County Museum of Natural History, *Museum Alliance Quarterly* 6, no. 2 (Fall 1967): 16.

5. Cited in Henry Shih-shan Tsai, *The Chinese Experience in America* (Bloomington: Indiana University Press, 1986), 105. In Ronald Takaki's estimate, 12,559 out of 45,614 were laundry men, and therefore there were probably more Chinese working in restaurants than in laundries. See Ronald Takaki, *Strangers from the Different Shore: A History of Asian Americans* (Boston: Little, Brown, 1989), 240.

6. Mai Liqian (Lai, Him Mark), *Cong huaqiao dao huaren: Ershi shiji meiguo huaren shehui fazhan shi* (From Overseas Chinese to Chinese Americans: A History of Twentieth-Century Chinese American Social and Economical Development) (Hong Kong: San Lian Press [joint publishing H. K. Co.], 1992), 85.

7. Takaki, *Strangers from the Different Shore*, 267.

8. Mai (Lai), *Cong huaqiao dao huaren*, 393.

9. For the recipe and menu of these two and other Americanized Chinese dishes, see Alice Miller Mitchell, *Oriental Cookbook* (Chicago: Rand McNally, 1950), 11–12.

10. Takaki, *Strangers from the Different Shore*, 421.

11. Zhuang Guotu, *Huaqiao huaren yu Zhongguo de guanxi* (Relationship between Overseas Chinese and China) (Guangzhou, China: Guangdong Gaodeng Jiaoyu Press, 2001), 480.

12. Karl Schoenberger, "Breathing Life into Southland from Mainland Millionaires to Grad Students, a 'New Wave' of Chinese Immigrants Is Invigorating the Economy," *Los Angeles Times*, October 4, 1993.

13. Min Zhou, *Chinatown: The Socioeconomic Potential of an Urban Enclave* (Philadelphia: Temple University Press, 1992), 14.

14. Tsai, *Chinese Experience in America*, 149.

15. Mai (Lai), *Cong huaqiao dao huaren*, 394.

16. Daryl E. Lembke, "And More Immigrants Pour In," *Los Angeles Times*, December 18, 1966.

17. Jerry Hulse, "Chinatown Changing as Suburbs Call Residents," *Los Angeles Times*, October 26, 1959.

18. Jean Murphy, "Chinese Immigrants Learning English," *Los Angeles Times*, December 19, 1969.

19. Penelope McMillan, "L.A.'s Chinatown Turns from Tourists to the Chinese," *Los Angeles Times*, September 18, 1977.

20. Ibid. However, the Golden Palace was later closed, and the Palm Tree Inn took its place.

21. We have learned this information from Gilbert Hom, a member of Chinese Historical Society of Southern California.

22. "Training Under Way to Ease Shortage of Chinese Cooks," *Los Angeles Times*, August 24, 1973.

23. Lois Dwan, "Restaurants," *Los Angeles Times*, May 11, 1980.

24. Barbara Hansen, "All Lucky Asian Lure," *Los Angeles Times*, June 11, 1981.

25. This number is based on information collected from *Chinese Consumer Yellow Pages 1997*; and *Chinese Yellow Pages 1997*. The actual number should be larger, as there were restaurants that did not advertise in these two telephone books.

26. Wei Li, "Building Ethnoburbia: The Emergence and Manifestation of the Chinese Ethnoburb in Los Angeles' San Gabriel Valley," *Journal of Asian American Studies* 2, no. 1 (February 1999): 7–8.

27. Ibid., 5.

28. Tim Fong, *The First Suburban Chinatown: The Making of Monterey Park, California* (Philadelphia: Temple University Press, 1994), 26. For the population, see Li, "Building Ethnoburbia," 5.

29. Penelope McMillan, "Influx in Monterey Park," *Los Angeles Times*, April 13, 1980.

30. Steve Harvey, "Sings the Blues without Locust's Song," *Los Angeles Times*, April 5, 1983.

31. Fong, *First Suburban Chinatown*, 43–44.

32. Mark Arax, "Monterey Park Nation's 1st Suburban Chinatown," *Los Angeles Times*, April 6, 1987.

33. Mike Ward, "Cities Report Growth—and Some Losses—From Asian Business Series: ASIAN IMPACT," *Los Angeles Times*, April 19, 1987.

34. Fong, *First Suburban Chinatown*, 62.

35. Arax, "Monterey Park Nation's 1st Suburban Chinatown."

36. Li, "Building Ethnoburbia," 9.

37. Shawn Hubler, "A Feeding Frenzy in the 'New Chinatown,'" *Los Angeles Times*, December 5, 1995.

38. Huping Ling, "Reconceptualizing Chinese American Community in St. Louis: From Chinatown to Cultural Community," *Journal of American Ethnic History* 24, no. 2 (Winter 2005): 65–101.

39. Hubler, "Feeding Frenzy."

40. Mark Arax, "Family Elders Cling to Old Ways as Young Look to New," *Los Angeles Times*, April 16, 1987.

41. Max Jacobson, "Top 10: A Guide to the Middle Kingdom," *Los Angeles Times*, October 26, 1986.

42. Arax, "Monterey Park Nation's 1st Suburban Chinatown."

43. Penelope McMillan, "Influx in Monterey Park," *Los Angeles Times*, April 13, 1980.

44. Mark Arax, "Selling Out, Moving On, Some Old-Timers Flee the Congestion, Density and Unfamiliarity of 'Little China,'" *Los Angeles Times*, April 12, 1987.

45. Los Angeles: Asian Pacific American Legal Center of Southern California, *The Diverse Face of Asians and Pacific Islanders in Los Angeles County* (2004), 49.

46. Ibid., 7. See also the 2000 census from www.census.gov. Accessed July 2007.

47. Schoenberger, "Breathing Life into Southland."

48. Hubler, "Feeding Frenzy."

49. Hubler, "Feeding Frenzy."

50. Stephanie Chavez, "New Look Reflects an Old Pattern," *Los Angeles Times*, July 25, 2004.

51. Ward, "Cities Report Growth."

52. Schoenberger, "Breathing Life into Southland."

53. Iris Chang, *The Chinese in American: A Narrative History* (New York: Penguin Group, 2003), 283.

54. Arax, "Family Elders Cling to Old Ways."

55. Stephanie Chavez, "New Look Reflects an Old Pattern," *Los Angeles Times*, July 25, 2004.

56. Charles Perry and Linda Burum, "Real Fireworks; A Burst of Innovation Has Electrified the Local Dim Sum Scene," *Los Angeles Times*, January 26, 2005.

57. Terrance J. Reeves and Claudette E Bennett, *We the People: Asians in the United States—Special Report* (Washington, D.C.: U.S. Census Bureau, December 2004), 11.

58. The *Los Angeles Times* 1997 survey indicated that 79 percent of the Chinese in Southern California spoke Chinese at home. K. Connie Kang, "Chinese in the Southland," *Los Angeles Times*, 27 June 1997.

59. David Pierson, "Selling the Taste of Chinatown," *Los Angeles Times*, June 16, 2004. However, the number of Chinese restaurants in Chinatown in this article is different from our estimate in Table 1 because Table 1 includes merely those restaurants that are listed in *Chinese Yellow Pages*.

60. See http://www.sanmarinochamber.org/directory. Accessed July 2007.

61. See Los Angeles County's Web site: www.lapublichealth.org. Accessed July 2007.

62. The rating information on the six P. F. Chang's restaurants is from www.lapublichealth.org, and one Pasadena rating is from www.cityofpasadena.net, accessed July 2007. The score for P. F. Chang's in Burbank is 96 out of 100; in El Segundo, 92; in Los Angeles, 92; in Pasadena, 100 (city inspection); in Santa Monica, 92; in Torrance, 97; and in Woodland Hills, 94.

63. "A Cultural Tour to Chinese Restaurants," *Zhongcan Tongxun* (Chinese Restaurant News) (June 2006), 164 (a journal published by Smart Business Services, Inc.). According to another source, the total number of Chinese restaurants in the United States is 36,000. See "Chinese Immigrants Keep U.S. Well Fed," *New York Times* News Service, October 9, 2005, http://www.taipeitimes.com/News/world/archives/2005/10/09/2003275064. The total number of McDonald's restaurants in the world is 30,000; Burger King, 11,100; and Wendy's, 6,600, for a combined total of 47,700. See http://www.mcdonalds.com/corp/invest/pub/2006; Burger King Holdings, Inc. Second Quarter Fiscal 2008 Earnings, 1/31/08, www.burgerking.com/bkglobal; and http://www.wendys-invest.com, all accessed February 4, 2008. Most of the McDonald's are outside the United States, and Burger King is trying to catch up as it only has 3,800 stores overseas.

64. http://www.restaurant.org/pressroom/. Accessed in July 2007.

Matthew Salesses recently published his first novel, *The Hundred Year Flood,* about a Korean-American living in Prague during an historic flood. He has published essays about his life as the adopted Asian son of white parents for publications such as *Code Switch, The New York Times,* and *The Toast.*

Different Racisms: On Jeremy Lin and How the Rules of Racism Are Different for Asian Americans
Matthew Salesses

My senior year in Chapel Hill, I finally got up the courage to take a course in Asian American literature. Stupidly, I treated it as a little experiment. As an adoptee, I had grown up with white parents in a white town in rural Connecticut. My only knowledge of Asian culture was Chinese food and, when I was growing up, a number of meetings of adopted children that still haunt me, though I realize that my parents had my best interests at heart. They had taken me to these meetings for connection, but what I remember was the disconnect: the awkwardness of forced interaction between children who thought of themselves as white and didn't want to be shown otherwise. We hated being categorized as adoptees, or I did and I read those feelings into the others, who to me did not seem friendly, or familiar, only more strange for their yellow faces.

Those meetings made me feel classified by my parents as *other.* One of the things I most remember from that time (and from books like *We Adopted You, Benjamin Koo*) is the common experience that the adopted child has when one day he looks into the mirror and all of a sudden realizes that his skin color is not the same as his parents'. Up until that moment, he sees himself as white (in the case that the parents are white). I saw myself as white. When I closed my eyes, or when I was in a conversation and seemed to be watching from above, I was a skinny white boy, a combination of my parents, just like other kids. Sometimes, if I am being honest, I still catch myself looking down at my conversations with white people and picturing myself, in that strange ongoing record in my head, as no different from them. As a boy, the one thing that nagged at me was the flatness of my nose. I was constantly tugging on it, thinking that I could stretch it out and thereby gain acceptance.

But let me pause here for a moment. This is going to be a difficult essay to write, and I want to prepare myself—and you, reader—by coming at this topic from a larger angle.

Right now, it seems to me that a similar type of self-contextualizing (through race) is happening on a grand scale in Asian America, as Jeremy Lin takes over sports news and much of AA media references. With Lin's rise, there has been a feeling, a swelling collective feeling, that we Asians are no different from the other people we see on national TV, almost exclusively white and black. That we are Jeremy Lin, able to play as well as they in "their" arena, the ability of Jeremy Lin pointing to a potential in all of us. The writer Jay Caspian Kang says something to this effect in his Grantland article: "The pride we feel over [Lin's] accomplishments is deeply personal and cuts across discomforting truths that many of us have never discussed. It's why a headline that reads 'Chink in the Armor,' or Jason Whitlock's tweeted joke about 'two inches of pain,' stings with a new intensity. Try to understand, everything said about Jeremy Lin, whether glowing, dismissive, or bigoted, doubles as a referendum on where we, as a people, stand." When the disparagements came—as we feared and maybe suspected they would but hoped they wouldn't—it was like that first time looking in the mirror. We realized that for all of Jeremy Lin's accomplishments, we as Asians are still different, are still seen differently than other races by the vast majority of Americans.

The truth is, racism toward Asians is treated differently in America than racism toward other ethnic groups. This is a truth all Asian Americans know. While the same racist may hold back terms he sees as off-limits toward other minorities, he will often not hesitate to call an Asian person a chink, as Jeremy Lin was referred to, or talk about that Asian person as if he must know karate, or call him Bruce Lee, or consider him weak or effeminate, or so on. Bullying against Asian Americans continues at the highest rate of any ethnic group. I remember, when I was taking the Asian American literature course, an article in a major magazine that ran pictures of (male) Asian models above the tagline, "Gay or Asian?" I remember a video that went viral last year in which people explained why men prefer Asian women and why women dislike Asian men. Some of the women on the video were Asian American.

As I said, I was treating the AA literature course as an experiment. There were a few white students in class who laughed at the "Gay or Asian?" tag and found little offensive about it, at least until pressed. Maybe the first sign that my experiment was working was the anger I felt toward them. The test, you see, was secretly how Asian I was, or maybe whether I was Asian at all. It was something to do with discovering myself, and how much that self was formed by my birth, which I knew nothing about, and by my birth mother, who had abandoned me, and by the country that had raised me while leaving scars of unknown origin on various parts of my body.

College can be a chance to remake oneself, or to get closer to the foundation of oneself that one gradually moves away from under the influence of peers. I had, in fact, as soon as I got to UNC, attempted to join the Asian American club, but I couldn't get over how cliquish they seemed, embracing their strangeness, while the truth is that I was trying to get away from those differences. Soon I found myself, with this second chance, once again trying to be accepted by people who looked like my parents, telling myself I didn't want to be Asian if this was what being Asian meant, being birds of a different feather, expected to be an automatic friend because of race. I had, as you can see, my excuses.

Yet somewhere inside of me, I must have felt that I was growing further from myself. Racist jokes were told with alarming frequency for a school billed the "most liberal in the South," and I was friends with two groups: one mostly white, mostly Southerners in the same dorm; the other mostly black, with whom I played pick-up basketball. They joked without censor. I had a girlfriend whose aunt and uncle lived in North Carolina, and when we went to visit, they would say that at least I wasn't black, often before some racist diatribe. This seemed the predominant sentiment then. At least I wasn't ____.

I was taking the AA course to find out what I *was*. I hadn't read much Asian American literature at that time—I think almost all I could add to the class discussion was Michael Ondaatje—and a couple of books planted seeds in me then that would grow into a certain self-awareness later in life. I will always be grateful to Don Lee's story collection, *Yellow*. In Lee's stories, Asian American characters experience racist incident after racist incident, but these incidents are mostly background to their lives as sculptors, surfers, lovers, etc. The characters are very much of the world in which they live, the world in which I lived and a different world than the one in which white people live with the privilege of their color. In class, the white students were incredulous. They claimed such acts of racism could never happen with such frequency. Yet if anything, to me, the racism seemed infrequent, and with minimal effect on the characters' lives. I had grown up constantly wavering between denying and suspecting that my skin color was behind the fights picked with me, the insults, the casual distance kept up even between myself and some of my closest friends. Sometimes—in retrospect: oftentimes—these incidents were obviously rooted in race. I have been called "chink" and "flat face" and "monkey" many many times. And it is the context of these words that make a child grow uncomfortable with who he is, that instill a deep fear in him. (As a side note: I am married now to a Korean woman who grew up in Korea, and when I mentioned the "flat face" slur to her, she said, "but your face is flat." Yet how different was this from the leering way it was said to me as a child, something she hadn't felt as a Korean in Korea.) I was afraid, back then, of myself, as if there were a little Asian person living within me that was corrupting my being, taking me away from the white person I thought I was.

There are still incidents from those days that I cannot get out of my mind. I remember watching, in one middle school class, a video meant to teach us that blackface and sculptures of big-lipped black people and stereotypes of watermelon and fried chicken were wrong. Later that same year, one of my best friends drew a picture of a square with a nose poking off of one side. I knew this was me even before he said it. Sometimes my friends would ask me to do the trick where I put my face against the table, touching both my forehead and my chin to the wood. I thought of this as a special ability, but underneath, I knew I should be ashamed.

I would bet that this friend does not remember drawing me in that one science class. We often drew together. He was in all of my classes that year, as we were allowed two friends to share a similar schedule, and I was the only one who requested him. That he wouldn't remember this drawing is part of the problem,

I know now. He thought of the picture as a joke, though I had never seen him draw caricatures or draw anyone else so simply. Surely a part of him knew what he was doing but didn't stop him. There was no video to tell him not to—there was no one to tell him not to, even me. I pretended it didn't bother me.

That was the same year my closest childhood friend suddenly cut me off. We had been inseparable, but at the start of that school year, he made fun of me and seemed to use this attack to springboard into popularity. I spent many nights during those first few weeks of school crying myself to sleep, not understanding why we weren't friends anymore. It is a wound that still hurts—as I type this, I find my face heating up and my breaths deepening. I still don't understand completely, but I can point to the fear that this was due to the color of my skin, more than anything, as an indication that it indeed was. I understood even when I didn't understand, as children can.

In response to the students who didn't believe the frequency/viciousness of the racism in *Yellow*, the professor showed us an interview in which Lee says every incident in the book has happened to him. Or perhaps I found this interview later, I don't remember now. As a matter of research, I thought I would ask a few Asian American authors I know about racist incidents in their books that are based on events that happened to them. Earlier this year, Salon ran a piece by Marie Myung-Ok Lee about a bully who made it into her novel and whom she finally, after many years, confronted. I heard from several writers about experiences making it into their books: how they were unable to get away from writing about those experiences, as unable as they were to stop thinking about them, but hardly anyone seemed to want to call out those past attackers. I spoke with one writer about the condition of anonymity, as the people who had hurt him most were those closest to him.

I think what all of this says to me is that 1. these things happen to all of us, and 2. they leave the type of mark that we cannot escape, that we return to again and again, as writers do.

A few years after UNC, when I was an MFA student at Emerson College (where Don Lee got his MFA and then later edited Ploughshares and taught), there was a rumor going around that in the original workshop stories from *Yellow*, the characters were white. That Lee made them Asian later. I'm not sure the truth of this statement. In fact, I'm not interested in the truth of it. I'm more interested in the fact that this was a rumor at all. This was something people wanted to talk about, and talked about as if the *truer* versions of the characters were white. If Lee did use white characters, originally, he is not alone. I know many Asian American writers who refuse to write about Asian Americans, out of a fear of being typecast, or a fear of being seen as "using" their ethnicity, or a fear of being an "Asian American writer," or something. And really, I understand that. I have been one of those writers. This may not come as a surprise, at this point in this essay, but for a long time, I wrote only about white characters. I wrote about them because I grew up with people like them, but also because they were the people in books and because I, too, feared the label, or at least told myself I did. What that fear really is, it seems to me now, is a fear of not being taken as seriously as the White Male Writer, who has so long ruled English literature.

The breakthrough came when I started to be able to read my own stories objectively. Something was not making sense. Why were my characters who they were? I inserted plenty of flashbacks and backstory to try to "explain" them. But in the end, I realized that what they were missing, in many cases, was a crucial piece of me that had gone into them. They were Asian, like me. Many of them were adopted, like me. The original characters were not the *true* characters. And "changing" them to Koreans made everything make sense.

For my day job, I organize a seminar at Harvard on the topic of Inequality. I attend these talks both out of responsibility and out of interest. But after two and a half years, I can only remember Asians being mentioned twice, once in direct response to a question by an Asian student. I remember sitting beside another Asian American student and listening to a lecture earlier this year. He said something like, "Nobody ever talks about Asians," and I said, "Asians don't exist in Sociology." We both laughed. It was a joke, but it stung with a certain truth. The time Asians were mentioned not in answer to a question was in reference to university admissions—a heated topic now in the AA community—as numbers show that students of Asian descent make up a disproportionately large percentage of admissions to top schools.

Often I have heard Asians talking about these percentages with pride, even in responding to racism. If attacked, they "point to the scoreboard" of college admissions. Yet it is a very real complaint that Asian descent seems to count against us in those same admissions numbers. Both Harvard and Princeton are currently under investigation on charges of racism toward Asians, whose grades and SAT scores, on average, must be higher than those of other races in order to gain admissions. Many Asian Americans are responding by marking the box on applications that declines to indicate race, something I cannot help but read symbolically. I confess that I would give my daughter that exact advice, in admissions: not to reveal her race. The accusation is that schools have capped their "quotas" of Asian students, and this is why Asians need to score higher, because they are competing amongst themselves for a limited number of spots. Most Asians accept the unwritten rules, pushing themselves or their children harder. But why should they, in a country that prides itself on equal *opportunity*?

To bring up college admissions is often to be met with the complaint that we should be happy with the success we have. In fact, success is often used as a justification for why Asians are ignored in discussions of inequality. I was forgetting a third mention of Asian Americans in the seminars: as a group other immigrant races should look toward as an example of successful assimilation. Why aren't we happy with our disproportionate admissions and the many children who grow up to be doctors and lawyers, pushed by their parents? (The more sarcastic answer: why aren't white people happy enough with EVERYTHING?) Jeremy Lin, early in his success, was called out by boxer Floyd Mayweather as only getting the attention he was getting because he is Asian, since every day black athletes accomplish what Lin has and receive no fanfare. Or something to this effect. Other journalists responded by saying Lin is getting the attention because he worked so hard and is the ultimate underdog. Both these points, it seems to me, have a lot to do with race. Why was Lin an underdog, ignored by scouts when he had succeeded at every level and outplayed the best point guards he faced (see: John Wall, Kemba Walker)? Writers always seem to mention how hard Lin works, and often mention this as a trait of Asian Americans. They mention that he went to Harvard, how smart he is. They mention that he is humble. When I wrote about the "Chink in the Armor" headline for the Good Men Project, a commenter responded by pointing to Asian Americans being too respectful to speak up against racism. This respectfulness, he said, was something he admired about Asians.

It is hard to call someone who thinks he is complimenting you a racist. But the positive stereotypes people think they can use because of their "positivity" continue (and worsen) the problem. Thinking you can call an entire race "respectful" is thinking you can classify someone by race, is racism. Which is what is happening to Jeremy Lin when he is called "hard-working" instead of "skilled," when his talent is marginalized by a writer who sees him as the Asian American stereotype, the child of immigrants who outworks and outstudies everyone else. Mayweather has one point, at least—other athletes work as hard or harder than Jeremy Lin. I've seen the videos of Lin's workouts, how intense they are, how long, but this is not unusual for a basketball star. Read about Kobe Bryant's work ethic, or Ray Allen's, either of which put Jeremy Lin to shame. Jeremy Lin is the success he is because of his individual talent, not because he is Asian American. His ethnicity, I would have to argue, was only a factor in him having to "come out of nowhere," since that was where Asians have been relegated to in sports.

After ESPN ran the "Chink in the Armor" headline, the writer of the headline made a very defensive apology in which he claimed to be a "good person" who didn't know the weight of the word he was using. He was fired, and this apology came afterward. When he was first fired, I felt sorry for him. I didn't think he deserved to lose his job but then his defensiveness came and took that sympathy away. Some on my Twitter feed suggested he didn't know the term because of his young age. He is 28. I am 29. "Chink" is a very common term, probably the most common slur against Asians, and this was a writer and (I'm assuming) a *reader* who made his livelihood online. I find it impossible to believe that he hadn't come across the term in some way. It bothers me to see people make excuses for him. "I'm sorry, but" is not "I'm sorry." If you believe you can get away with the excuse, then what is that telling me?

A few years after I graduated from UNC, I decided to go to Korea. I had never been back. I was still writing white characters, though I had let a Korean American slip into my novel in a supporting role, a character who never finished his sentences, who was always cut-off or cutting himself off. I was still searching for that Korean part of me. I had spent a long winter in Prague as one of the only Asians in the city, strange in a strange land. In Korea, I fell apart immediately. I ended up losing twenty pounds in two weeks, and I would have run back to the States if not for meeting my wife.

But then a strange thing happened. I got used to seeing Koreans, and was surprised whenever I saw a white person. And after some time, not like the sudden realization in the mirror but a gradual process, I began to see myself as a person from this country. I wrote my first story with a Korean character, and something in it, the vulnerability, the honesty, clicked. In Korea, I had different differences than in America. Not that race was out of the picture—the biggest shock to people was my culture, in spite of my skin color, my inability to speak Korean—but it was like looking at race from the inside out, the opposite of how I had been forced to see myself my whole life. It was a lesson: that I had control over my differences, that I could choose to build them up or break them down, that they were not simply genetic, something that had never been true in America.

S. Sayyid is a Professor of Social Theory and Decolonial Thought at the University of Leeds. His work deals with the ways rhetoric helps to craft societies; he is currently focused on the causes of radicalism among Muslim populations, tolerance, multiculturalism, racism, and Islamophobia.

A Measure of Islamophobia
S. Sayyid

The growing literature on Islamophobia is dominated by empirical studies, the analysis of media representations and socio-psychological approaches, while many of these studies have been valuable in illustrating the range of expressions of Islamophobia; they have been less successful in understanding the phenomena, and mapping its relationship with other forms of discriminatory practices such as racism and anti-Semitism. This article presents a conceptual examination of the category of Islamophobia and the work it is called upon to do in contemporary debates, as prelude to a discussion about what a theorization of this concept could contribute to the field of social analysis and policy.

Introduction

There is a film that I saw once or twice called *Things to Do in Denver When You're Dead* (1995). Maybe it was an in-flight movie or on late night TV. What I remember about it, though, is the criminal argot that the filmmakers invented for the demimonde characters of the movie to use. This decision to invent a new slang always struck me as rather curious, since there already exists a rich and well-known slang familiar to audiences of American gangster movies.[1] So why did the filmmakers think it was worthwhile investing in a new vocabulary? The invention of a vocabulary is only useful if it does some work, in other words, if it makes some difference to our practice, if it allows us to say and do things that we could not do previously. The invention of a gangster argot specific to *Things to Do in Denver* has the effect of placing the movie in a kind of never-never land of crime, turning a rather mundane story into something like a parable or a myth, in which Denver is not really an identifiable place and the characters not really people. In the world of *Things to Do in Denver When You're Dead* there is phrase that characters use frequently: "Give it a name …". This phrase is used as means of demanding an answer for any query.

Islamophobia is a concept that emerges precisely to do the work that categories like racism were not doing. It names something that needs to be named. Its continual circulation in public debate testifies to ways in which it hints at something that needs to be addressed. What it names, of course, remains a matter of dispute. This dispute has two sources: philosophical and political. By philosophical I mean that there is lack of clarity about the concept of Islamophobia. Any review of the growing literature on Islamophobia will show that it is dominated by empirical studies, by analysis of media representations and socio-psychological approaches. These ontic studies of Islamophobia do not (and cannot address) the ontology of the category. They cannot provide us with a theoretical clarification. By political I mean that the dispute about Islamophobia is not due to simply its conceptual lack of clarity, but also with the way it appears in a contested field where questions about national security, social cohesion and cultural belonging are played out. It is this field in which the relationship between national majorities and the post-colonial, ethnically marked minorities is being forged.

In other words, Islamophobia is rejected not only because there may be a disagreement about whether a particular practice or behavior meets the criterion of what constitutes Islamophobia, but also because there is a dispute that any such behavior could be considered to be Islamophobic, because the concept of Islamophobia lacks any validity. In what follows, I want to address what kind of phenomena are brought forth by giving them the name of Islamophobia, and what a theorization of this concept could contribute to the field of social analysis and policy.

The tension between policy and philosophy is expressed in a number of ways in social sciences: there is the common assertion that policy and philosophy belong to two distinct realms in which the abstract reasoning and complicated language of philosophers has nothing to add to the work of practical men and women dealing with complex social problems.

In this article I want to focus on one aspect of this general problem: that is, the production of "action-able knowledge", which is knowledge that policy makers, with sufficient political will and resources, could use to make things better. This is similar in a way to the classic "mirror for princes" literature, which existed in various historical civilizations, for example, Hellenic, Sinic and Indic. To give advice to the prince was the province of the philosopher, who would educate the prince in how to exercise what could be described as something akin to good governance. This conjoining of the speculative with the practical is what Aristotle described as *phronesis*. It is as contribution to phronetic social science that this examination of Islamophobia should be seen.[2] Specifically, I want to sketch out some of the possible ways in which we account for Islamophobia so that the exercise of accounting would be a prelude to its reduction.

Defining Islamophobia

Discussions about the legitimacy of Islamophobia take place in the context of various mobilizations and confrontations centered on the figure of the Muslim. These range from the series of "moral panics" that seem to regularly sweep over mainly Western plutocracies, but also other places in the world in which some cherished universal (or Western) values are threatened by the actions of Muslims (or their extremist fringes). These are values—such as the freedom of expression, gender equality or tolerance—most often brought into play as being threatened by actions of "some" Muslims.[3]

As a term, Islamophobia has a number of iterations: more consistently developed in French, in the colonial context and around the 1920s in particular. It appears somewhat more sporadically as used in English, with the occasional reference, such as Edward Said's 1985 reconsideration of *Orientalism*, before its enduring appearance in 1997 in the Runnymede report. The latter makes no reference to its early formulations, giving the impression that it is a neologism without any historical depth and completely inspired by the contingencies of "race relations" in Britain.[4] In particular, the context for the report is given as mobilizations against the publication of *The Satanic Verses* and the emergence of a Muslim political subject. Conventional uses of Islamophobia, at least in the Anglophonic world, follow the lead of the Runnymede Trust report of 1997. The concept of Islamophobia that appeared in its pages was one that was defined in terms of eight constituent parts. These components ranged from perceptions of Islam as an unchanging monolith, to the view of its inherent violent nature and its fundamental inferiority to the West. Six of the eight components refer to Islam, and the other two refer to Muslims. Muslims are seen as subject to Islamophobia primarily through the transference of hostility to Islam and the naturalization of that hostility. This definition combines insights from the critique of Orientalism (in particular the Orientalist characterization of Islam) to ideas of racism in Britain that focus on the unjust discriminatory practices directed at ethnically subordinated socio-historical groups. It is possible to read in the Runnymede report, a conceptualization of Islamophobia as a product of the articulation between Orientalism and racism. The report does this by surreptitiously (and perhaps inadvertently) confirming the emergence of new political subjectivity into the discourse of British race relations: Muslim. By translating hostility to Islam into an hostility against those described as Muslims in contemporary society, one can see in the report an implicit recognition of the racialization of Muslims.[5]

Scholars of racism had already moved to the understanding that racism was not predicated on the existence of race as understood in primarily biological terms, but rather that race was the product of the process of racialization. As such, a mix of elements including histories, cultures, geographies and bodies were articulated to forge "race" as the condition of possibility of the exercise of racism. The radicality of the Runnymede report was to point to the way in which religious affiliation could be a sufficient source of group formation. In the context of Britain's ethnoscape, which by the time of the publication of the report had come to be organized around three principal subject positions—White, Black and Asian—the introduction of a Muslim identity was disruptive. Muslims could be found along all the spectrum of ethnically subject positions in a significant number to subvert the racial logic of Britain's ethnoscapes. Contrary to the more frenzied charges of secular-minded critics, the emergence of the category of Muslim was not imposed by the multi-culturalist policies of the British state. Rather, its appearance in the pages of the Runnymede report was a reflection of the mobilization that had taken place in Britain against the publication of *The Satanic Verses* in 1989.[6]

This mobilization ruptured the immigrant imaginary that had governed the settlement and domestication of post-colonial migration to Britain.[7] It was a mobilization that was itself made possible by the phenomenon throughout the Muslim Ummah, in which Kemalist projects were shaken by Islamist advances (Sayyid 2003: 53–83). The conceptualization of Islamophobia that began to circulate in the wake of the Runnymede report shared a general understanding of racism that was positivist and saw racism as primarily a matter of attitudes and beliefs. Thus the report was unable to get across the subtlety of its formulation, and as such, Islamophobia emerged as a rather impoverished concept, uncertain and unclear about what work it was being asked to do. This enabled those who opposed the conceptualization of Islamophobia to see it as a portmanteau expression that had little purpose.

The opposition to Islamophobia has three overlapping strands. Firstly, it is argued that Islamophobia is not a valid category, since the phenomena it seeks to describe does not exist. That is, there is no significant specific discrimination against Muslims because they are Muslims.[8] Whatever discrimination or prejudice that may be said to exist against Muslims can be explained as racism—pure and simple—and as such does not require a special concept. Secondly, there are the set of arguments that maintain the deployment of Islamophobia is a means of stifling debate and free expression. In other words, Islamophobia is (to use popular expression) seen as another sign of "political correctness gone mad". Thirdly, it is argued that Islamophobia is a legitimate response to the threat, or perceptions of threat, produced by the radicalization of a significant number of Muslims.

What a term comes to mean is related to how it is used, how it is embedded in cultural practices and, in other words, the language game played around the term in question. For a concept as contested as Islamophobia, this means that the politics around its use are far more visible than the politics around the use of many other terms and an ostensive definition would not work. Nor would an approach that seeks to analyze Islamophobia into its constituent elements, which is a common way of trying to define a category.[9] To have a measure of Islamophobia, we need to be able to sketch out the main frontlines in the politics evoked by Islamophobia. The politics of Islamophobia are constituted by a struggle between the opponents of the concept and its advocates. The opposition to the category straddles the conventional differences between left and right. Similarly, the advocates of Islamophobia cannot be neatly grouped along pre-existing political allegiances and solidarities: in its ranks are included both conservatives and leftists. This rearranging of the normal axis of conflict in Western plutocracies, demonstrates the disruptive effect of the disclosure of a Muslim political subject position.

Those who favor the use of the category of Islamophobia argue that Islamophobia is a means of describing a situation that would otherwise go unreported and unattended. Arguments that support the concept of Islamophobia point to the work done by categories such as anti-Semitism and racism in mobilizing opposition to these forms of injustice. Islamophobia is then prized as the means by which to suggest a mechanism for the reduction of injustice directed at Muslims. Islamophobia is not about the "hatred and fear of Islam" or Muslims. The range of activities covered by Islamophobia exceed its common formulations; rather it occurs as a response to the problematization of Muslim identity. This is similar to the way in which Brian Klug (2013: 474–475) points out that what is important is not that anti-Semitism is simply an expression of intense hostility toward Jews or Judaism, but rather what is at stake is that anti-Semitism defines Jewishness in such a way that it impoverishes the ability of those designated as Jews to elaborate their sense of what it means to be Jewish. Similarly, more than an expression of hatred or fear, Islamophobia needs to be understood as an undermining of the ability of Muslims as Muslims, to project themselves into the future. The manner in which Islamophobia is expressed and made manifest are diverse. This makes it difficult to say that Islamophobia has one specific feature that is hidden behind all its various occurrences. There is no essence to Islamophobia; instead there is a series of overlapping elements that constitute a coherence based around a notion of what Wittgenstein described as a family resemblance.[10] It is possible to see how a gesture, a speech, and a police action can all be aspects of Islamophobia reflecting not an underlying unity, but a series of overlapping similarities. Thus the definition that this article introduces is to see Islamophobia through the range of its deployments, rather than through its purported essence or its constituent elements. The various ways in which Islamophobia is used to describe situations are conditioned by the specific cultural, socioeconomic and historical factors that have influenced the way in which Islam can be performed.

The performance of Islam is staged in four distinct theaters (Sayyid, 2010: 3). Firstly, there is Muslimistan, which is a group of countries socially and culturally dominated, either informally or formally, by the Islamicate. For all practical purposes, this means countries in which a very large percentage of the population would define themselves as Muslim.[11] Very often Islam would have some constitutional privilege accorded to it; for example, Islam defined as a state religion. Muslimistan approximates the membership of the Organization of Islamic Cooperation (OIC) with one or two anomalies, such as the inclusion of Mozambique, but the exclusion of Bosnia-Herzegovina. The second theater is formed by territories in which Muslims are a clear minority, marginal to the national narrative, even though their presence is simultaneous to or predates the formation of the state; for example, the Muslim populations of India, Russia, China and Thailand. The third theater where Islamophobia is performed, is in territories where Muslims are represented mainly as immigrants. Many of these countries are Western plutocracies, but this not exclusively so. The fourth theater, is one in which the Muslim presence is negligible and the Islamophobia that is performed is vicarious or virtual. Countries in large parts of Central Africa or most of South America would be included in this group. These four theaters condition the range of contexts and variety of forms that Islamophobia can take. The different ways in which Muslims are disclosed is crucial to the way in which Islamophobia is articulated.

The Repertoire of Islamophobia

In my discussion of *Things to Do in Denver When You're Dead* I said that when characters use the phrase "Give it a name" it is a call for an explanation. I came to this conclusion by seeing that various times throughout the film when the characters use the phrase, the response is an explanation. The meaning of the term could not have been understood analytically (by breaking it down its constituent parts), it could only be understood by seeing the range of its uses. In this section, I want to try and describe the various actions and attitudes that are most commonly described as being covered by the term.

The list is not exhaustive but indicative, and there is no claim that all these actions occur with equal intensity, or are comparable in terms of the level of harm that they may inflict. They are simply the types of things that can get described as being Islamophobic. The use of multiple examples of what is described as Islamophobia is a useful way of explaining (as opposed to just trying to define) this concept. Wittgenstein's discussion of family resemblance occurs as he gives one example after another of the meaning of the concept "game". He shows by a multiplicity of examples that even though there is no common property to various uses of the term, it is possible to see a network of associations by which we can understand that chess, solitaire, soccer, football and hop-scotch are all games. The purpose of drawing out the repertoire of Islamophobia, is to elucidate the kind of behaviors that can potentially be understood through deployment of the category. It is possible to group the activities described as Islamophobic in six main clusters.

Firstly, there are manifestations of Islamophobia through attacks on persons perceived to be Muslims. These attacks can be committed by random individuals or by semi-organized or organized groups acting together. These can include: shouting abuse, pushing, spitting, pulling hijabs from Muslim women, various forms of beating and, of course, can culminate in murder. What is common to all these incidents is that they target Muslims, the violence is unprovoked and that they occur in public settings such as the street or the park. Secondly, one can identify Islamophobia in attacks on property considered to be linked to Muslims: mosques, cemeteries, business premises. These attacks may include vandalism (broken windows, hurling pig's heads into mosques, graffiti), arson, desecration of Muslim graves. Thirdly, there is the Islamophobia represented by acts of intimidation. These actions would be organized since they would involve a number of persons acting in concert to intimidate a population that is perceived to be Muslim or friendly to Muslims.[12] The form of intimidation may include marches through areas with large Muslim populations. It may include advertising campaigns warning of the danger of Islam, as well as, the burning of Qur'an or demonstrations against building of mosques or cultural centers. What distinguishes these sets of actions is the degree of coordination requiring the expenditure of social and financial capital. The fourth cluster of Islamophobia can be described as that which may occur in institutional settings, in which those perceived to be Muslims receive less favorable treatment than their peers in comparative positions within the same organizations. Such behavior may take the form of harassment, bullying, pointed jokes, distribution of tasks, and assessments of performance in which those considered to be Muslims are subject to adverse treatment or comment. The range of examples could include (but would not be restricted to) the serving of ham sandwiches for Muslims in a university research center tasked with understanding Islam, or an implemented dress code that places greater burden on those perceived to be Muslims than other staff in the same organization. It can occur when the rationalization for decision-making in organizations includes elements that arise from tropes associated with Islam and its cognates. Thus, a Muslim may be refused promotion and the rationalization may be that he or she is radical, or does not know how to behave in a mixed gender workplace. Some of these organizations may be part of an institutional ensemble that makes up the state, while others may be private. Again, this cluster of Islamophobia is not necessarily directed or coordinated by a state project, rather its occurrence is a subject of absence of robust anti-discrimination legislation or culture, or the inclusion of Muslims within the ambit of such measures even if they exist. The fifth cluster of Islamophobia refers to incidents in which there is a sustained and systematic elaboration of comments in the public domain that disparage Muslims and/or Islam. This disparagement could be more or less subtle. For example, publishing the Qur'an with Muhammad listed as the author or recycling medieval Christian polemics as the "truth" about Islam or reading specific crimes as being motivated by Islam or Muslim culture.[13] This form of Islamophobia could be articulated on internet hate sites, newspapers, magazines, or other media. It may be in factual or fictional programs. The form of Islamophobia can also inform policy and opinion, and may be the ground for state interventions and regulations. It could also be part of the common sense of a society—that set of unexamined assumptions and beliefs that circulate in any society.

The above five sets of Islamophobia tend to be carried out by individuals or organizations (private or public). The state may facilitate them through benign neglect or refusal to provide adequate safeguards, or to challenge such actions, but it is not actively or openly involved in the perpetuation of these incidents. There are, however, other aspects of activities that are described as being Islamophobia in which the state (in the form of its functionaries) plays an active role.

These can include intensification of surveillance of Muslim populations using technology, agent provocateurs, and paid informers. Such surveillance may be carried out by what can be described rather loosely as the secret police (that is, state agencies tasked with clandestine operating procedures).[14] In addition to these secret police operations, there is an Islamophobia of the criminal justice system in which those deemed to be Muslims are perceived to be treated less favorably than others. This can be the result of differential sentencing, difference in the frequency of being stopped and searched by police officers. State policies could also be used to restrict expression of Muslimness—for example, limiting the building of mosques, regulating Muslim dress (bans on the burqa). What makes these sorts of activities appear to be Islamophobic is the degree to which they place extra burdens on sections of the population which are mostly Muslim.

What is clear about these performative clusters of Islamophobia is that most of the actions that constitute the repertoire of Islamophobia are not exclusive; they can be found in performances of anti-Semitism and racism in general. This raises the question about the exact relationship between Islamophobia, racism and anti-Semitism. To map out the contours of this relationship it is necessary for me to sketch out my understanding of racism.

The category of racism (as distinct from the category of race) first emerges in the 1930s to describe the experience of primarily people of Jewish heritage living under Nazi rule. Why was the concept of racism needed to describe these experiences? The Nuremberg Laws and the associated legal and extra-legal practices were very similar to what was going on throughout the rest of the world, in which European settlers or administrations regulated the conduct of what were deemed to be non-European peoples. One way of describing this ensemble of practices and institutions would be colonialism. The colonial frame refers not only to the empires of the British, French, and Dutch but also the "inner empires" in which European settlers confronted indigenous peoples of the Americas and Australasia. All the techniques of social exclusion, segregation and marginalization were already operating under the heading of colonialism: concentration camps, discriminatory legal codes, repression through native collusions, semi-official systems of violations—none of these were new to European practice or the innovation of the Nazis, so why not use the concept of colonialism to describe the phenomena, why the need for racism? One way of understanding Nazism is to understand it as the application of European colonial rule to the interior of the European continent. Racism emerges to account for the application of colonial rule in the heartlands of Europe, while still maintaining the difference between West and non-West, which was constitutive of the colonial world order.

This conceptualization of racism has a number of consequences. Firstly, it extrapolates from the policies of the Nazi regime the range of racist expressions and in doing so helps to foster a notion of racism as the antithesis of liberalism (Hesse and Sayyid, 2006: 13–31). Liberalism can be presented as an antidote to racism so that its complicity with racial logic is disavowed. This not only exceptionalizes racism, but also ideologizes it; that is, racism emerges as an abhorrent belief system, the product of an abhorrent regime that has ceased to exist (Hesse, 2007: 643–63). Thus the racism inherent in the European colonial enterprise—be it British, Spanish, French, Portuguese, Dutch, Russian, Belgian or American—is elided. The second consequence of this conception of racism is that it establishes the scientific and biological foundation of racism. Racism becomes centered on the existence of race understood as a biological phenomenon (this explains the effort made by biologists and others to deny that the category of "race" had any basis in science).

The split between racism and colonialism means that Islamophobia appears to be different from racism. It cannot be contained within the field of domestic policy, since one of the particularities of Muslims is that they are a transnational people. Thus, the borders of the nation-state are not adequate to contain all of them. Furthermore, it is difficult to find a biological locus for Muslims. Muslims are not a 'race' and being a Muslim is not the same as having a biological identity that cannot be easily changed. Thus Islamophobia, unlike classical assumptions of discriminatory practices such as anti-Semitism, sexism, homophobia, racism and so forth, seem to rest upon a subject that is not given by nature. Therefore, being Muslim is considered to be a matter of choice in a way that being a Jew, a woman, a Roma or gay is not (The conundrum of Islamophobia is that despite its expressions, which echo those found in anti-Semitism and racism in general, there is a degree of uncertainty about the construction of the subject of Islamophobia. If Muslims are not a race or even a lineage (which they clearly are not) then what are they? Is not being a Muslim similar to being a communist or liberal, that is, a matter of belief rather than fate? It is true that one may have a great deal of investment in a position one adopts, and this investment may seep into other aspects of one's life, but it is a position that can be abandoned or changed, it is not hardwired in human biology. The contrast with other forms of discriminatory practices and Islamophobia rests, to large extent, on the degree of voluntarism in being a Muslim that is perceived to be absent in racism or anti-Semitism.[15] If there is mutability to being a Muslim, then many of the acts that are presented as manifestations of Islamophobia can be seen as being expressions of other kinds of violations. The category of Islamophobia depends on the existence of a Muslim subject position. Muslims are not only targets of Islamophobia, but also those conscripted into resisting it.[16] What exactly is a Muslim?

Any answer to this question has to begin with an acknowledgment that being a Muslim is an over determined subject position; being a Muslim cannot mean being nothing else, and thus whatever a Muslim is, she is also many other things including racial or ethnically marked in various ways. The "throwness" of humans, however, is not simply reducible to the biological. For example, our diets are not based exclusively on what we can physically eat, but rather are culturally conditioned so that consumption of foods that are considered distasteful in particular cuisines can produce a visceral reaction. Human bodies are read through culture, history, science, geography—they never appear directly totally unmarked. Sometime during the long sixteenth century, a particular type of marking emerged as one of the main ways in which social identities were constructed. This social construction of collective entities began to take the form of races, a category that began to be dominated by scientific discourse. The discovery of races, however, remained rather imprecise and repeatedly failed to correspond to the idea of distinct species to be found in zoology. Not only were there frequent taxonomic disagreements, but the establishment of various miscegenation laws and taboos pointed to the difficulty of policing the frontiers between different 'races'. Thus from the very beginning the category of 'race' (like most other categories) was implicated in social and cultural imaginaries. Racial marking does not arise from a distinct biology. The process of forming a 'race' is not akin to the process of discovering new species of wildlife, races were not found but created. Racialization does not depend on biology. It is precisely the impossibility of biology to make races that makes it possible to see the construction of 'races' as collective identities produced by social processes.

The idea that Muslims have a choice to be Muslim or not, and that their failure to make the correct choice is based on fear or ignorance is a popular belief. The idea of choice, however, does not take into account why Muslims should, en masse, choose not to be Muslims. There have been three major instances of the de-Islamization of Muslim populations, that is, Muslim communities, en masse, ceased to perform as Muslims and often lost any sense of being Muslim or awareness of Islam. The first such instance refers to the conversions and expulsions carried out by the Iberian monarchs following the fall of Granada in 1492. Most Muslims became converts to Catholicism and, under the watchful eye of the Inquisition, lost most of the distinctive practices associated with Islam (e.g. prohibition on the consumption of pork). The Islamicate traces in Iberia are largely (but not exclusively) to be found in the language and architecture. The second instance refers to the process of de-Islamization among the enslaved of the Atlantic plantation economies.[17] It is estimated that perhaps one third to half of all enslaved Africans taken from Africa to the Americas were Muslim (Diouf, 1998:46–48). Under the harsh conditions of the plantation-slavery, assemblage of the traces of this Islamicate inheritance were erased; so much so that as Sherman Jackson points out, the emergence of the African–American Muslim community in the early twentieth century had no direct relationship with even the "memory" of its previous Islamicate traces (Jackson, 2005: 38–45). The third major instance of de-Islamization was carried out by communist authorities with varying degrees of success. In some countries, such as Albania, the secularization drive was able to produce a population in which the awareness of being Muslim was lost or marginal. Historically, the mass de-Islamization of Muslims has tended to only occur in the context of regimes that were inherently violent, and authoritarian.

Racialized Governmentalities

David Theo Goldberg's conceptualization of the racial state might be useful in understanding the institutional ensemble through which Islamophobia is disclosed. Goldberg's Althusserian reworking of Gramsci (Goldberg, 2002: 105) allows him to conceptualize a racial state as state that "defines populations in racially defined groups" (Goldberg, 2002: 110). These definitions are then used for the purposes of regulation (social, legal, economic, cultural registers) that make possible the shift from government to governmentality, which comes to define the modern state. Goldberg goes on to distinguish racial states from racist states. He argues that the former are basically state formations that have emerged in modernity and racial logics and are hardwired into the very infrastructure of these entities:

> Modern states and racial states are deeply entwined, the conditions of the latter bound up with possibilities of the former, the histories of the former at once accountable in terms of the projected spatialities and temporalities of the latter. Modern states are racial in their modernity, and modern in their racial quality, their raciality. (Goldberg, 2002: 7)

In contrast, racist states are those in which racist logics are "…explicitly defined as the principal (and 'principled') state project" (Goldberg, 2002: 114). With the end of the formal apartheid regime in South Africa we saw the dismantling of the last major racist state. The post-racial appears in the space vacated by the racist state. The end of racism that the post-racial announces is a reconfiguration of racial rule by abandonment of racist logics as a principle state project. Goldberg's emphasis on the state as the engine of racist rule is an important corrective to the view of racism that focuses on its emergence and regulation as an affair of civil society.

Islamophobia is a form of racialized governmentality. It is more than prejudice or ignorance; it is a series of interventions and classifications that affect the well-being of populations designated as Muslim. This does not mean that there are no emotional, cultural or religious investments and expressions in the articulation of Islamophobia, but rather that Islamophobia is a language game directed toward the undermining of a distinct Muslim identity. In other words, if we understand Islamophobia as the regulation and disciplining of Muslims by reference to a Westernizing horizon (Sayyid 2010, 15–17), it means accepting that this hostility to Muslims is neither necessarily emotional ("hatred") nor religious ("Muslims as infidels") or cultural ("Muslims as outsiders") but rather political.

Islamophobia has so far not been disclosed as the principal state project of any current state formation. This, however, does not mean that Islamophobia has not been integrated into the racial state. There is no reason why the incidence, range and intensity of Islamophobic phenomena cannot be calibrated. The logical extreme of Islamophobia would be the elimination of Muslims. This elimination can occur in two forms: one would be physical destruction of Muslims, which would be genocide. The other form would be what would be described as de-Islamization, which would involve the erasure of a Muslim identity. Based on the historical precedents mentioned above, it should be possible to isolate the various institutional arrays geared toward the elimination of a distinct Muslim identity.[18] The degree of de-Islamization would help demarcate a number of stages of Islamophobia, allowing it to be measured in ways that provide policy-makers with milestones against which they could assess the efficacy of measures to combat Islamophobia. In what follows, I provide thumbnail sketches of the manner in which Islamophobia has been crystallized in terms of its principal agents, arguments and attitudes.

i. One can imagine a society in which de-Islamization is explicitly pro-claimed and practiced. The de-Islamization policy is instutionalized in the machinery of the state as well as the organs of civil society. This would be analogous to Goldberg's racial state. Such an entity would approximate the post-Granada regimes in Spain, or the policies pursued in communist countries like Albania. Islamophobia is official policy.

ii. A state in which policies and practices are implemented that are deemed to be Islamophobic, even though the state denies that charge.

iii. A country in which there are significant and vocal organizations demanding measures that are considered to be Islamophobic. These organizations are no longer simply marginal and their opinions are echoed by senior politicians.

iv. A country in which there are demands for Islamophobic measures to be implemented, but these demands are continually challenged and organizations and opinions exist that challenge Islamophobia.

Let us recap: in this article, I started by arguing that the act of naming is essential to the process of problem formation. I then went on to show the way in which the invention of Islamophobia enables the analysis of various forms of violence, violations, discriminations and subordinations that are directed toward Muslims. By referring to the multiplicity of examples and contexts, I showed the range of experiences that can be marshaled by the category of Islamophobia. I then went on to draw a taxonomy of Islamophobic institutional ensembles. There remains, however, a lacuna between this taxonomy and the various experiences that can be described as Islamophobic. If I were of a foundationalist persuasion, I would either not see the lacuna or more likely, not consider it a problem. Alas, my faith in anti-foundationalism does not allow me this luxury. I want to draw out the dimensions of this lacuna by referring once again to the article by Brian Klug (2013). To show us the problem of identifying anti-Semitism, Klug imagines a bus journey where a number of characters witness a bus conductor asking a rabbi to get off the bus. The question arises as to whether such an act is anti-Semitic. Is the rabbi thrown out for infringing some rules (e.g. not smoking) or for being identified as a Jew or being misrecognized as a Muslim (Klug, 2013: 476–478)? The point of the parable is that there is "no algorithm" that determines for us whether the actions of the bus conductor were anti-Semitic (ibid: 477). Reading anti-Semitic behavior, like reading any behavior, is a doggedly interpretive activity that has to be learned. An example of this arises when people arrive in racial societies where they are ethnically marked. It can take years for them to make sense of the way in which others react and respond to them and understand those ways as being aspects of racism. How can we say with certainty that such an act is Islamophobic or racist or anti-Semitic? The short answer—and this is how I read Klug—is that we cannot. Often the first response to discovering the meaning of an action is to seek the intention behind it. An Islamophobic act is one behind which there is Islamophobic intent. This, however, not only defers the problem from action to intention, but also moves it to the terrain where there is no apodictic way of understanding anyone's intention. Imagine a murderer who claims that his actions were motivated by the orders he received from his neighbor's dog. It is unlikely that in contemporary society such an explanation would be considered valid. We would not accept that the motivation behind the murder was obedience to a demonic dog. Imagine, however, that these murders took place in medieval European society, in which case possession by a demonic dog would be a sufficient explanation. In contemporary Western society, the medicalization of "deviant" behavior would require an explanation that would emphasize perhaps psychic trauma and childhood abuse as motivating factors (and cunning murderers often resort to this sort of reasoning as a means of mitigating their guilt). Accounts of motivation and intention are culturally conditioned. As result of the anti-colonial struggles, the Holocaust, and the Civil Rights movement in the United States, there have been transformations in large parts of the world where anti-Semitism and racism have been recognized as forms of cruelty and there has been a general socialization about how to read these behaviors. For example in the United States, 300 years of racist rule has forced African–Americans and to some extent others to be able to read racism in its multiple complex and subtle forms. Racism has to be socialized, its conventions and constructions are internalized in the enunciation of particular forms of subject formation. To know whether the bus conductor who evicts a rabbi is endorsing anti-Semitism depends on the arguments that are made, the network of associations in play in the event; in other words, the occurrence of anti-Semitism is a rhetorical activity. This does not mean it does not have effects or that it is somehow trivial. Rather, in the absence of algorithms, only persuasion and interpretation can help us in understanding what is or is not anti-Semitic. There are some people who will always see anti-Semitism and there are those who will never see it. In between are those whose understanding of what actions constitute anti-Semitism would depend on being able to navigate the cultural codes and conventions that suggest whether a particular act is anti-Semitic or not. Learning to see anti-Semitism, racism or Islamophobia requires a skilled familiarity with particular language games. Reading racism or anti-Semitism (and I would argue Islamophobia) is the skilled following of networks of associations and making arguments; in other words it is a rhetorical activity.[19]

Reading Islamophobia

If being an Islamophobe (or if you prefer, committing Islamophobic acts) is a learned activity, then so is detecting it, pointing to it and condemning it. If it is a learned activity then there is something to be said for the level of proficiency an individual may acquire. One analysis of the way in which humans learn sets of skills is the so-called Dreyfus model. This model has gained wide acceptance in various fields including medicine and the military. The model is based on Heideggerian recasting of phenomenology. According to Dreyfus and Dreyfus, the process of learning a skill has five identifiable discrete stages: novice, advanced beginner, competent performer, proficient performer, and expert. Within each of these levels are not only differences in skills, but also differences in the way in which skills are acquired. The movement from one level to the next is neither certain (in some tasks very few will become proficient—such as playing a musical instrument, in others most people who undertake them will—such as driving), nor is it linear, that is being an expert is not a quantitative extrapolation of skills required at novice level, but rather a qualitative jump. The Dreyfus model makes a major distinction between the first three skill levels (novice, advanced beginner and competent performer) and the final two skill levels (proficient performer and expert). The first three levels are based on distinction among those whose acquisition of skills is increasingly skilled but explicit rule-following. The final two levels are based on distinction among those whose skill levels are based on intuitive, holistic mastery of context (Flyvbjerg, 2001: 21). The response to racism illustrates these two means of learning. Individuals and organizations become aware of racism through often crude and clumsy check-lists, which often leave those who are proficient in reading racism unsatisfied, since their understanding of racism and its effects is not based on rule-following but on a *coup d'oiel*. Setting up a rubric for assessing the configurations of Islamophobia does not (cannot) evade the necessity of interpretation. Interpreting Islamophobia (or anti-semitism or racism) is not a subjective practice, but rather a skilled one in which there has to be a sufficient degree of overlap between one's reading and the other readings in play in the culture at the time. One way to understand the different responses to the occurrence of Islamophobia is to focus on variations in skill levels of the reading on offer. Some people who have had intensive and frequent experience of Islamophobia can often detect it with great acuity, and share that knowledge with similarly skilled readers. This expert understanding of Islamophobia, however, is not the result of individual qualities, since what counts as Islamophobia is what a particular framing considers to be Islamophobic. This, of course, is a historically situated understanding.

I have indicated that the performance of Islamophobia is a complex multi-faceted operation that is simply not reducible to questions of the representations or whether images of Muslims and Islam reflect closed or open views. Islamophobia is not just idiosyncratic eruptions reflecting social or psychological profiles of the perpetrators, but rather its occurrence has to be seen in specific assemblages. By identifying these assemblages it should be possible not only to take a measure of Islamophobia, but also to take counter-measures against it. Conventional strategies for diminishing Islamophobia often take the well-intentioned but also well-worn form in which authoritative speakers are asked to make declarations along the lines that "Islam is a religion of peace" or that "Muslims are not homogenous" or "the majority of Muslims are moderates". While in a moment of urgency such declarations may have some part to play, on their own they are unlikely to counteract Islamophobia. These declarations apparently challenge the idea that Islam is a religion of violence, or all Muslims are extremists; but this exchange takes place in a context in which Muslims continue to be narrated in subaltern positions, and thus, are easily countered by assertions that Muslims are extremist or Islam is violent. The logic of Islamophobia in its various forms is a relationship of domination.

The end of Islamophobia will come about when the hierarchy that makes it possible dissolves. Countering Islamophobia requires the dismantling of the assemblages that make it possible. These assemblages are specific, and while any strategy would need to be as granular as the circumstances of the occurrence of Islamophobia, it may be useful to suggest that the most successful means of ending a relationship of domination—is to facilitate and empower those who are its subjects. Counter-measures against Islamophobia have to be more than just refutation of the claims made by Islamophobia; ultimately, they have to tell different stories not just in words but also in deeds. These alternative stories need to abandon a Westernizing horizon as a common destiny.

Conclusion

In this paper I have made three main claims: (1) that ontic approaches to Islamophobia cannot do justice to the concept, (2) that a Heideggerian –Wittgensteinian approach to Islamophobia is better than what is currently in play, (3) that it is possible to use such an approach to open a conversation with public policy. To describe a phenomena as Islamophobic is not to disclose a pre-existing pattern of behavior. To name something as being Islamophobic is a constitutive act; it enables the gathering of disparate elements into recognizable formations of cruelty and injustice, which is the first task of making demands for their rectification. To account for Islamophobia in a way that can make a difference in social policy requires an understanding of it that sees it as a definite issue, not simply as an amorphous mass of tangentially related attitudes and beliefs. The implicit demand is that Islamophobia should be measurable in ways that produce evidence, which could be the basis of a rational policy. The difficulty, of course, is that Islamophobia is so contested as a concept that any evidence for its occurrence is unlikely to be forthcoming as such. This is simply because there is little agreement on what Islamophobia entails and therefore what evidence would support or undermine it. In this article, I have argued that it is important to clarify the conceptual haze surrounding Islamophobia so as to better understand what kind of ameliorative measures can be taken. To this end, I have suggested that it is important to understand Islamophobia as belonging to the family of racism. I have also suggested a Heideggerian phenomenological understanding of knowledge acquisition, which ties in with a Wittgensteinian-inspired understanding of the language game, played around the category of Islamophobia which allows us to measure Islamophobia phronetically. The emergence of Islamophobia points to two key developments: firstly, Islamophobia posits a post-racial subject that is subjected to exclusionary practices. Secondly, Islamophobia marks the transformation in the balance of power and anxieties generated by the de-centering of the West. Naming something 'Islamophobia' is a way of alerting us to the persistence of the racial in the post-racial. Much of the opposition to the deployment of Islamophobia reminds us of the post in the post-racial.[20]

Acknowledgements

I would like to thank Abdoolkarim Vakil, Ian Law and Brian Klug for their comments and encouragement, like wise I would like to thank Shvetal Vyas-Pare for assistance in preparation of the manuscript.

Endnotes

1. To what extent cinematic representations mirror the actual use of slang by American criminal fraternity or to what extent American criminals use the language of fictional gangsters to sound like authentic gangsters is not that clear cut.

2. For details about phronetic social science see Flyvbjerg (2001).

3. It's not always clear whether it is some Muslims or potentially all Muslims who are the source of threat. One of the common tropes of Islamophobic discourse is the slippage from the few and the some to the many and then the all.

4. See Vakil (2010:23–44) for more details about the genealogy of Islamophobia.

5. The Runnymede Trust is registered charity and was founded in 1968 as independent think-tank dedicated to producing research for the furtherance of race equality. It has produced a number of landmark reports and research on the challenges of multi-ethnic and multi-cultural Britain.

6. See Khan 2006 for a succinct description of the interplay with international and national mobilizations which facilitate the opposition to the publication of *The Satanic Verses*.

7. For details of the immigrant imaginary see Sayyid (2004).

8. This position is most forcibly argued by Kenan Malik on many occasions and across many platforms, see Malik (2009). See also Hasan (2009) for similar critique of multiculturalism as facilitating conservative Muslim practices and groups.

9. See the discussion by Baker and Hacker on the prevalence of this analytical approach to the definition, which they trace within Western philosophy from Plato to the early Wittgenstein (2004: 184–190), as they suggest the legitimate use of a definition maybe no more than to circumscribe the range of an enquiry.

10. For an elaboration of the concept of family resemblance see Baker and Hacker (2004: 191).

11. Recently the OIC has declared that in future its membership will be restricted to countries in which at least fifty percent of the population is Muslim. This would halt attempts by India and Russia to seek full membership.

12. The Muslim–Marxist–Multiculturalist alliance that Brevik railed against to justify his massacre against young members of the Norwegian socialist party was not a just a personal delusion. The existence of such a *convergence is one of the key tropes of Islamophobic discourse found among neo-conservatives and their fellow travellers.

13. Websites such as Jihad Watch, Bare Naked Islam, Campus Watch, Atlas Shrugs, Gates of Vienna, just to name a few, are replete with these kinds of stories, allegations and assertions.

14. See Hatem Baizan's (2012) comparison of the FBI clandestine operations against Civil Rights organizations and individuals and recent counter-intelligence operations against those they consider to be Muslims terrorists.

15. See Meer and Modood (2010) for an elaboration of this argument.

16. I do not mean that all Muslims oppose Islamophobia but rather that most of them experience its effects, and that makes it difficult for them to be indifferent to it. The existence of Muslims who repudiate the concept of Islamophobia should not be more surprising than the existence of highly problematic liminal figures that are said to inhabit worlds produced by racialized hierarchies: the 'self-hating Jew', 'Uncle Tom' or 'vendidos' …

17. Diouf (1998) details the spirited manner in which enslaved African Muslims tried to maintain their religious identity in the Americas, thus the de-Islamization that occurred was not because of a weak attachment to Islam, but rather the enormous effort made to prevent these Muslims from being Muslim.

18. Francois Soyer (2013: 408–410) draws a chilling parallel between the quest of Philip II and his advisors for "a final remedy" to the Morisco problem and Nazi designs for a final solution.

19. I am using rhetoric in the sense that Stanley Fish deploys as being synomous with anti-foundationalism, see Fish, 1990, 343–340.

References

Bazian, Hatem, Bazian's 2012. Muslims- Enemies of the State: The New Counter-Intelligence Program (COINTELPRO). *Islamophobia Studies Journal*, Spring 2012. 1, 1 165–206.

Baker, Gordon P., and Peter M.S. Hacker. 2004. *Wittgenstein: Meaning and understanding: Essays on the philosophical investigations*. Oxford: Blackwell.

Diouf, Sylviane. 1998. *Servants of Allah: African Muslims Enslaved in the Americas*, New York: New York University Press.

Dreyfus, Stuart and Dreyfus, Hubert L. 1980. *A Five-Stage Model of the Mental Activities Involved in Directed Skill Acquistation*, Washington DC: Storming Media.

Fish, Stanley. 1990. *Doing What Comes Naturally*. Oxford: Oxford University Press.

Flyvbjerg, Bent. 2001. *Making Social Sciences Matter*. Cambridge: Cambridge University Press.

Goldberg, David Theo. 2002. The Racial State. Oxford: Blackwell Publishers.

Hall, Stuart. 1992. The West and the rest: discourse and power. In *Formations of Modernity*, ed. Stuart Hall and Bram Gieben, 275–331. Cambridge: Polity Press.

Hasan, Rumy. 2009. *Multiculturalism: Inconvient Truth*. London: Politicos.

Hesse, Barnor and S. Sayyid. 2006. Narrating the Postcolonial Political and the Immigrant Imaginary. In *A Postcolonial People: South Asians in Britain*, ed. Nasreen Ali, Virinder S. Kalra and S. Sayyid, 13–31. London: Hurst.

Hesse, Barnor. 2007. Racialized modernity: An analytics of white mythologies. *Ethnic and Racial Studies* 30, no. 4: 643–63.

Hirschkind, Charles, and Saba Mahmood. 2002. Feminism, the Taliban, and politics of counter-insurgency. *Anthropological Quarterly* 75, no. 2 (Spring): 339–54.

Jackson, Sherman. 2005. *Islam and the Blackamerican: Looking Toward the Third Resurrection*. Oxford: Oxford University Press.

Jacques, Martin. 2012. *When China rules the world*. London: Penguin Books.

Khan, Shela, 2006, "Muslims!" In *A Postcolonial People: South Asians in Britain*, ed. Nasreen Ali, Virinder S. Kalra and S. Sayyid, 182–186. London: Hurst.

Klug, Brian. 2013. "Interrogating the new anti-semitism". *Ethnic and Racial Studies* 36, no. 3: 468–82.

Malik, Kenan. 2009. *From Fatwa to Jihad: The Rushdie Affair and its Legacy*. London: Atlantic Books.

Meer Nasar and Tariq Modood. 2010. The Racialization of Muslims. *In Thinking Through Islamophobia*, ed.. S. Sayyid, and Abdoolkarim Vakil, 71–86. New York: Columbia University Press. d (2006 and 2012)

Said, Edward. 1985. *Orientalism*. London: Routledge and Kegan Paul.

Sayyid, S. 2010. Thinking Through Islamophobia *In Thinking Through Islamophobia*, ed. S. Sayyid, S. and Abdoolkarim Vakil, 1–4 , New York: Columbia University Press.

Sayyid, S. 2003. *A Fundamental Fear*. London: Zed Press.

Soyer, Francois. 2013. Faith, culture and fear: comparing Islamophobia in early modern Spain and twenty-first-century Europe." *Ethnic and Racial Studies* 36, no. 3: 399–416.

Felder, Gary (Dir.) *Things to Do in Denver When You're Dead* (1995)

Vakil, Abdoolkarim. 2010. Is The Islam in Islamophobia the Same as the Islam in Anti-Islam; Or, When is it Islamophobia Time? *In Thinking Through Islamophobia*, ed. S. Sayyid, S. and Abdoolkarim Vakil, 23–44 , New York: Columbia University Press.

Marcelo M. Suárez-Orozco is a Distinguished Professor of Education and Wasserman Dean of the University of Los Angeles's Graduate School of Education and Information Studies. His work focuses on psychological anthropology and cultural psychology as they relate to migration, globalization, and education. Carola Suárez-Orozco is a Professor and Co-Director of University of Los Angeles's Institute for Immigration, Globalization, and Education. Her research focuses on immigration, family, and education.

How Immigrants Become "Other"
Marcelo M. Suárez-Orozco and Carola Suárez-Orozco

Unauthorized Immigration

No human being can be "illegal." While there are illegal actions—running a red light or crossing an international border without the required authorization, one action should not come to define a person's existence. The terms *illegal, criminal,* and *alien,* often uttered in the same breath, conjure up unsavory associations.[1] Unsettling and distancing ways to label people, they have contributed to the creation of our very own caste of untouchables.

In many cases, "illegal status," or what we prefer to term unauthorized status, may not be voluntary. We prefer this term to *undocumented immigrant* as many have documents or could have documents but often find themselves in a limbo state pending a formal legal outcome.

In the mid-1990s, Sonia Martinez, mother of four children, all under the age of ten, became a young widow when her husband was stricken with cancer. With a limited education and no means to support her family on a rancho in rural southern Mexico, she reluctantly left her children behind in the care of her mother and crossed the border without papers. The week after arriving Sonia took up a job as a live-in housekeeper and nanny in the Southwest. Every month she faithfully sent money home to her family. She called them every week. Each time she called, they had less and less to say to her. Lovingly, she selected presents for each of her children over the course of the year. By Christmas she would make the pilgrimage back to her rancho to see her children and, Santa-like, shower them with American gifts. But the sweet visits home were always too short and she would soon have to face the dangerous and expensive crossing back to California, relying on the help of treacherous *coyotes* (smugglers) she hired each time. After September 11, as border controls tightened, she no longer dared to make the trek back and forth. She has stayed behind the trapdoor on this side of the border and has not seen her children since then.[2]

---

1. Santa Ana, O. (2002). *Brown tide rising: Metaphoric representations of Latinos in contemporary public discourse.* Austin: University of Texas Press. [All notes are the Suárez-Orozcos', except 13.]

2. Note that we have used a pseudonym; this case is from IS @ NYU data—see http://steinhardt.nyu.edu/scmsAdmin/media/users/ef58/metrocenter/Online_Supplemental_Notes.pdf.

Sonia found herself a young widow and in a post–NAFTA [North Atlantic Free Trade Agreement] Mexican economy with promised jobs that simply never materialized and in an unforgiving economy for poorly educated, unskilled, rural workers. Plentiful jobs in the Southwest economy in the mid-1990s, relatively comfortable working conditions as a live-in housekeeper and nanny in a middle-class neighborhood, and an extremely advantageous wage differential proved irresistible. Although not raising her children came at a high emotional cost, the ability to support them was its own reward.

In 1998, Hurricane Mitch devastated Honduras, leaving little in the way of work opportunities. Like many others, Gustavo Jimenez made his way north, dangerously riding atop trains through Central America and Mexico and then crossed with a hired *coyote* into Texas. He worked a series of odd jobs but found it difficult to find steady work. Then, yet another hurricane changed his fate. When Katrina devastated New Orleans in 2005, ample work opportunities opened—dirty work in horrific conditions were hard to fill over the long haul of the cleanup and reconstruction. Mr. Jimenez quickly found work: "Who but us migrants would do these hard jobs without ever taking a break? We worked day and night in jobs Americans would never do, so that the Gulf could be rebuilt." But he found that he would be treated with disdain. It left him mystified. On one hand, "I know that by coming here illegally I am breaking the law," but he added, "I did not come to steal from anyone. I put my all in the jobs I take. And I don't see any of the Americans wanting to do this work."[3] Gustavo's story is both old and new. Unauthorized immigrants have always been called upon to do the jobs on the dark side of the American economy. The post-Katrina cleanup is a fitting example. Adding insult to injury, these workers are the target of disdain and disparagement. The stigma of the work gets attached to them—as if those doing dirty, demanding, and dangerous jobs themselves by mimesis become dirty, despised, and dispensable.

Hervé Fonkou Takoulo is a college-educated professional with a knack for stock trading in his spare time. Mr. Takoulo arrived in the United States in 1998 on a valid visa from the troubled African nation of Cameroon. He took to New York like a duck to water. He graduated with an engineering degree from the State University of New York and married a U.S. citizen hailing from California. She was the vice president of a Manhattan media advertising company. The bi-racial professional couple was ecstatic when President Obama spoke of his dual African and American roots. Takoulo's wife, Caroline Jamieson, "recalled that she cried when Mr. Obama said during a 2008 campaign speech, 'With a mother from Kansas and a father from Kenya'—I said, 'Oh, Hervé, even the alliteration is right—with a mother from California and a father from Cameroon, our child could do the same!'" She cried again but for a very different reason when the letter

---

3. Gustavo's quotes are to be found in Orner, P. (Ed.). (2008). *Underground America: Narratives of undocumented lives.* San Francisco, CA: McSweeney's.

she wrote to President Obama resulted in her husband's arrest. The letter to the president "explained that Ms. Jamieson, 42, had filed a petition seeking a green card for her husband on the basis of their 2005 marriage. But before they met, Mr. Takoulo, who first arrived in the country on a temporary business visa, had applied for political asylum and had been denied it by an immigration judge in Baltimore, who ordered him deported." Surely, this president with his extensive personal experience in Africa would understand that Cameroon had a horrendous record of human rights abuses. Instead of the hoped-for presidential reprieve, the asylum seeking Obamista was met by two immigration agents, "in front of the couple's East Village apartment building. He says one agent asked him, 'Did you write a letter to President Obama?' When he acknowledged that his wife had, he was handcuffed and sent to an immigration jail in New Jersey for deportation."[4]

When she was four, Marieli's father was assassinated in front of his wife and children. Left as a widow responsible for her family, Marieli's mother reluctantly left Guatemala for the United States, as she put it, "in order to be able to feed my family." Once in California, she applied for asylum status and waited patiently for her papers to be processed. The unforgiving bureaucratic labyrinth took six years and a small fortune to complete. Only then could she begin the process of applying to reunite with her children. In the meantime, the grandmother, who had been raising the children in her absence, died. With no one to care for them and after having patiently waited for years, Marieli's mother made the drastic choice of having her children make the crossing without papers. Finally, at age eleven, after having spent more than half her childhood away from her mother, Marieli arrived in northern California after being smuggled into the country by *coyotes*. Recognizing she "owed everything" to her mother but at the same time angry she had been left behind for so long, the reunification with the mother she barely knew was a rocky and bittersweet one. Marieli is now an unauthorized immigrant waiting in limbo.

The Reagan-inspired U.S. wars of proxy in El Salvador, Guatemala, and Nicaragua of the 1980s resulted in systematic killings—largely of noncombatant civilians, massive displacements of people, and the beginning of an international exodus of biblical proportions not only to the United States but also to neighboring Latin American countries. The U.S. invasion of Iraq has made Iraqis top the list of formally admitted refugees in the United States in 2009. While those escaping our foreign policy debacles often make it through the legal maze, thousands of others fall through every year.

The cases reveal how war and conflict drive human migration. But the heart also plays an unanticipated but powerful role. Work, war, and love are behind almost every migrant journey—authorized or unauthorized.

---

4. Bernstein, N. (2010, June 18). Plea to Obama led to an immigrant's arrest. *New York Times*.

Many come here fully aware that they will be breaking a law by crossing without the proper documents, but in other cases accidents, misunderstandings, and an unforgiving bureaucracy can turn good faith errors into labyrinths without exit.

During his tour of duty in Iraq, Lt. Kenneth Tenebro "harbored a fear he did not share with anyone in the military. Lieutenant Tenebro worried that his wife, Wilma, back home in New York with their infant daughter, would be deported. Wilma, who like her husband was born in the Philippines, is an illegal immigrant.... That was our fear all the time." When he called home, "She often cried about it....Like, hey, what's going to happen? Where will I leave our daughter?" The Tenebros' story, like many others, began as a love story and an overstayed visa. They met several years ago while Wilma was on vacation in New York at the end of a job as a housekeeper on a cruise ship. Love kept her from returning to the Philippines, and ultimately she overstayed her visa. Today, the lieutenant and the wife face an unhappy choice: "Wilma is snagged on a statute, notorious among immigration lawyers, that makes it virtually impossible for her to become a legal resident without first leaving the United States and staying away for 10 years." Lt. Tenebro is not alone—thousands of U.S. soldiers facing dangerous tours of duty have the additional burden of worrying that loved ones close to them will be deported.[5]

Combined, these testimonies embody the varieties of unauthorized journeys into the United States. Synergetic "push" and "pull" factors coalesce, luring immigrants away from familiar but relatively scarce surroundings to an alluring unknown. Immigrant optimism springs eternal. While some fly in with documents and visas and simply overstay, more immigrants come undetected through the southern border. Often they hire dangerous *coyotes* (typically from Mexico or Central America) or *snakeheads* (working from as far away as China, India, or Russia). Immigrants pay a very high price for these unauthorized journeys. While the crossing from Mexico to the United States can run approximately $3,000, the costs of longer passages are substantially higher, running up to an exorbitant $30,000 per journey. Those who arrive under the long shadow of transnational smuggling syndicates often face a period of protracted indentured servitude, as they must pay back exorbitant crossing fees. Whether the journey begins in Fujian, China, or Puebla, Mexico, tough border controls have made the crossing more dangerous than ever before—on average more than a person a day dies at the southern border attempting to cross.

The Children of Unauthorized Immigrants

Unauthorized immigrants are neither from Mars nor Venus. The majority have roots in American society. While some are married to U.S. citizens, others partner with migrants already here. Nearly half of unauthorized immigrants

---

5. Preston, J. (2010, May 8). Worried about deploying with family in limbo. *New York Times.*

live in households with a partner and children. The vast majority of these children—79 percent—are U.S. citizens by birth.[6] The number of U.S.-born children in mixed-status families has expanded rapidly from 2.7 million in 2003 to 4 million in 2008.[7] Adding the 1.1 million unauthorized children living in the United States (like Marieli) means that there are 5.1 million children currently living in "mixed-status" homes.[8]

Nowhere is the story of the unauthorized immigration more dystopic than for the children who grow up in the shadows of the law. On an unbearable steamy afternoon in July 2010, Carola Suárez-Orozco found herself in a somber congressional chamber testifying on behalf of the American Psychological Association in front of an ad hoc committee of the United States House of Representatives headed by Arizona's Congressman Raúl Grijalva (D-Tucson). At her side were two children—precocious, overly serious. A congressional photographer afterward whispered to Carola that in over twenty years on the job he had never seen such young children testify before the U.S. Congress.

Eleven-year-old Mathew Parea was poised and collected as he spoke in the august chamber. At a tender age, he had already been active in social justice causes for several years including a four-day fast honoring the patron saint of migrant workers, César Chávez. Mathew spoke on behalf of thousands of children of migrant families. His steady voice was riveting: "I am here to tell you about my fears growing up in Arizona. Children want to be with their parents because we know that our parents love us. The laws in Arizona are just unjust and make me fear for my family. I am always worried when my family leaves the house that something might happen to them. I think about it when my dad goes to work that he might not come back or when I go to school that there might not be someone to pick me up when I get out."[9]

Heidi Portugal physically appeared younger than twelve, yet she carried herself in an unsettling serious manner. Her story embodies the immigrant dream turned nightmare: "At only 10 years of age I had a sad awakening the day of February 11th. When I woke up, I found out that my mother had been arrested . . . . My biggest preoccupation was my two little brothers and sister. What was going to happen to them? And what about my little brother that my mother was breast feeding?" She went on to explain how as the eldest sister, she took on the responsibility of caring for her younger siblings, how her mother was deported,

6. Passel, J. S., & Taylor, P. (2010). Unauthorized immigrants and their U.S.-born children. Washington, DC: Pew Research Center. Retrieved from pewhispanic.org/reports /report.php?ReportID=125.

7. Ibid.

8. Ibid.

9. See Testimony of Carola Suárez-Orozco before the United States House of Representatives, www.apa.org/about/gr/issues/cyf/immigration-enforcement.aspx.

and how she has never seen her mother again. She went on, "Before, I would admire all uniformed people that protect our country...[but they] took away the most precious thing that children can have, our mother. With one hit, they took away my smile and my happiness."[10]

Mathew and Heidi are part of an estimated one hundred thousand citizen[11] children whose parents have been deported. They face an impossible choice no child should have to make—staying in the United States with relatives or going with their parents to a country they do not know. These youngsters are a caste of orphans of the state, citizen children who day in and day out lose "the right to have rights"[12]—for them the protections of the Fourteenth Amendment[13] are an elusive mirage. Children whose parents are detained and/or deported by Immigration and Customs Enforcement exhibit multiple behavioral changes in the aftermath of parental detention, including anxiety, frequent crying, changes in eating and sleeping patterns, withdrawal, and anger. Such behavioral changes were documented for both short-term after the arrest as well as in the long-term at a nine-month follow-up.[14]

They also experience dramatic increases in housing instability and food insecurity—both important dimensions of basic developmental well-being. Such insecurities, while heightened for children whose parents are detained, is ongoing for children growing up in mixed-status households. These insecurities exist even though unauthorized immigrants have very high levels of employment; among men, fully 94 percent are active in the labor force (a rate substantially higher than for U.S.-born citizens—83 percent and legal immigrants—85 percent). At the same time, more than 30 percent of children growing up in unauthorized households live below the poverty line. Harvard psychologist Hiro Yoshikawa, in his detailed study of infants and their families, documents the range of penalties American-born preschool children of unauthorized parents face. First, the children's housing and economic situation was often quite fragile. Second, unauthorized parents were less likely to take advantage of a range of benefits to which their citizen children are entitled (like Temporary Assistance to Needy Families, Head Start, the Women, Infants and Children Nutritional Program, Medicaid, and others). Lastly, they had less access to extended social networks that can provide information, babysit, or lend money in a crisis.[15]

While the majority of children of unauthorized immigrants are citizen children (4 million), there are some 1.1 million children who just like Marieli have no

---

10. Ibid.

11. Ibid.

12. Arendt, H. (1966). *The origins of totalitarianism*. New York: Harcourt.

13. **the Fourteenth Amendment:** Provides equal protection and due process under the law. [Eds.]

14. Chaudry, A., Pedroza, J., Castañeda, R. M., Santos, R., & Scott, M. M. (2010). *Facing our future: Children in the aftermath of immigration enforcement*. Washington, DC: Urban Institute.

15. Yoshikawa, H. (2011). *Immigrants raising citizens: Undocumented parents and their young children*. New York: Russell Sage Foundation.

papers. Many arrive when they are very young, others in their teen years. These children grow up in America, attending American schools, making American friends, learning English, and developing an emerging American identity. Every year approximately 65,000 young people graduate from high schools without the requisite papers either to go on to college or to legally enter the work force.

Unauthorized immigrants live in a parallel universe. Their lives are shaped by forces and habits that are unimaginable to many American citizens. Work and fear are the two constants. They lead to routines, where the fear of apprehension and deportation is an ever-present shadow in their lives. Dropping off a child to school, a casual trip to the supermarket, a train or bus ride, expose them to the threat of appre-hension, deportation, and the pain of being separated from their loved ones.

Mass unauthorized immigration has become a social phenomenon with deep structural roots in American institutions. The responsibility must be shared beyond the immigrants themselves to the businesses that thrive on their labor, the middle-class families who rely on them for housekeeping, babysitting, landscaping, and other amenities, consumers who have come to expect their affordable produce and rapid delivery services, and all citizens who have con-sciously or unconsciously enabled a dysfunctional system to flourish. Above all the political class shares the bulk of the responsibility by oscillating between denial, grand-standing, and hysterical scapegoating. They have brought us demagogic, unworkable, and self-defeating policy proposals.

Broken Lines

Outcry over our broken immigration system is focused on the borderline. Frustrated and fearful, Americans ask, "Why won't these illegals get in line like everybody else?" On the surface that is a perfectly reasonable question.

The reality, however, is that there is no orderly line to join. The terrorist attacks of September 11 threw sand in an already rusty machinery of legal im-migration. In countless U.S. consulates and embassies the world over and in U.S. Citizenship and Immigration Services offices all over the country, millions wait in interminable queues. New security considerations brought an already inefficient system to a near standstill.

There are nearly 3.5 million immediate family members of U.S. citizens and permanent lawful immigrants waiting overseas for their visas.[16] In U.S. consul-ates in Mexico alone, approximately a quarter of a million spouses and minor children of U.S. citizens and permanent lawful residents wait to legally join their immediate relatives north of the border. In the Philippines, approximately 70,000 spouses and minor children are in the same situation. The average wait in line for these countries is from four to six years for spouses and under-age children. If you are a U.S. citizen and your sister is in the Philippines, you will have to wait

---

16. Anderson, S. (2010). Family immigration: The long wait to immigrate. Arlington, VA: National Foundation for American Policy. Retrieved from www.nfap.com/.

twenty years before she can join you. If you are a U.S. citizen and would like to sponsor your unmarried adult child in Mexico, you will wait sixteen years and spend considerable resources.

The visa allocation system for work permits is no more functional.[17] The annual quota for work visas is 140,000 per year; as this includes spouses and children, the actual number of workers is much lower. There is no systematic queue for low-skilled workers. There are a million people waiting in Mexico alone in any given year.[18] As Roxanna Bacon, the chief counsel for the United States Citizenship and Immigration Services in Washington, D.C., succinctly stated, "Our housing industry, our service industry, our gardening, landscape industry, you name it—it's been dependent for decades on Mexican labor. None of these people qualify for an employment-based visa. So when the hate mongers say, 'Why can't they wait in line? Can't they get a visa?'—there aren't any visas to get! There is no line to wait in! And that's why everyone who knows this area of law says without comprehensive immigration reform you really aren't going to solve any of these pop-up issues."[19]

Reasonable voices have been driven off stage, while demagogic venting, grandstanding, and obfuscation saturate the airwaves, the print media, the Internet, and town halls throughout the nation. Rather than offering new solutions, an amalgamation of cultural xenophobes and economic nativists has joined together to fuel the fire. Xenophobes see mass immigration, especially from Latin America, as a growing menace to the pristine tapestry of American culture that would be stained by new arrivals from the "Brown" continent. Economic nativists wring their hands: immigration presents unfair competition for ever-scarcer jobs as well as putting downward pressure on wages. For them, immigration has come to embody the globalization in all its pathologies. Immigrants are tangible representations of enormous and amorphous problems—the globalization of terror, the outsourcing of jobs, and the discomfort of being surrounded by strangers (dis)figuring the social sphere with exotic languages, cultural habits, and uncanny ways.

References

Anderson, S. (2009). *Employment-based green card projections point to decade-long waits.* Arlington, VA: National Foundation for American Policy. Retrieved from www.nfap.com/.

Anderson, S. (2010). *Family immigration: The long wait to immigrate.* Arlington, VA: National Foundation for American Policy. Retrieved from www.nfap.com/.

Arendt, H. (1966), *The origins of totalitarianism.* New York: Harcourt.

17. Anderson, S. (2009). *Employment-based green card projections point to decade-long waits.* Arlington, VA: National Foundation for American Policy. Retrieved from www.nfap.com/.

18. U.S. State Department (2009). Annual report on immigrant visa applicants in the family sponsored and employment based preferences registered at the National Visa Center as of November 1. Annual Report on Immigrant Visas. Washington, DC: U.S. State Department.

19. Bacon, R. (2010, May 22). One border, many sides. *New York Times.* Retrieved on 22 February 2012 from www.nytimes.com/2010/05/23/opinion/23deavere-smith.html?sc =8&sq=Deavere-Smith&st=cse&pagewanted=1.

Bernstein, N. (2006, May 22). 100 years in the back door, out the front. *New York Times.* Retrieved on July 31, 2011 from www.nytimes.com/learning/teachers/featured_articles/20060522monday.html?scp=10&sq=Ari%20Zolberg&st=cse.

Bernstein, N. (2010, June 18). Plea to Obama led to an immigrant's arrest. *New York Times.*

Chaudry, A., Pedroza, J., Castañeda, R. M., Santos, R., & Scott, M. M. (2010). *Facing our future: Children in the aftermath of immigration enforcement.* Washington, DC: Urban Institute.

Orner, P. (Ed.). (2008). *Underground America: Narratives of undocumented lives.* San Francisco, CA: McSweeney's.

Passel, J. S., & Taylor, P. (2010). Unauthorized immigrants and their U.S.-born children. Washington, DC: Pew Research Center. Retrieved from pewhispanic.org/reports/report.php?ReportID=125.

Preston, J. (2010, May 8). Worried about deploying with family in limbo. *New York Times.*

Santa Ana, O. (2002). *Brown tide rising: Metaphoric representations of Latinos in contemporary public discourse.* Austin: University of Texas Press.

David Treuer is a Professor of English at the Dana and David Dornsife College of Letters, Arts, and Sciences at the University of Southern California. He is best known for his work as a novelist.

From Rez Life: An Indian's Journey Through Reservation Life
David Treuer

I am not supposed to be alive. Native Americans were supposed to die off, as endangered species do, a century ago. Our reservations aren't supposed to exist either; they were supposed to be temporary in many ways, and, under assault by the Dawes Act[1] in the nineteenth century and by termination policy during the Eisenhower era[2] in the twentieth century, they were supposed to disappear, too.

But I am not dead after all, and neither is rez life despite the coldest wishes of a republic since two centuries before I was born. We stubbornly continue to exist. There were just over 200,000 Native Americans alive at the dawn of the twentieth century; as of the 2000 census, we number more than 2 million. If you discount population growth by immigration, we are the fastest-growing segment of the U.S. population. But even as our populations are growing, something else, I fear, is dying: our cultures.

Among my fellow Indians, this is not a popular thing to say. Most of us immediately sneer at warnings of cultural death, calling the very idea further proof that "the man" is still trying to kill us, but now with attitudes and arguments rather than discrimination and guns. Any Indian caught worrying that we might indeed vanish can expect to be grouped with the self-haters. While many things go into making a culture—kinship, history, religion, place—the disappearance of our languages suggests that our cultures, in total, may not be here for much longer.

For now, many Native American languages still exist, but most of them just barely, with only a very few living speakers, all of them old. On January 21, 2008, Marie Smith Jones, the last living fluent speaker of Eyak, one of about twenty remaining Native Alaskan languages, died at the age of eighty-nine. Linguists estimate that when Europeans first came to North America, more than 300 Native American languages were spoken here. Today, there are only about 150. Of those languages, only twenty are spoken by children. Only three languages—Dakota, Dene, and Ojibwe—have a vibrant community of speakers. Within a century, if nothing is done, hardly any Native languages will remain, though the surviving ones will include my language, Ojibwe.

Cultures change, of course. Sometimes they change slowly, in response to such factors as warming temperatures, differences in food sources, or new

---

1. **Dawes Act:** The General Allotment Act of 1887, sponsored by Senator Henry L. Dawes of Massachusetts, divided Indian land into individual allotments; "excess" land was purchased by the government and sold to non–Indians. Individual land ownership effectively diluted tribal power. [All notes are the editors', except 5, 8, and 9.]

2. **termination policy during the Eisenhower era:** From 1953 to 1966, over 100 tribes lost their tribal status, over a million acres of land were removed from trust, and over 33,000 native people were relocated from reservations to large cities.

migration patterns. At other times, cultural changes are swift—the result of colonialism, famine, migration, or war. But at some point (which no one is anxious to identify exactly), a culture ceases to be a culture and becomes an ethnicity—that is, it changes from a life system that develops its own terms into one that borrows, almost completely, someone else's.

To claim that Indian cultures can continue without Indian languages only hastens our end, even if it makes us feel better about ourselves. Our cultures and our languages—as unique, identifiable, and particular entities—are linked to our sovereignty. If we allow our own wishful thinking and complacency to finish what George Armstrong Custer began, we will lose what we've managed to retain: our languages, land, laws, institutions, ceremonies, and, finally, ourselves. Cultural death matters because if the culture dies, we will have lost the chance not only to live on our own terms (something for which our ancestors fought long and hard) but also to live in our own terms.

If my language dies, our word for bear, "makwa," will disappear, and with it the understanding that "makwa" is derived from the word for box, "makak" (because black bears box themselves up, sleeping, for the winter). So too will the word for namesake, "niiyawen'enh." Every child who gets an Ojibwe name has namesakes, sometimes as many as six or eight of them. Throughout a child's life, his or her name-sakes function somewhat like godparents, giving advice and help, good for a dollar to buy an Indian taco at a powwow. But they offer something more too. The term for "my body," "niiyaw" (a possessive noun: ni- = "I/mine"; -iiyaw = "body/soul"), is incorporated into the word for a namesake because the idea (contained by the word and vice versa) is that when you take part in a naming, you are giving a part of your soul, your body, to the person being named. So, to say "my namesake," niiyawen'enh, is to say "my fellow body, myself." If these words are lost, much will happen, but also very little will happen. We will be able to go to Starbucks, GameStop, Walmart, and Home Depot. We will still use Crest Whitestrips. Some of us will still do our taxes. Some of us still won't. The mechanics of life as it is lived by modern Ojibwes will remain, for the most part, unchanged. The languages we lose, when we lose them, are always replaced by other languages. And all languages can get the job of life done. But something else might be lost and there might be more to the job of life than simply living it.

At Waadookodaading Ojibwe Language Immersion School at Lac Courte Oreilles (LCO) Reservation in Wisconsin, people are doing something about this. You drive past a lot of natural beauty between Hayward and the school—a lot of maple and pine; deep, clear lakes—most of it owned by whites. At the school, in two yellow modular buildings built with tribal funds in what used to be the corner of the school parking lot, a cultural revival is occurring. On the hot day in May when I visited the school I saw silhouettes of students drawn in chalk on the wooden decking that connects the buildings. The third and fourth grades were studying solar movement as part of their science curriculum, all done in

Ojibwe, and done only here. Inside, the classroom walls are covered with signs in the Ojibwe language. A smartboard, linked to the teacher's laptop, provides state-of-the-art learning opportunities.

One of the teachers who helped start the immersion program is a lanky, tall, excitable man named Keller Paap. When these teachers started the school in 2000 they had only a few students in kindergarten. Now, there are about twenty students in the program between kin-dergarten and fourth grade. After greeting the fourth-grade students in the classroom, Keller brings them to the music room in the main school building, where they all sing along with Keller's guitar playing to welcome the new day. They speak, sing, argue, and flirt with each other in Ojibwe at a level that eludes most adults at LCO and every other Ojibwe reservation across the United States. After the morning singing they head back to the classroom and begin working on their science unit. "Ahaw," asks Keller. "Awegonesh ge-ayaayambam da-agawaateyaag?" [So. What do all you need to make a shadow?]

One girl says, shyly, "Andaatewin."

"Mii gwayak," says Keller. "Awegonesh gaye? Giizis ina?"

"Ahaw," says a playful boy, without a hint of shame or bashfulness.

"Mii go gaye apiichaawin," says another kid, in a spurt of intuition.

This classroom is light-years ahead of most tribal language programs, which are still stuck on "bezhig, niizh, niswi," and "makwa, waabooz, waagosh" ("one, two, three" and "bear, rabbit, fox"). They aren't listing things in Ojibwe at Waa-dookodaading; they are thinking in Ojibwe.

Keller; his wife, Lisa LaRonge; Alex Decoteau; and the other teachers at Waadookodaading are, together, saving Ojibwe culture. Keller Paap is one of a few activists who have devoted their lives to saving the Ojibwe language. He is an unlikely hero. Raised in a suburb of Minneapolis, college-educated, a recovering rock star (he is an accomplished guitarist), he has given up all financial security, all his other possible pros-pects, everything, in order to move to LCO to open an Ojibwe-language immersion school. He is a new kind of activist for a new kind of reservation community.

Indian activism used to be a tough guy's game. In the late 1960s and early 1970s the American Indian Movement (AIM) rose from urban Indian popula-tions across the country. Cleveland, Minneapolis, Chicago, Oakland, and Los Angeles had been destinations for Indians relocated during the 1950s, and they became the seed plots for a surge of Indian activism. Relocation, a government-sponsored program, yet another switchback in the U.S. government's long road toward freeing itself of Indians and of all responsibility toward us, was a policy that sought to integrate Indians into the mainstream workforce by severing their relationship to their reservation communities. The relocation program promised jobs, education, and housing in up-and-coming American cities. Very little of this was forthcoming. Instead, Indians were crowded into ghettos, fought for work, fought for education, and suffered. It should be said that many Indians flourished in cities in the 1950s and many still flourish there today; more than half of all Indians live in urban areas. Still, the common notion that reservations are prisons should be revised; it was the city that became a prison for many Indians. They were stuck in a city and could not get out. They hadn't the money to move back to the reservation and yet they had little reason to stay. Franklin Avenue, Gowanus Canal, Chicago's South Side—these became signifiers of rough life as important as the reservations the Indians had come from. Out of this situation, which was supposed to gradually make Indians as Indians "disappear," came AIM.

Clyde Bellecourt, Dennis Banks, George Mitchell, and Herb Powless, among others, founded AIM in 1968. Its rationale and goals were: the U.S. government has never had the interests of American Indians in mind or at heart, and any attempt to work within the system or with the system is bound to fail. Unlike the black civil rights movement, AIM had no great strength of numbers, economic capital, or visibility to use in getting its point across. The answer: bold, graphic takeovers and marches. Within seven years AIM had marched on and taken over Alcatraz Island (more accurately, a group of Bay Area Indians took over Alcatraz and some of the high-profile AIM leadership came toward the end of the takeover); the Bureau of Indian Affairs (BIA) headquarters in Washington, D.C.; Mount Rushmore; and a replica of the *Mayflower*. At each event the AIM-sters dressed in cowboy boots, tight jeans, buckskin jackets, and headbands and issued passionate, even poetic, statements about the continued mistreatment of American Indians. Often, light-skinned Indians were told they couldn't belong to AIM or had to march in the back. AIM was always concerned with its image. Its activism was a kind of art—street theater that was visual and often violent and that conveyed clear messages about the mistreatment of Indians.

The most shocking and visible moment for AIM, and the moment that marked its decline, was its standoff with the federal government at the Jumping Bull Compound on the Pine Ridge Reservation in South Dakota, which left two federal agents dead. Leonard Peltier was charged with and convicted of murder and is still serving a sentence at Leavenworth. Afterward, marked by vicious infighting and infiltrated by the FBI, AIM became, in the opinion of many, aim-less. And not everyone had approved of AIM in the first place. During the 1970s anger at the Red Lake Reservation chairman, Roger Jourdain, at his policies, and at embezzlement by other employees fueled riots at Red Lake. Jourdain's house was burned down and cars were shot through with bullets. AIM tried to muscle in on the unrest and was rebuffed. The traditional community of Ponemah took a stand against AIM. As Eugene Stillday recounts, a number of veterans (of World War II, Korea, and Vietnam) from Ponemah gathered at The Cut—a narrow place in the road, bordered by the lake on one side and a large swamp on the other. They barricaded the road, built sandbag bunkers, and kept constant guard, armed with deer rifles and shotguns. Carloads of AIMsters drove up the road, were stopped, and after looking at the faces of the Ponemah veterans chose to turn around and go elsewhere.

This was what passed for activism in the late 1960s and 1970s. Keller Paap, on the other hand, is an unlikely activist. He was raised in a comfortable suburb: White Bear Lake, on the north side of St. Paul. His mother is from Red Cliff Reservation in Wisconsin; his father is of German ancestry. After graduating from high school in White Bear Lake he started college, stopped, and devoted himself to becoming a rock and roller. Keller *looks* like a rock star. He's tallish (six feet and change), thin, and bony, with long black hair, wide cheekbones and lips, and long tapered fingers that were made to hold a guitar and to play it well. When someone is talking to him about the Ojibwe language, the glazed look that comes over his eyes must be the same look he had during a guitar solo. It is not difficult to imagine him wearing a bandanna, like Steven Van Zandt,[3] or the same purse-lipped expression when he is focused on his guitar. During the day the kids sometimes start spacing out during their lessons and Keller jumps up, thumbs his iPod while gushing at the kids in Ojibwe, finds Herbie Hancock's "Rockit," and gets his kids to kick off their shoes and try to do the "robot," the "scarecrow," and "the moon walk." During the early 1980s Keller spent a lot of time practicing his break-dancing moves. Later, he and his friends followed the Grateful Dead.[4]

I first met Paap in 1994 at the University of Minnesota, where he was finishing his undergraduate degree. He was a student in the Ojibwe-language class offered through the department of American Indian Studies. At the time he didn't seem all that interested in the language.

"Back then I thought it was sort of cool," he says. "I was Ojibwe, my people were from Red Cliff, and this was our language, and it felt good to study it."

That good feeling quickly became a passion.

"It all started with hanging out with Dennis Jones, the Ojibwe-language in-structor at the U. I traveled around with him and recorded his mom and worked on translating her stories. And, man! The intricacy! The crazy complexity of the language totally got me. I mean, hanging out with Nancy, and Rose Tainter, and Delores Wakefield—all those elders, sitting around the kitchen table drinking Red Rose tea and talking—it felt comfortable, like it was with my uncles and cousins and relatives up at Red Cliff when I was a kid. Even more than music, even more than the guitar, the complexity and music of the language and the feeling of belonging to something totally caught me."[5]

Catch him it did. Soon after graduating he worked as a teaching assistant for the language program. He met his wife there. Lisa LaRonge is from LCO Reservation, due south of Red Cliff. Like Keller she is tall, with long brown hair.

---

3. **Steven Van Zandt:** Rock musician and actor, best known as a member of Bruce Springsteen's E Street Band.

4. **the Grateful Dead:** Founded in 1965 in the San Francisco Bay area; one of the longest lasting rock bands with some of the most dedicated followers (Deadheads).

5. Interview with Keller Paap, August 2009, Scattergood Lake. [Treuer's note.]

Like Keller, she has gone through many incarnations before devoting herself to the language. They moved to Lisa's reservation in 1998 and, with a few others, opened an Ojibwe-language immersion school—Waadookodaading ("we help each other"). Waadookodaading has been in operation for ten years now, as one of only a few schools generating fluent speakers of the Ojibwe language. Strangely, many other Ojibwe-language activists have some kind of artistic pedigree. Leslie Harper—who along with her sister Laurie, Adrian Liberty, and elders like Johnny Mitchell founded the Niigaane Immersion program at Leech Lake—is a writer and a former Miss Indian Minneapolis. Liberty is a drummer—his band Powermad was featured in David Lynch's *Wild at Heart*.

The goal of these activists seems odd to many: in communities rife with drugs, violence, gangs, domestic abuse, suicide, and high dropout rates, Ojibwe-language immersion seems like a perverse luxury.

Odd or not, what these fighters are after is something very different from what AIM was after in the 1960s and 1970s. AIM wanted the world to stand up and take notice of the injustices we suffered and continue to suffer. By taking notice public opinion might actually sway policy. Language activists look in the other direction—instead of looking out at the government and the mainstream and trying to convince them of something, they are looking in and are trying to convince their fellow Indians of something else. As my brother has put it on a number of occasions, "The U.S. government has spent millions of dollars trying to take our language away from us. Why would we expect the government to give it back? It's up to us to give it back to ourselves."

The U.S. government did indeed spend millions of dollars and many years trying to stamp out indigenous languages, mostly through subtle discriminatory practices (such as hiring and education) but the government also used unsubtle means, the most destructive of which was the institution of Indian boarding schools. As Native American languages endured a sustained assault, Indian identity—those elusive bonds that wed self and society and that make a people—took the greatest number of hits. Many Indians see this as proof of the spiteful, harmful attitude the feds have always had toward Indians. But governments really aren't spiteful just to be spiteful. They are like animals—they do what they do out of self-interest. And for many years, Indians were a threat—a constant, powerful, very real, very physical threat—to American imperial expansion. We were, quite simply, either in the way or powerful enough to pose a threat if provoked. The process by which Indians were dealt with only sometimes took the form of war. In many other instances Indians were subjected to a process of "Americanization." In place from colonial days, Americanization was aimed at creating a uniform public body, one that shared the same values and lifestyles and put the same premium on work, saving, expansion, and accumulation of capital. However, for Indians, the late nineteenth century and the early twentieth century was a dark time, in many ways because of the boarding schools.

In 1878–1879, the U.S. government built and funded the first of twenty-six federally controlled Indian boarding schools. Carlisle Indian Industrial School, in Carlisle, Pennsylvania, came to epitomize the boarding school era, which for many Indians was one of the darkest times in our history. The idea of the boarding schools was to forcibly break the family bonds that, in the opinion of many, kept Indians from becoming civilized and part of the American public. Carlisle drew students from more than 140 different tribes. The students had their hair cut short. Their names were changed. They were forbidden to speak their Native languages. No Indian religions were allowed at the school—attendance at Christian services was compulsory. Students were beaten for speaking their languages. Many were abused. By 1902, with twenty-six schools in operation, more than 6,000 Indian children had been removed from their homes and sent hundreds of miles away from their communities. When boarding schools and the policies that supported them were finally abolished in the 1970s, hundreds of thousands of Indians had been sent there. Carlisle alone admitted more than 12,000 students by the time of its closing in 1918.

Attendance at boarding schools was not compulsory. Parents had to agree to let their children go. But their permission was often effected through coercion. Indian agents, who got bonuses for collecting children for school, threatened to withhold annuities or supplies. They black-listed Indian families who refused to send their children along. Some parents, like my great-grandmother, could not afford to feed their children, and while their Indianness was under assault at these boarding schools at least their children would have something to eat. After the schools had been in existence for a few decades the pressure to send children away became a norm. If you wanted your children to have a chance at a job or an education you sent them away. It simply was what was done. Agents from the BIA were extremely effective at coercing families into letting their children go....

Forced assimilation in the form of allotment[6] and boarding schools had terrible effects on reservation life and Indian lives. But as bad as the U.S. government has been in its treatment of Indians, sometimes Indians are as bad or even worse to one another. One really fucked-up aspect of Indian life is that, unlike any other minority, Indians have rules, based on genetics and "blood quantum," that determine whether or not someone is *officially* an Indian ....

"Blood quantum" is a strange way to determine who is and who is not officially Indian. And whatever impact this might have on how one feels about one's identity, such exclusions have direct and sometimes dire consequences.... There have been blood quantum laws on the books since the eighteenth century, most notably in Virginia, where it was illegal to mix with Indians and blacks. Ironically, "one drop" laws (one drop of black blood made you black) were reversed for Indians: they had to prove they had a certain fraction of Indian blood in order

---

6. **allotment:** Refers to the effect of the Dawes Act; individual land ownership was designed to encourage Native Americans to assimilate into American society.

to qualify for enrollment and membership and to receive their treaty rights. But it wasn't until the 1930s that blood quantum became a widespread marker for racial descent, on which hung the issue of an Indian's nationality. Until then, for hundreds of years, Indian tribes had various means of including or excluding someone. Many tribes, mine among them, practiced widespread "adoptions." Indian children (and often white children) were captured or kidnapped and formally adopted into Ojibwe families to replace children and men lost in war or lost to disease. That's what happened to John Tanner in the mid-eighteenth century. He was abducted by Shawnee in the Ohio River valley when he was about ten years old, was marched into northern Ohio and Michigan, and later was sold to an Ojibwe family. He grew up among the Ojibwe, spoke our language, married an Ojibwe woman, and made his life with us. Not that it was always a happy life for him—his Shawnee captors beat him, left him for dead, smeared feces on his face, and piled other humiliations on him during his captivity. His Ojibwe family was only marginally more loving, until he proved he could hunt and provide for them. Indians from other tribes were adopted or married in and they enjoyed not only an Indian identity but the rights secured by the tribes and bands they joined.

Such fluid cultural boundaries became more rigid in the twentieth century. As part of the IRA,[7] which brought constitutional government to many tribes, the tribes could set their own blood quantum requirements for enrollment (half, one-fourth, one-sixteenth, or whatever), but only in consultation with, and with the approval of, the BIA. Since its inception, even though Indians are the fastest-growing segment of the U.S. population, official Indians in some tribes are declining. That is, many tribes are getting smaller.

Now many tribes are shrinking by their own efforts. The Mdewakanton Sioux Community has roughly 250 enrolled members. This number has remained quite static for the last twenty years—interestingly, the period when the tribe has run multibillion-dollar Mystic Lake Casino. The Mdewakanton is supposed to be a community reserved for the descendants of Dakota Indians who sided with the U.S. government during the Dakota Conflict of 1862. In payment for their support and their reluctance to join their tribesmen they were given land near present-day Shakopee, Minnesota. However, a lawsuit working its way through the courts alleges that there are more than 20,000 eligible enrollees (according to blood quantum rules on the books) living in the United States and Canada who meet the tribal enrollment criteria and can prove membership to the band at Shakopee. These descendants have appealed to the tribe and been rejected. The tribe doesn't want them and doesn't want to enroll them. In their case this is not a matter of "identity" but a matter of resources. If enrolled they would be entitled, along with the 250 officially enrolled members, to per capita payments, which would drop from $80,000 a month down to $1,000 a month. It is easy to

---

7. **IRA:** The Indian Reorganization Act (1934) terminated the allotment system, limited the sale of American Indian lands, and granted limited tribal sovereignty.

see why the Indians in power and enrolled at Shakopee don't want to open their arms to their tribal brothers. They are as greedy as any other Americans; I can't think of many people who after a lifetime of struggle would gladly give up $1.2 million a year in exchange for the moral high ground.[8]

Who gets to be an official Indian and who is an unofficial Indian is sometimes a matter of identity and insecurity about that identity. Sometimes it is a matter of economics and greed. In both instances tribal enrollment confuses race (descent) and culture (environment). Being enrolled won't necessarily make you more culturally Indian. And not being enrolled won't make you less so. But enrollment and nonenrollment can make you more or less poor and can determine where and how you live.

One of the strangest and most fascinating instances of the question "Who is and who isn't Indian?" is the case of the Cherokee Freedmen.

The forced removal of Cherokee and the other four members of the Five Civilized Tribes from their lands in Georgia, Florida, Tennessee, Kentucky, and South Carolina in the 1820s and 1830s to the Indian Territories on what was known as the Trail of Tears has become a symbolic moment in American history. The Trail of Tears has come to signify American injustice, Indian-hating presidents, paternalistic Supreme Court justices, and the Indians' plight in general. It has been written about, sung about, painted, reenacted. The Trail of Tears was brutal. Of the 15,000 Indians who were forced to march to Indian Territory in the dead of winter, 4,000 died along the way—from starvation, hypothermia, typhus, or pneumonia. One can envision the long line of the down-trodden and disposed staggering through blizzards and fording icy rivers. The Cherokee and allied tribes were forced to march because they had been dispossessed. Their 5,000 black slaves were forced to march because they were the personal property of the Indians. Once they reached Oklahoma, the black slaves continued to be slaves until emancipation. During the Civil War the Cherokee Nation was divided. Some Cherokee sided with the Union, others with the Confederacy. After the Union victory the Cherokee Nation was forced to the negotiating table, largely as punishment for supporting the Confederacy, and forced to sign a treaty. One stipulation of the treaty of 1866 was that former Cherokee slaves, known as Freedmen, were to be given full citizenship in the Cherokee Nation. As members of the Cherokee Nation, the Freedmen would be entitled to all the rights and benefits of Cherokee citizens, such as allotments, the right to vote in tribal elections, the right to stand for office, and receipt of annuities.

A little over 100 years later the Cherokee Nation wanted to remove the descendants of the Freedmen from the rolls and deprive them of tribal membership. This meant that these descendants—who considered themselves culturally (if not completely racially) Cherokee, who had lived and worked on Cherokee

---

8. Kevin Diaz, *Minneapolis Star Tribune*, November 10, 2009, http://www.startribune.com/politics/state/69722942.html. [Treuer's note.]

lands, who had the same values and language as the Cherokee—would no longer be eligible to vote, hold office, receive federal housing assistance, or receive whatever casino profits might come their way. One can smell divisive greed in the air again, though one senses something else, too: the Cherokee in Oklahoma have long had one of the most welcoming, inclusive, and progressive enrollment policies. Unlike the St. Croix Band of Ojibwe in Wisconsin, the Cherokee Nation requires only proof of descent from the "Dawes rolls," a list of Cherokee and other Civilized Tribe members compiled in 1893 and closed in 1907 for the purpose of allotment. The Dawes rolls had included a few categories of tribal membership: by blood; by marriage; and, specifically, Freedmen or descendants of Freedmen, and Delaware Indians adopted into the Cherokee Nation. There is no minimum blood quantum requirement. Such a policy has been a blessing and a curse to the Cherokee. With more than 250,000 enrolled members living in almost every state in the Union, they have remarkable power of presence and numbers and a much more flexible understanding than any other tribe of what it might mean to be Indian. They also suffer from encroachment and the constant threat of cultural dissolution through acculturation—many who want to be Indian claim to be Cherokee, not because they are but because it's easy. Hence the popular refrain we all hear at parties: my grandmother was a Cherokee princess. (No one seriously claims to be descended from a Hopi princess, a Dakota princess, or an Inuit princess.)

In the late 1980s the Cherokee Nation tried to disenroll the descendants of the Freedmen. The case went to federal court, which ruled in *Nero v. Cherokee Nation* that tribes had the right to determine the criteria of their own tribal membership. This ran counter to a century of policy that said tribes could determine the criteria for membership but only in "consultation" with the BIA. Many members of the Cherokee Nation were (and are) divided over the issue, and in 2006 the Cherokee Nation Judicial Appeals Tribunal maintained that the Freedmen were potentially eligible for enrollment. The Cherokee Nation put the issue to a referendum, and as a result a constitutional amendment was passed in 2007 that limited membership in the Cherokee Nation to those who were Cherokee, Shawnee, or Delaware by blood, listed on the Dawes rolls.

The wheels on the bus go round and round. The Black Congressional Caucus got involved. It saw the exclusion of the Cherokee Freedmen as an instance of exclusion based on race. As the case worked its way through the courts, Representative Diane Watson of California introduced legislation that would block $300 million in federal funding and annul all gaming compacts between the Cherokee and the state of Oklahoma until the Cherokee Nation reinstated the Freedmen. The basis for the legislation is about as potent an irony as exists in the history of Indian-white relations: the Cherokee were being punished for breaking a treaty they made in "good faith" with the United States![9]

---

9. See http://www.time.com/time/nation/article/0,8599,1635873,00.html.

The U.S. government and the state government of Oklahoma don't want to be too hasty or too autocratic in dealing with the Cherokee Nation—if only because the Cherokee suffered so much, before, during, and after the Trail of Tears. But haven't the Cherokee Freedmen—not just disposed, but the dehumanized *property* of the dispossessed—suffered more? In 1828, leading up to the Trail of Tears, the Cherokee had standing in U.S. courts. Their slaves did not. Tribal enrollment has been, from the beginning, a way of determining who can claim economic benefits that devolve from treaties. From the start, enrollment and Indian citizenship have been institutions created by the U.S. government as a way of limiting its responsibility toward Indians and eventually getting out of the "Indian business." But it couldn't always control the ways in which tribes sought to define themselves. Blood quantum was supposed to be a way out for the government. But this has been tricky. The Dawes rolls (and this fact seems to have been lost) were created as a means of fractionalizing collective Cherokee landholdings and opening up the Indian Territories for white settlement. When the white bureaucrats made the rolls, they listed people who looked Cherokee as Cherokee, and those who looked black (even if these were mixed black and Cherokee) as black. The Dawes rolls were based on blood, but only on how blood "looked" (and here we remember the anthropologists scratching the chests of White Earth Indians and measuring their skulls). From the beginning, the rolls were flawed and were designed to cheat Indians. One wonders: why rely on them now for any purpose? Enrollment has become a kind of signifier for Indians that says (or is believed to say) what someone's degree of Indianness is. But this is a relatively recent development. One wonders: by fighting about enrollment at all, aren't we just adopting a system of exclusion that helps the U.S. government but doesn't help us? And couldn't the Cherokee have won a little something from everyone had they thought of the problems of race, identity, and enrollment differently? After all, very few nations in the world base citizenship on race. It can be based on many things—such as language, a naturalization process, an oath, residency, or all of the above. Couldn't the Cherokee Nation say: since we were slaveholders, we have a moral debt to the descendants of the people we wrongly enslaved? Couldn't the Cherokee say: in order to pay that debt we will allow the Freedmen to remain on the rolls as citizens of the Cherokee Nation (or even limited citizens, nonvoting citizens, or whatever), though they are not racially Cherokee? This way the Cherokee would have sacrificed some autonomy and spread some resources a little thinner but would have made right a historical wrong and emerged as the moral victors in the enrollment issue.

Many Indian tribes, many reservations, are stronger than they have ever been before. Gaming has something to do with that. So do numbers. But we are not so strong that we can afford to waste our people. We are not so strong that we can keep excluding one another. But that's exactly what tribes often do....

In part, impatience with the sometimes self-serving identity politics is what motivates language-immersion activists such as Keller Paap. They feel that if they are able to bring language back to the center of our sense of ourselves, all the other complicated politics of self, all the other markers of authenticity, will fall away. They feel that the government's attempt at assimilation created the destructive, diseased social fabric in which we are wrapped today. And so the work that Keller Paap, Lisa LaRonge,...Adrian Liberty, Leslie Harper, and others are doing to bring the Ojibwe language back is, essentially, an antiassimilationist movement. In many ways it turns around what AIM started. (One of AIM's cries was "Indian pride"—and AIMsters didn't style themselves as BIA bureaucrats with short hair and bolo ties.) The renewed interest in tribal cultures and tribal language runs against hundreds of years of government policy....

For language activists, the language is the key to everything else—identity, life and lifestyle, home and homeland. Most language activists are also traditional Indians, but very modern traditional Indians, as likely to attend a ceremony as they are to have smartphones on which they record language material and Indian ceremonial music they are trying to learn. This new traditionalism is not a turning back of the clock, but a response to it; modernism (and modern, global capitalism) is a great obliterator of cultural difference and a great infuser of a new kind of class difference, and language activism is one way Indians are not only protecting themselves and their rights but also creating meaning in their lives. For Keller Paap and his family, this means tapping maple trees, ricing, hunting, collecting wild leeks, blasting Hendrix and Chris Whitley from the tinny speakers of their VW Westy van, and competing every year in the Birkebeiner cross-country ski race held in Hayward, Wisconsin. It means choosing to live their modern lives, with all those modern contradictions, in the Ojibwe language—to choose Ojibwe over English, whether for ceremony or for karaoke....

If we lose our language and the culture that goes with it, I think, something more will be lost than simply a bouquet of discrete understandings about bears or namesakes, more than an opportunity to speak to my children and friends in public without anyone eavesdropping. If the language dies, we will lose something personal, a degree of understanding that resides, for most fluent speakers, on an unconscious level. We will lose our sense of ourselves and our culture. There are many aspects of culture that are extralinguistic—that is, they exist outside or in spite of language: kinship, legal systems, governance, history, personal identity. But there is very little that is extralinguistic about a story, about language itself. I think what I am trying to say is that we will lose beauty—the beauty of the particular, the beauty of the past and the intricacies of a language tailored for our space in the world. That Native American cultures are imperiled is important and not just to Indians. It is important to everyone, or should be. When we lose cultures, we lose American plurality—the productive and lovely discomfort that true difference brings.

George Yancy is a Professor in the Department of Philosophy at Emory University. His research focuses on critical philosophy of race, critical whiteness studies, and philosophy of black experience.

Dear White America
George Yancy

In 2015, I conducted a series of 19 interviews with philosophers and public intellectuals on the issue of race. My aim was to engage, in this very public space, with the often unnamed elephant in the room.

These discussions helped me, and I hope many of our readers, to better understand how race continues to function in painful ways within our country. That was one part of a gift that I wanted to give to readers of The Stone, the larger philosophical community, and the world.

The interviewees themselves—bell hooks, Cornel West, Judith Butler, Peter Singer, David H. Kim, Molefi Kete Asante among them—came from a variety of racial backgrounds, and their concerns and positions were even more diverse. But on the whole I came to see these interviews as linked by a common thread: They were messages to white America—because they often directly expressed the experience of those who live and have lived as people of color in a white-run world, and that is something no white person could ever truly know firsthand.

That is how I want to deliver my own message now.

•

Dear White America,

I have a weighty request. As you read this letter, I want you to listen with love, a sort of love that demands that you look at parts of yourself that might cause pain and terror, as James Baldwin would say. Did you hear that? You may have missed it. I repeat: *I want you to listen with love*. Well, at least try.

We don't talk much about the urgency of love these days, especially within the public sphere. Much of our discourse these days is about revenge, name calling, hate, and divisiveness. I have yet to hear it from our presidential hopefuls, or our political pundits. I don't mean the Hollywood type of love, but the scary kind, the kind that risks not being reciprocated, the kind that refuses to flee in the face of danger. To make it a bit easier for you, I've decided to model, as best as I can, what I'm asking of you. Let me demonstrate the vulnerability that I wish you to show. As a child of Socrates, James Baldwin and Audre Lorde, let me speak the truth, refuse to err on the side of caution.

This letter is a gift for you. Bear in mind, though, that some gifts can be heavy to bear. You don't have to accept it; there is no obligation. I give it freely, believing that many of you will throw the gift back in my face, saying that I wrongly accuse you, that I am too sensitive, that I'm a race hustler, and that I blame white people (you) for everything.

I have read many of your comments. I have even received some hate mail. In this letter, I ask you to look deep, to look into your souls with silence, to quiet that voice that will speak to you of your white "innocence." So, as you read this letter, take a deep breath. Make a space for my voice in the deepest part of your psyche. Try to listen, to practice being silent. There are times when you must quiet your own voice to hear from or about those who suffer in ways that you do not.

What if I told you that I'm sexist? Well, I am. Yes. I said it and I mean just that. I have watched my male students squirm in their seats when I've asked them to identify and talk about their sexism. There are few men, I suspect, who would say that they are sexists, and even fewer would admit that their sexism actually oppresses women. Certainly not publicly, as I've just done. No taking it back now.

To make things worse, I'm an academic, a philosopher. I'm supposed to be one of the "enlightened" ones. Surely, we are beyond being sexists. Some, who may genuinely care about my career, will say that I'm being too risky, that I am jeopardizing my academic livelihood. Some might even say that as a black male, who has already been stereotyped as a "crotch-grabbing, sexual fiend," that I'm at risk of reinforcing that stereotype. (Let's be real, that racist stereotype has been around for centuries; it is already part of white America's imaginary landscape.)

Yet, I refuse to remain a prisoner of the lies that we men like to tell ourselves—that we are beyond the messiness of sexism and male patriarchy, that we don't oppress women. Let me clarify. This doesn't mean that I intentionally hate women or that I desire to oppress them. It means that despite my best intentions, I perpetuate sexism every day of my life. Please don't take this as a confession for which I'm seeking forgiveness. Confessions can be easy, especially when we know that forgiveness is immediately forthcoming.

As a sexist, I have failed women. I have failed to speak out when I should have. I have failed to engage critically and extensively their pain and suffering in my writing. I have failed to transcend the rigidity of gender roles in my own life. I have failed to challenge those poisonous assumptions that women are "inferior" to men or to speak out loudly in the company of male philosophers who believe that feminist philosophy is just a nonphilosophical fad. I have been complicit with, and have allowed myself to be seduced by, a country that makes billions of dollars from sexually objectifying women, from pornography, commercials, video games, to Hollywood movies. I am not innocent.

I have been fed a poisonous diet of images that fragment women into mere body parts. I have also been complicit with a dominant male narrative that says that women enjoy being treated like sexual toys. In our collective male imagination, women are "things" to be used for our visual and physical titillation. And even as I know how poisonous and false these sexist assumptions are, I am often ambushed by my own hidden sexism. I continue to see women through the male gaze that belies my best intentions not to sexually objectify them. Our collective male erotic feelings and fantasies are complicit in the degradation of women. And we must be mindful that not all women endure sexual degradation in the same way.

I recognize how my being a sexist has a differential impact on black women and women of color who are not only victims of racism, but also sexism, *my sexism*. For example, black women and women of color not only suffer from sexual objectification, but the ways in which they are objectified is linked to how they are racially depicted, some as "exotic" and others as "hyper-sexual." You see, the complicity, the responsibility, the pain that I cause runs deep. And, get this. I refuse to seek shelter; I refuse to live a lie. So, every day of my life I fight against the dominant male narrative, choosing to see women as subjects, not objects. But even as I fight, there are moments of failure. Just because I fight against sexism does not give me clean hands, as it were, at the end of the day; I continue to falter, and I continue to oppress. And even though the ways in which I oppress women is unintentional, this does not free me of being responsible.

If you are white, and you are reading this letter, I ask that you don't run to seek shelter from your own racism. Don't hide from your responsibility. Rather, begin, right now, to practice being vulnerable. Being neither a "good" white person nor a liberal white person will get you off the proverbial hook. I consider myself to be a decent human being. Yet, I'm sexist. Take another deep breath. I ask that you try to be "un-sutured." If that term brings to mind a state of pain, open flesh, it is meant to do so. After all, it is painful to let go of your "white innocence," to use this letter as a mirror, one that refuses to show you what you want to see, one that demands that you look at the lies that you tell yourself so that you don't feel the weight of responsibility for those who live under the yoke of whiteness, your whiteness.

I can see your anger. I can see that this letter is being misunderstood. This letter is not asking you to feel bad about yourself, to wallow in guilt. That is too easy. I'm asking for you to tarry, to linger, with the ways in which you perpetuate a racist society, the ways in which you are racist. I'm now daring you to face a racist history which, paraphrasing Baldwin, has placed you where you are and that has formed your own racism. Again, in the spirit of Baldwin, I am asking you to enter into battle with your white self. I'm asking that you open yourself up; to speak to, to admit to, the racist poison that is inside of you.

Again, take a deep breath. Don't tell me about how many black friends you have. Don't tell me that you are married to someone of color. Don't tell me that you voted for Obama. Don't tell me that *I'm* the racist. Don't tell me that you don't see color. Don't tell me that I'm blaming whites for everything. To do so is to hide yet again. You may have never used the N-word in your life, you may hate the K.K.K., but that does not mean that you don't harbor racism and benefit from racism. After all, you are part of a system that allows you to walk into stores where you are not followed, where you get to go for a bank loan and your skin does not count against you, where you don't need to engage in "the talk" that black people and people of color must tell their children when they are confronted by white police officers.

As you reap comfort from being white, we suffer for being black and people of color. But your comfort is linked to our pain and suffering. Just as my comfort in being male is linked to the suffering of women, which makes me sexist, so, too, you are racist. That is the gift that I want you to accept, to embrace. It is a form of knowledge that is taboo. Imagine the impact that the acceptance of this gift might have on you and the world.

Take another deep breath. I know that there are those who will write to me in the comment section with boiling anger, sarcasm, disbelief, denial. There are those who will say, "Yancy is just an angry black man." There are others who will say, "Why isn't Yancy telling black people to be honest about the violence in their own black neighborhoods?" Or, "How can Yancy say that all white people are racists?" If you are saying these things, then you've already failed to listen. I come with a gift. You're already rejecting the gift that I have to offer. This letter is about *you*. Don't change the conversation. I assure you that so many black people suffering from poverty and joblessness, which is linked to high levels of crime, are painfully aware of the existential toll that they have had to face because they are black and, as Baldwin adds, *"for no other reason."*

Some of your white brothers and sisters have made this leap. The legal scholar Stephanie M. Wildman, has written, "I simply believe that no matter how hard I work at not being racist, I still am. Because part of racism is systemic, I benefit from the privilege that I am struggling to see." And the journalism professor Robert Jensen: "I like to think I have changed, even though I routinely trip over the lingering effects of that internalized racism and the institutional racism around me. Every time I walk into a store at the same time as a black man and the security guard follows him and leaves me alone to shop, I am benefiting from white privilege."

What I'm asking is that you first accept the racism within yourself, accept all of the truth about what it means for you to be white in a society that was created for you. I'm asking for you to trace the binds that tie you to forms of domination that you would rather not see. When you walk into the world, you can walk with assurance; you have already signed a contract, so to speak, that guarantees you a certain form of social safety.

Baldwin argues for a form of love that is "a state of being, or state of grace—not in the infantile American sense of being made happy but in the tough and universal sense of quest and daring and growth." Most of my days, I'm engaged in a personal and societal battle against sexism. So many times, I fail. And so many times, I'm complicit. But I refuse to hide behind that mirror that lies to me about my "non-sexist nobility." Baldwin says, "Love takes off the masks that we fear we cannot live without and know we cannot live within." In my heart, I'm done with the mask of sexism, though I'm tempted every day to wear it. And, there are times when it still gets the better of me.

White America, are you prepared to be at war with yourself, your white identity, your white power, your white privilege? Are you prepared to show me a white self that love has unmasked? I'm asking for love in return for a gift; in fact, I'm hoping that this gift might help you to see yourself in ways that you have not seen before. Of course, the history of white supremacy in America belies this gesture of black gift-giving, this gesture of non-sentimental love. Martin Luther King Jr. was murdered even as he loved.

Perhaps the language of this letter will encourage a split—not a split between black and white, but a fissure in your understanding, a space for loving a Trayvon Martin, Eric Garner, Tamir Rice, Aiyana Jones, Sandra Bland, Laquan McDonald and others. I'm suggesting a form of love that enables you to see the role that you play (even despite your anti-racist actions) in a *system* that continues to value black lives on the cheap.

Take one more deep breath. I have another gift.

If you have young children, before you fall off to sleep tonight, I want you to hold your child. Touch your child's face. Smell your child's hair. Count the fingers on your child's hand. See the miracle that is your child. And then, with as much vision as you can muster, I want you to imagine that your child is black.

In peace,
George Yancy

Acknowledgements *(continued from copyright page)*

Bartlett, Donald, L. and Steele, James. "Monsanto's Harvest of Fear," originally published in *Vanity Fair*, April 2, 2008. Copyright © 2008 by Donald Bartlett and James Steele, used by permission of The Wylie Agency, LLC.

Cockrall-King, Jennifer. "Chicago: The Vertical Farm" from *Food and City: Urban Agriculture and the New Food Revolution* (Amherst, NY: Prometheus Books, 2012), pages 263–282. Copyright © 2012 by Jennifer Cockrall-King. All rights reserved. Used with permission of the publisher; www.prometheusbooks.com

Doan, Petra. "The Tyranny of Gendered Spaces: Reflections from Beyond the Gender Dichotomy" from *Gender, Place & Culture: A Journal of Feminist Geography*, vol. 17, issue 5, 2010. Copyright © 2010. Reprinted by permission of the publisher (Taylor & Francis Ltd, http://www.tandfonline.com) via Copyright Clearance Center.

Fine, Cordelia. "The 'Seductive Allure' of Neuroscience" from *Delusions of Gender: How our Minds, Society, and Neurosexism Create Difference* by Cordelia Fine. Copyright © 2010 by Cordelia Fine. Used by permission of W.W. Norton & Company, Inc.

Gay, Roxane. "Some Jokes Are Funnier Than Others" [as appeared in salon.com July 12, 2012 article] from *Bad Feminist* by Roxane Gay. Copyright © 2014 by Roxane Gay. Reprinted by permission of HarperCollins Publishers.

Gerstel, Naomi and Sarkisian, Natalia. "The Color of Family Ties: Race, Class, and Gender, and Extended Family Involvement" from *American Families: A Multicultural Reader*, 2nd ed., edited by Stephanie Coontz. Copyright © 2008. Reprinted by permission of the authors.

Gillam, Ken and Wooden, Shannon R. "Post-Princess Models of Gender: The New Man in Disney/Pixar" from *Journal of Popular Film and Television* 36, no. 1 (2008): 2–8. Copyright © 2008. Reprinted by permission of the publisher (Taylor & Francis Ltd, http://www.tandfonline.com) via Copyright Clearance Center.

Goldstein, Diane. "I'm a Cop and I Support Black Lives Matter" from *Vice*, July 12, 2016. Reprinted with permission.

Holtzman, Linda and Sharpe, Leon. "Theories and Constructs of Race" from "Racing in America: Fact or Fiction," *Media Messages: What Film, Television, and Popular Music Teach Us About Race, Class, Gender, and Sexual Orientation*, pg. 534, pp. 242–249, and 305–308. Copyright © 2014 by Taylor & Francis. Reprinted by permission of the publisher (Taylor & Francis Ltd, http://www.tandfonline.com) via Copyright Clearance Center.

Hurst, Blake. "The Omnivore's Delusion: Against the Agri-intellectuals" From *The American*. Reprinted with permission of the American Enterprise Institute.

Idov, Michael. "When Did Young People Start Spending 25% of The Paychecks on Pickled Lamb's Tongues?" from *New York Magazine*, March 25, 2012. Copyright © 2012. Reprinted by permission of Michael Idov/New York Magazine.

Karkazis, Katrina. "Taxonomies of Intersexuality to the 1950s" in *Fixing Sex* by Katrina Karkazis, pages 31–46 . Copyright © 2008 Duke University Press. All rights reserved. Republished by permission of the copyright holder. www.dukeupress.edu

Kimmel, Michael. "'Bros Before Hos': The Guy Code" [pp. 44–69] from *Guyland: The Perilous World Where Boys Become Men* by Michael Kimmel. Copyright © 2008 by Michael Kimmel. Reprinted by permission of HarperCollins Publishers.

Kingsolver, Barbara. "You Can't Run Away on Harvest Day" [pp. 219–37] from *Animal, Vegetable, Miracle: A Year of Food Life* by Barbara Kingsolver, Steven L. Hopp and Camille Kingsolver. Copyright © 2007 by Barbara Kingsolver, Steven L. Hopp, and Camille Kingsolver. Published by HarperCollins Publishers.

Levy, Ariel. "Either/Or" from *The New Yorker*, November 30, 2009. Copyright © 2009. Reprinted by permission of Ariel Levy, The New Yorker.

Lui, Haiming and Lin, Lianlian. "'Food, Culinary Identity, and Transnational Culture" from *Journal of Asian American Studies* Volume 12, Number 2, June 2009, pages 135–162. Copyright © 2010. Reproduced with permission of THE JOHNS HOPKINS UNIVERSITY PRESS in the format Republish in a book via Copyright Clearance Center.

McGonigal, Jane. "Becoming Part of Something Bigger Than Ourselves" from Jane McGonigal, *Reality Is Broken: Why Games Make Us Better and How They Can Change the World* (New York: The Penguin Press, 2011), pp. 95–107, 112–115 + notes on pp. 370–372. Copyright © 2011. Reprinted by permission of Jane McGonigal. janemcgonigal.com

McKibben, Bill. "The Only Way to Have a Cow" from *Orion Magazine*, April 2, 2010. Copyright © 2010 Bill McKibben. Reprinted with permission from the author.

Nestle, Marion. "Eating Made Simple" from *Scientific American*, September 1, 2007. Reprinted with permission. Copyright © 2007 Scientific American, Inc. All rights reserved.

Paarlberg, Robert. "Attention Whole Food Shoppers" from *Foreign Policy*, April 26, 2010. Copyright © 2010. Reproduced with permission of Slate Group LLC; permission conveyed through Copyright Clearance Center, Inc.

Padawer, Ruth. "When Women Become Men at Wellesley" from *The New York Times*, October 19, 2014. Copyright © 2014 The New York Times. All rights reserved. Used by permission and protected by the Copyright Laws of the United States. The printing, copying, redistribution, or retransmission of this Content without express written permission is prohibited.

HRH the Prince Wales. "On the Future of Food." Excerpts from *The Prince's Speech* by HRH The Prince of Wales. Copyright © 2012 by AG Carrick, Ltd. Permission granted by Rodale, Inc., Emmaus, PA.

Prinz, Jesse J. "Gender and Geometry" (Chapter 9) from *Beyond Human Nature* by Jesse J. Prinz. Copyright © 2012 by Jesse J. Prinz. Used by permission of W. W. Norton & Company, Inc.

Salesses, Matthew. "Different Racism: On Jeremy Lin and How The Rules of Racism Are Different for Asian Americans." Excerpt from *Own Story* by Matthew Salesses, reprinted under a license arrangement originating with Amazon Publishing, www.apub.com.

Sayyid, S. "A Measure of Islamophobia" from *Islamophobia Studies Journal* Vol. 2, No. 1, Spring 2014, pages 10–25. Published by Islamophobia Research and Documentation Project, Center for Race and Gender, University of California, Berkeley. Copyright © 2014. Reprinted with permission.

Schmidt, Eric. "Our Future Selves." Excerpts from *The New Digital Age: Reshaping the Future of People, Nations and Business* by Eric Schmidt and Jared Cohen. Copyright © 2013 by Google Inc. and Jared Cohen. Used by permission of Alfred A. Knopf, an imprint of the Knopf Doubleday Publishing Group, a division of Penguin Random House LLC. All rights reserved. Any third party use of this material, outside of publication, is prohibited. Interested parties must apply directly to Penguin Random House LLC for permission.

Schneider, Susan. "Mindscan: Transcending and Enhancing the Human Brain" from *Science Fiction and Philosophy: From Time Travel to Superintelligence*, edited by Susan Schneider, pages 241–256. Copyright © 2009 Blackwell Publishing, Ltd. Reproduced with permission of Blackwell Publishing, Ltd.

Schwartz, Pepper. "The Social Construction of Heterosexuality" from *The Sexual Self: The Construction of Sexual Scripts*, edited by Michael Kimmel (Vanderbilt University Press, July 10, 2007). Copyright © 2007. Reprinted by permission of Pepper Schwartz.

Solomon, Akiba, "Thugs. Students. Rioters. Fans: Media's Subtle Racism in Unrest Coverage." *Colorlines*, April 28, 2015, Copyright © 2015. Originally published at Colorlines.com. Reprinted by permission of Race Forward.

Sommers, Christina Hoff. "The Boys at the Back." From *The New York Times*, February 3, 2013. Copyright © 2013 The New York Times. All rights reserved. Used by permission and protected by the Copyright Laws of the United States. The printing, copying, redistribution, or retransmission of this Content without express written permission is prohibited.

Steinkuehler, Constance and Duncan, Sean. "Scientific Habits of Mind in Virtual Worlds" from *Journal of Science Education and Technology* (2008) 17, pages 530–543. Copyright © 2008. Reprinted with permission of Springer.

Suarez-Orozco, Marcelo M. and Carola. "How Immigrants Become 'Other.'" From "Immigration in the Age of Global Vertigo" from *Arizona Firestorm*, ed. by Otto Santa Ana (2012). Used by permission of Rowman & Littlefield Publishing Group. All rights reserved.

Talbot, Margaret. "Brain Gain: The Underground World of 'Neuroenhancing' Drugs." Excerpt from "Brain Gain" by Margaret Talbot, originally published in *The New Yorker*. Copyright © 2009 Margaret Talbot, used by permission of The Wylie Agency, LLC.

Treuer, David. Excerpt from *Rez Life*. Copyright © 2012 by David Treuer. Used by permission of Grove/Atlantic, Inc. Any third party use of this material, outside this publication, is prohibited.

Twilley, Nicola and Graber, Cynthia. "Why the Calorie Is Broken" Mosaic.com, January 26, 2016. http://mosaicscience.com/story/why-calorie-broken. CC-BY 4.0 license. Republished with permission.

Wells, Taylor M. and Dennis, Alan R. "To Email or Not to Email: The Impact of Media on Psychophysiological Responses and Emotional Content in Utilitarian and Romantic Communication." Reprinted from *Computers in Human Behavior*, Volume 54, January 2016, pages 1–9. Copyright © 2015, with permission from Elsevier.

Wuest, Bryan. "Stories Like Mine: Coming Out Videos and Queer Identities on YouTube." From *Queer Youth and Media Cultures*, edited by Christopher Pullen, pages 19–33. Copyright © 2014 by the author. Reprinted by permission of Springer Nature, Macmillan Publishers Ltd.

Yancy, George. "Dear White America" from *The New York Times*, December 24, 2015. Copyright © 2015. Reprinted with permission of the author.